GRADUAL FAILURE

THE AIR WAR OVER NORTH VIETNAM
1965–1966

JACOB VAN STAAVEREN

Originally published by
Air Force History and Museums Program
United States Air Force
Washington, D.C. 2002

Cover art and promotional text (c) 2011 Booklife
ISBN 978-1-257-90462-4
This publication is subject to Title 17, United States Code, Sections 101 and 105. It is in the public domain and may not be copyrighted.
Third commercial reprint

Library of Congress Cataloging-in Publication Data

Van Staaveren, Jacob.
   Gradual failure : the air war over North Vietnam, 1965-1966 / Jacob Van Staaveren.
      p. cm. -- (The United States Air Force in Southeast Asia) Includes bibliographical reference and index.
  1. Vietnamese Conflict, 1961-1975--Aerial operations, American. 2. United States. Air Force--History--Vietnamese Conflict, 1961-1975. I. Title. II. Series

Foreword

The United States Air Force reached its nadir during the opening two years of the Rolling Thunder air campaign in North Vietnam. Never had the Air Force operated with so many restraints and to so little effect. These pages are painful but necessary reading for all who care about the nation's military power.

Jacob Van Staaveren wrote this book in the 1970s near the end of his distinguished government service, which began during the occupation of Japan; the University of Washington Press published his book on that experience in 1995. He was an Air Force historian in Korea during the Korean War, and he began to write about the Vietnam War while it was still being fought. His volume on the air war in Laos was declassified and published in 1993. Now this volume on the air war in North Vietnam has also been declassified and is being published for the first time. Although he retired to McMinnville, Oregon, a number of years ago, we asked him to review the manuscript and make any changes that seemed warranted. For the most part, this is the book he wrote soon after the war.

Readers of this volume will also want to read the sequel, Wayne Thompson's *To Hanoi and Back: The U. S. Air Force and North Vietnam, 1966–1973*, which tells the more encouraging story of how the Air Force employed airpower to far greater effect using a combination of better doctrine, tactics, technology, and training.

RICHARD P. HALLION
Air Force Historian

The Author

Jacob Van Staaveren (1917–1999) served as a historian for over twenty years with the Air Force history program, both in Washington and in the field. He earned a B.A. degree from Linfield College, Oregon, and an M.A. in history from the University of Chicago. From 1946 to 1950, Mr. Van Staaveren served with the Allied occupation forces in Japan, initially as an adviser on civil reforms, then as a historian preparing studies on Japanese economic reforms. The University of Washington Press published his account of this period, *An American in Japan, 1945–1948: A Civilian View of the Occupation*, in 1994. During his long career with Air Force history, he wrote numerous studies, including several on the war in Southeast Asia. He was co-author of *The United States Air Force in Southeast Asia, 1961–1973: An Illustrated Account* (1977) and the author of *Interdiction in Southern Laos, 1960–1968* (1993).

Contents

Foreword iii
Author iv
Introduction 3

Chapter 1

Flaming Dart 9
   The United States Considers a Reprisal Attack 10
   Flaming Dart I 14
   Flaming Dart II 22

Chapter 2

Planning 27
   Paramilitary Activities and Bombing Plans 28
   Rising Pressure from the Services to Bomb the North 39
   Selecting Major North Vietnamese Targets 43
   The Gulf of Tonkin Incident 48
   Washington Forbids Follow-on Strikes 52
   The Bien Hoa Incident 59
   Beginning of a Limited, Two-Phase Program 61
   Washington's Resistance to a Bombing Program Ends 64

Chapter 3

Rolling Thunder Begins 69
   The Air Challenge in North Vietnam 69
   Command and Control of Air Resources 72
   Preparations for a Rolling Thunder Program 76
   The First Two Rolling Thunder Strikes 83
   Initial Analysis of Aircraft Losses 86
   An Air Strategy Emerges 89
   Beginning of Weekly Rolling Thunder Strikes 92
   Supporting Operations for Rolling Thunder 95
   Contingency Planning for a Larger Conflict 97

Chapter 4

Gradual Expansion 101
    Further Decisions on Prosecuting the War 102
    Initial Bridge-Busting Attacks 104
    Countering the North's Air Defenses 113
    The Honolulu Conference of April 1965. 119
    Rolling Thunder's Moderate Pace Continues. 123
    Expansion of the Leaflet Program 129
    Cautious Optimism on Bombing Results 130

Chapter 5

Pause and Escalation 133
    The First Bombing Halt 134
    Rolling Thunder Resumes 135
    Hanoi Expands its Air and Ground Defenses 141
    The Air Force Organizes for Extended Combat. 145
    Washington Rejects a More Air-Oriented Strategy 149
    Beginning of Two-Week Bombing Cycles. 157

Chapter 6

The SAM Threat 163
    Initial anti-SAM Operations. 164
    The First Iron Hand Missions. 167
    Improving Detection of SAM Sites. 174
    Continued Air Strikes on non-SAM Targets 176
    Establishment of a Target Intelligence Center. 185
    Deepening Service Concern about Strike Restrictions 185
    The First SAM "Kill" and the anti-SAM Campaign in Late 1965. ... 192
    The Air Force Increases its anti-SAM Capability 195

Chapter 7

Toward the Thirty-seven Day Bombing Halt 199
    Additional Interdiction Changes and Planning for Negotiation ... 202
    Continuation of the Leaflet Program. 210
    Beginning of a Thirty-seven Day Bombing Halt. 211

Chapter 8

Diplomacy Fails. 215
   Hanoi Rejects American Peace Overtures 215
   Debate on Resuming the Bombing 218
   Rolling Thunder 48 224
   More Deployment Planning 229
   Rolling Thunder 49 236

Chapter 9

Rolling Thunder 50. 243
   Westmoreland's "Extended Battlefield" Area 243
   Selecting Rolling Thunder 50 Targets 248
   Rolling Thunder 50 Begins. 252
   The Air Munitions Shortage 263
   Circumventing Bad Weather With MSQ–77 Radar 265
   Countering the North's Air Defense System 267
   Improving MiG Watch and Border Patrol 276

Chapter 10

The Strikes 279
   The POL Debate 279
   Approval of a Few POL Strikes 284
   Gradual Expansion of POL Strikes. 288
   Strikes on Major POL Sites Begin 289
   The Honolulu Conference, July 1966 294
   The POL Strangulation Campaign 297

Chapter 11

Summary and Reappraisal 309

Notes 325
Glossary 355
Bibliography 359
Index 367

Illustrations

Maps

Southeast Asia, Principal U.S. Airbases. xvii
Armed Reconnaissance Route Packages 240

Figures

1. Rolling Thunder Sorties, Ordnance, and Targets
   March–June 1965 13
2. Redeployment of Aircraft
   August 5–9, 1964 50
3. Redeployment of Aircraft by CINCSTRIKE
   August 8–21, 1964 51
4. Location of USAF Combat Squadrons
   February 1965 77
5. RollingThunder Sorties, Ordnance Delivered, and Principal Targets
   March 2–June 24, 1965 142
6. Troops and Equipment in South Vietnam and Thailand
   February and June 1965 146
7. Targets and Air Strikes
   As of June 24, 1965 152
8. Increase in Conventional Antiaircraft Weaponry
   July 5–September 30, 1965 186
9. Personnel Shortfalls
   February 1966 231
10. Air Force Deployments
    1966 234
11. Sortie Effectiveness
    April, May, and June 1966 263
12. Aircraft Destroyed or Damaged
    April, May and June 1966. 267
13. Storage Capacity of Major North Vietnamese POL Installations
    1964–1966 280

14. Prestrike and Poststrike Storage Capacity of POL Targets,
Route Package 1
August 1966 302
15. Prestrike and Poststrike Storage Capacity of POL Targets,
Route Package 6A
August 1966 302

Photographs

F–105 Thunderchief 4
Infiltration route in Laos 5
EC–121s at Tan Son Nhut Air Base 6
North Vietnamese military barracks area under attack 7
U.S. dependents leaving South Vietnam in 1965 8
President Lyndon B. Johnson 10
Gen. Curtis E. LeMay 12
President Johnson and advisers 14
USS *Ticonderoga* 15
A–4 launching from USS *Hancock* 16
F–102s at Tan Son Nhut Air Base 17
Da Nang Air Base 19
Gen. William C. Westmoreland 20
Farm Gate aircraft at Bien Hoa Air Base 21
F–105s at Da Nang Air Base 23
Secretary of State Dean Rusk 24
South Vietnamese A–1s and T–28s 26
Laotian General Vang Pao 28
South Vietnamese President Ngo Dinh Diem 29
President John F. Kennedy 33
Gen. Earle G. Wheeler 34
Secretary of Defense Robert S. McNamara, Gen. Maxwell D. Taylor, and
  Ambassador Henry Cabot Lodge at Tan Son Nhut Air Base, 1964 ... 36
Gen. Maxwell D. Taylor 39
B–57 in flight 41
B–57s at Da Nang Air Base 43
Shipping in Haiphong Harbor 44
Burning North Vietnamese Swatow boat 50
Joint Chiefs of Staff, 1965 54
Gen. Hunter Harris 57
B–57 destroyed in Viet Cong mortar attack at Bien Hoa, November 1964 ... 58

Laotian T–28 65
Saigon hotel bombing, December 1964. 66
Air attack on North Vietnamese barracks 68
F–105s at Takhli Royal Thai Air Base............................. 70
MiG–17 71
Gen. Curtis E. LeMay and Gen. Paul D. Harkins................... 73
F–105s at Korat Royal Thai Air Base 75
Gen. John P. McConnell arriving at Tan Son Nhut Air Base 79
Tan Son Nhut Air Base... 80
Secretary of Defense McNamara at a Pentagon press conference 84
Secretary of the Air Force Eugene M. Zuckert 87
Antiaircraft fire at night 90
F–100 attacking enemy target 96
Damaged bridge, Laos, 1965..................................... 100
U.S. ground troops unloading C–130 102
Kim Cuong bridge, North Vietnam 104
Dong Phuong Thuong bridge, North Vietnam 105
F–105 with Bullpup missiles.................................... 106
F–105 refueling receptacles 107
Qui Vinh bridge, North Vietnam................................. 108
RF–101 landing 110
RF–101 nose camera... 110
Xom Ca Trang bridge, North Vietnam............................. 112
Bullpup missile in flight 113
U–2 at Bien Hoa Air Base....................................... 114
F–8 launching from USS *Hancock* 115
F–4 in flight 117
F–104s at Da Nang Air Base..................................... 119
Phu Dien Chau bridge, North Vietnam 122
My Duc bridge, North Vietnam................................... 123
DC–130 and drones 124
Damage at Tan Son Nhut Air Base after attack on April 14, 1966 ... 126–127
KC–135 refueling F–105s.. 132
Ambassador Taylor and General Westmoreland..................... 134
KC–135 refueling an F–4 138
Dien Bien Phu airfield, North Vietnam, after attack 139
North Vietnamese supply area under attack...................... 140
Il–28 aircraft in revetments at Gia Lam airfield............... 143
President Lyndon Johnson, Gen. William Westmoreland, Vietnamese

Chief of State Nguyen Van Thieu, and Premier Nguyen Cao Ky	150
Trai Hoi bridge, North Vietnam	151
F–4 attacking enemy position	159
Air Force crews credited with downing first MiGs	160
SA–2 surface-to-air missile in flight and detonation	162
SA–2 missile on launcher	163
EC–121 in flight	164
SA–2 site, empty and with missiles	166–167
Lang Met bridge, North Vietnam	168
Navy ordnancemen moving 500-pound bombs	170
Lt. Col. Robinson Risner	172
EB–66 in flight	175
Air Force photo interpreters	176
North Vietnamese SA–2 site	177
Destroyed bridge on Route 6, North Vietnam	178
B–52 releasing bombs	180
Air Force crew members loading bombs on B–52	181
F–105 with 750-pound bombs on fuselage centerline	183
North Vietnamese antiaircraft gun site	187
North Vietnamese 57-mm antiaircraft gun and crew	188
F–105 bombing North Vietnamese bridge	189
Rocket attack on a North Vietnamese surface-to-air missile site	190
North Vietnamese train after attack	194
F–100F in flight	196
Udorn Royal Thai Air Force Base	198
Bac Can bridge, North Vietnam	200
A–6 launching from USS *Kitty Hawk*	202
North Vietnamese patrol boat repair area under attack	204
Secretary of the Air Force Harold Brown	205
North Vietnamese bridge repairs and bypass	207
Ground crew removing film from RF–4	208
Crew members attach a 500-pound bomb to an F–4	209
Destroyed bridge on Route 19, North Vietnam	211
President Johnson and Secretary of State Rusk	213
Southeast Asia Conference in Manila, the Philippines	214
Lt. Gen. Nguyen Van Thieu greets U.S. airmen at Da Nang Air Base	217
Pontoon bridge bypass around destroyed bridge	218
Destroyed bridge bypassed with a ford	220
MiG–17s at Phuc Yen airfield, North Vietnam	223

F–4 launching from USS *Franklin Roosevelt*........................ 226
KC–135s at Takhli Royal Thai Air Base 227
HU–16 rescue seaplane at Tan Son Nhut Air Base 228
HU–16 rescuing downed pilot 229
Air Force Secretary Brown and Premier Ky 232
Runway construction at Cam Ranh Bay 233
F–105 fires rockets at a North Vietnamese target 238
North Vietnamese camp near Mu Gia Pass 242
MiG–21 in flight... 244
North Vietnamese truck park after attack 245
Air Force Secretary Brown and General Westmoreland................ 246
Phu Ly bridge, North Vietnam 247
Lt. Gen. Nguyen Chanh Thi and Nguyen Van Thieu 249
O–1 forward air control aircraft and pilot 253
Yen Bai railyard, North Vietnam 254
Thai Nguyen railyard, North Vietnam 255
Capt. C. Glen Nix.. 256
Bac Giang bridge, North Vietnam.................................. 257
Than Hoa bridge, North Vietnam 258
North Vietnamese bridge with three bypass routes 259
Mu Gia Pass after bombing.. 261
Bomb rack for B–52s 262
Modified B–52 releases load of 108 bombs 263
EB–66 leads F–105s on bombing mission............................ 264
MSQ–77 facility at Dong Ha, South Vietnam 268
North Vietnamese 37-mm antiaircraft gun and crew 269
F–105 with Shrike air-to-surface missile.......................... 270
Air-to-surface missile launched at missile site................... 271
North Vietnamese gunners running to man their positions............ 272
MiG–17 hit by cannon fire 273
Kep airfield, North Vietnam 275
Underground petroleum storage area burning 278
Underground petroleum storage area under construction............. 281
Petroleum supplies in drums...................................... 287
Hanoi petroleum storage facility after attack.................. 290–292
Dong Hoi petroleum storage area after attack 294
Soviet tanker *Buguruslan* outside Haiphong Harbor................. 295
Badon petroleum storage area 296–297
Hanoi railyard... 298

A–4 launching from carrier.................................... 299
Adm. U.S. Grant Sharp and Lt. Gen. William W. Momyer.............. 301
Surface-to-air missile contrail.................................. 303
Chieu Ung railroad bridge................................ 304–305
F–105 bombing a rail line...................................... 306
F–105s refueling en route to North Vietnam 308

PRINCIPAL U.S. AIR BASES

1. Udorn
2. Nakhon Phanom
3. Takhli
4. Korat
5. Don Muang
6. U-Tapao
7. Ubon
8. Binh Thuy
9. Tan Son Nhut
10. Bien Hoa
11. Phan Rang
12. Cam Ranh Bay
13. Nha Trang
14. Tuy Hoa
15. Qui Nhon
16. Pleiku
17. Phu Cat
18. Chu Lai
19. Da Nang

Note 1: Map originally published in color
Note 2: Numbers in circles on map lost due to government printing process

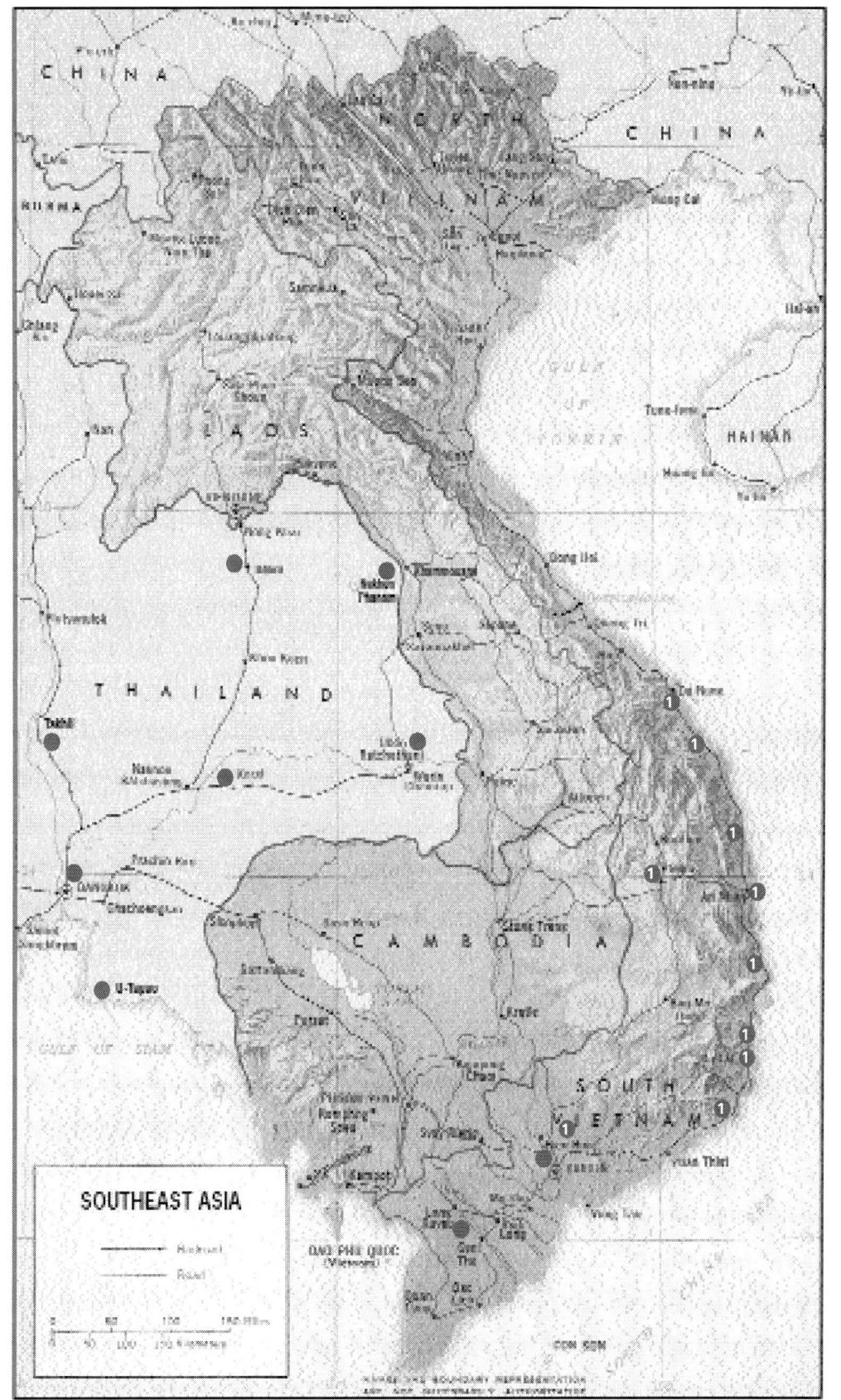

Introduction

Of the many facets of the American war in Southeast Asia debated by U.S. authorities in Washington, by the military services and the public, none has proved more controversial than the air war against North Vietnam. The air war's inauguration with the nickname Rolling Thunder followed an eleven-year American effort to induce communist North Vietnam to sign a peace treaty without openly attacking its territory. Thus, Rolling Thunder was a new military program in what had been a relatively low-key attempt by the United States to "win" the war within South Vietnam against insurgent communist Viet Cong forces, aided and abetted by the north.

The present volume covers the first phase of the Rolling Thunder campaign from March 1965 to late 1966. It begins with a description of the planning and execution of two initial limited air strikes, nicknamed Flaming Dart I and II. The Flaming Dart strikes were carried out against North Vietnam in February 1965 as the precursors to a regular, albeit limited, Rolling Thunder air program launched the following month. Before proceeding with an account of Rolling Thunder, its roots are traced in the events that compelled the United States to adopt an anti-communist containment policy in Southeast Asia after the defeat of French forces by the communist Vietnamese in May 1954.

The Geneva Agreements of July 1954 formally ended the first Indochina war, but led to a Vietnam divided into a communist north and a noncommunist south, with the United States committed to ensuring that the latter had the political and military strength to defend itself. The United States encountered intractable difficulties in establishing a viable new nation in a South Vietnam wracked by chronic social, political, and military instability and poor leadership, all aggravated by an incipient Viet Cong insurgency within its borders. Despite these problems, Washington authorities believed that this policy of communist containment had to be won first in South Vietnam, whose defense required ever-increasing numbers of American forces for training, counterinsurgency and regular military operations from all branches of the armed services. Many in Washington feared possible intervention by communist China or the Soviet Union, the main military suppliers of the north, if the war was extended to North Vietnam proper. It was a fear not shared by Air Force and Navy leaders, who believed that the conflict could be won only by vigorously striking the north and who were confident that the risk of intervention by the two large communist powers was minimal.

American policy included attempts to stabilize Laos, one of the former Indochina states, by very limited air and covert ground actions, while sending Air Force and Navy air strikes to stem the flow of North Vietnamese troops and

The Republic F–105 Thunderchief was the Air Force aircraft used most often in bombing missions over North Vietnam. Originally designed as a tactical nuclear bomber, it was big, tough, and carried a large load of munitions.

supplies through southern Laos and into South Vietnam to bolster the Viet Cong insurgency there. These limited air actions, with nicknames like Barrel Roll and Steel Tiger, also represented attempts to "signal" the North Vietnamese government of stronger U.S. military action unless it desisted from its efforts to destabilize South Vietnam with its continued support for the Viet Cong.

Meanwhile, an emboldened communist north began instigating major hostile "incidents," which forced Washington to modify its military strategy of confining the war largely to South Vietnam. Most important was an attack on a U.S. Navy patrol in the Gulf of Tonkin in August 1964, resulting in the first air strike on the north, and the enactment by the U.S. Congress of a "Tonkin Gulf Resolution" empowering the U.S. President to take whatever action he deemed necessary to prevent further communist aggression in Southeast Asia. Then in late 1964 and early 1965, three more attacks on American and Vietnamese military installations in South Vietnam led to the retaliatory Flaming Dart air attacks on the north.

In March 1965, Washington inaugurated a highly restricted and carefully controlled series of numbered Rolling Thunder air programs against the north. Conducted by U.S. Air Force and Navy carrier aircraft with the small Vietnamese Air Force making "token" air strikes, Washington dictated the number of combat sorties that could be flown and the number, type and location of targets that could be struck. Avoiding civilian casualties was emphasized repeatedly. Sometimes alone, and frequently with the Navy, Air Force leaders attempted—without success—to persuade Washington authorities that the regime would only be brought to the negotiating table by a more robust attack on all of the north's industrial sites, logistic centers, road and rail network, port

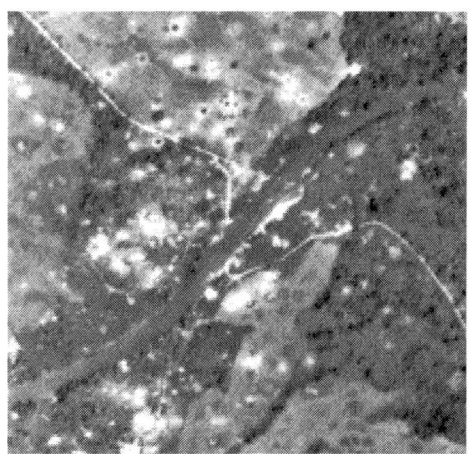

A destroyed bridge on an infiltration route in Laos.

facilities, and by mining the harbors. When they failed to convince Washington, Air Force and Navy units nonetheless carried out their Rolling Thunder mission within the tight constraints imposed from home. This included an adjustment to a highly complex air command and control system in the Southeast Asia theater. The system consisted of an Army-controlled Military Assistance Command in Saigon, and a Navy-controlled Pacific Command in Honolulu, with the commanders of each having considerable air authority, in contrast to a single air commander having overall control of all air operations in a war theater as Air Force doctrine specified.

As the air campaign against the north gradually expanded and the permissible targeting area moved northward incrementally towards Hanoi-Haiphong and the Chinese border, the Air Force used a variety of specially equipped aircraft—such as F–100Fs, RB–66Bs, RB–66Cs, and EC–121Ds—to locate and/or neutralize the hundreds of enemy radar-controlled antiaircraft guns and Soviet-built SA–2 surface-to-air missile sites that appeared in the spring of 1965 around the north's industrial areas, key logistic centers, and road and rail routes. Air Force fighters had to engage in aerial battles with MiGs as the Soviet-built fighters began to challenge strike aircraft. The Air Force and the Navy adjusted their aerial tactics as a consequence of Washington's tight combat constraints while devising navigational safeguards after occasional violations of Chinese air space.

Even as they approved the Rolling Thunder program, many in Washington believed "air power" could never win the war in the north. Still, they expected the air strikes, in conjunction with ongoing American military action against the Viet Cong in South Vietnam and southern Laos, to inflict sufficient "pain" on the Hanoi regime to force it to negotiate. When this goal was not immediately realized, Washington embarked upon—over the objections of military commanders—a vigorous "negotiating strategy" to convince the Hanoi regime

Lockheed EC–121 Constellations at Tan Son
Nhut Air Base, South Vietnam, in 1965.

it could not win the war. To persuade Hanoi to begin "talks", Washington declared bombing halts. One, lasting five days in May 1965, was part of a diplomatic initiative code-named Mayflower; the second, lasting thirty-seven days in late 1965 and early 1966, was part of a diplomatic initiative code-named Marigold. Both efforts failed to persuade Hanoi to begin discussions to end the war.

With Washington's negotiating strategy in recess—although "peace feelers" continued with the help of other nations—Rolling Thunder resumed, initially with more restrictions than before, but these restrictions were slowly relaxed in the first half of 1966 to permit the Air Force and Navy to strike more northerly targets. However, most air combat and combat support sortie constraints remained. All the while, losses of aircraft, pilots and other aircrew mounted because of the ferocity of the north's growing arsenal of antiaircraft guns, automatic weapons and SA–2 missiles, many of which could not be struck because of their proximity to the Hanoi-Haiphong area and the Chinese border. In permitted bombing areas, the Air Force and Navy deployed more sophisticated armament, such as the Air Force's newest Wild Weasel F–105Fs with the Navy's improved Shrike AGM–45 air-to-surface missiles, to attack or neutralize Soviet-built SA–2 SAM sites whose numbers continued to increase.

Finally, the Joint Chiefs of Staff and commanders in the field succeeded in obtaining Washington's approval to strike the principal petroleum, oil and lubrication (POL) storage sites in North Vietnam. These operations, beginning on June 29 and ending in October with many sites destroyed or damaged, raised hopes briefly they would measurably reduce the flow of North Vietnamese troops and supplies into South Vietnam. The impact of the POL attacks was

A North Vietnamese military barracks area after an Air Force F–105 attack with 750-pound bombs.

diminished, however, by the long delay in authorizing them, which gave the Hanoi regime time to disperse its POL supplies in barrels throughout towns and villages that Washington had exempted from bombing to avoid civilian casualties. In addition, Soviet ships had begun offloading POL onto barges lest the Navy mine Haiphong harbor and other ports.

After the failure of POL strikes to slow to any appreciable degree the movement of the north's supplies—logistic and road and rail repair personnel by now numbered several hundred thousand—or to bring the Hanoi regime to the negotiating table, Washington approved a new "barrier strategy" for reducing communist infiltration through southern Laos and the demilitarized zone. This would include air support and the use of special mines and sensors. Concurrently, Washington asked the military services to study ways to make the Rolling Thunder program more effective and to reduce aircraft attrition. The substance of the Air Force and the Joint Staff replies was that while bad weather, antiaircraft fire, and other factors hindered Rolling Thunder operations, only by striking all remaining significant targets in the north and by mining its harbors could aircraft losses be reduced and victory be assured in the conflict. Washington remained unswayed in its belief, however, that an all-out air campaign against the north and the mining of its harbors not only could not win the war, but threatened a serious military confrontation with communist China, the Soviet Union, or both.

Dependents leaving South Vietnam in February 1965.

CHAPTER 1

Flaming Dart

At approximately two in the morning of February 7, 1965, a small band of Viet Cong (VC) insurgents, numbering between six and ten men, breached the last strands of barbed wire protecting the small U.S. Advisory Detachment of II Corps, popularly known as the MACV compound, about 4.5 kilometers north of Pleiku in the central highlands of South Vietnam. Entering the compound, they placed several small demolition charges with delay fuses of four to five seconds along the north wall of the main building and against the entrance gate. A U.S. sentry, Jesse Pyle, who was on duty in a sandbagged area near a billet, moved to investigate. Suddenly a charge four feet away exploded prematurely, mortally wounding Pyle. Proceeding with their stealthy attack, the Viet Cong quickly detonated three more charges, which blasted off the entrance gate, hit a mess office, and tore a hole through the roof of the main building. They threw sixteen more charges through the damaged wall and windows of the building, then sprayed it with fire from 7.62-mm automatic weapons. In the attack, which lasted from ten to fifteen minutes, the Viet Cong killed Pyle and wounded twenty-four other Americans and destroyed five rooms and damaged twelve more. There were no Vietnamese casualties.

Almost simultaneously, about 6.5 kilometers distant but still close to Pleiku, two small assault teams consisting of five to six Viet Cong and each armed with demolition charges and 81-mm mortars, entered the runway and aircraft parking area at Camp Holloway, the headquarters of the U.S. Army's 52d Aviation Battalion. One team placed demolition charges on the landing gear and under the fuselages of several aircraft while the other broke through a barbed wire fence near the helicopter ramp and placed charges on helicopter skis. As the charges exploded, the Viet Cong fired their mortars at nearby billets, engulfing them in flame and mortar fragments. This assault, which also lasted between ten and fifteen minutes, caused much greater carnage than the one at the MACV compound: 7 American soldiers were killed and 104 were wounded. Again, there were no Vietnamese casualties. On or near the airfield, five Army UH–1B helicopters had been reduced to smoldering ruins. The toll of major or minor damage further included eleven UH–1B helicopters, two CV–2 transports, three O–1F forward air control (FAC) aircraft, and one Vietnamese air force (VNAF) O–1F stationed temporarily at the airfield.

At about the same time, near the coastal town of Tuy Hoa, the Viet Cong fired 81-mm mortars into villages and two gas storage tanks near a VNAF airstrip, destroying the tanks. A fourth attack was carried out on a village about fifteen miles northeast of Nha Trang. No Americans were injured in the last two incidents.

At the MACV compound and Camp Holloway, the scenes of the major assaults, the Americans responded immediately with firearms and search but they were not able to capture any of the infiltrators. A postaction report attributed

President Lyndon B. Johnson.

the surprising and successful onslaught chiefly to lack of vigilance on the part of security units of the South Vietnamese Army (popularly known as ARVN, for the Army of Vietnam) in the Pleiku area. While officially the chief guarantor of safety for American installations, the ARVN's habitual state of undermanning and low level of alertness were further diminished by the week-long Lunar New Year Tet celebrations that had ended the previous day. Another factor was the attitude of the populace of Pleiku Province. Consisting largely of Montagnard tribal groups whose loyalties were to family and tribe rather than to the Saigon government or to the Viet Cong, they were not inclined to sound an alarm.[1]

The United States Considers a Reprisal Attack

It was the afternoon of February 6, 1965, in Washington when news of the Viet Cong depredations at the MACV compound and Camp Holloway reached the White House. Faced with this last and most serious in a chain of "significant" Viet Cong "incidents," President Lyndon B. Johnson braced for renewed pressure from some of his advisers to conduct an air strike on North Vietnam in reprisal. When he learned of the extent of devastation at Pleiku, he ordered a meeting of the National Security Council (NSC) for 7:45 that evening.[2]

Meanwhile, the President awaited further reports from American officials in Saigon. By coincidence, his special adviser on National Security Affairs, McGeorge Bundy, was in the South Vietnamese capital assessing the faltering military and political fortunes of the Saigon government with Ambassador Maxwell D. Taylor, Deputy Ambassador U. Alexis Johnson, and Gen. William C. Westmoreland, Commander of the U.S. Military Assistance Command,

Vietnam (COMUSMACV). Bundy's recommendation, endorsed by Taylor, Johnson, and Westmoreland, was that the two attacks at Pleiku called for an immediate air riposte on North Vietnam.[3]

Despite the unanimity of views in Saigon, the President and some of his advisers were apprehensive. On February 4, a few days before the assault at Pleiku, Soviet Premier Alexei N. Kosygin, arrived in Hanoi accompanied by military and economic advisers. It was assumed, and soon confirmed, that the Soviets would offer more aid to North Vietnam. Their presence in the capital prompted American officials to delay and then cancel a special patrol by the U.S. Seventh Fleet, planned earlier and nicknamed De Soto, off the coast of North Vietnam, and to order the *Coral Sea* and the *Hancock*, two of three Seventh Fleet carriers, to "stand down" from a "fully alert" status and head for the American naval base at Subic Bay in the Philippines. Only the carrier *Ranger* was instructed to remain "on alert" at the Yankee Station area in the Gulf of Tonkin off the North Vietnamese coast. The main purpose of the De Soto patrol, normally a one-destroyer type of operation to collect electronic intelligence and harass the North Vietnamese,* was to make a "show of force" and elicit a military response that might justify a retaliatory air strike by the United States. In preparation for this eventuality, at the request of the Joint Chiefs of Staff (JCS), the Commander in Chief, Pacific Command (CINCPAC) had compiled a list of North Vietnamese targets. It contained three strike options for Seventh Fleet carrier aircraft and for Pacific Air Force (PACAF) aircraft based in South Vietnam and Thailand.[4]

The NSC members and attendees who assembled with the President on February 6 to review the attack on American installations at Pleiku included Robert S. McNamara, the Secretary of Defense; Gen. Earle G. Wheeler, Chairman of the JCS; George Ball, Under Secretary of State (sitting in for the absent Secretary, Dean Rusk); senate majority leader, Mike Mansfield; and house speaker John McCormack. General Wheeler unequivocally urged a quick reprisal air strike on the north. His recommendation was supported by and had been made repeatedly in previous months by all of the service chiefs, especially by Gen. Curtis E. LeMay, the Air Force Chief of Staff who had just retired.† The service chiefs were convinced that air strikes against the Hanoi regime were the quickest way to arrest the political and military decline of the Saigon government. Other advisers, particularly McNamara and Rusk, had insisted that Saigon's military and political problems should be ameliorated before an air program was begun against the northern adversaries. The magnitude of the Viet Cong's attack at Pleiku forcibly changed opinions.

---

* De Soto patrols had been conducted infrequently by the Seventh Fleet off the North Vietnamese coast since April 1962.

† Gen. John P. McConnell succeeded Gen. LeMay on February 1, 1965.

Gen. Curtis E. LeMay,
Air Force Chief of Staff,
1961–1965.

With the strongly supportive views of Bundy, Taylor, and Westmoreland before them, the NSC members and attendees now agreed that a reprisal air strike was mandatory. Senator Mansfield alone was not persuaded. He feared that an air strike on the north might trigger a war with China or heal Sino-Soviet disputes. In the President's opinion, the senator offered no alternative American response to the attack at Pleiku. The NSC conferees were heartened by the latest U.S. intelligence assessment that China would not intervene in the war unless the United States invaded the north or the Hanoi regime was in danger of being overthrown. Encouraged by the call for action by his principal officials in Saigon and Washington, the President concurred. For the chief executive, the hour was a dramatic one for intelligence assurances could not completely dispel lingering uncertainties concerning the way in which the communist countries would respond to the proposed air strike. The President later recalled:[5]

> As we talked, there was an electric tension in the air. Everyone in the room was deadly serious as he considered the possible consequence of this decision. Each man around the table knew how crucial such action could be. How would Hanoi react? Would the Chinese Communists use it as a pretext for involving themselves? What about Kosygin and the Russians in Hanoi?

From the original three-option target list compiled by CINCPAC, the President selected four targets in southern North Vietnam associated with communist infiltration into the south, and directed U.S. aircraft to hit three and the Vietnamese air force (VNAF) to strike one. The importance of VNAF participation in action against the north to demonstrate U.S.-Vietnamese solidarity of purpose had been stressed by Ambassador Taylor and General Westmoreland in earlier planning.

In addition to strike options, the target list prepared for the Air Force and Navy contained the approximate number of aircraft required for "strike" and "cover" for each of seven targets (figure 1).[6]

Figure 1

Rolling Thunder Sorties, Ordnance, and Targets, March–June 1965

JCS Target No.	Name of Target	No. of Strike A/C	No. of Flak/CAP A/C	Service
Option I				
33	Dong Hoi Barracks	24	16	CINCPACFLT
36	Vit Thu Lu Army Barracks	24	12	CINCPACFLT
39	Chap Le Barracks	40	16	CINCPACAF
Option II[a]				
24	Chanh Hoi Barracks	28	24	CINCPACFLT
32	Vu Con Barracks	10	12	CINCPACAF
Option III[b]				

[a] To include Option I targets
[b] To include Option I and II targets

The target list was easily adjusted to include Vietnamese aircraft. CINCPAC's operational order accompanying the list for a possible reprisal air attack triggered by the De Soto patrol was nicknamed Flaming Dart.* The name was retained to meet the crisis occasioned by the Viet Cong's attack at Pleiku.[7] Notwithstanding the weeks and months of planning to prepare for an

---

* Redesignated Flaming Dart I soon thereafter.

President Johnson meets with advisers, (from left) Maxwell D. Taylor, Ambassador to South Vietnam; Secretary of State Dean Rusk; Johnson; and Secretary of Defense Robert McNamara.

air attack, as the hour grew near, Air Force, Navy, and VNAF commanders possessed an inadequate picture of the assigned targets. There had been no tactical reconnaissance of North Vietnam thus far and, to ensure maximum surprise, none was ordered prior to the impending strike. The only photos available were those taken by high altitude SAC Trojan Horse U–2 aircraft.*[8]

Flaming Dart I

It was nearly midday on February 7 when the President's order, sent by the JCS to Admiral U.S.G. Sharp, CINCPAC in Honolulu, reached the principal Air Force and Navy commanders in Southeast Asia. Sharp's command chain for the Navy consisted of Admiral Thomas H. Moorer, Commander, Pacific Fleet (CINCPACFLT) who was also in Honolulu, and Rear Admiral Joseph W. Williams, Commander, Seventh Fleet (COMSEVENTHFLT) who was located in the coastal waters off South and North Vietnam. The command chain for the Air Force began with Gen. Hunter Harris, Jr., Commander, Pacific Air Forces (CINCPACAF) in Honolulu. Under General Harris was Maj. Gen. Sam Maddux, Jr., Commander, Thirteenth Air Force at Clark AB, Philippines. Subordinate to General Maddux was Maj. Gen. Joseph H. Moore, Jr., Commander, 2d Air

---

* Regular U–2 missions in Southeast Asia began in February 1964 (see Chapter 2).

USS *Ticonderoga*

Division at Tan Son Nhut Air Base, Saigon. The 2d Air Division, which was also a component command of General Westmoreland's MACV headquarters, was removed temporarily from COMUSMACV by Admiral Sharp, who had command and control authority for U.S. air operations in North Vietnam and Laos, so that Sharp would be able to notify U.S. and VNAF aircraft of the impending Flaming Dart strike through his subordinate PACAF and PACFLT commanders. Sharp assigned coordinating authority to General Harris, a task that was soon further delegated to General Moore in Saigon. The carriers *Coral Sea* and *Hancock* reversed course to take up their positions at Yankee Station, the nickname for the area in the Gulf of Tonkin where the carriers prepared for a strike on the north.[9]

Sharp's operational order called for Air Force F–105s based in Thailand to hit the Chap Le barracks, and the Navy's carrier aircraft to strike the Vit Thu Lu and Dong Hoi barracks.[10] As a precautionary measure, the JCS directed certain commanders in the United States and Asia to alert their air and ground units for possible deployment to Southeast Asia or nearby Pacific bases: ten tactical fighter squadrons from the Commander in Chief, Strike Command (CINCSTRIKE); thirty B–52s for conventional bombing from the Commander in Chief, Strategic Air Command (CINCSAC); and the Marine airbase defense battalions based in Okinawa, two Marine amphibious groups, and the Army's 173d Airborne Brigade from CINCPAC.[11]

The first U.S. aircraft were scheduled to hit their targets at about three in the afternoon Saigon time. However, with the onset of the northeast monsoon, which each year from mid-October to mid-March battered the coastal and delta regions from about 12 degrees north in South Vietnam northward into North

15

An A–4 on the deck of the USS *Hancock*.

Vietnam and made for poor flying weather, General Moore was forced to cancel the scheduled Farm Gate* air strikes by the Air Force and VNAF on Chap Le and Vu Con respectively. The Vit Thu Lu barracks, one of two Navy targets, was also scrubbed due to bad weather after a fleet of thirty-four aircraft had been launched from the attack carrier *Ranger*. The second Navy target at Dong Hoi was struck, however. Lying slightly north of the demilitarized zone (DMZ) that divided North and South Vietnam, the target area consisted of 275 barracks and administrative buildings and housed 12,500 troops of North Vietnam's 352d Division as well as four other battalions.

Supported by twenty other aircraft, twenty-nine A–4s were launched from the carriers *Coral Sea* and *Hancock* and briefly blasted the barracks with 250-pound bombs, 2.75-inch rockets, and a few Zunis. The JCS had prohibited the use of napalm. Subsequent bomb damage assessment (BDA) showed sixteen buildings destroyed and six damaged. The Flaming Dart strike was not without penalty: apparently on the alert for air strike, the North Vietnamese downed one A–4E with pilot and damaged seven other aircraft with antiaircraft and small arms fire.[12]

Although the JCS and the service commanders in Honolulu and Saigon wished to continue the air strikes, the President held his decision in abeyance. At eight o'clock on the morning of February 8, he again conferred with the NSC to determine whether the three targets that had not been struck should be

---

* Farm Gate was the name for the Air Force personnel and aircraft that deployed to South Vietnam in 1961. Based at Bien Hoa AB, the original purpose was training of South Vietnamese, but Farm Gate began to conduct combat missions more frequently as the war intensified. Flown by U.S. Air Force pilots, the aircraft carried South Vietnamese insignia and had a South Vietnamese crew member on each flight.

F–102s at Tan Son Nhut Air Base, 1966.

attacked. The NSC consensus was "no" and he agreed. "We all felt," the President recalls, "that a second daytime strike by U.S. planes might give Hanoi and Moscow the impression that we had begun a sustained air offensive." But mindful of the importance Ambassador Taylor and General Westmoreland attached to VNAF participation in attacks on the north, he authorized the VNAF to strike its originally scheduled target, the Vu Con barracks. The Vietnamese government concurred.[13]

Bad weather once more foreclosed an attack at Vu Con, so a weather alternate was chosen, the Chap Le barracks near Vinh Linh, which had initially been earmarked for the Air Force. The area was a suspected enemy center for radio communications, coding, training, and liaison activities, and consisted of about 140 barracks and administration structures for North Vietnam's 270th Regiment with approximately 6,500 troops. The JCS order emphasized the importance of a successful first strike by the VNAF. To ensure its success, the service chiefs directed Farm Gate and other aircraft to provide navigational assistance, flak suppression, combat air patrol (CAP), reconnaissance, and rescue. Farm Gate pilots were directed to replace the VNAF markings on their aircraft, which had signified their combat training role in South Vietnam, with USAF insignia. They would carry no Vietnamese "student" pilots.

In preparation for the strike on Chap Le, an armada consisting of fifty-five aircraft from the VNAF, Farm Gate, and the U.S. Air Force assembled at Da Nang in northern South Vietnam. It included F–100 Super Sabres of the 90th Tactical Fighter Squadron (TFS) of the 3d Tactical Fighter Wing (TFW) which arrived on February 8 from Clark Air Base, the Philippines. The twenty-six A–1Hs from the VNAF were led by Air Vice Marshal Nguyen Cao Ky, the VNAF commander. Upon reaching the target area at 1530 Saigon time, the Skyraiders dropped 260 500-pound general-purpose bombs on the barracks. Air Force aircraft provided support in the form of six Farm Gate A–1Es, three RF–101s, six F–102s, and twenty F–100s, principally to provide BDA, cover for rescue, and flak suppression. Although JCS guidance directed only the VNAF to attack the target, the Farm Gate A–1Es of the 34th Tactical Group, led by Lt. Col. Andrew

H. Chapman, flew an unscheduled strike to ensure the success of the VNAF mission. Behind the VNAF aircraft, Farm Gate pilots hit portions of the Chap Le barracks, while supporting F–100s flying in an antiflak role dumped about 30,000 pounds of ordnance on enemy antiaircraft sites. This was the first Air Force strike on North Vietnam and the only time when A–1E Skyraiders were used against the north.

Although visibility was good, the first VNAF-Farm Gate effort inflicted relatively little damage on the Chap Le barracks, destroying nine buildings and damaging thirteen. This was roughly 16 percent of the 140 buildings in the area, well below the 68 percent destruction and damage figure that was hoped for considering the size of the ordnance loads. In a poststrike assessment, Colonel Chapman said the VNAF erred by splitting its forces so that it became impossible to achieve total target destruction.

For their part, North Vietnamese gunners penalized the VNAF by shooting down one A–1H with pilot, who was quickly rescued, and damaging sixteen other Skyraiders, chiefly with 30- and 50-caliber small arms fire. Only one of Colonel Chapman's A–1Es suffered damage, a hole in the right wing flap caused by a 30-caliber shot.[14]

The announcement by Washington of the U.S. and Vietnamese reprisal air strikes elicited reaction from abroad and at home. As the strikes began, a White House statement charged Hanoi with the Viet Cong attacks at Pleiku and elsewhere, because it had taken "a more aggressive course of action against South Vietnam and American installations," and Americans assisting the South Vietnamese people to defend their freedoms. "We have no choice now," ran the statement, "but to clear the decks and make absolutely clear our continued determination to back South Vietnam in its fight to maintain its independence." Simultaneously, the President announced that all American dependents (numbering about 1,800) would be withdrawn from South Vietnam and that a Marine Hawk air defense battalion would reinforce the air defense of the important Da Nang Air Base.[15]

In an emotionally charged televised news conference on February 7, Secretary McNamara characterized the Viet Cong attacks as "a test and challenge to which the United States could not fail to respond without misleading the North Vietnamese of the American strength and purpose." He charged that captured documents and prisoner of war reports showed how Hanoi stepped up infiltration. Twice the number of infiltrators entered the south in 1964 compared with 1963, he said, and intelligence sources indicated that the attacks at Pleiku, Tuy Hoa, and Nha Trang were "ordered and directed, and masterminded directly from Hanoi."[16]

The next day, before a Boy Scout delegation in the Capitol, the President stressed the dangers of miscalculating the character and strength of young Americans, adding: "We shall take up any challenge...answer any threat...pay any price...to make certain freedom shall not perish from this earth."[17]

Da Nang Air Base, 1965.

Communist reaction to the Flaming Dart strikes was defiant. The Hanoi government denounced the air attacks as "a new and utterly grave act of war," for which the United States "must bear full responsibility for all consequences arising from its aggressive and war-seeking policy in this area."[18] In Peking, one million Chinese reportedly demonstrated against the United States.[19] In Moscow, a mob of about 2,000, led by Asian and Russian students, attacked the American Embassy;[20] and in separate statements the Chinese and Soviet governments vowed that they would not fail to aid North Vietnam.[21] A few days later, U Thant, Secretary General of the United Nations, attempted to dampen the fire of escalated warfare. He called on all parties in the conflict "to move from the field of battle to the conference table," inside or outside the United Nations, and to refrain from any new acts that could lead to further expansion of the conflict.[22]

In Washington on the morning of February 8, the President met with NSC members to assess domestic and foreign reaction to Flaming Dart, and to review a report prepared by McGeorge Bundy and his group following their conferences with Ambassador Taylor and General Westmoreland. Bundy's report provided a rationale for continuing the air strikes. It characterized the internal situation in South Vietnam as "grim" and "deteriorating," and warned that without new U.S. measures defeat appeared "inevitable" within a year or so. To halt the military and political decline, the report proposed a "graduated and continuing reprisal" against North Vietnam:

Gen. William C. Westmoreland, Commander, U.S. Military Assistance Command, Vietnam.

We believe that the best available way of increasing our chance of success in Vietnam is the development and execution of a policy of sustained reprisal against North Vietnam policy in which air and naval action against the north is justified by and related to the whole Viet Cong campaign of violence and terror in the south.

The report stopped short of recommending an all-out air campaign:

[The] reprisal policy should begin at a low level. Its level of force and pressure should be increased only gradually and as indicated above it should be decreased if VC terror visibly decreases. The object would not be to "win" an air war against Hanoi but rather to influence the course of struggle in the south.

The NSC endorsed the report unanimously. However, Bundy and some of the President's other advisers remained sharply divided regarding the pace and purpose of the initial air strikes. While he agreed with Bundy that the strikes should begin gradually, Ambassador Taylor believed that their ultimate objective should be to force North Vietnam to "cease its intervention" in South Vietnam. The Joint Chiefs, particularly General McConnell, the Air Force Chief of Staff, favored a series of air strikes that would begin vigorously and would knock the Hanoi regime out of the war.[23]

President Johnson adopted the gradual approach favored by Taylor and Bundy. On the same day, February 7, he informed the Ambassador that he planned to begin a program of "continuing action" against the north "with

Farm Gate aircraft at Bien Hoa Air Base in 1962: on the right,
a T–28; next to it, a B–26; and in the background, a row of T–6s.

modifications up and down in tempo and scale in light of your recommendations...and our own continuing review of the situation." He asked the Ambassador to inform key South Vietnamese leaders of his thinking and his hope that the United States could work out its plans and actions with a unified and operating government.[24]

The President did not specify when the graduated strike program would begin, but on February 10, the tenacious Viet Cong again forced his hand. That evening (Saigon time), they bombed an American Army enlisted men's barracks at Qui Nhon, about 80 miles east of Pleiku, killing twenty-three Americans and wounding twenty-one, and killing seven Vietnamese. President Johnson again summoned the NSC. After reviewing the details of the attack, McNamara, the JCS, and General Westmoreland (from Saigon) all urged another prompt retaliatory air strike. However, some NSC attendees, notably Under Secretary of State George Ball and Ambassador Llewellyn Thompson, suggested that it be postponed until after Soviet Premier Kosygin had left Hanoi. Vice President Hubert Humphrey expressed "mixed emotions" about a fast response. After weighing the arguments, the President determined that another air strike was necessary. In deference to Kosygin's presence in Hanoi, the President deleted a bridge target only seventy-five miles south of the North Vietnamese capital.[25]

The strike order, again relayed by an execute message from the JCS to CINCPAC, contained two primary targets, the Chanh Hoi and the Vu Con barracks, and two alternate targets to allow for bad weather, the Dong Hoi and Chap Le barracks areas. All were in the southernmost part of North Vietnam. In the operational order to his subordinate commanders, CINCPAC nicknamed the upcoming assault Flaming Dart II and designated Navy air to strike the barracks at Chanh Hoi and the VNAF to attack Vu Con. As in the first strike, the Air Force's Farm Gate unit was directed to fly cover for the VNAF. Last-minute changes in the target selection process, mostly in Washington, created havoc with planning at PACOM, PACAF, Thirteenth Air Force, MACV, and 2d Air Division headquarters. The 2d Air Division was again responsible for coordinating joint operations by the Navy, the Air Force, and the VNAF. At the same time, the JCS directed four and one half Air Force tactical squadrons to deploy to Southeast Asia on February 10.*[26]

Flaming Dart II

The Flaming Dart II strike was not launched until late on February 11 Saigon time and, as noted, it was again principally a U.S. Navy and VNAF operation. Ninety-seven Navy aircraft, of which seventy-one had a strike role, left the carriers *Coral Sea*, *Hancock*, and *Ranger* for Chanh Hoi. They hit the area at two forty in the afternoon. About two hours later, twenty-eight VNAF A–1H Skyraiders carried out a second strike on Chap Le barracks, supported by thirty-two USAF aircraft, mostly F–100s flying flak suppression and combat air patrol and RF–101s. The attack at Vu Con had again been postponed due to poor weather. The Skyraiders dropped about 168 260-pound fragmentation bombs, an equal number of 250-pound fragmentation bombs, and an equal number of 250-pound general-purpose bombs on the target area. In their supporting role, the Air Force F–100s struck several enemy antiaircraft sites containing 37-mm and 57-mm guns.[27]

As with Flaming Dart I, the task of coordinating the strike was immensely complex for General Moore's 2d Air Division headquarters. MACV exercised operational control of Air Force activities in South Vietnam but, as noted ear-

---

* The deployments consisted of one squadron each of F–100 Super Sabres and F–105 Thunderchiefs from Japan and Okinawa respectively to Da Nang AB, South Vietnam; two similar squadrons to the Thai airbases at Takhli and Korat; eight B–57s from Clark AB in the Philippines to Bien Hoa AB, South Vietnam. Less than 24 hours later, the JCS ordered the Strategic Air Command (SAC) to deploy thirty B–52s of the 2d and 320th Bomb Wings at Barksdale AFB, Louisiana, and Mather AFB, California, all modified for conventional warfare, to Andersen AFB, Guam, and to deploy thirty KC–135 refueling tankers of the 913th and 904th Refueling Squadrons to Kadena AB, Okinawa. Nicknamed Arc Light, the SAC Bombers were prepared to conduct high altitude, all-weather strikes against the north. SAC airmen arrived in Guam with twenty high priority targets in their folders and complete plans for attacking two of them: Phuc Yen airfield near Hanoi and a petroleum, oil, and lubricant (POL) facility near Haiphong. However, the SAC bombers were eventually used mainly in South Vietnam, beginning on June 18, 1965. They did not make an initial strike on Laos until December 10, 1965, and did not strike North Vietnam until September 16, 1966

F–105s on the ramp at Da Nang Air Base in 1966.

lier, CINCPAC possessed authority for operations in North Vietnam and Laos. Thus, in both Flaming Dart I and II, control was transferred briefly from MACV to CINCPAC, and back to MACV upon completion of each mission.[28]

The air strikes required that Navy and VNAF strikes be coordinated with Air Force support aircraft, with the latter flying flak suppression and cover for the A–1Es. The decision by CINCPAC to limit Air Force participation in Flaming Dart II to support for the VNAF and not to use the newly arrived F–105 Thunderchiefs at Da Nang AB, South Vietnam, perturbed the Air Force. The omission prompted protest from PACAF headquarters, but to no avail.[29]

While the decision by CINCPAC not to use USAF aircraft based in South Vietnam could be explained as an air commander's prerogative, it was political considerations that compelled the JCS to order the PACOM commander not to use USAF aircraft based in Thailand. It was disclosed later that Ambassador Graham A. Martin in Bangkok did not request the approval of the Thai government to employ the aircraft for a direct strike on North Vietnam. Since on August 7, 1964, the government had agreed to allow combat missions from its bases if they could be "plausibly denied," for diplomatic reasons Martin was reluctant to approach the Thai authorities for permission. In Vientiane, Laos, Ambassador William H. Sullivan needed the approval of the Lao government for overflights of its territory by U.S. aircraft flying from Thai bases to strike the north, but he was also reluctant to seek concurrence unless a specific U.S. request to do so was received and he could explain to Lao officials the "larger plan" of which air action would be a part.[30]

Dean Rusk, Secretary of State, 1961–1969.

The Navy attack on the Chanh Hoi barracks destroyed approximately twenty buildings and damaged three while the VNAF destroyed approximately eleven buildings and damaged thirteen at Chap Le. The results were based largely on pilot reports rather than BDA, which was poor because of smoke, haze, dust, and low clouds in the target areas.[31]

Both attacks were costly. The Navy lost three aircraft (two A–4s and one F–8). While no VNAF aircraft were lost, eighteen were damaged, and not all by enemy groundfire: in several instances, VNAF pilots bruised their aircraft by flying into their own bomb blasts. The Air Force experienced no losses and only slight damage to two F–100s. As in Flaming Dart I, North Vietnamese casualties were judged to be light or negligible.[32]

Unlike Flaming Dart I, the administration indicated that Flaming Dart II took place in retaliation not for a single enemy attack, but for a series of Viet Cong depredations since February 8, such as the attack at Qui Nhon, the mining of and attacks on the South Vietnamese rail system, the overrunning of a district town in Phuoc Long Province, and ambushes and assassinations of American and South Vietnamese civilian and military officials.[33]

Two days after Flaming Dart II, Ambassador Taylor in Saigon asserted that the aim of the air attacks was political rather than military. Thus, rather than trying to achieve "great military effect," the strikes were conducted to suggest the possibility of other and "bigger forms of reaction." American limits on air action against North Vietnam, he said, could be "set by the behavior of the Hanoi government." The objective was limited, namely "to oblige Hanoi, to persuade Hanoi to desist in its efforts to maintain the insurgency in South Vietnam."[34]

In Washington, President Johnson had already determined that there should be "bigger forms of reaction." He had so informed Ambassador Taylor on the 8th, and on the 13th he issued a memorandum outlining a plan to begin regular and measured bombing of North Vietnam in the near future.[35]

To reassure himself that he was making the right decision, the President met with most of his senior advisers on February 17, to listen to the views of former President Dwight D. Eisenhower who had been invited to attend the meeting. Eisenhower stressed the need to contain communism in Southeast Asia and said that, while bombing the north would not end infiltration into South Vietnam, it would help to achieve the goal and "weaken Hanoi's will to continue the war." Thus American policy should shift from conducting retaliatory strikes to a "campaign of pressure." The former President supported all U.S. measures to prevail, from using as many as eight U.S. divisions if necessary, to warning the Chinese and Soviets of "dire results" (such as nuclear bombing) if they openly intervened in the war. Secretary of State Dean Rusk strongly supported Eisenhower's position.

On February 19, the President finally decided to begin a campaign of regular bombing of the north, though he chose not to announce it publicly for the time being, apparently to protect his domestic programs, and to shield himself from criticism from military "hawks" in Congress and among the public, and an immediate sharp response from China, the Soviet Union, or both.[36]

South Vietnamese A–1s and T–28s.

CHAPTER 2
Planning

The two Flaming Dart strikes in February 1965 ended a protracted debate within the Johnson administration concerning the political and military risks of bombing the Democratic Republic of Vietnam (DRV). Although air strikes had not been considered seriously until Premier Ngo Dinh Diem's Saigon government was overthrown on November 1, 1963, their desirability had been under discussion since the late 1950s.

The discussions arose from several American concerns regarding activities of the DRV. Initially, they focused on the materiel and moral support provided by Hanoi to the Viet Cong in South Vietnam, and later on its support for the communist-led Pathet Lao (PL) insurgents in Laos, who threatened the Neutralist government in Vientiane. Hanoi's close relationship with the Peking and Moscow governments also gave cause for concern. Desirous of neighbors having political policies congruent with its own, China provided a continuing flow of military and economic aid to the DRV during the latter's successful war against the French in 1954, which ended with the Geneva Agreements on Vietnam, Laos, and Cambodia the same year. The Soviet Union was seeking a foothold in Southeast Asia and was accordingly increasing its military and economic assistance to the Pathet Lao and North Vietnamese.

Meanwhile, the United States had replaced the French as the dominant foreign influence in Southeast Asia after 1954, and provided South Vietnam, Laos, and Cambodia with most of their military and economic needs. Its stake in preserving the independence of the new countries was growing.

The first serious American confrontation with communists in the region occurred in Laos in the early 1960s. To settle the internal political rivalry between the Neutralist and the Pathet Lao factions, the United States led an effort to stabilize Laos by means of another Geneva Agreement, eventually signed on July 23, 1962, by fourteen nations including the United States, the People's Republic of China, the Soviet Union, and the United Kingdom. The Declaration on the Neutrality of Laos, as the agreement was called officially, recognized the existence of a coalition government of rightists, neutralists, and communists under Premier Souvanna Phouma; it also called for the withdrawal of all foreign troops, and forbade a neutral Laos from joining a foreign military alliance, granting military bases, or taking other actions that could directly or indirectly "impair the sovereignty, independence, neutrality, unity or territorial integrity" of the country. The new Laotian Agreement would be enforced by the International Control Commission, which had been established in 1954 to enforce the provisions of the 1954 Geneva Accords on Indochina and consisted of representatives from India, Canada, and Poland.[1]

Unfortunately, mutual suspicions and the actions of the foreign antagonists in Laos could not be overcome. The United States withdrew its military mission

Gen. Vang Pao,
Laotian Meo commander.

from Vientiane but quietly continued to support a Laotian guerrilla army commanded by Meo Gen. Vang Pao and a small neutralist military group headed by a Capt. Kong Le. The Hanoi regime withdrew only some of the 9,000 to 10,000 men deployed in Laos. By September of 1962, an estimated 6,000 North Vietnamese Army (NVA) troops were still encamped throughout the country and continued to exert considerable influence over the Pathet Lao faction headed by Prince Souphanouvong, a half-brother of Neutralist Premier Souvanna Phouma. Although the Pathet Lao maintained a liaison mission in Vientiane after 1962, it refused to cooperate with Souvanna's government and, indeed, attempted to undermine it with forays against government ground units. As a consequence, the United States resumed its military assistance to Vientiane, but to prevent an open breach of the 1962 agreement, the aid was limited and unannounced.[2]

Paramilitary Activities and Bombing Plans

Besides the assaults of the PL-NVA on the Vientiane government, Washington was also perturbed that Hanoi was funneling manpower and supplies through southern Laos to insurgents in South Vietnam. To discourage this activity, and to collect intelligence and harass the new communist government in Hanoi, in 1954 the United States, in concert with the British, the French, and other allies, began to carry out small paramilitary activities against the north. American activities were conducted by a Saigon Military Mission, which was supported by the CIA and headed by Edward G. Lansdale, an Air Force

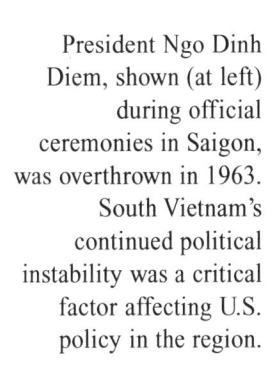

President Ngo Dinh Diem, shown (at left) during official ceremonies in Saigon, was overthrown in 1963. South Vietnam's continued political instability was a critical factor affecting U.S. policy in the region.

colonel.[3] However, the activities in the ensuing months and years did not appreciably deter the leaders in Hanoi from strengthening their position in the north and providing assistance to Viet Cong insurgents in South Vietnam.

By 1960, as the military and political travails of the Saigon government worsened, the United States had decided to step up paramilitary operations "to do to the north what it was doing to the south." From June 1960 until the early summer of 1962, the CIA office in Saigon, headed by William E. Colby, trained more South Vietnamese paramilitary personnel for limited assaults on the north. To perform this task, Colby's office was augmented by former members of the U.S. Air Force, Navy, and Army Special Forces who were variously skilled in night flying, coastal landings, and "living off the land" in enemy territory. Two air organizations were enlisted for the operations: the South Vietnamese Air Force, trained by the USAF and commanded by Nguyen Cao Ky, and a newly organized CIA proprietor called the Vietnamese Air Transport, Inc., or "VIET," which recruited aircrews from among Chinese pilots who had been trained by the USAF and were living in Taiwan.[4]

By early 1961, the VNAF and VIET aircrews were occasionally dropping specially trained and equipped South Vietnamese personnel into isolated North Vietnamese areas. The personnel expanded intelligence-collecting activities where possible and engaged in small-scale sabotage of industrial and transportation facilities, as did South Vietnamese "frogmen" who landed in coastal areas. The frequency of missions flown to drop leaflets containing anticommunist and anti-infiltration propaganda increased, as did "black" radio broadcasts from South Vietnam. There was one aerial mishap when a plane was downed in the north and some members of the aircrews and paramilitary personnel were captured. Hanoi managed to obtain highly publicized confessions from them all.[5]

The small but slowly expanding CIA operations against the north were accompanied by deepening U.S. concern about the military and political viability of the Diem government. There was also high-level debate in the administration concerning harsher measures against the north, possibly the threat of bombing. Some officials believed that such a threat might persuade Hanoi's leaders to cease and desist from their support of insurgent factions in South Vietnam and Laos. Gen. Maxwell D. Taylor, President Kennedy's Special Military Representative, and Walt W. Rostow, Deputy Assistant for National Security Affairs, led a presidential mission to Saigon in October 1961. The mission studied Diem's requirements and concluded that American ground commitment could be held to a maximum of six divisions or 205,000 men, because the north was "extremely vulnerable to conventional bombing." The mission also informed Mr. Colby, the CIA chief in Saigon, that the CIA's recently expanded air, sea, and ground forays against the north should be transferred gradually to Defense Department agencies, with CIA operatives limited to a supporting role. According to General Taylor, this decision flowed from an important "lesson" of the unsuccessful Bay of Pigs operation organized by the CIA in April 1961 against the regime of Premier Fidel Castro of Cuba. The lesson was that the CIA possessed neither the staff nor the logistic backup to undertake large and difficult military-style operations.*[6]

Taylor's decision was not immediately implemented, however, and interagency debate over the merits of the transition continued for many months. MACV did not assume control of the covert operations until the beginning of 1964.

Other important recommendations of the Taylor mission called for the dispatch of additional U.S. Air Force, Army, Navy, and Marine advisory units and more assistance for the economic and pacification programs to bolster the embattled Diem regime in Saigon. Secretary McNamara generally endorsed the mission's recommendations and sent them to President Kennedy on November 8, 1961. As the military deployments began, the Defense Secretary advised the President that Hanoi should be informed that "we mean business" and warned "that continued support of the Viet Cong will lead to punitive retaliation."[7]

---

* At the request of President Kennedy, Taylor had conducted the official postmortem of the Bay of Pigs operation [see Taylor's *Swords and Plowshares* (New York, 1972), Chap 13]. Colby observes that the CIA planned and supported rather sizeable and successful operations in Laos on behalf of Meo Gen. Vang Pao's troops and guerrillas and also aided in recruiting, training, and supervising tribal teams for intelligence collection and air targeting, which disproved Taylor's conclusion about the CIA's capabilities [William E. Colby and Peter Forbath, *Honorable Men: My Life in the CIA* (New York, 1978), pp 174 and 200–201].

Other officials and analysts were less sanguine about altering Hanoi's behavior by more visible American support for the Diem regime or a bombing threat. Some in the Office of the Secretary of Defense (OSD) believed that the dispatch of additional U.S. military units to the south would prompt Hanoi's leaders to increase their assistance to the Viet Cong, to which the United States would react, in turn, by deploying three or more divisions to South Vietnam. The authors of a special national intelligence estimate (SNIE) of November 5 viewed a U.S. threat or decision to bomb the north as a mistake. This, they said, would not only fail to end Hanoi's support for the insurgency, but would also probably strengthen determination on the part of Peking and Moscow to defend their ally.[8]

Despite uncertainty over how the DRV and its two principal communist allies would view increased American military pressure on the north, at an early date administration leaders had compiled a series of possible actions. A conference in Honolulu in December 1961 attended by McNamara and other ranking officials reviewed these actions, including aerial photoreconnaissance to detect any significant DRV military buildup, harassing strikes patterned after North Korea's Bedcheck Charlie flights of the Korean War,* interdiction of logistics routes between Techepone and South Vietnam used to resupply the Viet Cong, airdropping of "booby trap" and other ordnance in selected areas, and airlifting more South Vietnamese or Chinese nationalist special forces teams into and out of the north for intelligence gathering and more intensive sabotage and harassing operations. Apparently, small-scale air activity could be conducted safely as Hanoi appeared to have no air force or ground-controlled intercept capability, and its thin air defense radar system could be avoided by flying below 5,000 feet.[9]

A decision on these options was deferred pending a more concerted American effort to deal with the Viet Cong within South Vietnam. In December 1961, in accordance with the recommendations of General Taylor, Mr. Rostow, and Mr. McNamara, President Kennedy directed the deployment of the first U.S. air, ground, and naval combat advisory units to South Vietnam to bolster the Diem government's military and internal security forces. One of the first units was an Air Force special air warfare detachment nicknamed "Farm Gate." On February 8, 1962, the Kennedy administration displayed further determination to deal forcefully with the Viet Cong insurgency by establishing the

---

* These were missions flown by North Korean pilots in a flimsy Po–2 propeller aircraft over the Seoul area, usually after midnight. By flying at very low altitude, the aircraft usually escaped detection on antiaircraft radar scopes. Although they dropped bombs, the pilots accomplished little, yet were considered "a small but very agonizing thorn in the side of the United Nations force." Air Force and Marine pilots succeeded in shooting a few of them down. See Robert F. Futrell, *The United States Air Force in Korea, 1950–1953* (Ofc AF Hist, 1983), pp 310–11 and 662–66.

U.S. Military Assistance Command, Vietnam with Army Lt. Gen. Paul D. Harkins as commander and Air Force Brig. Gen. Rollen H. Anthis as commander of the 2d ADVON (advanced echelon), soon thereafter renamed 2d Air Division, as the Air Force component in General Harkins' command. For a brief period in the ensuing months, the increased advisory training for South Vietnam's armed forces and other internal security organizations appeared to augur eventual success.[10]

Of course, prudence dictated the preparation of contingency plans in the event that North Vietnam or China or both attempted to overrun South Vietnam and other parts of the region. As was customary, the Joint Chiefs assigned this task to Adm. Harry D. Felt's Pacific Command (PACOM) headquarters which prepared a series of plans. Operations Plan 33-62 called for direct and progressively heavier Air Force and Navy operations against the north but was sufficiently flexible to permit a wide range of covert activities. To stabilize the military situation in Laos should the need arise, in 1963 PACOM prepared Operations Plan 99-64, which required selective air and naval assaults against Hanoi. A more comprehensive Operations Plan 32-64 provided for air, naval, and ground defense against a combined Chinese and North Vietnamese thrust against mainland Southeast Asia, defined as the countries of South Vietnam, Laos, Cambodia, Thailand, Malaysia, and Singapore. The manpower, aircraft, and materiel needed by CINCPAC to execute the plans were spelled out in considerable detail in supporting plans prepared by PACOM's service components, Pacific Air Forces (PACAF), Pacific Fleet (PACFLT), and U.S. Army, Pacific (USARPAC).[11]

Throughout 1962, American officials believed the outlook for containing the Viet Cong was promising, despite occasional military setbacks. However, the weakness of the Diem government's armed forces contrasted sharply with the energy and perseverance of the insurgents, backed by the Hanoi regime's political and limited materiel support. As a consequence, in January 1963 the JCS sent an investigative team to South Vietnam to review the military situation. The teams were led by Gen. Earle G. Wheeler, Army Chief of Staff, and Lt. Gen. David A. Burchinal, Assistant Chief of Staff for Plans and Operations, Headquarters USAF.

After its return to Washington, the JCS team warned that Hanoi possessed the resources and "latitude of choice," in aiding the Viet Cong, and could readily increase its supporting role. The disquieting circumstances in the south warranted more American actions against the northerners "...it is not realistic," the team said, "to ignore the fact we have given Ho Chi Minh [no] evidence...we are prepared to call him to account for helping to keep the insurgency in South Vietnam alive." The North Vietnamese should be made to "bleed." What should be done? The CIA's small intelligence-gathering and sabotage forays were too minor, but a precipitous air attack would be "too grave" a step. The alternative was for MACV to develop a South Vietnamese unconventional warfare capabil-

President John Fitzgerald Kennedy.

ity for launching "a coordinated program of sabotage, destruction, propaganda, and subversive missions against the north. This would "consume communist resources" and prevent the north from giving its undivided attention to the southern insurgency. In short, it was a restatement of Taylor's recommendation in late 1961 to transfer CIA's expanding paramilitary operations to the services.

The JCS team chafed over existing U.S. political restrictions that barred unilateral activities in the theater. The Viet Cong and its supporters enjoyed a "privileged sanctuary" in Laos and Cambodia, it observed, and in December 1962 Washington halted RF–101 photoreconnaissance missions over Laos and along the North Vietnamese border.*[12]

As no immediate action was taken on the JCS team's recommendations, the services continued to examine ways to combat the Viet Cong insurgency more effectively. An Army study, completed in April 1963, proposed airborne and amphibious "hit and run" raids under the cover of a "National Liberation Army of the North," which the United States would help organize. The purpose of the raids would be more psychological than political. Admiral Felt noted, however, that the study complemented part of his Operations Plan 33-62, providing for American and South Vietnamese personnel to conduct limited overt operations. Under the Navy plan, specially trained Navy units would harass the North Vietnamese

---

* In April 1961, the Air Force began flying intermittent RF–101 reconnaissance missions along the border between Laos and North Vietnam to determine the extent of communist movements into Laos and South Vietnam. (See Jacob Van Staaveren, *Interdiction in Southern Laos, 1960–1968,* (Center AF Hist, 1994), p 5.

Gen. Earle G. Wheeler,
Chairman, Joint Chiefs of Staff,
1964-1970.

coastal installations by mining or possibly sinking a ship in Haiphong channel, and the Air Force would use its Farm Gate or other aircraft for airdropping personnel into North Vietnam and subsequently retrieving them. A few important North Vietnamese targets might also be struck by VNAF or U.S. aircraft.[13]

In the same month, in conjunction with a review of the military situation in Laos, where PL-DRV units had recently made gains against Laotian government forces, the Joint Chiefs urged President Kennedy to convey a sharp warning to Hanoi by bombing eight key targets in the north: Dong Hoi and Vinh airfields, a Haiphong thermal power plant, a steel rolling mill, separate chemical and POL storage facilities, and two highway bridges. The attacks would be conducted by USAF aircraft based in Thailand and some carrier-based aircraft. However, the President withheld his assent.[14]

Nonetheless, the bombing proposal remained alive and was discussed again, along with plans to step up covert activities against the Hanoi regime, on May 6, 1963, during another conference in Honolulu, which was attended by Secretaries McNamara and Rusk, JCS Chairman Taylor, General Wheeler, Admiral Felt, General Harkins, Frederick C. Nolting (U.S. Ambassador to Saigon), and other officials. Felt and Nolting strongly believed that circumstances warranted a series of air strikes, possibly against more than the initial eight targets. The Ambassador predicted that the air assault might hinder activities by the north in Laos. McNamara indicated that the President still believed such action was untimely, but asked Felt to include the targets in his contingency planning documents.

In a review of the ongoing covert air, ground, and sea operations against the north, it was evident that the CIA's involvement had not been phased out, as ordered by General Taylor in late 1961.* In fact, the issue was still being debated. General Wheeler believed MACV (i.e., the Army) should control such activities using non-U.S. personnel, and he clearly stated the difficulty of establishing any South Vietnamese support movement in the north such as the Viet Cong had in the south. On the other hand, Admiral Felt believed the CIA station in Saigon should continue to have chief responsibility for applying covert pressure on the Hanoi regime, noting that it had placed nine specially-trained teams in the DRV and had trained twenty-five teams for airdropping. The agency accomplished this, he noted, while complying with Washington's injunction not to use Laotian territory as a "back door" for attacking the north. If MACV were to take over these activities, he averred, this would contravene present American policy, which stated that U.S. commanders and forces were assisting South Vietnam solely in an advisory role. McNamara indicated that the existing policy might be changed and directed another review of the restrictions imposed on special military activities against the north.[15]

Two days after the conclusion of the conference, long simmering internal dissent against the Diem government flared into Buddhist protest marches in Saigon, and then in other cities, and disorder spread to the universities and high schools. Numerous monks and students were killed and wounded, and others were arrested in clashes with police. American officials in Saigon and Washington were divided over the best way to suppress the Viet Cong insurgency. Some believed that the United States could no longer "win with Diem" whose powers were being increasingly preempted by his brother Nhu.[16]

In the ensuing weeks, as South Vietnam's instability increased and U.S. concern grew over a resurgence of PL-DRV activities in neighboring Laos, the JCS cooperated with CINCPAC and his component commanders to step up planning against North Vietnam. On May 22, the Joint Chiefs approved a concept for "hit and run" raids, although Gen. Curtis E. LeMay, the Air Force Chief of Staff, believed considerably stronger measures were required. Admiral Felt updated his Operations Plan 33-62 against the north, now renumbered Plan 33-63, and at the request of McNamara and the JCS he prepared a new Operations Plan 99-64.[17]

Operations Plan 99-64 called for another series of actions to strengthen the combat capabilities of the Laotian and South Vietnamese governments in the face of enemy infiltration and to penalize the north with threatening or punitive action. The last envisaged air and naval gunfire strikes, aerial mining of certain harbors, airborne and amphibious raids, and at its most severe, a maritime

---

* Taylor left his post as military representative of the president to become Chairman of the JCS on October 1, 1962.

Secretary of Defense Robert S. McNamara speaking during a visit to Tan Son Nhut Air Base in 1964. Gen. Maxwell Taylor, chairman, Joint Chiefs of Staff, and Henry Cabot Lodge, U.S. Ambassador to Vietnam, are to his left.

blockade of North Vietnamese ports. As usual, PACAF, PACFLT, and USARPAC prepared supporting plans.[18]

To the relief of administration officials, the Laotian crisis subsided quickly, the annual monsoon rains helping to dampen military operations. South Vietnam's tribulations continued, however, although McNamara, JCS chairman Taylor, and others still believed that most "war progress" indicators augured eventual success for the U.S. combat advisory, economic, and other measures introduced over the past 18 months. To underscore their optimism, they announced plans to reduce the advisory force by 1,000 men by the end of 1963. Against the north, South Vietnamese and Chinese Nationalists, trained and supported by the U.S. continued their low-level intelligence collecting, sabotage, leaflet dropping, and harassment activities in cooperation with the U.S. Air Force and Navy. Admiral Felt and his component commanders made sure their contingency plans for an overt attack on the country remained current.[19]

Unhappily, South Vietnam's internal problems after mid-1963 only intensified, peaking on November 1 when a group of South Vietnamese officers, led by Maj. Gen. Duong "Big" Minh overthrew the Diem regime. President Diem and his brother Nhu were killed, leaving General Minh and a collegium of fellow officers to take over the government. Washington underwent its own trauma twenty-two days later when President Kennedy was assassinated and Vice President Lyndon B. Johnson succeeded to the presidency. On November 26, after a quick review of the situation in South Vietnam, Mr. Johnson issued National Security Memorandum (NSAM) 273, which presaged further actions against the communists in Laos as well as in North Vietnam.[20]

NSAM 273 demonstrated the continuity of American policy in Southeast Asia and authorized more military and economic assistance for the new Minh government. It also solicited plans from the JCS for stepping up clandestine activity against the north, and for launching ground incursions up to 50 kilometers across infiltration routes in southern Laos.[21]

In mid-December, President Johnson sent McNamara and John McCone, the CIA director, to Saigon to meet with General Harkins, the MACV commander, and Henry Cabot Lodge, who had succeeded Nolting as ambassador in August, to assess the new government's ability to combat the insurgency, and then to determine what additional pressures could be applied to North Vietnam. On his return to Washington on December 21, the Defense Secretary warned Mr. Johnson that unless the United States immediately reduced the infiltration of men and weapons through Laos, there was real danger of neutralization or communist control of the country. He recommended measures that exceeded those mandated by NSAM 273, such as bolstering the new Minh regime with more advisory assistance, mapping the Laotian and Cambodian borders using SAC U–2 reconnaissance aircraft, and launching a twelve-month program of increased intelligence collection, sabotage, and psychological warfare activities against North Vietnam, to be carried out chiefly by MACV rather than CIA. In preparation for this responsibility, MACV, with CIA assistance, had prepared an Operations Plan 34A, dated December 15, 1963, which described four major categories of activities: harassing, attritional, punitive, and aerial. As before, the operations would be conducted by specially trained South Vietnamese tribesmen, South Vietnamese special forces, Chinese Nationalists, and other personnel. The military assets of the 2d Air Division, MACV, and the Vietnamese Air Force, Army, and Navy would all be enlisted directly to execute the plan.[22]

President Johnson approved most of Secretary McNamara's recommendations. To oversee the implementation of the measures outlined in the plan 34A, Mr. Johnson created an interdepartmental committee, composed of representatives of the Defense and State Departments and the CIA and chaired by Marine Maj. Gen. Victor H. Krulak, Special Assistant for Counterinsurgency and Special Activities in the JCS. He instructed the new organization to select activities that promised the greatest return with the least risk.

In January 1964, the committee proposed an initial four-month program against North Vietnam consisting of eighteen sabotage missions by teams that would enter either by airdrop or on foot, special naval operations, nineteen U–2 reconnaissance and four aerial communications electronic missions performed by SAC, and more intensive leaflet distribution and radio propaganda broadcasts. The President quickly approved these measures. The U.S. National Board of Estimates predicted that Peking's reaction to these activities would be slight as long as they avoided Haiphong and China. Some Washington analysts speculated (wrongly in retrospect) that the Hanoi regime might construe the measures as a threat, and perhaps agree to convene an international conference to settle the conflict before it grew any further.[23]

To carry out its new mandate for covert operations, on January 24, 1964, MACV established a Special Operations Group (MACSOG) with CIA in a supporting role. MACSOG was accorded the status of a special staff section under the oversight of MACV J-5. The new section quickly divided its activities into five categories: air and airborne, maritime, psychological, intelligence, and logistic. As already noted, manpower, aircraft, and other resources for the special organization would be drawn from all of the services.[24]

With the approval of the Minh government and its successor, headed by Maj. Gen. Nguyen Khanh, who replaced Minh in a bloodless coup on January 30, 1964, on February 1, the United States with its South Vietnamese and other allies began to apply further, low-level military and psychological pressure on the north. Starting on the 13th, two SAC U–2 aircraft, nicknamed Lucky Dragon, were used to fly two sorties a day over parts of Laos, Cambodia, and South Vietnam. The aircraft belonged to the 4080th Strategic Wing, and had deployed from the United States to Clark AB in the Philippines. Their purpose was to map more accurately the boundaries of these countries and to pick up intelligence on communist activity in the photographed areas. On March 5, the U–2 unit moved to Bien Hoa AB in South Vietnam. Photography quickly provided new evidence of DRV military activities close to the Plain of Jars in northern Laos, and confirmed the inaccuracy of recent government statements that 8,000 strategic hamlets had been established in the pacification program.[25]

In another action, starting on February 28 and continuing into March, the Seventh Fleet resumed De Soto* patrols, using the destroyer USS *Craig*. The patrol was intended to provide "a show of force," and to collect visual, electronic, and photographic data on infiltration by sea from the north into South Vietnam. The ship was authorized to approach within four nautical miles (n.m.) of the North Vietnamese mainland, but instructed to remain fifteen n.m. from the Chinese mainland and twelve n.m. from Chinese-held islands.[26]

By March and April of 1964, with Washington watching closely, the low-level activities of Plan 34A were conducted as regularly as weather conditions permitted. SAC U–2s continued mapping and intelligence-gathering missions. VNAF RT–28s and RC–47s flew photo and electronic reconnaissance missions respectively, and its C–47s, T–28s, A–1Hs, and H–34s airdropped and supplied small intelligence and harassing teams and distributed propaganda leaflets and gift kits. During one night operation in early April, for example, the aircraft dropped 1,350,000 leaflets and 2,000 gift kits. Farm Gate T–28s, B–26s, C–47s, and C–123s occasionally participated in these activities, though pilots were very careful not to venture too deeply into North Vietnamese airspace. Supported by Seventh Fleet personnel and resources, the Vietnamese Navy

---

* De Soto patrols had been conducted off the North Vietnamese coast periodically since April 1962 (see Chapter 1).

Gen. Maxwell D. Taylor, Chairman, Joint Chiefs of Staff, 1962–1964, and Ambassador to South Vietnam, 1964–1965.

stepped up its maritime operations. These consisted of commando raids by PT boats to blow up rail and highway bridges and bombardment of coastal installations.[27]

Operation Hardnose was also intensified. This was a program of attacks by specially trained South Vietnamese on DRV men and supplies as they moved down the Ho Chi Minh Trail toward South Vietnam. U.S. officials briefly encouraged the South Vietnamese and Laotian governments to cooperate more in these intelligence-gathering and harassing activities, but the political and military weaknesses of both, as well as Laos' traditional distrust of the Vietnamese, brought an early end to such joint operations. American officials were further disquieted by the considerable publicity that accompanied the planning of the anti-infiltration program. Although sporadic air and ground attacks along the Trail increased, they were the result of separate programs backed by the United States, rather than joint operations by the Vientiane and Saigon governments.[28]

Rising Pressure from the Services to Bomb the North

However, the expansion of MACV Plan 34A against the Hanoi regime failed to reduce pressure for more aggressive measures against the communists, inside and outside of South Vietnam. On January 22, 1964, in a delayed response to the President's NSAM 273 of November 26, 1963, the Joint Chiefs outlined a ten-point program of "bolder actions." The program required that the United States virtually take over the war in South Vietnam, that it commit whatever forces were necessary for this purpose, and that it increase air, ground, and sea training for the South Vietnamese. Against North Vietnam, the service chiefs called for the bombing of key military targets, larger commando raids, and the mining of sea approaches. They believed these measures could be carried out under South Vietnamese "cover," while the MACV commander assumed complete responsibility. In Laos, they recommended that South Vietnamese ground operations be of sufficient size to impede the movement of men and supplies southward, and that the United States carry out tactical reconnaissance of Laos and Cambodia to obtain whatever "operational intelligence" was needed.[29]

The ten-point program was too drastic for the administration, particularly after Maj. Gen. Nguyen Khanh, the I Corps commander, and a new group of rebel officers overthrew the Minh regime in a bloodless coup on January 30, 1966. Khanh charged that Minh and his associates were contemplating the neutralization of South Vietnam in accordance with a plan outlined by President De Gaulle of France several months earlier. The coup underscored again South Vietnam's political and military weaknesses. A U.S. special national intelligence estimate of February 12 quickly warned that, unless the new government demonstrated "marked improvement," it had, at best, only a 50 percent chance of surviving the Viet Cong insurgency for the next few weeks or months.[30]

President Johnson wanted more moderate measures against the enemy and solicited the views of the JCS on revitalizing the counterinsurgency program and possible alternative military actions against North Vietnam. As McNamara explained to the service chiefs, the President wanted to examine a range of overt and covert air and sea actions that would be most likely to end Hanoi's support for the insurgencies in South Vietnam and Laos, but unlikely to escalate the conflict and draw adverse "third country" reaction.[31]

The JCS pondered the options separately and jointly. General LeMay still advocated immediate U.S. bombing of North Vietnamese targets. In the preceding month, he had made a similar proposal in more colorful and blunter language before a committee of the House of Representatives: "We are swatting flies," he said, "instead of going after the manure pile." But in their formal, joint reply on March 2, the Joint Chiefs recommended that U.S. cooperation with the South Vietnamese in military activities against the north become more direct, but remain limited. They said the Air Force's Farm Gate or regular Air Force and Navy aircraft should fly low-level reconnaissance missions over the north and Laos and armed reconnaissance missions against bridges, airfields, POL installations, and other targets along North Vietnamese supply routes leading to Laos. Work began on a combined Air Force and Navy plan to stop the aggression of Hanoi and Peking (in the event the Chinese entered the war).[32]

Martin B–57 over South Vietnam, 1966.

The joint reply had obviously muted the views of individual service chiefs. General LeMay, for example, considered the recommendations weaker than he desired, and Gen. Harold K. Johnson, the Army Chief of Staff, would have preferred to delay further military action against the north until the Saigon government's most recent efforts, with American assistance, had been given a trial. Gen. Wallace M. Greene, Jr., who succeeded Gen. David M. Shoup as Commandant of the Marine Corps at the beginning of the year, agreed with LeMay. The views of the Air Force and the Navy were not identical but the differences between them were less significant than between the Air Force and the Army.[33]

Secretary McNamara "noted" the reply and promised to consider its contents in higher level deliberations. Then, at President Johnson's request, he again traveled to Saigon in early March and conferred with General Harkins and Ambassador Lodge and their staffs concerning the U.S. advisory effort. McNamara's report to the President, made on March 16, was a detailed and doleful account of the Khanh government's military, political, and economic woes and warned that the military situation had worsened considerably since September 1963. The decline contrasted with Viet Cong territorial gains in a context of growing public apathy, increased military desertions, waning morale, and setbacks in the pacification program.

As for remedial action, the Defense Secretary said that he and his associates in Washington and Saigon "have given serious thought to all the implications and ways of carrying out directly military action against North Vietnam in order to supplement the counterinsurgency program in South Vietnam." Three categories of action were reviewed: additional border control, retaliation, and graduated overt military pressure. As the severity of the respective responses increased, each would entail more direct Air Force, Navy, and Army operations and the indirect support of the South Vietnamese military forces. The most important transition would be from the retaliatory or "tit for tat" air attacks on important industrial and other targets in North Vietnam. These would be conducted by combined VNAF, USAF Farm Gate, and three USAF squadrons of B–57s based in Japan. In advance of the last actions, which risked an escalation of the war, the United States should strengthen its military presence in the Pacific and improve air defense in South Vietnam.

When weighing alternative measures, McNamara believed the Khanh government was too weak to risk a higher level of conflict. Accordingly, he proposed a twelve-point program to arrest the government's decline. The first ten measures would improve Saigon's civil and military structure and personnel training, provide the South Vietnamese with guerrilla and paramilitary forces, and equip the VNAF with twenty-five A–1H Skyraider aircraft instead of the present force of T–28s. The last two measures provided for cautious "outcountry" actions. Under point 11, the United States would continue to fly high-altitude reconnaissance flights, using U–2s to map South Vietnam's borders. "Hot pursuit" activities by South Vietnamese forces, which followed the enemy into Laos for the purpose of border control, would be expanded, but still limited. Under point 12, military commanders were authorized to plan numerous border control actions inside Laos and Cambodia and a program of "graduated overt military pressure against North Vietnam" on thirty-days' notice. President Johnson quickly approved McNamara's recommendations that were issued on March 17 as NSAM 288. The JCS directed Admiral Felt to prepare contingency plans for conducting operations.[34]

The Defense Secretary's recommendations reflected a pervasive administration fear of an untimely escalation of the war. Secretary Rusk foresaw the possibility of Soviet diversionary moves in Berlin, the Middle East, or elsewhere if the United States applied too much pressure on the Hanoi government. The President later explained: "We did not know what secret agreements Hanoi might have worked out with Peking and Moscow." On the other hand, the President saw another justification for exercising restraint against North Vietnam in the difficult relations between the Chinese and the Soviets. The expectation of an imminent confrontation between the two communist countries, he informed Ambassador Lodge, meant that action against the north would be more "practicable" after such an event had played out.

American domestic politics also stayed the President's hand. Barry Goldwater, the Republican nominee in the presidential race, favored a considerably more aggressive policy for U.S. military involvement in Southeast Asia. On the other hand, Mr. Johnson had made numerous promises not to involve the United States in a larger war. This commitment could not be breached easily without damaging consequences for the President and his political party.[35]

There were other high officials who were more willing to risk escalation. In Saigon, Ambassador Lodge wanted to take strong punitive measures against the North Vietnamese, especially for instigating terrorist acts in South Vietnam,

A line of B–57s at Da Nang start their engines with black powder cartridges.

and make them "cease and desist from their murderous intrusion" into the country. John A. McCone, Director of CIA, was a staunch advocate of heavy air and naval strikes against the north now rather than later. The Joint Chiefs, especially General LeMay, believed the twelve-point program was inadequate and called for more vigorous air action against the communists in both North Vietnam and Laos.[36]

During mid-April, however, the consensus among the Joint Chiefs lost strength, and another paper to McNamara bore witness to the divided opinion. Generals LeMay and Greene still recommended air strikes against the north, attributing them to the VNAF if necessary, and that low-level photoreconnaissance continue. But in a shift of opinion toward that of the White House, General Taylor, the JCS Chairman, Gen. Harold K. Johnson, the Army Chief of Staff, and Adm. David L. McDonald, Chief of Naval operations (CNO), now believed heavy pressure on the north was not warranted for the time being.[37]

Selecting Major North Vietnamese Targets

As the Saigon government grew weaker, still riven with political factions and the malaise of its fighting forces, General LeMay's concern grew. In late May, in a meeting with his service colleagues, he warned that the war was being lost. He called for an end to the policy of sending "messages" in the form of the low-level military actions, in the hope that Hanoi would change its policy, and insisted on action that would destroy the regime's capability to aid the Viet Cong. In spite of more than two years of effort to convince the communists of America's will, he observed, the VC-DRV had clearly improved their military position. It was time to convey a "message" sharply and directly, and he proposed striking two targets supporting the Viet Cong and the Pathet Lao. One

Shipping in Haiphong harbor.

was the city of Vinh, just north of the demilitarized zone (DMZ), and the other was Dien Bien Phu in northeastern North Vietnam, famous as the site of the last stand of the French army in the spring of 1954. The Army, Navy, and Marine Corps chiefs agreed with the proposal and, as the acting JCS chairman (General Taylor was not in Washington at the time), LeMay sent the recommendation to Secretary McNamara on May 30.[38]

Upon his return to the Pentagon, Taylor disagreed with the JCS views submitted in his absence and prepared his own. He said the two targets, Vinh and Dien Bien Phu, were too large, required too many sorties, and hitting them would be fraught with too many risks. There were three ways, he said, to strike the north: by massive attack on all significant targets, rendering them unusable for the Viet Cong or the Pathet Lao, by smaller attacks on some significant parts of the north's target system to persuade Hanoi to cease its support for the Viet Cong and Pathet Lao or to obtain its cooperation in calling off the insurgency, and by limited attacks on smaller installations to impress upon Hanoi U.S. willingness to move to the first and second alternatives.

Taylor rejected the first alternative as unnecessarily destructive if the purpose was to change the will of the adversary as it reduced the likelihood of winning Hanoi's cooperation and "could challenge the Communist bloc and raise considerable possibility of escalation." He favored the second alternative, but sensed that political considerations would incline the President's civilian advisers to opt for the third. Thus, the JCS should prepare a plan for its possible execution.

McNamara agreed generally with Taylor's views, and on June 10 asked the JCS to prepare a three-phase strike plan ranging from "demonstrative" attacks showing U.S. readiness and intent to attacks on all significant targets within the country.[39]

The first two days of June 1964 found all of the principal U.S. military and civilian officials conferring again in Honolulu, with Secretary Rusk serving as chairman. There was more lengthy and agonizing debate over Saigon's internal problems and how to resolve them. Aside from the three service chiefs, who were not present and whose chairman, General Taylor, did not share their view, one of the loudest voices in favor of an attack on North Vietnam was Ambassador Lodge. At the plenary session of the conference, the Ambassador expressed the belief that most support for the VC would fade as soon as counter-terror measures were begun against the Hanoi regime. He called for a selective bombing campaign against military targets in the country and also in Laos, citing Techepone as an example, predicting this would bolster the morale and a feeling of unity among the South Vietnamese people and reduce quarreling among its leaders. On the other hand, Westmoreland and Taylor believed that the deterioration in the south had been arrested, obviating the need to launch a bombing campaign. McNamara and CIA Director McCone were considerably less sanguine about Saigon's future stability.[40]

The conferees discussed the possibility of Chinese intervention in the event that the United States began bombing the north. McNamara surmised that tactical air strikes might reduce the effectiveness of invading Chinese troops by 50 percent, this would not stop a large Chinese force of up to eighteen divisions. Another participant estimated that it would take five to seven U.S. and allied divisions to hold mainland Southeast Asia, but Admiral Felt said these divisions were out of "practical reach" and, in any event, the United States would deplete its bomb supply before it could defeat the Chinese. U.S. commanders would then have to resort to tactical nuclear weapons. Rusk countered that the use of nuclear bombs would be "a most serious matter," and could induce the Soviets to take diversionary military action. The discussion produced a consensus that it would be too risky to escalate air and naval action against the communists in the north and Laos for the time being, and that measures to ensure the survival of the Khanh government should have first priority. Two immediate goals were imperative: the government must be made more politically secure and the armed forces must be made more effective. Until these goals were attained, probably not before the end of 1964, U.S. military and economic programs should be strengthened. In the interim, Admiral Felt should continue to review his contingency plans for dealing with an unexpected Chinese entry into the war.[41]

In the ensuing weeks, however, planning activities for more drastic action against Hanoi and Peking were not diminished by the administration's decision to concentrate on bolstering the Saigon government. At McNamara's request, in early June the Joint Chiefs prepared data on shipping entering Haiphong harbor, plans to mine the harbor, alternate ports if Haiphong were closed, military requirements to sustain "escalation phases" of CINCPAC's Operations Plans 32-64 and 37-64, a U.S.-Thai military plan for the defense of the Mekong Delta, and plans for conducting more punitive attacks on the communists in Laos. The service chiefs also sent General Taylor a study on the ability of U.S. and allied air power to blunt a possible force of eighteen North Vietnamese and Chinese divisions advancing towards the Mekong River. At the request of both the Defense Secretary and the JCS chairman, the Joint Chiefs collaborated with CINCPAC in the preparation of a three-phase air attack plan against the north, ranging from a massive air strike on all significant military targets to limited "demonstrative" air strikes on a few targets. To carry out the latter option, Taylor asked for the number of sorties that would be needed per target if bombing was conducted solely by the VNAF; jointly by the VNAF, Farm Gate, and B–57 units; and by a combined effort of the VNAF, Farm Gate, B–57s, and other USAF and Navy aircraft.[42]

On June 15, in response to a request by McNamara, an ad hoc study group within the JCS and composed of representatives of the services and the Defense Intelligence Agency (DIA), completed an initial list of ninety-one of the most important "JCS designated" targets, and another three-phase attack scenario for use against North Vietnam. The scenario was suffused with details of types of ordnance, ordnance delivery tactics, prestrike reconnaissance needs, and anticipated aircraft attrition. Following further revisions requested by McNamara, on July 11, the study group issued a list of ninety-four targets and a four-phase attack scenario.*[43]

While supporting the list of ninety-four targets, the Air Force was nonetheless highly disenchanted with the administration's air planning.[44] Observing that some of the alternate attack plans provided for the covert use of USAF's Farm Gate aircraft and B–57s based in South Vietnam, PACAF planners argued strongly for overt attacks on the north, citing some salutary results in Laos where armed escorts of Yankee Team aircraft were now permitted to return enemy fire. PACAF was also concerned about the status of pilots captured in covert strikes, whose fate could cost the United States considerable international political capital. Gen. Jacob E. Smart, who was retiring as commander of PACAF,† believed Washington was injecting itself too deeply into the details of military activity. In a report on the worldwide military problems of the United States, but with Vietnam specifically in mind, he averred there was too much "dedicated and misguided" effort over detailed operations from too high and remote a level to permit "adequate judgment of dynamic events...."[45] For his part, General LeMay insisted that the military problems in South Vietnam

---

* A final version of the list of ninety-four targets identified by the JCS was sent to McNamara on August 24. The list also contained several hundred less important targets.

† Gen. Hunter Harris, Jr., succeeded Gen. Smart as PACAF commander on August 1, 1964.

and Laos could not be solved satisfactorily without striking the north and ensuring a "credible impact" on the Hanoi regime.[46]

As the debate continued, U.S. officials suddenly faced the possibility that Saigon's generals might make a unilateral attack on the north. On July 18, speaking before 100,000 Vietnamese in Saigon on the tenth anniversary of the division of their country (known as National Shame Day), General Khanh led the call to "Bac Tien" or "Go North." He declared that a million refugees, Buddhists, Catholics, and students wished to liberate their compatriots in the north and unite the country. The next day, the government formally made an identical threat. On July 22, Vice President Ky committed a diplomatic faux pas, stating publicly that South Vietnam had sent sabotage teams into North Vietnam and that Vietnamese pilots were receiving training on jet bombers in preparation for large-scale attacks.*[47]

General Taylor, who resigned as JCS chairman on July 2, 1964 to replace Henry Cabot Lodge as U.S. Ambassador to Saigon—and arrived there with an unusually broad presidential writ of authority for conducting the war in the south†—sought to forestall the Saigon government's "go-it-alone" policy by promising joint U.S.-South Vietnamese military planning against the Hanoi regime. A worried State Department thought South Vietnam's morale might be raised and Khanh's attention diverted if the VNAF struck communist supply lines in the Laos panhandle. But Ambassador Leonard Unger in Vientiane vetoed that proposal. He doubted whether Prime Minister Souvanna Phouma would approve participation by the Vietnamese and, if he did consent, Unger feared the air strikes would have only a marginal effect, would deepen U.S. involvement in Laos, and complicate Laos' overall political problems. The Soviet Union, Unger noted, had threatened to resign its cochairmanship (with Great Britain) of the Geneva Agreement on Laos, signed on July 23, 1962. To the relief of U.S. officialdom, the danger that Khanh's government might conduct a strike on the north soon subsided.[48]

Even as military planning continued in June and July 1964, the administration tried to strengthen its political and diplomatic hand. In speeches and news conferences, President Johnson, Secretaries Rusk and McNamara, and others sought to allay public and congressional doubts about U.S. objectives in Southeast Asia. They discussed the need for a Congressional Resolution to support U.S. policy, and William P. Bundy, Assistant Secretary of State for Far Eastern Affairs, prepared

---

* On May 9, the JCS approved B–57 training for six VNAF pilots. The first two pilots completed their training on June 27, 1964.

† Taylor was succeeded as JCS chairman by Gen. Earle G. Wheeler, the former Army Chief of Staff. Taylor's broad authority and prestige in the White House inevitably made his voice one of the most influential on every aspect of the war, including the scope and tempo of the Rolling Thunder program once it began.

drafts of such a resolution. On June 18, through J. Blair Seaborn, Canadian Representative to the International Control Commission, the administration conveyed to Hanoi its determination to maintain a noncommunist regime in Saigon and the threat of "greater devastation" to the north. Hanoi's rejoinder, also made through Mr. Seaborn, was that the government would continue its support of the Viet Cong, and the United States should withdraw from South Vietnam and permit the installation of a "neutral" regime. Between June 1964 and June 1965 Mr. Seaborn would serve as intermediary between Washington and Hanoi on five occasions, but none of his efforts to initiate discussions or negotiations to end the war proved successful.[49]

The Gulf of Tonkin Incident

The preoccupation of the United States to make the Khanh government more effective militarily and politically was interrupted briefly by a new crisis, triggered by intelligence gathering and covert actions. On July 14, 1964, to gather more North Vietnamese and Chinese communication data in the area of the Gulf of Tonkin, a detachment of specially equipped Air Force C–130Bs of the 6091st Reconnaissance Squadron deployed from Japan to Don Muang Royal Thai Air Force Base (RTAFB). Under the nickname Queen Bee, the aircraft began flying communications intercept missions. Following this, on the night of July 30–31 and under the aegis of Oplan 34A, four South Vietnamese patrol boats shelled a North Vietnamese radar station on Hon Me Island and a communication transmitter on Hon Ngu Island. Both islands lay off the coastal town of Vinh and were considered waypoints for men and supplies en route to South Vietnam.

Also on July 31, the Seventh Fleet's destroyer *Maddox* began sailing close to the North Vietnamese coast in another De Soto patrol, last conducted between February 28 and March 10. The destroyer's mission was to make a "show of force" and to collect visual and electronic intelligence. The probings of the *Maddox* were uneventful until August 2. Evidently provoked by the South Vietnamese attacks on Hon Me and Hon Ngu islands or by the intelligence collection activities of the *Maddox*—or both—the North Vietnamese sent three high-speed, armed Swatow boats to meet the American ship. They were beaten off by the *Maddox*'s guns and F–8E aircraft from the carrier *Ticonderoga*. At the time of the attack, the *Maddox* claimed it was 28 n.m. offshore and moving away from the North Vietnamese coast line.

In Washington, after discussing the attack with his advisers, the President dispatched a protest to Hanoi and ordered reinforcements for the De Soto destroyer patrol, with the *C. Turner Joy* joining the *Maddox*. On the night of August 3–4, South Vietnamese patrol boats attacked a radar station on Cape Vinh Son and a security station near Cuo Ron. Twenty-two hours later, on the night of August 4, the *Maddox* and the *C. Turner Joy*, which were then about seventy miles to the northeast, were thought to have come under fire again from North Vietnamese Swatow patrol boats. Although subsequent analyses indicated the attack probably did not occur, at the time Admiral Ulysses S. G. Sharp, who had succeeded Admiral Felt as CINCPAC on July 1, 1964,* and General Harris recommended an immediate retaliatory air strike on the north. After reviewing the details of the incident and intercepted North Vietnamese messages, the NSC and other presidential advisers were unanimous in their recommendation, and the President agreed, Hanoi must be punished with air strikes on several military targets. At the same time, the President asked Congress to pass a resolution supporting his policy in Southeast Asia.†

On August 5 (Saigon time), under code name Pierce Arrow, Navy A–1 Skyraiders, A–4 Skyhawks, and F–8 Crusaders from the *Ticonderoga* and *Constellation*, flying sixty-four sorties, struck four torpedo bases at Hon Gay, Loc Chao, Phuc Loi, and Quang Khe and an oil storage facility at Vinh. The bombs destroyed eight boats, damaged twenty-one, and wiped out about 90 percent of the oil facility, which held about 10 percent of the north's oil storage capacity. One A–1 and one A–4 were shot down over Hon Gay, resulting in the death of one Navy pilot and the capture of the other, Lt. Everett Alverez, Jr., the first U.S. airman to become a prisoner of war in North Vietnam. Two other aircraft were hit, but returned safely to their carriers. No Air Force aircraft were employed as Ambassador Martin had not secured the approval of the Thai government to use USAF aircraft based in Thailand for strikes on North Vietnam.

---

* For Adm. Sharp's account of the Gulf of Tonkin Incident and his role as CINCPAC during the war, see his *Strategy For Defeat* (San Rafael, Calif., 1978).

† Many students of the Gulf of Tonkin Incident are convinced that the United States provoked the attack on U.S. Navy ships on August 2 and 5, 1964, through its clandestine support for the operation by the South Vietnamese Navy and its own intelligence collection activity. In any event, the incident prompted both houses of Congress to pass the fateful Southeast Asia Resolution (popularly known as the Gulf of Tonkin Resolution) by overwhelming votes. The resolution voiced strong congressional support for the President should he deem it necessary to take more forceful military action against aggression in Southeast Asia. The incident has been studied intensively by Congress, newsmen, and scholars. Two congressional studies are: Hearings before the Senate Committee on Foreign Relations, *The Gulf of Tonkin, the 1964 Incidents*, 90th Cong, 2d Sess, with the Hon. Robert S. McNamara on February 20, 1968, and Part II (with supplementary documents to the study of February 20, 1968), February 16, 1968. The subject is also addressed in the following six books: Joseph C. Goulden, *Truth is the First Casualty: The Gulf of Tonkin Affair—Illusion and Reality*, (Chicago, 1969); John Galloway, *The Gulf of Tonkin Resolution* (Rutherford, N.J., 1970); Eugene G. Windcy, *Tonkin Gulf* (New York, 1971); Anthony Austin, *The President's War* (New York, 1971); Stanley Karnow, *Vietnam: A History* (New York, 1983), pp 369–76; and Robert S. McNamara and Brian VanDeMark, *In Retrospect: The Lessons and Tragedy of Vietnam* (New York, 1995), pp 132–36.

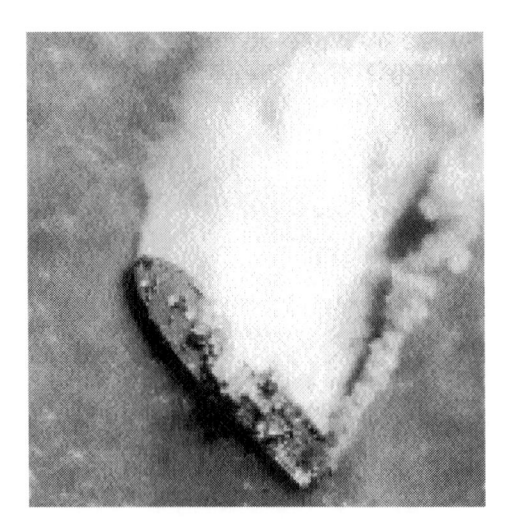

Burning North Vietnamese Swatow boat, August 1964.

As the air assault began, President Johnson publicly warned the communist nations not to support or widen aggression in Southeast Asia and, with his approval, the JCS ordered the immediate deployment of additional air, sea, and ground units to Pacific bases. Between August 5 and 9, more than eighty Air Force fighter, reconnaissance, and refueling aircraft were redeployed from the Philippines, Okinawa, and Japan to bases in South Vietnam and Thailand (figure 2).

Figure 2

Redeployment of Aircraft, August 5–9, 1964

Units	Type	Number	Bases
509th TFS	F–102	6	Clark, Phil Is to Da Nang, SVN
16th TFS	F–102	6	Naha, Okinawa to Tan Son Nhut, SVN
615th TFS	F–100	8	Clark, Phil Is to Da Nang, SVN
8th and 13th TFB	B–57	36[a]	Clark, Phil Is to Bien Hoa
15th TRS	RF–101	6	Misawa, Japan to Kadena, Okinawa
405th TFW	F–100	10	Clark, Phil Is to Takhli, Thailand
36th TFS	F–105	8	Yakota, Japan to Korat, Thailand
421st ARS	KB–50	8	Yakota, Japan to Tan Son Nhut,

SVN, and Takhli, Thailand

a Because of rain and a slick runway at Clark AB, one B–57 was destroyed and two damaged.

In addition, the JCS directed the Commander in Chief, Strike Command (CINCSTRIKE) to send the following TAC (Tactical Air Command) composite strike force and supporting SAC refueling tankers from the United States to Pacific bases (figure 3).

Figure 3

Redeployment of Aircraft by CINCSTRIKE, August 8–21, 1964

Units	Type	Number	Bases
522 TFS	F–100	Unk	Clark, Phil Is
614 TFS	F–100	Unk	Clark, Phil Is
363 CRU	RF–101	6	Kadena, Okinawa
314, 463, and 516 TCW	C–130	48	Clark, Phil Is, and Kadena, Okinawa
SAC	KC–135	56	Andersen, Guam, and Clark, Phil Is

These deployments were carried out between August 8 and 21. In preparation for additional attacks, on August 6 General Moore created a command post for the 2d Air Division at Tan Son Nhut, separate from the Vietnamese-USAF operations center to assure a tighter command link between all USAF units in South Vietnam and Thailand.

From its First Fleet on the Pacific Coast, the U.S. Navy sent the carrier *Ranger*, twelve destroyers, an antisubmarine task force, and selected Marine units to the Asian Pacific area. The Army sent additional aviation and ground units to South Vietnam. Tours of duty for personnel assigned to theater tactical forces were extended indefinitely, and the total U.S. manpower authorization in South Vietnam was raised to 23,308.[50]

On August 7, at President Johnson's request, the Congress overwhelmingly approved a resolution of support calling for him "to take all necessary measures to repel any armed attack against the forces of the United States and to prevent further aggression." Popularly named the Gulf of Tonkin Resolution and signed by the President on August 10, it was similar to resolutions passed by the Congress during the crises in the Formosa Strait in 1955, in the Middle East in 1958, and in Cuba in 1962.[51]

Washington Forbids Follow-On Strikes

Predictably, the principal communist countries reacted strongly to the retaliatory air strike of August 5. China and the Soviet Union threatened to intervene in the war and promised more aid for Hanoi.[52] Flexing its air muscle, North Vietnam flew about thirty of its MiG–15s and MiG–17s from bases in South China to Phuc Yen airfield near the capital. General Harris urged quick destruction of the aircraft to eliminate their threat to Air Force bases in South Vietnam, and to teach China a "sharp lesson" lest it send more MiGs to the north and continue its "aggression."[53]

To the dismay of General Harris, Admiral Sharp, and other military commanders, the President failed to order a follow-up strike. In fact, the actions that were approved by the administration represented a short step backward. Seventh Fleet patrols in the Gulf of Tonkin and all Oplan 34A operations against the north were suspended temporarily and support for Royal Laotian Air Force (RLAF) T–28 attacks on the Pathet Lao forces and their North Vietnamese allies was reduced. In consonance with decisions taken at a high-level conference in Honolulu in early June, Ambassador Taylor informed the President and other Washington officials this was no time to escalate the war. Although the air strikes on August 5 had left General Khanh, Saigon's military chief, in a "euphoric" state, Taylor warned that Khanh had "at best" only a 50-50 chance of surviving until the end of the year. His government was ineffective, and the populace confused and apathetic. Taylor wanted the energies of the United States mission in Saigon devoted principally to shoring up Khanh's government both politically and militarily, improving the pacification program, and, with CINCPAC, preparing contingency plans for operations against the north which probably could not begin until January 1965.[54]

The President's principal advisers accepted Taylor's views, which were formalized in a new and pivotal policy paper prepared by William P. Bundy, Assistant Secretary of State for Far Eastern Affairs. The document, endorsed by the NSC on August 14, outlined a three-phase program for pursuing American objectives in Vietnam over the next few months. Phase I called for the suspension of further U.S. action against the communists in Laos or North Vietnam until the end of August 1964, to avoid providing them with a pretext for escalating the war. In phase II, from September through December 1964, military pressure was to be used in the two countries sufficient only to maintain the

---

* Interestingly, circumstances would prompt the United States to begin "heavier" military pressure on North Vietnam in February 1965, only a month later than had been envisaged in August 1964.

morale of the Saigon government. This might consist of new cross-border incursions into Laos by land (to determine the extent of infiltration and detect targets), renewed U.S. Navy De Soto patrols off the North Vietnamese coast, and "tit for tat" military reprisal attacks. Beginning in January 1965, phase III consisted of heavier air and naval pressure on North Vietnam.*[55]

Within the JCS, Generals LeMay and Greene were highly distressed by the NSC's languid provisions for the remainder of the year. They believed that it did not send clear, recurring signals of U.S. determination to remain in Asia. Nonetheless, the principal thrust of the NSC paper, which postponed any major air pressure on the north until early 1965, was destined to prevail.[56]

Further details were added to the cautious military policy, however, including more planning for changing circumstances that warranted strikes on the north or against the event that Hanoi and Peking declared open war. On August 7, after conferring with the Deputy Defense Minister of Thailand, U.S. Ambassador Graham A. Martin, persuaded the Thai government to allow USAF combat aircraft based in Thailand to be used against North Vietnam should this become necessary. "All concerned must recognize this as a major departure from previous Thai policy," Martin said, "and authority is granted with considerable reluctance." While authority to use the aircraft was unlimited, the degree of restraint the U.S. demonstrated in their use would probably affect future decisions by the Thai government. The ambassador also declared that no further deployments to Thailand for contingency purposes should take place until he personally had obtained Bangkok's consent.[57]

On August 9, the Departments of State and Defense approved "in principle" limited air and ground operations against the North Vietnamese in the Laos corridor as soon as they were politically and militarily feasible.[58] In regional defense planning, on August 17, the JCS informed McNamara that CINCPAC was readying Oplan 37-64 for the defense of South Vietnam, and Oplan 99-64 for the defense of Laos. On the 24th, the service chiefs sent the Defense Secretary a contingency planning facilities list (CPFL) of about 650 targets in North Vietnam that included the earlier ninety-four JCS targets. The list divided targets into five categories: airfields, lines of communication (LOCs), military installations, industrial sites, and targets suitable for armed reconnaissance. In submitting the document, the JCS affirmed that from a military viewpoint, the most effective application of military force would result from a sudden "sharp blow" to convey to Hanoi the penalty for violating international agreements and the resolve of the United States to end the north's support of the insurgencies in South Vietnam and Laos.[59] When he received the list, McNamara asked for more information on the likely impact of the proposed air strikes, the sufficiency of POL and stocks, and other possible measures if the destruction of the initial ninety-four targets failed to undermine the capability and will of the North Vietnamese to continue the war.[60]

On August 26 the Joint Chiefs, with General LeMay as acting chairman, sent McNamara another paper based on a review of the document prepared by

The Joint Chiefs of Staff, February 1965. Seated, left to right: Adm. David L. McDonald, Chief of Naval Operations; Gen. Earle G. Wheeler, USA, chairman; Gen. Harold K. Johnson, Chief of Staff, USA. Standing, left to right: Gen. John P. McConnell, Chief of Staff, USAF, and Gen. Wallace M. Greene, Commandant, USMC.

Bundy and recent analyses of the conflict by Admiral Sharp, General Westmoreland, Ambassadors Taylor and Unger, and the DIA. Its overall and gloomy conclusion was that "accelerated and forceful action with respect to North Vietnam is essential to prevent a complete collapse of the U.S. position in Southeast Asia." With recommendations obviously tailored to what might be acceptable, the paper urged the immediate resumption of De Soto patrols off the coast, covert Oplan 34A, sea and air operations against selected targets, and retaliatory air strikes in response to the increased activity by Viet Cong or Pathet Lao actions in South Vietnam and Laos. In the Laotian panhandle, the paper recommended that the RLAF and South Vietnamese ground forces (with U.S. support) attack enemy LOCs, and U.S. armed reconnaissance strike infiltration targets. For the campaign in South Vietnam they favored "hot pursuit" of Viet Cong insurgents into Cambodia; strict controls of traffic on the Mekong and Bassac Rivers; continuation of the pacification program, especially around Saigon; "direct action" against the Viet Cong leadership; and additional "forward deployments" of U.S. combat units. Should this prescription fail to end Hanoi's support for the insurgencies—and the Joint Chiefs were convinced it would—more American forces should be sent to Southeast Asia in accordance with CINCPAC's Oplan 37-64 (for the defense of South Vietnam), and air strikes on the north in accordance with "current planning (i.e., the list of ninety-four targets)."[61]

As usual, the Joint Chiefs' views were considered only in conjunction with higher White House deliberations on the war. In view of the continued disarray in Saigon in early September 1965, the President began another reassessment of U.S. policy in Southeast Asia, with the persuasive and influential Ambassador Taylor briefing the President and his principal advisers. The advisers accepted with little debate Taylor's pessimistic evaluation of the situation in South Vietnam, which had deteriorated since August. In essence, the ambassador reported that for the next two to three months the Khanh government would be unable to strike the north or face the communist response to U.S. air attacks. Believing that some punitive military pressure should be continued, the advisers agreed upon, and the President approved, a number of low key measures that were spelled out in NSAM 314 on September 10. The measures were more limited than those advocated by the JCS on August 26: prompt resumption of U.S. Navy De Soto patrols off the coast of North Vietnam with naval air cover initially outside the international limit of twelve nautical miles; resumption of Oplan 34A; maritime, airdrop, and leaflet operations, to be conducted separately and covertly by South Vietnamese forces; and preparations to "respond as appropriate" to a NVA or VC attack on U.S. or South Vietnamese units or facilities. In Laos, U.S. and Lao officials should quickly arrange for the beginning of limited South Vietnamese air and ground operations, RLAF air strikes, and U.S. armed reconnaissance in the southern corridor. In South Vietnam, U.S. policy should concentrate on providing economic and political programs having an "immediate impact" without resource restrictions. These decisions, NSAM 314 stated, were based on "a prevailing judgment that the first order of business ... is to take actions which will help strengthen the fabric of the Government of South Vietnam ...."[62]

General Wheeler immediately informed McNamara that the Joint Chiefs considered the NSAM 314 measures inadequate. Going beyond the JCS proposals of August 26, he personally advocated more extensive air and ground operations against infiltration in the Laos corridor and U.S. air strikes to respond to any attack on U.S. units and units of the government of South Vietnam (GVN). The other service chiefs, Wheeler reported, were not of one mind about what to do. There was a congruence of views between himself, the Army Chief of Staff, and the Chief of Naval Operations with Taylor's recommendation not to create an incident that would trigger military escalation but to respond only and "appropriately" if the communists attacked a U.S. unit. Moreover, the Air Force and Marine chiefs (i.e., LeMay and Greene) believed otherwise. According to Wheeler, both had concluded:

> time is against us and military action against the DRV should be taken now. They concur that the American public should support any action taken by the United States government against the DRV. They consider

that, linked to the next significant incident, we should commence a retaliatory GVN and U.S. air strike program against the DRV in accordance with the 94 target plan. In this regard, they consider that a battalion-size VC attack on South Vietnam should be construed as significant.[63]

LeMay's disenchantment with administration policy in prosecuting the war in Southeast Asia was already total. He concluded earlier that the "message" delivered to Hanoi by the air strike on August 5 in response to the north's attacks on U.S ships in the Gulf of Tonkin had been nullified by subsequent American actions. For example, a CIA study indicating that the United States wanted to negotiate had been leaked to the press, and he perceived a cutback in RLAF T–28 strikes on communist targets in Laos. He believed Washington's highest officials were overly concerned about escalating the war and unrealistic in their efforts to strengthen Saigon politically before hitting the north. As LeMay saw it, air strikes would help strengthen Saigon's political base and he urged that the JCS' recommendations of August 26 be implemented soon, that these strikes be carried out, and that more U.S. ground troops be deployed to Thailand (where most Air Force aircraft would be based for strikes on the north) to bolster that country's defenses.[64]

The upshot of the latest presidential review was a decision not to exceed the measures outlined in NSAM 314. The administration's apprehension over Saigon's instability increased on September 13 when two Vietnamese brigadier generals and 2,000 followers tried unsuccessfully to topple the Khanh government in a "minicoup."[65] There was reluctance to risk provocative operations. On the night of September 17 (Saigon time), a U.S. Navy De Soto patrol consisting of two destroyers flashed it had made enemy contact. (The patrols had resumed two days earlier.) With JCS authority, Admiral Sharp alerted his Air Force and Navy commanders for a possible retaliatory air strike on the north. Probably mindful of the difficulty in collecting and assessing the facts surrounding Hanoi's attack on a similar patrol early in August, which had led to just such an air strike, Washington demanded "positive evidence" that enemy craft had again fired on the destroyers. However, the U.S. Navy was unable to provide the evidence and a strike was not conducted. To avoid another incident, on Ambassador Taylor's recommendation, Washington's highest authorities

---

* The next De Soto patrol was not scheduled until early February 1965. This patrol was also suspended in deference to the arrival in Hanoi of Soviet Premier Kosygin and his military and economic aides on February 4.

† Typical covert operations in October consisted of two coastal South Vietnamese probes of enemy defenses near Vinh, an unsuccessful effort to capture a junk, and bombardment of a radar site and an observation post at Vinh and Mui Dai, respectively [Robert F. Futrell, *The Advisory Years to 1965* (Ofc AF Hist, 1981), p 460].

Gen. Hunter Harris,
Commander in Chief,
Pacific Air Forces

again suspended the patrols in the Gulf* and covert operations in the north. The latter would be resumed under tighter control on October 4.† Several USAF RB–47s were permitted to continue collecting electronic intelligence, however, and they were shortly flying weekly missions off the North Vietnamese coast.[66]

Saigon's political and military travails did not ease in October. Both Taylor and Special National Intelligence Estimate (SNIE) 53264 reported that the morale and effectiveness of the South Vietnamese forces continued to decline. In mid-October, the ambassador said that the north was sending more men into South Vietnam, including regulars from the Peoples Army, Vietnam (PAVN). Before the end of October, Saigon's leadership again reorganized, culminating on the 30th in the designation of a civilian premier, Tran Van Huong, who replaced General Khanh, although Khanh retained control of the armed forces. Events would soon reveal that the new premier was also unable to ameliorate the government's intractable internal difficulties.[67]

Unable to take forceful action against the DRV, the services busied themselves with more contingency planning. Apprehensive lest the United States find in Saigon an unfriendly government or no government at all, on September 25, Admiral Sharp asked General Harris and Admiral Moorer, his Air Force and Navy component commanders, to provide him with plans ranging from possible American disengagement to taking a "stronger hold" of the government and conducting joint U.S. and South Vietnamese strikes on the north. Sharp also completed, and the JCS approved, his Oplan 39-64 (redesignated Oplan 39-65) to counter an attack on South Vietnam, South Korea, and other parts of

Airmen of the 13th Bomb Squadron at Bien Hoa Air Base
clean up the remains of a B–57 aircraft destroyed in the
Viet Cong mortar attack on November 1, 1964.

Southeast Asia by China alone or with North Vietnam and North Korea. In the Air Force's view, it was PACOM's first truly offensive plan providing for the proper use of air power to destroy China's main economic, military, and logistic targets. Previously, the Army and Marine chiefs had raised objections on the grounds that air power could not entirely replace ground forces.[68]

On October 14, the services derived some satisfaction from the inauguration of limited air operations by the T–28s of the fledgling Royal Laotian Air Force against an initial list of thirteen enemy targets on the Laotian side of Mu Gia Pass, a key infiltration point from North Vietnam into Laos, and along several routes of the Ho Chi Minh Trail. In compliance with NSAM 310, which had been issued on September 10, the attacks were aimed at bridges, supply sites, and barracks. The purpose of the strikes was to inflict military and psychological pain on the North Vietnamese and thereby boost the morale of Laotian and South Vietnamese armed forces. Air Force F–100 combat aircraft normally assigned as escorts for RF–101 Yankee Team reconnaissance missions accompanied the South Vietnamese strike aircraft.

Although the initial interdiction plan called for the USAF combat escorts to fire back at enemy antiaircraft sites and to supplement the attacks on heavily defended targets, Washington's nervous planners decided at the last moment not to hazard such U.S. participation except for USAF search and rescue missions. Between October 14 and November 2, the RLAF struck all thirteen targets plus three others, then continued to hit new targets along the Trail. While there was evidence that the attacks "seriously damaged" some of the targets, there was no immediately discernible impact on Hanoi's leaders.[69]

The Joint Chiefs were still exasperated and dismayed by the reluctance of Washington's civilian leadership to sanction more forceful military pressure. In late October, they dispatched additional memoranda to McNamara, one document warning that the United States was "fast running out of time," and another expressing apprehension about a possible "collapse of the American position in Southeast Asia." The memoranda again urged stronger measures to curb the infiltration of enemy manpower and supplies into South Vietnam and for stronger action against the Hanoi regime. As before, Generals LeMay and Greene argued for heavier air strikes than the other service chiefs in response to communist depredations in South Vietnam.

On November 1, McNamara met with General Wheeler, who said that the service chiefs felt so strongly that, "if the President decided against additional military action, most of them believed the United States should withdraw from South Vietnam." On the other hand, Ambassador Taylor believed that the JCS proposals constituted an effective departure from the longstanding principle of the Kennedy and Johnson administrations that the South Vietnamese must fight their own war. Westmoreland was of like mind and, in fact, he had recently predicted that without a fairly effective government in South Vietnam, no amount of U.S. offensive action in or outside of South Vietnam could "reverse the deterioration now under way."[70]

The Bien Hoa Incident

The administration's forbearance, in the face of extreme "provocation," was remarkable. On November 1, 1964, a Viet Cong mortar squad audaciously entered the perimeter of Bien Hoa Air Base and, in a twenty-minute barrage, left enormous carnage. Four Americans were killed and seventy-two wounded. On the airfield, seven Air Force aircraft were destroyed (six B–57s, one H–43 helicopter) and sixteen were damaged (thirteen B–57s, three H–43s). South Vietnamese losses totaled two personnel killed, five wounded, and three aircraft destroyed (all A–1Hs) and five damaged (three A–1Hs, two C–47s). Three houses, a mess hall, vehicles, and fuel tanks were also destroyed or badly damaged.[71]

The attack on Bien Hoa ended disagreement among the services regarding the magnitude of retaliatory air strikes. The Joint Chiefs, now backed by General Westmoreland, Admiral Sharp, and Ambassador Taylor—who had counseled for months against precipitous action until the Saigon government displayed more stability—unanimously urged a rapid tactical riposte against the Hanoi regime. The service chiefs also proposed using SAC's B–52s based in Guam to bomb Phuc Yen airfield near Hanoi, where most of the North Vietnamese Air Force (NVAF) aircraft were based. But President Johnson, finding that most of his civilian advisers, particularly McNamara and Rusk, were still opposed to such action, withheld his approval. The administration consensus was that the "concerns of September" over Saigon's unsteadiness and military weaknesses were still valid and the United States should avoid provoking a Viet Cong attack on U.S. civilian and military dependents still in Saigon. The officials were also reluctant to retaliate for an enemy attack directed chiefly against U.S. rather than South Vietnamese aircraft and installations.[72]

These were the official reasons for not responding in kind to the Bien Hoa "incident." There was another obvious reason. The attack came two days before the U.S. national elections, and in the 1964 presidential campaign President Johnson had frequently vowed that he would not enlarge the war by going "north" and "dropping bombs."[73] The only exception to this policy had been his approval on August 5 of U.S. Navy air strikes on North Vietnamese targets in retaliation for attacks on two destroyers in the Gulf of Tonkin. Thus, presidential restraint was undoubtedly dictated by political necessity, and it was so understood by General Westmoreland and particularly by Ambassador Taylor, who had pressed frequently for "immediate retaliation of the kind we...often discussed in Washington...."[74]

The attack on Bien Hoa also inflamed a smoldering dispute between the Air Force and Army over the inadequate base protection provided by South Vietnamese security units. Generals LeMay and Harris and other Air Force leaders urged immediate action to ensure more protection. LeMay went so far as to recommend that the United States-South Vietnamese military agreement be revised to permit special U.S. Army or Marine security forces to establish an 8,000-meter security perimeter around the most important airbases, particularly Tan Son Nhut, Bien Hoa, and Da Nang.[75] But Westmoreland and Taylor opposed such a deployment on the grounds that the troops would lack language and area knowledge to search local dwellings, and create political problems and encourage the South Vietnamese to relax their security activities. The MACV commander and Admiral Sharp recommended the addition of 300 and 502, respectively, Air Force, Army, and Marine police personnel to bolster airbase defense, but these appeals likewise failed to win administration approval.[76] In fact, OSD was unwilling to admit officially the shortcomings of South Vietnamese defensive duties. Not until Viet Cong attacks on Army facilities in February 1965, which triggered the first two Flaming Dart air strikes on the north, and the onset of Rolling Thunder operations in March,* which in turn increased the likelihood of larger Viet Cong assaults on airbases, did MACV recommend and Washington approve the dispatch of the first contingent of U.S. combat-ready Marines to protect Da Nang and the "beefing up" of American security personnel around other Air Force bases.†[77]

---

* See Chapter 1.
† For a discussion of airbase defense during the Southeast Asia war, see Roger P. Fox, *Air Base Defense in the Republic of Vietnam* (Ofc AF Hist, 1979).

In the meantime, in Laos a lesser "provocation" also resulted in no retaliatory action. On November 19, a USAF F–100 was shot down and the pilot killed. The aircraft was escorting RLAF T–28s as they attacked infiltration targets on roads leading to the Mu Gia Pass on the Laotian-North Vietnamese border. This very limited air program began on October 14. Two days later, a USAF RF–101 on a Yankee Team reconnaissance mission was also downed by groundfire, but in this case the pilot was rescued.

Within the JCS, General LeMay urged rapid retribution for the aircraft losses by air strikes on five infiltration targets in the Laotian panhandle, but had to settle for a more moderate JCS consensus. The Joint Chiefs asked McNamara to approve flak suppression missions along and in the vicinity of Routes 12 and 23 from the North Vietnamese border to the junctions of Routes 8 and 121 in Laos. The Defense Secretary, preparing for another NSC review of the war, did not reply formally. To reduce the risk of additional shootdowns, he issued new operational guidance requiring all U.S. medium-altitude missions in Laos to fly no lower than 10,000 feet, well out of range of most communist antiaircraft guns.[78]

Beginning of a Limited, Two-Phase Program

Thus, once again, contrary to JCS recommendations, communist attacks in South Vietnam and Laos failed to elicit high-level support for "tit for tat" or any other type of retaliatory action. The main reason was the deepening administration anxieties concerning Saigon's military and political insolvency. Each new internal crisis appeared to reinforce Washington's military paralysis. Marking time, the President asked for another review of the war by the National Security Council.[79]

The new review was conducted by an "NSC Working Group" on South Vietnam and Southeast Asia established by the President at the beginning of November with William P. Bundy, Assistant Secretary of State for Far Eastern Affairs, as chairman. Over the next three weeks, the working group, staffed with personnel from key State and Defense agencies, painstakingly assessed and reassessed the situation in South Vietnam, the American stake in Southeast Asia, military options, and negotiating possibilities. A working group paper, dated November 21, summarized, with some modifications, the principal courses of action previously considered to induce Hanoi to call off the insurgency in South Vietnam and to accept the reality of a noncommunist South Vietnamese nation. The first option was for the U.S. to conduct reprisal air strikes on North Vietnam (not necessarily just for the spectacular Viet Cong "provocations" as had occurred at Bien Hoa), intensify coastal raids as provided in covert Oplan 34A, resume destroyer (De Soto) patrols in the Gulf, step up air strikes by RLAF T–28s against infiltration targets in Laos, and seek reforms in South Vietnam. The second option was "a fast/full squeeze" bombing of the north at a fairly rapid pace without interruption with early air raids on Phuc Yen airfield near Hanoi and key bridges on road and rail links with China until American demands were met (supported by the JCS but regarded by Bundy as virtually a reckless invitation to the Chinese to intervene). The final option was a "slow squeeze" series of air strikes on infiltration targets, first in Laos, then in North Vietnam, to convey the impression of a steady, deliberate approach, but allowing the United States the alternatives of proceeding at this pace, increasing the pace, or escalating in other areas.

Although the Joint Chiefs were represented on the NSC working group, their voice was only one of many. In response to direct questions from the group or from McNamara, the service chiefs boldly expressed their disagreement with administration policy. Having studied the group's military-political options, they replied that there were five, not three, ranging from terminating the American commitment to South Vietnam and Laos and withdrawing as gracefully as possible, to a controlled program of intense military pressures accompanied by appropriate diplomatic pressure. The last, they insisted, entailed the least risk, the fewest casualties, and the lowest costs; entailed less danger of enemy miscalculation or intervention; and would most probably achieve American objectives. In another contingency plan, they expressed confidence that the United States could deal with any direct military response from Hanoi and Peking. They proclaimed Southeast Asia an area of major U.S. strategic importance, the loss of which would lead to "grave" political and military consequences, not only in the Pacific, but worldwide.[80]

An exhaustive, high-level review of the working group's assessment began in late November. The principal attendees, McNamara, Rusk, Wheeler, Taylor, George Ball (Under Secretary of State), and John P. McCone (Director of the CIA) were divided. On this occasion, Ambassador Taylor, who normally played a highly influential role in such proceedings, found that he and Wheeler, who represented JCS views, were alone in arguing for air strikes on North Vietnam and infiltration routes in southern Laos. The others, Taylor found, were not ready to abandon the dictum that "stable government in the south must precede military action in the north despite the improbability of ever getting stable government without the lift to the national spirit which military action against the homeland of the enemy could provide." In essence, Taylor's position was that while conducting air strikes on the north, in Laos, or in both areas, he would try harder to persuade Saigon's leaders to institute political and administrative reforms leading to more effective and stable government. The attendees fully agreed, on the other hand, that in the event the administration approved some type of air program outside of South Vietnam, no negotiating opportunity should be overlooked.[81]

As the high-level review of military options neared an end, Taylor suggested, and the conferees agreed, to lay before President Johnson a limited two-phase military program for South Vietnam, Laos, and North Vietnam for the ensuing weeks. The program's concept, pulled from several working papers, consisted of revised and somewhat softened provisions contained in the three options drawn up by the NSC working group. The NSC principals then presented the concept to the President on December 13, 1964.

The President accepted the concept. Phase I, lasting for thirty days, would consist of heavier air strikes against infiltration in the Laotian panhandle and intensified covert Oplan 34A operations against North Vietnam, principally by U.S.-trained South Vietnamese personnel. The air strikes would be conducted by RLAF T–28s and U.S. Air Force and Navy aircraft flying armed reconnaissance missions. The objective was psychological rather than military, to warn Hanoi of American strength. After a period of thirty days, U.S. commanders could continue flying armed reconnaissance or take other measures to "signal" Hanoi. For example, they could withdraw American dependents from South Vietnam or, for the first time, conduct air strikes on North Vietnamese targets a short distance above the DMZ.

If the Hanoi regime failed to heed these warnings, the United States would launch phase II operations, with the President's approval. These would be US-VNAF coordinated air strikes on North Vietnam beginning in the southernmost sector of the country. The strikes would increase in number and intensity for two to six months until all significant targets had been hit. Meanwhile, the United States might exert other pressure such as mining or blockading North Vietnam's seaports, all the while seeking opportunities to negotiate an end to the conflict. Despite his approval of the two-phase concept, the President's position had not changed fundamentally since September 1964, when he had concluded that the United States could do little until Saigon's leaders pulled together. Before Johnson approved the two-phase program, a draft NSAM 319 was prepared, but never issued, apparently because the concept differed little from the provisions in NSAM 314 of September 10, 1964.[82]

Ambassador Taylor returned to Saigon on December 6 with authority to implement the phase I military actions and to discuss with Saigon's leadership joint U.S.-South Vietnamese bombing plans against North Vietnam, along with more economic and other assistance. On December 10, in Vientiane, Ambassador William H. Sullivan, who had replaced Unger the previous month, secured Prime Minister Souvanna Phouma's consent to limited U.S. armed reconnaissance along certain Laotian routes, provided there was no publicity. In Washington, the Joint Chiefs completed a scenario for conducting missions, and on the 12th, Deputy Defense Secretary Cyrus R. Vance briefed the President's principal Southeast Asia advisers on the air objectives. U.S. aircraft, he explained, would strike targets of opportunity along segments of Routes 8, 121, and 12, or strike secondary targets, such as barracks areas and military strongpoints. If an aircraft was downed in Laos, the United States would adhere to its official position that the loss occurred while the plane was escorting Yankee Team reconnaissance flights requested by the Laotian government.[83]

On December 14, six Air Force F–105s, eight F–100s, two RF–101s, all from Da Nang, plus two refueling KC–135 tankers, flew their first mission in the Laotian panhandle. Nicknamed Barrel Roll, the aerial program was directed against infiltration targets along Route 8 from the border of North Vietnam southward in Laos toward South Vietnam. Navy F–4Bs and A–1Hs launched their initial missions on the 17th. Because the bombing tempo was intentionally low, only six Barrel Roll missions had been flown by January 2, 1965, three each by the Air Force and Navy. As part of phase I, on behalf of Secretaries Rusk and McNamara, Ambassador Sullivan asked the Laotian government to intensify the bombing of routes and targets in the Laos corridor near the DRV. RLAF T–28s, with USAF F–100s flying combat air patrol, had been bombing infiltration targets in Laos since October 14.

With only a handful of T–28s available, the RLAF could do little to increase its sortie rate. By the end of 1964 it had flown seventy-seven sorties and the Hanoi government was complaining about the strikes to the International Control Commission, the three-nation supervisory body established to oversee compliance with the 1962 Geneva Agreement on Laos' neutrality. Hanoi alleged that the RLAF attacks sponsored by the United States were also hitting North Vietnamese territory.

Not included in the phase I operations were Air Force and Navy Yankee Team reconnaissance missions, which began on May 18, 1964, to photograph Pathet Lao and North Vietnamese dispositions and movements in Laos. Including escort, weather, and electronic intelligence operations, the United States flew a total of 1,500 missions over Laos in 1964, a not inconsiderable number, warning the Hanoi regime of a gradual increase in aerial surveillance.[84]

Washington's Resistance to a Bombing Program Ends

Before the end of 1964, another "significant" incident, presumably conducted by the Viet Cong, increased pressure for a retaliatory strike on North Vietnam. On Christmas Eve, a 300-pound explosive charge detonated in the Brink Hotel, a billet for U.S. personnel in Saigon, killing two and wounding sixty-four Americans and wounding forty-eight South Vietnamese. Ambassador Taylor, Deputy Ambassador Johnson, and General Westmoreland in Saigon; Admiral Sharp in Honolulu; and the JCS in Washington all urged an air strike. Admiral Sharp alerted PACFLT air (but not PACAF) to make the riposte. But President Johnson refused, advancing the familiar arguments that Saigon's political base was too shaky to withstand a possible communist reaction, and he did not wish to provoke an attack on American dependents in Saigon. There was also uncertainty as to whether the Brink Hotel bombing was instigated by the Viet Cong. The President was willing to dispatch more U.S. troops to South Vietnam, but Ambassador Taylor believed that increasing their presence at this time would only slacken the government's military efforts.

Laotian Air Force T–28.

Following a severe defeat of the South Vietnamese by the Viet Cong at Binh Gia during the last few days of December 1964, Taylor, Deputy Ambassador Johnson, and Westmoreland again warned Washington of the worsening military situation, increasing anti-Americanism, and possible civil disorder. Concerned lest these developments spawn a new Saigon government hostile to the United States, they again urged an immediate air attack on the north. But the President refused to alter his no-strike stance, or to implement those parts of the phase I and phase II programs approved in late November 1964 that provided for air strikes on North Vietnamese targets lying above the DMZ.[85]

The political disarray in Saigon only served to exacerbate the military problems. Throughout December 1964 and January 1965, Taylor and his embassy staff were confronted with a three-cornered, largely public conflict, between Premier Tran Van Huong's government and South Vietnam's generals, the generals versus Taylor, and the Buddhists versus the Huong government and the Ambassador. It seemed the United States was "playing a losing game."[86]

Within the JCS, no service chief was more anguished than General LeMay. In mid-January 1965, he asserted: "I don't understand how we can go on as we have...." He feared for American lives in South Vietnam, but observed that when the JCS recommended moving dependents from the country, Headquarters

---

* In his memoir of the war, Gen. Westmoreland describes his position on the issue at this time as follows: "To a Joint Chiefs' proposal that the U.S. military's dependents go home and a U.S. Marine force land at Da Nang, I replied that either or both would reflect lack of confidence in the Vietnamese and would seriously affect their morale." *A Soldier Reports* (New York, 1976), p 112.

Interior of the Brink Hotel after the attack in December 1964.

MACV objected because of "serious defeatist" implications.* LeMay continued:

> For a long time I've said we should go north. Our present strategies aren't working. The coups are getting worse. Dissatisfaction with the government in South Vietnam is growing. The military is the only viable and cohesive force. It is possible to do things with them. But these things smolder. Who knows when rioting will spread to the Army? Everything else would then go up. We would lose our people who are dispersed and not... able to get to an airfield.

In advocating an attack on North Vietnam, the "source" of the aggression, LeMay did not fear Chinese intervention.[87]

CIA Director McCone was also very pessimistic. In conversations with the President he predicted that General Khanh was heading for another crisis. On the international scene, he believed an impending trip by Soviet Premier Alexei N. Kosygin to Hanoi only presaged more trouble. He added that, after removing Nikita Khrushchev from power on October 14, 1964, Kosygin and the new chief of the Communist Party, Leonid I. Brezhnev, appeared ready to reverse the policy of relative inaction in Southeast Asia. McCone conjectured they had concluded Hanoi would win the war and wished to share credit for the anticipated victory. The CIA Director joined the JCS and Taylor in advocating the bombing of selected targets in North Vietnam, beginning with initial strikes above the 17th parallel, and intensifying them as the attack program moved northward.[88]

On January 27, 1965, the President's Special Assistant for National Security

Affairs, McGeorge Bundy, informed the President that he and Secretary McNamara agreed that present U.S. policy would lead to a disastrous defeat. They saw two alternatives: employ military power to force a change in Hanoi's policy or deploy more manpower and other resources in concert with a "negotiation track" and salvage what little was possible without significant risk. Bundy added that Secretary Rusk knew things were going badly but did not think the deterioration could be stopped. Rusk believed that the consequences of both escalation and withdrawal were so bad that we simply must find a way of making our present policy work. In contrast, Bundy and McNamara were convinced present policy could no longer work.[89]

In the light of Bundy's memo and further discussions with his advisers, President Johnson asked Mr. Rusk to consider again all ways for finding a peaceful solution to the war. At the same time, he asked Bundy to fly to Saigon immediately with a team of military and civilian experts "for a hard look at the situation on the ground."

Bundy and his experts departed Washington quickly for Saigon. Before they completed their review of South Vietnam's military and political crisis, the Viet Cong attacked the MACV compound and Camp Holloway at Pleiku in the central highlands. Within twenty-four hours, President Johnson approved a retaliatory air strike, Flaming Dart I, that was conducted on February 7. On February 11, after a second attack on an American Army barracks at Qui Nhon, Flaming Dart II was launched against several North Vietnamese targets, ushering in a new phase of the war.

An attack on a North Vietnamese barracks area, 1965.

CHAPTER 3
Rolling Thunder Begins

The Flaming Dart air strikes in February and the President's decision to continue them represented a significant milestone in America's containment policy in Southeast Asia. Having led the other services in pressing home the need to deter the Hanoi regime with air power, initially the Air Force felt vindicated. But disenchantment quickly followed as the service chiefs found administration officials intent on controlling the scope and tempo of the bombing to an unprecedented degree. The strictures on air operations by civilian rather than military men violated basic Air Force doctrine and created severely frustrating problems for professional airmen.

The Air Challenge in North Vietnam

The tight oversight of the bombing program stemmed from an administration fear that an overwhelming aerial assault on the north, an assault that could quickly turn the major industrial and population targets to ashes, could impel the Chinese and the Soviets to engage in diversionary activities or enter the conflict openly, thus opening the door to the possible use of nuclear weapons. The fear was underscored by the stark disparity in aerial strength between the United States and the small, Soviet-trained and -equipped North Vietnamese Air Force.

At the beginning of February 1965, USAF's combat force in South Vietnam consisted of 200 aircraft. The largest single units were the 1st and 602d Air Commando Squadrons and their 48 A–1Es. About 7,000 of 24,000 U.S. personnel assisting the Saigon government's military effort were Air Force. Although the force was geared for advisory operations in the south, many aircraft could and were used against the north. Eighty-three aircraft, mostly jets, were based in Thailand, as well as 1,000 Air Force personnel.[1] Three aircraft carriers of the U.S. Seventh Fleet with about 200 aircraft lay in the Gulf of Tonkin off the South Vietnamese coast, and all were available for operations in North or South Vietnam or Laos. In fact Navy and Air Force aircraft had been flying very limited tactical aerial reconnaissance missions over Laos since late 1961.[2]

As has been noted, on the eve of the Flaming Dart II strike on the north, the Air Force's aircraft inventory in Southeast Asia was reinforced by the deployment of four and a half tactical squadrons that were moved quickly to airbases in South Vietnam and Thailand.[3] In addition, two B–52 squadrons and two KC–135 squadrons were ordered to bases in Guam and Okinawa, respectively.[4] The small Vietnamese Air Force was ready to fly a limited number of strikes in North Vietnam over and above daily missions in South Vietnam. In early 1965, the VNAF's combat arm consisted of fifty-three A–1E Skyraiders. Five were based at Tan Son Nhut, thirty-two at Bien Hoa, eleven at Da Nang, and five

F–105s at Takhli Royal Thai Air Base.

were on other bases. The Skyraiders that were used in Flaming Dart I and II[5] flew from Da Nang, the northernmost base, and subsequent VNAF strikes on the north would also start from there.

Although many U.S. tactical air squadrons at airbases in Southeast and East Asia were on four-month temporary duty (TDY) tours, which obviously degraded their potential effectiveness, their aggregate number gave the United States overwhelming air superiority. In contrast, North Vietnam possessed a minuscule force of 117 to 128 Soviet aircraft, of which only thirty-five were MiG–15 or MiG–17 fighters. The rest were transports, trainers, liaison aircraft, and helicopters. The MiGs were based at Phuc Yen airfield near the capital. Of the twenty-one airfields in the north, only Phuc Yen was suitable for jet aircraft operations although several other airfields were being readied for jets.[6]

More formidable was the Hanoi regime's antiaircraft defense system, which was expanding rapidly. One of several American intelligence estimates in early 1965 indicated that the regime possessed 1,039 antiaircraft guns: 322 14.5-mm and 37-mm, 709 57-mm, and eight 85-mm. There were 298 antiaircraft sites, of which 161 were considered active. The sites were located mainly around the Hanoi-Haiphong area and along important rail lines, roads, and bridges north and south of the two cities.[7]

The threat from China's air force was more ominous. In February 1965, the Chinese possessed about 310 MiG fighters and twenty light bombers on airfields in the Kunming and Canton Military Regions adjacent to North Vietnam. From there they could easily redeploy to Phuc Yen and the other jet bases nearing completion.[8]

The communists had two other valuable allies against U.S. air power: tropical vegetation and weather. As a consequence of the counterinsurgency operations from 1961 to 1965, many U.S. airmen were familiar with the aerial problems

The MiG–17.

associated with jungle growth in various sectors of the country. In Laos, jungle growth and forested, mountainous terrain covered most of the country. SAC U–2 pilots and those who undertook reconnaissance as part of Yankee Team operations, or strike operations in Barrel Roll, were aware of the considerably greater obstacles such terrain posed for interdiction and armed reconnaissance. U.S. aerial experience over North Vietnam had been limited to a single air strike in August 1964 and the two Flaming Dart strikes.

North Vietnam's terrain was somewhat less forbidding for airmen than that of South Vietnam and Laos. Nonetheless, roughly 50 percent of the country's 61,300 square miles was forested, 37.5 percent was wasteland, and only 12.7 percent was under cultivation to feed a population of about 17,800,000. The transportation system, meager by western standards, included slightly more than 6,000 miles of roads suitable for motor vehicles, about 44,000 miles of poorer secondary roads, 3,380 miles of navigable waterways (the Red River the principal artery) and a rail system stretching 561 miles. The forested and tropical areas provided cover for the small roads and waterways. On the other hand, the rail system, which was rebuilt after it had been largely destroyed during the French-Viet Minh war, was highly visible. It consisted of four main lines. Two ran between Hanoi and China, one to the northwest and the other to the northeast, to Lao Cai and Dong Dang respectively. At the border, the two lines connected directly with China's rail system. A third line, reopened in 1964, ran southward for 156 miles to Thanh Hao, and a fourth spanned the 65 miles between Hanoi and Haiphong, the north's principal seaport.

The effect of the weather on air operations was considerable. It was responsible for thousands of canceled or aborted missions, it delayed takeoffs or lengthened takeoff intervals, which in turn delayed formation after takeoff, and it prevented aerial refueling or created difficulties for aircraft attempting to rendezvous for aerial refueling. Poor weather forced aircraft to deviate from planned routes or planned targets, leaving pilots with the option of hitting targets by radar, striking a secondary target, or aborting the mission. Bad weather often precluded the release of ordnance at the preferred 30- to 45-degree angle to minimize aircraft exposure to flak, forcing release at a lesser angle—or even a level release—allowing maximum exposure to enemy gunners; it made spotting small, transitory targets impossible; and as the war progressed, the weather was a factor in the determination of ordnance used. Finally, all pilots knew that bombing through cloud cover at low altitudes created hazards, such as "low blows" (self-inflicted damage to aircraft), "short rounds" (strikes on friendly or wrong targets), or flying into the ground.

Another impediment to visibility throughout Southeast Asia was the effect of vegetation burned by natives to clear land. Smoke, dust, and haze accompanying such burnings, often aggravated by weather and the effects of American bombing, seriously hampered attempts to locate small targets by visual or photoreconnaissance, keep them in view for an air strike, and photograph them for bomb damage assessment. Darkness also hampered air operations and, when combined with weather and the effects of burning, made night operations in Southeast Asia exceedingly difficult.[9]

As the scope of the war expanded, American technicians introduced improved airborne and ground radar, infrared (IR), side-looking radar (SLAR), forward air controllers (FACs) and other devices and techniques to overcome the difficulties in conducting air operations in North Vietnam and Laos. Their use by the Air Force will be described in later chapters.

Command and Control of Air Resources

Another vexing problem, especially for the Air Force, was the command and control structure for aircraft engaged in the Rolling Thunder program. The structure that had evolved, first for operations in South Vietnam, then in Laos, and finally in North Vietnam, conflicted sharply with the Air Force's roles and missions doctrine. Briefly, this doctrine required that a single air commander, preferably Air Force, control and coordinate all service aircraft in a combat theater. Such an arrangement appeared most appropriate for Southeast and East Asia where China was perceived to be the main threat to U.S. interests.[10]

From the Air Force's viewpoint, however, the command and control arrangements in South Vietnam had been unduly complex and inefficient since the United States' combat advisory involvement began in that country in the early 1960s. The problem was compounded by the establishment on February 8, 1962 of Headquarters MACV in Saigon as a sub-unified command of PACOM. MACV's first commander, Lt. Gen. Paul D. Harkins, exercised overall command and control authority for all military operations in the south. Air Force control over its own air assets, let alone those of other services, was diluted first by the initial assignment of the principal air units to the 2d ADVON, a component of MACV, and then because MACV was staffed predominantly with Army personnel. Not only were most of the staff drawn from the Army, they also held most of the key positions. In the Air Force's chain of command, 2d ADVON/2d Air Division was also a component of Thirteenth Air Force in

Gen. Curtis E. LeMay, Air Force Chief of Staff, and Gen. Paul D. Harkins, Commander, U.S. Military Assistance Command, Vietnam.

the Philippines, which in turn, was a component of PACAF in Honolulu, which, along with PACFLT and USARPAC, was a component of PACOM.[11]

However, as South Vietnam had been the principal theater of military operations since the early 1960s and had first claim on available air assets, the MACV commander would also have considerable influence on air operations in Laos and North Vietnam when they began in those countries, in 1964 and 1965, respectively. With the establishment of MACV, the Air Force attempted to obtain greater representation in the unified command structure. Initially, General LeMay attempted to place an Air Force general officer in the post of MACV Chief of Staff and then in the post of MACV Deputy Commander when it was created for the first time in January 1964. Despite support from the Navy and Marine chiefs, LeMay's efforts were unsuccessful because McNamara supported the Army. Air Force frustration over its subordinate role in South Vietnam was exacerbated by the PACOM's refusal to permit a Navy component to be assigned to MACV.

Thus, from the beginning MACV leadership reflected Army ideas concerning the role of air and ground forces in combating the Viet Cong and the North Vietnamese insurgency. Whereas the Air Force stressed the importance of air power in counterinsurgency activities, the Army insisted that only ground forces, with appropriate air support, could fashion a victory against the enemy. In fact, Army leaders claimed counterinsurgency was an Army mission. In June 1964, when General Westmoreland, then MACV Deputy Commander, succeeded the retiring General Harkins and debate about who was to take over as

Deputy Commander was revived, General Taylor, still JCS chairman, averred that it was "hardly conceivable" a member from any service other than the Army could fill the post. General LeMay strongly believed otherwise and was again supported by the Navy and Marine chiefs, especially since the Army's decision two months earlier to replace the outgoing Chief of Staff, who had been a Marine general officer, with an Army general officer. The disagreement among the JCS about who should occupy this post was resolved once more by McNamara who supported the Army's position, as did many other high administration officials. Thus, in mid-1964, the Army held the top three MACV posts.[12]

The question of who should have overall command and control authority over "outcountry" combat operations, namely in Laos and North Vietnam, was largely avoided until May 1964 when the United States began regular tactical reconnaissance of Laos, using Air Force and Navy Yankee Team resources. Then, the principal contenders were the commanders of the two unified commands, Admiral Felt and General Harkins. Felt claimed that he had operational control of Laotian operations and intended to exercise his authority through his PACAF component commanders, bypassing MACV. The commanders of PACAF, the Thirteenth Air Force, and the 2d Air Division supported Felt's position, convinced that Harkins' authority should be strictly limited to military operations in South Vietnam.

Harkins disagreed. Because he controlled the aircraft of the 2d Air Division, based in South Vietnam, some of which would be diverted to Laos (and soon to North Vietnam), he claimed the right to issue operational orders "solely" to General Moore, the 2d Air Division commander. The disagreement was ameliorated when Gen. Jacob Smart,* then PACAF commander, suggested that Felt pass "execute" orders for Yankee Team reconnaissance in Laos through MACV to General Moore. This was done in the ensuing months for Laotian missions and for the initial air strikes against the north in August 1964 and early 1965. Under this arrangement, the PACOM commander remained the principal authority for allocating Air Force, Navy, and Marine aircraft for operations in Laos and North Vietnam, taking into account the daily needs of the MACV commander. He delegated air coordinating authority through MACV to General Moore and his 2d Air Division. Mission coordination was facilitated by exchanges of Air Force and Navy liaison officers between Moore's headquarters at Tan Son Nhut AB in South Vietnam and the Seventh Fleet in the Gulf of Tonkin.[13]

Meanwhile, command and control arrangements for air operations outside of South Vietnam were further modified in July 1964. To meet Thailand's desire to avoid being perceived as directly belligerent in the war in the south, General Moore established the office of Deputy Commander, 2d Air Division,

---

* Gen. Harris succeeded Gen. Smart on Aug. 1, 1964.

Two F–105s at Korat are readied for a mission over North Vietnam.

at Udorn Air Base in Thailand. Moore appointed Brig. Gen. John H. McCreery as Deputy Commander and at the same time established an Air Operations Center (AOC), and a Command Reporting Post (CRP) at Udorn. With secure communication links to the 2d Air Division's AOC in Saigon, to USAF tenants at Thai bases, and to the Royal Laotian Air Force AOC in Vientiane, Laos, McCreery was technically capable of maintaining operational control of Air Force operations in Laos, and if necessary in North Vietnam, by USAF aircraft based in Thailand. Administrative and logistic support for USAF units was provided by Detachment 2, 35th Tactical Group, established at Udorn in June. Although the arrangement ended the appearance that an Air Force commander based in South Vietnam controlled USAF aircraft in Thailand, it increased the complexity of the command and control system in the Southeast Asia theater.

In practice, no substantive change was made, since McCreery normally deferred judgment on all Air Force operational matters to Moore, who coordinated (but did not control) air operations of the other services. However, McCreery served actively as Moore's point of contact with the U.S. Embassy in Vientiane, which exercised oversight of Yankee Team reconnaissance and several small covert air and air-ground activities in Laos and with the U.S. Embassy in Bangkok, which obtained permission for all Air Force deployments to or within Thailand, as well as operations in Laos and, beginning in 1965, in North Vietnam of aircraft based in Thailand.[14]

Air Force commanders chafed over the diffused nature of authority in the Southeast Asia command and control system as it existed at the start of Rolling Thunder, believing that many of the systemic mistakes made in World War II and the Korean War were being repeated.[15] Although they accepted PACOM's overall authority for air operations in Laos and North Vietnam, they objected to the stream of detailed operational guidance issued by the headquarters. The best operational expertise, they believed, resided in the PACAF and PACFLT component commands and their subordinate organizations, and in the geographically compact Southeast Asia war theater, the preferred command and control arrangement was to have one local theater commander in charge, preferably an Air Force officer.[16] In General Moore's opinion, the PACOM commander was

> a little too far away from the scene of action...to [conduct air operations] effectively. You just can't have more than one commander controlling the air in a geographical area even a...bit larger than Vietnam.... Aircraft move mighty fast. You've got great flexibility. You can go anywhere. And to get the most efficient, most effective use of it, it should be under the control of one man, one commander.[17]

Maj. Gen. Gilbert L. Meyers, who would serve as the 2d Air Division's first Deputy Air Commander from July 1, 1965 to August 31, 1966, agreed that efficient air control could not be exercised from Hawaii, let alone from Washington.[18]

General Harris, the PACAF commander, believed that the Air Force was uniquely equipped to exercise overall command and control and coordinating authority in the war theater. The principal Air Force organizations, beginning with PACAF in Hawaii, the subordinate Thirteenth Air Force in the Philippines, and the 2d Air Division in South Vietnam, he observed, possessed adequate tactical air control center facilities and aircraft, control, and warning systems. The 2d Air Division also possessed a command post and an air operations center to control strike, air defense, airlift, and other operations.[19]

However, these resources could not overcome the desire of each service to maintain as much control as possible over its own aircraft. In fact, as Rolling Thunder operations expanded, the jerrybuilt command and control system would undergo yet more changes in 1965 and would become even more complex.

Preparations for a Rolling Thunder Program

There was no immediate follow-up to the Flaming Dart I and II strikes in early February 1965. In Washington, administration officials waited for Hanoi, Peking, and Moscow to react while service planners in the major commands worked on new air deployment and strike plans. On February 11, as Flaming Dart II was under way, the JCS urged OSD to immediately dispatch nine more Air Force squadrons to bases in the western Pacific and solicited Admiral Sharp's views on deploying six more at a later date. The most definitive planning document was prepared by General Harris' staff at Headquarters PACAF. This showed the location of the Air Force's thirteen combat squadrons in South

Vietnam, Thailand, the Philippines, Okinawa, Japan, and Korea and proposals for the addition of fifteen more (figure 4).

Figure 4

Location of USAF Combat Squadrons, February 1965

Existing Military Assistance Command Vietnam PACAF Posture (squadrons)

Takhli, Thailand F–100	1	Kunsan AB, Korea F–100	1
Korat, Thailand F–105	1		2 B–57
Osan AB, Korea F–105	1	Kadena AB, Okinawa F–105	2
		Yokota AB, Japan	2

Proposed Augmentation (9 squadrons)

Ubon, Thailand	1 F–4C	F–100	
Korat, Thailand	1 F–105	Kadena AB, Okinawa	2 F–105
Tainan AB, Taiwan	2 F–100	Naha AB, Okinawa	1 F–4C
Kung Kuan AB, Taiwan	1	Kunsan AB, Korea	1 F–100

Proposed Augmentation (6 squadrons)

Itazuke AB, Japan	2 F–4C	Osan AB, Korea	1 F–105
Yokota AB, Japan	1 F–105	Kunsan AB, Korea	1 F–100
Misawa AB, Japan	1 F–100		

As Harris explained to higher authorities, PACAF's deployment plan generally followed the force structure of CINCPAC's plan 39-65, with U.S. air power to be deployed along the Chinese border to deter that government from intervening in the war.[20] As events unfolded, all new deployment proposals were weighed carefully by Washington's highest officials and approved incrementally based on theater-wide need, base saturation, and plans to enlarge existing bases or construct new ones.

Meanwhile, in Saigon, General Moore warned Harris that Hanoi might send its small fleet of MiGs to challenge further Flaming Dart missions over the north or to challenge the Yankee Team reconnaissance and Barrel Roll interdiction operations in Laos. To thwart such an eventuality, he advocated a prompt "overwhelming blow" against North Vietnam's MiG bases.[21] From Honolulu, Admiral Sharp sent the JCS a new list of targets below the 20th parallel and bombing options for a Flaming Dart III strike.[22] He also proposed an attack by the Air Force on the Mu Gia Pass, a key infiltration point between Laos and North Vietnam border. A force of twelve B–57s, twelve F–100s, and twenty F–105s, he said, would assure a 90-percent damage level to military facilities in the area, permit "seeding" the pass with delayed-action bombs, and "clearly imply America's interest in preventing subversion in Laos as well as in South Vietnam."[23]

General Moore, Admiral Sharp, and the JCS pressed for a more rapid escalation of the air program against the north, but Westmoreland was more inclined to a program of "graduated reprisal" that would be a "most powerful persuader." He believed that the intensity of reprisal air strikes should be determined by the level of Viet Cong atrocities, outrages, and incidents committed against U.S. or South Vietnamese personnel or facilities. A special MACV project nicknamed Fish Net would compile a daily summary of provocative Viet Cong actions justifying U.S.-GVN air strikes on the north. The U.S. Embassy in Saigon would transmit the data to Washington and coordinate the project with the Saigon government. The MACV commander said graduated air reprisals would complement the other four military programs (Yankee Team reconnaissance and Barrel Roll interdiction in Laos, covert 34A operations, and U.S. Navy De Soto patrols) exerting pressure on the DRV.*[24]

On February 8, immediately following the first Flaming Dart strike, McNamara asked the JCS to submit a tentative eight-week bombing program. The request implied that a short period of air assaults would convince Hanoi to end its support of the insurgencies in South Vietnam and Laos. McGeorge Bundy, the President's Special Adviser on National Security Affairs, believed Hanoi would come to terms within three months after bombing began.[25]

Three days later, the JCS submitted an eight-week program, deliberately mild since it was apparent that the administration would not accept more aggressive recommendations. The program called for a series of U.S. and Vietnamese air strikes ascending in intensity and risk, initially on targets lying along Route 7 and south of the 19th parallel. They would begin at a rate of two to four per week in coordination with Barrel Roll operations in Laos, U–2 reconnaissance coverage of the north, ground cross-border incursions into Laos (still awaiting approval), U.S. Navy De Soto patrols off the North Vietnamese

---

* Gen. Westmoreland briefly summarized his views in late 1964 and early 1965 on bombing North Vietnam in his memoir, *A Soldier Reports* (New York, 1978), pp 142–46 and 152–57.

Air Force Chief of Staff Gen. John P. McConnell arriving at Tan Son Nhut Air Base, October 1965.

coast, heavier coastal bombardment by the Navy, and covert 34A activities.

There would be no air strikes on MiG airfields unless North Vietnamese and Chinese pilots interfered with the U.S.-VNAF assault, an eventuality that would obviously signal an escalation of the war and alter the eight-week bombing scenario. On balance, however, the Joint Chiefs foresaw that only Hanoi would enter the war openly, at least for the time being. They urged the immediate adoption of the program and cited examples of Viet Cong "provocations" that could trigger its implementation.[26]

The program remained under study, however, and although soon overtaken by events, many of the proposed targets were struck soon after Rolling Thunder operations began on March 2, 1965. The preferred tactic of the JCS, enunciated several times in 1964, was to launch a sudden blow against the north. Gen. John P. McConnell, the new Air Force Chief of Staff,* was convinced that this would be the most appropriate military response to the situation facing the United States in South Vietnam.[27]

With the endorsements of General Westmoreland and Ambassador Taylor, on February 11 General Wheeler also sent an air attack plan to McNamara.† The plan was designed to impede movements of materiel and personnel from North to South Vietnam with at least 201 air strike sorties against five rail bridges and "classification yards" at Vinh, all well below the 20th parallel. This

---

* Gen. McConnell succeeded Gen. LeMay as Air Force Chief of Staff on February 1, 1965.
† Hastily put together, Gen. Wheeler's plan was not staffed through the JCS.

Tan Son Nhut Air Base.

would make it easier to trap and destroy rolling stock. Wheeler argued that the attacks by the Viet Cong on the south's rail system throughout 1963 and 1964 justified such a program. McNamara was interested in Wheeler's plan and asked for more details, but after they were provided, he continued to consider the plan in conjunction with others submitted to him.[28]

Disregarding service views on how to proceed with the bombing, the White House wrote its own scenario. On February 13, President Johnson issued a three-point military and political proposal that was cautious and suffused with political considerations, in contrast with the views of the JCS and the air commanders who wanted no more delay in launching a major air program. It recommended intensifying attempts at pacification in South Vietnam "by all available means," conducting only "measured and limited" action in the north using U.S. and GVN aircraft against targets south of the 19th parallel (at a rate of one or two attacks per week and against two or three targets on each day of operation), and "proving" Hanoi's "aggression" before the United Nations Security Council, while leaving no doubt that the United States was ready for "talks" to terminate it. The President asked Ambassador Taylor to obtain approval from Saigon on these three points. He failed to specify precisely when the bombing would continue.

Taylor, who with Bundy was a persuasive advocate of gradual bombing of North Vietnam, received the President's directive "with enthusiasm," but warned of the difficulty in obtaining Saigon's concurrence while it remained in a state of "virtual nongovernment." Nevertheless, Taylor promised to inform authorities in Saigon that a "dramatic change" was occurring in U.S. policy, one highly favorable to their interests but demanding a parallel "dramatic change" on the part of the government.[29] Between February 13 and 18, President Johnson continued to review the hazards and difficulties of conducting a regular bombing campaign against the north. Seeking advice that supported his policy, he consulted with former President Dwight D. Eisenhower, who endorsed a "campaign of pressure" against the DRV to make it pay a price and backed the use of six to eight divisions in South Vietnam if circumstances dictated. Eisenhower's overall support of the war undoubtedly gave Mr. Johnson confidence that his tentative policy was on the right track.[30]

The President was also reluctant to quickly follow the two Flaming Dart air strikes with more action for another reason. Always hopeful of a negotiating "breakthrough," he wished to await the outcome of the Soviet Union approach to the British government on February 7, on possibly reactivating the British-Soviet cochairmanship of the 1954 Geneva Conference established to deal with the Vietnam crisis. After mid-February, however, it became apparent that the "peace feeler" was without substance.[31]

Events revealed that the most compelling reason for not proceeding rapidly with further bombing was the governmental disarray in Saigon. "My advisers had long argued," the President later recalled, "that a weak government in Saigon would have difficulty surviving the pressures that might be exerted against the south if we bombed the north." There was also apprehension that South Vietnam's restless generals might impulsively act on their own. Westmoreland and Taylor alerted Washington that General Khanh (who resigned on February 26) might order a VNAF strike against the north rather than wait to coordinate it with U.S. aircraft as had been agreed.[32]

The fears were not realized. On February 18, persuaded that a modicum of political stability had been restored to the south, the President made his fateful decision to resume bombing. On his order, the JCS quickly issued an execute directive to Admiral Sharp to launch Rolling Thunder 1 on the north from "dawn to dusk" on February 20. Sharp dispatched instructions to the commanders of PACAF, PACFLT, and MACV and assigned Navy carrier aircraft to strike a naval base at Quang Khe and the VNAF to hit the Vu Con barracks, both of which were in the southernmost part of North Vietnam. If weathered out, pilots were authorized alternate targets. As in the two Flaming Dart strikes, the Air Force was restricted to flying support for the VNAF. As Sharp's coordinating authority for the U.S.-VNAF strike, General Harris again redelegated the responsibility to General Moore. To the commander, Thirteenth Air Force, at Clark AB in the Philippines, he assigned responsibility for coordinating Air Force aircraft based in Thailand should they be needed.[33]

No sooner had the JCS flashed the President's strike decision to Sharp than a new political crisis erupted in Saigon. At one in the afternoon February 18, Saigon time, Col. Pham Ngoc Thao, a participant in a previous coup attempt, tried to oust General Khanh, though not the ruling Armed Forces Council. He was aided by Brig. Gen. Lam Van Phat, a former interior minister. The troops under Thao and Phat occupied the military headquarters of the army, the radio station, and several other buildings. To prevent intervention by Gen. Nguyen Cao Ky and his air force, they rolled tanks onto the runway at Tan Son Nhut airfield on the outskirts of the capital and occupied Ky's headquarters and air communications center.[34]

Eluding the coup leaders, General Ky flew to nearby Bien Hoa Air Base and there joined forces with ARVN general Nguyen Chanh Thi. At this juncture, Brig. Gen. Robert R. Rowland, chief of the Air Force's advisory group in Saigon, contacted the VNAF commander and, in a "man to man" conversation, urged Ky to avoid bloodshed. His plea was successful, as Ky and Thi, without any killings, managed to regain control of the situation in Saigon the next day.[35]

Washington, at Ambassador Taylor's urgent request, canceled the proposed Rolling Thunder 1 strike.[36] A reshuffle of the political structure in Saigon brought to the fore a new power factor: General Ky and the Vietnamese Air Force. Ky remained on the alert for further internal struggle, despite General Westmoreland's efforts to get him to end it and direct the VNAF's energies toward the war against the communists.[37]

Meanwhile, preparations resumed for another air strike on the north, with the Air Force and Navy on alert to do so. Rolling Thunder 2 was scheduled, then Rolling Thunder 3, but each was canceled as Saigon worked toward a political resolution. It was achieved on February 26 when General Khanh resigned to assume a hastily arranged and nebulous post of Ambassador-at-Large. He was replaced by Maj. Gen. Tran Van Minh, popularly known as "Little Minh." At the same time, a civilian premier, Phan Huy Quat, whose appointment was announced on the 16th, was installed by the junta, and Taylor informed Washington it should proceed with the air strikes. Rolling Thunder program 4 was readied for execution, but bad weather blanketed most of North Vietnam for the next four days, again postponing a launch of U.S. and Vietnamese aircraft. The first Rolling Thunder strike did not get off the ground until March 2.[38]

While Saigon's politics and bad weather frustrated efforts to bomb the north, the administration attempted to strengthen its domestic and foreign support and signal Hanoi that more military pressure was imminent. In a news conference on February 25, Secretary Rusk averred that the United States would not negotiate an end to the war unless Hanoi agreed to terminate its aggression and "leave its neighbors alone."[39] Other high U.S. and South Vietnamese officials in Washington and Saigon alerted the news media to the "virtual certainty" of a limited air war against the north to assure an honorable negotiated settlement.[40] On the 27th, the State Department issued a paper summarizing "massive" evidence of Hanoi's aggression. It alleged that since 1959, more than 20,000 Viet Cong officers, soldiers, and technicians had entered South Vietnam on orders from Hanoi, and that their numbers had been swelled by a further 17,000 supporters. It declared that Hanoi's military high command was responsible for training these personnel and for their infiltration.[41] The intensive public information campaign, led by Rusk, continued into the first week of March.[42]

The Hanoi government was under no illusions about what to expect. Near the end of February, the Central Committee of the ruling Lao Dong (Labor) Party publicly declared that the primary task of the party and the people would be to maintain communications and transportation and to expect the complete destruction of the entire country, including Hanoi and Haiphong. On the 28th, the government issued its first nationwide order to citizens in the larger cities to disperse. All those not engaged in production of combat materiel (meaning, apparently, the very young and the very old) should leave the cities. Although not enforced vigorously at first, the government's action established evacuation criteria and procedures that were soon applied to other North Vietnamese areas bearing the heaviest American air attacks. By autumn 1965, an estimated 50,000 residents of Hanoi had departed, assisting American airmen in complying with their directives to minimize civilian casualties as far as possible.[43]

The First Two Rolling Thunder Strikes

After nineteen turbulent days of false starts, on March 1 the JCS ordered Admiral Sharp to proceed with the first Rolling Thunder strike, designated program 5. Once again, the air commanders were constrained by the execute and other implementing directives, since these specified both the strike day and the number of sorties to be flown; they required participation by the VNAF prior to or concurrent with U.S. air strikes; they limited strikes to targets approved by Washington; they directed pilots to dump unused ordnance in the China Sea; and they prohibited the use of napalm. In addition, reconnaissance aircraft were barred from flying over a target area immediately before an attack and, if sent on a bomb assessment mission, they had to fly unescorted and at medium altitude. There were other operational restrictions: pilots were instructed to exercise "extreme caution" in attacking North Vietnamese vessels to avoid hitting nonmilitary personnel and to inflict the "maximum feasible damage level" on authorized targets, but not to conduct restrikes without Washington's consent.*[44]

Initially, four targets designated by the JCS were earmarked for the attack,

---

* Washington's control of the first Rolling Thunder strikes early in 1965 was virtually total. Gen. Moore, the 2d Air Division commander recalls: "...I was never allowed in the early days to send a single airplane North [without being] told how many bombs I would have on it, how many airplanes were in the flight, and what time it would be over the target. And if we couldn't get there at that time for some reason (weather or what not) we couldn't put the strike on later. We had to...cancel it and start over again (Intvw, Maj. Samuel E. Riddlebarger and Lt. Col. Valentino Castellina with Gen. Moore, Nov 22, 1969, p 12).

Secretary of Defense Robert S. McNamara conducting a press briefing at the Pentagon, February 7, 1965.

but by aircraft takeoff time on March 2, the number was reduced to two: JCS target 64 at Xom Bang, an ammunition depot about ten miles above the DMZ, covering roughly thirty-five acres and containing forty-nine barracks, administration, and support structures and JCS target 74A, the north's southernmost naval base at Quang Khe, sixty-five miles above the 17th parallel and possessing berthing, repair, dry-dock, and logistic facilities.[45]

Thus, the attack on Xom Bang was the first Rolling Thunder strike and, except for the six Farm Gate A–1Es used during the VNAF-Farm Gate strikes on February 8, it was also the first conducted solely by Air Force tactical aircraft. The assault force consisted of twenty-five F–105s and twenty B–57s with a "mix" of supporting aircraft: sixteen F–105s and eight F–100s for flak suppression; F–100s for MiG and rescue combat air patrol (CAP); two RF–101s for reconnaissance, and six SAC KC–135s for refueling. Most of the F–105s and some of the F–100s came from Korat and Takhli in Thailand. Strike aircraft carried 250-pound and 500-pound general-purpose bombs and CBU–2A fragmentation bomblets. No MiGs were encountered and the attacks destroyed or damaged an estimated 75 to 80 percent of the target area, with thirty-six to forty-nine structures completely demolished. Personnel casualties were undetermined.[46] B–52 bombers on Guam were alerted, this time for a night strike on the ammunition depot, but were not used.[47]

Almost simultaneously, twenty South Vietnamese A–1Hs, supported by about sixty F–105s, F–100s and RF–101s from the 2d Air Division hit the naval base at Quang Khe. VNAF pilots dropped 250-pound fragmentation and 500-pound general-purpose bombs and CBU–2A ordnance. As with the air strike on Xom Bang, bomb damage assessment disclosed that about 75 to 80 percent of the target area, consisting mainly of buildings, was destroyed or damaged. Again, there was no information on personnel casualties. The cost of the air strikes was high: the Air Force lost three F–105s in the assault on Xom Bang and two F–100s over Quang Khe. With the exception of one Thunderchief pilot, all airmen were rescued.[48]

Unlike the Flaming Dart sorties I and II in February, the double air strike was not launched in retaliation for a specific attack on U.S. installations in the south. In fact, communist activity in the preceding week had been at a very low level. According to officials in Saigon, the purpose of the strike was "to make clear to Hanoi that North Vietnam will be held fully responsible for continuing aggression against South Vietnam."[49] Secretary McNamara explained the new bombing policy before a House appropriations subcommittee: "We will not limit our bombing to respond to their attacks on U.S. personnel or property. We will attack the north when it seems necessary to respond properly to their level of infiltration or support of aggression in the South." The principal military effort, he added, would remain in South Vietnam.[50]

On March 9, the President approved a second Rolling Thunder strike, designated program 6. The execute message from the Joint Chiefs to Admiral Sharp directed two separate daylight strikes on the 11th, Saigon time. On the same day, administration officials allowed the Air Force and the Navy to make daily photo and weather reconnaissance flights over North Vietnam south of the 19th parallel. Nicknamed Blue Tree, the new program would follow the targeting and reporting procedures employed in the Air Force-Navy Yankee Team reconnaissance operations. The initial photo missions over the north were also tightly controlled by Washington officials. After program 6, reconnaissance pilots would be restricted to a "single pass" mission at low level to assess target damage.[51]

However, it would be five days before Rolling Thunder program 6 was flown, mainly because VNAF pilots were not on alert at Da Nang, although bad weather also contributed to the standdown. Air rules still required that the VNAF participate with U.S. (specifically Air Force) missions. General Ky claimed that his A–1H Skyraiders were not ready and needed inspection, although American officials in Saigon were inclined to attribute the VNAF's hesitation to the danger of another coup. Ambassador Taylor expressed the frustration of the services: "We are failing to give the mounting crescendo to Rolling Thunder," he said, "which is necessary to get the desired result."

On the 14th, with improved but still marginal weather and the VNAF again on alert, Rolling Thunder program 6 was launched. General Ky led the attack against a barracks area containing seven buildings that housed an estimated 250 to 300 troops on Hon Gio (Tiger) Island, about twenty miles off the North Vietnamese coast and slightly above the 17th parallel. Ky's strike force consisted of twenty A–1Hs loaded with 250-pound, 500-pound, and 750-pound bombs and 2.75-inch rockets. The VNAF commander's force was supported by twenty-three Air Force F–100s and F–105s to suppress flak and guard against possible MiG interception. As a result of the strikes, two buildings were destroyed by fire and five were damaged. Neither the VNAF or the USAF aircraft sustained damages or losses from groundfire.[52]

The next day (March 15) a joint Air Force-Navy force struck the Phu Qui ammunition depot that covered about forty acres some one hundred miles southwest of Hanoi. Of 137 aircraft dispatched, 84 flew a strike profile (20 Air Force F–105s and 64 Navy A–1Hs, A–4Cs, and A–4Es). Air Force ordnance consisted of 250-pound and 750-pound general-purpose bombs, 2.75-inch rockets, and napalm, which was authorized for the first time. As on the previous day, the missions were flown in marginal weather. About 33 percent of the target area was hit and bomb damage assessment photos confirming that at least three ammunition structures and one support building were destroyed and seventeen damaged. Bombs also inflicted damage outside of the target zone. The only loss was a Navy aircraft that crashed short of a carrier on its return flight, apparently as a result of a mechanical problem rather than from enemy groundfire.[53]

Initial Analysis of Aircraft Losses

Although gratified by the results of the Flaming Dart-Rolling Thunder strikes, the services and administration authorities, especially McNamara, were deeply concerned about the aircraft attrition inflicted by enemy groundfire. By March 2, eleven aircraft had been shot down (five Air Force, four Navy, and two VNAF) and forty-one damaged (seven Navy and thirty-four VNAF) during the strikes. The Defense Secretary asked the Joint Staff to analyze the loss rates quickly, compare them with those of World War II and the Korean War, and to submit recommendations for reducing losses.[54] At the same time, with McNamara's approval, General McConnell quickly established a USAF Analysis Team, headed by Maj. Gen. Gordon M. Graham, Vice Commander, Tactical Air Command (TAC), to undertake a second and more comprehensive study of aircraft attrition.[55]

Air Force concern about the north's antiaircraft defenses was pervasive. Secretary of the Air Force Eugene M. Zuckert foresaw a "credibility" problem arising from the loss of tactical aircraft to "unsophisticated" weapons. Combat crews of USAF's 18th and 469th TFSs attested to the effectiveness of the enemy's small arms and automatic weapons. To some aircrews, it seemed that nearly every foot soldier had an automatic weapon "so barrage capability of small arms fire is a threat up to 1,000 feet in or near target complexes." In fact, most of the aircraft destroyed or damaged were hit by small arms fire under this altitude. A change in tactics was imperative: fewer aircraft—no more than sixteen—should be sent against a defended target complex in a single attack and cluster bombs, dropped from no lower than 1,000 feet whenever possible. In another study, Admiral Sharp's analysts noted that bad weather seldom permitted dive bombing. They observed that pilots could expect cloud layers at 3,500 feet more than 50 percent of the time and usually did not have good strike weather until the middle of the afternoon, a circumstance not lost on the North Vietnamese who knew when to be on the alert for most of the attacks. The analysts also noted the complaint of air commanders, who believed higher authorities did not allow them sufficient operational "flexibility" to conduct the air

Eugene M. Zuckert,
Secretary of the Air Force,
1961–1965.

strikes, which contributed to the high aircraft losses.[56]

The Joint Chiefs' initial findings were compiled with the studies by the Air Force and Navy analysts and sent to McNamara by General Wheeler on March 10. They were based on 505 missions totaling 2,565 Air Force and Navy sorties (Farm Gate and VNAF sorties were excluded) flown in 1964 and 1965 over Laos and North Vietnam. Loss rates (based on 1,000 sorties) compared favorably with those sustained in previous wars: World War II; 0.9 percent; Korea, 0.3 percent; and Southeast Asia, 0.6 percent. Wheeler believed improved tactics and equipment would eventually reduce the loss rate, as in previous wars.

The report listed several items to lower the loss rate: the recommendations by Air Force and Navy air commanders for reducing aircraft attrition in North Vietnam and Laos; lifting the ban on napalm and other types of improved ordnance; random reconnaissance and more prestrike reconnaissance at medium and low altitudes to preclude "signaling" air missions; better security, cover, and deception activities at Vietnamese and American-occupied airbases; and greater operational "flexibility" for air commanders on the timing of air strikes and in the selection of alternate targets. The last recommendation was crucial to compensate for poor weather and enemy antiaircraft defenses.[57]

A few days after Wheeler submitted his report, Dr. Harold Brown, OSD's Director of Defense Research and Engineering (DDR&E) ordered the Weapons System Evaluation Group within the JCS to establish a study unit to conduct further analyses of aircraft destruction. Dr. Brown believed this would aid research and development efforts to reduce combat aircraft losses.[58]

Meanwhile, General Graham's analysis team was completing its study of aircraft attrition in Southeast Asia. For statistical purposes, the team's database was limited to one Barrel Roll mission and one Rolling Thunder mission in which Air Force and Navy aircraft sustained considerable damage. In a preliminary report to Secretary McNamara, sent through Air Force Secretary Zuckert in April, Graham endorsed virtually all of the changes recommended by Wheeler and added others: fewer "flash" precedence messages from Washington, especially those containing last-minute changes to missions; more uniform rules of engagement in the war theater (the rules for the air programs in North Vietnam and Laos varied widely); deployment of Air Force reconnaissance RB–66s equipped with electronic countermeasures (ECM) gear* to conduct missions against radar-controlled antiaircraft guns; use of delayed-fuse bombs; better night interdiction capability; modifications in the dive bombing training programs in the United States paralleling the development of new types of ordnance nicknamed Snake Eye, Dragon Tooth, and Gravel.

In separate briefings and reports for the Air Force, General Graham stressed the need for pilots to receive more realistic training before their assignment to combat duty. Their training, he said, should go beyond gunnery school patterns, and airmen flying in squadron formation should relearn the technique of flying and fighting as a squadron. A follow-on study by TAC operations analysts who interviewed officers of the 2d Air Division in May 1965 further emphasized the need for more practice in gunnery and weapons delivery. The analysts concluded that combat preparation should require the use of bombing ranges containing camouflaged real targets such as vehicles, bridges, and gun emplacements; practice with 750-pound bombs, napalm, CBUs, and newer types of ordnance such as Snake Eye and Lazy Dog, but without the use of run-in headings and ordnance release altitudes; and using tactics, dive angles, and release altitudes that minimized aircraft exposure to groundfire. These findings would change TAC's training program over the coming months.[59]

General Graham's final report, which was processed through the Joint Staff, was submitted to the Defense Secretary on May 22. The Joint Staff addressed the operational restrictions imposed by Washington that prevented air commanders from engaging in "optimum" tactics to reduce aircraft attrition, including restrictions on bombing target areas, restrikes, use of advanced ordnance, and selection of secondary targets. Further, the injunction to achieve "maximum feasible damage" in single strikes encouraged air commanders to dispatch more strike aircraft than was prudent given the strength of enemy antiaircraft positions. Frequent detailed guidance on air routes and entry into a target area often eliminated the element of surprise. The command and control system was cumbersome,

---

* Initially, Air Force personnel did not differentiate carefully between RB–66 reconnaissance aircraft equipped with cameras and infrared detectors and those equipped to detect and jam enemy radars in electronic countermeasures (ECM) operations. Eventually a distinction was made between RB–66Bs and RB–66Cs, although the B models might engage in reconnaissance rather than ECM. In the spring of 1966, the Air Force began to designate

complex, and unrealistic. In brief, aircraft attrition could be reduced most readily in the same manner that operational effectiveness could be enhanced: by allowing Air Force and Navy air commanders greater flexibility in planning and executing air strikes.[60]

Although Mr. McNamara did not reply formally to the JCS report, the services were already revising some of their aerial tactics. However, air commanders still did not have the operational flexibility they considered essential that, in their view, would shorten the war and save many aircraft and American lives.

An Air Strategy Emerges

As had happened with the Flaming Dart strikes, the first Rolling Thunder strikes on March 2 reverberated in world capitals. In Paris there was renewed anxiety, in Tokyo criticism, and in Moscow communist leaders attending a conclave predictably condemned the attacks.[61] Domestic and worldwide concern increased when, four days after Rolling Thunder 5, the Defense Department announced that 3,500 Marines of the 9th Marine Expeditionary Brigade were on their way to Da Nang to provide additional security for the military center serving as the springboard for most Air Force attacks on the north, for Barrel Roll operations in northern Laos, and for many Air Force-Marine operations against the Viet Cong in the south. After the first contingent of "leathernecks" reached Da Nang on March 8 (by mid-April, 8,000 would be stationed there), Hanoi charged that their arrival was "an open declaration of war on the entire Vietnamese people," and vowed to defend itself, and Peking saw "a grave move to further expand the war in Indochina."[62]

Against these events, the Secretary General of the United Nations appealed to the principal nations involved in the conflict (the United States, the Soviet Union, Great Britain, France, China, and South and North Vietnam) to convene a preliminary conference to discuss the issues. The United States' response was a rejection of U Thant's offer until North Vietnam stopped its aggression against South Vietnam.[63] In support of this stance, the State Department circulated a memorandum proclaiming that U.S. and South Vietnamese air attacks on the north were "fully justified" under international law, and consonant with the United Nations charter and the 1954 Geneva agreements on Vietnam.[64]

As Washington officials saw it, the bombing policy could not be suspended, at least for the time being, in light of the continued military and political reports of deterioration in South Vietnam. Before more strikes were carried out,

---

all RB–66s engaged in ECM as EB–66s. For the sake of consistency, the latter designation will be used as applicable throughout this narrative (See Bernard C. Nalty, *Tactics and Techniques of Electronic Warfare: Electronic Countermeasures in the Air War Against North Vietnam, 1965–1973* (Ofc AF Hist, 1977), p 19.

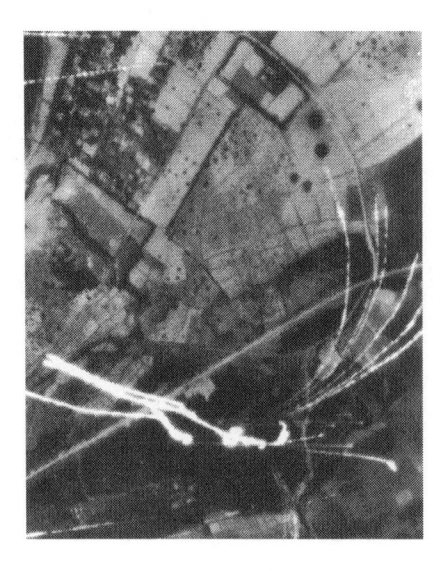

Appearing to curve as they streak skyward, these tracers from small and medium antiaircraft guns were filmed during a reconnaissance flight over a staging area ten miles south of Dong Hoi.

the first strikes were examined closely, but Admiral Sharp and his analysts could not determine the total impact. Nonetheless, the PACOM commander conjectured that Hanoi was playing a "waiting game" until American intentions toward the north were clearer. His confidence in the potential of air power was complete:

> The damage inflicted by these attacks on LOCs and military installations in North Vietnam will cause a diminution of the support being rendered to the Viet Cong. Successful strikes on bridges will degrade the transportation system and an attendant reduction in its capability to transport food and materials from production to storage areas. Manpower and supplies will undoubtedly be diverted toward the recovery and rebuilding process. While the effect may not be felt immediately by the VC, this increased pressure will demonstrate our strength of purpose and at the same time make support of the VC as onerous as possible.

Sharp's latest "optimum" air program called for attacks initially below the 20th parallel on eleven targets designated by the JCS, wider ranging reconnaissance, harassment of rolling stock and truck shuttling, and then more bombing of other primary and secondary LOC targets. He proposed sending two to four aircraft on each daylight mission and beginning night operations. This tactic would be followed by "maximum intensity" air strikes on ten JCS targets above the 20th parallel (not in the Hanoi-Haiphong area) and by armed reconnaissance on five North Vietnamese supply routes.[65]

While high administration officials moved slowly toward a decision on the scope and tempo of Rolling Thunder, Ambassador Taylor, increasingly apprehensive about the declining fortunes of the Saigon government, strongly urged that air operations be intensified. He believed Hanoi had construed the initial strikes merely as "a few isolated thunderclaps" whereas their objective was to convince the DRV of "progressively severe punishment." The ambassador declared there was "an urgent need" for a consensus on "measured and limited air action" lasting several weeks, with one or two air attacks per week on two or three targets, and retaining the option of heavier strikes in more northern areas. Taylor thought that the eight weeks of bombing proposed tentatively by the JCS, while very useful, was limited to targets too far south of the 19th parallel. But to avoid giving Hanoi a misleading signal, U.S. aircraft should also hit targets immediately north of the 19th parallel in "a slow but steadily ascending movement." He foresaw no difficulty in coping with the north's MiGs.

The ambassador decried international pressure on the United States to negotiate with Hanoi without "clear evidence" that Hanoi (and Peking) were "prepared to leave their neighbors alone." He cited a recent observation by Blair Seaborn, Canada's representative to the International Control Commission* who found in Hanoi an air of confidence and an impression that the bombing was limited to improving the United States' bargaining position and "hence of no great cause for immediate concern." Significantly, Taylor's views on the scope and intensity of an air program and on negotiations had the explicit endorsement of General Westmoreland.[66]

Gen. Harold K. Johnson, Army Chief of Staff, made further recommendations. General Johnson had been sent to Saigon at the personal request of President Johnson and Secretary McNamara to make a comprehensive evaluation of Saigon's sagging military and political situation, and on March 15, he presented the President with a pivotal 21-point program for alleviating South Vietnam's internal difficulties and improving the limited bombing programs in North Vietnam and Laos. The air war thus far against North Vietnam, he said, was inadequate "to convey a clear sense of U.S. purpose to Hanoi." He recommended increasing the scope and tempo of operations, canceling the requirement for Washington's approval for each alternate target, selecting targets from a narrow geographical area, flying U.S. and VNAF strike missions concurrently, and using only unclassified or older types of munitions. He also called for more covert (i.e., plan 34A attacks) air, ground, and seaborne activities against the north. In Laos, he proposed limiting the Barrel Roll program to the northern part of the country and inaugurating a new, anti-infiltration attack program along infiltration routes in the Laotian panhandle. The Army Chief of Staff conceded that these stronger military measures, especially against the north, could escalate the war, but they also promised to induce Hanoi to cease and desist in

---

* Since June 18, 1964, Mr. Seaborn visited Hanoi periodically to convey the American view of the war and on negotiations.

its support of the Viet Cong.[67]

Beginning of Weekly Rolling Thunder Strikes

The President immediately approved most of General Johnson's recommendations for the north. However, he and most of his advisers, including Secretary McNamara, agreed that a regular bombing program should proceed very cautiously and with continued tight controls from Washington. This was made clear in the Joint Chiefs' directive to Admiral Sharp on March 16 that informed him the next series of Rolling Thunder strikes, scheduled to begin on March 19, would be planned on a weekly basis. South Vietnamese and VNAF aircraft, USAF units based in Thailand, and Navy carrier aircraft would all be involved in the missions. All operations by USAF aircraft from Thai bases would continue to be cleared through the U.S. Embassy in Bangkok. In addition to strikes on fixed targets, one U.S. and two VNAF armed reconnaissance missions would be permitted weekly, although concurrent USAF-VNAF missions were no longer mandatory. USAF advisors could accompany Vietnamese airmen, but only in aircraft marked with USAF insignia, USAF combat pilots could "fill out" VNAF sortie requirements beyond the capability of the Vietnamese.[68]

On the same day, the service chiefs raised the northernmost limit of Air Force and Navy Blue Tree reconnaissance missions from the 19th to the 20th parallel and allowed them to be accompanied by fighters for combat air patrol. Pilots were ordered not to pick a fight with the North Vietnamese Air Force MiGs, and if any were sighted, should withdraw. The fighters were authorized to engage in combat only to protect reconnaissance aircraft from an attack. Two days later, as an additional precaution, air commanders were directed to fly photo, visual, infrared, radar, and other sensor-equipped aircraft at or above 10,000 feet and to remain south of the 20th parallel. Although General Harris, the PACAF commander, insisted that the need for low-level reconnaissance missions was "imperative," Sharp, who fully agreed, noted that the political "climate" in Washington was "not right" to press the issue. He counseled patience and expressed confidence that approval would be obtained eventually.[69]

General McConnell, the new Air Force Chief of Staff, viewed the administration's bombing policy with considerable disquiet. Convinced it was far too restrictive, on March 17 he sought JCS endorsement of an air and naval offensive plan that had been devised to allow the Air Force to strike the ninety-four JCS-designated targets over a period of twenty-eight days. Like General LeMay, and other Air Force commanders, and General Greene, the Marine Commandant, he believed air power should be applied more quickly against the north's vital targets. Otherwise the United States might find itself in a prolonged ground war in South Vietnam or forced to invade North Vietnam.[70]

The Joint Staff quickly expanded McConnell's proposal into a tentative four-phase plan. In phase I, air commanders would reduce the flow of manpower and materiel moving southward with an intensive, three-week bombing campaign against the north's transportation network below the 20th parallel. The campaign would also send a "signal" to Hanoi concerning the United States' ability to widen the scope and intensity of the bombing. Phase II would be a six-week campaign to cut the northeast and northwest rail lines into China, bringing the war closer to the regime's government and people. Phase III, lasting two weeks, would introduce the mining of the north's seaward approaches, all of its ports, and the ammunition and supply centers in the Hanoi-Haiphong area. This would complete the attacks on most of the ninety-four targets, and hopefully convince Hanoi that the takeover of South Vietnam was no longer worth the price. Finally, phase IV would last two weeks and would be directed against whatever industrial targets remained outside of the populated areas and any targets that had not been fully destroyed or had been repaired.[71]

Three days after McConnell sent his plan forward, the Joint Staff prepared a twelve-week bombing proposal requested by McNamara. Other proposals from the field were also examined by the Joint Staff. All required comments by Admiral Sharp's PACOM headquarters, his PACAF and PACFLT component commands, and MACV. The short-range and long-range planning exercises revealed that recent JCS agreements on the need for a more intensive Rolling Thunder program had glossed over long-standing differences among the services. As in the previous year, Generals McConnell and Greene still championed a series of rapid attacks on all of the north's major industrial and transportation targets while the Army's position, articulated by General Westmoreland, called for gradually escalating strikes, initially below the 20th parallel, until their impact could be assessed carefully. This approach would also reduce the danger of Chinese intervention in the war, and the Administration had already aligned itself with this view.[72]

Meanwhile, as plans were being laid for the bombing scheduled to begin on March 19 as Rolling Thunder program 7, Admiral Sharp proposed a massive "radar busting" day in southern North Vietnam. He said that this would dramatize the United States' ability to destroy the north's air defense command and control network at will. However, McNamara decided only three radar sites should be struck initially. A JCS directive, based on McNamara's guidance, spelled out in considerable detail how the services should proceed. Three radar sites at Vinh Son, Vinh Linh, and Dong Hoi should be struck in conjunction with three armed reconnaissance missions over segments of the coastal north-south Route 1, with all targets well below the 20th parallel. U.S. aircraft should strike the first two JCS targets and one radar site and the VNAF the third target and two radar sites. All Air Force aircraft in Thailand scheduled for operations in North Vietnam and Laos still had to be "cleared" by the U.S. Embassy in Bangkok.[73]

Nonetheless, the restrictions were somewhat less confining than for the first two Rolling Thunder attacks. PACAF pilots were no longer limited to flying missions only in conjunction with the VNAF and could "fill out" VNAF operations as necessary against military vehicles and rolling stock, and air commanders had seven days in which to complete their strikes on authorized targets. As in the initial attacks, pilots were ordered to achieve the "maximum feasible damage" against their objectives.[74]

Navy carrier aircraft flew the first Rolling Thunder 7 mission on the 19th, striking the Phu Van ammunition depot and the Vinh Son army supply depot. The Phu Van target, about 20.5 n.m. northwest of Vinh, consisted of eighty-two buildings. The Navy launched eighty-six aircraft, fifty-seven in a strike role, with damage estimated at 50 percent. Only six Air Force strike aircraft were used for an attack on twelve buildings in the Vinh Son area, but they damaged an estimated 70 percent of them.

There were no attacks on the 20th, but on the 21st, twenty-four VNAF A–1Es hit the Vu Con army barracks one mile north of the DMZ. The supporting Air Force planes included Farm Gate "pathfinders," which led VNAF pilots to the target areas, and aircraft providing reconnaissance, flak suppression, combat air patrol, bomb damage assessment, and rescue. As in previous attacks on the north, the Farm Gate aircraft bore USAF insignia.[75]

On March 22, flying the first of three armed reconnaissance missions, the Air Force hit a radar site seven miles north of Vinh Son, the first mission not flown in conjunction with the VNAF. Eighteen aircraft were dispatched, with eight F–105 Thunderchiefs in a strike profile. One Thunderchief was lost when the squadron flight commander's aircraft was hit. The flight commander bailed out and was rescued in fifteen minutes.[76]

Over the next two days, with Air Force support, the VNAF twice attacked radar sites. In the first mission, seventeen aircraft (eight VNAF and nine Air Force) struck a coastal early warning site near Vinh, about three miles above the DMZ. In the second, eighteen aircraft (eight VNAF, ten Air Force) flew against an early warning site near Dong Hoi. Enjoying clear visibility at Vinh, VNAF pilots claimed "100 percent" site damage, but the second mission encountered bad weather and was unable to reach the target. Pilots dropped their ordnance on an antiaircraft position a mile west of the radar site. No aircraft were lost or damaged in the twin attacks. In accordance with McNamara's guidance,[77] Rolling Thunder program 8 (March 26–April 1) authorized strikes or restrikes on eight radar sites and on the Vit Thu Lu barracks. CINCPAC allocated four sites each to the Air Force and Navy and scheduled three armed reconnaissance missions, two to be flown by U.S. and one by VNAF aircraft. The rules for program 7 applied except that pilots were granted slightly more authority. When attacking the radar sites, they could hit ancillary military installations, support facilities, targets of opportunity, vehicles and DRV water patrol craft. The armed reconnaissance area was extended slightly northward toward the 20th parallel.[78]

Last minute changes altered strike plans. Because of weather, missions were flown only on March 26, 30, and 31, and six of eight radar sites were struck. These were at or in the vicinity of Cap Mui Ron, Ha Tinh, Cua Lo, and on the coastal islands of Bach Long, Hon Ngu, and Hon Matt. The Navy flew seven missions, the Air Force two, and the VNAF one, with Air Force support. The VNAF was scheduled to hit the Vit Thu Lu barracks, but selected the Dong Hoi airfield as an alternate target. In the first strike on an airfield, the VNAF destroyed four of fifteen buildings and cratered the runway and parking area.

Results of Rolling Thunder 8 were based largely on pilot estimates. Navy claims ranged from 43 to 100 percent destruction or damage to target areas while the Air Force reported damage to 50 percent of its targets at Hon Matt. No damage was inflicted on Hon Ngu, as all bombs missed the target. The VNAF-Air Force assault on Dong Hoi airfield was judged to have been 81 percent effective. Intelligence analysts found some evidence that the North Vietnamese had moved radar equipment at several sites just prior to or immediately after the air strikes.[79]

The North Vietnamese exacted a severe penalty for program 8, especially from the Navy, which lost nine aircraft: four A–1Hs, two A–4Es, and three F–8Ds. The Air Force lost one F–105 and the VNAF none.[80] There was some consolation in the valuable experience gained over the north. By the end of March, they had struck eighteen of the targets designated by the JCS south of the 20th parallel, as well as many smaller ones. Several lessons on the usefulness of different types of ordnance had been learned. Napalm was most effective against barracks and supply buildings, general-purpose bombs against revetted and concrete structures, and rockets against manned antiaircraft sites and watercraft.[81] In his assessment of the initial Rolling Thunder operations, Ambassador Taylor believed they had brought about "a clear lift in morale" in South Vietnam.[82]

Supporting Operations for Rolling Thunder

Washington's insistence on restricting Air Force and Navy reconnaissance aircrews to medium-altitude missions impeded Rolling Thunder operations throughout March. As noted, General Harris, had emphasized the need for low-level pre- and poststrike reconnaissance, and Admiral Sharp had heartily agreed. On the 21st, in outlining a two-phase program to cut lines of communication, Sharp informed the JCS that weather over the north in April would probably render 40 to 60 percent of medium-level reconnaissance missions nonproductive. When he visited Washington late in the month, Ambassador Taylor sided with the air commanders in their requests to remove the altitude restriction. On March 30, the authorities at last permitted photoreconnaissance at lower altitude and simultaneously extended the authorized reconnaissance area from the 20th to the 21st parallel. For the first time, Sharp could also schedule photo missions at his discretion.[83]

The removal of the altitude limitation was not without strings. The PACOM commander could schedule no more than ten two-aircraft missions per week or

F–100 flying flak suppression fires rockets at an enemy gun position.

a total of twenty sorties, aircraft were forbidden to intrude within forty n.m. of Phuc Yen airfield and Haiphong, and the JCS would decide on a case-by-case basis whether to approve requests for supporting flak suppression.[84]

These restrictions notwithstanding, Washington authorized more reconnaissance for North Vietnam and Laos, speeding plans by General Moore and his staff to redeploy and augment the 2d Air Division's RF–101 force. On March 6, several personnel of the 15th Tactical Reconnaissance Squadron (TRS) at Tan Son Nhut flew to Udorn, Thailand, to arrange for the redeployment of some of the Voodoos at that base, and on the 31st the first four RF–101 units of the 15th TRS arrived there. Nicknamed Green Python, the unit flew its first Yankee Team mission over Laos the next day, and in April they began Blue Tree missions over the north. A month later, the Thai government authorized eight more RF–101s at Udorn, bringing the total to twelve, providing regular reconnaissance for Rolling Thunder. The 2d Air Division was soon flying about two-thirds of the tactical reconnaissance missions over the north while the Navy flew the remainder.[85]

The Air Force took other actions in support of the Rolling Thunder program. Thirty-four MiG–15s and MiG–17s were based at Phuc Yen airfield near Hanoi, and the Air Force requested a squadron of F–4s to provide cover for reconnaissance and strike missions over the north. On April 1, McNamara approved the JCS recommendation to move this squadron to Udorn. The two-seat Phantoms were the newest and most sophisticated fighters in the Air Force's inventory. Responding quickly, Tactical Air Command dispatched the 45th TFS of the 15th TFW from the United States to Udorn, where it arrived on April 7. Aircrews immediately began flying combat air patrol.[86] Also at the Air Force's request, the JCS authorized TAC to begin modifying several RB–66 reconnaissance aircraft to provide an electronic intelligence (ELINT) and countermeasures capability against Hanoi's expanding ground communication intercept (GCI) system and possibly Soviet-built SA–2 surface-to-air missiles (SAMs).[87] In Honolulu and Saigon, military and civilian psychological warfare specialists prepared for a major overt leaflet dropping program against the north's populace and leadership. Specially equipped Air Force and Vietnamese fighters would distribute the leaflets.[88]

On the night of April 3, in an effort to reduce the infiltration of manpower and supplies through southern Laos, General Moore launched two missions against enemy truck traffic on segments of three truck routes. Each mission consisted of a navigation and flare-carrying C–130 Blindbat and two strike B–57s. Recommended by General Johnson in mid-March and approved by the President shortly thereafter, these missions began a new Air Force and Navy anti-infiltration interdiction program nicknamed Steel Tiger,* that was intended to supplement the Rolling Thunder program against the north.[89]

Contingency Planning for a Larger Conflict

The beginning of Rolling Thunder triggered more JCS planning to counter any strong military reactions by Hanoi, Peking, or Moscow. In their eight-week bombing scenario, drafted at McNamara's request early in February 1965, the Joint Chiefs speculated that:

> the DRV, communist China, and the Soviet Union will make every effort through propaganda and diplomatic moves to halt the U.S. attacks. The DRV will defend itself, and open, overt aggression in South Vietnam and Laos by the DRV might occur.... Hanoi would probably elect to maintain the very intense levels of activity of the past few days.

As the bombing intensified, however, the Joint Chiefs foresaw that the Chinese and Soviets might take additional measures. The Chinese might send "volunteers" into North Vietnam and northern Laos, thereby raising "the specter of further escalation to underline their commitment to assist the North Vietnamese, and to challenge the Soviets to extend corresponding support." The Soviets would probably intensify their diplomatic and propaganda effort "to bring the United States to the conference table," and step up their shipments of antiaircraft artillery, radars, and perhaps SA–2 missiles to Hanoi.[90]

The most likely threat was open intervention by the Hanoi and Peking governments rather than the Soviets, but the Joint Chiefs were confident the United States and its allies could deal with such an eventuality.[91] On hand were CINCPAC's Operations Plan 32-64 or CINCPAC's Operations Plan 39-64. The

---

* For a discussion of the origins and initial operations of the Steel Tiger program, see Jacob Van Staaveren, *Interdiction in Southern Laos, 1960–1968* (Washington, 1993), p 147.

first was basically defensive, requiring large numbers of American and allied ground forces to prevent a Chinese takeover of mainland Southeast Asia; the second was an Air Force and Naval plan to deter, or if necessary, halt a major Chinese thrust into Southeast Asia or into South Korea, Taiwan, or Burma. Not surprisingly, the services were divided on the merits of the two plans. The Army, always ground-oriented, favored the first, while the Air Force and Navy, opposing large-scale use of American troops on the Asian mainland, supported the second.[92]

General Wheeler considered both plans inadequate, plan 32-64 because it was not logistically sustainable in the short term, and plan 39-64* because it was not politically feasible. He doubted that the authorities in Washington were capable of making a quick decision to use the Air Force and Navy to prevent Chinese troops from moving into South Vietnam, Thailand, or Burma or from making diversionary actions against South Korea or Taiwan. He directed the Joint Staff to determine the minimum number of ground and air units needed in Southeast Asia and the Pacific to keep the Chinese from taking over the countries defended by or allied to the United States.[93]

General McConnell disagreed strongly with Wheeler's assertion that plan 39-64 was not politically viable, and lent his planning support for a possible land war in Asia. He was convinced that the most prudent action was to deploy the fifteen Air Force squadrons to bases in Southeast Asia and the Pacific as envisaged in plan 39-64. This was not only possible logistically, but was the best strategy to meet the twin threats of Hanoi and Peking.[94] General Harris articulated the Air Force's strategic view more precisely:

> While we are hurting both VC and Hanoi by increased air strikes in SVN and DRV, it would be prudent to convey a concurrent message to Peking. This can be done quickly by significant deployments of air power around the periphery of China rather than large-scale ground deployments to SEA. I see...major ground deployments as inconsistent with sound strategy which could take advantage of our superiority in air and naval strength. We've already noted a buildup of Soviet strength in Vladivostok area and see [a] continuing shift of China air strength to the south. If we place the principal emphasis in Southeast Asia, we may mislead Peking and, in fact, encourage concentration of their support for Hanoi rather than forcing a China posture to cope with other possible actions on China's periphery. We should make it unmistakably clear to Peking that the United States will not restrict action as we did in Korea.

Harris cited the Berlin and Cuban missile crises as precedents where signif-

---

* The plans were updated frequently and soon renumbered 32-65 and 39-65.

icant Air Force deployments provided deterrence and made all but a few other combat forces unnecessary. Within the JCS, General McConnell reminded his colleagues that they had previously approved CINCPACs air-oriented Air Force and Navy plan 39-64 and considered it feasible, as it would allow the U.S. government to engage or disengage its forces in the Pacific as necessary. Preparing still another concept as desired by General Wheeler, he said, would take time.[95]

Of course, it was not possible to override the request of the JCS Chairman for the Joint Staff to also examine about ten alternate U.S. and allied deployment proposals for South Vietnam and Thailand that had surfaced in recent days with sizeable ground forces. The principal concepts called for the deployment of one or two U.S. Army divisions in northeast Thailand or one Army division around Saigon or near Pleiku in the central highlands, a U.S. or multinational force under the aegis of the Southeast Asia Treaty Organization (SEATO)* in South Vietnam below the DMZ, a South Korean division near Saigon, and U.S. ground units for beach enclaves along South Vietnam's coastal areas.[96] Except for the coastal ground enclave concept, the Air Force strongly opposed the dispatch of division-level forces to Thailand and South Vietnam and, with the Navy, believed that the United States should rely principally on air and naval power for either defensive or offensive operations against China and North Vietnam. The Army, on the other hand, staunchly believed neither major defensive nor offensive operations were possible without sizeable ground forces. The Marine Corps shared the Army's view regarding South Vietnam because of the instability of the government and the unreliability of its leaders.[97]

As China would not enter the war, contingency planning for the "worst case" military threat remained only an exercise, but high-level debate on strategy and planning continued over the size of U.S. and allied forces that would be required to stop the deteriorating situation in South Vietnam.

---

* Signed on September 8, 1954, by eight Asian and western nations, including the United States, to prevent the further spread of communism in Southeast Asia, the SEATO Pact came into force on February 20, 1955.

Bridge damaged by bombing in 1965.

CHAPTER 4
Gradual Expansion

Washington's decision to inaugurate the Rolling Thunder and Steel Tiger programs in North Vietnam and Laos, respectively, did not end debate on how to prosecute the war. In late March and the first two days of April, when the National Security Council addressed the subject, high officials expressed conflicting views. The Joint Chiefs believed that direct action was "imperative" to halt the decline in South Vietnam. They recommended the deployment of three ground divisions (two American, one Korean) to bolster Saigon's military effort and four more Air Force squadrons to apply "more forceful...pressure on the north."[1] John P. McCone, the Director of the CIA, conceded that more U.S. troops were needed but believed that the major emphasis should be on bombing.[2] Conversely, General Westmoreland proposed sending more troops to South Vietnam and then waiting until June 1965 to determine whether the Rolling Thunder program was successful. If not, the United States should send additional combat manpower, but not substantially more aircraft.*[3]

Ambassador Taylor was also pessimistic about the potential effect of the Rolling Thunder program, and he insisted that it could not win the war. He played down the threat of the North Vietnamese MiGs based at Phuc Yen airfield. On the other hand, he was in favor of the mining of Haiphong harbor by the VNAF and credited the bombing with having raised the morale of the South Vietnamese people. With John T. McNaughton, Assistant Secretary of Defense for International Security Affairs, he opposed a major increase in U.S. troops in the south.[4]

McNaughton hoped that the military situation in the south had "bottomed out" and would not propel the United States into using "extreme measures" against Hanoi. He suggested redefining America's Southeast Asia objectives, which he said were to avoid a humiliating defeat (70 percent), to keep South Vietnam and adjacent territory out of Chinese hands (20 percent), and to permit the South Vietnamese people to enjoy a better and freer way of life (10 percent).[5] George W. Ball, Under Secretary of State, was in favor of cutting American losses with no further commitment to the war.[6] But William P. Bundy, Assistant Secretary of State for Far Eastern Affairs, who supported the bombing, believed that after two or three months of Rolling Thunder, Hanoi might begin "making noises" about negotiations. By then, there should be "clear evidence" the United States had the means to win in South Vietnam.[7]

---

* For more discussion of the various views on the planning and implementation of Rolling Thunder strikes, see Mark Clodfelter, *The Limits of Air Power: The American Bombing of North Vietnam* (New York, 1989), chap 2; Earl H. Tilford, Jr., *Crosswinds: The Air Force's Setup in Vietnam* (Texas, 1993), chap 3; and Robert S. McNamara with Brian VanDeMark, *In Retrospect: The Tragedy and Lessons of Vietnam* (New York, 1995), pp 171–77.

In April 1965, President Johnson increased the number of ground troops deployed to South Vietnam. Here, arriving troops unload gear from a C–130.

Further Decisions on Prosecuting the War

After examining these views and numerous studies and memoranda on the bombing, the NSC, after its meetings of April 1 and 2, sent new recommendations to President Johnson. These sought to accommodate three diverse views on the war: those who wished to move more rapidly against the communists in both South and North Vietnam; those who would proceed more prudently, chiefly in the south, without significantly increasing the bombing in the north; and those who opposed any increase in the American commitment.[8]

The President's decision, embodied in NSAM 328 and issued on April 6, was the most fateful of his administration. He sanctioned a modest increase in U.S. ground troops in South Vietnam—two Marine battalions and one Air Force squadron plus support—and altered the mission of the U.S. Marines from defense to "more active use" or offense. In short, the change signaled the beginning of open U.S. ground warfare, a strategy strongly opposed by the Air Force. The President also authorized 18,000 to 20,000 more support personnel, stepped up nonmilitary assistance and USIA programs, and more bombing of North Vietnam.

The air assault on the north, however, continued very cautiously:

> We should continue roughly the present slowly ascending tempo of Rolling Thunder operations, being prepared to add strikes in response to a higher rate of VC operations, or conceivably to slow the pace in the unlikely event [the] VC slackened off sharply for what appeared to be more than a temporary operational lull.

The target systems should continue to avoid the effective GCI range of MiGs. We should continue to vary the types of targets, stepping up attacks on lines of communication in the near future, and possibly moving in a few weeks to attacks on the rail lines north and northeast of Hanoi.

Leaflet operations should be expanded to obtain maximum practicable psychological effect on the North Vietnamese population. Proposals to blockade or mine North Vietnamese ports from the air, while offering many advantages, required further study as such action augured major political complications "especially in relation to the Soviets and other third countries." To reduce infiltration through southern Laos, Mr. Johnson repeated his endorsement of "aerial route blocking" at the "maximum remunerative rate" in Steel Tiger. At the President's request, officials publicly downplayed the decisions in NSAM 328 to avoid any suggestion there had been a sudden change in American policy on the war.[9]

NSAM 328 emerged against a background of separate, harsh warnings in late March voiced by China's newspaper, *People's Daily*, and by Premier Chou En-Lai and Foreign Minister Chen Yi. They affirmed support for the National Liberation Front's demand for the withdrawal of American troops from South Vietnam; promised the insurgents more arms, materiel, and if asked, Chinese troops; and predicted that the Chinese and Soviet peoples would close ranks and fight side by side if the United States precipitated a major war in Southeast Asia.[10] In a television interview in early April, McGeorge Bundy, the President's Special Assistant for NSC Affairs, replied that if China intervened in Southeast Asia, it would not enjoy a "privileged sanctuary" as it did in the Korean War.[11]

The administration's effort to minimize public fears of a larger conflict failed to quiet the crescendo of dissent. India, France, Sweden, and other noncommunist countries and large segments of the American public, Congress, and the press expressed apprehension over the conflict or outright disapproval of the bombing. Meeting in Belgrade, Yugoslavia on 1 April, an assembly of nonaligned nations appealed for negotiations without preconditions among interested parties as soon as possible.[12]

President Johnson had considered making another major public statement on U.S. policy in the war. He seized this statement, signed by seventeen nations, as an opportunity to answer these nations and other foreign and domestic critics. With the approval of the NSC, the President selected as his forum Johns Hopkins University in Baltimore, where he delivered an address on April 7. There, he reaffirmed the United States' determination to halt Hanoi's attacks on the south, but offered to begin "unconditional discussions" for peace and asked the U.S. Congress for one billion dollars for investment in a vast Southeast Asia regional development program that might eventually include North Vietnam. This was the administration's first significant effort to negotiate with Hanoi, and the President subsequently considered his offer to do so without preconditions as his fourth major decision on Vietnam.

Kim Cuong highway bridge after attack.

The address was applauded generally in the Congress and the country, but the reaction in Hanoi, Peking, and Moscow was negative. After an initial tirade against the President's offer, Premier Pham Van Dong quickly announced a four-point peace plan which demanded the basic rights of the Vietnamese people.* The rights were defined as independence, sovereignty, unity, and territorial integrity; withdrawal of all foreign military personnel in accordance with the 1954 Geneva Agreement; settlement of South Vietnam's internal affairs with the program of the National Liberation Front; and peaceful reunification of the two Vietnam zones without foreign interference.[13] Subsequently, Hanoi also rejected the appeal by the seventeen nonaligned nations, asserting that the Premier's four points could be the only basis for a settlement of the Vietnam problem, a position supported by Peking.[14]

Initial Bridge-Busting Attacks

With the administration's peace initiative firmly rejected by the three communist capitals, the Rolling Thunder campaign continued as envisaged in NSAM 328. Air strikes remained well below the 20th parallel, to minimize the risk of a wider war with Hanoi and Peking. Under the aegis of Rolling Thunder program 9, which

---

* Various dates have been given for the four-point peace plan. It is believed to have been announced initially by Premier Pham Van Dong during an internal government meeting in Hanoi on April 8, but was not distributed officially until April 13, 1965 (see *New York Times*, Apr 14, 1965, p 1).

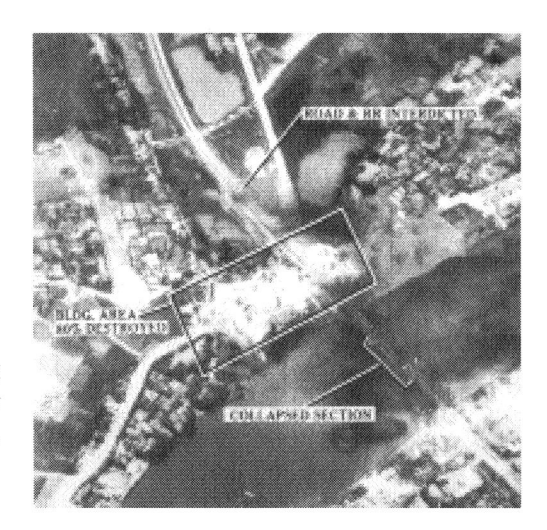

Dong Phuong Thuong railroad and highway bridge after attack.

lasted from April 2 to 8, attacks were made on four fixed targets, of which, for the first time, three were highway and rail bridges. The bridges at Thanh Hoa, Dong Phuong Thuong, and Dong Hoi each carried rail and vehicle traffic and were considered vital for the transportation of materiel for guerrilla operations in South Vietnam. The Thanh Hoa bridge was the most prestigious, having been destroyed during the French-Viet Minh war, rebuilt, and dedicated by Ho Chi Minh in 1964. CINCPAC assigned one bridge each to the Air Force, the Navy, and the VNAF. The bombing directive authorized a limited number of armed reconnaissance missions and once again eased operational restrictions somewhat by allowing Air Force and Navy aircraft to drop unexpended ordnance on rolling stock in the permissible bombing areas or on military targets on Hon Gio (Tiger) Island off the North Vietnamese coast rather than dumping it at sea. At the same time, the new Steel Tiger program was launched against troops and supplies in Laos heading toward South Vietnam.

Admiral Sharp directed the Air Force to attack the Thanh Hoa bridge, also known by the Vietnamese as the Hong Rong (the Dragon's Jaw). Spanning the Song Ma River about seventy-six miles south of Hanoi, it was 540 feet long, 54 feet wide, and 50 feet above the water, the longest bridge below the 20th parallel. It would prove to be one of the toughest targets in North Vietnam. Bombed repeatedly in subsequent years, the bridge's two spans were not dropped until May 14, 1972.*

---

* For a detailed account of the bombing of Thanh Hoa (and later the Paul Doumer bridge) in North Vietnam, see Maj. A. J. C. Lavalle, ed., *The Tale of Two Bridges* and *The Battle for the Skies Over North Vietnam*, USAF Southeast Asia Monograph Series, Vol I (Air University, 1976).

A F–105 carrying Bullpup missiles on a mission to North Vietnam refuels from a KC–135.

The initial assault on April 3 was planned and coordinated by the 67th TFS, which was commanded by Lt. Col. Robinson Risner. Seventy-nine aircraft were assembled, with forty-six F–105 Thunderchiefs forming the principal strike force. Sixteen were loaded with a pair of AGM–12B Bullpup missiles with 250-pound warheads, and the remaining thirty carried eight 750-pound bombs each. Support aircraft consisted of twenty-one F–100 Super Sabres for flak suppression, weather reconnaissance, MiG and rescue CAP; two RF–101s for photoreconnaissance; and ten KC–135 tankers. The F–105s were based in Thailand, the other tactical aircraft in South Vietnam, and the SAC tankers in Okinawa.

Launched in the afternoon, the strike aircraft hit the bridge with 254 750-pound bombs and 266 2.75-inch rockets, inflicting considerable damage on the bridge's roadways and structure. However, they failed to drop the spans. Heavy enemy groundfire exacted a penalty, downing one reconnaissance aircraft and a Super Sabre flying flak suppression, and damaging other aircraft, including Colonel Risner's F–105. Despite crippled aircraft and smoke in the cockpit, Risner continued to direct the attack and landed safely at Da Nang.[15]

At about the same time, Navy carrier aircraft attacked the Dong Phuong Thuong bridge twice in three hours. Fifty-seven aircraft flew in the first attack, thirty-eight in a strike role, and sixty-eight flew in the second, with thirty-five in a strike role. Using general-purpose bombs and 2.75-inch rockets, the aircraft dropped the center span and inflicted other damage at the cost of one A–4 that was shot down. The strike was enlivened when, for the first time since Rolling Thunder began, three North Vietnamese MiGs rose to challenge the attackers. In a brief encounter, one MiG scored four or five hits on the tail and two hits on the wing of a Navy F–8E. The MiGs escaped before fighters could engage them. The F–8E pilot made an emergency landing at Da Nang.[16]

Deeply perturbed over the failure of the first strike to disable the Thanh Hoa bridge, General McConnell personally directed General Moore to put adequate sorties on the target. The next day, Moore dispatched sixty-eight aircraft, of

The F–105 had a probe for probe-and-drogue refueling and a receptacle for boom refueling, one of only a few Air Force aircraft to be equipped for both modes of refueling.

which forty-eight were F–105s, again loaded with 750-pound general-purpose bombs, the remainder were F–100s for MiG and rescue CAP and weather reconnaissance. No flak suppression strikes were ordered, reflecting the previous day's unsuccessful attempt to silence enemy gunners. Colonel Risner again led the mission, and for his "extraordinary heroism" in both strikes, in May he received the first Air Force Cross awarded in the war, from Gen. John P. McConnell, the Air Force Chief of Staff.* The Thunderchiefs attacked the stubborn target with 384 750-pound bombs and Bullpups. This attack cratered both approaches to the bridge, blasted out large chunks of concrete, holed the rail trestle, and caused one span to sag. North Vietnamese traffic was halted, but only temporarily. Some aircraft struck nearby secondary targets, destroying an estimated 74 percent of the Thanh Hoa power station facilities, thirteen pieces of rolling stock, and some trucks.

The State Department immediately flashed Taylor that the attack on the plant was unauthorized, but the charge was denied by PACAF and 2d Air Division. General Wheeler soon cleared up the mystery by confessing, much to the President's displeasure, that he had personally authorized the attack. Also beyond dispute was the cost of the strikes on the bridge and secondary targets: three F–105s and their pilots downed, one by antiaircraft fire and two others by

---

* In recognition of the award and his exploits in both the Korean and Vietnamese wars, Colonel Risner was the subject of *Time* magazine's cover story on April 23, 1965.

Qui Vinh railroad bridge after an attack in April 1965.

four North Vietnamese MiG–17s that appeared suddenly for the second time in two days to challenge Air Force and Navy fighter-bombers.[17]

A MiG attack was not totally unexpected, but as General Moore explained later, preparations to meet one were not entirely adequate. Flying at about 500 knots, the MiG–17s struck in two waves against four F–105 Thunderchiefs that were circling at 14,000 to 17,000 feet and 375 knots about ten miles south of the target area, waiting to strike the bridge. Pilots of the two lead Thunderchiefs, laden with ordnance and surprised by the attack, could not maneuver swiftly enough to shake off the attackers. They were shot down and lost with their aircraft. Other Air Force and Navy fighters flying cover were too far away to assist. Poststrike debriefings indicated that the MiG pilots demonstrated good training and were probably guided by the north's GCI system. One PACAF pilot believed he scored a hit. As the air-to-air incident appeared to be unduly inflammatory, President Johnson informed the service chiefs he did not want any more MiGs shot down, although circumstances would soon dictate otherwise.[18]

The next day, VNAF and PACAF aircraft struck the 400-foot bridge at Dong Hoi, the third bridge on the authorized target list. Twenty VNAF A–1Hs flew strike and the PACAF aircraft flew support. General-purpose bombs collapsed the center span and heavily damaged other parts of the bridge. The Defense Department declared that the bombings had made all three bridges impassable.

The fourth fixed target in program 9 was a repeat strike against a coastal early warning radar station near Vinh Linh, the southernmost radar site in North Vietnam. The strike was carried out on April 15 by forty-four Navy aircraft, twenty-six in a strike profile, but only a few buildings were damaged. Reports on the type and manner of enemy antiaircraft fire in these early strikes suggested to General Moore that some of it was controlled by radar.[19]

In armed reconnaissance, Navy aircraft flew two missions on April 4 over the coastal railroad and national highway 1, the main artery from Thanh Hoa southward to Vinh. Pilot reports, unconfirmed by BDA, claimed twenty-one vehicles destroyed, four probably destroyed, eight vehicles damaged, and eight rail cars and one locomotive damaged. The next day, PACAF flew an armed reconnaissance foray with sixteen aircraft from the coast north of Vinh to the Laos border, then up to the Plain of Jars and over Route 8 from Vinh to the Laotian border at Nape Pass. The aircraft hit a truck convoy and two trains. In the first attack, results were undetermined, and in the second, pilots claimed the destruction of two locomotives and two nearby trucks. One F–105 was shot down. Program 9 armed reconnaissance missions were completed on April 7 when Navy aircraft flew along the coastal railroad and highway 1 from Dong Phuong Thuong to Vinh. Pilots reported three vehicles destroyed and eight damaged, along with one antiaircraft and one aircraft warning site probably damaged.[20]

As the second weekly Rolling Thunder program neared its end, McNamara verbally requested and Wheeler submitted an evaluation of the bombing through April 4. Except for "damaging blows" against three major rail and highway bridges, which slowed traffic and destroyed some enemy ammunition and other supplies stores, Wheeler said, the air strikes "have not reduced in any major way the capabilities of the NVN," and the impact on Hanoi's economy was minimal. While the country's military leaders were "keenly aware" of American power, they were prepared to use their ground defenses to make the United States "pay a good price," and he noted, the North Vietnamese Air Force MiGs "showed daring" in their first two attacks on U.S. Navy and Air Force planes. The North Vietnamese navy had dispersed and its crews had been ordered not to fire on U.S. aircraft unless attacked. Although the Hanoi regime acted as if it were not influenced by the air strikes, intercepted messages indicated that it was adopting a range of counterbombing measures. It had partially evacuated some population centers, launched air raid exercises and the construction of air raid shelters, and expanded its air defenses. Wheeler avoided recommending a faster paced Rolling Thunder program, although he implied he favored it, apparently so as not to place himself at variance with the President who, that day, issued NSAM 328, enjoining the services to continue operations in the north at "roughly the present slowly ascending tempo."[21]

Air Staff officials objected to the tenor of Wheeler's singular evaluation of Rolling Thunder, observing he had not coordinated it with the other service chiefs. The JCS chairman, they noted, particularly failed to address "the political

The McDonnell RF–101 Voodoo was the mainstay of the Air Force's reconnaissance effort in 1965 and 1966. Above, a RF–101 lands at a Thailand base. Left, the nose camera of the RF–101.

restraints and limited scope of air operations by type, location, and the number of targets" in the bombing program.[22]

Rolling Thunder 10 (from April 9 to 15) authorized strikes on five more bridges and two radar sites. CINCPAC assigned three bridges and the radar sites to the Air Force, two bridges to the Navy, and authorized more armed reconnaissance. Of ten armed reconnaissance missions flown, the Air Force flew five, the Navy three, VNAF-Air Force one, and VNAF one. On April 10, the JCS increased to twenty-four the number of armed reconnaissance sorties allowed in a 24-hour period. All air missions remained well below the 20th parallel.

Still relying on the F–105 Thunderchiefs as the principal strike aircraft, the Air Force completely destroyed the Khe Kiem highway bridge and dropped one span of each of the other bridges, the Phuong Can highway bridge and the Qui Vinh bridge. The Navy, using A–1Hs and A–4s in a double strike, dropped the north and center span of the Tamada rail bridge and, in a single attack, one span of the Kim Cuong highway bridge. Approaches to the latter were cratered and nearby buildings left burning. During the first strike on the Tamada bridge, an engagement with MiGs off of Hainan Island cost the Navy an F–4B and the North Vietnamese a MiG. Groundfire claimed an A–4C in the second strike. A single Air Force strike on radar sites at Hon Matt Island and Cuo Lao caused moderate damage to eleven buildings on the island, but results at Cuo Lao were uncertain.[23]

The clash between the Navy and the MiGs, occurring almost simultaneously with the Navy's attack on the Tamada bridge on April 9, was the third aerial battle since Rolling Thunder began, but the first with a Chinese aircraft. It began when four MiG–17s based on Hainan Island pounced on four Navy F–4B Phantom IIs on "barrier combat patrol" in the Gulf of Tonkin. In the ensuing battle, the MiGs, armed only with cannons, failed to score a hit, but the Phantom crew downed one of the Chinese aircraft with a Sidewinder air-to-air missile. This was the first aerial "kill" of the war. Unfortunately, on the return flight to the carrier *Ranger*, the four Phantoms became separated, and the aircraft and the two-man crew responsible for the shootdown were lost. The responsibility for the aerial engagement and the circumstance of the Navy's loss were immediately the subject of conflicting American and Chinese claims. Peking said the Navy aircraft intruded into Chinese air space, but Navy pilots reported that the MiG–17 attack occurred about thirty-five miles southeast of Hainan Island; Peking further asserted that an American missile, fired at a MiG, downed a Navy plane. The Navy initially attributed the loss of its Phantom to insufficient fuel while it was returning to the carrier. Later, however, the Navy conceded that its air loss was apparently caused by another Sidewinder, as the Chinese had claimed.[24]

The State Department received news of the aerial engagement near or over Hainan Island—the facts were not clear—with considerable unease, as the rules of engagement explicitly stated that "no [aerial] pursuit is authorized at this time into the territorial waters or airspace of Communist China." Acting Secretary of State George Ball sought renewed assurances from Deputy Defense Secretary Cyrus R. Vance and General Wheeler that the rules would be "precisely followed."[25]

Results of program 10 armed reconnaissance missions were meager. On a double mission on April 10, Air Force pilots claimed two trucks destroyed and three damaged. On the 15th, the Air Force hit a ferry landing and damaged a boat, while the Navy attacked two small bridges and set ancillary buildings ablaze, but the results of several joint Air Force-Navy strikes on gun positions, radar sites, and trucks were unknown. On several missions, no targets were sighted. With support from the Air Force, VNAF A–1Hs, flew one night armed reconnaissance mission between the DMZ and Vinh, but made no target sightings, dropping their bombs on a road with unknown results.[26]

Program 11 (from April 16 to 22) targeted five more bridges. Three were assigned to the Air Force (one a restrike), one to the VNAF-Air Force, and one to the Navy. Armed reconnaissance missions were again increased: twenty-three were flown over part or all of Routes 1, 15, 101, 102, 111, 113, and 117. As before, targets were principally military vehicles, infiltration points or sites, and highways. The latter were cut by ordnance where possible. A special air strike was directed for the first time against the Mu Gia Pass staging area, a vital border point

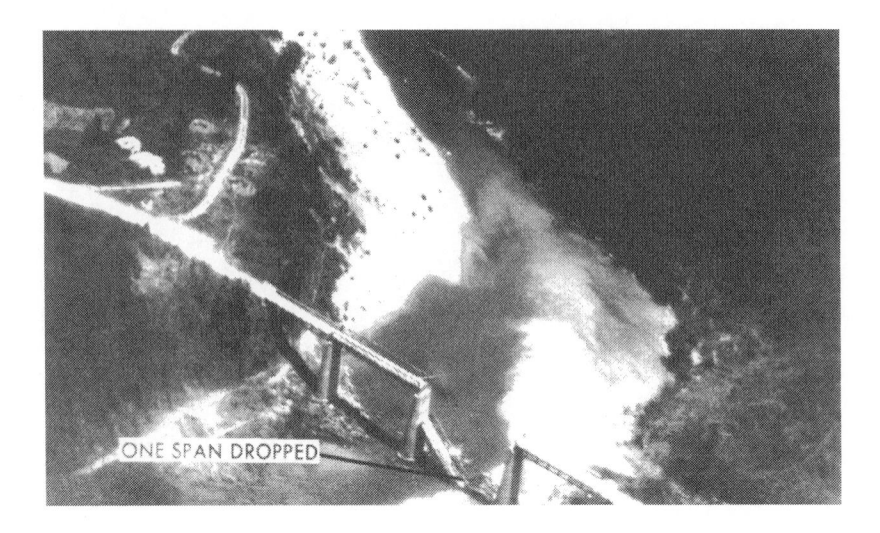

Measuring 350 feet in length, the four-span Xom Ca Trang highway bridge was situated between the convoy staging areas along Route 12 and the Mu Gia Pass. The bridge was struck on April 16, 1965, with one span completely destroyed.

for infiltrating men and supplies into Laos. The maximum authorized number of armed reconnaissance sorties for any one day remained at twenty-four.[27]

On April 16, the services launched their largest one-day effort against the north in a series of strikes against bridges. Air Force F–105 Thunderchiefs hit the heretofore unscathed Dien Chau railroad bridge and the Thai Hai highway bridge with 296 750-pound bombs. The bombs dropped the center span and forty feet of a second span on the first bridge and the single span of the second. A restrike on the Kim Cuong highway bridge also destroyed a span. On the same day, twin air strikes by the Navy against the Bai Duc bridge, recently completed and used for sending supplies into Laos, dropped one span and left a forty-foot gap in the other. In another Navy attack, an AGM–12B Bullpup missile dropped the span of the Xom Ca Trang highway bridge. On the 20th, eight VNAF A–1Hs were joined for the first time by eight Air Force F–100 Super Sabres in an attack on the My Duc highway bridge. The bridge was destroyed, but groundfire claimed one of the Vietnamese Skyraiders.[28]

Twenty-six armed reconnaissance missions were flown during program 11, and a small number of trucks, buildings, boats, and boxcars were destroyed or damaged. The most lucrative target, spotted by Navy pilots, was a convoy of 80 to 100 trucks that stretched over eight to ten miles. A smaller convoy of 16 to 20 trucks was also spotted. Results of many of the armed reconnaissance strikes were unknown. Losses during the week of 16–22 April consisted of an Air Force F–105 on the 17th and one VNAF A–1H on the 19th.[29]

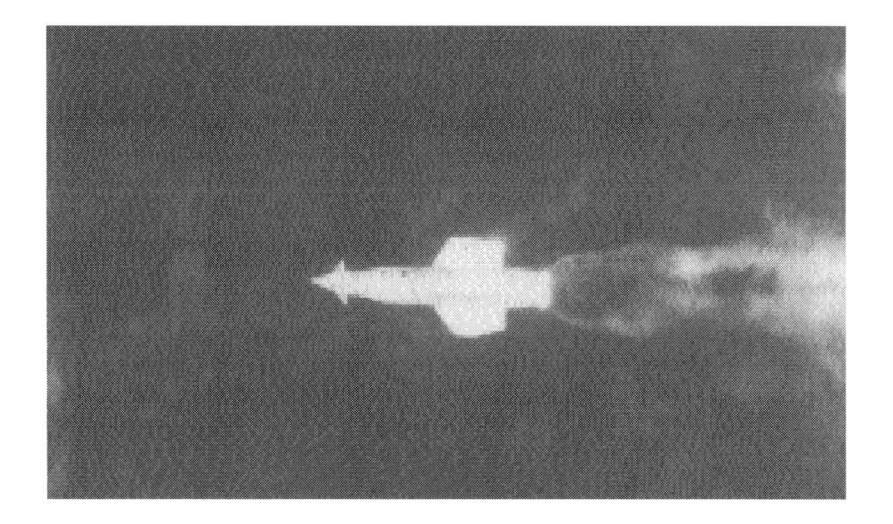

A Bullpup missile launched from an F–105 over North Vietnam.

As usual, Hanoi continued to make extravagant claims, stating that seven U.S. aircraft were shot down and many others damaged during the large-scale raids on bridges on the 16th. In fact, North Vietnamese newspapers and journals, which were almost totally propagandistic and engaged in domestic morale building, provided little substantive information on the impact of Rolling Thunder operations. American "air pirates" reportedly struck mostly homes, schools, hospitals, dikes, and other civilian targets, and casualties invariably were only women, children, the elderly, and the wounded. If roads, bridges, factories, and other military installations were hit occasionally, civilian workers repaired them in record time, thus minimizing any traffic or production slowdowns.[30]

Countering the North's Air Defenses

However, Hanoi's actions belied much of its propaganda: in late March and early April, its air defense forces were attempting to blunt the impact of the bombing. In addition to augmenting their automatic weapons and artillery units, the forces deployed a new weapon. Photos taken by a U–2 high-altitude reconnaissance aircraft on April 5, 1965 disclosed for the first time an SA–2 surface-to-air missile site under construction about fifteen miles southeast of Hanoi.*[31] The JCS

---

* Two high-flying U–2s of SAC's 4080th Strategic Wing arrived at Bien Hoa AB, South Vietnam, on February 13, 1964, to begin reconnaissance missions over Cambodia, Laos, and North Vietnam. Over North Vietnam, except when haze, clouds, and bad weather interfered, the U–2s could acquire usable, oblique coverage of SAM sites and other targets from a distance of about seventeen n.m.

A U–2 at Bien Hoa Air Base in 1965.

unanimously urged the destruction of the site and others that might be detected before they became operable.[32] McNamara deferred a decision pending discussions with the State Department and the White House, but authorized the services to maintain a 48-hour alert for a strike on the site.[33] A strike order was not forthcoming. Washington's civilian authorities were still committed to limiting the bombing well below the Hanoi-Haiphong area and were inclined to discount the seriousness of the SA–2 threat. One high-ranking civilian, John T. McNaughton, Assistant Secretary of Defense for International Security Affairs, believed that the sole purpose of the Soviet Union in placing missiles around Hanoi was to bolster the sagging morale of the North Vietnamese, not to fire them against aircraft, an assumption that was proved incorrect on July 23, 1965, when the first missiles downed a PACAF F–4C Phantom.[34] Only then were Air Force and Navy pilots authorized to attack missile sites.

In the interval between initial detection and the first air strike against the SA–2 sites, the services undertook a series of measures to increase the protection of their aircraft from a possible SAM attack. On April 8, SAC was instructed to install "System 12" electronic countermeasures equipment in its U–2s in Southeast Asia. This equipment was designed to warn pilots if they were being tracked by the SAM's Fan Song radar, but it had very limited jamming capability. Pending the installation of improved "System 15" ECM equipment, U–2 pilots were directed not to fly within thirty n.m. of known SA–2 sites.[35]

However, SAC was permitted to launch some of its unmanned reconnaissance drones over the Hanoi area for the first time. First known as the model 147B Lightening Bug, and produced by the Ryan Corporation, the early drones were improved by lengthening their fuselage and extending their wing span until they achieved a speed of Mach .74, an altitude of 60,000 feet, and a range of 1,200 n.m. These models, redesignated 147D and assigned to SAC's 4080th Strategic Wing, were first tested in early 1962 and sent to Southeast Asia in

An F–8 launching from the USS *Hancock*.

1964, where they began operational reconnaissance missions. Launched from a DC–130A based at Bien Hoa AB in South Vietnam, at first the drones did not penetrate deeply into North Vietnam.[36]

Blue Spring operations consisted of four elements: an Air Force DC–130A "mother ship" for launch and control, the drone itself with reconnaissance gear, a ground control station for drone recovery, and a helicopter for drone retrieval. By the end of 1964, SAC had launched nineteen drones, of which thirteen were considered very successful in terms of launch, photography, and retrieval, while six failed to return. By the spring of 1965, Blue Spring photography had added significantly to the gathering of targeting and other data in North Vietnam.[37]

However, the drones were not used to assist in locating SAM sites by electronic means until mid-1965. This task, and the related task of locating a growing array of other North Vietnamese air defense radars was conducted almost entirely by tactical aircraft. The Navy led off on April 16 when several of its carrier-based EA–1Fs flew their first ECM mission over the north. The Air Force followed on April 29, using three RF–101 Voodoos, hastily refitted with QRC–160-1 ECM pods designed to jam the SA–2 Fan Song radar. The retrofit began in the middle of April, with the pods drawn hastily from Fifth Air Force bases at Misawa, Japan, and Kadena, Okinawa. After May 5, PACAF's ECM effort was augmented by five EF–10B ECM aircraft of the Marine Composite Reconnaissance Squadron based at Da Nang, and Air Force, Marine, and Navy ECM operations were normally coordinated by the 2d Air Division.

115

PACAF's use of the QRC–160-1 pods was brief. The pods were not built to endure in-flight vibrations, which loosened internal parts and caused the RF–101 wing tips to tuck, creating a safety hazard. They were soon removed and sent to the United States. Meanwhile, in April, a first group of four Douglas Destroyer RB–66Bs and two EB–66Cs of the 9th Tactical Reconnaissance Squadron at Shaw AFB, South Carolina arrived at Tan Son Nhut AB. Three of the RB–66Bs with night photo and infrared sensor equipment were put to work immediately on reconnaissance missions over South Vietnam. The EB–66Cs began flying missions against the north's air defense radars on May 7. Before the end of May, two more EB–66Cs arrived from Shaw AFB, and all of the Douglas Destroyers then redeployed from Tan Son Nhut to Takhli in Thailand. Normally carrying a pilot, a navigator, and four electronic warfare officers, the EB–66Cs alerted strike pilots to the approximate location of enemy radars, analyzed the signals, and frequently attempted to jam them with chaff.

The EB–66s were most effective in reducing the ability of North Vietnamese antiaircraft gun crews to direct fire by radar. ECM operators reported frequent successes in breaking Fire Can radar lock-ons, but disrupting SA–2 missile radar was another matter. Although the EB–66C crews—and aircrews of Navy and Marine ECM aircraft—later developed the ability to warn other aircraft of some SAM areas when conducting a strike, aircrews generally found the ECM equipment only marginally effective or, in some instances, obsolescent. After a SAM destroyed an Air Force F–105 Thunderchief on July 23, heralding the enemy's intent to use them, the services separately embarked on crash programs to correct many of the deficiencies of the airborne ECM equipment in use in Southeast Asia.*[38]

Meanwhile, the overall air defense threat became more formidable. At least twenty different types of "radar threats" were soon identified and included radars for early warning, height finding, SA–2 target acquisition, tracking and guidance, gun laying, and airborne intercept. The most difficult to defeat were the north's early warning and GCI radars with their frequent signal diversity, good overlapping coverage, and cross-tell communications net. The frequency diversities required U.S. ECM aircraft to carry a wide variety of jammers to provide full spectrum capability against all of the frequency bands. However, the north's principal EW/GCI radars were equipped with antijam features and were not very vulnerable to the equipment on a single ECM aircraft. As a result, several

---

* For further discussion of the antiaircraft radar and SA–2 threat and Air Force electronic countermeasures, see Lt. Col. Robert M. Burch, *Tactical Electronic Warfare Operations in Southeast Asia, 1962–1968* (Proj CHECO, 1969); Bernard C. Nalty, *Tactics and Techniques in Electronic Countermeasures in the Air War Against North Vietnam, 1965–1973*, (Ofc AF Hist, 1977); and Earl E. Tilford, *Crosswinds: The Air Force's Setup in Vietnam* (College Station, Tex: 1993), pp 81–84.

A McDonnell Douglas Phantom II armed with air-to-air Sparrow missiles.

EB–66Cs were launched against a single target or group of targets employing a combination of electronic jamming, chaff, and crossing tracks. They could degrade EW/GCI in a given area, but could not render it entirely ineffective.[39]

The north's air defense system included its small force of Soviet-built MiGs that had been based at Phuc Yen airfield near Hanoi since the U.S. Tonkin Gulf air strike of August 5, 1964. As noted earlier, a squadron of F–4C Phantoms was based at Udorn to challenge the Phuc Yen MiGs if necessary.[40] For more defense against the MiGs, on March 18, General Harris, the PACAF commander, asked Admiral Sharp to approve the deployment of five Air Force Lockheed EC–121D Big Eye aircraft to provide a "MiG watch," while American aircraft flew missions over the north. Admiral Sharp's initial response was to claim there was insufficient logistic and unit "beddown" information about the EC–121Ds to warrant soliciting JCS support for the deployment of the aircraft.[41] However, the MiG attack on a Navy F–8E on April 3 and the loss of two Air Force F–105D Thunderchiefs the next day during a strike on the Thanh Hoa bridge sparked the decision-making process. Washington immediately authorized the deployment of Big Eye aircraft.[42]

The F–4C Phantoms of the 45th Tactical Fighter Squadron of the 8th Tactical Fighter Wing, from George AFB, California, arrived at Udorn RTAFB on April 7. Like most air units, they were assigned for a 120-day TDY. The Phantoms flew their first MiG combat air patrol for the workhorse F–105s on the 9th (they did not fly a primary strike mission until May 30).[43] On April 4, five Big Eye EC–121 aircraft with 153 aircrew and supporting personnel of the 552d Airborne Early Warning and Control (AEWC) Wing began to deploy to Southeast Asia from McClellan AFB, California. The first two aircraft, each with a normal seven-man crew and eleven radar operators, analysts, and maintenance personnel, arrived at Tainan Air Station, Taiwan on April 16, then redeployed quickly to Tan Son Nhut AB, South Vietnam, their forward operating base, and began flying missions during the week of April 16–22. Employing a water-reflecting AN/APS–95 search radar, the EC–121Ds initially flew in a racetrack pattern at an altitude of only 50 to 300 feet about fifty miles off the North Vietnamese coast. Soon afterwards, they adopted the tactic of flying in groups of two, one at high altitude, the other low, although single missions were sometimes flown at either high or low altitude. Although the radar equipment in the aircraft was designed principally for operations over water, it also permitted surveillance over land areas. Besides providing early warning of hostile aircraft, the EC–121Ds served as airborne communications relay centers and assisted in the search for targets and rescue of downed pilots. If necessary, they could provide on-station support twenty-four hours per day. Later, as Rolling Thunder strikes were conducted closer to the Chinese border, the Big Eye aircraft provided border warning for Air Force and Navy combat pilots.*[44]

About fourteen F–104 Starfighters of the 476th Tactical Fighter Squadron of the 479th Tactical Fighter Wing from George AFB were deployed with the Big Eye aircraft. Earmarked to fly cover for the EC–121Ds, they began to arrive at Kung Kuan AB, Taiwan, on April 7. From there, many were sent to Da Nang AB as their forward operating base. Most of the squadron's Starfighters were normally stationed there.[45]

Although the F–4Cs and EC–121s reduced the MiG threat somewhat, the most effective countermeasure, namely the bombing of the principal North Vietnamese airfields, was still prohibited by Washington authorities. Phuc Yen, which sheltered most of the MiGs, lay well above the current bomb line at the 20th parallel. It was further protected by the zone of forty nautical miles around Hanoi and Haiphong established by Washington authorities near the end of March to prevent intrusion into this sensitive area. Since authorization to bomb the MiG airfields appeared highly remote for the time being, air commanders fashioned a plan to conduct ostensibly separate Air Force and Navy air strikes on two North Vietnamese targets as a ruse to "flush" the MiGs into the air where they could be destroyed. Prepared by CINCPAC in coordination with PACAF, PACFLT, and the JCS, the plan went to McNamara on April 22, but elicited no immediate response. Frequently revised, it was not used for many months.[46]

---

* Several special studies have described in considerable detail the procedures employed by Big Eye (redesignated College Eye on March 9, 1967) aircraft in airborne control of fighters in Southeast Asia. See especially Capt. Carl W. Reddell, *College Eye, Special Report* (Proj CHECO, 1968), and Grover C. Jarret, *History of College Eye, Apr 1965–Jun 1969* (ADC, Ofc of Command and Hist, 1969).

Lockheed F-104 Starfighters at Da Nang Air Base, December 1965.

Washington's prohibition against MiG base attacks lasted until April 1967 when the North Vietnamese Air Force began large-scale attacks on Air Force and Navy Rolling Thunder aircraft and could no longer be ignored. Until then, the services were frustrated that they were not allowed to strike more important military targets. The Washington-imposed strictures highlighted the widely divergent viewpoints of high civilian officials and military commanders, with the former clearly reluctant to permit air strikes that might be considered unduly provocative.[47]

The Honolulu Conference of April 1965

Another divisive issue affecting bombing strategy was whether more U.S. and allied troops were needed immediately in South Vietnam. Ambassador Taylor had left Washington for Saigon late on April 2 after the NSC deliberations that produced NSAM 328. The basic U.S. objectives of the NSAM were the continuation of "the slowly ascending tempo of Rolling Thunder operations," more military and nonmilitary assistance for the Saigon government, and, most significantly, "a change in mission" for the U.S. Marines guarding Da Nang Air Base. This meant that for the first time the Marines were permitted to engage in offensive as well as defensive operations.

Between April 8 and 18, however, numerous JCS and Department of Defense dispatches to Taylor and Westmoreland indicated that President Johnson and his advisers were increasingly alarmed about the deteriorating situation in the south. Convinced that "something new" had to be added to achieve victory, the President believed the South Vietnamese Army could be revitalized by the insertion of U.S. troops into its ranks, and by the participation of more U.S. and allied battalion-size units. He specifically cited the possible deployments of the U.S. Army's 173d Brigade and combat units from Australia and Korea. Although Taylor and NSC members had discussed these and other options at the NSC meetings on April 1 and 2, none were approved at that time. Now, Taylor was asked to obtain immediate approval of the additional deployments from Premier Phan Huy Quat, who assumed leadership of a new Saigon government on February 16. The ambassador subsequently characterized the switch in administration policy as "the product of Washington's initiative, flogged to a new level of creativity by a President determined to get prompt results."[48]

Asking for clarification, Taylor noted the Quat government was still digesting a mountain of military and nonmilitary programs imposed by the United States. He expressed alarm over the administration's "far greater willingness to get into [a] ground war," than he discerned during his recent trip to the capital to participate in the NSC deliberations. Believing Vietnam's internal situation still did not warrant a large infusion of U.S. and allied troops, he urged that the proposed deployments be discussed at a conference scheduled for April 20–21 in Honolulu.[49]

The two-day conclave met as scheduled. In attendance were Secretary McNamara; General Wheeler; John T. McNaughton, Assistant Secretary of Defense for International Security Affairs; William P. Bundy, Assistant Secretary of State for Far Eastern Affairs; Ambassador Taylor; General Westmoreland; and Admiral Sharp. Other ranking officials, including General Harris, were present, but they were excluded from the principal meeting held on April 20.

The conference's minutes and McNamara's summary of the decisions reached and sent to the President on April 21 indicated that South Vietnam's problems remained paramount. The seven principal conferees agreed that the DRV-VC could not be expected to capitulate or provide acceptable terms for ending the war in less than six months and that a war settlement would come as much or more from VC failure in the south as DRV "pain" in the north. Taylor, Wheeler, Sharp, and Westmoreland agreed that the strategy should be "to break the will of the DRV by denying it victory. It was thus vital to hold on in the south and avoid a "spectacular defeat" of the Saigon government or U.S forces. The recent lull in the war was the quiet before the storm.

The majority view called for the addition of 100,000 to 160,000 to South Vietnam's existing armed forces, then at 450,000 men. Also, overriding Taylor's position, the U.S. military presence in the south should be increased from 33,500 to 82,000, with the further addition of 7,250 troops from Korean, Australian, and New Zealand contingents. A U.S. Army airmobile division of about 15,800 men, Korean troops equal to a full division, and a U.S. Marine expeditionary force totaling 24,800 men were also planned for later deployment.

In addressing the Rolling Thunder program, the conferees assigned it a role subordinate to air and ground operations in South Vietnam. According to the record, no one argued for a more aggressive program, at least for the time being. According to the Defense Secretary:

> They all think...the present tempo is about right, that sufficient pressure is provided by repetition and continuation. All of them envision a strike program continuing at least six months, perhaps a year or more, avoiding the Hanoi-Haiphong-Phuc Yen areas during that period. There might be fewer fixed targets or more restrikes, or more armed reconnaissance missions.

Taylor expressed a shared view that it was important "not to kill the hostage" by destroying the North Vietnam's "assets" inside the "Hanoi donut" or sanctuary area. While all believed that the strike program was essential psychologically and physically, "it cannot be expected to do the job alone." The seven principals also agreed that strikes against the north should continue during any "talks" between Washington and Hanoi with a view to finding a solution to the conflict. However, with regard to the allocation of air power in the war theater, Rolling Thunder should be accorded only second priority; first priority was assigned to South Vietnam. If there were insufficient aircraft to perform all tasks, then more air units should be deployed.[50]

Admiral Sharp quickly dispatched the air priority decision to his Air Force and Navy commanders, adding that Rolling Thunder requirements, in turn, would take precedence over the Barrel Roll and Steel Tiger interdiction and the Yankee Team reconnaissance air programs in Laos.[51]

Needless to say, the Air Force would have given Rolling Thunder first priority in the war and opposed a ground-oriented strategy in the south. Reviewing the implications of the Honolulu decision for General McConnell, General Harris warned that there might not be sufficient airbases in South Vietnam to permit the Air Force to quickly increase air support for ground operations. He solicited the assistance of the Air Force Chief of Staff in securing fast approval of a PACAF request for the emergency construction of a new jet base. The use of USAF jets based in Thailand was not very practical because of their distance from the battlefield and, in any event, their use in South Vietnam was still prohibited by the Thai government. Service interest, said Harris, also dictated rapid expansion of South Vietnam's bases for USAF aircraft. Unless this was done "we will find both [the] Marine Corps and carrier based aircraft taking over a portion of USAF responsibilities and missions." In fact, the current shortage of airbases prompted the Navy to stress the "political flexibility" of the carrier.[52]

Approving the decisions taken at the Honolulu conference, President Johnson directed the deployment of more U.S. Army, Marine, and allied units to South Vietnam. In a news conference on April 27, he restated America's commitment to stand firm against the communists, condemned the provocations of

The Phu Dien Chau railroad bridge after it was attacked
on April 17, 1965, and the main span destroyed.

the Viet Cong, and said only military targets in the north would be hit until aggression ceased. He reaffirmed a willingness to "talk to any government, anywhere, anytime, without conditions," to achieve a settlement of the war.[53]

In news conferences in Honolulu and Washington, Secretary McNamara also discussed the communist threat and the administration's strategy for defeating it. He stressed the "very high level" of infiltration of men and materiel by land through Laos, by sea across the beaches of South Vietnam, and the delivery of weapons to the Viet Cong by China and other communist countries. Justifying the "South Vietnamese first" strategy, he said that the south's military, paramilitary, and police forces needed to be enlarged because it was in the south where the "war against the guerrilla is being fought and it's there we must direct our primary attention."

The Defense Secretary defended the limited nature of Rolling Thunder operations being conducted largely below the 20th parallel. The air strikes, he said, had already reduced the movement of men and materiel "significantly" and "adversely" affected the morale of the Viet Cong. Strikes against bridges in the DRV had proved successful and of twenty-seven highway and rail bridges struck

My Duc highway bridge photographed by an RF–101 that also recorded the shadow of its passing, April 1965.

thus far by American and South Vietnamese aircraft, twenty-four were destroyed or so severely damaged as to render them unusable. Targets were restricted to bridges, transit points, barracks, supply and ammunition depots, and lines of communication. The aerial objective was "to force [the North Vietnamese] off the rails onto the highways and off the highways onto their feet." If the Soviets introduced antiaircraft SAMs into the north as anticipated, "we have ways and means of taking care of them." The Defense Secretary said that he and Secretary of State Rusk agreed on the danger of halting the bombing as some foreign governments desired lest it be interpreted as a major American military defeat and bring about the collapse of the Saigon government.[54]

Rolling Thunder's Moderate Pace Continues

The administration's commitment to a gradually escalating bombing program was manifested in Rolling Thunder program 12 for April 23–29. The JCS approved attacks on eight bridges and seven ferries along major road and rail lines. The directive also relaxed operating rules somewhat by approving a few

A DC–130 releases a reconnaissance drone (top), and reconnaissance drones with the DC–130 carrier behind them (above).

more night missions and lifting a ban on flying more than twenty-four armed reconnaissance sorties in a 24-hour period, enabling pilots to hit trucks and rolling stock that had been missed during preplanned missions. Also, for the first time, the JCS permitted pilots to fly in "successive waves" of aircraft (rather than to conduct single strike missions) against primary targets, and to use any unexpended ordnance on targets of opportunity along specified routes in addition to dropping it on the North Vietnamese-held Hon Gio (Tiger) Island off the North Vietnamese coast.[55]

At the end of the week, Air Force, Navy, and VNAF pilots reported they had destroyed or seriously damaged all of the authorized bridges and had hit hard several ferries and ferry ramps. They also claimed to have destroyed or damaged an estimated 150 buildings, dozens of railroad cars and trucks, a number of enemy antiaircraft sites, and to have made numerous road cuts. F–105 Thunderchiefs remained the Air Force's principal "workhorse" for these operations.

Meanwhile, on April 22, two Air Force B–57s of the 3d Bombardment Wing at Clark AB, the Philippines, attached to the 34th Tactical Group at Bien Hoa, South Vietnam, flew their first night armed reconnaissance missions over North Vietnam, damaging an estimated six trucks and six buildings. In the last week of April, six B–57s were dispatched on four different nights to search for trucks and other targets of opportunity and to cut enemy roads with bombs and "seed" them with mines. On the night of May 4/5, the Air Force made its first use over the north of Blindbat C–130 flare and navigation aircraft. They were used as pathfinders for B–57s that normally carried 500-pound and 750-pound general-purpose bombs and 2.75-inch rockets.* Since most C–130/B–57 night operations produced uncertain or unknown results, not many were flown in the ensuing weeks and months. Not until the arrival of the better equipped F–4C Phantom jets of the 68th TFS in September 1965 did the Air Force launch Night Owl operations and significantly step up its night activities over the north. In the interim, the Navy flew most night missions.[56]

The cost of the week's strike effort was fairly heavy. Enemy gunners damaged seven Air Force aircraft—five F–105s and two F–100s—the VNAF lost one A–1H and suffered damage to another, and the Navy sustained damage to ten aircraft.[57] Rolling Thunder 12 ended the initial air campaign against the north's major road and rail targets, especially bridges, south of the 20th parallel that began with program 9 on April 2.[58]

The next two Rolling Thunder programs, 13 (from April 30–May 6) and 14 (May 7–13) singled out fewer primary fixed targets and placed greater emphasis on day and night armed reconnaissance missions. Pilots were directed to

---

* For an account of Blindbat and other Air Force night operations in Southeast Asia, see Maj. Victor B. Anthony, *The Air Force in Southeast Asia, Tactics and Techniques of Night Operations, 1961–1970* (Ofc AF Hist, 1972).

On April 14, 1966, the Viet Cong mounted a surprise mortar
attack against Tan Son Nhut Air Base. A firetruck sprays
foam on a burning storage tank (left), and flames
engulf another tank hit by mortar fire (right).

concentrate on rail and road traffic, ferries, lighters, radar sites, secondary bridges, road repair equipment, and staging areas. Beginning with program 13, the number of preplanned armed reconnaissance aircraft authorized for a single day was raised from 24 to 40, with a maximum of 200 during the week. The total authorized sorties could be exceeded by six sorties per day to hit trucks, rolling stock, and naval craft that were discovered late. To exceed the maximum authorized numbers, Air Force and Navy air commanders had to obtain permission from CINCPAC.[59]

Program 14 concentrated more armed reconnaissance against the north's coastal regions to destroy more enemy naval boats and other types of watercraft in estuaries, at moorings, and in the vicinity of coastal islands. Return fire was authorized on any air mission, and henceforth, pilots could jettison their loads on Tiger Island, radar sites on Hon Nieu and Hon Matt Islands, and on the Dong Hoi barracks.

About twenty Rolling Thunder missions were flown in program 13 and twenty-two in program 14. Attacks on significant fixed targets included a restrike on the enduring Thanh Hoa bridge, an initial strike on Vinh airfield, and a restrike on the Xom Trung Hoa barracks. Again, numerous smaller bridges were targeted.

For the restrike on Thanh Hoa bridge, whose defenses had been increased, on May 7 General Moore dispatched a composite strike force of sixty-four aircraft coordinated by Maj. Charles A. Watry of the 354th Tactical Fighter Wing based at Korat. The force included twenty-eight F–105s that pounded the bridge and the surrounding area with 356 750-pound bombs and 304 2.75-inch rockets. While Major Watry was leading the first attack element, groundfire hit a Thunderchief whose pilot was able to reach the Tonkin Gulf, where he bailed out and was quickly rescued. Several other aircraft were also damaged, including Watry's. Hit in the wing by flak, Watry's plane began leaking fuel. Despite

The remains of a C–47 destroyed in the April 14 attack at Tan Son Nhut.

uncertainty about his own aircraft's chances of survival, he continued to direct other strike aircraft to the target area, radioing all the while to other aircrews the location of antiaircraft guns, intensity of fire, and other bombing information. For his heroism and leadership, he won the Silver Star.

The attack severely cratered the eastern approach to the bridge and railroad, and moderately damaged the eastern end of the truss and abutment, but the two spans remained standing. Later that day, General Moore dispatched two more strike aircraft against the bridge, but their ordnance caused no further visible damage. Nonetheless, the attacks again halted all traffic across the bridge temporarily.[60]

General Moore and his fellow commanders were chagrined over the losses sustained in bombing the Thanh Hoa bridge and the failure to drop the spans completely. A poststrike assessment offered several lessons. First, much ordnance was wasted on the bridge, chiefly because the 750-pound general-purpose bombs normally exploded into fragments and had little penetration capability. Second, pilots and operations personnel generally had little knowledge about fusing bombs.* Third, large numbers of aircraft attacking the bridge at the same time led to excessive bombing errors with some circular error probabilities (CEPs) reaching 700 feet. Skip bombing, which required pilots to drop their bombs at low altitude, was considered too risky. In view of these problems, Moore and his aides decided not to bomb Thanh Hoa bridge again until the Air Force obtained an improved AGM–12C Bullpup missile with a 1,000-pound

---

* Maj. Gen. Gilbert L. Meyers subsequently underscored the general lack of Air Force training in fusing bombs properly. "I am amazed...how few people know weapons and effects ...It's understandable if you think about it. The average pilot never drops a...live bomb until he goes to war. There are a few expended in the United States for demonstration purposes...that's the only time we...expend live munitions....The fusing is so critical as far as the damage that [the] bomb is going to do vis-à-vis a given target." (Intvw, Maj. Richard B. Clement and Capt. Ralph G. Swentson with Gen. Meyers, May 27, 1970, pp 73–74).

warhead (delivery was expected by about July 1, 1965), and to limit future attack missions to only four to eight aircraft.[61]

On May 8, an Air Force restrike on the Xom Trung Hoa barracks and supply area produced better results. Sixty-two planes, led by twenty-eight F–105s, destroyed between thirty-four and forty buildings, leaving most of the barracks area in ruins. On the same day, the Navy hit a North Vietnamese airfield at Vinh, which contained radar equipment and warehouses. This was a double strike, with about eighty-four aircraft dispatched for each mission, and forty-six and forty-eight in strike profiles. Dropping about 160 tons of bombs in the two raids, the assaults cratered the runway in fourteen places, damaged six of seventeen buildings in the area, inflicted further damage on the nearby Vinh radar site, and destroyed eight buildings in a warehouse area. Two aircraft were lost and two damaged in the attacks. Both the Air Force and the Navy attacks also struck numerous secondary bridges.[62]

Rolling Thunder program 14 completed about eight weeks of bombing that began on March 2, 1965 with program 5. By now, all of the north's primary and principal secondary roads south of the 20th parallel had sustained the loss of one or more bridges. Most of the sorties were scheduled for armed reconnaissance, as relatively few were needed against fixed targets. Every day, armed reconnaissance pilots looked for trucks, rail cars, locomotives, boats, small bridges, and hidden radar and antiaircraft sites. State Department officials carefully scrutinized each Rolling Thunder program, often deleting certain targets and modifying early drafts of proposed strike execute orders to CINCPAC, to avoid any precipitous increase in the bombing tempo. The President continued to make the final decisions on the intensity of the aerial assault on the north in coordination with Secretaries McNamara and Rusk and other advisers.

BDA results were most easily obtained from fixed targets. However, for the hundreds of armed reconnaissance missions flown, destruction and damage results were based principally on pilot "eyeball" observation or surmise. Secondary explosions, for example, suggested a successful strike on fuel or ammunition stores.

North Vietnamese gunners continued to exact a heavy price for the Rolling Thunder attacks. In programs 13 and 14 combined (April 30–May 13), the Air Force lost one RF–101, one F–105, and sustained damage to six aircraft. The Navy lost three aircraft and nine were damaged.[63]

Although generally gratified by the authorizations to strike more targets in the north, the Joint Chiefs—and especially Air Force and Navy commanders—chafed over the restrictions against bombing more important targets in the Hanoi-Haiphong area, well above the 20th parallel. Two highly desirable objectives still off limits to pilots were the first SA–2 site near Hanoi, photographed by a U–2 aircraft on April 5, and Haiphong harbor. In late April, the State Department denied permission for overt attacks on both. Hitting the SA–2 sites, it said, would be "a big step up the escalation ladder" and increase the hazard of a direct confrontation with Hanoi and Peking.[64]

Haiphong harbor, now hosting many more Soviet and other communist ships laden with supplies, was obviously a more sensitive target. Seeking an indirect way to reduce shipping, McNamara queried the services about the feasibility of using air strikes to sink the dredges that maintained harbor depths. Admiral Sharp opposed sinking the dredges from the air. He feared the numerous antiaircraft guns in the area would take a high toll and believed the harbor could be closed more easily by mining.[65] However, the JCS considered an air strike feasible, noting that of seven known dredges in the area, only one, a large SC–8 suction dredge, was used to keep the channel clear. If this dredge were eliminated, the harbor channel would silt up in about six months, effectively closing Haiphong harbor to shipping. The service chiefs estimated that six aircraft, plus antiflak and other air support, could sink the dredge and ordered Admiral Sharp to prepare a plan to do so.[66] When the plan was completed, however, McNamara made no further decision on the proposal. In fact, except for a few targets, Haiphong and its harbor would remain untouched by U.S. fighter-bombers until May 1972.[67] Only then, in the wake of a large-scale North Vietnamese invasion of South Vietnam, would President Richard M. Nixon impose an air and naval blockade on all of the north's major seaports and order its harbors mined.

Expansion of the Leaflet Program

With the gradual expansion northward of Rolling Thunder strikes during April and early May, American planners decided to expand leaflet dropping operations in the north. Although millions of leaflets had already been scattered under the aegis of MACV's covert Operations Plan 34A, their impact on the North Vietnamese was not yet perceptible. The new and expanded program, authorized by NSAM 328 of April 6, 1965, would be overt with no attempt to disguise the nationality of the aircraft employed for the missions.[68]

Officials placed great store in the new leaflet program, which was assigned the nickname Fact Sheet. With the concurrence of MACV and the United States Information Service (USIS) representatives in Saigon, Ambassador Taylor advised Washington that the leaflets, together with the air strikes, promised to have a "dramatic psychological impact" on the Hanoi regime. The messages, he said, would make credible U.S. policy not to destroy the DRV, warn Hanoi's leaders of the ability to drop bombs as easily as leaflets, and demonstrate the United States' willingness to intensify the bombing until Hanoi ceased its support of the insurgencies in South Vietnam and Laos.

The first major leaflet mission, flown on April 14, was conducted by four F–100 Super Sabres over the cities of Dong Hoi, Ha Tinh, Vinh, and Thanh Hoa, all well below the Hanoi-Haiphong area. Leaflet messages underscored China's role in the war, the slavish relationship of the north's leadership with the Chinese, and the necessity for air strikes to blunt China's aggression and VC-NVA killing of South Vietnamese people.

They warned the populace to avoid military installations, industrial plants, and communication centers. The F–100s also dropped translations of President Johnson's Johns Hopkins University address of April 7, in which he proposed "unconditional discussions" to terminate hostilities.

The second and third leaflet missions were conducted on April 17 and 19 over the same four cities, plus Bai Thuong, Ha Trung, Phu Qui, and Phu Diem Chau. The fourth leaflet drop, on April 28, again carried out by four F–100s, scattered about one million leaflets on Cua Rao, Khe Bo, Muong Seng, and Cong Cuong. These told the populace to stay away from military targets and promised that strike aircraft would try to avoid harming North Vietnamese civilians. In the following weeks the leaflet drops increased in volume and frequency and extended over larger areas of North Vietnam.[69]

Cautious Optimism on Bombing Results

In early May, as authorities in Washington prepared to test Hanoi's willingness to begin peace negotiations, American civilian and military officials expressed varying degrees of optimism about the war. McNamara believed that the U.S. and VNAF strikes on the north, the new Steel Tiger program, and the recent arrival of four battalions of U.S. Marines had halted the military and political deterioration of the previous eighteen months in South Vietnam and had improved military and civilian morale. However, he considered it premature to assess the impact of all military actions on the Hanoi regime's morale and capability.[70]

Commanders and analysts at PACOM and PACAF were likewise guardedly "upbeat" in their assessments. Admiral Sharp saw progress in both North Vietnam and Laos and urged Washington to approve more targets and speed up the pace of the bombing. Air strikes, he said, had disrupted road and rail movements in the north and had completely changed the pattern of logistic support to Laos as the Pathet Lao were more dependent than the Viet Cong on DRV support. PACAF intelligence analysts were quite optimistic, observing that in addition to destroying bridges, trucks, rail cars, and other targets in the north, the air program had forced the Hanoi government to relocate some of its agencies, divert manpower to road and rail repair work, caused food shortages, and eroded morale. In Laos, bombing had disrupted supply shipments to South Vietnam, and in both Laos and North Vietnam, the DRV had been forced to deploy more antiaircraft weapons and institute other air defense measures. In the next few months, it appeared likely that Hanoi would have to choose between accepting Soviet and Chinese domination, because of its excessive dependency of their supplies, or the possibility of defeat in South Vietnam.[71]

PACAF's operations analysts took a more sober view of Rolling Thunder's achievements thus far, noting that "bridge busting" and armed reconnaissance operations below the 20th parallel had not damaged Hanoi's logistic system too severely. Poststrike reconnaissance of bridge bombings, they said, revealed the DRV's skill at adapting. Of twenty-three bridges struck between April 4 and May 10, five were bypassed within one to five days and eight between one and thirty days, chiefly by repairing the bridges, using ferries, and fording streams. The DRV also made frequent use of floating spans at water crossings, of men and animals to carry supplies, and they built many points for staging, rest, and refueling on key routes located within one day's walking distance from each other. Nine such points were spotted on Routes 12 and 101. Although aerial attacks had apparently reduced supply movements, the DRV could still readily transport the estimated 101 tons of supplies required daily by VC-NVA forces in southern North Vietnam, southern Laos, and South Vietnam. Indeed, the DRV's supply capability considerably exceeded its current rate of supply movements and was sufficient to transport up to 300 tons of supplies per day to the DMZ and 175 tons daily into Laos. To thwart interdiction, the Hanoi regime recruited thousands of laborers—the number would eventually reach an estimated 500,000—to repair its rail lines, roads, and bridges.[72]

Although there was sufficient poststrike photography for PACAF to make early assessments of the impact of Rolling Thunder operations, its BDA interpreters very soon faced increasing difficulty in determining what all of the Air Force, Navy, and VNAF air strikes were accomplishing. A growing profusion of BDA photos and insufficient numbers of adequately trained photo interpreters quickly led to a glut of unanalyzed photos. This problem would be exacerbated as more strike and armed reconnaissance missions were approved by Washington in the coming months. Another problem, especially for the Air Force, was that the JCS relied principally on analysts with the Defense Intelligence Agency (DIA) in Washington, who represented all four services in assessing strike results and their impact on the Hanoi regime in moving troops and supplies towards South Vietnam.[73]

A KC–135 refuels a flight of F–105s during a mission to North Vietnam.

CHAPTER 5
Pause and Escalation

In May 1965, President Johnson took a new approach in the air war against North Vietnam. He temporarily halted the bombing to induce Hanoi's leaders to negotiate for peace. A second but more compelling consideration was to mollify, if possible, domestic and foreign critics of the war and particularly of the Rolling Thunder program.

Hanoi's Premier Phan Van Dong, supported by Peking and Moscow, demanded the unconditional cessation of U.S. bombing as a precondition to ending hostilities, so Mr. Johnson doubted that a suspension would lead to meaningful bargaining. But he reasoned that a demonstration of Washington's willingness to parley might "correct" the wishful thinking of some critics who believed that a reduction or even the complete termination of bombing would bring Hanoi to the negotiating table.*

Mr. Johnson made his decision on May 10 after receiving assurances from General Wheeler and other military advisers that a short bombing halt would not seriously harm the United States or the allied cause. He quickly received the assent of Premier Quat in Saigon, and privately informed the Peking and Moscow governments of his intentions. Administration officials assigned the code word Mayflower to this military and diplomatic ploy.[1]

On the 11th, Secretaries McNamara and Rusk jointly advised Admiral Sharp, General Westmoreland, and Ambassador Taylor that armed reconnaissance and other strikes against the north would cease for several days beginning midnight, May 12, Saigon time. To conceal the fact that Washington planned to conduct secret negotiations with Hanoi during the period, the two secretaries asked the ranking officials in Southeast Asia to state that the main purpose of the halt to bombing was to permit aerial reconnaissance of the DRV's rail and road transportation activity.[2]

Sharp quickly informed General Harris and Adm. Roy L. Johnson, who had succeeded Admiral Moorer as PACFLT commander on March 30, 1965, to intensify Air Force and Navy "eyeball" and photoreconnaissance of the north. However, the air commanders should schedule no more than two aircraft at a time, and pilots should fly only at medium or high altitude below the 20th parallel, and conduct as little flak suppression as possible. He said that aircrews and photoanalysts should look for evidence of enemy truck movements, shuttling and transshipment points, portering, ferrying and fording by vehicles, repair activities on bridges and ferries,

---

* For a discussion of events leading to the brief bombing halt in May 1965, see George C. Herring, *LBJ and Vietnam: A Different Kind of War* (Austin, 1994), pp 96–97 and 125; and Robert S. McNamara with Brian VanDeMark, *In Retrospect: The Tragedy and Lessons of Vietnam* (New York, 1995), pp 184–86.

Ambassador to Vietnam Maxwell D. Taylor consults with General William C. Westmoreland, Commanding General, U.S. Military Assistance Command, Vietnam, at Tan Son Nhut Air Base.

coastal traffic, camouflaging and dispersion actions, alternate routes, shifting air defenses, and POL, bivouac, and other fixed targets. Sharp singled out about forty separate routes and route segments below the 20th parallel for concentrated Air Force and Navy visual and photosurveillance. Strike sorties normally scheduled for the north should be diverted temporarily to targets in South Vietnam to the extent practicable, and Yankee Team reconnaissance operations in Laos should be reduced to allow concentrated reconnaissance of the north.[3]

To comply with Sharp's directive, PACAF diverted some of its RF–101s normally reserved for Laotian missions to the Blue Tree program over the north, and raised the strength of the reconnaissance unit in Udorn from eight to twelve aircraft, the maximum permitted by the Thai government.[4]

The First Bombing Halt

The bombing pause began as scheduled, without public announcement from Washington or Saigon. Launching his negotiation effort, President Johnson asked the Soviet Union to relay a message to the Hanoi government. When they refused, the message was dispatched to Hanoi through the U.S. Embassy in Moscow and the British Consul in Hong Kong. The message called for a reduction of armed action against South Vietnam, asserted that peace could be achieved only by a complete end to armed acts, and warned of American determination to demonstrate clearly, after the bombing pause, that it would not accept further aggression. The message expressed hope that Hanoi would not misunderstand the purpose of the pause, and would respond in a manner that would allow its extension. In a public address on May 13, the President, avoiding any reference to his diplomatic gambit, said that there was no purely military solution to the war, reiterated America's willingness to come to the conference table, and accused China of wishing to continue the war at whatever cost to its allies: "It's target is not merely South Vietnam: It is Asia."[5]

Meanwhile, the Air Force and the Navy had launched the special reconnaissance effort, and in the ensuing five days flew about eighty-five photo missions. Unfortunately, much of the photography was wasted as the volume quickly exceeded the capability of personnel to process and interpret the film. Air Force F–105 pilots flew 175 additional visual reconnaissance sorties and the Navy about 36. On May 16, Sharp advised the Joint Chiefs that while much of the data was valuable, it was becoming repetitive. He urged a quick resumption of the bombing to prevent Hanoi from gaining further advantage from the halt.[6]

Initial photo and visual reconnaissance disclosed little rail or road traffic from Thanh Hoa to the junction of Routes 1 and 17, but yielded substantial indications that the North Vietnamese were taking advantage of the strike-free period to increase daylight road and river movements from the Vinh area southward. Approximately 329 vehicles, 263 railroad cars, 221 barges, 387 boats of all types, and 24 ferries were sighted below the 20th parallel. Except for 55 trucks spotted in one convoy, most vehicles appeared to travel in small groups. Traffic on highways 1, 8, and 12 crossed rivers at fords where the bridges had been destroyed, and there appeared to be no traffic obstacles along Route 7. Most of the daylight air sightings were obtained in the first three days, then—presumably in anticipation of renewed bombing or to minimize aerial detection—the North Vietnamese reverted to moving most of their vehicles and watercraft at night.[7]

As the President expected, Hanoi's reaction to the bombing halt and negotiating initiative was negative. The notes sent to the government were returned unopened.[8] The DRV's news media characterized the American offer as "an old trick of deceit and a threat" and charged the President with imposing "arrogant conditions." The Foreign Ministry insisted that its four-point peace program, made public on April 13, 1965, was the only sound basis for a settlement of the Vietnam problem. Peking likewise denounced the offer and alleged that there had been no bombing pause.[9] In Washington, a State Department spokesman decried Hanoi's lack of proper response to the bombing halt,[10] and President Johnson concluded that he had opened the door to negotiations, only to have Hanoi slam it shut. After just five days, the Rolling Thunder strikes were resumed.[11]

Rolling Thunder Resumes

Before bombing resumed, the future scope and tempo of Rolling Thunder was debated intensely in Saigon, Honolulu, and Washington. In mid-May, Ambassador Taylor and General Westmoreland sent Washington a flexible bombing proposal. Still believing that Rolling Thunder strikes could be used as a coercive instrument, they suggested that they be linked to the level of Viet Cong activity in the south. For example, a downward trend in Viet Cong incidents would be rewarded by reduced bombing and an upward trend would signal more. The United States worked out a number of such *quid pro quo* arrangements in response to any peace initiative from Hanoi. These included offers to reduce the level of air strikes, stop them altogether, or reduce the U.S. military presence in South Vietnam. If there was another pause in the bombing, for example, Hanoi could take some form of action leading to the termination of hostilities on U.S. terms without formally engaging in negotiations.[12]

Both Sharp and the JCS opposed the Taylor-Westmoreland prescription on the grounds that the United States needed a stronger military position in South Vietnam before it could undertake any negotiations. They felt that discussions should take cognizance of America's future posture in Southeast Asia and the western Pacific. Transmitting their views to Secretary McNamara, the service chiefs cited their memorandum of March 15, 1965, which stressed the same point and added: "We must maintain a position of strength to thwart communist aggression and expansion in these areas."[13] They reaffirmed the need for heavy bombing throughout North Vietnam. A rationale for more bombing was also proffered by Walt W. Rostow, Chairman of the State Department's Policy Planning Council, who said that an historical analysis of recent guerrilla wars in Greece, China, North Vietnam, Malaya, and the Philippines suggested that Hanoi's military and political progress would recede in the face of more bombing of the north and military successes in the south. Mr. Rostow believed that Hanoi's hopes of winning the war in February had changed to the prospect of "clear-cut" defeat, higher military costs, increasing U.S. strength, and improved morale in South Vietnam.[14]

The President adopted none of the competing proposals. Instead, he decided not to alter significantly the pace of either reconnaissance or strike activity. This decision translated into a JCS directive to CINCPAC for program 15 (May 18–24). Yankee Team and Blue Tree reconnaissance missions would resume in Laos and North Vietnam, and Rolling Thunder attacks would resume in North Vietnam. One of the nine targets identified was Quang Soui barracks, the first target authorized above the 20th parallel (notwithstanding State Department objections), which was assigned to the Air Force. The State Department feared that a strike above the 20th might be interpreted negatively: Hanoi would conclude that the United States had made a "change in signal" and planned to bring the war closer to MiG bases, and the American press would see "the opening of a new phase" of the war. Program 15 also permitted more armed reconnaissance of coastal areas, harassment of offshore shipping, and more night reconnaissance. However, reconnaissance was restricted to 40 sorties a day and no more than 200 sorties in a week. Twelve more sorties could be flown to destroy suddenly discovered trucks, rolling stock, and naval craft not hit within the week's sortie allocation. Finally, the directive enjoined the services once again to exercise "utmost caution" and avoid populated areas in close proximity to the targets.[15]

The Navy led off the week's strikes with three missions on May 18 and one on the 20th. An attack on Hoan Lao barracks by thirty-two strike aircraft destroyed or damaged an estimated 79 percent of seventy-eight major buildings in the area. The Chanh Hoi military radio station, which was hit by six aircraft, suffered an estimated 86 percent level of damage or destruction. Twenty-two aircraft hit the Phu Qui POL storage area again, with damage estimated at 73 percent, and eighty-six carrier strike and support aircraft hit the Phuc Lao naval base near Vinh, inflicting an estimated 84 percent destruction level.

The Air Force's first strike mission for the week beginning May 20 (the Quang Soui barracks, above the 20th parallel) was canceled because of bad weather. As a result, it selected a secondary target, several military installations on Hon Matt Island, but an attack by twenty-four aircraft produced unknown results. On the same day, four F–105 Thunderchiefs dropped leaflets on Ninh Binh, only fifty miles south of Hanoi, the deepest penetration into the north since the Flaming Dart I strike on February 7, 1965. The F–105s dispensed eight canisters containing half a million leaflets that appealed to the North Vietnamese people not to let their leaders or the Chinese communists use them in the fratricidal war against South Vietnam and said that the purpose of the air strikes was to compel the Viet Cong to cease their sabotage and other aggressive acts in the south.

On May 22, improved weather finally permitted forty F–105s to fly against the Quang Soui barracks, a few miles south of Ninh Binh and fifty-five to sixty miles from Hanoi. The attack achieved moderate results, hitting about twenty of seventy-one buildings in the target complex, with three destroyed and the rest damaged to varying degrees. Simultaneously, some aircraft also attacked the Phu Qui ammunition depot, destroying six buildings and damaging three. The rest of the target area containing barracks buildings was attacked on May 22. Twenty-seven buildings were demolished and forty-eight were damaged. On the same day, VNAF A–1Es distributed about 400,000 leaflets over Ron and Ba Den in conjunction with the armed reconnaissance missions over four separate routes. The leaflets urged DRV soldiers to end their support for the war in South Vietnam. Joint VNAF A–1E and USAF F–105 strikes were conducted on May 21 and 22 against NVA barracks at Phu Le and Vu San, with destruction and damage at the two sites estimated at 48 and 83 percent, respectively.[16]

The next series of Rolling Thunder programs, numbers 16 to 21 and encompassing the period from May 25 to July 8, continued the gradual northward trend of Air Force and Navy strikes and included restrikes against fixed targets and armed reconnaissance missions. The VNAF was now flying about twenty-four sorties against fixed targets and four armed reconnaissance sorties in southern North Vietnam every week, although aircraft aborts and weather sometimes caused variation in this figure. The weekly cycle of Washington's authorization for U.S. attacks on the north's targets was uninterrupted except for program 16, which lasted ten days, from May 25 to June 3.

An F–4 en route to North Vietnam refuels from a KC–135.

Still under orders to achieve "maximum feasible damage," air commanders often scheduled large armadas of thirty, forty, or more aircraft against a single target area. Operational rules for aircrews continued to be relaxed gradually, but OSD, the State Department, and frequently the President still dictated target selection and the overall sortie rate. Administration authorities also maintained a ban on strikes in populated areas, MiG bases, and SA–2 missile sites.[17]

Among the important targets struck in this six-week period was the Hoai An ammunition depot on May 30, 31, and June 1, with the Air Force's F–4C Phantoms first used over the north in a strike role. Assigned to the 45th TFS, the Phantoms joined a number of F–105s in blasting the depot. In a series of separate strikes during the same three days, the Thunderchiefs again hit the Thanh Hoa bridge, reversing an earlier Air Force decision not to strike the bridge again until AGM–12C Bullpup missiles with 1,000-pound warheads became available in the theater. One mission consisted of five aircraft, the others were four-aircraft missions. As before, the bridge's spans remained standing although traffic was halted temporarily.[18] Beginning with Rolling Thunder programs 20 and 21 (from June 25 to July 8), Washington approved a series of targets west and northwest of Hanoi, all of which were struck by Air Force Thunderchiefs and Phantoms. The three most important targets were the Ban Nuoc Chieu depot, the Son La army barracks, and the Dien Bien Phu airfield and barracks area. The targets were about 70, 110, and 170 miles respectively west or northwest of Hanoi. The Son La area straddled Route 6, which ran south from China and connected with Route 7 at Sam Neua in Laos. This route was used for much of the infiltration traffic in support of the Pathet Lao and the North Vietnamese in Laos, and the area was blasted several times in the last week of June. Dien Bien Phu, the site of the last major resistance by the French before they capitulated to the Viet

Dien Bien Phu airfield after an Air Force attack.

Minh on May 27, 1954, was both a military and psychological target. Near the airfield was a barracks area containing several hundred structures with an estimated troop capacity of 10,000 and the headquarters of the NVA's 316th Infantry Brigade. The complex was believed to be a staging area for NVA units assigned to support the Pathet Lao in Laos. In an initial attack on July 2, twenty-eight Air Force F–105s and F–4Cs struck the airfield and barracks twice, destroying twenty-three buildings and damaging seven. The planes also hit an antiaircraft site and cratered the airfield. On July 8, thirteen Thunderchiefs and Phantoms conducted a second strike, but because of marginal weather, the attack achieved only further cratering of the airfield.[19]

However, the majority of Air Force and Navy missions were for armed reconnaissance over the growing area of authorized road and rail routes. Pilots searched constantly for a variety of targets: bridges, structures, ferries, trucks, rolling stock, watercraft, barracks, supply areas, and antiaircraft sites, and they made hundreds of road and rail cuts. The standard armament for an F–105 on an armed reconnaissance mission at this time consisted of six 750-pound general-purpose bombs on the centerline rack, two outboard rocket pods, and 20-mm high explosive incendiary ammunition.[20]

From the beginning of Rolling Thunder, air commanders considered North Vietnam's road and rail bridges to be primary targets, whose destruction, they hoped, would significantly slow the movement of men and supplies into Laos and South Vietnam. By early June, PACAF analysts had studied strike results on twenty-seven of the most important bridges. Their data showed that the Air Force had hit twelve, the Navy eleven, and the VNAF four. Destruction (defined as dropping at least one bridge span) was achieved on all but the Thanh Hoa bridge. Although comparison of service performance against the bridges was admittedly imprecise because of the different types of ordnance carried by strike aircraft, the analysts nonetheless offered the following statistics: the Air Force used 22.7 aircraft per bridge, the Navy 40, and the VNAF 21.5. The

Bombs from Air Force F–105s explode in a North Vietnamese supply area southwest of Hanoi.

Navy's larger total was attributed to the relatively light ordnance loading requirement for carrier aircraft. Air Force F–105s carried an average ordnance load of 3 tons, the VNAF's A–1Hs about 2.5 tons, and Navy A–4Cs and A–4Es less than either the Air Force or the VNAF, while Navy A–1Hs carried about the same load as the VNAF's Skyraiders. The analysts concluded that the 750-pound general-purpose bombs were better against bridges than had been expected and the AGM–12B Bullpup missile, with its 250-pound warhead, was less than satisfactory except against small bridges.[21]

Another statistical finding, as of June 24, was that the Air Force's larger F–105s and F–4Cs were dropping about 55 percent of all conventional bomb tonnage in the north, while the Navy dropped about 32 percent and the VNAF 13 percent.[22] However, the PACAF analysts did not address the impact of bridge and other bombing on the north's manpower and supply movements.

At the same time, Air Force and VNAF pilots were escalating their delivery of psychological warfare leaflets to undermine the morale of the populace and government leaders. On June 28, for example, the two services scattered leaflets on five towns: Phat Diem, only fifty-six miles south of Hanoi, and the more distant towns of Pai Thuong, Thanh Hoa, Dong Phuong Thuong, and Minh Binh. The leaflets charged Hanoi's leaders with taking rice from the people to purchase arms in China and continuing the oppression of South Vietnam.

They urged the people to demand that their leaders end the war. On July 2, a new type of leaflet was dropped on Mac Chou, about eighty miles southwest of Hanoi, warning the populace that the air strikes would continue "violently" and "unceasingly" until the leaders in North Vietnam and China stopped their invasion of South Vietnam.[23]

By mid-1965, the Rolling Thunder program was still expanding in scope and intensity. From a combined total of 585 attack sorties by the Air Force, Navy, and VNAF in March 1965, the level of effort had reached 5,901 attack sorties in June. The Navy and Air Force each flew about half the sorties, with the VNAF contributing only a small percentage. Several thousand additional sorties were flown for MiG combat air patrol, rescue patrol, escort, bomb damage assessment, and other types of support. Although the damage inflicted on enemy manpower, trucks, and supplies in both the north and in southern Laos was steady, even if difficult to quantify, and the north's transportation system was suffering, the Hanoi regime had failed to signal a willingness to negotiate on American terms. In fact, the regime was rapidly augmenting its air defense system and downing more U.S. and VNAF aircraft with a consequent rising loss of airmen killed or captured.[24]

Hanoi Expands its Air and Ground Defenses

By June 24, 1965, Hanoi's air defense system had been responsible for the loss of fifty-seven U.S. and VNAF aircraft: the Navy lost twenty-six, the Air Force twenty-four, and the VNAF seven. Except for two Air Force and one Navy aircraft downed by MiGs, they were victims of groundfire. In addition, enemy gunners had inflicted damage on 161 aircraft: the Navy eighty-two, the Air Force seventy-two, and the VNAF eight.

Intelligence analysts at PACOM and the Defense Intelligence Agency (DIA) maintained a close watch on the north's antiaircraft arsenal. In February 1965, they counted about 943 guns of various caliber and in May raised the estimated total to 978: 327 light 14.5-mm and 37-mm guns, 635 light 57-mm and 85-mm guns, 8 ZSU self-propelled 57-mm guns, and 8 guns of medium but unspecified caliber. There were a total of 180 active and 319 inactive sites. Additionally, there were undetermined numbers of air defense personnel with automatic hand weapons capable of inflicting loss or damage on low-flying aircraft. There was also a sharp upswing in air defense radar strength. In February 1965, forty-four radars had been confirmed and sixteen were suspected. In early May, the figures were sixty-six and eleven respectively, grouped in the following categories: early warning, forty-one; height finders, five; GCI, one; fire control, seventeen; and surface search, two.[25] The extent to which the estimated numbers of larger guns, sites, and radars represented true increases or were simply the result of a more intense reconnaissance effort was unknown. Whatever the size of the air defense system, ground gunners were becoming more proficient in damaging and downing aircraft.

Figure 5

Rolling Thunder Sorties, Ordnance Delivered, and Principal Targets
March 2–June 24, 1965

SORTIES

Type of Sortie	PACAF	PACFLT	VNAF	Total
Strike	2,072	2,393	384	4,849
Flak support	286	660	—	946
MiG-rescue CAP/Escort	1,649	896	40	2,585
BDA and other	282	323	—	605
	4,289	4,272	424	8,985

ORDNANCE DELIVERED

	PACAF	PACFLT	VNAF	Total
Conventional bombs	3,651	2,009	920	6,580
Rocket pods (19/pod)	1,205	1,365	618	3,188
Anti-Pam bombs (napalm)	—	52	127	179
AGM weapons	—	142	195	337
Zuni rockets	—	3,495	—	3,495
Lazy Dog containers	—	8	—	8
CBU–2A pods	48	36	24	108

TARGETS

	PACAF Des	PACAF Dam	PACFLT Des	PACFLT Dam	VNAF Des	VNAF Dam
Structures	465	522	227	390	59	257
Bridges	52	128	33	93	8	9
Trucks, RR Rolling Stock, and Boats	121	93	191	450	24	23

Source: Hq USAF Rpt, *Stat Sum, Air Ops SEA*, Vol VIII, 11–24 June, 65, tab 3B.

Gia Lam airfield with Il–28s in revetments.

To pilots who flew over the north daily, the MiG–15s and MiG–17s on bases protected by Washington's self-imposed restraint were understandably a threat. In May, several Soviet-built Il–28 bombers arrived at Phuc Yen airfield near Hanoi, creating apprehension about their possible use against airbases in South Vietnam. On May 25, 2d Air Division hosted an air defense conference in Saigon, and PACOM held another in Honolulu three days later, both for the purpose of examining the state of air defense readiness or deficiencies in the south. The consensus was to upgrade the air defense capabilities of the 2d Air Division and the 1st Marine Air Wing around , which was heavily populated with Air Force and Marine aircraft, and to adopt a variety of other defensive measures.[26]

In Washington, the Joint Chiefs considered the MiGs, the Il–28 bombers, and the SA–2 sites highly disquieting. They warned McNamara that the bombers added a "new dimension" to the north's threat to South Vietnam and raised the specter of a combined MiG and Il–28 strike on Da Nang that could destroy or damage 100 to 150 aircraft and inflict 500 to 600 casualties. This would enhance the communist cause, reduce American prestige, and hinder the achievement of U.S. objectives in the war. The SA–2 sites, numbering two by June with evidence that others were under construction, augured a more serious problem. A protective ring of missiles around Hanoi would endanger all air operations within 80 to 125 miles of the capital, jeopardize SAC U–2 reconnaissance flights, and restrict tactical reconnaissance for gathering data on the north's troop and logistic movements. General Moore's staff briefed Westmoreland on an attack plan against the missile sites that the MACV commander considered "feasible and sound." All Southeast Asia commanders and the JCS regarded the elimination of the three threats—the MiGs, the Il–28s, and the SA–2 sites—as "a matter of military urgency."

A JCS plan to destroy the enemy aircraft, backed by Admiral Sharp and General Harris, envisaged the use of low-level night strikes by B–52s on Phuc Yen airfield, followed by early morning armed reconnaissance of all airfields in the Hanoi-Haiphong area to finish off Phuc Yen and any dispersed MiGs. Just prior to or concurrent with the Phuc Yen attack there should be air strikes on all known SA–2 sites. According to the planners, anticipated aircraft loss rates would not be higher than those for Rolling Thunder interdiction, but would increase the longer the administration procrastinated.

The Joint Chiefs conceded that an attack was not without risks. It could intensify domestic and foreign controversy over the war, provoke the Soviet Union and China to step up support for Hanoi, and increase U.S. commitment to Southeast Asia. Nevertheless, they advocated destroying as many aircraft and missiles as possible before the Soviet Union embarked on a policy of more generous assistance to Hanoi and the political obstacles to a Washington decision to destroy Phuc Yen airfield and the SA–2 sites became insurmountable.[27] In early June, at the instigation of General McConnell, the service chiefs reaffirmed their recommendations.[28]

The administration remained unpersuaded. In mid-June, McNamara informed the service chiefs that Deputy Ambassador U. Alexis Johnson and General Westmoreland in Saigon opposed a strike on the Il–28s on the grounds that Hanoi was unlikely to use them for offensive purposes. The Defense Secretary also refused to lift the ban on striking SA–2 sites or MiG airfields, observing that neither enemy missiles nor planes had interfered with Rolling Thunder operations.[29]

Although the Il–28s would never attack the south, thus confirming the administration's benign view of their purpose, the MiG threat was another matter. On June 17 and 20, MiG pilots again challenged U.S. aircraft. The first clash occurred when two Navy F–4B Phantoms on "high barrier" patrol between MiG bases near Hanoi and Thanh Hoa encountered a flight of four MiG–17s.* As the rival aircraft closed, pilots of the Phantoms fired their Sparrow III missiles. Each struck a MiG and both aircraft, enveloped in orange flame and smoke, plummeted to the ground. Only one enemy pilot was observed descending by parachute. These were the first two "kills" of North Vietnamese aircraft in aerial combat and followed the downing, also by a Navy Phantom, of the first Chinese MiG off of Hainan Island on April 9.[30]

On the 20th, in a unique engagement, a flight of four Navy A–1H Skyraiders led by Lt. Cmdr. Edwin A. Greathouse, was flying at about 11,000 feet searching for an Air Force pilot downed during an attack on the Son La barracks when two MiGs suddenly appeared and fired missiles that failed to score. The Skyraider pilots immediately dropped to treetop level to evade the faster MiGs but were pursued. After circling for about five minutes the Americans separated the enemy aircraft. Two A–1H pilots, coming out of a 90-degree bank, saw a MiG on the tail of Commander Greathouse's aircraft. One of them fired his 85-mm gun at the MiG which plunged into the forest as the other enemy aircraft fled. Lt. (JG) Charles W. Hartman and Lt. Clinton B. Johnson

---

* Pilots and radar intercept officers of the two Navy aircraft were Cmdr. Louis C. Page and Lt. John C. Smith, Jr., and Lt. (JG) E.D. Batson and Lt. Cmdr. Robert B. Dormus.

were credited with half a MiG each. It was the only instance in the war in which a propeller aircraft downed a jet.[31]

The MiGs made a third challenge on June 24, during the Air Force's fourth strike on the Ban Nuoc Chieu ammunition depot. A flight of four F–105s, with one element flying at 17,000 feet and another at 22,000 feet, were approached from a six o'clock position by two MiG–15s. As the lower Thunderchiefs broke right and up to engage the MiGs, one of the enemy aircraft broke off. The second MiG was pursued by the topside Thunderchief pilots, who fired their guns but failed to score. After a 270-degree turn, the second MiG also disengaged. All Air Force aircraft returned safely to base without damage.[32] Thus, as the first four months of Rolling Thunder operations ended, the North Vietnamese Air Force had clearly signaled its intent not to let the daily Air Force and Navy attacks go unchallenged.

The Air Force Organizes for Extended Combat

As the tempo of Rolling Thunder attacks and North Vietnamese reaction to them increased in the first half of 1965, the Air Force made more changes in personnel, air units, and the administration of those units to facilitate the prosecution of the air war largely from airbases in Thailand. In May, Brig. Gen. John R. Murphy succeeded Brig. Gen. John H. McCreery as the deputy commander of 2d Air Division at Udorn. From Udorn, the 2d Air Division deputy commander maintained close contact with the American Embassy staffs in Bangkok and Vientiane on all Air Force combat operations affecting the Thai and Laotian governments. Since July 1964 the 2d Air Division deputy commander administered the units through the 35th Tactical Control Group, which by early 1965, was located at Don Muang RTAFB near Bangkok. However, the arrival of four F–105 squadrons, an F–4C squadron, and additional RF–101, EB–66, and other aircraft in Thailand in the spring of 1965 demanded wing-size organizations. Consequently, on April 5, 1965, the Air Force activated the 6234th TFW (Provisional) at Korat. The wing exercised operational and administrative control over all Air Force units based in Thailand until permanent wings were established later in the year. The 35th Tactical Group was then converted to a purely support organization. On May 8, in a further reorganization, the 6234th and 6235th Combat Support Groups were organized at Korat and Takhli, respectively.[33]

The rapid increase in Air Force and other service personnel and aircraft in South Vietnam and Thailand created other administrative and operational problems. The extent of the buildup in the first half of 1965 can be seen in figure 6.*[34]

---

* In the same period, U.S. Navy carrier aircraft strength rose from about 200 to 463 aircraft with two of three carriers positioned at Yankee Station in the Gulf of Tonkin for strikes on North Vietnam and Laos.

Figure 6
Troops and Equipment in South Vietnam and Thailand
February and June 1965

February 1, 1965

	South Vietnam	Thailand
U.S. military personnel	24,000	4,300
Air Force personnel	7,000	1,000
U.S. aircraft (including helicopters)	Unknown	Unknown
Air Force aircraft	200	83

June 30, 1965

	South Vietnam	Thailand
U.S. military personnel	59,000	9,796
Air Force personnel	10,000	6,039
U.S. Aircraft (including helicopters)	1,047	141
Air Force aircraft	319	141

The Air Force experienced major difficulties because of the short 120-day temporary duty (TDY) tours of many recently arrived Air Force combat and combat support units. They were most severe in Thailand where, at the end of June 1965, about 59 percent of all Air Force personnel were on TDY, compared with 30 percent in South Vietnam. An Air Force officer assigned on a one-year permanent change of station (PCS) tour in Southeast Asia underscored the shortcomings of the TDY assignments:[35]

> Generally, the four month TDY personnel cannot be considered efficient enough to justify their being sent to Vietnam. Both TDY and PCS personnel require similar periods of orientation...the PCS man is useful for 11 months whereas the TDY person is only useful for 75 percent of his tour.... Millions of extra dollars are spent creating a vast decrease in efficiency. We could endure the situation if it applied only to airmen, but we of the PCS variety had to endure many TDY staff policy makers, each with new ideas, procedures, policies, and regulations. Just as they grasped the situation they were ready to go home and another man, with other desires and different methods of winning the war rolled in. If any single factor contributed to lack of continuity and bad morale, this was it.

All four F–105 squadrons in Thailand, for example, were on TDY status, and in mid-1965 the rapid turnovers continued: on June 12, the 357th TFS replaced the 354th TFS, and three days later the 12th TFS replaced the 44th TFS. On June 26, at Takhli the 80th TFS replaced the 35th TFS. The 563d TFS arrived at Takhli on April 7, 1965 and was replaced by the 47th TFS, another Phantom unit, on July 26. RF–101 and EB–66 reconnaissance and ECM units suffered from the same administrative, personnel, and operational turbulence.[36]

The Air Staff in Washington and Generals Harris, Maddux, and Moore were, of course, fully aware of this problem. Throughout the spring of 1965, they prepared plans to deal with it. The sheer size of the 2d Air Division, approaching that of a numbered Air Force, and the probability that more Air Force units would deploy to Southeast Asia, prompted attempts to establish a structure geared to longer operations. In July, Moore established the first permanent tactical fighter wing, the 6234th at Korat, which replaced the 6234th (Provisional). The replacement of TDY with PCS units received impetus in late July when President Johnson ordered a sharp increase in U.S air, ground, and Navy units to Southeast Asia to prevent the collapse of the Saigon government's military efforts. A special CINCPAC deployment conference, hastily convened in Honolulu from August 2 to 6, made plans to dispatch the first PCS Air Force F–105 and F–4C tactical fighter squadrons to South Vietnam and Thailand by late 1965.[37]

There were other changes in the Southeast Asia command and control structure. The staff of Headquarters 2d Air Division needed to expand to meet its growing responsibilities for waging war in three countries and for managing the Air Force's expansion program in South Vietnam. On July 8 General McConnell ended the 2d's status as a component of the Thirteenth Air Force and placed it directly under PACAF. Air Force units on six principal Thai bases were assigned to the Thirteenth for administrative and logistic purposes only, while operational control was retained by the 2d Air Division. General Murphy assumed a second responsibility as Deputy Commander, Thirteenth Air Force, and his office was redesignated Deputy Commander, 2d Air Division/Thirteenth Air Force. The leadership of the Thirteenth Air Force also underwent change when Maj. Gen. James Wilson succeeded Maj. Gen. Sam Maddux as commander on July 15.[38]

In Saigon, General Moore's position also underwent a change. On June 25, with JCS and McNamara's approval, General Westmoreland appointed Moore MACV Deputy Commander for Air Operations in addition to his post as commander of the 2d Air Division. On the same day, in recognition of the change, Moore was promoted to Lieutenant General and assigned a deputy commander. The latter post was filled on July 1 by Maj. Gen. Gilbert L. Meyers, formerly commander of the Air Force's Tactical Air Warfare Center at Eglin AFB, Florida.[39]

Although Westmoreland claimed General Moore's new status as MACV Deputy Commander for Air Operations enlarged his authority and would promote interservice harmony, the Air Staff saw little practical significance in the new title. In fact, it regarded the change as unwise organizationally as it divided Moore's energies between the two headquarters, his own at Tan Son Nhut and that of MACV in downtown Saigon. In addition, he remained outside of the MACV headquarters staff structure.[40] Nonetheless, Moore and his successors retained the new position for several years.

Another organizational adjustment occurred on July 10 when General Westmoreland, Commander, MACV since June 1964, relinquished his second "hat" as Commander, U.S. Military Assistance Command, Vietnam/Thailand (COMUSMACVTHAI) to an Army commander in Bangkok. The COMUS-MACVTHAI post was initially created as a vehicle for U.S. participation in military planning by the eight-nation SEATO countries, of which Thailand was a member. Once again, political rather than military considerations dictated the reorganization: to allay the concern of the Thai government that it may be identified too closely with American military activities in support of South Vietnam. The new post, designated U.S. Military Assistance Command, Thailand (COMUSMACTHAI) would be the focal point for U.S. military participation in SEATO planning. The creation of the post triggered another debate with General McConnell, supported by the Navy and Marine Corps chiefs, advocating the appointment of an Air Force general officer. But the new JCS chairman, Army Gen. Earle G. Wheeler, who had replaced Taylor in June, favored an Army incumbent. McNamara selected Brig. Gen. Ernest F. Easterbrook, already in Bangkok as Chief of the Joint U.S. Military Assistance Advisory Group, Thailand, who would assume the duties of COMUSMACTHAI as an additional duty. Air Force Brig. Gen. Thomas B. Whitehouse was appointed Deputy Commander, COMUSMACTHAI.* As a result of this change, theater command and control relationships became more complex as General Murphy, now Deputy Commander, 2d Air Division/Thirteenth Air Force, at Udorn, dealt directly with General Easterbrook and with the staffs of the American Embassies in Bangkok and Vientiane regarding Air Force and other service matters associated with the U.S. military presence in Thailand.[41]

Thus, in mid-1965, changes in the Southeast Asia command and control system failed to strengthen the Air Force's role in planning and conducting air operations in North Vietnam as well as in Laos and South Vietnam. In truth, the system was more elaborate than ever and, in the Air Force's view, augured less efficient use of available air power in the theater. In July 1965, General Harris wistfully sent a proposed command and control arrangement to the Air Staff, which he believed would be simpler, more effective, and more in consonance

---

* Gen. Easterbrook was succeeded by Army Maj. Gen. Richard G. Stillwell on August 14, 1965. Gen. Whitehouse was promoted to the rank of major general in August, and assumed his post on September 2, 1965.

with Air Force doctrine. According to this arrangement, control of all service air operations in South Vietnam would be transferred from the MACV to the 2d Air Division commander which would assure the PACOM commander of undisputed control of air operations in Laos and North Vietnam (unencumbered by operational directives and requests from Washington, MACV, and the U.S. Embassies in Saigon, Vientiane, and Bangkok). The PACOM commander would exercise his authority solely through his PACAF and PACFLT component commanders, relying principally on USAF aircraft in Thailand and with Navy carrier aircraft playing only a minimal role.[42] Of course, if submitted officially, Harris' proposal would have been totally unacceptable to the Army-oriented MACV commander, who was about to assume responsibility for a greatly expanded air and ground war in South Vietnam, and to the Navy-oriented PACOM commander, who would never seriously countenance a subordinate role for Navy air operations.

Washington Rejects a More Air-Oriented Strategy

By mid-1965, it was clear that the earlier expectations of some high administration officials that Rolling Thunder would bring Hanoi quickly to the negotiating table would not be realized. Military and political developments in South Vietnam continued to favor the insurgents. A Viet Cong "monsoon offensive" forced Saigon's army to abandon six district capitals, and there were many military reverses offset by only occasional successes.[43] Communist destruction and disruption of the road and rail system in South Vietnam was widespread. Prime Minister Quat was embroiled in a dispute with President Phan Khac Suii over cabinet appointments and was caught in the struggle between Catholic and Buddhist factions. On June 11, Quat resigned. Political power returned to an all-military National Leadership Council, with Maj. Gen. Nguyen Van Thieu as acting chief of state and Brig. Gen. Nguyen Cao Ky as *de facto* prime minister. With the collapse of the fourth government and the fourth constitution in twenty months, a new regime emerged on June 19 with General Ky, the colorful chief of the Vietnamese Air Force, as prime minister. Thus did the Thieu-Ky team come into being. Together, they would give Saigon a semblance of political stability in the coming months. But they could not halt the deterioration of the ground forces.[44]

Meanwhile, on June 6, General Westmoreland and Ambassador Taylor agreed that more troops were needed to contain the VC-NVA in South Vietnam. However, in Westmoreland's opinion, the South Vietnamese Army's excessively high desertion rates, casualties, and occasional heavy losses, made further enlargement of the Army impossible until November 1965. With the ratio of military manpower tilting progressively in favor of the communists, he doubted that the Saigon government would be able to withstand a VC-NVA military and political offensive for more than six months. To rectify the imbalance, he proposed the addition of 45,000 more U.S. troops to the 50,000 already in the

President Lyndon B. Johnson, Gen. William C. Westmoreland,
Vietnamese Chief of State Nguyen Van Thieu, and Premier
Nguyen Cao Ky salute the colors during the President's
visit to Cam Ranh Bay Air Base, South Vietnam, 1965.

south and four more Air Force tactical squadrons. The Army's additional manpower, he believed, should include the 1st Cavalry Division (Air Mobile) plus support for the emplacement near Pleiku in the central highlands. Concurrently, the JCS made plans to send the equivalent of twenty-three U.S and nine Korean battalions to the south, and for "more intense" air operations against the north to underscore U.S. perseverance in the war.[45]

During the high-level deliberations on Westmoreland's proposals in Saigon, Honolulu, and Washington, the Air Force opposed the evolving strategy requiring more ground troops rather than air power to halt enemy advances in South Vietnam. On June 8, General Harris again emphasized to the Air Staff—which needed no persuading—the need for raising the tempo of the air war against the north and striking more key targets above the 20th parallel. This, he said, would be a simpler, more easily controllable, and less risky course of action than "the introduction of…U.S. troops into the jungles and mountain areas of RVN." The PACAF commander conceded that additional troops should be deployed to protect military bases and to establish enclaves to assure the effective use of air power, but he strongly opposed their engagement principally to defeat the Viet Cong. Placing a force of 20,000 to 30,000 men in the highlands near Pleiku, he warned, invited another Dien Bien Phu or a "retreat from the Yalu [River]" and would generate major logistic problems.[46]

Contrary to the Air Force's view, on June 16, Secretary McNamara announced the dispatch of 20,000 more U.S. troops to the south, bringing the number of men there to between 70,000 and 75,000. He said that this was dictated by the growth in Viet Cong strength, now totaling about 165,000 guerrillas,

Poststrike photo shows results of an F–105 strike against the Trai Hoi highway bridge in April 1965. One span of the bridge was dropped and the ferry docks were destroyed by direct hits.

which threatened Saigon's regular and pararegular forces of about 500,000 men and created an unsatisfactory ratio of roughly one to three between the guerrillas and the south's regular forces. He had little to say about the Rolling Thunder campaign in the north, but indicated it had been effective in reducing the flow of men and supplies from North to South Vietnam. Aircraft were striking barracks, supply and POL depots, and rail and highway bridges, he noted, and efforts were under way to keep twenty-two of twenty-three bridges struck thus far impassable to traffic.[47]

Events would show that McNamara's decision of June 16 was merely the initial increment of still larger ground reinforcements for the embattled South Vietnamese government. Within the JCS, during interminable debate on the declining fortunes of Saigon and nature of additional U.S. assistance, General McConnell expressed his discontent with the administration's slow pace in approving strikes for important targets. Of the ninety-four fixed targets in the north designated by the JCS, he informed his colleagues, only twenty-two had been struck, and many targets subsequently added to the master list (which totaled 235 targets by June 17) were unimportant. Thus it would be wasteful to hit them. Many targets approved by the administration, he observed, had not been endorsed by the Joint Chiefs. In view of recent DIA bombing assessments indicating that air strikes in South Vietnam were not hurting the VC-NVA sufficiently, he characterized as incongruous the stringent bombing restraints that kept planes out of the Hanoi-Haiphong area and the buffer zone near China. For McConnell, there was an inherent contradiction in the United States' objective of destroying the will and capability of the Hanoi regime and the refusal to employ enough air power to do so.[48]

To underscore his argument, the Air Force Chief of Staff gave the other service chiefs and McNamara a targeting chart (figure 7) showing the number of important changes as of June 24, 1965.[49]

Figure 7
Targets and Airstrikes as of June 24, 1965

FIXED TARGETS	No. Targeted	No Hit	No. of Attacks	Strike Sorties
Barracks	42	29	51	1,014
Ammunition depots	16	8	17	575
POL storage	12	3	3	50
Supply depots	11	6	17	259
Power plants	17	3	4	345
Airfields	9	3	4	180
Railyards & shops	57	25	34	1,097
Ferries	5	1	3	30
Communications installations	13	11	5	40
Radar sites	27	10	13	223
Naval bases and ports	11	3	6	116
Total	**220**	**102**	**157**	**3,929**

ARMED RECONNAISSANCE	Destroyed	Damaged
Water vessels	105	164
Vehicles	132	194
Railroad stock	55	248

Total fixed targets and armed reconnaissance sorties plus other sorties against targets not listed   7,029

PERCENT OF NATIONAL CAPACITY REMAINING OF SELECTED FACILITIES

FACILITIES	
Major jet airfields	100
Other small airfields	93
Bridges	60
Railyards and shops	94
Ferries	78
Military barracks and headquarters	98
Locks and dams	100

PERCENT OF REMAINING CAPACITY

Ammunition depots	82
POL storage	86
Supply depots	97
Communication installations	50
Naval facilities and ports	94
SAM sites	100
Radar sites	75
Electricity power plants	91

In another memorandum, McConnell said he was "more convinced than ever," that air strikes on the north were essential to the defeat of the Viet Cong in the south. Rather than destroying the insurgents' will and capability, the current attack level provided them with an opportunity to strengthen themselves. A JCS recommendation sent to McNamara in November 1964 urging strikes on all key military and industrial targets, he noted, had yet to be adopted.[50] In another meeting with the service chiefs on June 25, McConnell said that if the United States sent fighting troops to the south without first "completely knocking out the North Vietnamese with air power," the Joint Chiefs would be "criminally responsible."[51]

The fact that not all of the service chiefs agreed fully with these fervent arguments was evident two days later when they provided McNamara with another memorandum reflecting a compromise of service positions. The document retained the thrust of McConnell's views, calling for increased activity against the north: more armed reconnaissance missions; strikes on POL installations, the major rail and highway bridges between Hanoi and China, airfields, and newly constructed missile sites; and the mining of the major seaports. To accomplish these objectives, the number of Rolling Thunder sorties should rise from the current 2,000 to 5,000 per month. However, the document also supported the dispatch of more U.S. ground troops to the south as desired by the Army and Marine Corps.[52]

Nonetheless, persuaded by Westmoreland, the administration again refused to accelerate drastically the strike tempo against the north. Convinced that the war had to be won in the south, its sole concern at the moment was the number of additional U.S. and allied air, ground, and sea units necessary to assist South Vietnamese forces and when they should be sent. At the President's request, Secretary McNamara, General Wheeler, and Ambassador-designate, Henry Cabot Lodge* and their staffs arrived in Saigon on July 16 to confer with MACV and embassy authorities concerning the problems of the war, and to

---

* Lodge would officially succeed Taylor as ambassador to South Vietnam in August 1965. This was Lodge's second tour as ambassador, having served previously from mid-1963 to mid-1964.

determine more precisely the scope of Saigon's additional needs. General Moore would serve as the senior Air Force representative at the meetings.

In briefings for the high-ranking visitors, MACV officials said the Viet Cong had increased its strength from forty-two to sixty-eight battalions in the eighteen months from January 1964 to July 1965 (McNamara thought the total was higher), possessed a manpower pool of one million, and could expand its strength by 100,000 men per year. In comparison, infiltration from the north (consisting of southern returnees and DRV personnel) into South Vietnam was small, totaling about 5,000 since February 1965. Travel time varied from a few months to two years.

Viet Cong supply needs from outside South Vietnam were estimated at fourteen tons per day (a figure used by the JCS), based on the Viet Cong strength and combat level. Ambassador Taylor conjectured that it would take about 12,000 personnel to support a daily requirement of fourteen tons per day. The Viet Cong did not appear to be suffering from an ammunition shortage and had probably fired forty-one tons during a recent two-day battle at Dong Xoai. There was general surprise over the ability of the communists to get along with so few materiel resources.

McNamara did not expect the present Rolling Thunder program to reduce the requirement, and noted that the Viet Cong were taking over the country with that level of support, and could acquire even more territory if they received twenty-eight tons per day of supplies from sources outside the country. Because the insurgents had needed so few supplies in the past, at present, and probably in the future, the Defense Secretary doubted if the bombing could seriously degrade communist logistics, although he did not advocate stopping the attacks. The military situation dictated more manpower in the south, and because the Viet Cong could readily obtain more recruits locally, the U.S. and South Vietnamese governments should be prepared to increase their own troop strengths accordingly.

McNamara evinced considerable interest in obtaining more information from communist prisoners of war on the effect of bombing on Viet Cong recruitment, infiltration from the north, and the movement of the South Vietnamese populace from one area to another. He characterized a recent RAND study that provided a rationale for stepping up the bombing* as an "initial meek effort," although it threw some light on air strike results.

In reviewing additional U.S. and allied needs for the war, the conferees considered two basic plans. One, prepared by the JCS, would raise the overall level

---

* See Leon Goure and C.A.H. Thompson, *Some Impressions of Viet Cong Vulnerabilities: An Interim Report*, memo RM-4699-ISA/ARPA. After interviewing 215 Viet Cong military and civilian cadres and rank and file, the authors concluded tentatively that the Viet Cong had military, political, and psychological vulnerabilities that could be exploited further by intensified interdiction and psychological warfare programs. This promised to generate more Viet Cong deserters and defectors and add to the discontent of the populace who would be encouraged to withhold men and supplies from the insurgents.

of U.S. and allied troops in the south to 176,000 personnel by the end of 1965, providing thirty-four infantry-type "maneuver" battalions, and six to nine more USAF squadrons, contingent on the completion of more airfields. A second plan prepared by MACV would raise troop levels in the south to 196,000 men by the end of 1965 and provide forty-four "maneuver battalions." A second phase of the plan, extending into 1966, would raise the number of U.S. and allied forces in-country to 270,927.

In further discussion of the Rolling Thunder program, Ambassador Taylor, whose views were highly influential, now argued for maintaining the current bombing tempo rather than increasing it as he had earlier in the program. Amplifying his position later in response to specific questions from McNamara, Taylor averred that vigorous air attacks would not bring Hanoi to terms immediately, but promised to have a greater "climactic" effect later. He cautioned that the United States should avoid bringing China into the war and avoid alienating its friends. The best way to apply maximum pressure on Hanoi, he said, was to achieve military success in the south coupled with air pressure on the north.

Taylor observed that in Laos the limited data from aerial reconnaissance and road watch teams made it difficult to assess the effect of the bombing. Thus far, it did not appear to be great. He said that there was data showing that from April 26 to May 24, 1965 it took an average of six sorties to destroy one truck, and studies of eight choke points revealed that they were closed less than one third of the time.*

The principal result of strikes on choke points was to delay and harass communist traffic. Taylor favored no major change in the level of armed reconnaissance or choke point missions but recommended more attacks on river traffic and fixed targets. These would increase air needs from about forty to sixty-eight sorties per day. He also urged that ground-based incursions into the Laotian border regions, supported from the air, be organized by MACV and launched as soon as possible to provide more intelligence on infiltration and the impact of air strikes.

The upshot of the conference was that Secretary McNamara, whose views were essentially congruent with Taylor's, decided to maintain a tight rein on out-country bombing while concentrating on winning the war in the south. He reiterated the standing policy giving military operations in South Vietnam first claim on available air power:[53]

> I want to make clear... that I do not want one plane dropping bombs on North Vietnam if it can be used advantageously for air operations in South Vietnam.... There is to be no bombing in Laos or in North Vietnam if we can use that sortie effectively in South Vietnam. Now this is clearly estab-

---

* Msg, CINCPAC to AmEmb Vientiane, COMUSMACV, 260330Z Jun 65.

lished U.S. policy. I want to make sure that is understood and followed.

On his return to Washington, McNamara immediately sent his recommendations to President Johnson. Declaring that the situation in South Vietnam was worse than a year previously (which, in turn, was worse than a year before that) he considered the odds "less than even," that the Saigon government could last out the year. Pacification was making little progress, and the communists believed South Vietnam was on the run and near collapse and were determined to try for "a complete takeover." The Defense Secretary posed three alternate courses of action: cutting U.S. losses and withdrawing in as orderly a fashion as possible but under conditions humiliating to the United States and damaging to U.S. effectiveness throughout the world; continuing at the present level while limiting U.S. forces to about 75,000 in the south, holding on and playing for the breaks, a policy that would almost certainly force a choice between withdrawal or emergency expansion of forces when it might be too late to do any good; or expanding "promptly and substantially" U.S. pressure on the Viet Cong in the south, maintaining pressure against the north, and launching a vigorous political effort to lay the groundwork for "a favorable outcome by clarifying our objectives and establishing channels of communication." Amplifying the third alternative, which he favored, he noted Ambassador Lodge's view that an American effort to negotiate an end to the war before South Vietnam was strong militarily would simply harden communist resolve to fight. He said that Ambassador Taylor and Deputy Ambassador Johnson agreed with this position but also believed that the United States should maintain discreet contacts with the Soviet Union. The Defense Secretary continued:

> [The third] alternative would stave off defeat in the short run and offer a good chance of producing a favorable settlement in the longer run; at the same time, it would imply a commitment to see a fighting war clear through at considerable cost in casualties and materiel and would make any later decision to withdraw even more difficult and even more costly than would be the case today.

The most propitious time for launching another diplomatic effort for peace, he counseled, was after the United States and third countries had deployed forty-four more battalions (as proposed by MACV) to the south and subjected the north to heavier bombing—such as destroying key bridges north of Hanoi. The United States might then consider a six- to eight-week bombing pause as part of that initiative. He thought five considerations should guide future bombing: to capitalize on Hanoi's fear of destruction that could be avoided if it agreed to negotiate or agreed to some type of settlement; to make it politically easy for Hanoi to enter into negotiations and make concessions—as when no bombing was taking place on its territory; to maximize bombing effectiveness and minimize political repercussions arising from methods used; to coordinate with whatever factors that might induce Hanoi to consider a settlement with the United States as preferable to continuing the war; and to avoid a program of air attacks with a high risk of war with the Soviet Union or China or which would alienate America's friends and allies.[54]

On July 21, to review McNamara's recommendations, the President began a series of meetings with his principal advisers, with General Wheeler the sole representative of the armed forces. The sessions continued intermittently until the 27th when the President briefed the congressional leaders on his tentative decisions, which were announced the next day at a news conference.[55] Accepting most of McNamara's views, he said that U.S. troop strength in South Vietnam would rise almost immediately from 75,000 to 125,000 men and include the Army's 1st Air Mobile Division. He promised to send more men later as needed. Military draft calls would rise gradually from about 17,000 to 35,000 men per month, but there would be no call-up of reserve units. He said that Ambassador Lodge would initiate reform programs in South Vietnam, and Ambassador Arthur Goldberg at the United Nations would launch new efforts to bring peace. Denying that the substantial new deployments constituted a change in U.S. policy in the war, the President strongly reaffirmed America's support for the Saigon government and its determination to prevent the communist domination of Asia.[56]

Thus, three years and nine months after the first American counterinsurgency units entered South Vietnam, the U.S. government, faced with the possible loss of its Saigon ally, embarked on a conventional air and ground war. During this period, despite support from Admiral Sharp, CIA Director McCone, Walt W. Rostow, the State Department's Policy Planning Chief, and a few other officials, the Air Force had failed to persuade higher authorities to pursue an air-oriented rather than a ground-oriented strategy to bring the Hanoi regime more quickly to the negotiating table. However, it would carry out the administration's directives.

Beginning of Two-Week Bombing Cycles

The President's July decisions did not significantly alter the current tempo of air attacks on North Vietnam, and left any further gradual changes hostage to a variety of political and military developments. However, the administration supported one important change desired by air commanders for planning and executing Rolling Thunder programs. This was the extension of the bombing cycle from one to two weeks. Generals Moore and Westmoreland and Admiral Sharp had all called for this adjustment in June to ease the problems inherent in aircraft scheduling and weather aborts and to assure greater flexibility in the separate air programs in North Vietnam, South Vietnam, and Laos. The two-week cycle was adopted beginning with Rolling Thunder programs 22/23 (July

9–22). Air commanders were instructed to apportion the level of air effort for each seven-day period as equally as possible.[57]

Several other tactical changes promised to enhance somewhat the effectiveness of Rolling Thunder operations. Pilots were granted authority to strike more targets above the 20th parallel, to fly upwards of 550 armed reconnaissance sorties for a fourteen-day period, and to hit designated road segments in Laos with ordnance not expended in North Vietnam while returning to bases in Thailand. As before, Admiral Sharp assigned about half of the allocated sorties to the Air Force and VNAF, and half to Navy carrier air.[58]

Of seven targets above the 20th parallel designated by the JCS and authorized for programs 22/23, several had been attacked previously. Air Force F–105s and F–4Cs hit four of the northernmost targets between July 9 and 14, leading off with air strikes on the Yen Son and Yen Bai ordnance depots, about sixty-five and seventy miles northwest of Hanoi respectively. The larger of the two, Yen Son, encompassed about sixty acres, contained twenty-five buildings believed to hold ammunition, and represented about 10 percent of national capacity. As the major depot in the northwest, it supported military activities in the Red River Delta area above Hanoi and was assumed to be an important supply depot for the Pathet Lao via Dien Bien Phu and for the Viet Cong in South Vietnam via Moc Chau. Both Yen Son and Yen Bai depots were also suspected storage areas for supplies from China. Five Air Force missions against Yen Son and seven against Yen Bai wrought destruction estimated at 54 and 60 percent of capacity of the two targets. Several restrikes were also conducted by Air Force aircraft against the Dien Bien Phu and Son La military areas.[59]

On July 11, during restrikes on Dien Bien Phu and the Yen Bai and Yen Son ordnance depots, for the first time F–105 Thunderchief pilots of the 12th TFS dropped MLU–10 time-delay fused land mines along the Hanoi-Lao Cai rail line. On the same day, Hanoi and Peking charged that two formations of U.S. aircraft also struck Lao Cai, 160 miles northwest of Hanoi and near the Chinese border, several nearby populated areas, and entered Chinese air space over Hakow in Yunnan Province opposite Lao Cai. Hanoi protested to the International Control Commission and Peking denounced the alleged air intrusion short of threatening outright intervention. American officials denied the allegations.[60] On July 14, four F–105s severely damaged two trucks thirty-seven miles north of Dien Bien Phu, the furthest penetration yet into North Vietnam.[61]

The Navy's initial strikes on the Tri Dong highway bridge dropped one span and damaged three others. Navy aircraft also hit the Hamp Rong port facility for the first time and conducted a restrike on the Ban Xom Lam barracks area. Air Force and Navy aircraft carried out restrikes on several targets below the 20th parallel, the most notable consisting of four separate Navy missions against the hardy Thanh Hoa bridge. Radar-directed bombs scored hits near the bridge and its approaches, but the spans remained intact. No clear-cut BDA

An F–4 fires 2.75-inch rockets at a North Vietnamese target.

was achieved.[62]

An Air Force mission above the 20th parallel on July 10 was enlivened by an aerial engagement with North Vietnamese MiGs in which the Air Force made their first two MiG kills of the war. The engagement occurred about twenty-five to thirty-five miles northwest of Hanoi, where F–105s were pounding enemy targets in the Yen Bai area. A flight of four Phantom F–4Cs of the 45th TFS of the 8th TFW at Ubon, commanded by Maj. Richard Hall, were flying cover for the Thunderchiefs. Hoping not to alert the MiG pilots, they maintained complete radio silence during their flight and rendezvous with KC–135 refueling tankers and flew at Mach .85 at about 20,000 feet, a flight profile similar to that of the strike aircraft. A radar officer in an EC–121 Big Eye early warning and control aircraft sighted two MiG–17s and alerted the USAF crews. Shortly after entering orbit near Yen Bai, the lead Phantom established initial radar contact with a MiG and the number three Phantom locked on a few seconds later. In the ensuing maneuver and evasion by the contestants, in which all jettisoned their fuel tanks, the MiG pilots fired their cannons and missed, but two Phantom aircrews released eight Sidewinder air-to-air missiles, two of which found their mark, destroying both aircraft. All four Phantoms returned safely to Ubon.

The first MiG kill was credited to Capts. Thomas S. Roberts and Ronald C. Anderson, the pilot and radar intercept officer respectively, and the second to Capts. Kenneth E. Holcombe and Arthur C. Clark, who held the same assign-

Members of the first USAF flight to down MiGs over North Vietnam celebrate after receiving their medals. Capts. Thomas S. Roberts and Ronald C. Anderson, credited with the first MiG kill, are among the flight crew members raising the flight commander, Maj. Richard Hall, on their shoulders.

ments in the second Phantom. Soon afterwards, General Moore awarded Silver Stars to the four men and the Distinguished Flying Cross to the other two Phantom aircrews, who had assisted by visually identifying the enemy aircraft. The aerial battle brought to five the number of North Vietnamese MiGs destroyed in the war, the first three by Navy pilots on June 17 and 20.[63]

During the fourteen-day period of Rolling Thunder 22/23, the Air Force flew 233 sorties, the VNAF 28, and the Navy 471.[64] Antiaircraft fire continued to take a toll, downing two Navy planes and damaging three Air Force F–105s and six Navy planes.[65] Hanoi's news media claimed 370 America aircraft shot down from August 5, 1964 (the date of the first attack on the north during the Gulf of Tonkin crisis) to July 10, 1965.[66]

The real U.S. aircraft and pilot losses, while considerably more modest, nonetheless strained the Air Force's search and rescue resources, now thinly spread to save as many U.S. and Vietnamese aircrews as possible in the three-theater air war. As a result, the Air Force's Military Air Transport Service, the operating agency for rescue activities, established the 38th Air Rescue Squadron, with Lt. Col. Edward Krafka as commander at Tan Son Nhut AB,

---

* For further discussion of Air Force SAR deployments and operations, see Capt. Earl H. Tilford, *The Development of Search and Rescue Operations in the United States Air Force in Southeast Asia, 1961–1975* (Ofc AF Hist, 1980).

South Vietnam, on July 1. The new unit, which would soon receive additional manpower, helicopters, and aircraft, replaced temporary units of the Pacific Air Rescue Center that had performed SAR in Southeast Asia since early 1962. A total of seven detachments were established under the 38th—five in Thailand at Nakhon Phanom, Takhli, Ubon, Korat, and Udorn and two in South Vietnam at Bien Hoa and Da Nang.*[67]

The slowly increasing strike tempo in the north in July was accompanied by more widespread leaflet distribution by the Air Force and VNAF. About 9,888,000 leaflets were scattered from the DMZ to Dien Bien Phu in the first fourteen days of the month. In the last half of July, about 6,450,000 leaflets were released over nineteen separate areas, with the largest single leaflet distribution of the war on July 22, the eleventh anniversary of the partition of South and North Vietnam as a consequence of the 1954 Geneva Agreement. Fourteen Air Force aircraft were employed to dispense the messages for Hanoi, Haiphong, Nam Dinh, Ninh Binh, Thanh, Phat Diem, Vinh, and Phu Dien Chau. Because of the forty n.m. restricted zone around Hanoi and Haiphong, pilots relied on wind drift to scatter leaflets on the two cities. VNAF A–1Hs dropped leaflets on towns in southern North Vietnam on the same day.[68]

Although air commanders obtained satisfaction in striking a few more important targets in the north, however piecemeal the authorization to do so, they remained highly frustrated over Washington's ban on knocking out the north's SA–2 missile sites. Since U–2 photography had detected the first site near Hanoi on April 5, 1965, three more had been pinpointed by the end of June, all in the sensitive Hanoi-Haiphong area. Washington permitted only occasional reconnaissance of the sites by reconnaissance drones and U–2 pilots, although the latter, instructed to remain thirty n.m. miles away from the sites until their planes received better missile radar warning devices, took only oblique photographs.[69]

On July 4, 1965, photography disclosed work on a fifth site about twelve miles southwest of Hanoi. Secretary McNamara, again pressed by the services to strike the sites before they became operational, asked the JCS to compare the anticipated aircraft attrition rate if the sites were hit quickly with the rate after the sites became an integral part of the north's air defense system. The service chiefs replied quickly that the price of postponing an attack would be a significant rise in aircraft attrition. On July 7, McConnell informed the administration through the JCS that three of the five SA–2 sites might be ready to receive the necessary operational equipment within any 48-hour period. But the administration still refused to issue a strike order. In a news conference on the 11th, Secretary Rusk announced that there were no plans "at this time" to attack the sites, justifying the administration's stance, as McNamara had earlier, on the grounds the missiles were not interfering with Rolling Thunder operations. Thirteen days later, however, Hanoi would dramatically change the administration's no-strike policy by firing its first missiles, and with devastating effect.[70]

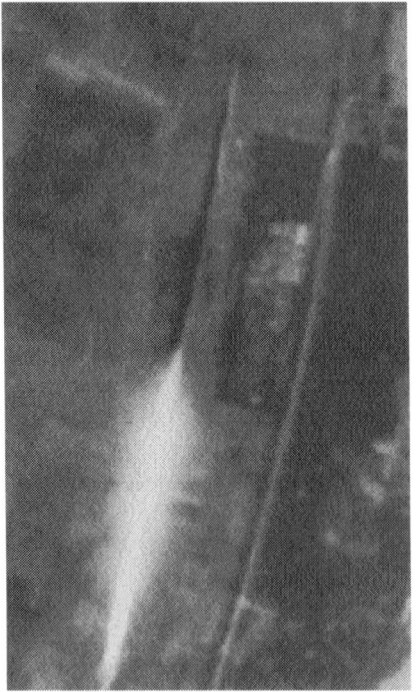

SA–2 surface-to-air missile in flight (left). SA–2 missile explodes underneath RF–4, downing it (above).

CHAPTER 6
The SAM Threat

On July 24, to the apparent surprise of some administration officials, the North Vietnamese fired their first SA–2 surface-to-air missiles from near the Hanoi sanctuary, downing an Air Force F–4C Phantom and its two-man crew. Thus the SAMs were allowed to draw "first blood" despite earlier appeals by the JCS, Admiral Sharp, General Harris, and other military commanders to Washington's highest authorities for permission to destroy the sites before they became operational. Defense Secretary McNamara initially opposed striking suspected or known SA–2 sites while Rolling Thunder was confined largely below the 20th parallel because he feared killing Chinese or Soviet technicians working at the sites.

A U–2 aircraft spotted the first SA–2 missile site under construction on April 5, 1965, and by late July, five were in place roughly in a circle within twenty n.m. of Hanoi. Each consisted of six firing, one guidance control, and one missile-holding revetments plus associated roadways. The diameter of the firing revetments and sites averaged about 75 and 750 feet respectively. The configuration was similar to that employed by the Soviet Union.[1]

However, no SA–2 missile had been demonstrably operational until 0805 Saigon time on July 24 when an Air Force EB–66 Destroyer intercepted for the second time in as many days a Fan Song radar signal from a missile site twenty-three n.m. west of Hanoi. A crew member flashed a warning to four F–4C Phantoms that were flying cover at about 20,000 feet for several F–105 Thunderchiefs en route to strike the Lang Tai explosive plant. Lt. Col. William A. Alden, aboard one of the Phantoms, suddenly saw two, perhaps three, missiles rising towards the flight. One exploded directly beneath the Phantom opposite Alden's. Flames erupted from the wing, then the plane rolled over and spiraled into the clouds. The pilot of the stricken plane, Capt. Richard P. Keirn, parachuted safely, but was to spend nearly eight years as a prisoner of war in North Vietnam. His radar intercept officer, Capt. Roscoe H. Fobair, apparently

SA–2 on launcher.

Lockheed EC-121 Constellation.

died in the crash. The other one or two missiles detonated near the flight and peppered the remaining Phantoms with shrapnel, damaging them severely. The surviving aircrews likened each SAM to "a telephone pole with fins," judged they had been set with proximity fuses, and were fired from two previously undetected sites quickly numbered sites 6 and 7. Admiral Sharp flashed the JCS that the initial enemy SAM attack from outside of Hanoi's strike-free perimeter demanded the abandonment of all political considerations heretofore precluding attacks on missile targets.[2] Ambassador Taylor in Saigon likewise backed a prompt response and urged simultaneous attacks against all of the north's known SAM sites.[3] The lethality of the SA–2s was punctuated the next day when another downed a SAC reconnaissance drone flying at 59,000 feet.[4]

Initial anti-SAM Operations

For several days, high administration and military officials pondered what the American response to these missile firings should be. In a JCS meeting on the 26th, General McConnell proposed attacking all known SA–2 sites in the north, including those in the sanctuary area around Hanoi, and bombing Phuc Yen airfield. As civilian officials were unlikely to approve such action, the service chiefs recommended a less drastic measure.[5] After weighing the missile threat to the Rolling Thunder program, President Johnson approved a retaliatory air strike against the offending site or sites outside the Hanoi-Haiphong sanctuary. The JCS quickly sent the order to Admiral Sharp who assigned the task to the Air Force. On July 27, under the code name Spring High, General Moore sent forty-six F–105s, carrying napalm and CBUs, supported by fifty-eight other aircraft (three EB–66s, six Marine EF–10Bs, two EC–121s, eight F–105s, eight F–104s, four RF–101s, twelve F–4Cs, and fifteen KC–135s) to the offending missile installations. Eleven Thunderchiefs struck site 6 and twelve struck site 7. At the same time, twenty-three aircraft hit barracks areas suspected of housing SAM air defense personnel at nearby Cam Doi and Phu Nieu. In their bombing runs, pilots flew 50 to 100 feet above the terrain, four abreast, to deliver their napalm and CBU ordnance.* The attack was very costly. The North Vietnamese had ringed the sites with 37-mm, 57-mm, and 85-mm antiaircraft guns, and aircraft flying into and out of the target areas faced intense groundfire for seven and a half minutes. Enemy gunners damaged one F–105 striking site 6. During the approach to Udorn with an escort, the damaged aircraft rammed its escort and both planes and pilots were lost. Two more Thunderchiefs were shot down with their pilots while attacking site 7. A fifth F–105 and pilot were lost in an associated strike on the Cam Doi barracks. A sixth was downed after hitting the barracks at Phu Nieu, but the pilot was rescued, the sole survivor of the antiaircraft barrage. The heavy attrition was even more distressing in light of electronic evidence that Fan Song radars were emitting before, during, and after the air strikes and that bomb damage assessment photos disclosed that there was a dummy missile in site 6, placed there as a trap, and that site 7 was empty.[6]

There were also diplomatic repercussions. A United Press International news story, based on information provided by a USAF spokesman in Saigon, stated that the two USAF aircraft that had collided had been on a Rolling Thunder mission. The disclosure greatly agitated Ambassador Martin in Bangkok who was honor-bound to enforce the Thai government's request not to acknowledge that USAF aircraft based in Thailand were bombing North Vietnam. Such "unthinking utterances," he informed U.S. officials in Saigon and elsewhere, could cost the United States the use of Thai airbases, lead to Soviet accusations against Thailand for allowing Americans to operate from their territory, and possibly have other serious consequences. He said that the embassy had planned to treat the plane collision as an unfortunate accident without relating it to Rolling Thunder operations. Martin personally asked General Harris to prevent any future untimely security leaks.[7]

A poststrike study of the first anti-SAM attack that cost six aircraft and five lives was launched immediately. PACAF analysts quickly ascertained that a more careful readout of U–2 photography taken on July 20 could have pinpointed the sites. Other factors militating against success were insufficient low-level prestrike photography of the target area, an inadequate antiaircraft

---

* For additional details of the initial SAM firings and Air Force and Navy tactics to counter them, see Capt. Melvin Potter, *Air Tactics Against NVN/Air Ground Defenses* (Project CHECO, 1967), p 114; Bernard C. Nalty, *Tactics and Techniques of Electronic Warfare: Electronic Countermeasures in the Air War Against North Vietnam, 1965–1973* (Ofc AF Hist, 1977); and Earl H. Tilford, Jr., *Crosswinds: The Air Force's Setup in Vietnam* (College Station, Texas, 1993), pp 81–83.

Unoccupied SA–2 missile site near Hanoi.

order of battle, pilot difficulties in finding the targets at low altitude from fast-flying jets, and the likelihood that North Vietnamese air defense personnel anticipated the air strike. This last factor, plus the time lag in responding to the SA–2 attack, enabled the defenders to place more antiaircraft weapons near the sites.[8] These included light- and medium-caliber guns, automatic weapons, and an antiaircraft installation, confirmed by photoreconnaissance on July 29, consisting of eight 100-mm guns, each with an altitude range of about 39,000 feet.*[9]

Although all but one of the aircraft losses were caused directly or indirectly by conventional antiaircraft fire, air commanders were most concerned about the proliferating SAM sites. On July 29, Admiral Sharp directed his Air Force and Navy components to conduct at least one electronic intelligence flight every three hours against SAM-associated radars until further notice. The sorties could be flown separately or in conjunction with other reconnaissance or strike missions over the north. To expedite the electronic coverage, the Air Force should conduct missions from midnight to noon and the Navy from noon to midnight Saigon time.[10] Five known SAM sites within the Hanoi-Haiphong sanctuary area were exempt from surveillance to avoid possible strong counteraction by North Vietnam, China, or the Soviet Union.[11]

Sharp also directed a more careful study of aerial photos of the north by target analysts, believing that the extra effort would reveal more sites and wider distribution among the services of information about the installations. For its part, Washington took some steps to relax the air rules.[12]

---

* Estimates of North Vietnamese antiaircraft weapons varied widely. In early July, PACAF believed that the DRV possessed about 2,306 light and medium guns and 639 smaller-caliber automatic weapons (PACAF DI rprt, *Effects of Air Ops, SEA*, 6th ed, 5 Jul 65, p 9).

Same SA–2 site as page 166, with missiles.

Not surprisingly, SAM installations were first priority targets in the next series of Rolling Thunder strikes, program 26/27 for August 6–19. The sudden detection of another site, number 8 northwest of Hanoi, again outside the sanctuary area, was cleared for a strike. On August 9, a force of twelve F–105 Thunderchiefs with Maj. William J. Hosmer of the 12th Tactical Fighter Squadron as mission commander, headed for the installation accompanied by many supporting aircraft flying MiG and rescue CAP, ECM, and ELINT. Because the area was heavily defended by 37-mm, 57-mm, 85-mm, and 100-mm guns, Hosmer split his force into three flights of four aircraft each. The lead flight, led by Hosmer, winging at minimum altitude and high speed from divergent directions, dropped 173 CBUs on radar-directed and other antiaircraft guns. Behind them, flying in train, came the remaining Thunderchiefs, dropping their 750-pound general-purpose bombs in a series of low-altitude, pop-up strikes. The tactic of targeting the gun emplacements first, of which several were hit, and of drawing away fire allowed the follow-on aircraft to strike the missile area more accurately. No aircraft were lost and only one Thunderchief was damaged. For his leadership, Major Hosmer won the Silver Star. Unfortunately, as in the assault on July 27, bomb damage assessment disclosed that the missile revetments were unoccupied, indicating that the DRV was able to anticipate an attack and to disperse missiles and associated equipment quickly.[13]

The First Iron Hand Missions

On August 11, with administration approval, the JCS directed Admiral Sharp to step up attacks and extend the boundary for armed reconnaissance slightly northward to 20°30'N . Strikes on selected targets above this line, such as SAM

The Lang Met highway bridge on Route 1A north of Hanoi, October 1965.

site numbers 6, 7, and 8 and bridges northwest of Hanoi were permitted. However, armed reconnaissance pilots could not fly within an extended radius of Hanoi, within 10 n.m. of Haiphong, nor within the twenty-five to thirty n.m. buffer zone between North Vietnam and China (strikes close to the buffer zone would begin later in 1965). The service chiefs exempted sorties flown by specialized aircraft earmarked for anti-SAM missions—nicknamed Iron Hand by PACOM—from the sortie limitations imposed on the biweekly Rolling Thunder program.[14]

General Harris quickly selected a number of F–105Ds as Iron Hand aircraft and PACFLT designated a few A–6A Intruders and A–4E Skyhawks for the same purpose.* The Air Force Thunderchiefs, loaded with ordnance, would rely initially on photos or ELINT data gathered by reconnaissance planes in searching for known or suspected SAM installations. If weather or operational problems canceled an anti-SAM mission, they could strike other targets.[15]

Meanwhile, Hanoi's air defense units were far from intimidated. On August 12, within hours of Sharp's receipt of the Joint Chiefs' latest strike authorization,

---

* In the ensuing months, other aircraft would be assigned to fly Iron Hand missions. For example, in November 1965, four F–100F Wild Weasel aircraft, capable of detecting SA–2 radar emissions, arrived in Southeast Asia to fly test "hunter-killer" missions with strike F–105s against SAM targets. In 1966, the F–100s would be replaced by F–105s with improved electronics for the hunter-killer missions.

another SA–2 missile downed a Navy A–4E Skyhawk and damaged a second about fifty-five miles southwest of Hanoi. As no parachute was observed, the pilot of the first Skyhawk was presumed killed. Both aircraft were part of a flight engaged in armed reconnaissance along Route 119 at about 9,000 feet, outside the range of known SAM sites. The other Skyhawk pilots believed they saw a second missile fired.

Sharp immediately dispatched his first Iron Hand search and destroy directive to PACAF and PACFLT commanders. But in selecting Navy aircraft for the initial missions, he ordered PACAF to "stand down" its Rolling Thunder operations for the remainder of the day while aircraft from the *Coral Sea* and *Midway* undertook a massive hunt for the offending SAM site or sites. During the next two days, the Navy flew 124 missions, with an outcome not unlike the Air Force's first anti-SAM effort on July 27: high cost and no verifiable results. Intense groundfire downed five Navy aircraft and damaged seven. Two pilots were lost. Once again, North Vietnam's air defense cadres had camouflaged the sites, positioned many antiaircraft weapons in the surrounding area, and dispersed their missile equipment prior to the Navy's search.[16]

The downing of a second U.S. aircraft by a SA–2 missile and the Navy's five losses during its retaliatory search sent shock waves throughout the JCS and the services. In Washington, the Joint Staff, the Air Force, and the Navy quickly established separate committees to examine the missile threat and propose ways to counter it.[17] As the in-depth studies began, the anti-SAM campaign continued. On August 16, the Air Force flew its first Iron Hand mission while attacking the Binh Linh barracks, the Bai Du Thon highway, and Kbu Mai staging areas. To assure quick reaction to ELINT or other data pinpointing a SAM site, it established an Iron Hand F–105 ground alert force. But the tactic proved ineffective. As a consequence, Iron Hand planes were henceforth dispatched with regular daily missions against fixed or armed reconnaissance targets. By August 19, there was more evidence to indicate that the DRV had embarked on an expansive SAM emplacement program: nine sites were confirmed and ten suspected.[18]

Like the Air Force, the Navy quickly compiled its own study of the costly anti-SAM operation on August 12–13. One clear lesson was that the Navy had overreacted, as had the Air Force on July 27 when it lost its first aircraft to an SA–2. A second lesson showed that JCS and Navy intermediate command directives on conducting the eye-for-an-eye response, while intending to be helpful, unfortunately drew an excessive number of Navy aircraft at low altitude (about 800 feet) over a relatively small area that was heavily defended by the North Vietnamese. A wiser riposte would have been a retaliatory strike on the Haiphong POL storage area with tactics left to the local air commander. As a result of the study and other analyses, shortly thereafter the JCS rescinded an earlier directive requiring Air Force and Navy strike aircraft to remain below the effective range of the SAMs.[19]

Rolling Thunder program 28/29 (August 20–September 2) was the first to include Iron Hand missions. In another significant change, the biweekly JCS operational directive increased the level of preplanned armed reconnaissance from 500 to 1,000 sorties. As usual, Sharp allocated the sorties evenly between the Navy and the Air Force-VNAF. However, pilots were allowed to fly additional sorties to destroy trucks, rolling stock, and naval craft that were detected accidentally. Non-Iron Hand aircraft were instructed to fly outside of the effective range of installations containing SA–2 missiles.[20]

In the following weeks, search and attack missions against SAM installations continued without success. When Air Force Iron Hand searches on August 23 and 24 uncovered no missile sites, the aircraft struck the barracks areas at Xom Ban and Ban Na Pew as secondary targets.[21] On the 23d, the Navy attacked a suspected site about thirty-five miles northeast of Hanoi. Sixteen A–4Es, escorted by six F–8s, zoomed in at low level to drop Snake Eye ordnance. Once more, poststrike photos disclosed an empty site and the cost was considerable. DRV gunners damaged six aircraft, filling two with so many holes in their wing tanks they had to fly back to their carrier plugged into refueling tankers.[22]

The next day, one of two PACFLT F–4B Phantoms flying at 12,000 feet on barrier combat air patrol (BARCAP) was lost to a salvo of about seven SAMs from a site about fifty miles southeast of Hanoi and ten miles north of the Thanh Hoa bridge. One missile detonated directly behind the doomed aircraft and a second narrowly missed a wingman. Of the two-man crew in the downed Phantom, one was believed killed and the second, who parachuted safely from his aircraft, was apparently captured. It was the fourth U.S. loss to SAMs.[23] Very upset, Admiral Sharp informed the JCS that the chances of finding the mobile SAM equipment and concealed site were remote, and that the DRV gunners were probably waiting for a special U.S. air effort to find the offending weapon. Sharp said that the continued missile firings indicated that the present Rolling Thunder targets were not of great value to the Hanoi regime. He strongly urged hitting a more vital target, such as Haiphong's principal POL installation, as soon as possible. However, administration officials were not prepared to endorse such provocative action.[24]

Because of the aircraft destroyed and damaged by SAMs, Air Force and Navy commanders understandably considered the missiles a grave threat.[25] The rapid proliferation of the sites was also a matter of serious concern. The number of known sites rose from seven at the end of July to eighteen confirmed and a further eighteen suspected by September 2. Furthermore, DRV air defense personnel demonstrated an ability to construct missile installations quickly. One appeared to have been built in forty-eight hours. In consonance with a mobility concept, the sites considerably outnumbered available missiles and missile launchers. Air defense crews demonstrated that they could move missiles, launchers, and associated equipment in or out of a site in a few hours.[26]

Navy ordnancemen roll 500-pound bombs across a carrier deck.

Throughout September, pilots witnessed more missile firings. On the 9th, an SA–2 was fired against four F–105 Thunderchiefs returning from a strike mission about twelve miles from the Laotian border and sixty-two miles west of Hanoi. The missile passed between the flight leader and the wingman, but caused no damage. A pilot believed he saw square fins on the missile, raising considerable speculation at the time, later discounted, that the Soviet Union had introduced an advanced SA–3 SAM into North Vietnam. Reports of at least a dozen firings in the first half of the month alone attested to the increasing activity of the SAM crews.

The Navy was flying most of the SAM search and destroy missions. On September 4, a Navy aircraft detected an enemy Fan Song radar emission and struck a suspected site, which was believed to be camouflaged within buildings near a canal. However, poststrike reconnaissance failed to verify its existence. Frustrated in their search, from September 12 to 14 Navy pilots launched another intensive effort to locate and destroy sites, flying 338 Iron Hand sorties without success.[27] On the morning of September 16, the Air Force attacked a site near Thanh Hoa, resulting in the downing of two Thunderchiefs and their pilots, one of whom was captured. He was Lt. Col. Robinson Risner, who had won the Air Force Cross for his exploits in April. After his release in February 1973, he wrote a book about his experiences that included a graphic account of his fateful anti-SAM mission on September 16:

> We had four two-ship flights going out. For maneuverability, we wanted only two-ship flights because we were looking for SAM sites. The lead aircraft in each of the two-ship flights was loaded with napalm and the other with 750-pound bombs. As lead, when we found the SAM sites,

171

Lt. Col. Robinson Risner

I would go in and drop napalm on the control trailer from where they launched the missiles. Then the other man would go to afterburner (which gave him half again as much power), climb to the proper altitude and dive-bomb the SAM missiles with those 750-pound bombs.

This morning, our mission was to hit a SAM site about ten miles north of the provincial capital of Thanh Hoa. Just as we came in over Highway 1, I heard one of my flight commanders, leading another flight about fifteen miles to my left to say: 'Heads up, they're shooting!' I knew we were going to get groundfire.

As we approached we turned left to go right up the highway. It was cut through a little hill perhaps a hundred feet high. We were right down on the deck. I had to lift to go over the hill, and as I topped it, the first thing I saw were tracers. I was hit immediately. My engine shuddered, followed by several quick explosions in the cockpit, which immediately filled with smoke. Fire was coming in behind me from the right side, and I couldn't see anything else.

As soon as I was hit, I said, 'Oak Lead—I'm hit,' Within a second or two my wing man was shouting 'Get Out, Lead, Get Out, Lead, You're burning. You're burning all over.' He kept hollering but I didn't intend to get out....

I was already in a right pull up and only two or three miles from the ocean. The nose was coming up when the engine quit, but I had about 550 knots by then because I had gone to afterburner. Suddenly my stick came right back into my lap and the aircraft pitched forward, throwing me up against my shoulder straps toward the canopy. My options were gone—I was out of control. I reached for the handle to eject the canopy. After it went, I squeezed the trigger and ejected...before I realized it, I was almost ready to hit the ground. I frantically shoved the radio back in the pocket. I was headed for a rice field between two hamlets. I could see people running toward me.

The man who had said he would never be captured was down in enemy territory. And I had just dropped a load of napalm on them.[28]

On the same day, Navy pilots flying A–4Es equipped with ALQ–51 radar deceptive devices claimed a "first" in "breaking" a Fan Song radar "lock-on" on an aircraft. Another first was achieved on the 20th when pilots of similarly equipped Navy A–4Es believed they diverted the aim of six SAMs fired at them and other aircraft in the vicinity. Elsewhere that day, a non-Iron Hand mission along the Northeast Hanoi-Lang San rail line elicited a barrage of ten SAMs and heavy antiaircraft fire, but no aircraft were hit or sustained damage. The Navy's SAM detection capability was enhanced on September 5 when it began flying its own EC–121 airborne command and control aircraft—nicknamed Big Look—over the Tonkin Gulf to coordinate air strikes in North Vietnam. Similar in purpose to the Air Force's Big Eye EC–121s, the Navy plane also carried an APS–20 radar for detecting the DRV's SA–2 Fan Song radar.[29]

On September 23, while attacking an ammunition depot at Tai Xouan northwest of Hanoi, Air Force Thunderchief pilots observed two SAMs heading towards them. As one missile soared toward an aircraft, the pilot made a "SAM Break" maneuver that allowed him to elude it.[30]

Meanwhile, the Air Force's loss of two planes and the capture of a pilot on September 16 led McNamara to inquire if the mission was worth the risk. He also asked for the rationale of the strike and if the planning and the tactics were sound. General Moore, the commander of the 2d Air Division, defended the mission vigorously. He warned higher authorities of the operational hazard posed by the SA–2 missiles, cited the Air Force's "severely limited" capability to locate, photograph, and attack the sites and insisted that the risk was no greater than for other types of missions. Observing that eighty-seven U.S. aircraft had been lost over the north since January 1, 1965, the majority to groundfire while flying below 5,000 feet, he said that SA–2 missiles precluded medium-altitude air operations. Thus, aircraft losses at low altitude would probably rise. "We must accept the risks or losses involved in the SA–2 campaign," he emphasized, "if we are to take the initiative away from the enemy."[31]

On September 30, the Air Force lost its second F–105 to a SAM during a Rolling Thunder strike near a bridge at Ninh Binh. It was the lead aircraft of a flight and was destroyed at 18,000 feet. Another SAM was also observed in the area, and an F–4C on the same mission was shot down by antiaircraft fire.[32]

Improving Detection of SAM Sites

Meanwhile, neither conventional aerial photography nor the intensive electronic intelligence effort directed by Admiral Sharp on July 29 had produced much data to help in pinpointing SAM locations. The new threat to the Rolling Thunder program did have one salutary impact on air operations, at least from the viewpoint of air commanders and aircrews. It forced administration officials to relax some of the more stringent air rules in the north which enabled the services to become more innovative in searching for SAM sites.

On August 3, for the first time, the Joint Chiefs authorized Air Force and Navy air commanders to conduct low-altitude photoreconnaissance, except over the sanctuary areas, to confirm SAM site locations and to strike them immediately. Another welcome change was an end to the inclusion of anti-SAM operations in the established bimonthly Rolling Thunder sortie ceilings.[33] In mid-August, Admiral Sharp, saying that better dissemination of electronic intelligence was needed, directed the Air Force and Marine Corps to collaborate more closely in employing one or more of the Marine EA–3B Skywarriors with Air Force tactical reconnaissance and strike missions. He urged the use of several Marine aircraft at one time to obtain "optimum flight tracks" for intercepting Fan Song and other SAM-associated radars. Sharp also asked the Air Force to undertake periodic joint strike and SAC reconnaissance drone operations to determine if they would activate SAM radars, leading to their more precise location.[34]

The use of SAC Ryan 147D drones for photographic or electronic reconnaissance, begun in April 1965, was still very much in the experimental stage, however. Launched from DC–130 mother ships, the drones, flying at low or high altitude, emitted signals that were picked up by RB–47s, whose aircrews then recorded and studied the signals. Of twenty-five drones launched between July and September 1965, only eleven returned to the recovery areas. Nonetheless, some drone launches and recoveries were successful, even if the mission objective was not attained. On August 21, for example, a drone was sent to a target area accompanied by a Marine EA–3B electronic and Air Force photo and strike aircraft. The Marine aircraft twice succeeded in "exciting" Fan Song radars, but the signals ceased before the aircrew could flash their location to the photo and strike aircraft. As a result, alternate targets were struck. The operation underscored a basic problem in locating missile radar sites: the short duration of Fan Song transmissions.[35]

On August 31, another drone operation was somewhat more successful. This witnessed the use of two drones escorted part of the way by twelve F–105 Thunderchiefs. Sixty other Air Force aircraft, including EC–121s, EB–66s, F–105s, F–4Cs, and KC–135s along with Marine EF–10Bs were launched separately. As the drone began its "coast in" period, an RB–47 began recording the anticipated Fan Song radar signal. After an eleven-minute break, Fan Song signals were received continuously for one hour and twenty minutes. This data permitted three fixes on SAM site installations within a five-mile circle. An SA–2

A Douglas EB–66.

missile destroyed the drone, but a flight of F–105 Thunderchiefs was dispatched quickly to the area. The strike pilots were unable to find the sites and finished their mission by striking a bridge as an alternate target. Antiaircraft guns downed one of the planes, but the pilot was rescued.[36]

The use of drones to find SAM sites diminished in the ensuing weeks. On October 16, a drone was unable to elicit the desired SAM radar signals, two drones launched on October 20 and November 5 fell victim to the north's antiaircraft guns, and three low-altitude drones launched in October never returned to the recovery area. SAC then halted the operations temporarily until the reliability and survivability of the drones could be improved.[37]

Other measures were instituted to facilitate the search for new SAM sites. At the end of August, the JCS authorized the first low-altitude armed reconnaissance of sites detected by electronic intelligence or U–2 photography.[38] They also approved an Air Force proposal to deploy a specially equipped RB–57F reconnaissance aircraft, with six supporting officers and twelve airmen, for intensive photo coverage of suspected sites. The 2d Air Division had emphasized that weather conditions made repeat photography mandatory. Assigned to the 6250th Combat Group at Tan Son Nhut in South Vietnam, the aircraft and personnel deployed quickly to Udorn. Because of the aircraft's vulnerability to missile and conventional antiaircraft fire, however, the JCS limited missions to authorized reconnaissance areas, prohibited direct overflights of known or suspected sites, and permitted the use of fighter escorts. However, an initial series of fifteen missions in September to mid-October, provided little useful data. A second effort from December 1965 to February 1966 was no more successful. After this, the project was discontinued.[39]

Air Force photo interpreters at Tan Son Nhut Air Base.

In August, the Navy began testing a new air-to-surface, stand-off, antielectronic radiation weapon, the AGM–45 Shrike, with a 141-pound warhead and a maximum range of twenty-five miles. Later used by the Air Force as well, the weapon was designed principally to home in on S-band and C-band guidance radars for the SA–2s, but they could also be adapted to counter radar-controlled antiaircraft guns and early warning and GCI radars.

During a few weeks of testing, the Shrike generally failed to perform as expected, although aircrews quickly gained firing experience, but the north's SAM crews learned how to neutralize the weapon's homing capability. When an aircraft performed a maneuver commonly employed just prior to the Shrike's release, they turned off the radar which the weapon used to home to its target. In addition, aircrews found it difficult to judge the Shrike's performance because of the long release distance, the need for aircraft to take quick evasive action after firing it, and the possibility that the missile would err and follow a wrong signal. By September 25, the results of twenty-five Shrikes fired at radiating targets were as follows: seven probable and two possible hits, two probable misses, and fourteen unknown results. Because of the limited number of missiles, testing ceased in September and the remaining weapons were set aside as a reserve.[40] After further development, an improved Shrike became combat ready early in 1966 and Air Force and Navy aircrews began using it on a regular basis.

Continued Air Strikes on non-SAM Targets

Although air commanders were largely concerned about the evolving SAM threat—and still awaiting solid confirmation of a first SAM kill—most air missions were still scheduled for non-SAM targets. For Rolling Thunder program 24/25 (July 23–August 3), for example, the JCS authorized 13 fixed targets and 500 armed reconnaissance sorties.[41]

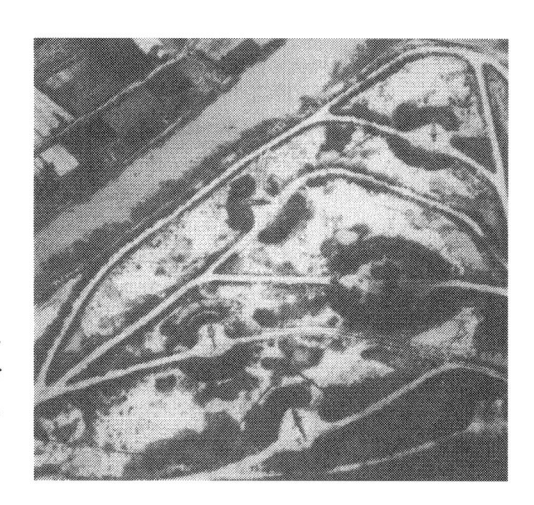

North Vietnamese surface-to-air missile site with four missiles in place.

The Air Force's most important targets during this period were the Ban Pham Lat and Phu Huong bridges above Hanoi on the northwest Hanoi to Lao Cao rail line. The strikes destroyed both bridges and such ancillary objectives as boxcars and river barges and cut segments of the rail line. In armed reconnaissance, Air Force operations were highlighted by the first use (on July 28) of 3,000-pound general-purpose blockbusters by F–105 pilots of the 12th TFS against the durable Thanh Hoa bridge. The spans did not collapse, but pedestrian traffic across the bridge again came to a temporary halt. With Air Force support, the VNAF flew a restrike on the DRV army barracks at Vinh and the ammunition depot at Xom Rung.

Many of the Navy's missions were against several earlier targets in the Nam Dinh area. These included a POL site, a railyard, six nearby antiaircraft sites, and the Nam Dinh thermal power plant. Additional attacks were mounted against the Thanh Hoa power plant (a restrike); radars on Hon Matt Island; the barracks areas at Dong Hoi, Quang Suoi, and Bai Thuong; and the Roa Leky bridges. The power plants at Nam Dinh and Thanh Hoa, now judged destroyed, were believed to have reduced the DRV's electrical capacity by 7 percent. During a night attack on the Thanh Hoa power plant, Navy pilots reported tracking by twelve to twenty-four searchlights, the first known instance of the north's use of air defense illumination. About forty-eight hours later in another target area, two Navy aircraft on ECM missions were also tracked with searchlights. Pilots were unable to determine if the searchlights were controlled by radar.[42]

For Rolling Thunder program 26/27 (August 6–9), the Joint Chiefs proposed striking a number of new and more significant targets, but administration authorities again overruled their selection in favor of targets deemed less provocative. These included the barracks and SAM installations around Dien Bien Phu, warehouses at Long Giem Da and Dang Thanh, two bridges, and the Long Chi explosives plant. The Air Force made seven separate assaults on the

Bridge on Route 6 southeast of Dien Bien Phu destroyed by Air Force F–105s.

targets around Dien Bien Phu, and on August 10 Thunderchiefs destroyed the Vinh Tuy bridge employing a 3,000-pound bomb and, for the first time, an AGM–12C Bullpup missile with a 1,000-pound warhead. Until the latter weapon became available, the Air Force had used the AGM–12B Bullpup with a 250-pound warhead.

The Navy's principal fixed targets in this period were the frequently bombed Vinh army barracks, railyards, and a supply depot that endured eight separate strikes. The Navy also struck the barracks areas at Son La and Than Chai and the Ban Nuoc Chieu ammunition depot.[43]

For program number 28/29 (August 20–September 2), the JCS authorized strikes and restrikes on nine fixed targets and slightly expanded the boundaries for armed reconnaissance. SAM sites 1 and 9 and airfields used by attacking MiGs remained off limits to Air Force and Navy commanders because of their proximity to Hanoi.*[44] Air Force pilots hit the Bai Thuong barracks area, the Xom Truong Hoa barracks and ammunition complex, and the Long Ban rail bridge. The bridge was a vital link on the northwest Hanoi to Lao Cao rail line and was located on a segment northwest of Yen Bai that had been hit numerous times since July 11. By August 25, six bridges on the line had been destroyed and five damaged. Nevertheless, in a sustained repair effort, DRV work crews restored the bridges sufficiently to keep traffic moving over them. U.S. analysts observed that repair time averaged two to six weeks per bridge. The railyard at Yen Ba, heavily damaged on July 17, was also serviceable again by late August, permitting rail traffic to pass through the city.[45]

The Air Force's most important targets were the Ban Thach dam and hydroelectric plant and the associated Bic Thuong locks located about eighty miles

---

* This meant that SAM sites 6 and 7, having been attacked once, could not be attacked again.

southwest of Hanoi. These targets were struck five times between August 21 and 23. On the 23d, Air Force aircraft dropped eight 3,000-pound bombs on the generator building and the dam. The attacks created news headlines and speculation there would be more bombing of dams, dikes, and locks in the flood-vulnerable Red River Delta. Although the two targets were not part of the DRV's river irrigation system, their bombing alarmed the State Department. Taking seriously Hanoi's allegations that such targets had been hit before, State directed OSD to desist from targeting dams and locks. The assault on the Ban Thach power plant, the fifth DRV power plant struck thus far, and on other targets on August 22, made it the largest one-day Air Force effort of the war. A total of eighty-seven strike sorties dropped 228 tons of bombs.

On August 2, the Air Force scheduled its F–4C Phantoms for armed reconnaissance missions for the first time. Newer and more sophisticated than the F–105 Thunderchiefs, the Phantoms of the 47th TFS (which replaced the 45th TFS at Ubon RTAFB in July) had been used for combat air patrol since April and for strikes on fixed targets since the end of May. During their initial armed reconnaissance mission, the F–4Cs hit bridges, trucks, a radar site, and the Kim Cuong barracks area. The beginning of August also coincided roughly with a transition point in the Rolling Thunder program when air commanders began scheduling more sorties for armed reconnaissance than for fixed targets. There were two principal reasons for the change: the intensive search for SA–2 SAM sites and deteriorating flying weather. In the period from August 6 to 19, for example, eighty-eight scheduled Air Force sorties were canceled because of weather before takeoff and ten were aborted after launch due to poor weather. Flying under somewhat better weather conditions in coastal areas, the Navy claimed a lower cancellation rate and reported no weather aborts during the same period. In late August, an anticipated shortage of 750-pound bombs, used largely by the Air Force, resulted in reduced bomb loads. Bomb stockpiles were depleted much more rapidly after June 18, 1965, when SAC began B–52 Arc Light bombing in South Vietnam. The bombers were voracious consumers of ordnance, capable of carrying more than fifty-one of the 750-pound bombs. When studies showed that both 500-pound and 750-pound bombs would be in critically short supply by February 1966, Washington authorities ordered the production lines to be reopened, but predicted no new bomb supplies before August 1966. The Air Force adjusted to the impending munitions shortfall by relying more on CBUs and napalm. When a safety problem arose with the CBUs, PACAF used more 2.75-inch rockets and other types of ordnance.*[46]

---

* For a discussion of the sharpening munitions shortage in 1965 and measures to overcome it, see Herman S. Wolk, *USAF Logistic Plans and Policies in Southeast Asia, 1965* (USAF Hist Div Liaison Off, June 1967), chapter III.

B–52 releasing bombs over South Vietnam.

Rolling Thunder's tempo increased only moderately, despite the increase in air activity in August against SA–2 sites and the escalation of U.S. air and ground operations in South Vietnam to save that country from collapse. Air Force, Navy, and VNAF combat sorties in August totaled 1,263 compared with 1,001 in July, while ordnance expenditures decreased somewhat from 2,540 to 2,357 tons during the two months. Although the permissible bombing line had been extended northward, Air Force and Navy pilots still flew most of their missions below the 20th parallel. After six months of the Rolling Thunder program, they had struck or restruck 82 of the 91 targets designated by the JCS below the 20th parallel, but only 28 of 121 designated targets above it. The VNAF, usually supported by the Air Force, still limited its operations to below the 19th parallel and flew relatively few missions. In the four-week period from August 6 to September 2, for example, it completed twenty-eight armed reconnaissance and eight leaflet sorties.[47]

For Rolling Thunder program 30/31 (September 2–17), the JCS again selected more important targets, but administration authorities vetoed seven, added two of their own, and again permitted only a modest increase in the bombing level. They raised the biweekly sortie rate for armed reconnaissance from 1,000 to 1,200 to allow more attacks on SA–2 sites, trucks, rolling stock, naval craft, and other targets of opportunity. They also approved a slight extension westward of the armed reconnaissance area, from the coast at latitude 20°30'N to longitude 105°20'E, then north to a point 30 n.m. from the Chinese border, then southwest to the Laotian border, retaining a 25 n.m. distance from China.

Administration authorities also eased strike operations by making an exception to the rule prohibiting aircraft from entering the 25 n.m. to 30 n.m. buffer zone between North Vietnam and China. In the future, strike aircraft maneuvering to hit a target close to the northern edge of the zone could penetrate as far as 15 n.m. from the Chinese border.[48] As an indication of the gradually increasing

Ground crew loading bombs on underwing pylon of B–52.

pace of Rolling Thunder, during the week ending September 17, the Air Force flew 524 combat sorties and dropped 1,105 tons of bombs. In the following week the totals were 638 combat sorties and 1,105 tons of bombs.[49]

The most intensive missions of the month were against the Yen Khaoi army base and ammunition supply area about 40 n.m. west of Hanoi. Three strikes were conducted on September 9, 11, and 12. The mission leader in each instance was the redoubtable Lt. Col. Robinson Risner, commander of the 67th TFS at Korat RTAFB, and winner of the Air Force Cross for his exploits in April. To assure a surprise attack against a heavily defended target, Colonel Risner led his F–105 flights toward the area at low altitude and high speed each time. Attacks were conducted with aircraft approaching from different directions and angles, tactics particularly hazardous because of bad weather.

On the 9th, after leading his flights to the barracks and ammunition area and expending his own bomb load, Colonel Risner took on fuel from an SAC KC–135 tanker, then finished his mission by flying combat air patrol for a downed Thunderchief pilot. On the 12th, with the target area more heavily defended than before, he again completed a bomb run but as he pulled away the canopy of his Thunderchief was shattered by automatic weapons fire. Nevertheless, he managed an aerial refueling and landed at his home base. The three-day effort left about 100 barracks and other buildings destroyed or damaged. For his courage and professionalism, Colonel Risner was awarded the Silver Star. Unfortunately, he received his second award in absentia. On the 16th, as noted earlier, he was shot down and captured after completing an assault on a suspected SAM site near Thanh Hoa.[50]

Because the Air Force was suffering from a lack of aircraft with good night capability, it flew relatively few nocturnal sorties, leaving most of the task to the Navy. But in September it began launching more night operations, nicknamed Night Wind, using, as it had earlier in 1965, C–130 Blindbat navigation and flare ships in conjunction with two B–57 Canberra light bombers. Under flare illumination, the B–57s searched principally for trucks, attacking them when possible with 260-pound fragmentation ordnance.* During the period September 3–30, Air Force crews flew twelve night missions, compared with nineteen by the Navy.[51]

Beginning with Rolling Thunder program 33 in late September, the Air Force augmented its night interdiction effort by introducing specially equipped F–4C Phantoms of the 68th TFS whose two-man aircrews were trained in nighttime flying techniques. The squadron deployed to Korat RTAFB from George AFB, California on August 27. Nicknamed Night Owl, the missions consisted of two Phantoms flying in tandem with the lead aircraft carrying MK–24 flares and the second, about five miles behind, loaded with 750-pound bombs. Initially six missions, then eight, were scheduled nightly, but after mid-October monsoon weather began to curb operations drastically. In the period from October 29–November 11, for example, only 90 of 260 scheduled sorties were completed. Weather and darkness also obscured strike results, and the enemy was very elusive. At the first drop of a flare, truckers pulled off the roads. However, the night missions were believed to have a harassing effect.[52]

Given the frequently poor flying weather and the large areas of jungle in the north, occasional bombing accidents were inevitable. On September 16, an Air Force F–100 Super Sabre from Korat erroneously hit the northern end of a bridge spanning the Ben Hai River, the demarcation line between the northern and southern sectors of the DMZ. The strike destroyed the bridge and killed three Vietnamese civilians. The next day, a flight of four F–105 Thunderchiefs struck a hamlet in the southern sector of the DMZ, killing twenty-one Vietnamese, including eight policemen, and wounding many others. Because the 1954 Geneva Agreement prohibited military activity in the DMZ, the International Control Commission, made up of Canadian, Indian, and Polish representatives, conducted an investigation. Both incidents were attributed to pilot error in identifying targets. PACAF quickly tightened operational procedures, stipulating that in future all aircraft should confirm their positions by radar when flying within 20 n.m. of the DMZ and conduct no air strikes within five n.m. of the northern portion of the zone.[53]

On September 20, the Chinese shot down an Air Force F–104 Starfighter over Hainan Island, capturing its pilot, Capt. Philip E. Smith.[54] Captain Smith had been flying escort for four Silver Dawn C–130Bs that had arrived recently at Da Nang AB. Assigned to the 6091st Reconnaissance Squadron in Japan, the C–130Bs flew electronic and communications intercept missions off the North Vietnamese and Chinese coasts. Following midair refueling for his mission, Captain Smith reported navigational difficulty and drifted over Hainan Island.

---

*For an in-depth study of Air Force night operations see Maj. Victor B. Anthony, *The Air Force in Southeast Asia, Tactics and Techniques of Night Operations, 1961–1970*, (Ofc AF Hist, 1972).

750-pound bombs on a centerline pylon of an F–105.

His Starfighter was the second American aircraft lost to the Chinese since the beginning of the war.* Exploiting the propaganda value of their captive, the Chinese trumpeted that Captain Smith was given a bath and a hearty meal of Chinese noodles, then alleged that he had stated: "I hate this war. But I was made to come." Captain Smith's sudden disappearance led to another costly near tragedy. After completing a quick search for him, two Starfighters collided in mid-air over Da Nang and were destroyed, but both pilots bailed out and were rescued.[55]

Because dams and locks associated with North Vietnam's irrigation system were exempt from attack, Hanoi's claims in late August and early September that U.S. aircraft had struck four dams and a lock prompted a State Department inquiry. William P. Bundy, Assistant Secretary of State for Far Eastern Affairs, pressed the Defense Department to amend JCS Rolling Thunder guidance. He asked that dams, canal locks, flood-control levees, and hydroelectric plants be excluded from air attack, except as approved in Washington on a case-by-case basis.[56]

Responding for the JCS, General Wheeler believed that, except for flood-control levees and dams, waterway dams and locks were fair game for bombing, as were power plants. Of five plants struck thus far, he observed, all but one had prior interagency concurrence. He vigorously opposed the imposition of yet more restraints on the Rolling Thunder program. Nonetheless, Mr. Bundy's concerns were soon translated into a new bombing guideline. Starting in late October and early November (programs 38/39), locks and dams were specifically excluded from attack (certain exceptions were made shortly thereafter).[57]

---

* The first U.S. loss to a Chinese MiG occurred on April 9, 1965, during a PACFLT-Chinese aerial engagement near the Chinese-held Hainan Island in the eastern part of the Gulf of Tonkin.

Worried lest further violations of bombing rules lead to more restrictions and the establishment of additional sanctuary areas, Air Force leaders ordered their subordinates to comply fully with the bombing rules. At the end of September, General Harris directed his subordinates to make the "strongest effort" to tighten flight discipline and "insure that all crews are imbued with the seriousness of violations of restricted zones." He also ordered the establishment and monitoring of standard flight procedures to reduce the possibility of bombing infractions.[58] Several weeks later, addressing an Air Force commanders' conference, Air Force Brig. Gen. John W. Vogt, Director, Policy Planning Staff, Office of the Assistant Secretary of Defense, International Security Affairs, who in April 1972 would become Commander of the Seventh Air Force, further urged air commanders to observe Washington's operational restraints. He cited the most important "don'ts" for strike aircraft:

> Don't attack MiG airfields, even if you see MiG airplanes coming...to attack you. Don't go within thirty miles of Hanoi unless you are directed to do so. We have been directed twice, I think, not to go within the thirty-mile border. Don't go within ten miles of Haiphong unless you are directed. Don't hit SAMs in the thirty and ten-mile restricted areas unless you have specific authorization in advance, even if the SAMs are firing at you while you are in there. Don't hit SAMs elsewhere in the northeast restricted area outside the thirty-mile limit or ten-mile limit unless you have positive evidence that they are occupied beforehand...if you attack an empty SAM site, you are subject to criticism. Don't go closer than thirty miles to the Chinese border in the northwest. Don't go closer than twenty-five miles to the Chinese border in the northeast. We can go as close to twenty miles in both areas only if you are a strike airplane and positioning yourself for attack, and then you must drop your bombs twenty-five miles...and not twenty miles away [from China's border].
>
> Don't hit dams and locks unless you are sure they are associated with nonirrigational purposes. You can attack them if they are involved with navigation. Don't hit barges unless you think they are engaged in carrying supplies and equipment to support the war effort.
>
> I could go on and on, but the point is that the restrictions apply and we have to get them to the pilots. They change almost weekly. New restrictions are imposed, others are lifted. We are engaged in a constant discussion with CINCPAC and Joint Chiefs of Staff trying to get these things changed, and it is amazing to me that General Moore and his people are able to fight the war as effectively as they do under the rules and restrictions that apply.
>
> In addition, we have to provide constant justification for the manner we are fighting the war...to justify our Rolling Thunder operations to prove that they are doing some good. We have countless commissions and groups out here to investigate these things.[59]

Establishment of a Target Intelligence Center

By the summer of 1965, the need for more targets for Air Force and Navy aircrews, especially for armed reconnaissance missions, obliged the 2d Air Division to expand its targeting capability in the Directorate of Intelligence. On September 15, Col. Rockly Triantafellu,* Deputy for Intelligence, established a target intelligence center (TIC) with Lt. Col. James C. Enney as its chief. Staffed by personnel from the 13th Reconnaissance Squadron and the 2d's Intelligence Directorate, the TIC was divided into separate photo support, target recording, and target development branches. To improve targeting, the target development branch bisected the north at about the 19th parallel and divided Laos between the Barrel Roll and Steel Tiger sectors. Photoreconnaissance remained the basic source for enlarging the target base, but intelligence personnel made a concerted effort to use data from other sources.

The TIC began to pinpoint more targets, both short-term and long-term, for operational units on September 20. As before, when targets had been plotted and developed, the data was sent to all strike, reconnaissance, and other using units. Liaison among the TIC and aircrews, debriefing officers, and other personnel involved in operations improved markedly. In the ensuing months, the continuing search for all kinds of enemy targets resulted in further expansion of the TIC. Of course, most targets recommended for strikes were sent to the JCS, which forwarded them to McNamara and his staff for final approval.[60]

Deepening Service Concern about Strike Restrictions

Despite the gradual increase in strike sorties against more targets in North Vietnam throughout August and September 1965, Hanoi's press and radio and VC-NVA battlefield performance in the south showed no loss of determination to fight on. Intelligence assessments of Rolling Thunder also raised questions about its impact. A DIA-CIA report covering the period through the end of August 1965 concluded that the DRV's capability to defend its homeland, train its forces, and infiltrate men and supplies to the Viet Cong in South Vietnam and the Pathet Lao in Laos had "not diminished to any appreciable degree." The economic impact of the bombing thus far, the study showed, caused some disruption and strain within the country, but overall it did not "amount to much."[61] PACAF's intelligence analysts arrived at a similar conclusion. Bombing had caused some morale erosion, limited food shortages, evacuation of populated areas, and transportation problems, the latter because of destroyed roads and bridges, but the DRV showed no sign of giving up. Rather, its press and radio expressed a desire for revenge and maintained a confident attitude.[62]

---

* Col. Triantafellu was promoted to brigadier general on November 1, 1965.

There was mounting concern among air commanders over the cost of the constricted Rolling Thunder program. In the last three weeks of August the DRV's air defense shot down 19 aircraft (9 Air Force, 10 Navy), and damaged many more. In the following twenty-eight days (September 3–30), they downed 21 more aircraft (Air Force 11, Navy 8, VNAF 2) and damaged 66 (Air Force 31 and Navy 35). As of September 26, U.S. losses over the north totaled 114, the Air Force and Navy having lost 57 each. On the same day, Hanoi climaxed its propaganda effort by "celebrating" its "600th" shoot-down of American aircraft.[63]

The DRV's conventional antiaircraft capability was increasing, though how rapidly was uncertain. PACAF intelligence saw a fairly fast expansion of the DRV's antiaircraft weapons (figure 8).

Figure 8
Increase in Conventional Antiaircraft Weaponry
July 5–September 30, 1965

	Light Guns	Medium Guns	Automatic Weapons	Total
Jul 5, 65	920	1,386	639	2,945
Sep 30, 65	1,183	1,747	1,229	4,159

The DIA's estimates of the DRV's antiaircraft strength was considerably more conservative, although it too noted an increase. On November 3, 1965, it credited the North Vietnamese with 700 light and 900 medium guns, but made no estimate of the number of smaller automatic weapons.* Most antiaircraft guns were concentrated around important towns and cities, industrial sites, rail and road bridges, and transportation points. Intelligence analysts agreed that the DRV placed great emphasis on the mobility of their air defenses, sometimes constructing as many as four alternate antiaircraft battery sites around a vital target area.[64]

A Joint Staff aircraft attrition study, using data through mid-September 1965, confirmed previous estimates that the majority of hits and nearly 50 percent of all U.S. air losses over the north were inflicted by automatic weapons

---

* The antiaircraft estimating task was extremely difficult and depended on a number of variables: whether estimates were based solely on air reconnaissance or air reconnaissance plus data from POW and other sources, inclusion or exclusion of automatic weapons, the extent to which air search of antiaircraft sites had been stepped up and the extent to which more and better trained photoanalysts were being used for readouts, and the time lag between the acquisition and reporting of antiaircraft data.

North Vietnamese anti-aircraft artillery site with seven 57-mm weapons in place.

14.5-mm or smaller. The study noted that DRV gunners were trained to use small arms against all aircraft within range and regardless of speed. There were "firing cells" that aimed at an aircraft until it was out of sight. A trained platoon, it was judged, could shoot up to 1,000 rounds at a high-speed jet in three to five seconds. Other tactics included barrage-firing of automatic weapons and the larger 37-mm and 57-mm guns at a particular azimuth and altitude and setting up tempting targets as bait and surrounding them with a heavy concentration of guns (as was demonstrated in the initial Air Force and Navy strikes against SAM sites in July and August). An estimated 60 percent of the 57-mm and 85-mm guns were located within a 30 n.m. radius of Hanoi and Haiphong and many others encircled the towns of Vinh, Thai Nguyen, Thanh Hoa, Yen Bai, and elsewhere. The lethal air defenses generally forced pilots to remain above 4,500 feet and to limit the size of their missions to two, three, or four aircraft. Wingmen often flew one-half to one mile behind the lead aircraft and all were weaving constantly.[65]

There was evidence that many aircrews were disquieted about their daily missions and believed they were taking unwarranted risks in hitting targets of little value. Except for armed reconnaissance, they faulted Rolling Thunder guidelines requiring largely repetitive biweekly air programs that seemed more than anything else to benefit the enemy gunners. Following meetings with Air Force and Navy commanders in Southeast Asia, Adm. David L. McDonald, Chief of Naval Operations, documented these opinions in a report issued in September 1965. General Westmoreland agreed with his criticism of Rolling Thunder, but Admiral Sharp was reluctant to admit to any serious misuse of air resources, although he conceded that aircraft could be used more efficiently against more profitable targets in northeastern North Vietnam.[66]

North Vietnamese 57-mm antiaircraft weapon and crew.

Illustrative of service discontent was the planning for Rolling Thunder program 26/27 (August 6–19). The JCS sent Secretary McNamara proposals for attacking twelve new "significant" non-SAM targets (including Phuc Yen airfield near Hanoi, now harboring sixty-three MiG–15s and MiG–17s and eight Il–28 bombers), an accelerated and systematic campaign against all SAM installations regardless of location (i.e., including SAM sites within the Hanoi-Haiphong sanctuary area), and more sustained interdiction of LOCs supporting the SAM system. However, Mr. McNamara and State Department and White House officials drastically pruned the Joint Chiefs' requests, deleted all twelve targets, substituted nine others of lesser importance, and reduced the planned sortie rate accordingly.[67] They approved an increase only in attacks on SAM sites that were outside of the sanctuary area.

Such decisions deepened the disenchantment of many service leaders, especially in the Air Force. To a man, Air Force commanders remained convinced that the full weight of available air power should be brought to bear on all of the SAM sites and MiG bases in the north, the entire DRV air defense net, and those storage facilities and power stations that had not yet been bombed. The Air Staff was convinced that effective strikes against the last two target categories could "shut down the highways and turn off the lights throughout the DRV." Expounding on the air problems, Maj. Gen. Seth J. McKee, Chief of Plans for the Air Staff, conveyed to General Harris the shortcomings of the current war strategy:

An F–105 bombs a bridge in North Vietnam, 112 miles northwest of Vinh, November 1965.

Since the role of the U.S. ground forces was changed in SVN, the overall trend of U.S. actions has been toward greater imbalance of effort. The continuing emphasis on efforts within...SVN while refusing to destroy the source and direction and support of...NVN must be changed before we find ourselves unwillingly involved in an interminable and indecisive ground war on the Asian land mass.

McKee concluded that if the United States was disinclined to adopt a more balanced military program that included wider and more intense air operations against the north, "then we should not commit more U.S. troops to a war in the jungles of Vietnam from which we cannot extricate ourselves and...may have no chance of winning."[68]

Interestingly, Admiral Sharp took a more sanguine view of the Rolling Thunder program. Accepting the program's limited objectives, in late August he informed the Joint Chiefs that he considered the air campaign "successful," and predicted "we are on the threshold of realizing the full impact of a cumulative effect." "It is a campaign of pressure," he said. "Immediate and spectacular effects were not intended." He proposed two alternative bombing programs for the weeks ahead. The first, and the one preferred by all the services, was to strike targets designated by the JCS in the prohibited north and northeast sectors of North Vietnam to isolate Hanoi-Haiphong from China. If this was not politically feasible, he urged greatly increased armed reconnaissance with pilots assigned many "pre-briefed" targets. Whatever course Washington decided on, he believed it could be attained by flying a maximum of 5,500 sorties per month, a level to be attained by November 1965. About 70 percent of the sorties would be for target strikes and 30 percent for support.[69]

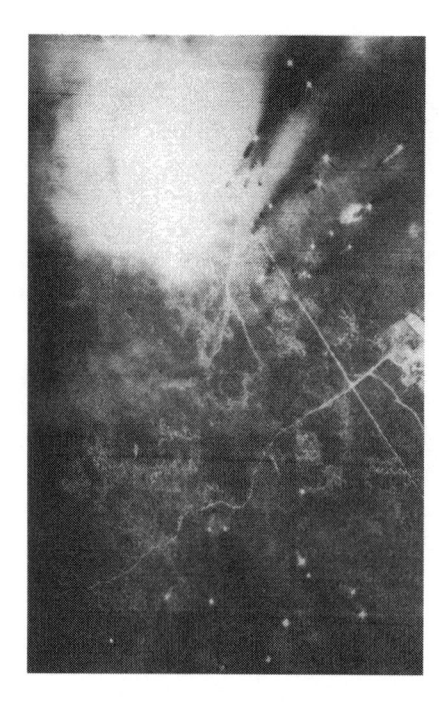

A salvo of rockets fired at a North Vietnamese missile site thirteen miles northwest of Dong Hoi.

Not surprisingly, for the next Rolling Thunder program 30/31 (September 2–17), the Joint Chiefs recommended immediate strikes on rail, highway, and waterway routes, traffic between Hanoi and Haiphong, and between the two cities and southern China; on POL storage facilities at Haiphong (holding about one-half of the remaining DRV POL stores); and four more thermal power plants (generating about half of the DRV's thermal power). They again asked for authority to strike all SAM sites regardless of location, and Phuc Yen airfield near Hanoi. The MiGs and Il–28 bombers at Phuc Yen, they warned, were within range of Da Nang AB and other South Vietnamese installations. If these were attacked, estimates predicted upwards of 2,000 casualties and 200 aircraft damaged or destroyed. The service chiefs asked that their views be placed before the President "without delay."[70]

As usual, the President and his civilian advisers refused to sanction a precipitous air assault on the north and approved a series of targets of lesser importance.[71] They relaxed the air rules again, however, approving a maximum of 1,200 armed reconnaissance missions (although this number could be exceeded if necessary), the highest number thus far for a two-week period, unrestricted strikes on JCS targets that had been struck previously, and strikes on secondary targets in the north by pilots flying Barrel Roll and Steel Tiger missions in Laos who might be carrying unspent ordnance.[72] Pilots on Rolling Thunder missions had previously been permitted to drop unexpended ordnance on secondary targets in Laos while returning to their bases in Thailand. The two-week strike effort was highlighted by a "flap" over public reports that Air Force planes had bombed a rail bridge only seventeen n.m. from the Chinese border. As the buffer zone extended from twenty-five to thirty n.m. from China, this was in clear violation of the air rules. An investigation quickly revealed that the bridge's coordinates had been misread and that the bridge was located within the authorized bombing area. Nevertheless, General Moore took steps to tighten the strike reporting system and avoid a similar incident in the future.[73]

McNamara shortly explained to the Joint Chiefs why some of their targeting proposals had been vetoed. There was "other" intelligence, he said, indicating that MiG or Il–28 bomber attacks on South Vietnamese installations were "unlikely" as Hanoi had reasons to fear strong American retaliatory action. Further, he doubted that heavier air strikes would persuade Hanoi that the price for assisting the Viet Cong was too high, or forestall the insurgents in the south. In fact, Hanoi's reaction might be the reverse and lead to actions more supportive of the Viet Cong. The Defense Secretary also disagreed with a DIA evaluation, made in May 1965 and accepted by the JCS, that predicted Chinese reaction to a U.S. air strike on Phuc Yen airfield was "unlikely," and a response by the Soviet Union would probably be "limited." On the contrary, he said, such a bombing might lead to a confrontation between the United Sates and China, but he left the door open for further discussion.[74]

Mr. McNamara's reasons for regarding a more aggressive Rolling Thunder program as neither wise nor feasible at this time were already a matter of public record. In the aggregate, they reflected a conviction that heavier strikes would prove counterproductive and provoke a stronger military reaction by Hanoi, or Chinese intervention in the war, or both. Nor did the Defense Secretary conceal his view of the efficacy of air power. "We never believed and we don't believe today," he averred in an interview in August, "that bombing in the north will drive the North Vietnamese to the bargaining table or force them to cease their terror tactics and harassment and subversion of political institutions...." The only way to stop this was "to prove they can't win in the south," and the strategy was directed to that end. It was the antithesis of the Air Force's view.[75]

A further reason for the administration's refusal to expand Rolling Thunder rapidly in the summer of 1965 was not articulated. As events soon disclosed, the President, Mr. McNamara, and other officials were considering another serious negotiating effort with Hanoi to terminate hostilities. For bargaining "chips," they planned to use the carrot of a prolonged bombing pause and the stick of heavier air attacks on more vital targets if negotiations failed. By fall, debate within the administration over another bombing halt had increased markedly. By the end of the year, the halt would become a reality.[76]

Political constraints and the arrival of the monsoons in October thus led to a reduction in Rolling Thunder operations. The only increase in air activity was against the growing number of SA–2 missile sites outside of the Hanoi-Haiphong sanctuary.

The First SAM "Kill" and the anti-SAM Campaign in Late 1965

On October 17, five Navy Iron Hand aircraft, accompanying a joint Air Force and Navy Rolling Thunder mission against the Bac Can and Thai Nguyen bridges on the northeast rail line, prepared to strike a missile site near Kep airfield, not far from the rail line. The missile installation, assigned number 32, had been detected two days earlier by a drone. As the Rolling Thunder mission neared the target, the Iron Hand aircraft, consisting of one A–6A Intruder and four A–4E Skyhawks, all from the carrier *Independence*, broke off, popped up to 8,000 feet, and attacked the missile and associated equipment from two directions. As the lead aircraft, the A–6A strung eighteen Mark V 500-pound bombs across a missile transporter park, each of the A–4Es dropped 500-pound and 1,000-pound bombs from about 4,500 feet on the revetments. One missile was destroyed by a bomb, and the second missile, after snaking on the ground, burned itself out. The attack also destroyed ten missile transporter vehicles, damaged four others, and left three vans in flames. All five aircraft returned safely to the *Independence*.[77]

This was the first confirmed destruction of missiles and related equipment since the Air Force conducted an initial authorized strike on a missile site on July 27, 1965. Although the two services had only marginally effective equipment for detecting and pinpointing SAM installations, tactics were improving. Another collaborative Air Force and Navy effort followed. On October 31, in a "hunter-killer" experiment, a Navy pilot, Cmdr. Richard Powers, flying one of several specially equipped A–4E Skyhawks, flew as a pathfinder for USAF F–105 Thunderchiefs in an attack on missile sites. On the day preceding the mission, Commander Powers flew his Skyhawk from the carrier *Oriskany* to the 355th TFW at Takhli RTAFB to make coordinating arrangements. The next day, during another regular Rolling Thunder mission on the Kep highway bridge about thirty-five miles northeast of Hanoi, Powers guided two flights of Air Force F–105s to the target area. While Navy jets hit the Kep bridge, destroying it, Powers picked up a Fan Song radar from one SAM site and then observed two SAMs fired from a second site about two miles away. He quickly directed the Thunderchiefs to the latter target, then headed back to the first, dropping MK–82 high-drag Snake Eye bombs on it. Powers' Skyhawk was hit by groundfire, forcing him to bail out. He was observed descending and landed apparently unhurt. Rescue efforts followed immediately, but as these proved unsuccessful, Powers was presumably captured (officially listed as missing in action). Meanwhile, four USAF F–105s ascended to about 8,000 feet and expended their ordnance on the second missile site. Then one Thunderchief pilot spotted a third site and attacked it.

Next, Navy "pouncer" aircraft went into action, dropping their Snake Eye bombs on all three SAM sites. They used both low-level and dive-bombing techniques and experienced withering groundfire including about thirteen SAMs. After the attacks, pilots of the two services believed they had destroyed radar and control vans in two and possibly in all three sites. This was widely reported in the press, although lingering smoke and haze precluded any conclusive BDA. Losses were minimal, and consisted of Commander Powers and his Skyhawk and one F–105 Thunderchief gun which blew up while firing. Pilots credited the low attrition to timely warnings from ELINT and other aircraft of approaching SAMs, which enabled them to take speedy evasive action. One USAF pilot reported that he was tracked by a SAM at 700 to 800 feet while executing a 90-degree turn and finally eluded the missile by flying behind a hill. Because the Navy had insufficient numbers of the specially equipped A–4E Skyhawks such as the one flown by Powers, no further Air Force/Navy hunter-killer experiments were conducted in the ensuing months.[78]

In one instance, search and rescue proved more costly than a strike operation. On November 5, an armada of fifty-six Air Force aircraft en route to a SAM support facility at Guoi Bo and the Phu Ly bridge were diverted to armed reconnaissance because of bad weather. Near Thanh Hoa, a SAM missile downed an F–105, and this single loss led to several more. An A–1E Skyraider, searching for the pilot the next day, was shot down by groundfire, as was a USAF CH–3 helicopter with a crew of four, which was launched to rescue the Skyraider pilot. Another rescue effort succeeded in saving one of the four helicopter crewmen. On the 6th, another A–1E searching for the downed pilots and crews was hit by antiaircraft fire and crashed. The pilot could not be rescued.

In another anti-SAM mission, also on November 6, twenty Navy aircraft first conducted a restrike on the Hai Duong bridge located in a restricted area between Hanoi and Haiphong (although outside the prohibited radius of both cities). Intercepting a SAM radar signal, three Iron Hand A–4Es found the site and scored a direct hit on a missile launcher causing a secondary explosion, but poor weather prevented most visual and photo assessment. Three SAM missiles were fired against the attackers but all missed. However, heavy flak from 37-mm and 57-mm guns damaged one of the aircraft, which then silenced one of the antiaircraft emplacements.

November 7, 1965, witnessed the largest one-day Air Force-Navy Rolling Thunder assault of the war. While twenty Navy aircraft, including accompanying Iron Hand A–4E's, were attacking the Me Xa highway bridge on the morning of the 7th, pilots spotted an SA–2 missile ascending north of Thanh. Two firing installations were quickly found and attacked. Five Skyhawks damaged a missile van and left two missiles burning in a revetment of the first installation. Another flight of five Skyhawks hit the second installation, destroying one or more missile control vans. However, poststrike photos disclosed that eighteen missiles on launchers or movers had escaped detection. Groundfire downed one Skyhawk, but the pilot was saved, as was the crew of a rescue helicopter that was forced down on a nearby mountaintop.

On the afternoon of the 7th, while fifteen Air Force F–4C Phantoms attacked the Phu Ly bridge and a nearby antiaircraft site, twenty more jets headed for two

In November 1965, A–4s from the carrier USS *Oriskany* struck this railroad siding located about 40 miles south of Thanh Hoa, destroying five railroad cars with 500-pound bombs.

SAM sites near the Guoi Bo bridge. Four aircraft destroyed a radar van at one site and hit two nearby antiaircraft emplacements. The attack on the second site destroyed ten buildings, damaged two, and caused secondary explosions, however, clouds prevented good bomb damage assessment. The Air Force incurred no losses on the last strike, but the aggregate three-day effort proved costly. The North Vietnamese downed five fixed-wing aircraft and two helicopters, damaged numerous others, and seven crewmen were missing. Although a good part of the SAM installations near Guoi Bo bridge were found to have escaped destruction, Admiral Sharp was unable to obtain immediate Washington authorization to conduct a restrike.[79]

Air Force F–105s struck four SAM sites on November 16 and 22, bringing to seventeen the number of sites attacked by U.S. aircraft since July 27. As usual, pilots reported some destruction and damage, but weather again precluded satisfactory photo verification. The attack on the 16th cost the Air Force one Thunderchief, which was downed by a SAM. It was the eighth U.S. loss to the SAMs and the 160th U.S. aircraft lost over North Vietnam since August 1964. On the 22d, four Thunderchiefs, employing terrain masking at minimum altitude and flying in a line-abreast formation, popped up ten miles from the target and released rockets from 5,500 feet while flying at 450 knots. The absence of flak suggested that the strike surprised enemy gunners. In a similar attack on the second site, despite SAM and MiG warnings, the Thunderchiefs encountered only flak leaving the target area while flying at 6,600 feet.

On November 27 at Dong Em, about twenty-two miles from Hanoi, USAF aircraft first hit a suspected SAM assembly and maintenance facility that was believed to support three nearby SAM sites. Pilots reportedly destroyed at least eight buildings and damaged eight others. An SA–2 missile, although struck by 2.75-inch rockets, became airborne and exploded at about 1,000 feet. The aircraft also dropped several 3,000-pound bombs on two cave entrances, but with unknown results.[80]

Air Force and Navy pilots conducted no major SAM strikes in December, although pilots reported numerous SAM firings and the North Vietnamese crews scored three times.

On December 19, during an Air Force raid on the Bag Can highway bridge, a JCS target, the communists fired two SAMs at the aircraft. One exploded near an F–4C Phantom, disabling it, but the crewmen ejected and were rescued. On the 22d, during a Navy strike on the Uong Bi thermal power plant, SAMs downed a combat A–5A and a reconnaissance RA–5A.[81]

The Air Force Increases its anti-SAM Capability

According to a Joint Staff review of the adequacy of ECM and ELINT equipment, the most "serious deficiency" was the inability of Iron Hand and other specialized aircraft to provide timely warning of SAM firings to aircrews. Issued in mid-October 1965, the study was prepared in cooperation with the scientific and industrial community and itemized the improvements needed in electronic intelligence, electronic countermeasures, all-weather navigation, reconnaissance, attack capability, and cameras, the last to insure more effective immediate poststrike assessment capability. The Air Force's Big Eye EC–121s, EB–66s, F–100s, and F–105s especially needed more sophisticated electronic equipment.

A separate Air Force study, conducted by a group headed by Brig. Gen. K.C. Dempster, Deputy Director for Operational Requirements, DCS/R&D, listed the requirements for countering SA–2 missiles: a warning system to alert air crews when they were under enemy radar surveillance, better pinpointing of enemy radar locations, timely processing of intelligence data, prompt air strike decisions, adequate ECM for all fighter aircraft, precise navigation for aircraft flying at high speed and low altitude into a target area, and suitable tactics for strikes in areas defended by antiaircraft weapons. The Dempster group divided remedial measures between those to be completed in the short term (6 months) and the long term (6 to 18 months). A Navy task force compiled a similar list of technical changes needed by Navy and Marine aircraft.[82]

By October, many of the recommended improvements were under development, some on a crash basis, but months would elapse before most of the new

A two-seat F–100F approaching a KC–135 for refueling.

equipment became available. As a consequence, the Air Force and Navy continued to employ existing systems and experimented further with tactics against the SAM installations with existing aircraft. The Air Force augmented its EB–66 force variously equipped with radar detection, jamming, and infrared equipment and cameras. Three more of the aircraft were sent from Shaw AFB in North Carolina TDY to Takhli, where they arrived on September 8 to join six similar planes already there and assigned to the 9th TRS. Then on October 7, the JCS directed that five EB–66s with aircrews and equipment of the 25th TRS at Chambley Air Base in France—part of the United States Air Force, Europe (USAFE)—likewise deploy to Takhli. They arrived on October 21, providing General Moore with fourteen EB–66s. In late November 1965, the 41st TRS moved to Takhli from Shaw, taking over all aircraft and personnel from the 9th TRS, which was discontinued.[83]

More specialized than the first EB–66s, each of the five USAFE aircraft carried a crew of three. Although not equipped for gathering electronic intelligence, all were very well suited for performing passive ECM. They possessed twenty-three jammers configured to counter all known North Vietnamese air defense radar emitters. The 2d Air Division developed anti-SAM radar tactics that called for the use of destroyers and jammers within 15 n.m. of an installation. A minimum of two aircraft were assigned to each ingress route. While one EB–66C (for active ECM) was placed in an orbit outside of the SAM ring, another penetrated the target's air space. The tactic proved quite successful.[84]

As a result of the Joint Staff and Air Force crash efforts instituted in August 1965 to equip special aircraft with advanced electronic gear, the Air Force deployed a detachment of four Wild Weasel two-seat F–100Fs from Eglin AFB, Florida, to Korat, Thailand, on November 25. Commanded by Maj. Garry A. Willard, Jr., the detachment was assigned to the 6234th TFS at the same airbase. Each aircraft had a radar homing and warning (RHAW) system, a panoramic

SCA Receiver (IR–133), and a missile guidance warning receiver (WR–300) that were controlled by an electronic warfare officer in the rear cockpit. The front cockpit had a duplicate scope of the RHAW for the pilot.[85]

From November 28 to 30, the detachment flew orientation missions with F–105 Thunderchiefs in preparation for operational tests. Bad weather delayed the initial flight tests, but on December 19, two Wild Weasel aircraft piloted by Major Willard and Capt. Leslie J. Lindemuth, accompanied by their respective electronic warfare officers, Capts. Truman "Walt" Lifsey and Robert D. Trier, ventured into SAM territory in North Vietnam. The two aircraft picked up no Fan Song missile radar signals, but the next day was fateful. After locating and then leading a strike attack on a SAM site about five nautical miles southeast of Kep airfield, a Wild Weasel piloted by Capt. John J. Pitchford was shot down by antiaircraft fire. Pitchford parachuted to safety, but was captured and remained a prisoner of war until February 1973. His electronic warfare officer, Captain Trier, died in the crash, a loss magnified by the unsuccessful attack. Three days later, electronic instruments in another Wild Weasel plane carrying Capts. Allen T. Lamb and John E. Donovan, pilot and electronic warfare officer respectively, picked up a Fan Song signal in the vicinity of Yen Bai. Captain Lamb quickly verified the location visually, sighting a radar van and three missiles partially concealed under a thatched hut. He marked the area with a smoke bomb and called in a flight of four Iron Hand F–105Ds. The Thunderchiefs struck the target area with seventy-six 2.75-inch rockets, creating numerous explosions and sending smoke and dust 300 to 400 feet into the air. Although not immediately confirmed, the missile site was presumed destroyed, demonstrating the potential of the specially equipped Wild Weasels.

By year's end, the operational tests had provided several useful tactical lessons. The aircrews learned that in the heavily defended sectors of North Vietnam, hunter-killer tactics worked best when one F–100F led three strike Thunderchiefs into a suspected SAM target area at 8,000 feet with five miles visibility. Maneuvering required a minimum of 4,000 feet. The tests also showed how operations could be improved considerably by employing special frequencies for inflight Iron Hand communications and assigning two rather than one KC–135 tankers to Wild Weasel missions, to expedite refueling and extend loiter time. In a separate but related action, Wild Weasel pilots were authorized at year's end to use BLU–27B finned napalm to mark targets.[86]

Although still engaged in testing at the end of 1965, and despite their vulnerability to groundfire, the F–100F Wild Weasels led the way in the Air Force's effort to improve its anti-SAM capability, hitherto borne solely by the Destroyer EB–66s. However, the F–100Fs would be replaced in the spring of 1966 by several two-seat F–105Fs, currently undergoing modification at Eglin AFB, with improved radar detection and suppression equipment.[87]

Udorn Royal Thai Air Force Base

CHAPTER 7

Toward the Thirty-seven-Day Bombing Halt

The air commanders' preoccupation with finding, neutralizing or destroying SA–2 missiles and their sites tended to obscure the fact that most sorties were still being flown against non-SAM targets. At the beginning of October 1965, the authorities in Washington permitted bombing of the northeast quadrant in the north, which included a large segment of the rail line from Hanoi to Ping Hsiang, China. Approved targets for the first half of the month were listed in JCS Rolling Thunder program 34/35 (October 1–14). The most important were bridges at Long Het, Xom Phuong, and Vu Chua and an ammunition depot near Long Het. In program 37/38 for the last half of the month (October 15–28), the key targets were bridges at Bac Can, Choi Moi, Thai Nguyen, and Lang Luang. Restrikes on bridges on the northwest line between Hanoi and Cai Cao were also authorized, but JCS directives limited the services to "a single coordinated attack" on each bridge during a seven-day period. Unhappily for aircrews, this rule would enable repair crews to nullify much of the bombing impact.

Other rules for striking fixed or armed reconnaissance targets remained largely unchanged for the remainder of 1965. Directives authorized a maximum of 1,200 armed reconnaissance sorties for each biweekly period: six hundred sorties were allocated to the Air Force and VNAF-Air Force operations, and the other 600 were allocated to the Navy. These figures could be exceeded if necessary. As indicated earlier, beginning with Rolling Thunder programs 38/39 (October 29–November 11), locks and dams were exempt from attack unless they were related solely to navigation.[1]

On October 5, in a major effort against the highway bridge at Long Het, eighteen PACAF F–105s dropped one end of the structure, damaged the other, and cratered the southern approach and a nearby road, leaving the bridge unserviceable. Groundfire downed one Thunderchief and damaged three, while an accompanying reconnaissance RF–101 was destroyed attempting to land at Da Nang Air Base. In a separate mission, eight F–4C Phantoms hit the Long Het ammunition depot with seventy-five 750-pound bombs with undetermined results. This too cost an aircraft and two airmen, although both were observed ejecting safely. Ten Phantoms, immediately diverted to rescue CAP, were unable to locate the pilots.

During the Long Het mission on October 5, five MiGs intercepted an EB–66C flying ECM support about fifteen miles east of the bridge, deep in the north's northeast sector. Two enemy aircraft made firing passes at the aircraft, but missed. The EB–66C pilot believed he saw Chinese markings on the planes, which flew due north after the attack. Speculation that the planes were Chinese increased when Peking publicly charged that an American aircraft had violated Chinese air space over Kwangsi Province, and in a dogfight that ensued, a Chinese fighter pilot shot it down. Peking also alleged that in a separate incident, U.S. aircraft strafed Chinese fishing boats in the South China Sea.

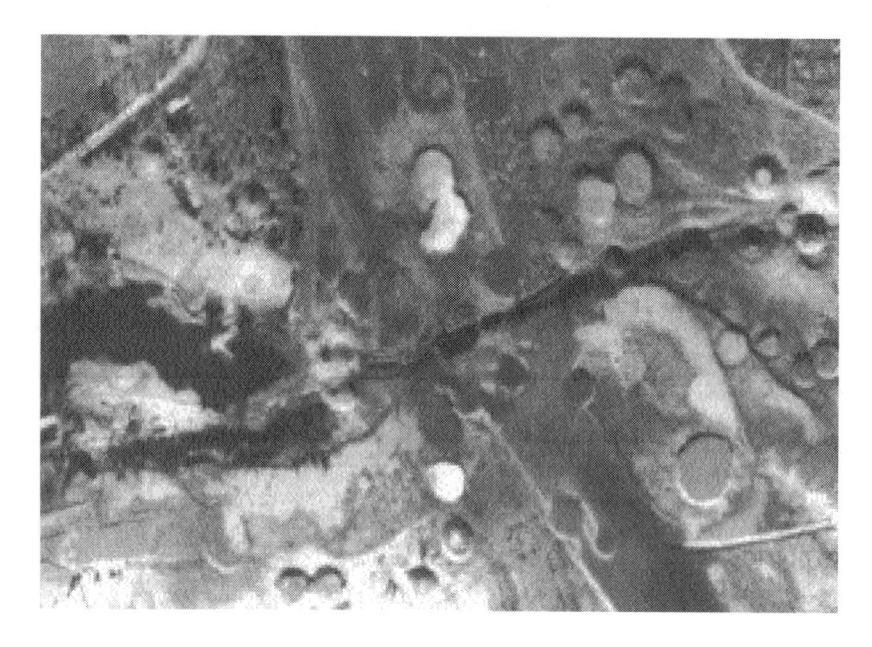

The Bac Can highway bridge, located about seventy-five miles
north of Hanoi, after an F–105 strike in December 1965.

American officials denied both allegations, and the Chinese failed to produce either aircraft parts or the pilot of the supposedly destroyed plane. However, an Air Force investigation of the incident indicated that the EB–66C had intruded to within 15 nautical miles of the Chinese border. The pilot and other Air Force officials believed it was permissible to make a nonbombing penetration this close to China, but Admiral Sharp responded that the 15 n.m. limit, authorized in September, was only for strike pilots who might have to maneuver to hit a target on the edge of the buffer zone established by Washington earlier in the year.

On October 5, Air Force planes struck the Kep highway bridge and hit the Vu Chua railroad bridge on the 7th. Bombs missed the Kep bridge, but cratered its southern end, while the Vu Chua bridge was destroyed. During the Kep bridge attack, pilots observed numerous bursts of fire, apparently SAMs. One flash was seen in the target area and others appeared about fifteen miles east and southeast of Haiphong. A Navy F–8E was hit by a SAM and disabled. The pilot was forced to eject offshore and was rescued.

On October 17, sixteen F–105s hit the Bac Can bridge, dropping thirty-two 3,000-pound bombs that cratered the south approach and left two holes in the bridge's deck. No aircraft were lost. The attack was coordinated with the Navy's strike on the heavily defended Thai Nguyen bridge that, in turn, served as a cover for the first successful air strike on an SA–2 site near Kep airfield, roughly adjacent to the northeast rail line some distance from Hanoi. For the bridge assault, the Navy used about thirty-two strike and support aircraft with the attackers dropping forty 500-pound bombs, thirty-one 1,000-pound bombs, and twenty-six 2,000-pound bombs. These damaged the bridge severely, left a large traverse crack on the deck, damaged the southern pier, and cratered the abutments and approaches. However, the mission was costly, with three aircraft downed and three damaged.[2]

The air campaign against the northeast rail and some road targets continued until the end of 1965, although its effectiveness was diminished by the monsoon season, a prodigious repair effort, and bombing rules that allowed only intermittent attacks. In the last two weeks of October, for example, weather forced the Air Force to cancel about 30 percent of its planned sorties. By early November, repairs on six rail bridges, two railyards, and rail cuts were sufficient to permit limited traffic on the rail line. Consequently, on November 6 Admiral Sharp directed his Air Force and Navy commanders to conduct more armed reconnaissance strikes on selected track segments. This was a difficult assignment: in the four-week period from October 28 to November 25, 354 Air Force sorties were aborted due to the thickening monsoon weather.[3]

Nonetheless, the missions were of sufficient frequency to draw the North Vietnamese Air Force (NVAF)—quiescent since July 10—into action to counter U.S. attacks near and above Hanoi. On November 15, two MiGs pounced on two Air Force RF–101s near Yen Bai, but the Voodoos eluded them. The next day, two other RF–101s spotted two MiGs northeast of Hanoi and made their escape. There were no further incidents until November 25 when four to six MiGs were observed about sixty-seven nautical miles northwest of Hanoi. The enemy pilots fired their guns at the reconnaissance aircraft which evaded the MiGs by flying at high speed and low altitude and returned safely to their base at Udorn.

On the same day, three or four MiGs twice engaged the second wave of Navy aircraft conducting a strike on the Me Xa bridge. One fired an air-to-air rocket and its cannons, but without effect. In a second attack, two MiGs made firing passes at two A–4Es, damaging one, possibly with 23-mm cannon fire. The second MiG engaged in low-altitude air-to-air combat for about five minutes before withdrawing. These attacks, made at about 2,000 feet, suggested a new enemy tactic to evade Air Force Big Eye EC–121s circling over the Gulf of Tonkin. Despite the NVAF's resurgence, analysts conjectured that Hanoi gave highest air defense priority to the installation of SAM sites and would rely on its MiGs only when the odds appeared favorable.[4]

Additional Interdiction Changes and Planning for Negotiation

In late November, with Washington's approval, Admiral Sharp again asked his Air Force and Navy commanders to shift their interdiction emphasis.

An A–6 launches from the deck of the USS *Kitty Hawk*.

Judging that armed reconnaissance of rail and road LOCs in the north had increased communist dependence on inland and coastal waterways to transport their supplies, he directed more attacks at watercraft. To enable pilots to distinguish more readily between military and nonmilitary cargoes, the PACOM commander said that watercraft were suspect if they were motorized (as the DRV owned most of the north's motorized vessels), carried large cargoes, engaged in night traffic, were camouflaged, and moved between points connecting different modes of transportation. Along coastal waterways, all vessels were suspect, including small groups of junks if they moved point-to-point in contrast with seaward movements for fishing. As usual, air crews were warned to minimize civilian casualties.[5]

November also witnessed a renewed JCS effort to get administration backing for a harder hitting campaign in both North Vietnam and Laos. On the 10th, in a "Concept for Vietnam" paper, the service chiefs sent Secretary McNamara a proposal calling for 7,000 combat and combat support sorties per month with 5,500 sorties allocated to Rolling Thunder and 1,500 to Laos, chiefly against infiltration routes. These sortie levels, they said, could be carried out by the Air Force aircraft already based in Thailand and two Navy aircraft carriers at Yankee Station in the Gulf of Tonkin. They believed it would take only "three to four" months to destroy most of the significant fixed targets. Thereafter, the services would need only 400 combat sorties per month to assure interdiction of the western and southern LOCs in North Vietnam and Laos respectively.

The Joint Chiefs' priority targets included POL facilities with an estimated storage capacity of 216,000 metric tons. Of thirteen storage sites, only four had been struck thus far. Further delay in striking the remainder, they warned Mr. McNamara, would permit Hanoi to continue its logistic support of Viet Cong-DRV forces in South Vietnam and to establish additional antiaircraft weapons around the POL sites. The alleged danger of retaliatory attacks by communist ground forces on POL installations in South Vietnam should not stand in the way of granting strike approval. The Joint Chiefs also backed "phase II" manpower and unit deployment schedules for South Vietnam in 1966, a callup of reserves, and extension of tours of duty.[6]

Nearly a month elapsed before OSD advised the service chiefs officially that their latest recommendations were being considered in conjunction with other views. As events disclosed, OSD's delayed reply was linked to high-level discussions in November on another political-military gambit to end the war. The President deferred a decision until Secretary McNamara, accompanied by General Wheeler, Admiral Sharp, and other officials had visited Saigon on November 28–29, again to assess the military situation and to determine what additional U.S. and allied manpower and other aid was needed to counter the growing strength of the VC-NVA.[7]

In the weeks preceding McNamara's trip to Saigon, a series of discreet activities by high-level U.S. and foreign diplomats and amateur peacemakers were under way to find a basis for Hanoi and Washington to begin talks or negotiations. The most prominent officials engaged in this effort were Secretary of State Rusk, Arthur Goldberg, U.S. Ambassador to the United Nations, and Amitore Fanfani, the Italian Foreign Minister. In May 1965, the President had encouraged Fanfani to help the United States seek a negotiated settlement.[8]

Presumably, the President and McNamara discounted the importance of these diplomatic maneuverings, for early in December, as part of Rolling Thunder program 44/45 (December 10–23), they approved the bombing of two sensitive targets hardly calculated to make Hanoi more amenable to negotiations. One was the Uong Bi power plant, only sixteen miles from Haiphong, and the other a highway bridge in the vicinity of Haiphong and thus within the sanctuary area. The power plant, which had a capacity of 24,000 kilowatts, supplied about 15 percent of the north's electricity, much of it consumed in Hanoi and Haiphong. It was the sixth electrical utility earmarked for attack and considered the DRV's most important industrial target.[9]

The strike on the Uong Bi plant was initially scheduled for December 10, but monsoon weather delayed several attacks, only part of many canceled missions. The Air Force and Navy would schedule more than 160 missions of which scores were canceled. The Air Force scratched completely all missions on seven days, the Navy on four. Many aircraft became weather aborts after launch or struck secondary targets in the north or Laos while returning to their bases in Thailand.[10]

After several weather cancellations, the Uong Bi attack finally began on December 15 with ninety Air Force aircraft. Twenty-three F–105s flew a strike profile, while sixty-seven other Thunderchiefs, F–4Cs, EB–66s, RF–101s, and KC–135s flew support. Poor weather forced all but seven of the strike F–105s to jettison their 750-pound, 1,000-pound, and 3,000-pound bombs. The other fighter-bombers dropped fourteen 3,000-pound bombs in a corner of the target area and expended 304 2.75-inch rockets on a nearby antiaircraft site. Enemy gunners shot

A riverside naval patrol boat repair area in North Vietnam, during an F–105 attack, October 8, 1965.

down one Thunderchief, although the pilot was rescued, and damaged five others. Secretary McNamara publicly called the attack "representative of the type we have carried out and will continue to carry out. I would not characterize it as retaliatory, but I think it is appropriate to the increased terror activity."

After poststrike data disclosed that, in fact, most of the power plant had not been hit, the Navy, with JCS permission, conducted a second strike on the night of December 19, while simultaneously attacking the Haiphong highway bridge. The Navy used six A–6A Intruders equipped with some of the latest night radar bombing systems. They dropped 2,000-pound bombs, but these too missed the power plant with one aircraft shot down by a SAM. After the JCS sanctioned a third strike on the 22d, the Navy dispatched thirty-five aircraft including several Intruders. These first hit the Haiphong bridge, then the Uong Bi plant. The bridge's deck was damaged, temporarily closing it. The pilots then dropped about twenty-five tons of bombs on the plant and fired three Bullpups with 1,000-pound warheads, finally destroying most of it. This brought the north's cumulative electricity generating loss to about 47,000 kilowatts, about 27 percent of national capacity. Antiaircraft fire brought down two A–4s and one RA–5. The aggregate Air Force-Navy loss in attacking the target thus totaled five aircraft destroyed and many others damaged. Another A–6A and an RA–5 were downed by SAMs in the strike on the Haiphong bridge. Struck once more by the Navy on the 23d, the bridge was left unserviceable.[11]

Highly disturbed by the excessive aircraft attrition in bombing a relatively small utility, Air Force analysts attributed the losses to Washington's over-control of operational matters. Admiral Sharp, they observed, had to obtain JCS assent

Dr. Harold Brown is sworn in as Secretary of the Air Force, October 1, 1965.

for each restrike and for the types of aircraft to be used. In addition, too much time elapsed between the restrikes, enabling the North Vietnamese to deploy many more antiaircraft weapons around the power plant. In the Air Staff's view, the Uong Bi operation underscored dramatically the need to let Navy and Air Force commanders rather than Washington control the strikes.[12] In the ensuing months, however, high administration officials showed no inclination to transfer significant authority for prosecuting the war, particularly for bombing North Vietnam, to general officers of the Air Force and Navy.

In late 1965, the Air Force deployed its first RF–4C all-weather and night reconnaissance unit to Southeast Asia. The specially equipped aircraft would augment the Blue Tree and Yankee Team reconnaissance programs over North Vietnam and Laos, respectively. Flying from Shaw AFB, South Carolina, nine RF–4Cs arrived at Tan Son Nhut AB on October 30 and were assigned to the 16th TRS. They flew an initial mission over Laos on November 16, and over North Vietnam the next day. Manned by a two-man crew, the aircraft were packed with sophisticated gear: infrared, side-looking, and forward-looking radars; cameras for day and night photography; high frequency and single sideband communications; a pinpoint inertial navigation system; and in-flight photographic film processing and film cassette ejection systems to ensure fast delivery of finished photos to field commanders. They also possessed an in-flight refueling capability.[13]

Initial reconnaissance results indicated a number of technical problems remained to be resolved. To assure good resolution of imagery from the infrared AN/AAS–18 system, the RF–4Cs had to fly at low altitude. There was difficulty in translating multisensor reconnaissance imagery rapidly to combat aircrews and inadequate target display in the cockpits. Downward-looking radar quickly proved more rewarding than side-looking. Highly specialized photointerpreters were needed to discriminate between good and poor data in reconnaissance film. Both Secretary of the Air Force Harold Brown (who replaced Eugene M. Zuckert on October 1), and General McConnell noted these shortcomings. Between mid-November and December 30, six RF–4C missions were flown in the north, thirty in Laos, and some in South Vietnam.[14]

In November, in conjunction with reconnaissance operations over the north, an RB–57E with infrared capability searched for enemy targets revealed by campfires, cooking fires, sentry fires, small manufacturing, and camouflage. Several EB–66Bs with infrared capability were also employed, but most of the RB–57E and EB–66B missions were flown over South Vietnam.

Despite the additional reconnaissance resources, it was evident that aerial detection of enemy infiltration from North Vietnam into Laos and southward into South Vietnam would have to be drastically improved if Air Force and Navy pilots were to be able to conduct more rewarding air strikes. The terrain, the darkness, and enemy concealment tactics made the interdiction task formidable. In December 1965, James Cameron, a British correspondent and the first westerner allowed by the Hanoi government to travel through southern North Vietnam, authored a graphic account of the way the DRV managed to avoid serious losses from road bombings:

> Through the hours of daylight practically nothing whatever moved on four wheels on the roads of North Vietnam; hardly a car or a truck; from the air, in the sunlight, it must have looked as though the country had no wheeled transport at all. That, of course, was the idea. It was the roads and the bridges that were being bombed; it was held to be no longer safe, after sunrise, to be near either.
>
> In the paddy fields in the sunlight the farmers were reaping their third harvest of the year, which had been especially abundant.... They moved among the rice bowed under a shawl of foliage, the camouflage that gave everyone kind of a carnival air, like so many Jack O' The Greens. At the corners of every field stood what looked like sheaves of iron corn, and which were stacks of rifles. The roads stretched long and empty, leading from nowhere to nowhere. One could have taken it for a charade; in this land does nothing *travel* from place to place?
>
> At dusk the roads became alive. From a thousand arbors and copses and the shelter of trees the traffic materialized; the engines were started and the convoys emerged from invisibility, began to grind away through the darkness behind the pinpoints of masked headlights. There were miles of them—heavy Russian-built lorries, antiaircraft batteries of guns, all deeply buried under layers of branches and leaves; processions of huge green haystacks. By day North Vietnam is abandoned; by night it thuds and groans with movement. It was an excessively fatiguing routine

These reconnaissance photos show the ability of the North Vietnamese to recover and reconstruct destroyed bridges and roads, sometimes in a matter of days after an airstrike. The top photo shows two destroyed bridges. A bypass system is under construction, complete with a river ford, around the bridge in the upper part of the photo. The dark spot near the fork in the road is a road grader. Below, an emergency span has been built to repair a railroad bridge 135 miles south of Hanoi.

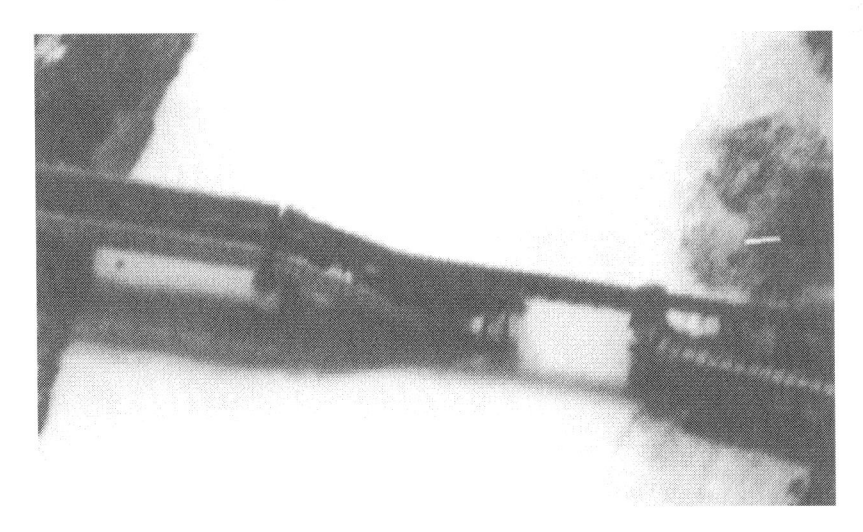

As the pilot gets out of the cockpit after a mission, the ground crew removes the film from this RF–4.

for those of us who were trying to capture this peculiar picture: moving always by night, and working always by day.

...by the time we inched through the darkness to the bombed area it seemed it was already passable, though only with difficulty. It was hard to see in the darkness what was happening though later, after many such experiences, I came to know: great multitudes of women had somehow been recruited or accumulated from the neighborhood and were filling in the holes and reconstituting some sort of a surface for the road, out of the piles of stones and gravel....It was impossible to count the number of women, but there were several hundred. This, they said, happened frequently; almost every major road in the country was a semi-permanent condition of running repair.

Two main bridges on the road head were gone long since; they had been destroyed in the early raids; they had been replaced with pontoons of bamboo rafts. Usually the replacement was a ferry; North Vietnam is a wilderness of ferries in the delta region; they take up a tremendous proportion of travelling time....Sometimes a pontoon bridge was alternated with a ferry, to cause confusion among the American reconnaissance aircraft. Frequently with makeshift bridges, when daylight came and traffic stopped, one end of the floating bridge was detached, so that the whole structure could drift down and lie parallel with the bank and become invisible. There never was a place where such importance was attached to invisibility.[15]

To tighten their loosely coordinated reconnaissance and bombing efforts over North Vietnam and Laos, in November the Air Force and Navy established the Rolling Thunder Armed Reconnaissance Coordination Committee. Like its

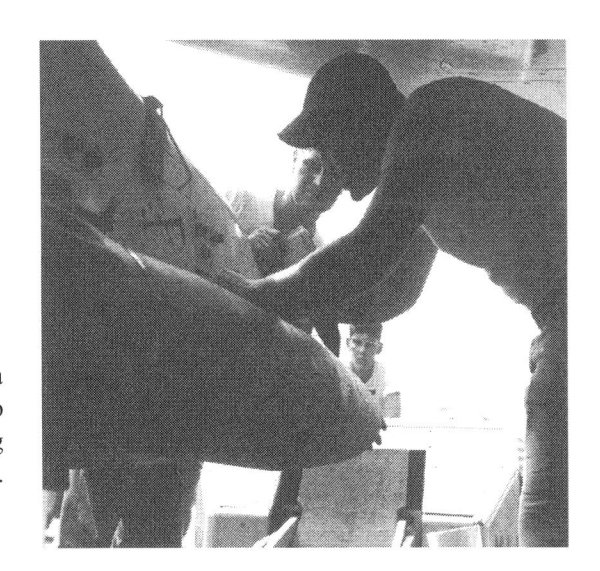

Crewmen attach a 500-pound bomb to an underwing rack on an F–4.

predecessor, the 2d Air Division-Task Force 77 coordinating committee established earlier in the bombing program, it was chaired by the Air Force. The rising number of armed reconnaissance sorties over the north, constituting about 86 percent of all combat sorties by late December, necessitated the change. The new committee tried to reduce overlapping and duplication of service missions by designating suitable LOCs and targets for armed reconnaissance, establishing special target and photo ELINT panels, developing route packages for each service over the north, and preparing common armed reconnaissance terminology. Plans called for the committee to meet once every two weeks, about five days prior to each biweekly Rolling Thunder period.

Although the new committee ironed out numerous problems, Admiral Sharp's desire to maintain command and control of operations over the north—with Navy air in a dominant role—soon made coordination of Air Force and Navy activities more nominal than real. The committee was reduced to a discussion forum, limited to exchanging information and ideas for essentially independent Air Force and Navy air activities in North Vietnam and Laos. Although the Air Force chairman strove to develop closer coordination for Rolling Thunder, he was unable to achieve it.

Admiral Sharp's insistence on maintaining Navy air independence was dramatized on December 10 when he unilaterally divided North Vietnam into six major geographical route packages for armed reconnaissance operations. He gave route packages 2, 4, and 5 to the Air Force, and route packages 1 and 3 to the Navy. The initial operational arrangement called for the two services to exchange their route packages every two weeks. In the event of poor weather, they could fly into each other's primary operating area after requesting and receiving permission from the other service. Missions flown in route package 6 in the northeast area of North Vietnam (divided into route packages 6A and 6B) would be authorized and assigned on a mission-by-mission basis. However, the Navy increasingly confined its strikes to the coastal route packages. The Navy's predilection for flying short-range sorties from its carriers was understandable, but the practice left the Air Force with responsibility for bombing the more distant and often more strongly defended inland targets. This highly hazardous task, General Moore believed, should have been shared by the Navy.[16]

In late 1965, the arrival of the first F–4C and F–105 tactical fighter squadrons on one-year permanent change of station (PCS) rather than 120-day TDY tours held the promise of improved combat capability for the Air Force. The 390th TFS arrived at Da Nang AB in November with F–4C Phantoms and was assigned to the 6252d TFW, while the 333d TFS with F–105 Thunderchiefs arrived at Takhli RTAFB on December 8, where it was assigned to the 355th TFW. In accordance with a decision by General McConnell in November, pilot tours were established at one hundred missions over North Vietnam or Laos or for one year, whichever was the lesser. Unless pilots completing one hundred missions could be used in a noncombat rated position in Southeast Asia to complete a year's tour, they would be returned to the United States. The change to PCS tours of duty, decided at a PACOM conference at Honolulu in August, promised to reduce the turmoil caused by continuing personnel turnover, lower orientation requirements, and to mitigate the reduced performance normally associated with 120-day TDY tours.[17]

Continuation of the Leaflet Program

The aerial distribution of psychological warfare leaflets over North Vietnam continued unabated in late 1965. Designed to undermine popular support for the war, most leaflets were dropped by Air Force F–105 Thunderchiefs. VNAF pilots made occasional drops in areas just above the DMZ. In a departure from normal delivery, on the night of September 10 an Air Force C–130 scattered about 9,000 packets of toys over the north in honor of the annual Vietnamese children's day. It was hoped that the populace would consider the toys a "goodwill" gesture from South Vietnam and its ally.[18]

By mid-October, approximately forty-four million leaflets had been spread over ninety areas and along major LOCs leading to population centers. Most were dropped between mid-July and mid-October under a program devised and carried out by the principal U.S. military, diplomatic, and information offices in Saigon. Although a MACV analysis of the six-month propaganda effort sent to Washington conceded that the operations did not threaten the Hanoi regime, they were nevertheless considered "successful" as measured by the DRV's press and radio reaction to the leaflets, newspapers, and gift packages. The reaction indicated that some citizens, believing what they read, had spread the propaganda and therefore needed more political indoctrination. A similar, but more expansive, leaflet program in South Vietnam to strengthen the south's morale and weaken that of the Viet Cong

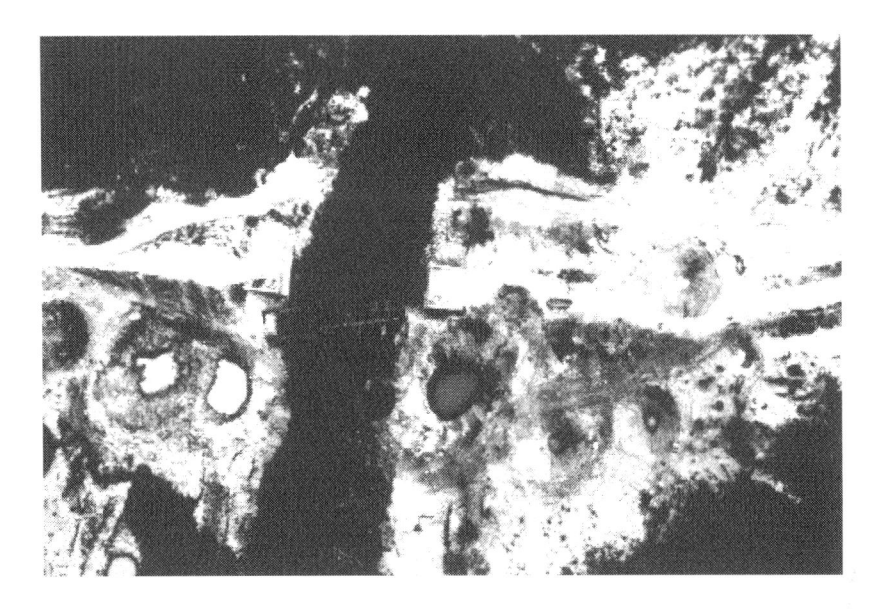

The remains of a bridge and the ford built to bypass it on
Route 19 northeast of Dien Bien Phu, October 1965.

was likewise judged "successful," although it failed to slow the rush of U.S. manpower and arms to the south to stop a possible communist takeover.[19]

Psychological warfare leaflet drops over the north continued at a steady pace throughout November and December. At Admiral Sharp's request, Washington relaxed somewhat the rules governing leaflet operations but continued to prohibit overflights of the Hanoi and Haiphong area and the buffer zone adjacent to China. On December 1, in a record-breaking mission, Air Force pilots released one million propaganda leaflets over cities and towns in the Red River Delta. They depended on wind drift to scatter the leaflets over the Hanoi-Haiphong sanctuary area. By December 24, seventy-seven million leaflets and fifteen thousand gift kits had been distributed. Based on reports that "in some instances" leaflet messages had forced Hanoi's authorities to take counter-propaganda actions, the leaflet program was considered worthwhile.[20]

Beginning of Thirty-Seven-Day Bombing Halt

The last Rolling Thunder missions in 1965 were flown on December 24. At 1800 Saigon time, with the approval of the Saigon government, President Johnson ordered a thirty-hour Christmas truce in the air and ground wars in South and North Vietnam and Laos.[21]

The end of the thirty-hour truce period, midnight on December 25, passed without a resumption of bombing over the north, although the tactical Barrel

Roll, Steel Tiger, and Tiger Hound* operations in Laos were quickly resumed, at the insistence of Ambassador Sullivan, but not from South Vietnamese bases. But all B–52 operations in South Vietnam and Laos ceased.[22] The truce continued into the 26th. On the 27th, Admiral Sharp informed his Air Force and Navy component commanders to be ready "on short notice" to resume Rolling Thunder armed reconnaissance missions on the 28th, weather permitting.[23] But before the day was out, President Johnson decided to extend the bombing halt indefinitely and to launch a major diplomatic effort to bring Hanoi to the bargaining table.[24]

The President's decision was the culmination of months of internal debate on how to force Hanoi to talk. In mid-July 1965, after the United States had deployed more ground forces to South Vietnam and subjected the north to heavier bombing, Secretary McNamara had suggested calling a halt to the bombing for six to eight weeks as part of a new peace initiative.[25] Westmoreland, Ambassador Lodge, Admiral Sharp, and the Joint Chiefs strongly opposed a cessation. In fact, the Joint Chiefs had objected to the Christmas truce and insisted that its continuance would only aid the North Vietnamese in their military buildup, regrouping, and road and rail repair activities and would expose the United States' determination and intentions in the war to criticism.[26]

In truth, domestic more than diplomatic considerations compelled the President to extend the Christmas truce. This became evident on the 28th when McNamara informed the Joint Chiefs of the reasons for the President's actions. One factor, he said, was the "thin" domestic support for the war. A high percentage of the public believed that the administration had failed to devise "a diplomatic equivalent to its military program" with half to three-fourths of the public desiring the United States to propose either a ceasefire or a complete cessation of bombing. Furthermore, in two to three weeks, the administration would ask the new Congress for an additional twenty-five billion dollars to support operations in Vietnam over the next eighteen months and to extend the bombing to POL depots and other targets that were important but as yet unscathed. Support for these proposals, "will be less than required unless we can show that an honest attempt has been made to test the effect of a bombing cessation on Hanoi's willingness to enter into negotiations."

For the Defense Secretary, there were other important reasons for stopping the bombing and trying to negotiate an end to the conflict. During his meetings with Ambassador Lodge, General Westmoreland, and their aides in Saigon on November 28–29, the MACV commander said that the Saigon government's

---

* Launched on December 5, 1965, Tiger Hound was another U.S. aerial anti-infiltration program and was confined to the extreme southeastern sector of Laos adjacent to the South Vietnamese border. For a discussion of the beginning of the Tiger Hound program, see Jacob Van Staaveren, *Interdiction in Southern Laos, 1960–1968,* (Center AF Hist, 1994), pp 80, 85, and 96–105.

President Johnson and Secretary of State Rusk.

instability had increased, pacification was stalled, and South Vietnamese army desertions had skyrocketed. He said he would need a total of 400,000 troops by the end of 1966 and possibly 200,000 more by the end of 1967. As a result of this somber assessment, when he returned to Washington, McNamara led a number of key presidential advisers who were convinced that, because military victory was not certain in South Vietnam, more vigorous diplomatic effort was necessary. Only Secretary of State Rusk strongly opposed the bombing halt.

McNamara also believed that a lengthy bombing pause would provide the Soviet Union with an opportunity to exert pressure on Hanoi to begin talks, test the "remote" possibility that its leaders would attend a negotiation conference, and possibly widen the breach between China and the Soviet Union. In the event that the pause was followed by more intensive military operations in South and North Vietnam, it would reduce the likelihood of a Soviet military response. McNamara and the principal presidential advisers marshaled all the foregoing arguments during the first three weeks of December 1965 to convince an initially reluctant President Johnson to approve a longer cessation of Rolling Thunder operations.[27]

As long as the Rolling Thunder pause continued, the Defense Secretary would receive daily photoreconnaissance findings of DRV movements from USAF Lt. Gen. Joseph F. Carroll, the DIA Director. If Hanoi took advantage of the pause, McNamara said he was "prepared to recommend [an] immediate bombing resumption." He also directed the services to transfer strike sorties normally scheduled for the north to the Laotian infiltration routes and asked for a plan for accomplishing this.[28]

As December 1965 ended and the north remained bomb-free for the first time since the five-day suspension in May, the President's diplomatic offensive to bring Hanoi to the negotiating table moved into high gear.

The leaders of seven nations met in 1966 for a conference on Southeast Asia. Gathered on the steps of the Congress of the Philippines are: (left to right) Prime Minister Nguyen Cao Ky of Vietnam; Prime Minister Keith Holyoake of New Zealand; President Park Chung Hee of Korea; President Ferdinand E. Marcos of the Philippines; Prime Minister Harold Holt of Australia; Prime Minister Thanon Kittikachorn of Thailand; and President Lyndon B. Johnson of the United States.

CHAPTER 8
Diplomacy Fails

New Year's Day 1966 dawned and North Vietnam was still free of American fighter-bombers as the administration's diplomatic initiative continued. Washington officials were unconvinced that the gambit would succeed, so they continued to develop plans to renew the bombing and to deploy large numbers of U.S. and allied air, ground, and naval units to the war theater. There was no surcease of lively debate on these two crucial subjects between Secretary McNamara and his aides on one side, and the JCS and top military commanders on the other. On the bombing issue, the services—especially the Air Force—still urged the immediate resumption of Rolling Thunder operations with fewer restrictions than in 1965.

Hanoi Rejects American Peace Overtures

The U.S. peace initiative, championed by McNamara and code-named Marigold, was orchestrated by President Johnson personally. It was a highly publicized effort, which entailed some of the nation's most distinguished officials winging their way around the world to consult with foreign statesmen and to solicit their understanding and support for America's military and political objectives. The most active traveler was Ambassador-at-Large W. Averell Harriman, while others were Hubert H. Humphrey, Vice President of the United States, Arthur Goldberg, U.S. Ambassador to the United Nations, and McGeorge Bundy, Special Assistant to the President for National Security Affairs. In total, thirty-four capitals in friendly, neutral, and communist countries were visited.* At the State Department, American officials met with numerous ambassadors to the United States. The President sent personal letters to several heads of state and to the chiefs of all 115 delegations to the United Nations, in which he emphasized the United States was prepared to negotiate with Hanoi "without prior conditions." In amplification of the American position for beginning negotiations, on December 23, 1965, Secretary of State Rusk proposed "twelve points"—enlarged to "fourteen points" on January 2, 1966—for transmittal to Hanoi.†[1]

---

* For brief summaries of different perspectives on the diplomatic initiative, see Lyndon B. Johnson, *The Vantage Point: Perspectives of the Presidency, 1963–1965* (New York, 1971), pp 233–40; George C. Herring, *LBJ and Vietnam: A Different Kind of War* (Austin, 1994), pp 99–111; and Robert S. McNamara with Brian VanDeMark, *In Retrospect, The Tragedy and Lessons of Vietnam* (New York, 1995), pp 227–31.

† Because the Hungarian government was serving as an intermediary between Washington and Hanoi in late 1965, Rusk's "fourteen points" were initially sent to Hanoi secretly through the Hungarian ambassador to the United States. They were summarized publicly in a White House statement on January 2, 1966 entitled: "The Heart of the Matter in Vietnam." See Janos Radvanyi, *Delusion and Reality Gambits: Hoaxes, and Diplomatic One-Upmanship in Vietnam* (South Bend, 1978), pp 101–12.

The fourteen points cited past U.S. statements on the Southeast Asia war that could be the basis for negotiations. In summary, the United States' position was that the peace could be based on provisions of the 1954 and 1962 Geneva Agreements or in the context of a Southeast Asia conference: unconditional discussions or negotiations would be possible, and a ceasefire arrangement would be the first order of business; Hanoi's four points could be discussed and the Viet Cong could be represented in discussions and meetings; and free elections could be held in South Vietnam to enable the people to choose their own government. In addition, the countries of Southeast Asia could choose to be nonaligned or neutral; there was no U. S. desire to maintain bases in Southeast Asia or troops in South Vietnam; the United States could make a minimum contribution of one billion dollars to a Southeast Asia regional reconstruction program; and there could be a permanent bombing halt if Hanoi took appropriate reciprocal action towards peace.[2]

Although the initiative was applauded at home and in many foreign countries, North Vietnam's truculent reaction offered no hope of success. On January 2, 1966, the newspaper *Nhan Dan* denounced the Goldberg and Humphrey diplomatic missions as "a noisy propaganda campaign." On the 4th, Radio Hanoi charged that the American peace effort was "a mere attempt to appease public opinion at home and abroad" and insisted peace could come only with an unconditional end to the bombing and acceptance of Hanoi's "four points" (made public on April 13, 1965).* On the 7th, a five-man Soviet mission, led by Alexander S. Shelepin, Secretary of the Communist Party Central Committee, arrived in Hanoi to arrange for more military and economic aid for the Hanoi regime. On the 24th, in a message to world communist leaders, President Ho Chi Minh reiterated his government's position requiring U.S. acceptance of the "four points," and also of the Viet Cong National Liberation Front as the sole representative of the South Vietnamese people as the basis for ending the war. Meanwhile, the Air Force and Navy, conducting special reconnaissance missions over the north, likewise found no evidence along roads and rail lines to suggest that Hanoi's leaders were amenable to "talks" or "negotiations."[3]

The special reconnaissance missions were launched immediately after bombing was halted on December 24, 1965. Air Force and Navy pilots concentrated on route packages 1 and 2 in the southernmost part of the country, although other areas were not wholly neglected. By February 3, four days after Rolling Thunder resumed and despite frequently poor weather, Air Force RF–101s and RF–4Cs had flown 498 sorties from their bases at Tan Son Nhut and Udorn; the

---

* On February 1, a DRV representative in Rangoon, Burma, would inform the United States that Radio Hanoi's statement of January 4, 1966, was his government's official response to the American peace initiative. Allen G. Goodman, *The Lost Peace: America's Search for a Negotiated Settlement of the War* (Stanford, 1978), p 35.

Lt. Gen. Nguyen Van Thieu, Vietnamese Chief of State, meets members of Detachment 4, 4th Air Commando Squadron, at Da Nang Air Base, January 1966.

Navy had flown 283 sorties. A number of RB–57Es and EB–66s also flew missions, the first to obtain photo and infrared data, the second to gather electronic intelligence and to conduct electronic countermeasures, chiefly against SA–2 SAMs. North Vietnamese air defenders, who considered U.S. reconnaissance to be as intolerable as combat aircraft, shot down one RF–101 on 26 January. The pilot ejected safely and was presumed captured.[4]

Although reconnaissance data was fragmentary, it confirmed that the North Vietnamese were taking full advantage of the bombing suspension and clearly expected air attacks to resume. On January 20, General McConnell informed a joint session of the House Armed Services and Appropriations Committees that the enemy was rebuilding routes and freely moving supplies and troops southward in daytime. He disclosed later that ten more SA–2 sites were detected during the suspension, bringing the total to at least sixty. Admiral Sharp's analysts found forty more air defense positions along or in the vicinity of the northwest rail line and twenty-six more antiaircraft guns to protect routes south of Vinh. Despite all of this reconnaissance data, McNamara remained committed to a lengthy pause to facilitate negotiations. On February 3, four days after bombing resumed, General Wheeler informed a House committee that the North Vietnamese "worked around the clock rebuilding bridges, building fords, and otherwise improving LOCs, and they were moving things...in daylight." The magnitude of the infiltration (during the thirty-seven-day period) was not yet clear, he noted, but the effect would show up in South Vietnam in the next sixty or ninety days. Asked to evaluate the consequences of the bombing halt, the JCS chairman opined, diplomatically, that the halt's adverse military impact had to be weighed against the President's effort to find peace and against the domestic and foreign relations gains that flowed therefrom.[5]

Trucks cross a pontoon bridge, bypassing downed Dong Lac highway bridge in North Vietnam, February 1966.

Debate on Resuming the Bombing

Concurrently with the peace initiative and reconnaissance operations, the JCS, Air Force, Navy, and administration officials debated the scope of Rolling Thunder operations if the President ordered their resumption. Throughout 1965, as noted, the services—except the Army—had been at sword's point with the administration over the weight of bombing, insisting on a harder-hitting program with fewer restraints. Except for an occasional JCS consensus, however, service disagreement over the war's strategy remained unresolved. The Air Force and Navy particularly desired to force the Hanoi regime to cease its support for the Viet Cong insurgency in the south by an air and sea campaign, in contrast with the administration, backed by the Army, which was inclined to defeat the VC-NVA in a ground-oriented war.

As the bombing halt entered its second week, the Air Staff launched another major effort to alter the thinking of the Army and the administration. General McConnell asked Air Force specialists at the Air University at Maxwell AFB, Alabama, for an "historical study" on opposition to a strategy envisaging the use of large U.S. ground forces in Southeast Asia and elsewhere on the Asian mainland. He also solicited the views of Lt. Gen. Glen W. Martin, the Inspector General of the Air Force, on ways to persuade the Johnson administration to alter its ground-oriented outlook.[6]

Responding quickly, General Martin observed:

> it is clear that both our strategy related to Southeast Asia and our tactics in South Vietnam have failed to achieve the desired results. In summary, we should consider the possibility we have committed a tactical blunder in the north through our piecemeal [bombing] approach and [committed] a major strategic error in the south by designing our plan fundamentally around ground operation concepts which reflect the enemy's greatest strength.

The Inspector General was not optimistic about the chances of change in the course of the war soon, as the President and his key advisers, he said, were convinced they had a "delicate problem" in dealing with American public support for the war. Nonetheless, he made five air-oriented proposals, which if judiciously worded and "not too radical and sweeping in nature," could conceivably influence the administration's position: encourage U.S. military discussions with the Thai government on making Thailand a stronger bulwark against communism; deploy or redeploy selected strategic and tactical units, including air defense, to Taiwan, Korea, and Japan to reassure those allies and deter Chinese air deployments south; interdict a minimum number of significant air, land, and sea transportation targets that could have a major, possibly decisive, impact on the north's access to supplies; request security for air units and airbases in South Vietnam in a manner that would emphasize the importance of air, rather than ground, operations; and underscore the opinions of most U.S. intelligence agencies that Chinese entry into the war was unlikely. The Air Force should also point out, he added, that if China entered the war, the services could initiate "highly selective" air attacks against the country in consonance with CINCPAC's Operations Plan 39-65 and demonstrate to Mao Tse-tung that he had far more to lose than to gain. The Air Force's position on the Soviet Union should be that, as they had a vested interest in keeping China out of the war, their reactions to a more assertive U.S. air policy would be political rather than military.[7]

Meanwhile, on January 6, McConnell informed Air Force Secretary Harold Brown that it would be very difficult for the Air Force to support the large ground forces in South Vietnam envisaged in deployment plans prepared by MACV and PACOM and sent to the JCS by Admiral Sharp in December 1965. These plans projected an escalation in movements of U.S. personnel to Southeast Asia, mostly to South Vietnam, in 1966. By the end of the year there would be 486,500 American air, ground, and navy personnel (of which 55,000 would be Air Force) in the south and 169,000 additional personnel in Thailand and other PACOM areas, notably Japan, Taiwan, and the Philippines. The Air Force would have to provide sixteen more tactical fighter squadrons (in addition to those already in the war theater) with four squadrons scheduled to arrive by the end of March. McConnell said this would require the withdrawal of some Air Force units from Europe, and transform most tactical fighter squadrons in

A ford, far left, bypasses this destroyed bridge.

the United States into training and rotation organizations. He feared a weakening of the visible U.S. deterrent around the periphery of China and elsewhere in the world. He called for the federalization of national guard units, as had the JCS. He continued:

> In my evaluation of additional force requirements, I'm concerned not enough consideration is being given to the problem of greatest importance: the maintenance of a viable, flexible, and credible military posture measured against the worldwide communist threat. The real threat to U.S. objectives and interest still remains China in the Western Pacific, and the USSR in Europe and against the continental United States. Therefore, while recognizing the immediacy and seriousness of the conflict in Southeast Asia, I believe we should view it in the perspective of the overall threat and examine alternate solutions and strategies to achieve our overall objectives.

He urged adoption of a strategy based on the concept of a Vietnam paper initially approved by the JCS on August 27, 1965.* The paper postulated three major objectives of equal priority in the war: force Hanoi to end its support for the Viet Cong; defeat the Viet Cong and extend the control of the Saigon government over all of South Vietnam; finally, deter the Chinese and, if necessary, defeat them. There should be continuous evaluation of progress toward these goals as a guide to future deployments.

The way to implement this strategy, McConnell continued, was to end the bombing pause over North Vietnam "dramatically" and "forcefully," relying on

---

* JCSM-652-65, 27 Aug 65.

American technical superiority—air power—for striking at the heart of the DRV-supported insurgency in the south rather than fighting a war of attrition. This could shorten the conflict by months, or possibly years, and arrest the decline of the U.S. military posture. He cited recent national intelligence estimates indicating that neither Hanoi nor Peking were likely to introduce substantially more combat troops into the war as a result of intensified air strikes. "I am... convinced," he concluded, "that before additional forces are deployed to Southeast Asia, serious consideration... be given to this proposal."[8]

In transmitting McConnell's views to McNamara on January 10, Secretary Brown characterized them as "revealing" and "challenging" and meriting "serious consideration" before a final decision was made to increase U.S. strength in Southeast Asia as Admiral Sharp had recommended. He also provided McNamara with an initial analysis of the Air Force's manpower, aircraft, and ammunition resources and of its training and field requirements to support Sharp's 1966 deployment proposals, noting the "lead time" and foreign government clearances needed for some units.[9]

The Air Force continued its challenge of the current strategy in late January. General William H. Blanchard, the Vice Commander of the Air Force, informed Deputy Secretary of Defense Cyrus R. Vance that the Air Force had not yet approved the Westmoreland-Sharp deployment proposals and that, without an evaluation of the effectiveness of forces in South Vietnam and until an intensified air campaign was conducted against the north, "the deployment of more American forces to Southeast Asia could not be justified." In his testimony before the House Armed Services and Appropriations Committee, McConnell urged a quick resumption of the Rolling Thunder program. The longer the bombing halt, the more costly it would be in American lives. "...a decisive military victory cannot be achieved," he emphasized, "unless military targets in both South...and North Vietnam are bombed...." McConnell also said that upwards of 600,000 U.S. and allied troops could not drive the enemy out of the south and keep them out.[10]

Meanwhile, McConnell joined the other service chiefs in advising McNamara on January 8 that the protracted bombing halt could prove costly in lives, as was learned in the Korean War. The intensified air campaign in South Vietnam and Laos could not compensate for no air attacks on the north. Thus, early resumption of Rolling Thunder was imperative to avoid any misinterpretation of America's resolve in Southeast Asia, to redress the military disadvantages, and to permit negotiations from a position of strength. A five-man delegation from the Soviet Union was in Hanoi to discuss more economic and military assistance for North Vietnam. The Joint Chiefs recommended that Rolling Thunder operations begin shortly after the delegation, headed by Alexander S. Shelepin, returned to Moscow and the results of its visit were communicated to Washington. In Saigon, Ambassador Lodge and General Westmoreland strongly supported JCS efforts to end the bombing halt and resume air strikes on the north.[11]

On the 18th, the Joint Chiefs suggested to McNamara four ways to resume the bombing and quickly exert more pressure on the Hanoi regime: by a "sharp blow," as recommended initially on November 23, 1964;* by closing Haiphong and other cities through which most of the "identifiable" imports reached North Vietnam in 1965, despite the sensitivity of mining operations;† by reducing the bombing sanctuary areas to a radius of ten nautical miles around Hanoi and Phuc Yen airfield, four nautical miles around Haiphong and twenty nautical miles along the border between North Vietnam and China, with exceptions permitted only by the JCS; and by the removal of armed reconnaissance sortie limits and air strike restrictions. Continued U.S. restraint, they said, probably increased rather than decreased the risk of Chinese intervention in the war and signaled American military vacillation to both communist and free world leaders.[12]

Other administration officials were more apprehensive about unleashing a heavy bombing program on the north. The most ominous view was expressed by George Ball, Under Secretary of State, who warned the President on January 25 "that sustained bombing of North Vietnam will more than likely lead us into a war with Red China—possibly in six to nine months." Further, it could trigger a possible limited war with the Soviet Union.

McNamara's position was less apocalyptic. He strongly recommended continued restraint with regard to bombing. Summarizing the war's progress for the President on the 24th, he urged that air attacks be confined largely to the north's routes, as in 1965. He cited the various ways in which limited bombing had diminished Hanoi's military capability and raised its war costs: the quantity of enemy supplies, delivered mostly in trucks, had dropped from 400 to 200 tons per day; between 50,000 and 100,000 personnel had been diverted to air defense and repair work; the mobility of the populace had been hampered; government activities had been decentralized, creating inefficiency and political risk; and military operations in Laos had been reduced. Continued (limited) bombing of the north and Laos would also weaken the VC-NVA's capability to launch frequent offensives against U.S., allied, and South Vietnamese troops and boost the latter's morale. If Rolling Thunder was resumed, the Defense Secretary suggested flying about 4,000 day and night armed reconnaissance sorties per month‡ in the north, more intense bombing of Laos, and better surveillance of the sea approaches to South Vietnam. In the latter country, there should be more harassment of the enemy's LOCs and destruction of its bases. He listed

---

* JCSM-982-64, 23 Nov 64.

† A DIA study of North Vietnam's imports in January 1966 indicated that about 67 percent arrived by sea and 33 percent by rail from China, while roads from China carried only a negligible amount (JCSM-41-66, 18 Jan 66).

‡ This would approximate the attack sorties flown in September 1965, the highest monthly total flown in that year.

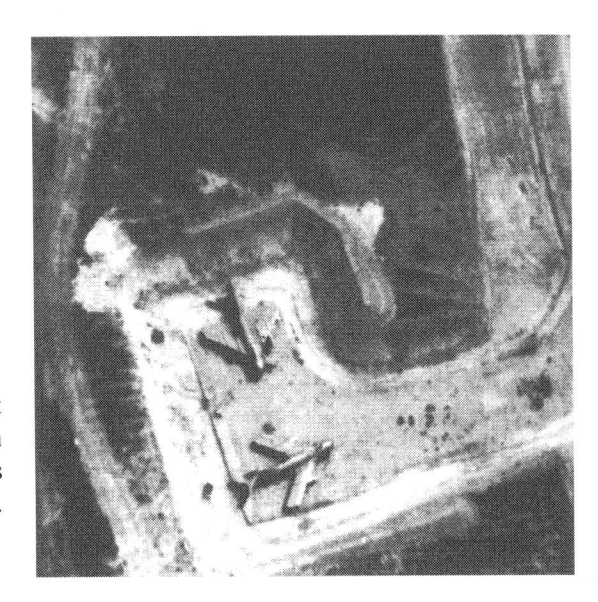

Two MiG–17 jet fighters at Phuc Yen airfield, twenty miles northwest of Hanoi.

several objectives for the south during 1966 that were quickly approved by the President and Prime Minister Nguyen Cao Ky at a meeting in Honolulu early in February.[13]

Before a House Subcommittee on Appropriations on the 26th, McNamara restated the administration's previous arguments against an all-out bombing offensive in the north: bombing alone could not force Hanoi to negotiate unless it was accompanied by military action in the south sufficient to prove it could not win there; Hanoi, Haiphong, and other ports and certain POL installations had not been and could not be bombed lest such action trigger a wider war (with China, the Soviet Union, or both); and targets would continue to be carefully controlled. Air Force Secretary Brown held essentially the same views. These views contrasted sharply with those held by the Air Force.[14]

The likelihood that the President would resume Rolling Thunder was signaled by Secretary Rusk on January 21 in a news conference where he expressed regret at his inability to report "any positive and encouraging response" from North Vietnam to end the war. The prospect of a less intense bombing campaign than prior to late 1965 was portended by William P. Bundy, Assistant Secretary of State for Far Eastern Affairs. He believed that for two or three weeks after bombing began, while the world was still "digesting" the impact of the bombing pause, the United States should do as little as possible to fuel likely communist charges that the pause was a prelude to a more volatile air campaign. John T. McNaughton, Assistant Secretary of Defense for International Security Affairs, agreed that the situation did not argue for a "noisy" resumption of bombing. He recommended bombing initially at the same level as before the pause, followed by an escalation in the tempo perhaps two weeks later.[15]

As for the precise geographical limits for the next Rolling Thunder program, Bundy recommended keeping Air Force and Navy aircraft below the 20th parallel. The State Department's intelligence office more precisely suggested confining the bombing to the region south and southeast of the Song Ca River in southern North Vietnam, a river which flowed into the Gulf of Tonkin just below Vinh. The smaller area, the office claimed, would assure more interdiction effectiveness and minimize the risk of Chinese intervention in the war. State's views would shortly prove generally congruent with President Johnson's thinking on where to reinstate the bombing program.[16]

The Joint Chiefs, painfully aware that their hard-hitting recommendations for renewing Rolling Thunder were unpalatable to the administration, sent three new bombing proposals to McNamara on January 25, all restrictive or escalating slowly. The first called for a "maximum" armed reconnaissance program throughout the north except for the Hanoi-Haiphong sanctuary area. All available USAF aircraft based in Thailand as well as planes from three Navy carriers would maintain a level of 450 strike sorties per day for twenty-four to seventy-two hours against major land and water LOCs, ferries, vehicles, pontoons, bridges, and similar types of targets. A second proposal envisaged an initial armed reconnaissance campaign of only 600 attack sorties per week in southern North Vietnam, then a gradually rising tempo until bombing attained the level recommended by the JCS on January 18. The third proposal provided for the use of only Navy aircraft from three carriers against the north's POL system for twenty-four to seventy-two hours and USAF and Navy armed reconnaissance against all LOCs. The least effective proposal, the Joint Chiefs said, would be the second one, as southern North Vietnam contained few important targets and the geographical restriction could be misconstrued by Hanoi as evidence that the United States had established a new sanctuary area above the permitted bombing area. Each proposal, they added, should begin without prior warning to the Hanoi regime. That McNamara leaned towards the adoption of some variation of proposal one was indicated the same day when General Wheeler requested, and Admiral Sharp quickly sent, a more detailed armed reconnaissance scenario in which POL targets associated only with rest stops, dispersal areas, and sites generally related to LOCs would be among the primary targets. The PACOM commander suggested apportioning the 450 strikes per day in the lower four route packages. General Westmoreland "sweetened" the proposal by flashing his willingness to give up fifty sorties in South Vietnam to assure a first-day level of 500 strike sorties.[17]

Rolling Thunder 48

As January neared its end and Hanoi's leaders remained totally unresponsive to Washington's peace overtures, President Johnson, after consulting with Congressional leaders and the National Security Council, ordered the resumption of Rolling Thunder. He approved a bombing scenario roughly in consonance with Admiral Sharp's hastily revised proposal and agreed to a little more flexibility for air commanders. Sharp's implementing directive to Admiral Johnson and Generals Harris and Westmoreland ordered the resumption of Rolling Thunder 48 on January 31, Saigon time. The precise moment was left to the Air Force and Navy commanders, except for the proviso that the first strike should be made before daylight and achieve surprise. However, the directive's guidelines were disheartening to the air commanders: both the tempo and permissible bombing area were more constricted than before the bombing halt had begun on December 24, 1965.[18]

Bombing for Rolling Thunder 48 was to be south and west of a line due west from the coast at latitude 20°31'N to longitude 105°20'E, then due north to 21°N, then due west to the Laos border. A maximum daily strike level of only 300 sorties—rather than 450 or 500—was established, Sharp allocating 120 sorties to the Air Force and 180 for the Navy's two carriers assigned to Rolling Thunder. Sorties would be apportioned, with route packages 2 and 3 receiving the majority of the sorties. Strike aircraft should concentrate on moving targets along infiltration routes leading into Laos and the principal north-south rail, highway, and waterway routes, with second priority for pontoon bridges, truck parks, and transshipment and dispersed storage areas. Targets designated by the JCS within the authorized area could be struck again if necessary. Iron Hand operations against SA–2 SAM sites would be limited to the authorized geographical area and collateral damage, as usual, kept to a minimum.

No VNAF strikes should be scheduled for the first day. Thereafter they could fly armed reconnaissance missions between the DMZ and the 19th parallel, as previously. Until further notice, all VNAF sorties should be included within the authorized ceiling of 300 sorties per day. Rolling Thunder 48 was unique in that it had no termination date, thus ending the one-week and two-week planning cycles that had existed throughout 1965.[19]

However, poor flying weather and the lack of good targets combined to yield an inauspicious beginning on the morning of January 31. The first five Air Force F–105 missions were weathered out, and the pilots returned to their bases with their ordnance.

A sixth Thunderchief mission finally broke through overcast skies to strike at targets along Route 1A in route package 1, expending 152 2.75-inch rockets with undetermined results. Four Navy A–4s and a single F–4 mission followed a few hours later, making two road cuts with 250-pound bombs while attacking a small bridge. Throughout the first day, only fifty-eight Air Force strike aircraft became airborne, but finding only ten targets, many diverted to Laos to hit secondary targets in the Steel Tiger area. A total of fifty-eight scheduled sorties were canceled because of weather. Navy pilots fared somewhat better. They flew sixty-six sorties and declared fifty "effective," while the rest, finding no suitable targets, jettisoned their ordnance over Tiger Island just off the North Vietnamese coast. By day's end, aircrews of the two services had struck

An F–4B launches from the USS *Franklin Roosevelt*.

a number of small bridges, vehicles, and cut and cratered many roads. Enemy air defense units, still vigilant, shot down an Air Force F–105, a Navy A–4, and a Navy F–4B. Operations personnel adjudged the first day's bombings as achieving little surprise and inflicting undetermined losses on the enemy.[20]

President Johnson made no public announcement regarding Rolling Thunder's resumption until February 1. "Our strikes... from the beginning have been aimed at military targets and controlled with great care. Those who direct and supply the aggression have no claim to immunity from military reply." Other administration officials informed the news media that, while bombing the north would be limited, military operations in South Vietnam against the VC and NVA would intensify. For example, they predicted heavier use of B–52s and ground artillery.[21]

The following days found no basic change in the low tempo and restricted bombing operations over the north. The 300 sorties per day rule remained in effect throughout February, although weather usually prevented pilots from achieving this total. To surmount the weather problem, the Seventh Air Force began employing a synchronous radar bombing procedure in which B–66Bs led F–105 and F–4C fighter-bombers on their bombing runs.[22]

Known as the "radar pathfinder buddy bombing technique," this tactic consisted of a B–66B pathfinder leading a formation of four, eight, or twelve aircraft across a target at an altitude above 15,000 feet. The B–66B navigator, using a K–5 bombing navigation system, determined the bomb release point for the formation. Throughout the bombing run, the pathfinder employed its S-band jammers to suppress radar-controlled antiaircraft (Fire Can) guns. After the formation released its bombs, the pathfinder continued its Fire Can jamming while circling over the target area. Meanwhile, the fighter-bombers broke away and, with unspent ordnance and weather permitting, completed their missions at a lower altitude, striking targets of opportunity. During the month, aircrews flew eighty-two of

KC–135 tankers at Takhli Royal Thai Air Force Base, January 1966.

these radar-guided strike missions, and they accounted for about 95 percent of all bombs dropped on the north. In addition to assuring more accurate bombing under adverse weather conditions, the B–66Bs obtained valuable radar coverage of the north, with the data sent to Headquarters USAF and SAC for inclusion in their respective radar film libraries. In late February, three SAC officers were sent to General Moore's headquarters to assist target planners in refining the technique for finding and bombing targets developed by radar. The Navy relied chiefly on its A–6As for bad weather and night operations.[23]

The only significant variation from routine armed reconnaissance missions in February was a series of strikes against Dien Bien Phu airfield and associated buildings, as well as installations in route packages. Ambassador Sullivan in Vientiane believed the airfield complex, a target designated by the JCS, was a major staging base for infiltrating men and supplies into Laos and should be struck. Air Force photo reconnaissance disclosed that the southern end of the runway had been graded and extended, and high-priority cargo, possibly airdropped, was stacked adjacent to the runway. After Sullivan's request was approved at the highest levels in Washington, General Wheeler directed Admiral Sharp to "neutralize the military activity there." Sharp gave the assignment to General Harris (who relayed it to General Moore) with instructions to await good weather to assure a successful strike and to ask Navy for strike support in the event that the Air Force could not attack both Dien Bien Phu and infiltration routes in route packages 2 and 4 within its daily allocation of 120 sorties.[24]

On February 6, the weather over northwest North Vietnam cleared sufficiently to permit General Moore to dispatch four morning and one afternoon strike missions against the Dien Bien Phu complex, employing a total of seventeen

An HU–16 at Tan Son Nhut Air Base in 1965, with a Navy A–3 and several F–8s behind it to the left and an Air Force F–4 and C–124 to the right.

F–105s, four F–4Cs, and several KC–135s. Pilots initially believed their 750-pound bombs severely cratered the runway and destroyed twelve or more structures. However, subsequent reconnaissance showed that the target area was only marginally damaged and the runway had not been cratered. As a result, Wheeler persuaded McNamara to include Dien Bien Phu henceforth in the authorized armed reconnaissance area and to continue the strikes. Accordingly, on February 15 General Moore sent eight more F–105s against the target area, and there were two more missions the next day, one consisting of four Thunderchiefs and another consisting of four Thunderchiefs and two Navy A–1 Skyraiders. The attacks destroyed some additional structures.[25]

In the latter part of February, General Moore made a concerted attempt to obtain approval for armed reconnaissance along the vital Hanoi to Lao Cai rail line, also in route package 5. Because of the extended bombing halt, he said, the North Vietnamese had been able to make this vital transportation artery from China operational again. He proposed beginning with strikes against the Yen Bai and the Phu Tho railyards, then cutting the rail line between Yen Bai and Lao Cai, but higher authorities insisted on keeping these targets "off limits."[26]

As in 1965, most estimates of attrition visited upon the North Vietnamese by air attacks were based on pilot reports, although little of it was verifiable by bomb damage assessment missions because of the poor flying conditions. For example, for one fourteen-day period (February 4–17), pilots claimed to have destroyed and damaged, respectively, the following targets: vehicles, 21 and 11; rivercraft, 29 and 37; bridges, 16 and 60; structures, 47 and 56; antiaircraft sites, 2 and 2. In addition, 4 radar sites were damaged, the Dien Bien Phu runway was hit twice, and 215 road cuts were made. As Admiral Sharp allocated the largest share of the authorized daily 300 strike sorties to the Navy (180 versus

A downed pilot swims to an Air Force HU–16.

120 to the Air Force), Navy reports of destroyed and damaged targets were larger than those of the Air Force.[27]

Both the relatively low level of air operations in February—2,809 Air Force and Navy attack sorties—and the confinement of most sorties to the lower four route packages, meant that aircraft attrition was low. The Air Force lost only two aircraft during the month, an F–105 to unknown causes and an EB–66E to an SA–2 SAM, fired from the vicinity of Vinh, the southernmost firing of a SAM yet. Although few SA–2 firings were observed, one missile scored on the 25th when it exploded behind the EB–66E flying an electronic countermeasures mission at about 28,000 feet. The weapon disabled the aircraft's control system, forcing the crew of six to bail out over the Tonkin Gulf. An Air Force HU–16 and several Navy helicopters reached the area of the downed men quickly and rescued all but one from the rough waters of the Gulf. North Vietnamese Air Force MiGs offered no challenges, although American pilots saw a number of them.[28]

More Deployment Planning

The debate leading to the resumption of Rolling Thunder in no way detracted from the administration's plans to send more air, ground, and sea units to the war theater. At the end of 1965, 184,346 American personnel were stationed in South Vietnam and 14,107 in Thailand, with the Air Force accounting for 20,620 and 9,117 respectively in the two countries. The Air Force had

536 aircraft on eight bases in South Vietnam, principally to prosecute the in-country war, although many missions were also directed against North Vietnamese and Laotian targets, and 205 aircraft on six bases in Thailand. For strike and strike support operations throughout the war theater, the Air Force had a variety of air commando, fighter-interceptor, tactical fighter-bomber, and tactical fighter squadrons. Until the bombing halt in December 1965, the Air Force relied principally on eleven tactical fighter squadrons for the air programs in North Vietnam and Laos: six F–4C Phantom squadrons (of which four were based in South Vietnam and two in Thailand), and five F–105 Thunderchief squadrons based in Thailand.[29]

A prerequisite for any rapid deployment of additional Air Force, Army, and Marine Corps units was airbase accommodation. In early 1966, airbase congestion was becoming severe, as slippage affected the improvement or new construction of four major bases in South Vietnam and two in Thailand. Work began on three of the six bases in 1965: Cam Ranh Bay (which possessed only an emergency air strip) and Phan Rang in South Vietnam and Sattahip in Thailand. Work had not begun at Tuy Hoa in South Vietnam, and two new major airbase sites, one each in South Vietnam and Thailand, remained to be designated.[30]

To some extent, especially in South Vietnam, expansion of airbases was temporarily hostage to a roles and mission conflict between the Air Force and the Navy. General McConnell believed that Admiral Sharp and other Navy leaders in PACOM were dragging their feet over construction decisions until they had decided whether to add a fourth aircraft carrier to the Pacific Fleet's force in the Tonkin Gulf. Air Force dependence on Army and Navy construction units for its major engineering needs represented a further problem. These two services were inclined to give higher priority to building ports and supply depots than to airfields. In May 1966, to overcome this obstacle, the Air Staff, with Secretary Brown's support, obtained OSD approval to hire a private U.S. construction firm to build one of the badly needed airbases at Tuy Hoa.[31]

However, the airbase problem did nothing to alter the administration's tentative plans, drafted in late 1965, to deploy upwards of 300,000 more U.S. and allied troops, plus supporting Air Force and other service air units, over the next twelve months. To determine more precisely how this should be accomplished, on January 17 Admiral Sharp convened an interservice deployment conference in Honolulu. To the dismay of the Air Force, the three-week proceedings again confirmed the administration's intent to pursue a ground-oriented strategy in the war.[32]

In early February, Admiral Sharp and other briefers summarized planning results for McNamara and his aides, who attended the closing sessions of the conference. The PACOM commander observed how estimates of future American air, ground, and naval strength in South Vietnam had evolved in 1965 through four planning phases: phase I, 220,000; phase II, 112,400; phase IIA, 57,500; and phase IIA (revised), 68,900. This would place nearly 459,000 U.S.

military personnel in the south by the end of 1966. A need for about 45,000 additional allied troops would boost the combined U.S. and allied total to 504,000. Subtracting those already in the country, a total of 274,700 U.S. and 23,900 allied (Korean, Australian, and New Zealand) personnel would have to be deployed during the year. U.S. forces in Thailand and other PACOM areas such as South Korea, Japan, Okinawa, and the Philippines, would rise to 172,000 personnel.[33]

On the basis of 459,000 U.S. personnel, Sharp calculated the possible contribution from each service to satisfy three "cases," each based on different "assumptions" of what the administration would approve to achieve three different manpower levels, and the likely "shortfalls" in each case (figure 9).

Figure 9
Personnel Shortfalls

	Case I		Case II		Case III	
	Programmed	Shortfall	Programmed	Shortfall	Programmed	Shortfall
Air Force	52,000		50,000	2,000	46,000	6,000
Navy	30,000		25,000	5,000	22,000	8,000
Marine Corps	70,000		70,000		70,000	
Army	270,000	30,000	254,000	53,000	197,000	119,000
Total	422,000	30,000	399,000	60,000	335,000	133,000

Case I assumed that manpower would come from the current force structure in the United States, new unit activations, some withdrawals from overseas, callups of selected reserve units, and extensions of terms of service. Case II was based on the same assumptions as case I, except that there would be no callups of selected reserve units or extension of terms of service. Case III was the same as case II and also assumed that there would be no withdrawals from overseas.

As the figures indicate, even case I would have a shortfall of 30,000 men compared with the 459,000 that MACV considered essential for prosecuting the war in South Vietnam by the end of 1966. MACV analysts believed only this number could assure a total of 122 U.S. "maneuver" battalions, of which 102 would be in South Vietnam and 20 in the PACOM reserve. Air Force, Navy,

Air Force Secretary Harold Brown (right) talks with South Vietnamese Premier Nguyen Cao Ky during Secretary Brown's visit to South Vietnam in January 1966.

and Marine manpower totals could be attained, at least on paper, although rapid deployments of supporting units, particularly aircraft, would create serious problems. One was insufficient airbase space; another was a growing shortage of air munitions.

Addressing theaterwide air planning, the PACOM commander said that about 648,000 tons of air munitions would be available, with 700,000 tons needed during the year. Taking this limitation into account, air planners would allocate air sorties as follows: 150 per month for each U.S. and allied maneuver battalion, 7,800 per month for South Vietnamese forces, 7,100 per month for North Vietnam, and 3,000 per month for Laos. To support this schedule and to maintain the desired American air posture, planners estimated that, in addition to the Navy's three aircraft carriers in the Tonkin Gulf, tactical fighter strength at the end of 1966 should consist of eighteen USAF and ten Marine Corps squadrons in South Vietnam, and eleven USAF squadrons in Thailand. To reach this goal, the Air Force would have to deploy sixteen more tactical fighter squadrons during the year, four of them by the end of March. The SAC B–52 force would have to be enlarged so that the sortie rate could increase from 400 sorties per month in February to 600 per month for the last six months of 1966. Thus far, all B–52 sorties had been flown in South Vietnam, except for one in Laos in December 1965. The first B–52 attack in North Vietnam would not take place until 1966.[34]

McNamara expressed few opinions during the briefings, but raised several

Runway construction at Cam Ranh Bay.

questions about the air program in North Vietnam. In the course of a colloquy, the PACOM briefers informed the Defense Secretary that a Rolling Thunder campaign limited only to LOCs in the two countries would probably not significantly degrade the Hanoi regime's capability to support the war in 1966, but would reduce it somewhat by mid-1967; striking the north's harbors, rail lines, thermal power plants, POL, and other "high value" targets in addition to the LOCs would have little effect on the enemy in the first half of 1966, but would have a significant impact in 1967; and it was not necessary to strike the north's airbases until the MiGs began to interfere seriously with U.S. air operations. Then, striking them would not draw the Chinese into the war.[35]

Admiral Sharp's closing observation was that the proposed increases and ground deployments would not vitiate predictions of a long war. There was uncertainty, he said, about the services' ability to meet the deployment goals, and major difficulties loomed in establishing adequate port facilities for handling the accelerated troop and unit buildups. He sent the official results of the three-week planning conference to Washington on February 12.[36]

On his return to Washington, McNamara discussed the options with the service secretaries, the JCS, and members of his OSD staff. He directed them to proceed with the planning and deployments in accordance with case I objectives, but with the proviso that there would be no callup of the reserves or extensions of duty tours, although he did not preclude further study of these two issues.[37] His order triggered a major service planning and data assembling effort. To guide it, the Defense Secretary established an OSD Southeast Asia Program Team, chaired by Dr. Victor K. Heyman, thus bypassing the JCS and assuring that he retained personal control over planning activities. The team immediately began preparing new deployment tables containing all essential information on available manpower, aircraft, logistic, and construction resources. McNamara also directed each service to establish counterpart teams to that of Dr. Heyman's. General McConnell quickly appointed Maj. Gen. John D. Lavalle, Headquarters USAF's Director of Aerospace Programs, to head the Air Force team, which was composed of representatives from all key Air Staff offices. At the request of Secretary Brown and General McConnell, the Air Staff also created an ad hoc study group* under Col. Leroy J. Manor of the Operations Directorate. Manor's group was assigned the task of scrutinizing Sharp's tactical air proposals for Southeast Asia. At the same time, the Directorate undertook an analysis of the Air Force's tactical fighter resources.[38]

In short order, the Air Staff's plans and operations analysts designated additional Air Force squadrons, supporting aircraft, and special units for deployment by the end of 1966 (figure 10).[39]

Figure 10
Air Force Deployments, 1966

Type of Aircraft	South Vietnam	Thailand
Tactical fighters	10 sqs	6 sqs
RF–101s	4 a/c	
RF–4Cs	1 sq	14 a/c
B–66Bs	8 a/c	
RB–66Cs	13 a/c	
O–1s	68 a/c	

Special Units	South Vietnam	Thailand
Tactical Control Party	1 [a]	
Airborne Battlefield Command and Control Center		1 1
Heavy Repair Units	3	1

[a] Consisting of 122 personnel.

The foregoing deployment actions, in which the Air Force played only a minimal role, heightened Air Staff vexation, already irritated by the adminis-

---

* After its expansion on July 15, 1966, this group was renamed the Operations Review Group within the Directorate of Operations.

tration's decision to restrict the Rolling Thunder operations that resumed on January 31. PACAF representatives at the Honolulu conference criticized the proceedings harshly in a report sent to the Air Staff by Maj. Gen. John W. Vogt, PACAF's Deputy Chief of Staff for Plans and Operations. According to Vogt's report, the three proposals were prepared almost solely by Westmoreland's staff, with little participation by the component services. Similarly, evaluations of past and future air operations in North Vietnam were readied principally by PACOM's staff. The report characterized the deployment data as "a purely mathematical development of the effectiveness of U.S.-Free World forces against the VC-NVA." PACAF attendees had only a day and a half to comment on the data and evaluations presented to McNamara and his aides, and no opportunity to change the ground rules for developing the three proposals. PACAF's comments were limited to injecting a more optimistic assessment of the air campaigns in North Vietnam and Laos and stressing the interrelationship of three separate air campaigns in the theater.[40]

General McConnell considered "unrealistic" the administration's refusal to call up reservists and extend terms of service and "insufficient" a proposed $1.2 billion allocation to support the air buildup. The Air Staff's view of the evolving deployment scenario was predictably in consonance with its strategic outlook: the trend towards U.S. and allied "matching" of enemy manpower was wrong, and proper use of air and naval power would make the sizeable troop deployments unnecessary. There were also practical considerations. The air munitions shortage (if exacerbated by a larger ground war in South Vietnam) would not be surmounted until the January–March 1967 period, and there would be slippages in the airbase construction and expansion program. If the case I deployment scenario was followed, the Air Force could meet its commitments only by withdrawing most of its reconnaissance aircraft from Europe (i.e., USAFE) and weakening the Air Force's posture there, by employing more Tactical Air Command squadrons in Southeast Asia, and by diverting many USAF personnel from around the globe.[41]

Air Force Secretary Brown, whose views on the prosecution of the war were generally supportive of McNamara's, nonetheless agreed with the Air Staff's position that case I deployments would require important adjustments in the Air Force's overseas posture. He said that this would mean replacing three F–100 squadrons with two PCS squadrons from the United States, in Turkey, retention for the duration of the Southeast Asia war of a Mace missile wing* in USAFE that had been scheduled for withdrawal, converting an F–5 Skoshi Tiger unit (engaged in combat testing in South Vietnam) to a full eighteen-aircraft squadron, converting an F–102 squadron on Okinawa from TDY to PCS, and sending two more F–102 squadrons to the war theater on PCS. Early in March,

---

* The Mace was an improved version of the Matador missile.

Brown warned the Defense Secretary that the Air Staff's analysis of the impact of the case I objectives showed that even if all sixteen tactical fighter squadrons were sent in 1966, assuming "beyond all optimistic hope" there would be sufficient airfields for them, some Air Force reservists would have to assist in maintaining an adequate training base in the United States. The JCS was blunter, advising the Defense Secretary at the beginning of March that even with a "maximum effort" all military units envisaged in Admiral Sharp's proposal could not be sent in 1966. They urged that deployments be stretched out over a sixteen-month period (i.e. to be completed by June 1967, rather than compressing them into South Vietnam and Thailand in the remaining ten months of the year).[42]

The warnings were partly effective. On March 10, McNamara informed the JCS and the service secretaries that their recent recommendations needed more study. Nonetheless, pending further notice, he insisted that they continue deploying men and units in accordance with case I guidelines without calling up reservists or extending terms of service. He said that OSD's Southeast Asia Program Division would continue to develop deployment data, expedite deployments, and indicate reasons for slippages in the deployment schedule. The Defense Secretary's next major deployment decision, on March 26, would consist of revised case I tactical aircraft requirements and combat sortie levels for South Vietnam, North Vietnam and Laos.[43]

Rolling Thunder 49

Meanwhile, there was further sparring between the Joint Chiefs and McNamara over the intensity of the next Rolling Thunder program, tentatively scheduled to begin in March. During a meeting with General Wheeler on February 12, the Defense Secretary indicated that if there were sufficient aircraft and weather conditions permitted, he might be willing to approve more attack sorties and invest air commanders with more bombing flexibility. He asked about Admiral Sharp's recommendation.[44]

Wheeler queried the PACOM commander, and his reply was incorporated in a JCS paper, supported by the Air Staff, to McNamara on the 19th. Sharp advocated a minimum authorized level of 10,000 to 11,000 strike sorties per month for North Vietnam and Laos, with upwards of 7,500 sorties allocated to Rolling Thunder. He arrived at the latter figure after recent intelligence disclosed construction of more SA–2 SAM sites and the apparent deployment of more antiaircraft artillery and other air defense weapons provided by the Chinese. The high number of sorties was needed, he said, against many small targets now being struck in compensation for the administration's ban on attacking more important ones. He fully agreed that air commanders needed more latitude to hit targets without regard to sortie ceilings.

In the event that the northeast quadrant (packages 6A and 6B) remained immune from attack (as in Rolling Thunder 48), it would be desirable either to extend armed reconnaissance over the same areas in the north as existed before the thirty-seven-day bombing halt, or to reduce the size of the sanctuary areas of Hanoi and Phuc Yen airfields, Haiphong, and the buffer zone between North Vietnam and China (as recommended by the JCS on January 18, 1966). The problem with the first alternative, however, was that the most important targets in earlier approved armed reconnaissance areas had been struck, and more bombing of small targets was unlikely to induce Hanoi to cease its support of the insurgency in South Vietnam. A third option was to make available to Air Force and Navy pilots about 5,000 square miles of territory just outside the northeast quadrant containing 650 miles of major rail, highway, and water routes and eighteen targets designated by the JCS. Sharp and the JCS strongly preferred the "balanced strategy" in the JCS paper of January 18, 1966 paper, which promised the greatest military return.[45]

On February 25, the administration approved a new bombing directive for Rolling Thunder 49. It had less weight than Sharp and the Joint Chiefs desired, but it provided for more bombing over a wider geographical area than was permitted under Rolling Thunder 48. It enlarged the armed reconnaissance area, including parts of route package 5, to the size existing on December 24, 1965—one of the options suggested by Admiral Sharp—and permitted the Navy to resume coastal armed reconnaissance north of 20°31'N to within twenty-five nautical miles of the Chinese border and to within three nautical miles of North Vietnamese territory. Air commanders were authorized to fly 8,100 strike sorties per month in North Vietnam and Laos, with a recommended allocation of about 5,100 and 3,000 sorties, respectively, between the two countries. Supporting MiG combat air patrol, reconnaissance, and electronic intelligence and countermeasures were exempt from the total. And, with McNamara's approbation, there was a marked improvement in operational flexibility for air commanders. For the first time they could vary the sortie level each day as weather and other factors dictated. Admiral Sharp quickly delegated his sortie allocation authority to General Harris and Admiral Johnson or their representatives. For the time being, the PACAF and PACFLT commanders would determine jointly the overall sortie level in North Vietnam on any one day and the sortie level in each of the five route packages. Sharp similarly delegated to General Westmoreland—and to his Air Force Deputy Commander, General Moore—and to Admiral Johnson the authority to determine service sortie allocations in Laos.[46]

Numerous irritating strictures remained. DRV naval craft outside of the authorized coastal area could not be attacked until they fired on American planes; Iron Hand missions could hit only SA–2 SAM sites located within the permitted armed reconnaissance areas, no new JCS-designated targets were approved, no North Vietnamese airfields, even those used by MiGs to attack American aircraft, could be struck, and route packages 6A and 6B, with their

Diving on a target in North Vietnam, an F–105
Thunderchief fires a volley of 2.75-inch rockets.

vital rail and road links between China and the Hanoi-Haiphong sanctuary, remained off limits. General Wheeler assured Admiral Sharp that the Joint Chiefs would keep up the pressure to relax further strike rules and gain permission to hit more significant targets.[47]

There was no operational break or public announcement as Rolling Thunder 48 ended in February and Air Force and Navy commanders inaugurated Rolling Thunder 49 on March 1. Nor did the heavy monsoon weather over the north relent in the next few weeks. Commanders were forced to cancel scores of scheduled missions, which made it very difficult to assess the results of many airborne missions.[48] On many days, pilots were confronted with a low cloud ceiling or light rain and drizzle that limited flying altitudes from 1,500 to 3,000 feet and visibility to two to four miles. Clouds and fog enveloped the inland river valleys, particularly the Red River valley to Lao Cai, and often persisted throughout the day. Thunderstorms sometimes blocked out the mountain regions. The most suitable flying weather was in the mountainous region of the northwest, east of 104 degrees longitude.[49]

Despite the monsoon weather, Air Force, Navy, and VNAF pilots succeeded in flying 4,551 strike sorties or about 87.5 percent of the total authorized for the month. The VNAF, almost totally preoccupied with the war in South Vietnam, contributed a token 12 sorties on two missions. Flying 57.5 percent of the sortie total, the Air Force concentrated on targets in route packages 1, 3, and 5, while the Navy hit route packages 2 and 4. More than 500 of the Air Force sorties were flown at night: fighters were accompanied by flare-dropping aircraft or B–66Bs with special radar bombing equipment to conduct buddy-bombing strikes. The Navy carried out somewhat fewer night sorties.[50] As in February, pilots searched for vehicles, rolling stock, rivercraft, coastal junks; such fixed targets as small bridges, military structures, and logistic and antiaircraft sites; and they cut scores of roads. In route package 1 the Air Force frequently struck routes leading to and in the area around Mu Gia Pass, the major entry point from North Vietnam into southern Laos. In route package 5, the favorite targets were segments of the northwest Hanoi to Lao Cai rail line, fully repaired and carrying rolling stock again. In route package 2, Navy pilots concentrated on segments of Routes 4, 8, 14, and 15; and in route package 4, they hit routes leading to Barthelemy Pass, another important entry point into Laos. They also continued their assault on coastal junks. In the absence of good flying weather and targets, Air Force and Navy pilots attacked vehicles and logistic sites and cut roads along the Ho Chi Minh Trail in Laos.[51]

Iron Hand missions, exempt from the authorized sortie ceiling, continued to search for and, when possible, hit SA–2 SAM radar sites. Air Force EB–66s performed some of the electronic detection and countermeasures tasks, but most were conducted by Marine EF–10Bs. From March 4 to 31, the Marines flew eighty-five of these sorties, escorted by their own or by Air Force fighters. When Iron Hand missions were canceled because of poor weather, accompanying strike aircraft were diverted to flying armed reconnaissance.[52]

Despite the weather and bombing restrictions, the services believed they took a considerably higher toll of enemy resources than in February. For the four-week period of March 4–31, the services claimed to have destroyed and damaged the following: vehicles, 103 and 103; rivercraft, 63 and 177; small bridges, 46 and 90; structures, 96 and 95; and antiaircraft sites, 18 and 5. In addition, they counted 28 damaged rail cars and made at least 145 road cuts.[53]

In inflicting this damage, the two services relied on existing ordnance. The Air Force continued to use chiefly 250-pound, 500-pound, and 750-pound general-purpose bombs, especially the latter, but frequently dropped 1,000-pound, 2,000-pound, and 3,000-pound bombs on more difficult targets, and fired thousands of 2.75-inch rockets. In route package 5, pilots tried to slow traffic on segments of the Hanoi to Lao Cai rail line and some key routes by dropping MLU–10 land mines. The Navy employed chiefly 250-pound and 500-pound bombs, but also substantial numbers of 1,000-pound bombs, and they used Zuni rockets heavily. Beginning in February and continuing into March, Navy pilots tested an improved AGM–45 Shrike air-to-surface missile against SA–2 SAM and other antiaircraft radar sites; but weather, combined with the mobility of the SAM and other air defense equipment, made damage assessment very difficult. General Moore's Seventh Air Force pilots would begin using the Shrike in April.[54]

More strikes over a larger geographical area resulted in greater aircraft attrition than in February. The Air Force's losses in March totaled thirteen aircraft (six F–105s, two F–4Cs, one F–100, three RF–101s, and one HU–16). Four air-

Armed Reconnaissance Route Packages

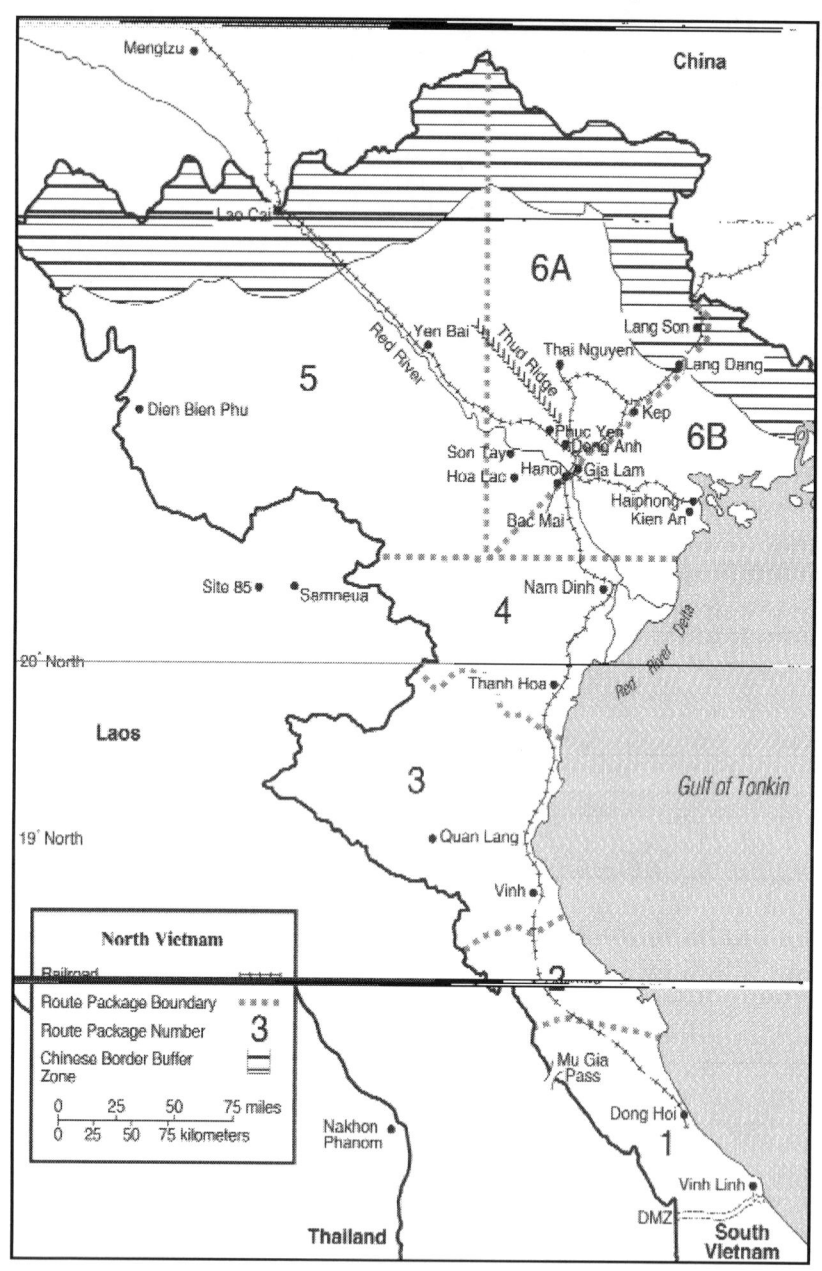

craft were damaged, but four planes (three F–105s and one RF–101) disappeared while flying Rolling Thunder missions, the cause of their loss unknown. The Navy lost at least five aircraft, and many others were damaged.[55]

The high level of aircraft attrition was easily attributed to the lethality of the north's air defense units along important routes. The heaviest concentrations were along rail lines and routes south of the 20th parallel. More SA–2 sites were also detected during the month, the total reaching in excess of one hundred throughout the country. With the mobility of the north's gun and missile units, however, the number of missiles and missile launchers was uncertain.[56]

Although there were no losses to enemy MiGs, air commanders anticipated more trouble from them if the authorized bomb line moved further northward and exposed more sensitive targets. MiGs were becoming increasingly aggressive, as was demonstrated on several occasions. On March 4, while circling at 13,000 feet on a combat air patrol mission for a strike on the Hanoi-Lao Cai rail line, four USAF F–4C Phantoms were challenged by a MiG pilot. Appearing from a 6 o'clock position, he made several firing passes. In several other instances, MiG pilots vectored near U.S. escort and strike aircraft, made visual passes, and threatened a number of RF–101s. The number of MiG warnings from Air Force Big Eye/Airborne Battlefield Command and Control Centers (ABCCCs) in March was substantially higher than in February.[57]

In late March, intelligence data indicated that there were about sixty-three MiG–15s and MiG–17s, plus fifteen MiG–21s, at Phuc Yen airfield. More MiG–21s, which had made their first appearance over North Vietnam in late 1965, were expected after photoreconnaissance indicated the presence of about fifty-three aircraft crates at Phuc Yen. Thirty crates were believed to contain aircraft fuselages, twenty-five of them MiG–21s and five MiG–15s, while twenty-three crates appeared to contain wings. The Air Staff believed that the recently arrived wings, frames, and parts, which could be assembled into operational aircraft in about six weeks, promised a significant increase in the air threat. The airfields were being improved and lengthened, and there were still a number of Il–28 bombers on the north's airfields that were capable of striking vital American and Vietnamese installations in South Vietnam. The Air Staff—in fact, all Air Force and Navy commanders—were still very frustrated by the administration's ban on attacking the crated MiGs and the airfields, especially the latter, as failure to do so now presaged higher American air losses later. From November 14, 1964 to March 1, 1966, the JCS, with occasional Army dissent, officially asked McNamara on eleven occasions for authority to strike all of the north's important airbases, convinced that this would not substantially increase the risk of Chinese intervention in the war, but Washington's refusal to allow such attacks would endure for many more months.[58]

Military camp near Mu Gia pass.

CHAPTER 9
Rolling Thunder 50

As Rolling Thunder 49 continued in March 1966, most Southeast Asia commanders and the JCS searched for new ways to convince the administration to step up the air and sea war against North Vietnam. Air Force and Navy leaders remained steadfast in their advocacy of "taking the wraps" off the bombing program. In Saigon, however, General Westmoreland made a counterproposal, which was quickly approved, to divert some air power from the upper regions of the north to areas closer to South Vietnam's battlefields and to adjust service responsibility accordingly from PACOM to MACV.

Westmoreland's Extended Battlefield Area

The MACV commander sent his proposal to Admiral Sharp and General Wheeler on March 17. He explained that a recent MACV study of VC-NVA activities in South Vietnam showed that manpower and supplies were being infiltrated on a "decidedly larger scale than experienced to date." Between October 1965 and February 1966, "at least" 11,280 infiltrators entered the south, and in the last two months "collateral reports and intelligence" indicated "possibly in excess of 15,000" NVA personnel had moved into Laos.

Westmoreland saw the Laotian panhandle as the "connecting link" between Hanoi's strategic base and the southern battlefields and expected the high troop and supply infiltration movements to continue until the monsoon weather in Laos, beginning in late May and June, made routes impassable. Thus, the United States and its allies had only a month and a half to improve air effectiveness against the north's routes leading to and adjacent to Laos's border.[1]

To deal with the increased infiltration, Westmoreland asked higher authorities to approve five related measures: a new, "national intelligence analysis" of the vulnerability of the north's transportation net from the Chinese border to South Vietnam; more armed reconnaissance in an "extended battlefield area" consisting of route packages 1 and 2, the Tiger Hound sector of Laos, and the demilitarized zone area west of 107°E; the transfer of command and control of the extended battlefield area from PACOM to MACV (and indirectly to the Seventh Air Force commander); the use of napalm in Laos (still banned except when authorized by the U.S. Ambassador in Vientiane) when directed by forward air controllers; more B–52 strikes along the eastern edge of the Laotian border with cover strikes in South Vietnam (as currently practiced); and the destruction of POL storage facilities, power plants, and other important targets in North Vietnam's "strategic rear" that had not yet been bombed. The Rolling Thunder Armed Reconnaissance Coordinating Committee would continue to provide the requisite field intelligence analysis and service coordination.

MiG–21 in flight over North Vietnam.

Westmoreland predicted that, if adopted, his proposals would enhance Sharp's operations against the north's "strategic resource base" because they would "relieve you of the day-to-day tactical concern related to those operations impacting directly on the battlefield in SVN." They would also insure optimum employment of available air resources. "General Moore concurs in the plan," he concluded, "and I request to put it into effect as a matter of operational urgency."²

Sharp agreed that NVA infiltration was growing and commended Westmoreland for his efforts to improve air operations in the north but rejected most of the proposals. The PACOM commander was skeptical of the recent estimate of 15,000 NVA entering Laos, reluctant to change command responsibility for the route packages, and disagreed that Hanoi's "strategic rear" was in North Vietnam; rather, he said, it was outside of the north. Further, he opposed allocating more air sorties in the panhandle at the expense of larger strikes further north and employing more B–52s against Laotian routes to create "choke points" since this tactic had previously proved unsuccessful. The Rolling Thunder Armed Reconnaissance Coordinating Committee, he continued, appeared to be allocating sorties satisfactorily, and any sortie shortages were the result of bad weather, which forced air commanders to cancel missions or divert aircraft to other areas. With better weather, the bombing tempo against the north would increase. Sharp had no quarrel with Westmoreland's desire to hit the remaining significant targets and sent him his own list of targets in order of importance: ports, POL storage facilities, supply storage sites along key routes from China, airfields, power plants, and locks and dams, the last two "relatively insignificant."³

The Air Force followed the Westmoreland-Sharp exchange with considerable interest, but its reaction was ambivalent. General Moore supported Westmoreland's proposals because MACV delegated much of its authority over

Truck park in North Vietnam after bombing by fighters.

air operations in South Vietnam to the 2d Air Division, and the extension of MACV's control into route packages 1 and 2 thus could lead to greater Air Force interdiction responsibility over this area.[4]

On the other hand, General Harris noted that the transfer from PACOM to MACV of command and control over the extended battlefield area would still leave all major policy decisions firmly in the hands of the Army. In the event that Sharp later transferred more authority to MACV, the PACAF commander foresaw that Rolling Thunder's tempo might be reduced, and worse, should PACOM headquarters receive a new Army "Commander, Southeast Asia," the Army would have complete control of all air operations in the war theater.* The last eventuality would leave the Air Force with little leverage to influence the use of air power generally in Southeast Asia, and specifically near China's borders, should that become necessary. Other Air Force officers were inclined to agree with Harris, believing that, on balance, the existing Rolling Thunder command and control arrangements were in the best interests of the Air Force. In Washington, a Joint Staff study likewise concluded that CINCPAC should retain operational control of bombing North Vietnam and that MACV should not be assigned any of the route packages.[5]

---

* First proposed by the Army in 1964, the concept of a new Southeast Asia Command that would replace MACV and bypass PACOM in the command chain between Saigon (or at some other Southeast Asia location) and Washington was still being discussed in 1966. The proposed command was never established. See McConnell Notebook, Item 113, 27 Apr 65; Maj. Gen. George S. Eckhardt, *Vietnam Studies: Command and Control, 1950–1969* (Dept of Army, 1974), pp 40–41.

Secretary of the Air Force Brown (left) and General Westmoreland during the Secretary's tour of Air Force installations in Vietnam in January 1966.

In discussions with General Wheeler on March 21 and 23, however, Secretary McNamara made it clear that he was highly supportive of Westmoreland's proposals, especially since Rolling Thunder was having "relatively little effect" on the enemy. He expressed "concern and wonderment" that the northwest Hanoi-Lao Cai rail line remained open after repeated bombings. Wheeler succeeded in allaying somewhat the Defense Secretary's skepticism about the bombing, at least to the extent that McNamara indicated that the northeast quadrant (i.e., route packages 6A and 6B) might shortly be reopened to air strikes.[6] Told of McNamara's desire to give first priority to whatever bombing Westmoreland requested, Admiral Sharp shifted primary responsibility for armed reconnaissance in route package 1—but not route package 2—to the MACV commander for his "extended battlefield area" (which already included the Tiger Hound section of Laos),* beginning with the next Rolling Thunder program on April 1, 1966. As before, General Moore's 2d Air Division, augmented occasionally by the VNAF, would conduct most of the route package 1 combat sorties, with the Navy assisting if weather or other circumstances precluded operations elsewhere in the north. The PACOM commander did not consider Westmoreland's request valid. He believed that there was ample in-theater air power to satisfy all of MACV's legitimate needs and that PACOM's existing command and control system checked the propensity of the MACV staff to inflate sortie requirements in and near South Vietnam and fritter away bombs on unjustified targets. However, the Defense Secretary had the last word, and Westmoreland received his new authority.[7]

---

*The Tiger Hound program began on December 5, 1965.

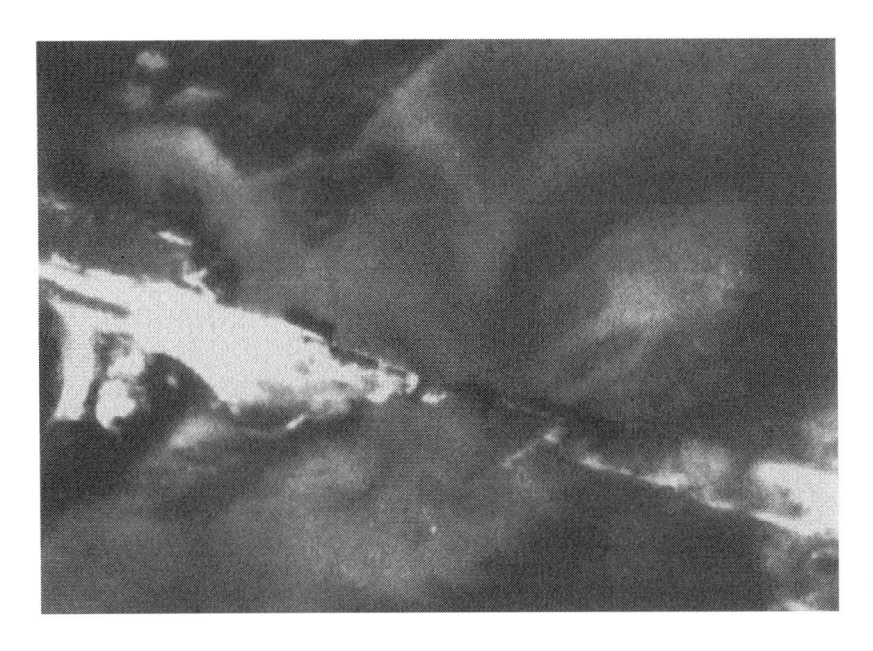

The Phu Ly railroad bridge, thirty-three miles southeast of Hanoi, immediately after an F–105 strike on April 17, 1966, that collapsed the south span and cratered the approaches to the bridge.

At the same time, Sharp decided to make other changes to Rolling Thunder operations. He reassigned the route packages, giving 5 and 6A to the Air Force and 2, 3, 4, and 6B to the Navy. He directed the Rolling Thunder Armed Reconnaissance Coordinating Committee, under the chairmanship of General Moore, to continue compiling data on armed reconnaissance of the north; MACV to recommend targets every two weeks in route package 1 and the authorized interdiction areas of Laos; and PACAF and PACFLT to submit a comprehensive status and analysis report of their respective bombing areas every two weeks. The PACAF-PACFLT report should describe the status of the main LOCs, traffic military support facilities, and list new targets. The Rolling Thunder Planning group, consisting of senior PACOM, PACAF, and PACFLT operations and intelligence officers would analyze fixed targets and, every Thursday, would recommend the targets that should be struck. Finally, the PACOM commander directed the U.S. Army Pacific (USARPAC) in Honolulu to perform a "detailed analysis" of all of North Vietnam's LOCs.[8]

Air Force leaders were highly disconcerted by Sharp's assignment of four route packages to the Navy and only two to the Air Force. Although the latter's assignment covered a sizeable geographical area, General Harris viewed the disparity as indicative of a diminished PACAF role in Rolling Thunder, and he particularly objected to the restrictions on PACAF with regard to attacking the north's coastal and inland waterways. Gen. George B. Simler, the Seventh Air Force's Deputy Chief of Staff for Plans and Operations, observed that the Navy could fly "neither the number nor the quality of reconnaissance missions needed in four route packages" and forecast a degradation in Rolling Thunder intelligence-gathering and tactical operations. Nor did he see any benefit to the Air Force from the adjusted functions of the Rolling Thunder Armed Reconnaissance Coordinating Committee, which at best practiced "nominal coordination of independent [service] efforts" in the bombing program. He believed that a better solution would be to transform the committee into a Southeast Asia Air Board, chaired by Moore, with authority to review all MACV and PACOM air planning and requirements in the Southeast Asia war theater. However, if the objections of the Air Force reached Admiral Sharp, they did nothing to deter him. Meanwhile, the JCS and McNamara were completing work on the target list for "Rolling Thunder 50," as the next bombing program would be called.[9]

Selecting Rolling Thunder 50 Targets

In late March, General Wheeler had attempted to assuage McNamara's skepticism about the Rolling Thunder program and to stress the need for more strikes on important targets even as more air power was shifted to Westmoreland's extended battlefield area. The JCS chairman described the difficulties Air Force and Navy pilots normally experienced over the north: poor flying weather (the monsoon did not usually abate until May), the heavy concentrations of antiaircraft weaponry along important segments of the Hanoi-Lao Cai and other rail lines, and the enemy's fast repair capability. In response, the Secretary indicated that, for the next Rolling Thunder program, he would be willing to approve 600 to 700 sorties per month for a "controlled armed reconnaissance program" in route packages 6A and 6B and for such JCS-designated targets as the Haiphong cement plant, the bridges at Viet Tri and Phu Ly, and a radar facility at Kep. On March 23, he informed Wheeler that he would allow attacks on POL storage facilities within the Hanoi-Haiphong sanctuary area, but would not sanction the mining of waters leading to Haiphong and other ports. He asked for specific Joint Staff bombing recommendations roughly within the foregoing guidelines.[10]

On March 26, the service chiefs sent McNamara a "bombing package" for execution beginning on April 1. They proposed 700 armed reconnaissance sorties against rail and highway routes in the northeast and strikes on nine important POL sites, six bridges (three would be restrikes), and four other important targets. For the twelfth time since November 1964, they also called for strikes on the north's jet-capable airfields. Their recommendation stated that from "a strictly military point of view," the sixty to seventy MiGs based near Hanoi posed a constant threat, and the airfields should take precedence over other proposed targets despite the risks of losing men and aircraft during such an air assault. Although

Lt. Gen. Nguyen Chanh Thi, I Corps Commander (left), and Lt. Gen. Nguyen Van Thieu, Vietnamese Chief of State, (center) at Da Nang Air Base, South Vietnam, January 1966.

the airfield recommendation had not been discussed with McNamara, the Joint Chiefs noted that overall, the bombing package was less escalatory than their "preferred" Rolling Thunder program outlined on January 18, 1966.[11]

Surprisingly, in the closing days of March, McNamara sent—with some modifications—an endorsement of the Joint Chief's bombing proposals to the President. Apparently influenced by a new CIA study that for the first time advocated heavier bombing in the north, the Defense Secretary said that Hanoi's loss of its only cement plant and most of its POL stores would harm its bridge and road repair activities and logistic movements. He minimized communist reaction to such strikes. Virtually paraphrasing earlier JCS assertions, he said that the Soviet Union would probably do nothing more than adopt "a somewhat harsher diplomatic and propaganda line" and that the Chinese "would not react to these attacks by active entry by ground or air" unless the United States took additional military steps. Such decisions "at each point would be largely within our ... control." The Defense Secretary did not abandon his long-held view, however, that Hanoi would not alter its policy until it concluded that its chances of winning the war in the south were so slim as to "no longer justify the damage being inflicted on the north." In the longer term, he said:

> The recommended bombing program...can be expected to create a substantial added burden on North Vietnam's manpower supply for defense and logistics tasks and to engender popular alienation from the regions should shortages became widespread. While we do not predict the regime's control would be appreciably weakened, there might eventually be an aggravation of differences within the regime as [to] the policies to be followed.[12]

Whether President Johnson was prepared to endorse McNamara's recommendations is uncertain. What is clear is that he felt constrained to withhold an endorsement at the moment because of another political upheaval in South Vietnam.[13] The latest crisis came on March 10 when Prime Minister Ky dismissed General Nguyen Chanh Thi, the rebellious commander of the South Vietnamese Army forces in the northernmost I Corps, which included five of the most strategic provinces. Ky and his ruling military collegium in Saigon charged Thi with insubordination. The I Corps commander was popular in the region, a hero because of his role in overthrowing the Diem regime in 1963, and he had the loyalty of his military and civilian appointees, most of whom resigned their posts in protest. Local Buddhist monks led anti-Ky demonstrations in Hue and Da Nang and were joined quickly by many other dissenters to Saigon's rule. Some condemned the presence of the United States in South Vietnam and called for negotiations with the National Liberation Front, the political arm of the Viet Cong. The disorder spread southward to Saigon where, on March 31, 10,000 Buddhists demonstrated against the Ky government. On April 5, Ky flew to Da Nang to quell the rebellion, threatening to use troops if necessary.[14]

In Washington, the unrest prompted renewed concerns about the war by critics within the administration, Congress, and the public about aiding an ally that appeared unwilling or unable to set aside domestic quarrels while fighting for its very survival. As a consequence, the President was obliged to defer his approval of the escalatory parts of the Rolling Thunder 50 package, namely the seven POL and two industrial targets. As a further precaution, he somewhat enlarged the principal sanctuary area by prohibiting any bombing within a thirty nautical miles of Hanoi and ten nautical miles of Haiphong. He made no change to the Chinese buffer zone, but he did shorten the maneuvering area for strike pilots flying over the zone: pilots were directed to remain at least twenty nautical miles from the border, not fifteen nautical miles, as before.

Nonetheless, the directive still gave Air Force and Navy commanders more targets and operational flexibility than they had enjoyed in the February and March operations. It permitted 900 (rather than 700) attack sorties (of 8,100 authorized per month for North Vietnam and Laos) in the reopened route packages 6A and 6B and retained in the target list four important rail and highway bridges and eight key rail and highway segments. Commanders were instructed to make a special effort to block train traffic along the northeast Hanoi-Dong Dang rail line.[15]

On April 1, Admiral Sharp, dispatched implementing orders to Generals Harris and Westmoreland and Admiral Johnson, allocating monthly armed reconnaissance sorties as follows: MACV, 3,500 for route package 1 and the Barrel Roll and Steel Tiger programs in Laos (most of which would be flown by the Air Force); Air Force, 1,100 sorties for route packages 5 and 6A; and Navy, 3,500 sorties for route packages 2, 3, 4, and 6B. He divided evenly between the two services the 900 sorties permitted for route packages 6A and 6B, allocating

450 sorties to each in their respective bombing areas. Each service was also assigned segments of four armed reconnaissance routes. The Air Force's segments totaled 134 miles, and the Navy's totaled 186. In addition, Sharp directed the Navy to continue flying armed reconnaissance of coastal areas in accordance with guidelines issued earlier by Washington. JCS targets in the north that had already been struck, he added, could be attacked at any time at the discretion of air commanders, but Iron Hand SA–2 SAM strikes in route packages 6A and 6B could be conducted only after photography confirmed the location of the sites. Attacks on fixed SAM sites, on the other hand, were permissible to protect aircraft and their aircrews.[16]

On the same day, Sharp issued a revised Rolling Thunder, Iron Hand anti-SAM, and Blue Tree reconnaissance operations order that assigned service responsibility for intelligence analysis for each of the route packages in a manner identical to service responsibility for attack sorties: MACV was assigned route package 1, the Air Force received route packages 5 and 6A, and the Navy route packages 2, 3, 4, and 6B. The PACOM commander insisted on retaining final control of these activities on the grounds that it was essential to have undivided authority over reconnaissance in North Vietnam.[17]

The foregoing attack and reconnaissance directives were issued only a week prior to the completion of a JCS study team report, requested by McNamara in February, on the results of Rolling Thunder's first year of operations (i.e., March 2, 1965 to March 2, 1966). Headed by USAF Brig. Gen. Jammie M. Philpott, the team concluded that the bombing program had achieved "a degree of success within the parameters of imposed restrictions." The team also determined that Hanoi was willing to absorb the present level of air-inflicted damage and would not cease its support of the insurgencies in South Vietnam and Laos.

The report also described Rolling Thunder's "unfinished business." Of 236 targets designated by the JCS in North Vietnam in early 1966, 134 had been struck, including 42 important bridges, but 102 remained untouched. Of these, 90 were in the northwest, including 70 in the sanctuary areas of Hanoi and Haiphong and within the Chinese border buffer zone. The team strongly recommended that the remainder of these top priority targets should be destroyed as a matter of urgency, in three attack phases. For each phase, Admiral Sharp would decide which targets should be struck, the weight of air effort, and the tactics. To assure maximum effectiveness, the operations should be conducted in concert with the air campaigns in South Vietnam and Laos.[18]

The team's conclusions had no discernible impact on the President's decision to permit only a moderate expansion of bombing under Rolling Thunder 50. A major shortcoming of the report was that it lacked Joint Staff endorsement, despite General McConnell's efforts to obtain it. When the report was sent to McNamara on March 9, the service chiefs merely "noted" it, stating that it was in consonance with their bombing recommendations of January 18, 1966, and would be useful in future Rolling Thunder planning.[19]

More important than the Philpott report were other events that obliged the President to withhold his approval of a major escalation of the bombing in late March and for the ensuing weeks. The internal strife in South Vietnam, precipitated by Prime Minister Ky's dismissal of General Thi, was not resolved in April, but would simmer throughout May and into June. On the diplomatic front, on April 28, General Taylor warned the President that heavier bombing and other possible U.S. military actions against the Hanoi regime were "blue chips" to be bargained away only at the negotiating table, not relinquished beforehand. More significantly, in May, United Nations General Secretary U Thant and the British government began separate peace initiatives, and in June, with Washington's concurrence, the Canadian government sent an emissary to Hanoi for the second time* to determine whether its leaders were prepared to scale down the fighting and begin discussions.[20]

Publicly, administration spokesmen would give oft-repeated reasons for the caution of the bombing program. On May 22, during an interview on NBC's "Meet the Press", Air Force Secretary Brown said that the use of additional air power against an expanded target list in North Vietnam might decrease infiltration, but would not "cut it off." Furthermore, it might well lead to a wider war, "and no responsible government can lightly step into such a situation." There was no significant change in bombing policy until late June, when the President finally approved strikes on several important POL targets.†[21]

Rolling Thunder 50 Begins

After receiving Admiral Sharp's "execute" message on April 1, Seventh Air Force‡ and Navy commanders quickly dispatched their fighter-bombers and support aircraft over the enlarged bombing area. Substantial numbers of strikes, in accordance with bombing guidelines, were flown in route package 1 and the Barrel Roll and Steel Tiger sectors of Laos. Targets in route package 1 alone absorbed 2,406 sorties in April, of which most were flown by the Air Force with the VNAF contributing a few. In mid-April, Secretary McNamara declared his interest in concentrating the air effort near South Vietnam's borders. "I want it clearly understood," he informed General Westmoreland, SAC Commander Gen. Joseph J. Nazzaro, General McConnell, and Admirals Sharp

---

* A Canadian emissary first visited Hanoi in March 1966.
† See Chapter 11.
‡ Because Headquarters, 2d Air Division, was now larger than that of a standard Air Force, on March 25, Gen. McConnell directed Gen. Harris to reestablish the division as Headquarters, Seventh Air Force, effective April 8, 1966. Headquarters, 2d Air Division, was discontinued. At the same time, the Deputy Commander, 2d Air Division/Thirteenth Air Force, at Udorn, Thailand, was redesignated Deputy Commander, Seventh Air Force/Thirteenth Air Force (msg, CSAF to CINCPACAF, 252211Z Mar 66).

An O–1 forward air control aircraft.

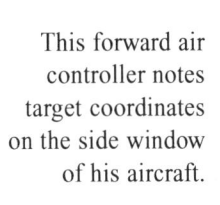

This forward air controller notes target coordinates on the side window of his aircraft.

and McDonald, "that all commanders are to give first priority...to fulfilling requirements...against targets in the extended battlefield." Operations in route packages 2, 3, 4, 5, 6A and 6B "are not to be carried out unless they can be performed without penalty" in the first priority area. The policy would remain in effect, he added, until a major field commander or a JCS member proposed a change, and he (McNamara) or Deputy Defense Secretary Vance agreed that a shift in air emphasis was warranted.[22]

In May, largely because of poor weather, strike sorties in route package 1 fell to 1,675 with the Air Force flying 1,391, the Navy 181, and the VNAF 103. In June, with monsoon weather easing, the three services recorded 4,070 strike sorties, with all but 243 flown by the Air Force. Targets consisted principally of small bridges, vehicles, structures, watercraft, ferries, supply and POL storage sites, and rolling stock along the rail line between Vinh and the DMZ. In addition, pilots cut and cratered hundreds of roads, especially along Routes 1A, 15, 101, and 137.[23]

Beginning on May 1 and continuing in June, some of the strikes in route package 1 were flown under the aegis of a new program. Patterned after the Tiger Hound operations inaugurated in December 1965 in southeastern Laos and controlled by an interservice Tiger Hound Task Force headed by Air Force Col. John F. Groom, Gate Guard was an "integrated interdiction" concept. As weather worsened in southern Laos but improved in North Vietnam, Air Force,

F–105 strikes on November 3, 1966, severely damaged the
railyards at Yen Bai, seventy-six miles northwest of Hanoi.

Navy, and Marine pilots shifted most of the their operations to the southern sector of route package 1. Attack sorties were supported by special aircraft: O–1 Bird Dog forward air controllers to direct strike pilots to their targets, C–130 ABCCCs, C–130 flare aircraft, EB–66Cs and EB–66Bs for electronic intelligence and countermeasures, and RF–101s for photoreconnaissance. Strike pilots concentrated on attacking "selected interdiction points" or "gates" in daytime and "fleeting targets," mostly vehicles, at night.[24]

Although the Gate Guard program initially promised to inflict more casualties on the enemy, especially at night, pilots found the operations in route package 1 more difficult and hazardous than in southeastern Laos. The low-flying O–1s were very vulnerable to the heavier antiaircraft fire in the area, the interdiction points on flatter terrain were easily bypassed, and there were more villages where the enemy could rest and service vehicles, secure in the knowledge that American airmen would not attack largely civilian targets. As a consequence, Gate Guard operations were soon terminated and were succeeded, on July 20, 1966, by Tally-Ho, a program designed to stem the increasing flow of manpower and supplies into South Vietnam through the demilitarized zone.*[25]

---

* For a detailed discussion of the Gate Guard and Tally-Ho programs, see Jacob Van Staaveren, *Interdiction in Southern Laos, 1960–1968* (Center AF Hist, 1994), pp 118–19, 152–58, and 181–84.

The Thai Nguyen railyard after strikes in May 1966.

In route packages 2, 3, and 4, assigned to the Navy, a total of 2,081 strike sorties were flown in April, with the Air Force contributing about 200. In May, sortie totals for the two services in these areas were 2,325 and 42, and in June 2,902 and 61 (the VNAF did not venture beyond route package 1). Most of the targets were similar to those in route package 1, with some special areas singled out for repeated attacks, including routes leading to the Barthelemy Pass, an infiltration entry point from North Vietnam into Laos; five important "logistic hubs" at Thanh Hoa, Vinh, Phi Din, Vinh Son, Phu Qui, and Bai Thuong; the Hai Yen and Phuc Loi naval bases; and the Son Chau POL storage area. In late April and May, following an air strike that blocked a canal, Navy pilots enjoyed a field day against an estimated 1,100 junks and sampans, with about 850 reported damaged or destroyed. In late June, Washington authorized additional strikes against dispersed and major POL storage areas located in these and more northern route packages.[26]

In route packages 5 and 6A, where only the larger and longer range Air Force planes ventured, numerous attacks were made against rail and highway bridges, rail tracks, and rolling stock along the Hanoi-Lao Cai and Hanoi-Thai Nguyen rail lines; the Yen Bai and Thai Nguyen railyards; logistic sites at Yen Bai, Son La, and Thai Nguyen; and, near the end of June, three major POL storage areas. Strike sorties in April, May, and June totaled 342, 237, and 98 respectively.[27]

The assault on the Thai Nguyen railyard was made in response to insistent requests by General Harris to Admiral Sharp to obtain the necessary strike authority. After administration officials assented, on April 29, thirteen F–105s conducted the attack, tearing up the tracks, cratering the yard, and destroying an estimated twelve railroad cars. Groundfire cost the attackers one plane and pilot. Air Force analysts

On May 5, 1966, F–105 pilot Capt. C. Glen Nix hit the center span of the Bac Giang railroad and highway bridge with a full bomb load, destroying that key bridge linking Hanoi with China.

believed that the destruction of the yard would hamper shipments from the north's only nearby steel mill—which remained off limits to the fighter-bombers. As usual, the North Vietnamese quickly began to repair the damage, assisted by a period of poor flying weather that prevented immediate restrikes.[28]

Air commanders were especially frustrated by Washington's refusal to approve an attack on 132 SA–2 SAM canisters, associated equipment, and a SAM maintenance installation at the Hanoi barracks northeast of Gia Thong Boe. Detected by a SAC Blue Spring reconnaissance drone at the beginning of May, analysts determined that the SAM assemblies could equip eleven North Vietnamese SA–2 battalions and contained missiles equal to the number fired at Air Force and Navy aircraft since December 1965. Admiral Sharp informed the JCS that an air attack on the target would constitute "a severe blow" to Hanoi's SA–2 capability.

General Wheeler was sympathetic to the PACOM commander's request, but advised him that it was not expedient "at this time" to ask higher authorities for the strike authority. The Joint Chiefs, he explained, were reluctant to jeopardize ongoing discussions with the authorities on bombing the important POL storage sites in the Hanoi-Haiphong area and reluctant to recommend a single strike on the missiles and equipment that would inevitably alert the north's air defenders to exercise greater vigilance in the vicinity of the POL targets.[29]

The fewest sorties in the three-month period were flown in route package 6B, an area assigned to the Navy, but shared with the Air Force. April sortie totals are unavailable, but in May, the Navy flew 116 and the Air Force 9, with the June totals 78 and 22 respectively. Both services concentrated on interdiction of bridges along the Hanoi-Dong Dang rail line, and in late June, Navy pilots struck four of seven major POL storage areas belatedly authorized by the President.*[30]

---

* See Chapter 10.

Bac Giang bridge after the May 5 attack. A pontoon
bridge and a ferry are above the destroyed bridge.

Air Force and Navy commanders expended considerable effort to knock out four rail and highway bridges designated by the JCS in the northern route packages authorized under Rolling Thunder 50. The largest bridge stood on the northeast Hanoi-Dong Dang rail line at Bac Giang. It possessed four steel trusses resting on three concrete piers and abutments, two center swing spans, each thirty-nine feet in length and two road lanes and one rail line.

After Admiral Sharp directed the Air Force to attack the Bac Giang bridge, General Moore dispatched four separate missions against the sturdy target. A total of twenty-three F–105 Thunderchiefs dropped 107 250-pound bombs on or near the bridge, but succeeded in damaging only one span and cratering the southwest approach. After numerous weather cancellations, a fifth strike was conducted on May 5 by two flights of four F–105s, all carrying 3,000-pound bombs, and these destroyed the two northern spans, closing the bridge to traffic. Twelve Air Force F–105s knocked out, for the second time, the Phu Ly railroad bridge on the same rail line (previously hit in 1965). Navy pilots likewise needed only single-mission attacks on two JCS bridges at Hai Duong and Haiphong on April 17 and 19 respectively, to make them unusable. All four bridges were struck again in May and June to keep them out of operation. Nonetheless, the indefatigable North Vietnamese did not cease their repair activity. In May, photoreconnaissance detected construction units building a rail bypass 2,300 feet north of the Hai Duong bridge.[31]

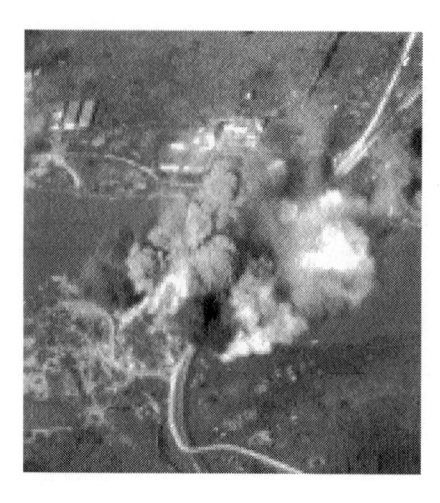

Thanh Hoa highway and railroad bridge under attack.

The most creative bridge assault during the three-month period was against the Thanh Hoa rail and road bridge in route package 3. Bombed repeatedly in 1965, the structure withstood Air Force and Navy bombs while groundfire inflicted considerable losses. To destroy its two heavy spans, the Air Force devised a special attack program nicknamed Carolina Moon. This called for dropping five huge 5,000-pound bombs from a Hercules C–130 cargo plane into the Song Ma River upstream from the bridge. The bombs would float towards the bridge and explode when they struck the superstructure. General Moore believed an upstream bomb drop was the only feasible method of attack, given the heavy air defenses in the vicinity of the bridge.[32]

Preparations for Carolina Moon began in late 1965 at the Air Force's Tactical Air Warfare Center at Eglin AFB, Florida. At the Center's Armament Development Laboratory, personnel constructed a number of high-explosive bombs, 96 inches wide and 31 1/2 inches high, with affixed sensors. The bomb weighed about 3,750 pounds, but the attachments increased the weight to about 5,000 pounds. During the extensive test and training period that followed, aircrews made about 80 test drops of the huge bombs from C–123 and C–130 aircraft, while two aircrews underwent special training in two C–130 Hercules planes that would conduct the mission in the war theater. One seven-man aircrew was headed by Maj. Richard T. Remers, the other by Maj. Thomas F. Case. Early in May, the two aircraft and their aircrews departed from Eglin and arrived at Da Nang AB, South Vietnam, on the 15th. They immediately began flying orientation missions and acquainting themselves with a Carolina Moon operational plan prepared by General Moore's staff and approved by Admiral Sharp in mid-April.[33]

Because of the weather, aircrews had to wait until late May to begin their mission. Finally, shortly after midnight on the 30th, Major Remer's aircrew of navigators, radio operators, and bombardiers took off from Da Nang. They flew a circuitous route towards Thanh Hoa that took them over the Gulf of Tonkin,

Repeated bombings led to the construction of three bypass routes around this destroyed bridge in North Vietnam.

then to a drop area about one mile upstream from the bridge. As the time neared to unload their five bombs, ten Air Force F–4C Phantoms made a diversionary strike on a highway ten miles north of Thanh Hoa while electronically equipped EB–66s engaged in jamming operations against antiaircraft radars in the vicinity of the bridge. Major Remer's bomb run was made at about 150 knots, 400 feet above the ground. After maneuvering safely through groundfire, his aircrew dropped the 5,000-pound blockbusters in the river. The mission was executed flawlessly. However, the results were nil. Photoreconnaissance the next day disclosed no new damage to the bridge or any trace of the bombs.[34]

Disappointed but undaunted, General Moore ordered Major Case's seven-man aircrew to fly an identical mission in the second Hercules the next night, with no changes in procedure. To provide additional navigational expertise for the mission, 1st Lt. William "Rocky" Edmundson, one of two navigators who had flown with Major Remer the night before, signed on with Major Case's C–130.

The plane left Da Nang without incident, then, presumably while flying over the Gulf of Tonkin towards the target area, Case's plane vanished. Also lost without trace was one of two F–4C Phantoms and its two-man crew which, as on the preceding night, made a diversionary attack just before the scheduled bomb drop above the bridge. After an extensive search failed to locate the plane and the eight-man aircrew, the Air Force decided to abandon the Carolina Moon project. Major Remer and his fellow airmen, plus support personnel, returned to Eglin AFB in June 1966.[35]

What happened to Major Remer's five bombs and Major Case's mission? Later, North Vietnamese sources provided conflicting accounts of Remer's bomb delivery. The first, in late 1966, indicated that four of the bombs exploded but caused little damage. According to the second account, obtained by the New York Times in 1972, the North Vietnamese "guards" who witnessed the drop leaped into the river and held the five bombs until they were defused by technicians. The main source of information about Major Case's mission came from a communist film obtained by the Japanese that was seen by Major Remer. This suggests that the plane was shot down about twenty miles west of the river, and that there were no survivors. However, U.S. authorities have never obtained conclusive evidence concerning the fate of Major Remer's five bombs or Major Case's mission.[36]

Another highlight of Rolling Thunder 50 was the first two strikes in North Vietnam by SAC's B–52s. The target was Mu Gia Pass, the north's principal entry point for troops and supplies into southern Laos. General Westmoreland had been pressing for an SAC attack on the area for many weeks and solicited the backing of Admiral Sharp and Ambassador Sullivan in Vientiane for the operation. Administration authorities reviewed the proposal intensively before concurring in early April 1966. On the 8th, the JCS sent an "execute" message to Sharp and General Nazzaro, the SAC commander. Unlike B–52 strikes in the eastern border regions of Laos, which were conducted under a veil of secrecy (despite occasional leaks to the press), there would be no effort to conceal Arc Light attacks in the north as Hanoi obviously would publicize them immediately.*[37]

On April 12, under the nickname Rock Kick II, the SAC commander ordered the bombers to strike the pass. Thirty B–52s and thirty KC–135s—the latter had been forced out of their home base on Okinawa by weather—consumed one hour and four minutes for take-off from Andersen AFB, Guam. Each bomber carried twenty-four 1,000-pound bombs internally and twenty-four 750-pound bombs externally. All of the 750-pound bombs were preset for subsurface burst while the thirty 1,000-pound bombs were fitted with long delay fuses. At the target area, twenty-nine bombers (one aborted because of a radar malfunction) released their ordnance from 35,000 to 37,000 feet. On the North Vietnamese side, the B–52s carpet bombed a three-mile segment of Route 15.[38]

Based on official briefings in Saigon, American newsmen characterized the attack as the largest single bombing mission of the war, and also the largest since World War II. Quoting "usually reliable sources," they said that the bombers also struck the Laotian side of the pass. The sources, on this occasion, were unreliable, as the final decision was to bomb only on the North Vietnamese side of the pass.[39]

---

* Considerable controversy surrounded the planning and implementation of the first two strikes on the Mu Gia Pass. See Jacob Van Staaveren, *Interdiction in Southern Laos, 1960–1968* (Center AF Hist. 1994), pp 135–37.

Cratering on Route 15 near Mu Gia Pass from B–52 bombing in April 1966.

U.S. spokesmen in Saigon hailed the raid as a "marked" success, as it created huge landslides leading to the pass. Within 24 hours, however, visual and photoreconnaissance confirmed that the communists were again shuttling traffic through the gateway into Laos. Westmoreland urged a second attack and, noting recent increased traffic sightings toward and through the pass, recommended Air Force and Navy follow-up tactical assaults, with the Air Force employing its B–66/F–105 buddy bombing pathfinder technique to assure accuracy. On Guam, Maj. Gen. William J. Crum, commander of the SAC's 3d Air Division, also desired to hit Mu Gia Pass again because several bomb drops during the first strike were marred because of a blurred radar image induced by the terrain. As usual, the MACV commander had to obtain the approval of Admiral Sharp and Ambassador Sullivan before the White House authorized another SAC strike on the Mu Gia area for April 17.[40]

The second SAC strike, nicknamed Big Kite was executed more smoothly than the first. SAC aircrews possessed better targeting data, the operational aiming points were more easily identified, and all of the aircraft delivered their ordnance as planned. The only untoward incident occurred when two SA–2 SAMs, launched from a site not far from Mu Gia Pass, scored a hit on an Air Force tactical escort, although the plane was not downed.[41]

Poststrike photography showed thirty-two craters along North Vietnam's Route 15 running towards the pass, but after eighteen hours, all of the craters were

A concept developed early in 1966 allowed loading of three racks of twenty-eight 500- and 750-pound bombs internally into B–52s, an increase of over 50 per cent.

filled and enemy trucks were again rumbling into southern Laos. In Westmoreland's view, the rapidity with which the North Vietnamese had reopened the route signaled the importance they attached to the traffic artery and justified more B–52 saturation bombing to keep it closed. And, with the annual monsoon weather approaching, he believed the pass should be struck frequently while weather permitted. Many bomb craters, filled with rain, would then frustrate enemy truck travel.[42]

However, Sullivan and Sharp now raised objections to further SAC bombing of the Mu Gia area. The Ambassador wished to avoid publicity about strikes on the Laotian side of the pass (Prime Minister Souvanna Phouma officially remained in the dark about SAC operations in his country), questioned the effectiveness of the bombing, considered wasteful the use of scarce munitions on Laotian targets that could be struck more easily and accurately by tactical aircraft, and worried about the safety of tribal road watch teams gathering intelligence in the targeted area. He also found control over strike aircraft to be inadequate, observing that on the night of April 25/26, several B–52s had "bombed through" a Navy mission apparently "working over" the SAM target along the Laos–South Vietnam border assigned to the Arc Lighters.[43]

Admiral Sharp's opposition to further B–52 strikes against Mu Gia Pass was based on their high cost, their excessive use of scarce ordnance, their ineffectiveness in cratering roads and blocking traffic, and the vulnerability of the bombers, which were ill-equipped to evade the SA–2 missiles sited not far from Mu Gia. He believed that SAC's primary mission should be to destroy war-making material, not to block routes.[44]

Westmoreland was unconvinced by these arguments, but in the ensuing weeks he was unable to persuade Sharp and Sullivan to renew the bombing using B–52s. Administration officials sided with the PACOM commander and the Ambassador, thus ending the operations for the time being. The bombers would not be employed against the Mu Gia area again until December 1966.[45]

A modified B–52 releases an internal load of 84 bombs during a test at Eglin Air Force Base, Florida. Increased use of B–52s intensified the bomb shortage.

The Air Munitions Shortage

With more targets available over a larger authorized bombing area, Rolling Thunder 50 operations inflicted more losses on the north's transportation, supply, and air defense systems than in February and March. Service tabulations showed hundreds of enemy vehicles, railroad cars, rivercraft, small bridges, antiaircraft sites, and structures damaged or destroyed. In addition, pilots continued to cut and crater hundreds of rail and road segments throughout the country.[46]

Operations were conducted in the face of a relatively new problem in the war theater: a growing shortage of air munitions. The likelihood that air munitions expenditures would eventually outpace production and deliveries became apparent in late 1965, and the trend became increasingly obvious in the first three months of 1966.[47]

In April, as the tempo of air operations gradually rose, Generals Moore and Westmoreland reported that the munitions shortfall had created "an emergency situation," forcing them to cancel many planned strike sorties. Shortfalls applied particularly to CBU–2s, 2.75-inch rockets, and 500-pound and 750-pound bombs. The supply of 750-pound bombs was diminishing most rapidly because of intensified B–52 operations in South Vietnam and the border areas of Laos. By mid-1966, there were inadequate inventories of thirteen types of air munitions, as well as components such as fuses. In addition to increased theater-wide consumption, munitions production in the United States was not keeping pace with demand, and there were unloading and delivery delays in South Vietnam. Meanwhile, the Air Force and Navy took separate actions to redistribute some of the munitions stocks at airbases throughout Southeast Asia.[48]

Twelve F–105s, led by an EB–66, bombing the Mu Gia Pass area, May 1966.

Seeking a solution to the munitions problem, Secretary McNamara sent Paul R. Ignatius, Assistant Secretary of Defense for Installations and Logistics, to Honolulu to meet with Admiral Sharp and other Navy and Air Force representatives. Two major actions resulted from the meetings. In Washington, President Johnson assigned "the highest national priority" to the production of 250-pound, 500-pound, and 750-pound bombs; 2.75-inch rockets; and 20-mm, 81-mm, and 105-mm cartridges and in Honolulu, with JCS approval, Admiral Sharp made tentative sortie allocations for all of the services for the remainder of 1966. Contingent on such factors as aircraft size and targets, each service was given temporary munitions loading limits. For example, the Air Force would carry 2.40 tons of munitions per sortie in North Vietnam and 1.65 tons per sortie in South Vietnam and Laos. For the Navy, the figures were 1.80 and 1.30 tons respectively. The Marine Corps and the VNAF were assigned 1.65 and 1.30 tons respectively.[49]

The April decisions on future service sortie allocations represented only the first step to deal with the problem. On May 24, Secretary McNamara again approved adjusted monthly sortie allocations for the remainder of 1966, based on estimates of available ordnance and the number of aircraft expected to be in the war theater by then. The Defense Secretary doubted if the services could use "effectively" more than 60,000 tons of air munitions per month. At bottom, he believed the munitions problem was partly a matter of insufficient production, but chiefly caused by inadequate distribution of available supplies.[50]

In a continuing debate on the munitions shortage, General McConnell and other JCS members consistently argued for a policy allowing full munitions loading of aircraft to assure successful missions. McNamara took a contrary position, asserting that large munitions loads were not warranted simply because aircraft could carry them. In June, he acquiesced temporarily when he directed a reduction in sortie rates rather than reduced aircraft loading. Then, following another high-level munitions conference in Honolulu in July, the Defense Secretary redefined "optimum" ordnance loads for aircraft as meaning loads based solely on mission and target requirements. On the basis of this and other guidance, planners worked out another revised ordnance and air sortie rate formula for the remainder of 1966, subject to further adjustment as circumstances dictated.[51]

The need to reduce the number of planned strike sorties and the unavailability of sufficient optimum munitions for Rolling Thunder and other air programs was a matter of considerable concern to air commanders and combat pilots. In their view, the twin deficiencies not only increased the danger of missions, but accounted for higher aircraft losses. The acute shortage of a variety of bomb fuses, frequently compounded by their unreliability, was deemed a particularly important factor. Although the losses were not easily documented, the airmen believed that their connection with an inadequate munitions supply was direct and real.[52] Surprisingly, General McConnell downplayed the importance of the munitions shortage, informing a Senate Committee on May 9 that the problem was overblown and could be rectified with better munitions management. His was a minority view, however.[53]

Circumventing Bad Weather with MSQ–77 Radar

More measurable was the impact of bad flying weather on bombing, especially during April and May. Normally, the monsoon over North Vietnam began to abate in the spring, but in 1966 the rain, drizzle, and overcast conditions lingered for many weeks. In fact, May proved to be the worst month, illustrated by sorties scheduled, canceled, and adjudged ineffective (figure 11).

Figure 11
Sortie Effectiveness
April, May, and June 1966

	Sorties Scheduled		Percent Canceled		Ineffective	
	USAF	USN	USAF	USN	USAF	USN
April	5,481	4,744	16.7	7.3	448	unk.
May	3,475	4,636	39.8	24.5	689	unk.
June	4,408	5,300	6.5	.5	1,095	unk.

In April, poor weather led to canceled operations for the following numbers of Air Force aircraft: 247 F–4Cs, 397 F–105s, and 1 F–100; in May, 743 F–4Cs, 1,060 F–105s, 18 A–1Es, and 30 B–57s; and in June, 196 F–4Cs, 130 F–105s, 14 A–1Es, 8 B–57s, and 12 F–104s. There are no comparable Navy figures.

The Navy flew fewer sorties over the north during the period mainly because, beginning in April, 30 or more sorties per day were diverted from route packages 2, 3, 4, and 6B to General Westmoreland's extended battlefield areas in route package 1 and in Laos.[54]

To reduce the impact of poor flying weather, the services continued to introduce new bombing methods and equipment. In March 1966, Seventh Air Force pilots began employing the radar pathfinder buddy bombing technique described earlier, in which a formation of B–57, F–105, or F–4C strike aircraft, flying at 15,000 feet or higher was led by a B–66B pathfinder, and the pathfinder's navigator determined the bomb release point for the formation using a K–5 bombing navigation system.

Early in June, combat pilots flying in route package 1 began relying on a new MSQ–77 radar system nicknamed Combat Skyspot, using special radar instruments in the aircraft and at ground installations at Nakhon Phanom, Thailand, and Dong Ha, South Vietnam. The same system had been introduced two months earlier in South Vietnam to assure more accurate close air support and B–52 strikes.*[55]

Adapted from MSQ–35, a radar bomb scoring system developed by the SAC which assured more accurate bomb dropping, the MSQ–77 was a pencil beam X-band radar and operated most effectively in conjunction with an SST–181 X-band beacon in an aircraft. Measuring about four inches on each side, the beacon received, amplified, and returned the signal from the MSQ–77. This greatly improved the navigation of both tactical and B–52 aircraft, assuring more accurate bombing. Without an SST–181 beacon aboard, the MSQ–77 radar could track an aircraft 40 to 50 miles using a "skin paint" technique; with the beacon, tracking could be extended upwards of 196 nautical miles. This would permit Skyspot bombing in the first three route packages, but left route packages 4, 5, 6A and 6B and northern Laos beyond the radar's range.[56]

Although an advance over other navigation and bombing systems, the MSQ–77 system was not without its limitations. Both the radar and associated UHF communications, on which MSQ–77 operations largely depended, were based on the line-of-sight principal. For the radar, this meant that operations were affected by the curvature of the Earth, or any obstacles between the radar site and airborne aircraft. For UHF communications, reliability generally did not exceed 140 nautical miles. The MSQ–77 system could control only one flight at a time against a single target. A five minute lapse was necessary before another flight could be con-

---

* A total of six MSQ–77 radar ground installations were activated on the following dates: Bien Hoa and Pleiku, South Vietnam, in April and May 1966, respectively; Nakhon Phanom, Thailand, and Dong Ha, South Vietnam, on June 3 and 12, 1966; and Da Lat and Binh Thuy, South Vietnam, on September 26, 1966 and April 3, 1967. See Van Staaveren, *USAF Plans and Operations: The Air Campaign Against North Vietnam, 1966* (USAF Hist Div Liaison Ofc, Jan 68), p 28.

trolled, and if the radar operator switched to another target, another five minutes were required in order to return to the original flight. Finally, an aircraft had to fly straight and level to ensure precision bombing using the radar system.[57] The results of the first month's use of MSQ–77 radar bombing in route package 1, totaling fifty-six strikes, could not be determined readily as cloud cover or darkness frustrated efforts to obtain good bomb damage assessment photography.

However, more than two month's experience with the Skyspot system in South Vietnam was encouraging. There, combat aircraft dropped ordnance safely within 1,000 yards of friendly troops, and tests showed that this figure could be reduced considerably. Skyspot promised to replace flareships and the B–66B pathfinders. By the beginning of July, 1966, General Westmoreland was sufficiently confident of the new radar bombing system to report that the pathfinders were no longer needed in southern North Vietnam.[58]

Countering the North's Air Defense System

While bad weather hindered or made bombing impossible, the north's growing antiaircraft defense capabilities continued to take a high toll of aircraft and aircrews. Figure 12 shows the numbers of Air Force, Navy, and VNAF aircraft destroyed or damaged for the period April to June 1966.[59]

Figure 12
Aircraft Destroyed or Damaged
April, May, and June 1966

	April Des	April Dam	May Des	May Dam	June Des	June Dam
USAF	15	13	13	7	12	1
USN	16	39	6	5	8	8
USMC	0	0	0	0	0	0
VNAF	0	0	1	0	0	1

With few exceptions, automatic weapons and antiaircraft artillery accounted for all of the enemy-inflicted aircraft attrition. Route 6A was a particularly hazardous area where the Air Force, flying relatively few sorties, lost five F–105s. The firing intensity was measurable. Prior to the bombing halt that began on December 24, 1965, one mission in twelve received enemy fire; in April the ratio

MSQ–77 Combat Skyspot facilities at Dong Ha, South Vietnam.

was one mission in four. The Air Force's monthly rate of aircraft loss (for every 1,000 combat sorties flown) was also rising. In February 1966, the rate was .0004, in March, .0034, and in April, .0037. The Navy began to experience a rate increase in April when it rose to .0035, almost matching that suffered by the Air Force.[60]

The north's inventory of conventional antiaircraft weapons also continued to grow. At the end of April, Air Force analysts made the following estimate of the active antiaircraft order of battle: automatic weapons, 672; 37-mm and 57-mm guns, 1,425; and 85-mm guns, 555. At the end of April, analysts plotted about 13,891 antiaircraft sites in the north, of which 4,047 were considered to be occupied.[61]

Conversely, the direct SA–2 SAM threat to Air Force and Navy pilots continued to fall. By mid-1966, of 376 U.S. aircraft lost in the north since the air war began, no more than 15 to 18 were shot down by SAMs. On March 31, General McConnell testified before a House Armed Services Committee that anti-SAM techniques had "reduced the effectiveness of the [SA–2 SAMs] and are expected to reduce it further." He added that the SAMs had not prevented any strikes against authorized targets in the north.[62]

The Hanoi regime's effort to construct more SAM sites and import more SAM equipment and missiles had by no means peaked. By July 5, 1966 (the last day of Rolling Thunder 50), about 115 sites had been detected and SA–2 firing battalions were believed to number between 20 and 25. This compared with 99 confirmed and suspected sites and 12 to 15 firing battalions at the end of 1965. U.S. pilots reported at least 24 single firings in May and 31 in June, but all missiles failed to score. The last confirmed SAM downing of an Air Force plane had occurred on April 24.[63]

North Vietnamese 37-mm antiaircraft artillery gun and crew.

The relative ineffectiveness of the SAMs could be attributed to a series of evolving countermeasures. These consisted of Iron Hand missions (with accompanying Air Force EB–66Cs, EB–66Bs, and F–100Fs as well as Navy EA–3s and Marine EF–10Bs, all variously equipped to detect or jam SAM radar emissions); pilots alerted to SAM firings (and MiG approaches) by Air Force EC–121Ds and Navy EC–121Ms, all heavily laden with communications and electronic gear; and pilot evasion tactics.[64]

The services were constantly improving their countermeasures by adding aircraft, better equipment, and refining tactics. In May, the Seventh Air Force's inventory of EB–66Bs was increased when five more arrived from the European theater. This gave the Seventh a total of eight EB–66Bs, in addition to twelve EB–66Cs. Also in May, the Seventh Air Force received an initial delivery of two-seat F–105F Wild Weasels from Eglin AFB, Florida. Carrying more sophisticated electronic equipment, these aircraft, known as Wild Weasel IIIs,* began anti-SAM operations immediately. Six more arrived in June, and all were assigned to the 388th TFW at Korat airbase in Thailand. The Wild Weasel Is returned to Eglin soon thereafter, after a change in their mission. Used primarily

---

* An experimental F–105F Wild Weasel II model, with homing and warning equipment mounted in the wing tips rather than in the fuselage, proved unsatisfactory.

An F–105 carrying a Shrike air-to-surface antiradiation missile.

as SAM hunter-killers in late 1965, by the spring of 1966 their role had changed to that of SAM and gun radar suppressors flying with the main strike force.[65]

In April 1966, Wild Weasel aircraft were equipped for the first time with the Navy's Shrike AGM–45 air-to-surface missile. The Navy had tested the weapon in the north in 1965, and in the spring of 1966 improved models arrived in the war theater. On the 18th, an F–100F Wild Weasel launched the first Shrike against a SAM site with undetermined results. More firings followed, and near the end of the month General Moore directed the first Shrike night attack against a SAM target as a riposte to several SAM night salvoes.[66]

Although the radars of known or suspected SAM sites were the principal targets for the Shrikes, they were also aimed at radars that controlled conventional antiaircraft positions. In May, in conjunction with Iron Hand missions, Wild Weasel aircraft fired fifty-five Shrikes, and in June there were thirty-two Shrike launches. In May, pilots reported at least one SAM radar and eighteen gun radars silenced by Shrikes, and in June they reported fifteen radars similarly silenced. Pilots assumed some of the radars and associated equipment were destroyed or damaged in these attacks, but assumptions were not facts. Between April 18 and July 15, 1966, the Wild Weasel Is and IIIs launched 107 missiles with only one hit confirmed as against 38 "probables."[67]

Although more Wild Weasel IIIs equipped with Shrikes would be deployed in the ensuing months—plans in April had called for up to 25 percent of Phantoms and six to eight Thunderchiefs in each F–105 wing to be equipped with the missile—the problems inherent in Shrike missions were quite apparent by mid-1966. The missile's ability to hold SAM and gun radar signals for hom-

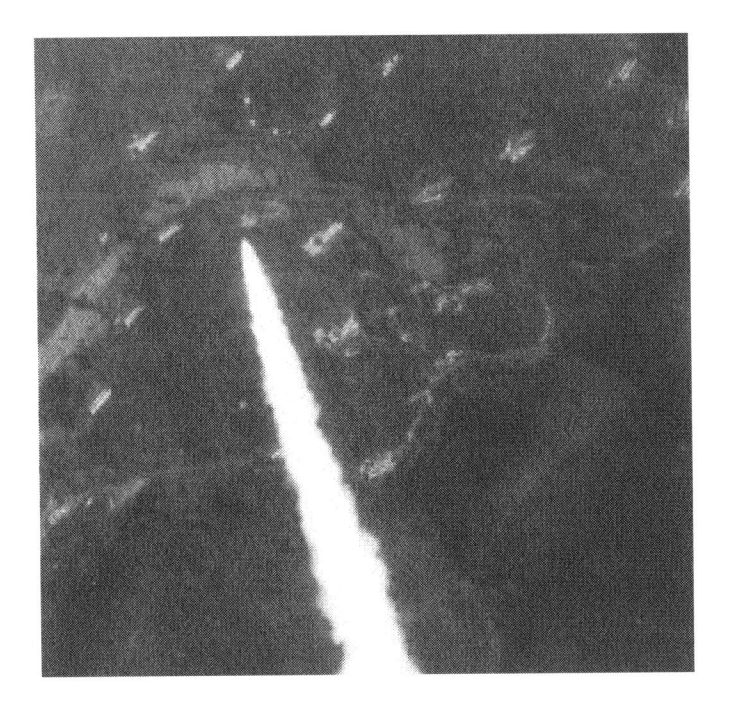

An air-to-surface missile launched by an F–105 at a missile site.

ing invariably ended when the air defenders, anticipating an air strike, turned off the signals; and with few exceptions, because of weather or terrain, aircrews could not visually locate enemy missiles and supporting equipment when a site had been located electronically. The Shrikes were also in short supply: on May 26, Shrike allocations to the Air Force were reduced and General Moore was instructed to conduct launches only against SAM radars.[68]

Meanwhile, the Air Force was planning to deploy additional EC–121Ds and, for the first time, KC–135 radio-relay aircraft. These two actions, completed in the latter half of 1966, promised to enhance further the Air Force's capability to alert pilots to SAM firings and MiG approaches.

The best and most frequently used measure against SAM firings, however, was simple evasion. The most common maneuver was the split-S while descending to a lower altitude or, in airman parlance, hitting the deck. "Our success in avoiding SAMs," Admiral Sharp reported at the end of April 1966, "has been almost entirely due to the fact [tactical aircraft pilots] have been able to take rapid evasive action...after receiving electronic intelligence warnings or seeing a missile approaching.... This prevented a SAM Fan Song radar lock-on to aircraft and the missiles usually detonated above them causing little or no damage. B–52 bombers, conversely, lacked maneuverability and this was why they should not be sent deeply into North Vietnam and risk being shot down by a SAM."[69]

271

Surprised by an RF–101 reconnaissance aircraft, North
Vietnamese gunners run to man their gun positions.

The diminishing direct threat of the SAMs was underlined on July 5, the last day of Rolling Thunder 50, when launching units fired at least twenty-six of the weapons against attacking aircraft northwest of Hanoi and failed to score a hit. Nonetheless, the SAMs continued to have a disruptive effect on operations and indirectly increased aircraft attrition. Col. William H. Holt, commander of the 355th Wing observed in mid-1966:[70]

> Although the loss rate to SAMs is relatively low compared to missiles fired, the SAMs are foiling the...strike plan and forcing the fighters down into range of other defenses. Strike aircraft are then susceptible to fire by all caliber guns; the attack plan is disrupted and additional fuel is consumed in reforming the attack.

Hanoi's third arm of air defense, its MiG fighters, had caused few problems before March 1966. Anticipating another surge of MiG activity, Admiral Sharp and his PACAF and Navy component commanders and the SAC commander had prepared a two-option strike plan against the major MiG airfields. According to option one, if administration authorities approved, the Air Force and Navy would strike the Phuc Yen and Kep airfields, where most MiGs were based. Under option two, twenty-five or thirty B–52s loaded with 750-pound

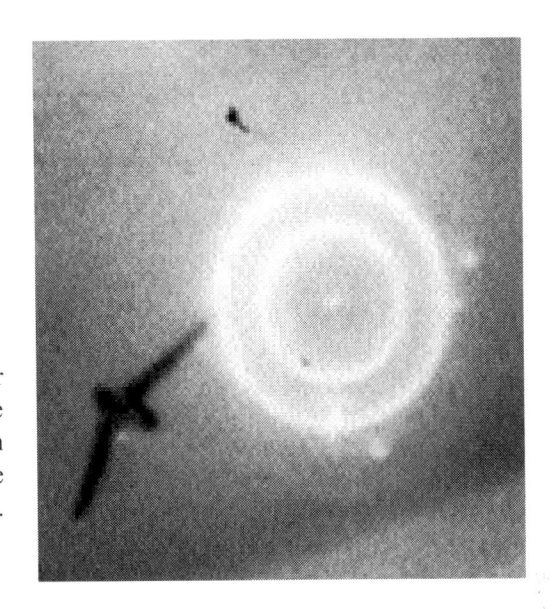

A MiG–17 shortly after being hit by cannon fire from an F–105, with flames starting to emerge at the left wing root.

bombs and BLU–3s would hit the airfields in a single low-level night attack. The bomber strikes would be followed by Air Force and Navy tactical "mopping up" sorties to destroy any MiGs remaining on any airfields.[71]

Because the airfields were within the Hanoi-Haiphong sanctuary area, administration authorities refused to approve either strike option despite a series of strong MiG challenges that began in late April. From the 23d until the end of the month, thirty-nine to forty MiGs periodically tried to break up Rolling Thunder missions. In each instance, they were intercepted by F–4C Phantoms and, in several air-to-air battles, Air Force aircrews downed six MiGs without a loss.[72]

The encounter on the 23d was triggered while four Phantoms of the 555th TFS of the 8th TFW were flying cover for F–105 Thunderchief flights en route to bomb the Bac Giang highway and rail bridge about twenty-five miles northeast of Hanoi. Phantom aircrews suddenly detected by radar four MiG–17s fifteen miles away. The planes met nearly head-on, then quickly engaged each other in a series of left-turning maneuvers at 10,000 to 18,000 feet. At first, neither side scored a hit. Then, Capt. Max F. Cameron and 1st Lt. Robert E. Evans shot down a MiG and Capt. Robert E. Blake and 1st Lt. S. W. George in a second Phantom scored on another. Throughout the battle, the MiG pilots fired several times but were unable to hit the Phantoms.[73]

Three days later, a flight of three Phantoms, flying cover for an EB–66 on an electronic countermeasures mission, were attacked by three MiG–21s. In the engagement that ensued—the first in the war with the more advanced Soviet-built aircraft—Maj. Paul J. Gilmore and 1st Lt. William T. Smith downed one of the enemy fighters with a Sidewinder. The two men had to disengage when low fuel forced them to return to their base. Aircrew reports that the enemy aircraft possibly had Chinese markings were quickly discounted by high administration officials.[74]

Two MiG–17s were destroyed on April 29 when Phantom aircrews of the 555th TFW, again flying MiG combat air patrol for a strike on the Bac Giang railroad and highway bridge, engaged the attackers north of the target area. Capt. William B. P. Dowell and 1st Lt. Hulbert Cossard downed one of the aircraft with a Sidewinder, while a second aircrew, Capt. Larry R. Keith and 1st Lt. Robert A. Bleakley, outmaneuvered another MiG, forcing its pilot to crash from about 2,500 feet. The enemy pilot, they conjectured, either lost control of his aircraft or attempted a split-S maneuver at insufficient altitude.[75]

The third battle occurred on April 30. A flight of four Phantoms was flying combat air patrol for an air rescue mission about 100 miles west and northwest of Hanoi. Two of the Phantoms had just completed midflight refueling while the other two were about to begin. At that moment, four MiG–17s, flying out of the sun and obviously hoping to catch the two Phantoms with low fuel, dove in for the attack. But Capt. Lawrence H. Goldberg and 1st Lt. Gerald D. Hargrove spotted the MiGs at about five miles. Calculating that they had enough fuel for a quick fight, they fired one Sidewinder that shot up a MiG tailpipe and exploded, destroying the aircraft. Goldberg and Hargrove then quickly returned to their base at Udorn, landing with only 400 pounds of fuel.[76]

For the next eleven days, the North Vietnamese Air Force was fairly quiet. Then, on May 12, an engagement took place that erupted into controversy. According to Air Force aircrews, the incident began when four MiG–17s jumped an electronic countermeasures mission, consisting of an EB–66 and three escorting F–4Cs, in the northern sector of North Vietnam. The aerial battle was precipitated when one of the MiGs headed for the EB–66 but was intercepted by an F–4 flown by Maj. William B. Dudley and 1st Lt. Imants Kringelis. As the MiG maneuvered towards the aircraft, the Dudley-Kringelis team unleashed a Sidewinder that missed as the MiG descended in what appeared to be a split-S maneuver for the purpose of regaining an offensive position. The Phantom aircrew fired a second Sidewinder as the MiG rolled out from behind the Destroyer. This time the missile flew into the MiG's tailpipe, destroying the plane. The pilot was not seen ejecting or parachuting and was presumed killed. The other Phantoms and MiGs continued the aerial duel a while longer, then both sides withdrew without further losses.[77]

The Peking government immediately claimed that five American fighters had penetrated its air space and fired guided missiles at several Chinese aircraft flying a training mission, with one missile downing an aircraft. The battle reportedly took place northeast of Makwan (about twenty miles north of North Vietnam's border) in Yunnan Province at 1617 local time. A Peking spokesman warned: "This is an extremely grave incident, a deliberate systematic act of provocation by the Johnson administration." Before the month was out, the Chinese

Kep airfield, North Vietnam, with an RF–101 above it.

published photographs showing fragments of a Sidewinder missile and auxiliary fuel tanks. The tanks were marked Mfg by Argent Fletcher Company, El Monte, California. Meanwhile, the Air Force and administration officials launched separate investigations that led to tightened Air Force "MiG Watch" and border warning and control.[78]

June witnessed three more MiG engagements, two involving the Navy, one involving the Air Force. The first occurred on June 12, when four MiG–17s jumped a Navy strike force. One MiG pilot, allowing himself to be attacked from the classic 6 o'clock position, was pursued immediately by a Navy pilot armed with Sidewinders. The first missile failed to connect, but the second struck and disabled the aircraft. The enemy pilot lost control and crashed with the plane. A second MiG was damaged, but not downed when hit by 20-mm fire. On June 21, several MiG–17s attacked two Navy F–8 Crusaders on combat air patrol for a downed Crusader pilot, and a dogfight ensued. One of the Navy pilots fired a Sidewinder that detonated near the tail of a MiG causing it to spiral downward, trailing black smoke, presumably crashing. The victor, flying with barely 200 pounds of fuel, then rendezvoused quickly with an aerial tanker and returned to a carrier.[79]

On June 29, a flight of four F–105s, completing an Iron Hand SAM suppression mission northwest of Hanoi, was attacked by four MiG–17s. After one MiG fired, the Thunderchief pilots took evasive action, pursued by all four enemy aircraft. As the American pilots jettisoned their ordnance and went to afterburners, one of the MiGs fired again, this time scoring several hits on the plane piloted by Maj. Fred L. Tracy. One 23-mm slug entered Tracy's cockpit, knocking his hand off the throttle, putting him out of afterburner, and damaging his gunsight, oxygen equipment, and other instruments. The attacking pilot overshot his American adversary and appeared suddenly at Tracy's 12 o'clock position. Tracy fired two hundred rounds from his 20-mm cannon and observed about ten hits. The MiG rolled over, flew a split-S at about two thousand feet, and crashed. Although Tracy left the battle area immediately, the fight was not over. A second MiG and two Thunderchiefs now engaged. The enemy plane scored once, and one Thunderchief pilot responded with two bursts of cannonfire but made no hits. This ended the dogfights. Tracy was credited with downing a MiG, the first F–105 pilot to do so.[80]

Despite the North Vietnamese Air Force's lack of success, it possessed ample aircraft at the end of June 1966. There were still fifty MiG–15s and MiG–17s and thirteen MiG–21s poised for action at Kep and Phuc Yen airfields. In South Vietnam, commanders continued to wonder if Hanoi intended to attack with the six Il–28 bombers at Phuc Yen.[81]

Improving MiG Watch and Border Patrol

The Peking government's allegation that its air space was violated by American fighters on May 12 prompted General Harris to order a thorough review of the incident. When questioned, aircrews associated with the mission insisted that there had been no border violation. At no time, they said, did they receive a warning of a SAM firing, approaching MiGs, or an alert that they were crossing China's border. Nor did the aircrews consider their navigation maps deficient.[82]

Unconvinced, Defense Secretary McNamara directed the Joint Chiefs to dispatch a special JCS team to South Vietnam and Thailand to conduct another investigation. The Joint Chiefs quickly appointed USAF Brig. Gen. Robert G. Owens of the JCS J-3 Operations Staff to head a team that included representatives of the Air Staff and the National Security Agency. As the team's preliminary findings pointed to a likely border violation, General Moore in Saigon took actions to assure closer Air Force and Navy coordination of their airborne control systems, tightened rules for fighter escorts of reconnaissance aircraft, issued new instructions for maintaining radio discipline, and explored the possibility of providing combat pilots with additional radios.[83]

The Owens report was completed in late May 1966 and concluded that "in all probability," because of a navigation error, an Air Force EB–66 and accompanying Phantom fighters had indeed entered China's air space on May 12. On June 9, General McConnell sent a special Air Force team, headed by Col. Charles E. Williams Jr., to Southeast Asia to conduct a thorough study of the reliability of the Air Force's command and control system for aircraft over North Vietnam. Before the Williams group had completed its study in South Vietnam and Thailand, the Peking government alleged that its border had again been violated by American aircraft, on June 29. As on May 12, the offenders were an EB–66 with three accompanying F–4C Phantoms. This time, the border crossing was verified by the EB–66's own photography, again causing alarm within the administration. Vice Adm. Lloyd M. Mustin, the JCS's Director of Operations, informed USAF Lt. Gen. Paul S. Emerick, PACOM's Chief of Staff, that the second incident created "extraordinary sensitivity" at high Washington levels and would impair service efforts to obtain future approval for attacks on important targets and for armed reconnaissance closer to China's border.[84]

The Williams team returned to Washington on July 6 and submitted its findings to General McConnell, the JCS, and the Air Staff. The team's major recommendation called for the establishment of an improved communications radio relay center in South Vietnam for receiving and correlating all aerial combat data, such as possible border violations, MiG approaches, and SA–2 firings. Because "lead time" was needed to procure all these items, the center, consisting of three interlocking installations, would be established in three phases: an improved central reporting system and relay center at Na Tra (or Monkey Mountain) about six miles northeast of Da Nang by July 15; a new manual Tactical Air Control Center at Na Tra by September 15; and a semiautomatic data processing and display facility at both Monkey Mountain and Udorn by September 1967. Other improvements would be added as warranted.[85]

The team also took three supporting actions. The first called for two more EC–121D airborne battlefield command and control center aircraft to augment the SAM firing and MiG surveillance and warning system. Two new high orbits would be maintained over the Gulf of Tonkin and Laos to supplement the low EC–121D orbits instituted in 1965. Second, specially-equipped KC–135s should be used over the north for radio relay operations at 35,000 feet. The converted SAC tankers would be equipped with ARC–89, 250-Watt UHF automatic relay equipment with a minimum of four communications channels. Two aircraft would be needed to ensure twelve-hour coverage and, if necessary, five could provide twenty-four-hour coverage. Finally, there would be procedural changes in flashing warnings to combat aircraft of possible violations within the border buffer zone.[86]

Following the second border violation on June 29, the JCS requested that the Air Force implement the recommendations made by the Williams team. The Air Force complied, assigning the nickname Combat Lighting to the project. Two KC–135s were equipped with communications gear and, on September 10, 1966, the JCS directed their deployment with aircrews and support personnel to U-Tapao whenever the Thai government agreed. As an interim measure, they were based at Kadena AB, Okinawa, from where they flew their first missions over the north in September.[87]

An underground petroleum storage area burning after strikes by F–105s in June 1966.

CHAPTER 10
The POL Strikes

On June 29, 1966, Air Force and Navy commanders began attacking a number of the north's major petroleum, oil, and lubricant storage areas. President Johnson's decision authorizing the attacks ended more than two years of intense debate between the services and high civilian officials over the value of these targets to the north's war effort and the possible political consequences at home and abroad of their destruction. The most important POL storage sites were located within the Hanoi-Haiphong sanctuary area, making them highly sensitive.

The POL Debate

The significance of POL targets in the north had been discussed by services and administration officials since the early 1960s, but a concerted effort to win authorization to destroy them did not begin until May 1964. At that time, General LeMay fashioned a JCS recommendation that called for attacks on all POL and other significant targets as soon as possible and was quickly sent to Secretary McNamara. The Defense Secretary's response was to ask the Joint Chiefs to prepare a list of key targets in the north. In June 1964, the JCS completed the list, which included thirteen important POL storage and facility installations.* Administration officials did not permit strikes on any targets on the list until March 1965, when they authorized Rolling Thunder operations. To avoid escalating the bombing too rapidly, officials ordered Air Force and Navy commanders to limit interdiction to southernmost North Vietnam and to move the bomb line northward gradually.

In subsequent months, a limited number of the JCS-designated targets were struck, but none within or above the Hanoi-Haiphong sanctuary area or near China. By the end of October 1965, only four of thirteen key POL targets had been attacked.[1]

Convinced that all of the POL sites could be destroyed without undue political risk, in November 1965, the JCS made clear to Secretary McNamara Hanoi's growing dependency on fuel supplies. The country's POL imports to date totaled about 170,000 tons, valued at $4.8 million, almost all of it shipped from the Black Sea area in the Soviet Union. After delivery to Haiphong, the only port with facilities for handling large oil tankers, the fuel was stored at that port in large tank farms, then transported by road, rail, and waterway to Hanoi and other areas of the country. The regime's reliance on POL revealed itself in increasing use of motorized watercraft and vehicles on an expanding network of small roads in North Vietnam and Laos. Thus, the destruction of

---

* See Chapter 2.

storage areas would more seriously damage North Vietnam's capability to move resources within the country and along infiltration routes than any other single large system.[2]

Figure 13
Storage Capacity of Major North Vietnamese POL Installations
1964–1966

Installation	Original Capacity (in metric tons)
Haiphong	45,200
Hanoi	31,250
Dong Nham	14,000
Phuc Yen	14,000
Nguyen Khe	13,000
Nam Dinh	12,000
Phu Qui	10,000
Vinh	10,000
Bac Giang	6,000
Don Son	4,000
Viet Tri	4,000
Phu Van	1,000
Kep	800
Total	**165,250**

Source: Msg, ADMINO CINCPAC TO JCS, 310121Z Jul 66.

Of the nine remaining key storage areas, the Joint Chiefs recommended attacking the one at Haiphong first. This would require about 336 strike and 80 flak suppression sorties. The cost would be about ten aircraft, some light collateral damage to the surrounding area, and fewer than fifty casualties. The operations should not be delayed, as Hanoi was strengthening its air defenses around the areas and dispersing supplies. Recent aerial photography of the Hanoi vicinity, they said, showed that the North Vietnamese were working around the clock burying groups of sixteen to twenty storage tanks with only vents and filling apparatus protruding above ground. Photography also disclosed considerable drum storage activity.[3]

Some petroleum was dispersed by storing it underground. Here, an underground petroleum storage facility is under construction.

However, U.S. intelligence offices and agencies did not share the services' conviction of the importance of the POL storage areas and the need to attack them quickly. In late 1965, the U.S. Board of National Estimates did not anticipate that VC-NVA activities in South Vietnam would be crippled if Hanoi lost its principal POL storage and distribution centers. The Board predicted that if the centers were bombed the Hanoi government would become more firmly entrenched, both in military terms and with respect to negotiations, and the bombing would be interpreted by the government and its communist allies as "a conspicuous change in the ground rules" for waging the war. A Special National Intelligence Estimate and a CIA intelligence analysis in December 1965 were inclined to favor more bombing of POL and other targets, but concluded the military impact would not last long. Individually, both reports stated that, at worst, Hanoi might find it more difficult to carry on the war and be forced to limit its support to the VC-NVA fighting in the south. The CIA doubted that the destruction of the major POL installations would readily undermine the determination of Hanoi's leaders to continue the war:

> Although there presumably is a point at which one or more turns of the screw would crack the enemy resistance to negotiations, past experience indicates that we are unlikely to have clear evidence when that point has been reached.[4]

Asked by McNamara to comment on the CIA's conclusion, in January 1966 General Wheeler reiterated the views expressed by the Joint Chiefs in November 1965. He said that the destruction of the major POL centers would have a "substantial impact" on the Hanoi regime's present and future military operations in the south, and compel it to rely largely on animals, porters, and motorless watercraft to move supplies. Wheeler went on to assert that the regime's dependency on POL was particularly evident in its inventory of 10,000 to 12,000 trucks and its request for 3,700 more from its Soviet allies. Although the U.S. services had destroyed about 800 trucks in the north in 1965, the losses were offset by imports of about 2,000.[5]

President Johnson's decision to suspend Rolling Thunder operations on December 24, 1965, to observe a thirty-hour Christmas truce stretched into an unsuccessful thirty-seven-day diplomatic initiative to convince Hanoi to begin negotiations. During the hiatus, the POL discussions were subsumed into the wider issue of the scope and tempo of future Rolling Thunder attacks. On January 8 and 18, 1966, the Joint Chiefs, strongly backed by all Southeast Asia commanders, urged McNamara to resume bombing with a "sharp blow" against the major POL, industrial, and other such targets if negotiations failed. However, when the President reinstituted the Rolling Thunder campaign on January 31, he sanctioned only armed reconnaissance missions below the 20th parallel for both political and military reasons.[6]

The President's decision to constrict Rolling Thunder operations brought no surcease in the debate over the major POL sites. On February 4, a special National Intelligence Estimate reaffirmed its earlier assessment that the destruction of the fuel facilities, as well as power plants and port targets, would not bring the country to its knees. According to the estimate, the loss of POL storage facilities could be readily offset by POL tankers unloading at Chan Ching in South China, from where the fuel could be transported by rail to North Vietnam's border, and from there by truck to Hanoi and elsewhere. Alternatively, POL supplies could also be moved by rail from the Soviet Union to Chan Ching and then shipped down the coast in shallow-draft boats.[7]

The highly restricted Rolling Thunder campaign continued through February and March 1966. During this two-month period, Generals Harris and Westmoreland, Admiral Sharp, other Southeast Asia commanders, and the Joint Chiefs again requested approval from the administration for strikes on important targets that had hitherto escaped bombing. The Joint Chiefs addressed the subject frequently in memoranda to Secretary McNamara. On March 1, they observed that striking POL sites remained "the highest priority action not yet approved." On the 10th, they appealed for authority to strike all important POL installations and the principal road and rail routes from China and to close Haiphong port by mining its waters.[8]

McNamara and other high officials rejected the military services' requests until late March, although there were indications that they soon planned to approve somewhat expanded bombing operations. The Defense Secretary's position appears to have been influenced by a change in the CIA's assessment of the progress of the war. In a new report, issued the same month, the agency—surprisingly—advocated intensified air attacks on the north, including the destruction of eight major POL storage facilities that had "a direct bearing" on Hanoi's ability to support the war in the south. In conversations with General Wheeler on March 21 and 23 concerning more air power for General Westmoreland's extended battlefield area, the Defense Secretary signaled that he was now inclined to allow striking important POL and other targets during the next bombing program, tentatively designated Rolling Thunder 50 and scheduled to begin on April 1.[9]

Gratified by the Defense Secretary's sudden support of heavier bombing—on condition that General Westmoreland's air needs would have first air priority—Wheeler requested, and Sharp quickly submitted, a new bombing scenario for destroying the key POL storage and distribution facilities. The PACOM commander challenged earlier intelligence analyses that played down the importance of POL to the north's warmaking capability:[10]

> I believe some influential views recently put forward understate [the] difficulty [the] enemy would have in mitigating [the] effects of [a] determined POL campaign. For example, [the] view that storage facilities at Haiphong are not required in order to pump POL to users on shore simply cannot be substantiated. Recently, [the] CIA estimated that bulk POL supplies could be lightened ashore as required, but we know from experience that offloading of public POL to lighters and then to shore is quite an operation. Storage facilities of some kind are required. Drumming operations take time and effort at each facility. Points where POL transfer must take place are more easily found by photoreconnaissance than many other types of activity. Even if POL is brought in already drummed, the offloading process would be tedious and time-consuming, and susceptible to disruption by armed reconnaissance.

Using Sharp's scenario, the Joint Chiefs assembled their recommended "bombing package" for the north. McNamara quickly endorsed it, and urged the President to do likewise, observing that the package included nine new JCS-designated targets, of which seven were key POL storage and distribution facilities, representing 70 to 80 percent of such facilities in the country. The Defense Secretary still believed that the destruction of the major POL sites would have less military impact than the service chiefs assumed. The losses, he said, would not cripple the regime as it possessed other POL stores, and it had recently doubled its POL orders with the Soviet Union. Still, Hanoi's overall military effort was bound to suffer.[11]

By late March, President Johnson appears to have concluded that attacks on the key POL and other targets near Hanoi and Haiphong could now be undertaken with minimum risk of expanding the war. However, renewed political strife in South Vietnam, triggered by Premier Nguyen Cao Ky's removal of General Nguyen Chanh Thi, Commander of South Vietnam's I Corps, and new diplomatic efforts in the ensuing weeks by the United Nations, Great Britain, and Canada to end the war delayed the President's decision until late June. In the intervening weeks, pressure to strike the POL sites continued to mount.[12]

Approval of a few POL Strikes

On April 1, 1966, Walt W. Rostow succeeded McGeorge Bundy as the President's Special Adviser on National Security Affairs. A noted student of international economic and political affairs, Mr. Rostow agreed with the Joint Chiefs of Staff that the destruction of the north's major POL sites could seriously cripple the communists' war effort. On May 6, he personally urged Secretaries McNamara and Rusk to back a quick assault on the targets, citing the impact of POL bombing in Germany in World War II:

> From the moment that serious and systematic oil attacks started, front line single fighter strength and tank ability was affected. The reason was this: it proved more difficult, in the face of general oil shortage, to allocate from less important to more important uses than the simple arithmetic of the problem would suggest. Oil moves in various logistic channels from central sources. When the central sources began to dry up, the effects proved fairly prompt and widespread. What look like reserves statistically are rather inflexible commitments to logistic pipelines.
>
> With an understanding that simple analogies are dangerous, I nevertheless feel it is quite possible the military effects of a systematic and sustained bombing of POL in North Vietnam may be more prompt and direct than conventional intelligence analysis would suggest. I would underline, however, the adjectives "systematic" and "sustained." If we take this step, we must cut clean through the POL system—and hold the cut—if we are looking for decisive results.

Earlier, he added, the United States calculated that 60 percent of the north's POL supplies were used for military purposes and 40 percent for the civilian sector, but that had grown to an estimated 80 percent of POL supplies for military use. Thus, Hanoi possessed only a small POL supply "cushion." Three days after Rostow dispatched his letter, General McConnell, a vigorous advocate of knocking out all POL sites, told a Senate Armed Services subcommittee that hitting the sites would have a "substantial" effect on the amount of supplies that the North Vietnamese could send to their forces in South Vietnam.[13]

President Johnson apparently believed that attacks on the north's entire POL system could not be delayed much longer, yet he was hesitant to flash the order to do so. The internal strife in South Vietnam still simmered and several foreign diplomatic initiatives to slow or halt the war were under way. Near the end of May, he decided he could risk a series of strikes on six less important storage areas south of Hanoi. At about the same time, he informed his closest European ally, British Prime Minister Harold Wilson, of his intent to bomb all of the major POL sites. But a new series of events—often marked by high drama—would delay the first attack on several major POL sites for another month.[14]

The usually supportive British Prime Minister quickly asked the President not to proceed with the POL assault. He warned that it would be construed abroad as further escalation of the war. The political disadvantages would far outweigh the military benefits and intensify the criticism by, and the disquiet among the United States' European allies. If the attacks were undertaken, he said, Britain would have to dissociate itself from the operations. The President tried (but failed) to change the Prime Minister's position.[15]

On May 31, Air Force and Navy fighter-bombers rained bombs on six dispersed sites in and around Vinh, Phuc Loi, Da Loc, Yen Duong, and Phu Qui, all located below Hanoi. These strikes and others on non-POL targets accounted for 313 sorties over North Vietnam, the largest number in one day since Rolling Thunder operations began in March 1965. Five days later, General Westmoreland asked Admiral Sharp and General Wheeler to maintain the air pressure. Citing an improved political situation in South Vietnam, he said the time was "ripe" for a "telling blow" against eight key POL storage sites at Haiphong, Hanoi, Nguyen Khe, Phuc Yen, Bac Giang, Don Son, Viet Tri, and Duong Nham. Further delay would reduce the bombing impact because of Hanoi's continuing dispersal activities.[16]

Admiral Sharp quickly endorsed Westmoreland's plea and, in a second cable to the Joint Chiefs, stressed the vital importance of destroying all of the major targets in the Hanoi-Haiphong area. The attacks, he averred, would have a "critical impact" on Hanoi at the moment its forces were about to launch another campaign in the south from their Laotian and Cambodian bases. Ambassador Lodge in Saigon also dispatched a cable to Washington, asserting that the present level of bombing was having an adverse effect on Hanoi and that heavier air strikes might force its leaders to come to the negotiating table. At the same time, Air Force intelligence analysts speculated that the destruction of the major POL targets would have a most profound impact on Hanoi's infiltration capability and could be conducted without severe civilian losses.[17]

By June 10, President Johnson was ready to give air commanders the go-ahead for strikes against the key POL sites and a few other JCS-designated targets. In the Pentagon, John McNaughton, the Assistant Secretary of Defense for Internal Security Affairs, had drafted a series of papers for release on the day of the operations, the JCS sent an "execute" message to CINCPAC, State Department sent cables to U.S. allies and "third countries" explaining the reasons for the strikes, and a public announcement of the bombings and "talking" papers were prepared for the use of high officials. However, a new political development again delayed the attacks.[18]

The Canadian Foreign Office informed the State Department that it had asked Chester Ronning, a retired Canadian ambassador, to make a second visit to Hanoi from June 14 to 18 to explore again the possibility of persuading Hanoi's leaders to negotiate with the United States. Secretary Rusk, who happened to be in Europe and approved of the Canadian initiative, immediately advised President Johnson to hold the POL strikes in abeyance. The President agreed. Both wished to avoid accusations by domestic and foreign critics of the war that the administration had struck sensitive targets deliberately to sabotage the Ronning mission.[19]

The strike postponement did not halt the frantic planning for the attacks. On June 13, McNamara informed Admiral Sharp that the initial strikes would be limited to four new targets: the two POL sites at Hanoi and Haiphong and a thermal power plant and a cement plant in Haiphong. However, final approval was contingent on the ability of American pilots to keep civilian casualties low. How many casualties would there be? What could be done to limit them?[20]

Vice Admiral Lloyd M. Mustin, Chief of the Joint Staff's operations section responsible for working out the tactical details of the proposed attack, made sure that Sharp had no doubt about the administration's profound concern over civilian losses. For example, a Joint Staff study projected about 48 casualties in bombing eleven POL targets, but CIA analysts concluded there might be up to 300. General Wheeler had already informed White House and State Department officials through McNamara that the services would minimize losses by employing only the most experienced pilots, by briefing those pilots extensively, by attacking only when the weather permitted visual targeting, and by using precision weapons consistent with mission objectives. "We know these [instructions]...are completely nauseous and tell you how to blow your nose," said Mustin, "but they were prepared as a 'sacrifice' to obtain strike authority."[21]

In response to McNamara's queries about casualties, Sharp indicated that Air Force and Navy pilots would adhere to the precise tactical guidelines already conveyed by Wheeler to higher officials and that they would select only the optimum axis of attack and use electronic countermeasures against radar-controlled SA-2 SAM and antiaircraft guns. Furthermore, air commanders would make certain that pilots were not distracted by communications not associated with their mission. Hanoi's excellent air alert system, the PACOM commander noted, would assist by giving the populace time to seek cover. All of these measures should minimize human deaths, which, he believed, would total less than fifty. McNamara was pleased with Sharp's response, but asked for, and quickly received, one additional assurance: that pilots would be extremely cautious while conducting flak and missile suppression missions.[22]

On June 15, while Canadian Ambassador Ronning was conferring with Hanoi's leaders, President Johnson approved for immediate execution attacks on a different series of targets, all outside of the Hanoi-Haiphong sanctuary area and the buffer zone bordering China. The three most sensitive targets were two POL sites at Don Son and Duong Nham, barely ten nautical miles outside of Haiphong, and

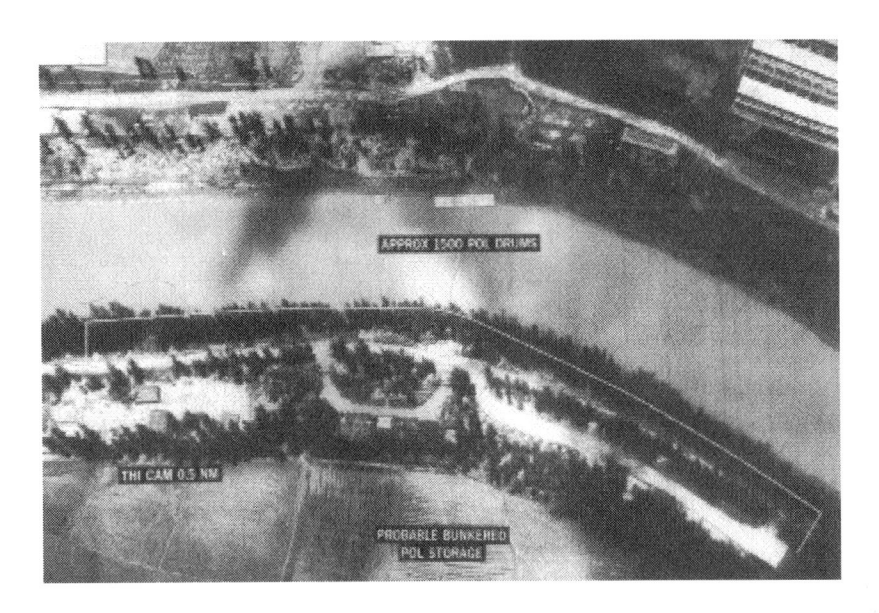

Dispersed petroleum supplies stored in drums alongside a stream.

a radar installation in the vicinity of Kep airfield, northeast of Hanoi. Slightly more than forty-eight hours later, the President ordered the three targets deleted from the approved list, although bad weather now delayed the planned air assaults. The deletion of the POL sites dismayed the service chiefs. General McConnell believed that the Joint Chiefs should seek another meeting with McNamara in order to underline the compelling need to attack "all segments of the POL system" in view of Hanoi's dispersal activities and the inevitably higher cost in aircraft and men if there was further delay in destroying the system.[23]

Meanwhile, Ronning had returned to Ottawa. North Vietnamese Prime Minister Pham Van Dong's "negotiating" position, as relayed by Ronning to William P. Bundy, Assistant Secretary of State for Far Eastern Affairs, was contradictory. The Prime Minister said his government would come to the conference table "unconditionally" and not insist, as previously, on U.S. acceptance of his government's Four Points, enunciated in April 1965, if the United States "unconditionally" stopped the bombing, a position in consonance with the Foreign Ministry's statement of January 4, 1966. Ronning realized that the Foreign Ministry's statement, which called upon the United States to halt the bombing "unconditionally" and to recognize the Four Points as the only basis for peace, could not be reconciled with the assurances he had just received from Bundy. He thus concluded, as did administration officials to whom he relayed his conversations with Ronning, that Prime Minister Dong had shown no new flexibility in his attitude towards peace. Thus, a change in Rolling Thunder planning and operations was not warranted.[24]

Gradual Expansion of POL Strikes

Thus it was that in a press conference on June 18, President Johnson signaled that heavier bombing in the north was likely. "We must continue to raise the cost of aggression at its source," he said, "and this is the sole purpose for striking selected targets." Three days later, as weather cleared, Air Force and Navy commanders again received the go-ahead to attack the dispersed POL sites and other targets authorized on June 15, minus the sites at Don Son and Duong Nham, and the radar installation at Kep. Attacks continued daily against POL sites near Vinh, Yen, Yen Hau, Bai Thuong, Thang Ha, and along routes 1A and 116. Eager to maintain the momentum, Air Force targeters plotted scores of "truck park/POL sites" for the fighter-bombers, assuming—with considerable justification—that every truck park harbored drums of POL. By now, the news media was rife with speculation that the major unharmed POL sites would be next.[25]

The speculation was well-founded. On June 22, White House and Pentagon officials were engaged in preparations to bomb the key POL sites and a few other sensitive targets. Admiral Mustin informed Sharp that the President and McNamara, were on the phone repeatedly and "have not seen the likes [of this] since [the] hours preceding, during, and after [the] Pierce Arrow strikes of August 1964."* The Joint Chiefs operations director attributed the frenetic activity to the "expected storm of reaction worldwide" and the fear of adverse reactions that had been "carefully implanted, nurtured, and amplified by those here who oppose more effective actions against the north." The latter group, he said, posed "the greatest danger to hope for future effective action against the north." Thus, future bombing approvals would be contingent on the manner in which the decisions of the President and Defense Secretary were fulfilled. He asked Sharp for "complete, exhaustive, minute details" of the strike operations before, during, and after their completion and for the data "any hour of the day or night." No effort should be spared in keeping McNamara and the President fully informed.[26]

The President's decision to proceed with the major bombing strikes was dispatched earlier in the day in a JCS execute directive to Admiral Sharp. The directive ordered air attacks "at first light" on the 24th against POL storage sites at Hanoi, Haiphong, Nguyen Khe, Bac Giang, Don Son, Viet Tri, and Duong Nham, plus the radar station at Kep. There were two pages of detailed operations guidance. The main instructions called for a surprise attack, no strikes in marginal weather, no strikes on Sunday, June 26, if weather delayed the fighter-bombers that long, no attacks on merchant shipping in Haiphong port (the Russian tanker *Komsomol* had been discharging its cargo near a POL facility), no attacks on other ships or watercraft unless they fired first and were

---

* Pierce Arrow was the code name for the first U.S. air strikes against North Vietnam in August 1964 in retaliation for patrol boat attacks on two U.S. destroyers in the Gulf of Tonkin. See Chapter 2.

unmistakably of North Vietnamese registry, and strict adherence to the tactical guidelines developed in mid-June to minimize civilian casualties.[27]

As Air Force and Navy commanders and hundreds of their aircrews and supporting airmen remained on alert, the Joint Chiefs flashed another bombing postponement. This time, a news leak on June 24—the date set for the attacks—aborted the planned take-offs. Philip Geyelin, a reporter for the Wall Street Journal, confirmed that the President intended to bomb the POL site at Haiphong. That evening the essential details of the decision appeared on a Dow Jones news wire. The Joint Chiefs considered the strike plan "thoroughly blown." However, bad weather had descended over the principal targets and, in all likelihood, would have canceled the attack. The postponed operation left administration spokesmen highly discomfited. In reply to press inquiries, they felt compelled to deny the President had made a decision to bomb the fuel dump at Haiphong. They found it easier to refute a highly erroneous CBS report that the installation would be struck by B–52 bombers.[28]

On June 28, Sharp informed Wheeler that favorable flying weather would permit the POL strikes, that his Air Force and Navy units were ready, and requested permission to conduct them beginning on the 29th. Wheeler flashed the President's approval, reinstating the directive of June 22 and asked that all messages pertaining to the strikes be sent "Special Category, Exclusive" to himself and Secretary McNamara.[29]

Strikes on Major POL Sites Begin

Thus, after several weeks of on-again, off-again decisions, on June 29 Admiral Sharp issued an execute order to his Air Force and Navy commanders. He instructed the Navy to hit the POL installations at Haiphong, Bac Giang, Don Son, and Duong Nham and a radar site near Kep airfield and assigned the Air Force the POL installations at Hanoi, Nguyen Khe, and Viet Tri and a highway and railroad bridge at Viet Tri.[30]

The Navy led off, not at "first light" as planned, but at 1350 Saigon time on the 29th because of weather. Sixteen A–6s and twelve support aircraft from the carriers *Constellation* and *Ranger* attacked the Haiphong site where they dropped one hundred nineteen 250-pound and twenty-four 1,000-pound bombs. Smaller missions hit the Don Son site, where pilots dropped eighteen 500-pound and six 250-pound bombs. Both sites escaped extensive destruction as many bombs fell off target, and the two sites were subsequently targeted for restrikes.[31]

Twenty-five minutes later, General Moore sent his Seventh Air Force planes against a POL tank farm three and a half miles from the center of Hanoi. The farm had a storage capacity estimated at 31,250 metric tons, or roughly 17 percent of the north's total POL reserves. Moore dispatched twenty-five strike F–105s, four EB–66s for electronic countermeasures, eight Iron Hand F–105s to attack radar-controlled SAMs and antiaircraft guns, and twenty-four F–4Cs and two

F–104s for combat air patrol and escort. The Thunderchief pilots dropped a total of 188 750-pound bombs on the storage tanks, triggered many explosions and sent smoke billowing 35,000 feet above the North Vietnamese capital. When the fires, smoke, and haze dissipated, only two of thirty-two tanks were left standing, although all appeared to have burned. The bombing was quite accurate, with about 90 percent of the target area destroyed. Poststrike photography showed only twenty-two bombs off target, and these fell mostly in rice fields. A few bombs accidentally destroyed five farming huts located within 300 feet of the storage area. As a "bonus," several bombs fell in the southwest corner of the Hanoi army barracks and supply depot, destroying and damaging four buildings.[32]

North Vietnam's air defenders, lying in wait, responded with a heavy barrage of SA–2 SAMs and conventional antiaircraft fire. The SAMs, none of which scored a hit, were less of a problem than the antiaircraft fire. Air Force Maj. Hallet F. Marsten, a veteran of 101 missions in Korea and more than 75 missions over North Vietnam, characterized the flak over Hanoi as very severe. One burst jolted his plane to a 90-degree angle. "It was worse than anything

The Hanoi petroleum storage facility shortly after the June 29, 1966, attack, opposite page and above. Strike pilots reported that flames were 12,000 feet high and that smoke rose to 35,000 feet.

I've experienced," he later told newsmen. By constant "jinking," or evasive action, all pilots except Capt. Murphy Neal and his Thunderchief made it back to their airbases. A group of four MiG–17s also challenged the attackers, zooming in against several Iron Hand F–105Ds. They paid a price. In a quick engagement, a plane piloted by Maj. Fred L. Tracy shot down one of the enemy aircraft, the first MiG "kill" of the war by a Thunderchief pilot.[33]

Captain Neal successfully ejected from his stricken plane, but he was captured and, according to the Soviet news agency Tass, paraded through the streets of Hanoi the same night with crowds shouting "down with the imperialists." He was then put on display before North Vietnamese and foreign newsmen and forced to express "contrition" for his "action against the Vietnamese people." Predictably, Radio Hanoi charged that the planes bombed indiscriminately and strafed residential and economic areas, causing human and material losses, but did not admit the destruction of the POL facilities. A Hanoi spokesman boasted that the air defenders shot down four planes and captured a number of Americans, but except for Captain Neal, failed to produce evidence that more than one plane was downed and one pilot captured.[34]

In Saigon, Maj. Gen. Gilbert Meyers, the deputy commander of the Seventh Air Force, characterized the strikes at Hanoi and Haiphong as "the most significant, most important of the war." In Washington, in a turbulent news conference, McNamara justified the POL attacks on the grounds that the Hanoi regime had increased its reliance on POL, a development clearly manifested by its expanding use of vehicles and powered junks. Truck movements in the first five

Damage to the Hanoi petroleum storage facility after the June 29 attack.
Approximately 80 percent of the facility's capacity was destroyed.

months of 1966, he said, were double those for the same period in the previous year and, with continuing truck imports and the construction of more and better roads, would probably double again by the end of 1966. As a consequence, over the past year, daily overland supply tonnages increased 150 percent, the infiltration rate increased 120 percent (averaging 4,500 men per month), and the number of NVA units in South Vietnam increased 100 percent.[35]

Over the next two days, U.S. pilots returned to hit the remaining key POL installations. General Moore dispatched two separate missions, each consisting of twelve F–105 strike and support aircraft, against the POL storage areas at Nguyen Khe and Viet Tri, seven miles north and twenty-eight miles northwest of Hanoi. The pilots rained sixty-two 750-pound bombs on the first and thirty-two on the second, with supporting aircraft plastering antiaircraft positions in each area with CBU–24 cluster bombs. Only one Thunderchief was damaged and the pilot, who ejected, was recovered safely. The dual mission proved only marginally successful, however, destroying only 20 percent of the target area at Nguyen Khe and 15 percent at Viet Tri.[36]

On the same day, Navy pilots from the carrier *Hancock* hit the Bac Giang POL facility twenty-five miles northeast of Hanoi, and the radar facility at Kep eleven miles northeast of Bac Giang. Forty-eight 500-pound bombs dropped from eighteen aircraft largely demolished the POL facility, while twelve aircraft inflicted heavy damage at Kep. Three radar vans and sixteen support buildings were destroyed.[37]

Air Force and Navy commanders continued the attacks into July. The Navy conducted restrikes at the Don Son and Haiphong POL sites, which had escaped heavy damage in the first attacks, and the Air Force bombed POL facilities twenty-eight and thirty-three miles north and northeast of Hanoi. By July 11, a total of twenty-five large and small sites had been struck, with Air Force and Navy planes dropping ordnance every day but one. Pentagon officials announced that

80 to 90 percent of the north's fuel storage areas and facilities had been attacked and 55 percent of all facilities had been destroyed.[38]

American officials made no estimate of the civilian casualties caused by the raids, but considered them small. Hanoi published no figures. But the strikes hastened the exodus of residents from the two cities, especially Hanoi. Foreign news sources reported 10,000 residents were leaving the city every day in addition to an estimated 700,000 residents who had left the capital in previous months.[39]

As expected, the POL bombings produced major domestic and foreign repercussions. In the United States some congressional supporters of the administration expressed unease about the danger of expanding the conflict, while well-known critics sharpened their attacks. Senator J. William Fulbright, Chairman of Senate Foreign Relations, who was holding special hearings on the war, cited a study prepared by academicians allegedly "proving" that peace hopes were dashed by U.S. military escalation on seven separate occasions since the beginning of the war. Senator Vance Hartke of Indiana charged that the bombings torpedoed Canadian Ambassador Ronning's mid-June mission to Hanoi. The United Kingdom, France, India, and other countries disapproved of the bombings, and there were violent anti-American demonstrations in several Indian cities, especially in Calcutta, where rioters attacked the U.S. information building. Peking, Moscow, and all East European countries predictably condemned the POL attacks and issued dark warnings about providing more overt assistance in the war, vowing unstinting aid to the Hanoi regime.[40]

Administration spokesmen vigorously defended the military operations. Under Secretary of State Ball denied that the strikes had frustrated the Canadian peace initiative, and the State Department observed that twenty-six Free World nations approved or indicated "understanding" of the action, while only twelve openly disapproved. State also emphasized that the attacks carefully avoided populated areas and that the United States did not intend to widen the war. In contrast, Hanoi was sending more men and supplies to South Vietnam and refusing to negotiate for peace.

In Des Moines, Iowa on June 30, President Johnson renewed his call for negotiations with Hanoi as "one way to end the killing in the south and the bombing of the north." "As long as [Hanoi's leaders] carry on the war" he warned, "we will persevere. They cannot wear us down and they cannot escape paying a very high price for their aggression." Walt W. Rostow, the President's Special Adviser for National Security Affairs, sought to allay domestic and foreign concern during a CBS "Face the Nation" broadcast. He stated that the POL strikes were "wholly consistent" with past U.S. military efforts to prevent a communist takeover of South Vietnam, they were not an attempt "to force North Vietnam to its knees, and they would not lead to a war with China." Interestingly, the overwhelming majority of congressional members supported the POL attacks. So did the American public. A Harris public opinion poll taken on July 11 showed that 62 percent backed the bombings, 11 percent opposed them, and 27 percent were undecided.[41]

Smoke rises from a petroleum storage area northwest of Dong Hoi after an attack in July 1966.

The Honolulu Conference, July 1966

With the POL strikes in full swing, Secretary McNamara and his aides flew to Honolulu where, on July 8, they conferred with Admiral Sharp and other Southeast Asia commanders. The purpose of the conference was to review the POL campaign, the pace of enemy infiltration into South Vietnam, future air, ground, and sea deployments to the war theater, and the progress of the war. After initial briefings by Sharp and his staff, McNamara said it was now President Johnson's desire that the services give "first priority" to complete the "strangulation" of the north's POL system. He went on to say that Admiral Sharp should not feel constrained by sortie limitations to accomplish this goal, which should be preceded by a thorough study of the north's land and sea POL system, the categorization of the targets, then their destruction. Concurrently and contributory, the services should step up air strikes on the main rail lines and selected bridges. He asked the PACOM commander to submit a POL strangulation plan in accordance with these guidelines.[42]

Current intelligence on the eve of the conference was sobering. Despite an estimated 137,800 killed from 1959 to mid-1966, mostly in South Vietnam, North Vietnam appeared as determined and resilient as ever. Its strength in South Vietnam was believed to total between 260,000 and 280,000. This contrasted with about 165,000 men a year earlier, and Viet Cong recruitment inside the south and infiltration from the north was unremitting. Further, the Hanoi regime was adjudged capable of training 75,000 to 100,000 troops annually to serve as combat replacements in the south and of fielding upwards of 500,000

The Soviet tanker *Buguruslan* anchored in Vung Ha Bay
outside Haiphong Harbor, transferring petroleum to
barges for transport to mainland North Vietnam.

troops without serious strain. Air Force and Navy bombing operations, which totaled about 3,000 combat sorties in December 1965, reached a monthly high of 7,500 in June 1966. In Laos, a yearly high of 3,000 combat sorties (including those of the Laotian Air Force) in December 1965 was eclipsed by monthly combat sortie totals of 6,000 to 8,000 during the driest months in the first half of 1966.[43]

In his briefing for McNamara, Sharp emphasized the burden of bombing restraints and requested permission to strike thirty-three significant North Vietnamese port and logistic sites used by the Soviets and Chinese for funneling supplies and enemy forces to the south and for other air attacks to reduce the southward movement of supplies and troops. He observed that about 28,000 North Vietnamese had entered South Vietnam in the first five months of 1966, and the infiltration rate of 4,500 per month at the beginning of the year threatened to reach 6,900 per month by the end of December. The VC-NVA were fielding more maneuver battalions, occasionally employed division-size forces, had increased their supply stockpiles, and had strengthened their support organizations.

Despite the many restrictions on Rolling Thunder, Sharp did not consider the program a failure. This was evident, he thought, by the rapidity with which the Hanoi regime built up its antiaircraft defenses. From March 1965, when Rolling Thunder operations began, Hanoi's antiaircraft gun inventory had risen from about 849 to 4,200, or an average of about 205 guns per month. In addition, there were now about 20 to 25 SA–2 SAM firing battalions, a respectable MiG force, and good early warning and GCI systems. Bombing had forced the north to divert upwards of 500,000 military and civilian personnel to its air

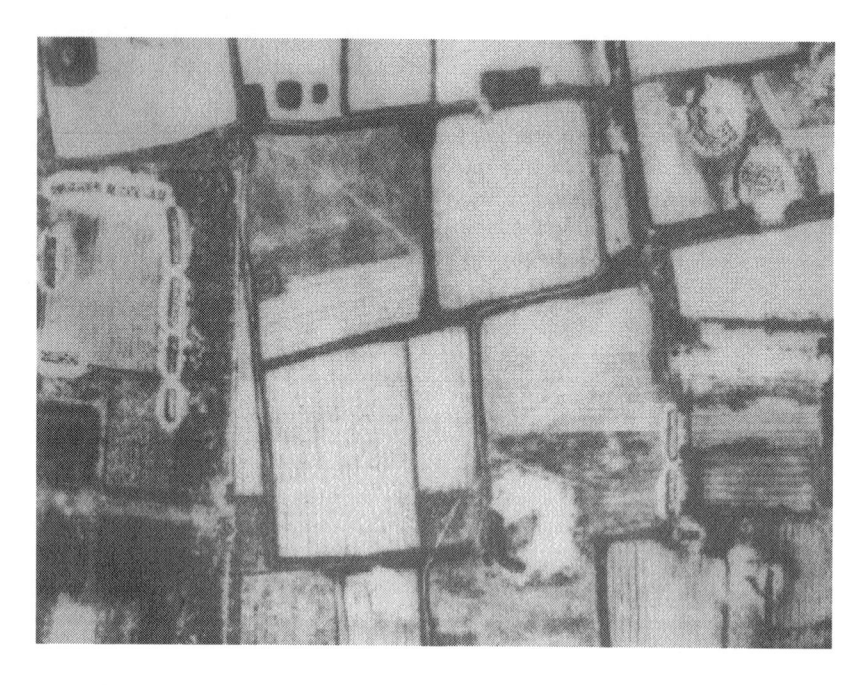

Trenches and craters from earlier attacks were used to store petroleum drums at the Ba Don storage area (above). A subsequent attack in August 1966 destroyed many of the drums and caused secondary explosions and fires (opposite page).

defenses and its repair and construction units stationed along roads, trails and rail lines. In addition, more than 2,000 watercraft had been destroyed by mid-1966. The PACOM commander did not expect air power to cut off sufficient supplies to "isolate the battlefield," but said he was convinced that air attacks against more significant targets would eventually undermine Hanoi's strength.[44]

Concerning future American deployments to Southeast Asia, Sharp proposed a force of 524,800 U. S. and allied personnel (50,000 Air Force) in South Vietnam and 147,800 personnel (20,000 Air Force) in Thailand and other PACOM areas by the end of 1966. For 1967, he proposed sending 121,000 more U. S. and allied personnel (18,300 Air Force) to South Vietnam and other PACOM areas. As future strategy promised to remain more ground than air oriented, Sharp proposed assembling a 136,800-man contingency corps for Southeast Asia for direct and indirect support of the war effort. This would raise U.S. and allied commitment to the war to 930,000 personnel (90,300 Air Force). Air combat sorties for North and South Vietnam would be increased to support the expanded military effort.[45]

Responding to the briefing by Sharp and others, McNamara said it was now President Johnson's desire that the services give "first priority" to complete the strangulation of the north's POL system. Accordingly, he wanted the PACOM commander to submit a POL strangulation plan. Second priority should be given to striking a few new bridges and rail line segments within the sanctuary area of Hanoi and Haiphong. He quashed any service expectations that he would approve a major change in other bombing restrictions within the buffer zone next to China and stressed the administration's "extreme sensitivity" to any further violations of China's air space, as occurred on May 12 and June 29.[46]

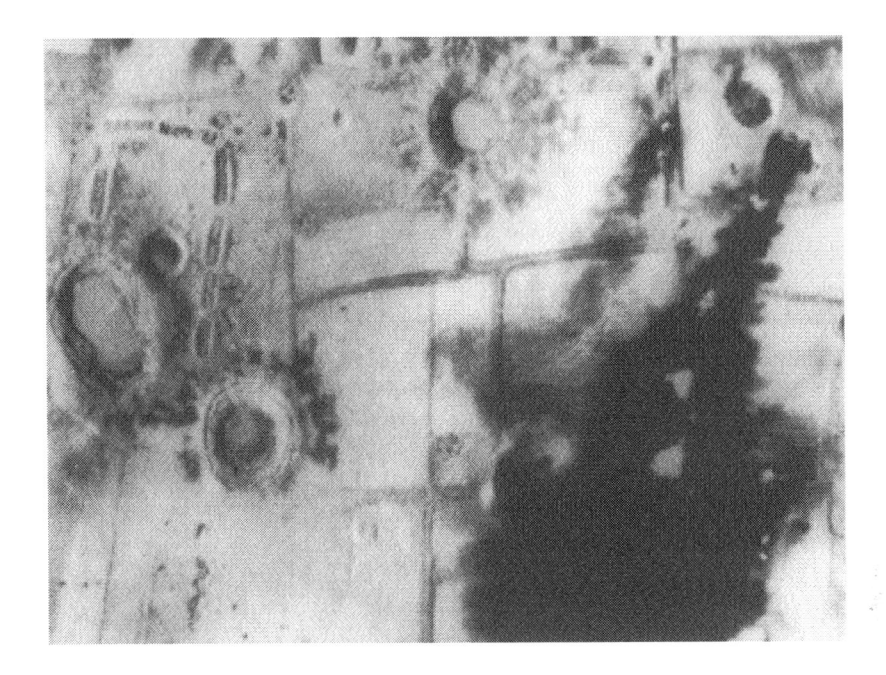

The POL Strangulation Campaign

The day following the end of the Honolulu conference, the JCS sent a new Rolling Thunder Program 51 to Admiral Sharp. This would become effective on July 9 and contained many of the guidelines indicated by McNamara just before or during the Honolulu conference. The program authorized additional strikes on selected targets within the Hanoi-Haiphong sanctuary area, principally on dispersed POL sites if identified positively with advance notice to the JCS of intent to strike. Also approved were armed reconnaissance strikes on seven segments of the two rail lines, ranging from 4 n.m. to 18 n.m. in length between Hanoi and China and Hanoi and Vinh, and five bridges. To support these modestly expanded operations of Rolling Thunder Program 51, McNamara authorized an increase in monthly armed reconnaissance sorties in North Vietnam and southeastern Laos from 8,100 (established in April 1966) to 10,100, an increase of about 25 percent.[47]

Because more armed reconnaissance operations were now authorized, Sharp quickly revised service sortie allocations. He assigned 4,500 sorties by Thailand-based aircraft to Westmoreland for his extended battlefield area of route

North Vietnam's railroads were used to disperse petroleum.
This railyard at Hanoi contains tank cars, rail cars carrying
petroleum tanks, and rail cars loaded with drums.

package 1 and the Tiger Hound sector of Laos; 4,100 sorties to the Navy for route packages 2, 3, 4, and 6B; and 1,500 sorties to the Air Force for route packages 5 and 6A.[48]

Meanwhile, Admiral Sharp's staff completed a POL strangulation plan in late July. Briefly, it called for the destruction of several types of remaining POL targets: port facilities; offshore lighterage; key road and rail routes from China, especially from the northeast; small sea craft moving POL from China or from point to point along the North Vietnamese coast; single and multiple POL tank complexes; dispersed drum storage areas; and vehicles and watercraft transporting POL along inland roads and waterways. The plan also called for special reconnaissance activities to detect POL and POL-associated targets to determine the amount of remaining POL, if any, after they were attacked. A new target list contained 225 POL sites, of which 100 had been photographed recently. Data indicated that about 90,000 metric tons of POL remained in the largest storage installations and 5,000 to 10,000 metric tons were in semipermanent drum storage areas. There was no estimate of the total amount of POL already dispersed in unknown sites throughout the country.[49] To carry out the plan, Admiral Sharp directed Air Force and Navy commanders to concentrate their POL operations against nine installations with the following estimated residual capacities in metric tons: Haiphong, 23,000; Nguyen Khe, 10,530; Duong Nam, 8,000; Viet Tri, 4,000; Don Son, 3,600; Phui Qui, 2,000; Vinh, 1,980; Hanoi, 1,700; and, Bac Giang, 1,380.[50]

An A–4 launches from the starboard catapult of a Navy carrier.

To meet the higher sortie requirements for the POL strangulation campaign and armed reconnaissance, the PACOM commander directed the PACFLT commander to transfer, on August 4, one aircraft carrier from the Dixie Station in the Gulf of Tonkin to the Yankee Station further north. This would permit the Navy to assign all three of its carriers to Rolling Thunder operations and to relieve the Seventh Air Force of its responsibility for bombing the Nape and Barthelemy Passes, both key infiltration points from North Vietnam into southern Laos. Additional Air Force sorties would thus be available for the POL campaign and, with newly arrived Air Force squadrons, for General Westmoreland's extended battlefield area in route package 1. Of the additional 1,000 authorized armed reconnaissance sorties for Rolling Thunder, the Navy would fly 900. Sharp's unilateral actions in realigning route package responsibilities and the unequal distribution of the additional armed reconnaissance sorties highly displeased the Air Force.[51]

Not surprisingly, Washington authorized far fewer POL targets than envisaged in Sharp's plan. By the end of July, the Air Force had attacked only sixteen dispersed POL sites holding an estimated 55,000 metric tons of fuel in route packages 1, 5, and 6A. Phantom and Thunderchief aircrews had concentrated their attacks on sites at or near Hanoi (Nguyen Khe, Dao Quan (west), Viet Tri, La Danh, Van Lung, and Duc Thang), all in route package 6A, destroying an estimated 42,600 metric tons of fuel. The fighter-bombers had also demolished a tank production plant at Thai Nguyen. Navy fliers had struck numerous sites with an estimated capacity of 114,800 metric tons of fuel in route packages 2, 3, 4, and 6B. They reported the destruction of many tons of fuel supplies at Haiphong, Don Son, Bac Giang, and Duong Nham, all of which had been attacked previously.[52]

In reality, the POL strangulation campaign was not a new program, but a continuation—with operational refinements and many restrictions—of the air effort against POL installations that began on June 29. Poststrike reports made no attempt to differentiate between the strikes conducted before or after the CINCPAC directive of July 24 that launched the program.[53]

Because the Defense Secretary quickly concluded that the POL strikes were not very effective—he refused to allow all POL sites to be struck—in August, Admiral Sharp sought Washington's approval to strike more "POL-associated" targets. These would include two lock and dam sites to render unusable about 200 miles of waterways for POL-carrying watercraft; new POL and LOC targets at the north's three main ports at Haiphong, Hon Gai, and Cam Pha; and harbor dredges at Haiphong used to keep the channel from silting up. Destruction of the dredges, initially and strongly urged in 1965, would make it impossible for Soviet and other foreign tankers to enter Haiphong harbor as soon as the harbor silted up. Again with service support, the PACOM commander also urged the destruction of the entire Thai Nguyen steel plant as it was producing, *inter alia*, barges used for the storage or movement of POL products.[54]

Except for the tank production facility, Washington refused to approve attacks on these large targets and on the POL sites at Phuc Yen and Kep, both of which were near the north's most important and politically sensitive MiG airfields. The State Department provided Washington's rationale for restraint: further bombing escalation might be construed by Peking as an American attempt to capitalize on confusion in China, which was in the initial throes of a "Cultural Revolution" led by the Red Guards, and trigger an "irrational" response. Also, Hanoi appeared "resolved" to stay the course in the war, at least until the next South Vietnamese elections, which were scheduled for November 1966. Thus, more bombing pressure would be hazardous in the first instance, wasteful in the second.[55]

Because of Washington's refusal to further expand the bombings, air commanders believed that the POL campaign had reached the point of diminishing returns. Lt. Gen. William Momyer, who succeeded General Moore as Commander, Seventh Air Force on July 1, 1966, informed Generals Harris and McConnell on August 12 that virtually all of the known POL caches in route package 1 had been bombed and he questioned the value of more attacks on small targets, especially those in heavily defended areas.

Despite the concentrated air attacks on small, dispersed POL sites, the North Vietnamese still seemed capable of moving their supplies from the Hanoi-Haiphong area through the demilitarized zone into South Vietnam. General Momyer characterized the POL strangulation campaign "as another piecemeal application of air power which left important targets unstruck." He recommended to Admiral Sharp that Air Force planes could be used more profitably against small POL and other targets in the Navy's route packages 2, 3, and 4, which contained about 1,480 miles of roads.[56]

Sharp agreed and permitted Seventh Air Force to fly an average of 50 sorties per day with peaks of 100 sorties per day, or 1,500 sorties per month, in the

Adm. U. S. Grant Sharp, Commander in Chief, Pacific Command (left),
and Lt. Gen. William W. Momyer, Commander, Seventh Air Force
(center), during a visit to Bien Hoa Air Base, South Vietnam.

western sectors of the three route packages. The PACOM commander then readjusted the services' armed reconnaissance responsibilities—still limited to 10,100 per month for North Vietnam and Laos—as follows: COMUSMACV, 2,500 sorties in North Vietnam (i.e., in route package 1) and Laos; CINCPACAF, 2,600 sorties in route packages 2, 3, 4, 5, and 6A; and CINCPACFLT, 5,000 sorties in route packages 2, 3, 4, and 6B.[57]

Inexplicably, as confidence in the restricted POL campaign waned among air commanders, Washington's interest grew. On August 11, McNamara, strangely, asked the service chiefs for additional briefings each Monday on the number of POL facilities destroyed, the residual capacity, the impact of bombing on the transport of POL into and within North Vietnam, and future POL bombing plans. Admiral Sharp and his PACAF and PACFLT commanders provided the available data as quickly as possible.[58]

In another report in late August, Admiral Sharp informed McNamara that air commanders had made little progress in reducing the size of the north's remaining POL capacity, now estimated at about 66,000 metric tons. Of this total, 17,000 metric tons were at sites not yet authorized for attack. Admiral Sharp had instructed his component commanders, to step up their aerial search for more POL sites, and to fly more reconnaissance missions against thirty-six small POL sites whose known or suspected locations had been plotted by DIA analysts in Washington. Some of these sites had been bombed previously. He added that it was not easy to obtain good BDA photography of these relatively small sites, which made it difficult to determine how much fuel remained after they had been struck.[59]

Operational data for August confirmed that dispatching large numbers of aircraft against small, dispersed POL sites was not very rewarding. In Westmoreland's extended battlefield area or route package 1, for example, the estimated capacity of five targets just before and just after air strikes is shown in figure 14:[60] Strikes against seven POL targets in route package 6A yielded similarly modest results (figure 15).

Figure 14
Prestrike and Poststrike Storage Capacity of POL Targets, Route Package 1
August 1966

Targets	Metric Tons Prior to Strikes	Metric Tons After Strikes
Ba Don Barracks/POL	420	252
Dong Hoi Barracks/POL	67	40
Thanh Thuy POL Storage	90	36
Xom Ve Truck Park/POL	94	68
Xom Duong Quan POL Storage	60	40

Figure 15
Prestrike and Poststrike Storage Capacity of POL Targets, Route Package 6A
August 1966

Targets	Metric Tons Prior to Strikes	Metric Tons After Strikes
Van Lung POL Products Storage (SSW)	297	219
Van Lung POL Products Storage (W)	75	75
Cu Van POL Products Storage	947	768
Dao Quan POL Products Storage	372	Unk
Hoang Mai POL Storage	252	202
Nguyen Ky Products Storage	7,500	6,346
Viet Tri POL Storage	1,400	215

Included in the 17,000 metric tons of POL still not authorized for strikes were the supplies at the Phuc Yen and Kep airfields. Meanwhile, reconnaissance photos were pinpointing numerous new, small sites, but many were in

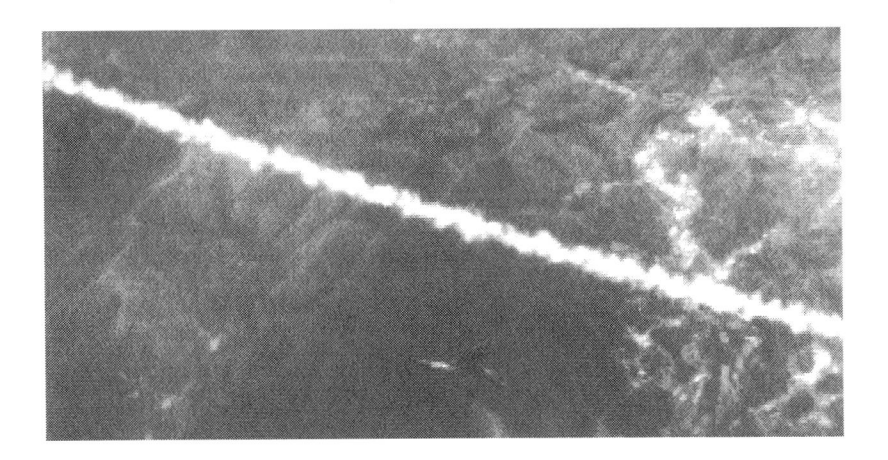

The strike camera of an F–105 Thunderchief recorded this contrail of a surface-to-air missile passing another Thunderchief (lower center) in the skies over North Vietnam.

populated areas. It was not unusual for photos to show streets in towns lined with POL drums, but fearful of causing civilian casualties, Washington officials forbade air commanders to attack the drums.[61]

Throughout September, service interest in the POL strangulation campaign continued to dwindle. "There are relatively few significant POL installations," General Harris observed, "that warrant a strike on a priority basis." Bombing a few important non-POL targets in conjunction with the POL campaign was perceived as a major shortcoming by the PACAF commander. "Until additional target complexes are authorized," he said, "no dramatic impact of a strategically persuasive nature seems likely."[62]

In contrast, Washington officials—especially McNamara—still viewed the campaign as important. They compelled the services to maintain a strenuous reconnaissance effort to find new POL sites within authorized areas and to continue submitting weekly reports on POL interdiction and the size of the residual POL capacity. During September, the Air Force and Navy reported striking thirty-five and eighty-two POL sites, respectively, in their assigned areas.[63]

Meanwhile, other ongoing assessments indicated that the restricted POL campaign was not seriously reducing Hanoi's ability to continue the war. Although the Air Force and Navy were not permitted to bomb or mine Haiphong and other harbors to cut off all POL and other shipping into North Vietnam, the tankers from the Soviet Union and other foreign suppliers took the precaution of offshore loading onto barges, usually at night. Strikes were authorized and a few were made against the barges, but with insignificant results. In September, an estimated 20,000 or more metric tons were unloaded successfully from two offshore tankers. There were also more oil shipments by

The 700-foot Chieu Ung railroad bridge is on the single-track line between Hanoi and China through the Red River valley, a major route for supplies to North Vietnam. Air Force F–105s destroyed the bridge on June 16, 1966, but the North Vietnamese repaired the bridge within a month (above). On July 22, F–105 pilots again destroyed the bridge (opposite page).

rail from China. In late August and early September, DIA and CIA analysts agreed that the country did not appear to be pinched for supplies and, with stocks on hand and a steady flow of imports, had enough to sustain military operations.[64]

A similar conclusion was reached by a group of forty-seven top U.S. scientists and engineers who had convened at McNamara's request to study enemy infiltration and bombing effectiveness. In a series of reports issued at the end of August 1966 through the JASON Division of the Institute for Defense Analyses, the study group foresaw no curtailment of infiltration into South Vietnam. They calculated that only 5 percent of Hanoi's fuel supply was used for truck operations through Laos, and they discerned no reduction in VC-NVA combat capability in the south, as enemy troops did not rely on fuel shipped from the north. Instead of heavier bombing, the JASON group recommended an innovative anti-infiltration system employing physical barriers and acoustic and seismic sensors. The JCS, Admiral Sharp, and other Air Force and Navy commanders opposed the barrier concept strongly on the grounds that it smacked of "Maginot Line thinking" and that its cost in terms of money and manpower would be enormous. However, Secretary McNamara quickly endorsed and the President approved the creation of the system. On September 15, McNamara appointed Army Lt. Gen. Alfred D. Starboard to head a task force to expedite the barrier's implementation. Nicknamed Igloo White, the sensors associated with the barrier became operational in late 1967.*[65]

Meanwhile, the POL campaign was not completely over. In October 1966, the Air Force struck an undetermined number of sites and the Navy twenty-nine. Occasionally, a restrike was conducted on one of the major POL installations, as at Bac Giang. Then, with the JASON reports in hand, McNamara and many aides made a three-day visit to Saigon during the second week of October 1966 to meet with Westmoreland, military and embassy officials, and several members of the South Vietnamese Government. Highlighting a seventeen-item agenda of briefings was the progress of Rolling Thunder program 51 and specifically the POL campaign. His report to President Johnson revealed his pessimism concerning the air campaign.[66]

Briefly, McNamara informed the President that the bombing of the north had neither reduced infiltration significantly nor diminished Hanoi's will to fight, a conclusion shared, he said, by the intelligence community. The North

---

* For a detailed discussion of the background of the Igloo White barrier concept and its initial implementation, see Jacob Van Staaveren, *Interdiction in Southern Laos, 1960–1968* (Center AF Hist, 1994), chap XI. The concept is also discussed briefly in *Gravel Pentagon Papers,* Vol IV, pp 115–24.

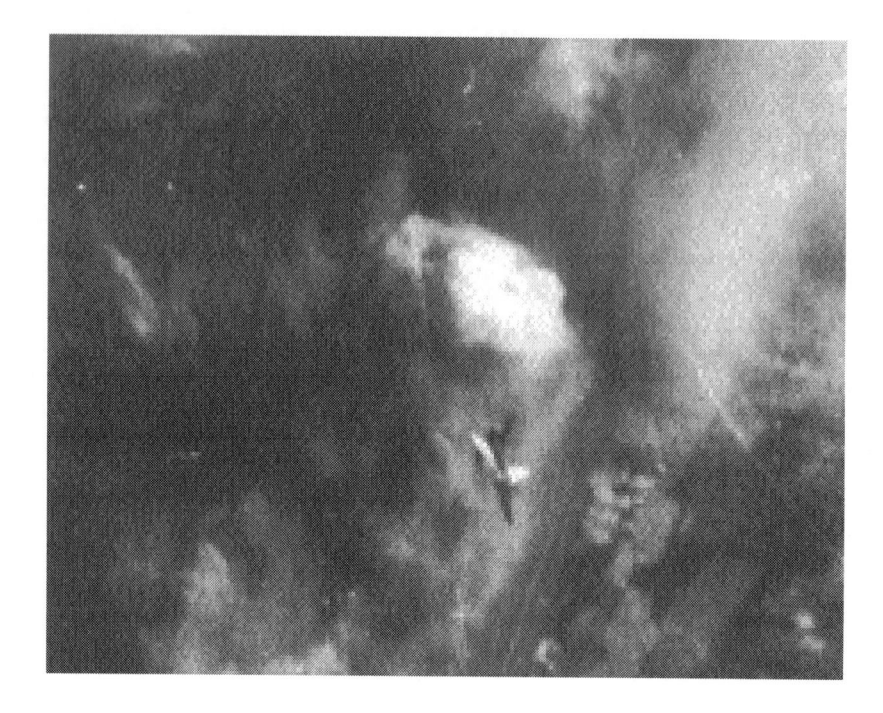

F–105 coming out of a bomb run against a rail line north of Hanoi.

Vietnamese-Laotian road network for military supplies was still capable of meeting communist needs in South Vietnam and attacks on the POL system had not seriously stanched the flow of essential supplies. He faulted the services for their over-optimistic estimates of what concentrated POL attacks could accomplish, although he praised close air support operations in South Vietnam. (Later, before Senate committees in January 1967, he would make much of the "failure" of the "unrestricted" POL campaign.) "It is clear," he said, that to bomb the north sufficiently to make a radical impact upon Hanoi's political, economic, and social structure "would require an effort we could make, but which would not be stomached either by our own people or by world opinion, and it would involve a serious risk of drawing us into open war with China."[67]

McNamara went on to say that the North Vietnamese had been forced to pay a price and assign about 300,000 personnel to their lines of communication to maintain the necessary flow of personnel and materiel to South Vietnam. He said that a large increase or decrease in the interdiction sortie level "would not substantially change the cost to the enemy of maintaining the roads, railroads, and waterways...." At the proper time, he believed, the United States should consider terminating the bombing of all of North Vietnam, or at least in the northeast zones "for an indefinite period in connection with covert moves toward peace." As an alternative to further bombing escalation, the Defense

Secretary recommended proceeding with the anti-infiltration barrier (the Igloo White project) across the DMZ and Laos that he had already endorsed and the President had approved.[68]

With regard to future increases in U.S. and allied forces in South Vietnam, McNamara said he would approve the deployment of only 40,000 more troops for an eventual end strength of 470,000. (This total would rise to 469,300 after the U.S. elections in November 1966.) This contrasted with Admiral Sharp's proposal in Honolulu on July 8 of 524,800 U.S. and allied troops by the end of 1966 (a figure that Sharp had recently raised to 570,000 for the end of 1967).[69]

In his strong criticism of the POL campaign, McNamara, of course, erred grossly in characterizing it as "unrestricted." Virtually all of the north's POL supplies delivered by Soviet and other foreign tankers were unloaded freely in Haiphong and other ports, exempt—except for a few storage sites—from mining or air attacks. Also, only minimum civilian casualties were tolerated. Despite the restrictions, Admiral Sharp believed that the POL campaign had exacted a price causing "destruction, greatly reduced capacity, or the abandonment of all major POL installations." The net effect, he averred, undoubtedly caused some temporary POL shortages, considerable inconvenience, and diverted more manpower and resources to POL dispersal activity.[70]

A flight of F–105s on their way to North Vietnam takes on fuel from a KC–135.

CHAPTER 11
Summary and Reappraisal

President Johnson's principal advisers, headed by Defense Secretary Robert S. McNamara, considered that the failure of the POL strikes to make obvious progress toward winning the war (even when combined with limited attacks against other targets) represented proof that bombing could not bring the Hanoi government to the negotiating table. They believed that the war first had to be won in South Vietnam, thus validating the administration's initial strategy. Top Army leaders in Washington and in Saigon generally supported this view.

Air Force and Navy leaders in Washington and tactical air commanders at PACOM in Honolulu, Saigon, and in Thailand saw the shortcomings of bombing POL sites and other targets differently. They believed strongly that, from the start of the American military buildup in South Vietnam in 1961, the new Kennedy administration should have begun attacking North Vietnam's most important targets and mining its harbors. They also objected strongly to Washington's tight control over targeting and the initial limited scope and tempo of air operations against the north.

The foregoing disparity in views on how the war in Southeast Asia should be fought had a long history. Following the French defeat at Dien Bien Phu in May 1954 and the signing of the Geneva agreements in July of that year, which led to the division of Vietnam into a communist north and a noncommunist south, the United States gradually assumed full responsibility for assuring the independence of South Vietnam and the neutrality of Laos and Cambodia. This responsibility was dictated by the Cold War between the United States and the Soviet Union and by the fall of China to a communist regime at the end of 1949. American policy was based on the premise that the fall of South Vietnam to communist rule would have a domino effect and lead to the communization of much of Southeast Asia, with serious consequences for the West, especially for the United States. This view received considerable impetus in June 1950 when communist North Korea suddenly attacked noncommunist South Korea, triggering a three-year war, during which China openly supported the North Koreans. An armistice finally ended the war in July 1953—less than a year before at Dien Bien Phu.

For eleven years after the official end of hostilities in the Indochina theater in 1954, the United States attempted to shore up the political and military infrastructure of the new South Vietnamese nation. It was a difficult task as the communist north, although a signatory to the Geneva agreement that divided Vietnam, nonetheless sought to destabilize South Vietnam by organizing and supporting communist Viet Cong insurgents within the new nation.

Despite the north's support of the Viet Cong insurgents, the U.S. Government refrained from overtly attacking North Vietnamese territory. Fearful of a wider war in Southeast Asia, which might involve the Chinese government and the Soviet Union, including possible nuclear confrontation with the Soviets, Washington opted to win the war in the south. Nonetheless, to make the Hanoi regime pay a price for its aggression, beginning in 1954 the United States tried mounting small-scale paramilitary activities to force the regime to cease and desist in its efforts to undermine the stability of South Vietnam. When these efforts failed, in 1960 the U.S. government approved in increase in paramilitary activities. Initially, the CIA, supported by the Air Force, Army, and Navy, was in charge of training South Vietnamese personnel for hit-and-run assaults on the north. However, these limited assaults proved unsuccessful in deterring the north's support for a small, but growing, Viet Cong insurgency in South Vietnam.

Primarily, but not solely, because of the growing insurgency, President Ngo Dinh Diem's government in South Vietnam remained unstable and the morale of its armed forces low. In 1961, a new administration under President John F. Kennedy undertook a series of more concerted actions. These consisted of an expansion of paramilitary activities against the north and the transfer of these activities to Defense Department agencies, with the CIA in a supporting role. Limited Air Force reconnaissance flights over the borders of Laos and North and South Vietnam were also begun to better determine the magnitude of the movement of troops and supplies into South Vietnam. In December 1961, President Kennedy ordered the deployment of the first combat advisory units to South Vietnam, which included an Air Force special air warfare unit named Farm Gate to provide combat training for the fledgling Vietnamese Air Force.

In February 1962, the Kennedy administration expanded its military training efforts by establishing the Military Assistance Command, Vietnam, Saigon, headed by (Army) General Harkins. Service components included an Air Force 2d ADVON with General Anthis as commander. The JCS also directed Admiral Sharp, Commander in Chief, Pacific, to develop operational plans for either graduated air attacks on the north or for thwarting a Chinese and North Vietnamese military thrust against other Southeast Asia countries. All the while, the chiefs of the military services, the Army excepted, urged President Kennedy and his key advisers, headed by McNamara, to begin air strikes against the north. General LeMay, Air Force Chief of Staff, was in the forefront of those arguing for an air-oriented campaign against the Hanoi regime, rather than a ground-oriented strategy within South Vietnam, to force Hanoi to desist in its support of the Viet Cong and to come to the negotiating table. Nonetheless, President Kennedy and his principal advisers in Washington, and at MACV headquarters in Saigon, continued to believe firmly that the war had to be won in the south. Only then would Hanoi sue for peace. Direct air strikes on the north were still ruled out lest they lead to a conflict with China, the Soviet Union, or both.

Throughout most of 1963, the Saigon government's chronic political instability and the poor performance of its ever growing army frustrated American combat advisory units in their efforts to defeat the Viet Cong. The culmination of the political instability came on November 1, 1963, when President Diem was overthrown and, with the approval of the United States, a military junta, led by Maj. Gen. Duong Minh, assumed control of the government. On November 22, President Kennedy was assassinated and Vice President Lyndon B. Johnson became President. One of his first important actions was to send Defense Secretary McNamara to Saigon to assess the political situation in the country.

McNamara's assessment was somber. Stressing the chronic weakness of the south's government and military forces, he recommended bolder covert air, sea, and ground attacks against the north. These soon found expression in an Operation Plan 34A prepared by MACV. In addition, SAC U–2 and Yankee Team tactical reconnaissance aircraft had already begun mapping more thoroughly the borders of North and South Vietnam and Laos, and the Royal Lao Air Force, with the U. S. Air Force flying support, had begun limited strikes on North Vietnamese infiltration targets in northern Laos. The Navy began De Soto patrols as its larger covert actions to harass the north. Meanwhile, most members of the JCS, especially General LeMay and other Air Force leaders and tactical commanders, continued to urge a series of quick, overt attacks on the north. They warned that the war was in danger of being lost.

The first seven months of 1964 witnessed more political instability in Saigon. In January 1964, the Minh government was overthrown in a bloodless coup by Maj. Gen. Nguyen Khanh. The new government soon demonstrated that it was also incapable of curing South Vietnam's chronic political instability. This fact, plus the constant infiltration of troops and supplies to support the Viet Cong in South Vietnam finally forced the Johnson administration to contemplate reversing its long-held policy of not openly attacking North Vietnam. On June 15, 1964, at the request of Secretary McNamara, the JCS completed a list of ninety-four of the most important targets in the north. The same month also saw the appointment of General Westmoreland as MACV's new commander in Saigon, replacing General Harkins.

Less than two months after the JCS completed its 94-target list, the Johnson administration used a naval incident as a pretext for attacking the Hanoi regime openly for the first time. On the night of August 3, North Vietnamese gunboats attacked a Navy De Soto patrol in the Gulf of Tonkin. A second attack was presumed to have occurred the following night, although it was never verified. The two incidents prompted President Johnson to authorize naval air strikes on several North Vietnamese targets in southern North Vietnam. At the President's request, on August 7, the U.S. Congress passed the Gulf of Tonkin Resolution that authorized the President to take all necessary measures to repel an attack on U.S. military forces and to prevent further aggression by the Hanoi regime.

To the distress of most service chiefs, especially the Air Force, now headed by General McConnell (who replaced General LeMay in February 1965), there were no immediate follow-up strikes, except in Laos, where in December 1964 Washington approved for the first time limited Air Force and Navy reconnaissance strikes. Nicknamed Barrel Roll, the strikes were intended to supplement ongoing

Royal Lao Air Force attacks on Laotian infiltration targets. (With limited strikes in Laos, the United States also sought—unsuccessfully—to signal Hanoi of the threat of more pain unless it agreed to negotiate an end to the war.) In fact, after the Tonkin Gulf air attacks, the President withheld approval of air strikes in the north for six months because of the weakness of the South Vietnamese government and the coming national election in the United States, scheduled for early November 1964. Not until Viet Cong attacks against an American airbase at Bien Hoa on November 2, a bombing at the American Brink Hotel on December 24, and an assault on a U.S. military compound in South Vietnam's II Corps on January 7, 1966—all causing death or injury to numerous Americans and South Vietnamese and considerable physical damage—did President Johnson, Secretary McNamara, and his other advisers in Washington and Saigon agree that Hanoi should be punished more severely for its provocations.

Another month of high-level agonizing in Washington elapsed, however, before the President decided to strike a series of North Vietnamese targets, albeit well below the 20th parallel. Called Flaming Dart I and Flaming Dart II, the air strikes were conducted on February 7 and 11 primarily by Air Force and Navy aircraft, with the VNAF making a few token strikes. Then, as the political and military viability of the south remained steadfastly unimproved, McNamara and other advisers called for, and the President authorized, a Rolling Thunder program against the north. The program began on March 2, 1966 in the form of numbered weekly packages of targets and sortie levels. Contrary to the recommendations of the service chiefs—the Army excepted—the targets were carefully selected and the number of combat and combat support sorties controlled by McNamara and his staff, although final approval rested with the President.

Also frustrating to the Air Force were the complex command and control arrangements for conducting the Rolling Thunder program. The JCS sent approved weekly strikes to CINCPAC, who determined the number of sorties to be flown jointly by the Air Force and the VNAF and by the Seventh Fleet from its three aircraft carriers in the Gulf of Tonkin. The Commander, Pacific Air Force, General Harris, also in Hawaii, would relay strike and target authorization to General Moore, the Commander, 2d Air Division, in Saigon. General Moore had earlier replaced General Anthis, and it was he who would then schedule aircraft based in South Vietnam. For aircraft based in Thailand, Moore's orders were relayed through the Thirteenth Air Force. Washington authorities also restricted air attacks on the north by creating a strike-free zone around the Hanoi-Haiphong area and another along the Chinese border and by mandating that civilian casualties be kept to a minimum.

The tight control over the initial air strikes against North Vietnam masked the overwhelming American air superiority in Southeast Asia. In February 1965, the Air Force possessed about 200 combat aircraft in South Vietnam and 83 aircraft of all types in Thailand. Offshore were three Navy aircraft carriers with more than 200 combat aircraft. In addition, the VNAF had about 53 aircraft. Ranged against them, the North Vietnamese Air Force possessed 35 MiG–15s and MiG–17s (and soon, a few MiG–21s), plus 20 light jet bombers. Above North Vietnam, however, loomed another potential threat: about 310 Chinese MiG fighters.

With the beginning of the constricted Rolling Thunder operations, the Air Force began to deploy many more aircraft and personnel to bases in South Vietnam and Thailand. Its principal combat aircraft were the F–100 Super Sabres and F–105 Thunderchiefs; but the higher performance F–4C Phantoms soon arrived in Thailand, although they would not be used immediately for striking the north. Air Force aircraft were already employed in an even more tightly controlled program against the movement of troops and supplies down the Ho Chi Minh Trail in southern Laos and into South Vietnam. In Laos, an American ambassador, the *de facto* military commander in that country, made the final decisions on the limited air strikes in coordination with Laotian government officials.

Taking advantage of long delay, by February 1965, the north had deployed nearly 1,000 antiaircraft guns of various sizes along many roads, railroads, logistic centers, bridges, power plants, and other likely targets, especially in the Hanoi-Haiphong area. As a consequence, enemy gunners immediately took a heavy toll during the two Flaming Dart and the initial Rolling Thunder strikes. A total of eleven aircraft were lost (five Air Force, four Navy, two VNAF) and forty-one were damaged, and one Air Force pilot was also lost. These losses would mount. Poor weather over the north, haze from slash burning, jungle terrain, and other factors usually forced combat and armed reconnaissance pilots to fly low and within range of antiaircraft guns. Frequent poor weather also frustrated efforts to obtain accurate bomb damage assessment of the targets struck.

Another major problem for Air Force and Navy pilots was Washington's decision to approve only a few of the ninety-four JCS targets in North Vietnam. In fact, most of the Rolling Thunder strikes in the ensuing weeks were confined to relatively unimportant targets below the 20th parallel—again to signal Hanoi of American determination to persevere in South Vietnam and force a negotiated end to the conflict. In early April 1965, a new Air Force and Navy strike program, nicknamed Steel Tiger, against more infiltration targets in southern Laos, likewise failed to motivate the Hanoi regime to negotiate. In the same month, the regime publicized its own four-point peace plan for ending the war that required *inter alia* the withdrawal of all foreign troops. The Johnson administration did not achieve any success with a new major propaganda campaign consisting of dropping leaflets over the north. A five-day bombing halt in mid-May 1965, codenamed Mayflower, to allow U.S. diplomats and other intermediaries to convince the Hanoi government to begin talks was likewise ineffective. Meanwhile, the Johnson administration decided to bolster internal security in South Vietnam against the Viet Cong insurgents. It approved funds for adding 100,000 more men to the south's military force of 450,000 men, increasing from 33,000 to 82,000 the number of American combat training and other types of forces in the country, plus the dispatch of 7,500 combat troops from South Korea, New Zealand, and Australia.

All the while, the Air Force, Navy, and VNAF aircraft—with the latter flying only limited sorties above the demilitarized zone separating the two Vietnams—continued to strike and restrike a large assortment of targets: rail and road lines, trucks, railroad rolling stock, bridges, watercraft, military barracks, ammunition depots, and antiaircraft sites. At the end of May, the Air Force's most modern fighter-bombers, the F–4Cs, also began bombing—to signal Hanoi of heavier bombings to come unless it was willing to negotiate. The air attacks destroyed or damaged hundreds of structures, trucks, railroad rolling stock, watercraft, and cut road and rail lines. Aircraft losses were high. By June 24, the Air Force had lost twenty-four, the Navy twenty-six, and the VNAF seven to North Vietnamese antiaircraft guns along with two Air Force and one Navy aircraft shot down by enemy MiGs that had first begun to challenge American pilots in April.

During June 1965 the Air Force, Navy, and VNAF flew about 2,300 strike, armed reconnaissance, and flak suppression sorties, compared with 585 flown in March, the first month of the Rolling Thunder program. Several thousand other sorties were flown for MiG combat patrol, rescue patrol, escort, bomb damage assessment, reconnaissance, and for other purposes. In July, at the request of the JCS, Washington authorized two-week Rolling Thunder targeting and sortie packages. Tight controls over targeting remained, but the pace of air operations increased slightly. The modest increase in the rate of bombings came in June of 1965, following another crisis in the South Vietnamese government and the emergence of Maj. Gen. Nguyen Van Thieu as Chief of State and Brig. Gen. Nguyen Cao Ky, the VNAF commander, as Prime Minister. Thieu and Ky, as Chief of State and Prime Minister, then as President and Vice President, gave South Vietnam political stability until the mid-1970s. Meanwhile, General Westmoreland obtained Washington's approval for substantially larger U.S. ground forces to deal with the still expanding insurgency.

General McConnell, the Air Force chief, and other tactical commanders such as General Harris, the PACAF commander, and General Moore, the 2d Air Division commander, continued to deplore Washington's policy of trying to win the war in South Vietnam rather than by bombing the north into submission. But McNamara and other key presidential advisers remained unwavering in their conviction that any precipitous bombing escalation could lead to open conflict with China and the Soviet Union or to some military diversionary action. China's angry reaction to an accidental intrusion of its airspace over Hainan Island in April, when a U.S. Navy aircraft clashed briefly with a Chinese MiG, fed Washington's enormous fear that Peking might openly enter the conflict. In addition, McNamara, most civilian presidential advisers, and Army leaders remained convinced that air power alone could not win the war in the north.

In addition to a daily toll of Air Force, Navy, and VNAF aircraft, two other threats to bombing appeared in the spring and summer of 1965. In April, North

Vietnamese MiGs began to challenge American pilots, first during separate Navy and Air Force attacks on the large Thanh Hoa bridge. The number of aerial engagements soon increased, with American pilots usually the victors. Because of the proximity of MiG airbases to Hanoi and Haiphong, and fearful of escalating the air war, Washington continued to withhold its approval for attacking the airfields. Another threat was posed by Soviet-built SA–2 missiles, which scored their first kill by downing an Air Force Phantom in July 1965. Although some newly built SA–2 sites outside of the sanctuaries near Hanoi, Haiphong, and China could be attacked, the sites inside could not.

For more precise targeting, to deal with the MiG threat, and particularly to lessen the threat from the north's deadly antiaircraft guns, in the spring and summer of 1965 the Air Force and Navy deployed increasing numbers of specially equipped aircraft: photo-equipped drones launched from C–130A aircraft; Wild Weasel F–100Fs, EB–66Bs and EB–66Cs with night photo or infrared equipment; and EC–121D airborne and early warning aircraft. After the first SA–2 missile site was discovered early in April, the Air Force deployed RF–101 reconnaissance aircraft equipped with QRC–160–1 ECM pods to neutralize the radar that controlled the guns and the missiles.

With the increase in confirmed SA–2 sites—five by the end of July and eighteen by the end of September—the Air Force and Navy also began to employ specially equipped Iron Hand aircraft: Air Force F–105 Thunderchiefs and Navy A–6A Intruders and A–4E Skyhawks. Both services also began testing the Navy's Shrike AGM–45 antiradar missiles, launching twenty-five against SA–2 sites. Withdrawn briefly for improvements, the Shrike AGM–45s entered into regular use in 1966. Washington authorities facilitated the anti-SAM campaign by allowing a slight northward extension of the authorized Rolling Thunder bombing area. Because of the danger from constantly heavier antiaircraft fire, as well as from light and medium guns and automatic weapons, the first confirmed SA–2 destruction was not achieved until October 17, by Navy aircraft. Other successful strikes followed in swift succession.

With the northward adjustment of the area open to bombing under Rolling Thunder in the last half of 1965, the Air Force and Navy were also able to strike and destroy or damage a few other targets heretofore off limits, such as small power plants, ammunition complexes, barracks, segments of new road and rail lines, and the like. However, the majority were still located below the 20th parallel, well south of the Hanoi-Haiphong area and the Chinese border. The beginning of the northwest monsoon weather in October often delayed or cancelled operations. The JCS periodically complained bitterly to McNamara and other presidential advisers for withholding approval of more important targets, such as the Phuc Yen airfield—where most North Vietnamese MiGs were based—and canal locks, flood control levees, and four thermal hydroelectric plants, all of which were within the Hanoi-Haiphong sanctuary area. The Defense Secretary asserted that the Hanoi government might view striking such targets as provocative and thus strengthen its resolve to fight and provide more support to the Viet Cong.

The latter months of 1965 witnessed only small increases in permitted monthly strike sorties. The period also saw two Air Force bombing errors. The first, due to pilot error, occurred when an F–105 Thunderchief struck the off limits demilitarized zone between North and South Vietnam, killing twenty-one Vietnamese and injuring others. The second, due to navigational error, occurred when another F–105 Thunderchief, flying escort for four C–130Bs, drifted over Hainan Island where it was shot down by a Chinese MiG and the pilot captured. This was the second time an American plane had been shot down by a Chinese MiG. Concerned lest both incidents lead to even tighter bombing restrictions, Air Force tactical commanders redoubled their efforts to prevent further mistakes. In November, the JCS sent to McNamara a paper titled Concept for Vietnam, which again stressed the importance of permission to hit more significant targets, including POL sites. Of thirteen of the most important, only four of the smaller targets had been struck.

The administration made no immediate reply as it contemplated another bombing halt to bring Hanoi to the negotiating table. In December, to consolidate his authority as Commander in Chief, Pacific, and the control over air operations over the north, Admiral Sharp unilaterally divided North Vietnam into six—and soon thereafter seven—geographical route package areas. He assigned route packages 2, 5, and 6A to the Air Force and route packages 1, 3, 4, and 6B to the Navy. The change displeased the Air Force, but it had no recourse but to accept the assignments.

Because of the highly restrictive Rolling Thunder rules of engagement, until December 24, 1965, when Washington halted all bombing of the north, combat pilots took many risks and often suffered high losses by striking and restriking a large number of relatively unimportant targets. Statistically, the number of sorties flown against the north during the year were impressive. Combat and combat support sorties totaled 54,791 (Air Force, 25,971; Navy, 28,168; VNAF, 652). Actual strike sorties totaled 23,194 (Air Force, 10,975; Navy, 11,656; VNAF, 563). The Air Force dropped 32,063 tons of explosives, the Navy, with smaller aircraft, 11,144 tons, while the total for VNAF was undetermined.

Assessing strike results was far more difficult. Sharp's analysts reported that by December 24, 1965, Rolling Thunder operations had destroyed or damaged an estimated 4,700 huts and buildings, 808 motor vehicles, 658 pieces of railroad rolling stock, 1,563 watercraft, 1,200 bridges, 115 antiaircraft installations, 51 radar facilities, 4 SA–2 missile sites, 6 POL storage tanks, and 5 electric power plants. Also hit were miscellaneous targets such as ferries and ferry slips, small airfield runways, and a few small locks and dams. Finally, the aerial assaults created about 846 significant road and 92 rail cuts along important traffic arteries. There were no reliable figures regarding civilian casualties, but they were relatively small. PACAF's computations were larger and credited

Rolling Thunder attacks with destroying or damaging an additional 2,700 buildings, 500 bridges, and 1,140 vehicles, railroad rolling stock, and watercraft. With photographic bomb damage assessment uncertain, many reports of destruction or damage were pilot estimates.

The cost in terms of aircraft was high. By December 24, Hanoi's air defense system had downed 171 aircraft (80 Air Force, 83 Navy, 8 VNAF) and damaged 450 (189 Air Force, 250 Navy, 11 VNAF). Losses were largely due to the north's large inventory of antiaircraft guns: by December 24, 1965, they numbered approximately 2,236, more than twice the number in February of that year, plus several thousand automatic weapons. Although few aircraft were lost to enemy aircraft and SA–2 missiles, they had a significant harassing effect on combat and reconnaissance missions.

On December 24, 1965, the Johnson administration announced that the Rolling Thunder program would cease temporarily for the express purpose of trying to persuade the Hanoi government to begin talks to end the war. The decision to halt the bombing arose primarily from McNamara's belief, born in July 1965 and belatedly shared by President Johnson, that the war could only be ended by negotiating with Hanoi. This constituted another major shift with regard to the Johnson administration's earlier strategies. The first was that the war had to be won within South Vietnam. When this strategy failed to move Hanoi, primarily because of South Vietnam's continuing political instability and the many desertions and poor morale of its army, the administration reluctantly approved a highly restrictive Rolling Thunder air program against the north. This strategy had also failed by late 1965. Thus, the Defense Secretary now counseled the President that only negotiations could end the war. The first step towards this objective required a lengthy bombing pause, coupled with a highly energetic diplomatic offensive.

This time, however, all of the service chiefs—Air Force and Navy tactical commanders, Admiral Sharp, and General Westmoreland—strongly opposed the halt, believing it to be a mistake. It would nullify whatever success the Rolling Thunder program had achieved thus far, and reduce pressure on the Hanoi government to parley. But their views were overruled. The bombing halt was to last thirty-seven days and witness frenetic activity on the part of the United States to entice Hanoi to the bargaining table. President Johnson's emissaries visited 35 foreign capitals and contacted 115 foreign governments to convey America's peaceful intentions if the Hanoi regime would cease and desist from its support of the Viet Cong insurgency in South Vietnam. The peace overture included a fourteen-point plan, which was relayed to Hanoi and provided for unconditional discussions and the promise of a contribution of at least one billion dollars to a Southeast Asia regional reconstruction program.

The Hanoi government rejected the plan out of hand and countered that the United States must first end all bombing of the north and accept the four-point peace plan of April 13, 1965, which required the withdrawal of all foreign troops. Washington's hopes that negotiations might end the war were struck still lower when a mission from Moscow arrived in Hanoi early in January 1966 to arrange more Soviet military and economic aid for its embattled ally. In addition, Air Force and Navy reconnaissance during the bombing pause showed that Hanoi was rebuilding its logistic routes, freely moving supplies and troops southward, and improving its antiaircraft defenses, which now included about sixty SA–2 sites.

The bombing hiatus also witnessed a concerted effort by top Air Force and Navy commanders to convince the Johnson administration to alter its ground-oriented strategy of first defeating Hanoi in South Vietnam. For the Air Force, this effort was led by General McConnell who was especially perturbed by tentative plans to boost American manpower in South Vietnam to 486,500 (of which 55,000 would be Air Force), and 169,000 military personnel (mostly Air Force) in Thailand by the end of 1966 (Admiral Sharp in Honolulu rapidly convened a three-week conference that prepared three manpower deployment options for McNamara, including an optimum of 459,000 military personnel in South Vietnam).

Objecting to this scenario, the Air Force Chief of Staff described the enormous problems that would arise. These would include an immense base construction effort, and the relocation of Air Force tactical units from around the world to provide sufficient air support for an ever-growing land army in South Vietnam. Despite their differences on military strategy, all of the services nonetheless strongly believed that Rolling Thunder operations should resume quickly with an unannounced sharp blow. More new targets should be authorized closer to China and within the Hanoi-Haiphong area, Haiphong's harbor should be mined to eliminate military imports, and restrictions on flying combat and armed reconnaissance missions should be reduced.

McNamara vetoed the recommendations, invoking again the danger of a war with China or the Soviet Union if the United States did not demonstrate restraint. Accepting the Defense Secretary's arguments, President Johnson did not authorize the resumption of bombing until January 31, 1966. With Rolling Thunder program 48, combat pilots found themselves more restricted than before. Only 300 strike sorties per day were permitted against targets located principally below the 21st parallel. Most strikes took place in route packages 1 through 4 and attacks were directed against vehicles, watercraft, rail and road lines, small bridges, structures, and a few antiaircraft and ground radar sites. Groundfire was intense, as Hanoi had taken full advantage of the bombing halt to move more troops and supplies to the south and to strengthen its antiaircraft defenses.

A total of 2,809 strike sorties were flown in February 1966 by the Air Force, Navy, and VNAF. Beginning with Rolling Thunder program 49 on March 1, McNamara relaxed bombing restrictions somewhat, authorizing 5,100 strike sorties for the north and 3,100 for Laos, the latter mostly against troops and supplies moving towards South Vietnam. Combat air patrol, reconnaissance, electronic countermeasures, and other sorties were not included in the authorized sortie totals. Despite the onset of monsoon weather, Air Force and Navy combat pilots flew about 87 percent of the permitted sorties. During March, the Air Force and Navy claimed to have destroyed or damaged respectively the following: vehicles, 103 and 103; rivercraft, 63 and 177; small bridges, 46 and 90; structures, 96 and 95; and antiaircraft sites, 18 and 5. In addition, they damaged 28 rail cars and made about 145 road cuts. Meanwhile, a growing munitions shortage of 250-pound, 500-pound, and 750-pound general-purpose bombs forced greater use of 1,000-pound, 2,000-pound, and 3,000-pound bombs.

In March, route package 1 was assigned to General Westmoreland in Saigon to serve as his extended battlefield to provide more air power against infiltration of North Vietnamese Army personnel from Laos into South Vietnam that was estimated at more than 11,000 and increasing between October 1965 and the end of February 1966. General Moore had some reservations, but still supported the change. Admiral Sharp did not, on the premise that South Vietnam's strategic rear was not within the country as Westmoreland claimed, but outside of North Vietnam (i.e., in China and the Soviet Union). McNamara sided with the MACV commander on the grounds that Rolling Thunder operations appeared to be having little effect on the Hanoi government. The change went into effect on April 1, 1966 (the start of Rolling Thunder program 50). At the same time, Sharp reshuffled service assignments over the north, giving route packages 5 and 6A to the Air Force and route packages 2,3,4, and 6B to the Navy. In the Air Force view, this change was not warranted as it gave Navy pilots a larger but less hazardous geographical area for their shorter range aircraft.

Rolling Thunder 50 began on April 1 and would continue through April, May, and June and end in early July 1966. In this program the scope of the air war in the north was modestly increased. Before it started, the JCS had proposed a new bombing package of targets, including nine POL sites, six bridges (three would be restrikes), one cement plant, and several other important targets not yet bombed. For the twelfth time since November 1964, they also made an urgent request to be allowed to strike the north's MiG airfields. They stressed that the sixty to seventy MiGs—among which there were now a number of MiG–21s—posed a constant military threat. McNamara surprisingly sent the recommendations with some modifications to the President, apparently influenced by a new CIA report advocating more severe bombing of the north. He also minimized the prospect of any Chinese ground or air action if Hanoi's only cement plant and some new POL sites were struck and said that the Soviet Union would do no more than adopt a harsher diplomatic line. Thus did the Defense Secretary suddenly modify his earlier thinking about strong Chinese and Soviet reaction to a more escalatory bombing policy.

The JCS recommendations, as approved by the Defense Secretary, sanctioned 700 monthly armed reconnaissance sorties, including strikes for the first time against rail and highway routes in the more northeastern sector of North

Vietnam. The recommendation also sanctioned strikes on nine new POL storage sites, six new bridges, and four other important targets. Program 50 would also provide for more strikes in route package 1, because of an upsurge in infiltration in that area, and which received first strike priority. To implement the last change, Westmoreland appointed General Moore as MACV Deputy Commander for Air Operations, but Moore's new title did little to increase his authority in conducting air operations. Almost at the same time, the 2d Air Division was redesignated the Seventh Air Force because of its huge size, and the Deputy Commander, 2d Air Division/Thirteenth Air Force in Thailand, became Deputy Commander, Seventh/Thirteenth Air Force.

The President briefly withheld approval of the new recommendations, however, following another political crisis in South Vietnam in early March triggered by President Ky's dismissal of a rebellious commanding general of South Vietnamese Army Forces in I Corps. The crisis would simmer until June. When he finally approved Rolling Thunder program 50, he imposed more restrictions than McNamara had recommended, although some earlier ones were dropped.

Authorized were the first two B–52 strikes on Mu Gia Pass (the main point of entry into Laos for the north's troops and supplies en route to South Vietnam), and an air program in Laos aimed at reducing infiltration into South Vietnam through the ten-mile demilitarized zone. Other highlights of program 50 were an initial strike on the Thai Nguyen railyard, the Bac Giang bridge, and the plan to attack the much-bombed Thanh Hoa bridge with five 5,000-pound bombs dropped from a C–130 that floated down the river to the bridge. Inexplicably, the bombs failed to explode. In a second attack, the C–130 and its eight-man crew were lost. The bridge would not be attacked again and destroyed until many months later.

Because radar-controlled antiaircraft guns and SA–2 missiles continued to proliferate, the Air Force again deployed more sophisticated aircraft in the spring and early summer of 1966 to detect and neutralize or destroy these weapons. Wild Weasel F–105Fs, equipped with Shrike AGM–45 antiradar missiles, replaced the earlier Wild Weasel F–100Fs. By mid-1966, of a total 376 Air Force, Navy, and VNAF aircraft lost in the north, only 15 to 18 were attributed to SA–2s, thus attesting to the efficacy of the anti-SAM measures. In addition, MSQ–77 Skyspot radar systems were installed in tactical and B–52 bombers and on ground sites to assure more accurate bombing. By mid-1967, six MSQ–77 ground installations had been activated in South Vietnam and Thailand, thus assuring more accurate bombing than theretofore.

In April 1966 the North Vietnamese MiG–15s, MiG–17s, and MiG–21s on airfields near Hanoi became more aggressive. In six aerial battles, however, Air Force F–4Cs downed six MiGs without loss. Once in May and again in June, China claimed that American aircraft had violated its air space. Because of Washington's extraordinary sensitivity, both PACAF and Joint Staff teams, the latter ordered by McNamara, conducted separate investigations of the violations. Both border intrusions were attributed to navigation errors. Air Force and

Navy commanders took immediate measures to improve communication and navigation control when flying near the Chinese border. Another problem affecting Rolling Thunder operations in the spring of 1966 was the increasing shortage of rockets, general-purpose bombs, and other ammunition for air operations in North and South Vietnam and Laos. President Johnson quickly gave highest priority to increasing production of certain types of ammunition.

Meanwhile, McNamara and the JCS continued to spar over the effects of bombing POL storage sites and associated targets. In recent months, the CIA's conflicting estimates of the possible impact had muddled the problem. On April 1, 1966 Walt W. Rostow succeeded McGeorge Bundy as the President's National Security Adviser. On May 6 he informed McNamara and Dean Rusk, the Secretary of State, that systematic and sustained attacks on Hanoi's POL supplies could seriously cripple its war effort, noting how attacks on Germany's petroleum resources compromised Germany's war operations in World War II. In the same month General McConnell informed a Senate committee that knocking out all of Hanoi's POL sites would have a substantial effect on the amount of supplies it could send to its forces in South Vietnam. General Westmoreland generally agreed, and soon called for the bombing of eight POL sites, warning that delay would allow Hanoi to continue its POL dispersal activities. Underlying these recommendations was a rising congressional and public concern about the course of the war.

Gradually, McNamara and the President were persuaded to approve more concentrated, albeit still limited, strikes on POL targets. The Defense Secretary justified attacking them because enemy truck movements in the first five months of 1966 were double those of 1965. Also compared with the previous year, daily enemy supply tonnage had increased 150 percent, the troop infiltration rate along the Ho Chi Minh Trail had increased by 120 percent (averaging 4,500 men per month), and the number of North Vietnamese Army units in South Vietnam had risen by 100 percent. Meanwhile, the usually inordinate fear of McNamara and most other presidential advisers in the face of excessive Chinese or Soviet reaction was again minimized. The President agreed, and in early June prepared to approve attacks on new POL and other targets. However, the President's final approval was delayed by a series of events, including a new Canadian diplomatic initiative to persuade Hanoi to negotiate (which proved unsuccessful), weather conditions, and a news leak about the impending bombings.

When the President made his final decision in late June, it was another compromise: some, but not all of the recommended POL sites and other new targets could be attacked. Finally, on June 29, Air Force and Navy aircraft struck the first authorized POL sites near Hanoi, Haiphong, and other areas previously off limits to combat pilots. Some radar sites in formerly restricted areas were also hit. By July 11, twenty-five large and small POL facilities had been attacked. Adding a few bombed previously, an estimated 80 to 90 percent of the north's POL inventory had been bombed and an estimated 55 percent destroyed. There was no estimate of civilian casualties, but analysts considered them small. As expected, the POL campaign triggered more domestic and foreign debate and concern that the war might expand. China, the Soviet Union, and other communist countries vowed to send more aid to the Hanoi regime.

On July 8, McNamara and his aides arrived in Honolulu to attend another series of briefings and discussions with military commanders. Current intelligence was sobering. Despite an estimated 137,000 enemy killed, the Hanoi regime had an estimated 260,000 to 280,000 insurgents in South Vietnam, compared with about 165,000 a year earlier. Although Admiral Sharp, who gave the principal briefing, believed that attacks on more significant targets would eventually undermine Hanoi's strength, he emphasized the frustration of the bombing restraints and noted that infiltration into South Vietnam, running at an estimated 4,500 men per month early in 1966, would continue to increase and that there were more antiaircraft guns and SA–2 battalions than ever before. Following earlier guidelines from McNamara, he also proposed sending more American troops to South Vietnam for an eventual force of 524,800 U.S. and allied personnel.

In response, McNamara asked the PACOM Commander for a POL strangulation plan as a first priority, plus plans to hit new road and rail targets within the Hanoi-Haiphong sanctuary area. In addition, he said more sorties would produce only marginal results, declared that the proposed new manpower totals for South Vietnam were too high and would create more economic inflation, considered the base construction programs in South Vietnam and Thailand too costly, and demanded that there be no more violations of Chinese air space.

Immediately after the Honolulu conference, Admiral Sharp's PACOM staff began preparing the strangulation plan. The next day, July 9, the JCS sent Rolling Thunder program 51 to Sharp, effective immediately. Program 51 would increase the number of authorized armed reconnaissance sorties in North Vietnam and Laos from 8,100 to 10,100 per month.

In late July, Air Force and Navy pilots began attacking the remaining POL targets approved by Washington in conformance with the new PACOM strangulation plan, as well as associated targets such as vehicles and watercraft. By the end of the month, the Air Force had attacked sixteen dispersed sites and destroyed an estimated 42,800 metric tons of fuel. Navy fliers also destroyed many thousands of tons of fuel in its areas of operation. However, Washington withheld permission to strike other POL sites and associated targets near Hanoi and Haiphong, such as two lock and dam sites, sites at the north's three major seaports, and a large steel plant. Nor did Washington approve the mining of the north's three main harbors to close them to shipping, as had long been advocated by both the Air Force and the Navy.

Although the tempo of air strikes against POL sites and associated targets had passed their apogee by early August, McNamara continued to ask for weekly reports on the campaign. Washington's rationale for not striking additional POL and other targets was that China, in the initial throes of a Cultural Revolution led by the Red Guard, might take irrational action (i.e., enter the war openly). In addition, Hanoi appeared resolved to continue the war until the next South Vietnamese election in November 1966. General William W. Momyer, who succeeded General Moore as Commander, Seventh Air Force on July 1, 1966, characterized the POL strangulation campaign as another piecemeal application of air power.

In late August, Admiral Sharp informed McNamara that little progress had been made in reducing further the north's POL storage capacity—much of it dispersed—estimated at 66,000 metric tons with sites containing 17,000 metric tons not yet authorized for bombing. The PACOM commander said weather and groundfire made it difficult to obtain good photos of strike results. He also informed the Defense Secretary that it was not worthwhile to send aircraft against small, dispersed POL sites as in MACV's route package 1 and, to avoid civilian casualties, pilots were prohibited from attacking POL drums on many streets in towns. PACAF concluded separately that few of the remaining authorized POL sites merited strikes on a priority basis. Still, McNamara considered the POL campaign important, and throughout September, he continued to ask for weekly reports.

By October, it was apparent that the highly restricted POL strangulation campaign had not reduced infiltration into South Vietnam. In fact, in late July and in subsequent weeks, U.S. Marines and South Vietnamese forces were battling elements of the north's 324th Division that had crossed the buffer zone into the I Corps area of South Vietnam. Other Viet Cong and North Vietnamese Army activity had also increased throughout the country. Uncertain if American POL bombing strictures would continue, Soviet and other foreign oil tankers, while still immune from a U.S. naval blockade and air strikes on port facilities, took the precaution of unloading onto barges. In Washington, the DIA and CIA had jointly concluded that the north's POL supplies remained adequate for transporting troops and supplies into South Vietnam, a conclusion that the JASON Division of the Institute of Defense Analyses had reached by the end of August.

Thus ended another unsuccessful special Rolling Thunder program intended to force Hanoi to the negotiating table. In a congressional hearing, McNamara faulted the services for their over-optimistic estimates of what unrestricted POL strikes could accomplish—not mentioning that the strikes were never unrestricted. And with no surcease in the political instability within South Vietnam, the lackluster performance of its Army, and the presence of several hundred thousand American troops, plus some allied units, the close of 1966 brought no sign that the war would end soon. All of the strategies tried thus far by the Johnson administration, devised and directed largely by McNamara and his principal associates in Washington, had proved to no avail. Despite the frequent warnings of the JCS and other tactical commanders, the Army excepted, that a ground-oriented strategy within South Vietnam could never win the war and that an incremental and highly restricted Rolling Thunder program on the north also could not bring Hanoi to heel, the Defense Secretary refused to acknowledge defeat. He never seriously considered unleashing the full might of Air Force and Navy aircraft against important targets in the north, including its seaports, since the specter of open conflict with China, the Soviet Union, or both was ever present.

Still believing that the war was winnable with more technology, McNamara now turned to a plan received at the end of August from the JASON Division of the Institute for Defense Analyses to establish a new anti-infiltration system. At his request, in the summer of 1966 forty-seven scientists and engineers under the aegis of the JASON Division had studied enemy infiltration and the impact of more bombing to reduce it. Rather than more bombing, the JASON group proposed, and McNamara quickly approved, the construction of a system of physical barriers and acoustic and seismic sensors in southern Laos and the demilitarized zone between the two Vietnams. Although the JCS, Admiral Sharp, and all other Air Force and Navy leaders and tactical air commanders strongly opposed the barrier concept as it reflected World War II Maginot Line thinking, sensor placement began early in 1967.

The end of the restricted POL strangulation campaign in October 1966 closed the first phase of Rolling Thunder operations that had begun on March 2, 1965. Although these air attacks had caused considerable pain to the Hanoi government, the gradualness of the air program had enabled the government to absorb its daily losses of military manpower, trucks, watercraft, and other materiel. It had marshaled an estimated 300,00 to 500,000 military and civilian personnel to maintain its logistic network and to man its antiaircraft guns and automatic weapons. Despite the Johnson administration's efforts to win the war using the carrot of diplomacy and eventual foreign aid, and the stick of limited military pressure, Hanoi clearly had not felt sufficient pain to begin talks on ending the war.

Notes

Chapter 1

1. *Report of Investigation, Pleiku Incident*, by Board of Officers to Investigate Incident at MACV Compound and Camp Holloway, Pleiku, RVN, Maj Gen Milton B. Adams, USAF, President, 16 Feb 65; Transcript of News Conference by McNamara and (Under Secy of State) Ball on Air Strike in VN, *Wash Post*, 8 Feb 65.

2. Lyndon Baines Johnson, *The Vantage Point: Perspectives of the Presidency, 1963–1969* (New York: Holt, Rinehart and Winston, 1971), pp 124–25.

3. *Ibid.*, p 124; Maxwell D. Taylor, *Swords and Plowshares* (New York: W.W. Norton & Co., Inc., 1972), p 335; Robert S. McNamara and Brian VanDeMark, *In Retrospect: The Tragedy and Lessons of Vietnam* (New York: Times Books/Random House, 1995), pp 172–74.

4. Hist, CINCPAC, 1965, Vol II, pp 317–18; CINCPACFLT rpt, The United States Navy in the Pacific, 1965, pp 13–14; *The Pentagon Papers: The Defense Department History of United States Decisionmaking on Vietnam. The Senator Gravel edition*, 12 vols. (Boston: Beacon Press, 1971), Vol III, pp 298–301; *New York Times*, 11 Feb 65; Adm. U.S. Grant Sharp, *Strategy for Defeat Vietnam in Retrospect* (San Rafael: Presidio Press, San Rafael, 1978) p 39; McNamara and VanDeMask, *In Retrospect*, pp 172–74.

5. Hist, CINCPAC, 1965, Vol II, pp 317–18; CINCPACFLT rpt, The United States Navy in the Pacific, 1965, pp 13–14; *Gravel Pentagon Papers*, Vol III, pp 298–301; *New York Times*, Feb 11, 65; U.S. Grant Sharp, *Strategy for Defeat: Vietnam in Retrospect* (San Rafael: Presidio Press, 1978) p 39; McNamara and VanDeMark, *In Retrospect*, pp 172–74.

6. Johnson, *The Vantage Point*, pp 121, 124–25.

7. *Ibid.*, p 124; hist, CINCPAC, 1965, Vol II pp 317–18; ltr, Harris to McConnell, 3 Jan 65.

8. Hist, CINCPAC, 1965, Vol II, pp 317–18.

9. Hq USAF rpt, *Analysis of Air Operations, Southeast Asia* (hereafter cited as *Analysis of Air Ops*), 26 Mar 65, Vol I, pp 3–9.

10. *Ibid.*, Vol I, pp 3-1 to 3-2; Hist, CINCPAC, 1965, Vol II, pp 319–20; CINCPACFLT rpt, *The U.S. Navy in the Pacific, 1965*, pp 14, 57, and 191–92.

11. *Analysis of Air Ops*, 26 Mar 65, Vol I, pp 3-1 to 3-2; msg, CINCPACAF to CSAF, 070535Z Feb 65.

12. Project CHECO Team, *Rolling Thunder* (Proj CHECO, 1966) (hereafter cited as *Rolling Thunder*), pp 8–9.

13. *Rolling Thunder*; hist CINCPAC, 1965, Vol II, pp 319–20; *Analysis Of Air Ops*, 26 Mar 65, Vol I, Mar 26 65, pp 3-1 to 3-10; Adm U.S.G. Sharp, CINCPAC, and Gen William C. Westmoreland, COMUSMACV, *Report on the War in Vietnam (as of 30 June 1968)* (Washington: GPO, 1969), pp 14–15.

14. Sharp and Westmoreland, *Rpt on the War in VN*, p 15; Johnson, *The Vantage Point*, p 126; hist, CINCPAC, 1965, Vol II, p 321.

15. Msg, JCS to CINCPAC, COMUSMACV, 071459Z Feb 65; *Analysis of Air Ops*, Vol I, pp 3-1 to 3-10; *Rolling Thunder*, pp 6–7; hist, CINCPAC, 1965, Vol II, p 321; Jacob Van Staaveren, *USAF Plans and Operations in SEA, 1965* (USAF Hist Div Liaison Ofc, 1966), p 7; intvw, with Lt Col Andrew H. Chapman, Hqs 2d AD, Feb 13 65; hist, 509th Ftr Int Sq; Jan–30 Jun 65, pp 9–10; Robert F. Futrell, *Chronology of Significant Air Power Events in Southeast Asia, 1954–1967,* (Maxwell AFB, Ala: Aerospace Studies Institute, 1968*)*, p 54.

16. *Public Papers of the Presidents of the United States: Lyndon B. Johnson, 1965* (Washington: Office of the Federal Register, National Archives & Records Service, 1966), Vol I, pp 153–54.

17. Transcript of News Conference by McNamara and Ball on Air Strikes in Vietnam, *New York Times*, Feb 8 65, p 15.

18. *Public Papers of the President*, Johnson, 1965, Vol I, p 166.

19. *New York Times*, Feb 9 65, p 1.

20. *Washington Post*, Feb 10 65.

21. *Ibid.*

22. *New York Times*, Feb 9 65.

23. *Ibid.*, Feb 13 65.

24. Johnson, *The Vantage Point*, pp 128–30; *Gravel Pentagon Papers*, Vol III, pp 271; 308–18; McNamara and VanDeMark, *In Retrospect*, pp 170–72.

25. Johnson, *The Vantage Point*, p 129.

26. *Ibid.*, pp 129–30; *Rolling Thunder*, pp 9–11.

27. *Rolling Thunder*, pp 9–12; hist, CINCPAC, 1965, Vol II, p 322.

28. Msg, PACAF to 13th AF, 5th AF, et al, 101934Z Feb 65; hist, PACAF, 1 Jul 64–30 Jun 65, Vol I, Pt 2, p 96, hist, SAC, Jan–Jun 65, Vol II, pp 238–39.

29. *Analysis of Air Ops,* May 64–65, Vol I, pp 3-1 to 3-16; *Rolling Thunder*, pp 9–12; Van Staaveren, *USAF Plans and Ops, SEA 1965*, pp 7–8; Hist, CINCPAC, 1965, Vol II, p 322; *Baltimore Sun*, Feb 12 65; *Washington Post*, Feb 12 65, p 1.

30. Fact Sheet, Subj: Operation Flaming Dart-Rolling Thunder, 16 Apr 65, Tab M in File, CINCPAC Agenda Fact Sheet for SECDEF Conference, 19–20 Apr 65; Futrell, *Chron of Significant Air Power Events, 1954–1967*, p 455.

31. Msg, CINCPAC to JCS, 062350Z Feb 65; msg, PACAF to CSAF 122330Z Feb 65; Gen Moore: Speech for Comdrs Conference, Gaguio, Phila, 22–25 Feb 65; PACAF rpt, *Out-Country Strike Operations in Southeast Asia,* Subtask 1A, *Strike Operations in NVN, Jan 1964–11 Feb 1965*, 30 Sep 70, (hereafter cited as PACAF rpt, *Strike Ops in NVN*, Vol I), pp 76–77; 2d AD rpt, *Sequence of Events (Flaming Dart I and II),* 6–17 Feb 65.

32. PACAF rpt, *Strike Ops in NVN*, Vol I, pp 76–77; msgs, Amembassy Bangkok to SECSTATE 133, 5 Aug 64 and 137, 7 Aug 64.

33. *Analysis of Air Ops*, Vol I, pp 3-1 to 3-10; *Wash Post*, Feb 12, 65, p 1.

34. *Analysis of Air Ops,* Vol I, pp 3-1 to 3-10 PACAF rpt, *Strike Ops in NVN*, pp 76–77; 2d AD rpt, *Sequence of Events,* 6–17 Feb 65.

35. *Documents on American Foreign Relations*, 1965, pp 130–31; *Gravel Pentagon Papers*, Vol III, p 306; *New York Times*, Feb 12, 65

36. *Deadline Data on World Affairs*, Feb 14, 65, p 44.

37. *The Pentagon Papers as Published by The New York Times* (New York: Bantam, 1971) (hereafter cited as the *New York Times Pentagon Papers*), pp 428–29.

38. McNamara and VanDeMark, *In Retrospect*, pp 172–73.

Chapter 2

1. Hearings before the Senate Subcommittee on United States Security Agreements and Commitments Abroad of the Committee on Foreign Relations, *United States Security Agreements and Commitments Abroad, The Kingdom of Laos*, 91st Cong, 1st sess, pt 2, pp 20–22, and Oct 28, 68, pp 367–74.

2. *Ibid.*; Senate Foreign Relations Committee Print, *Background Information Relating to Southeast Asia and Vietnam* (hereafter cited as *Background Info on SEA and VN*), 7th Rev Ed, 93d Cong, 2d sess (GPO, Dec 1974), pp 242–50; D. Gareth Porter, *After Geneva, Subverting Laotian Neutrality,* in *Laos: War and Revolution*, ed by Nina S. Adams and Alfred W. McCoy (New York, 1970), pp

183–95; Arthur J. Dommen, *Conflict in Laos: The Politics of Neutralization*, Rev ed, (New York: Praeger, 1971), pp 224–26 and 245–56; Maj Victor B. Anthony, Draft Study, *A Military History of the War in Northern Laos, 1945–1968*, chap IV.

3. House Cmte on Armed Services, Cmte Print, *United States-Vietnam Relations, 1945–1967, Study Prepared by the Department of Defense*, 12 vols, (GPO, 1971), (hereafter cited as *DOD Pentagon Papers*), Bk 2, IV.A.5. Tab 3, pp 60–64; *New York Times Pentagon Papers*, (New York, 1971), pp 53–56; *Final Report of the Select Committee Study on Governmental Operations with Respect to Intelligence Activities*, US Senate, Together with Additional Supplemental and Separate Views, Apr 26, 76, Report No. 94-755, 94th Cong, 2d Sess, *Foreign Military Intelligence* (hereafter cited as Senate Select Cmte on Intel Activities), Bk 1, p 147.

4. William E. Colby and Peter Forbath, *Honorable Men: My Life in the CIA* (New York: Simon and Schuster, 1978), pp 162–71.

5. *Ibid.*, pp 170–73.

6. *DOD Pentagon Papers*, Bk 2, IV, B 1, pp 117–18; Taylor, *Swords and Plowshares*, pp 216–44; Colby and Forbath, *Honorable Men*, pp 174–75.

7. *DOD Pentagon Papers*, Bk 2, IV, B 1. pp 122–23.

8. *Ibid.*, pp 120–21.

9. SECDEF Briefing Bk (for mtg in Jan 62), 16 Dec 61.

10. Jacob Van Staaveren, *USAF Plans and Policies in South Vietnam, 1961–1963* (USAF Hist Div Liaison Ofc, 1965), pp 14–18, 76–78.

11. Hist, CINCPAC, 1963, pp 38–43.

12. Rpt of Visit by JCS Team to SVN, Jan 63; Jacob Van Staaveren, *Interdiction in Southern Laos, 1960–1968* (Center for Air Force History, 1993), p 5.

13. Msg, CINCPAC to JCS (Exclusive for SACSA, Gen Harkins, Gen Collins, Adm Needham, Gen O'Donnell from Adm Felt), 300421Z Apr 63; msg, CSAF to PACAF (Personal, Gen Carpenter to Gen Martin), 222211Z Apr 63; memo, subj: GVN Ops in DRV-US Army Plan, in Summary of Defense Conference Bk (for May 1963 mtg), Blue Tab 5a.

14. Memo, 8 May 63, subj: Agenda Item 5 in Record of SECDEF Conference Held on 6 May 1963 at HQ CINCPAC.

15. *Ibid.*, msg, CINCPAC to JCS, 020048Z May 63.

16. Johnson, *The Vantage Point*, pp 60–61.

17. Van Staaveren, *USAF Plans and Policies in SVN, 1961–1963*, pp 69–72; hist, CINCPAC, 1963, pp 42–43 and 197–200.

18. *Ibid.*

19. Van Staaveren, *USAF Plans and Policies in SVN, 1961–1963*, pp 72–74; msg, JCS to CINCPAC, 312100Z Jun 63; msg, CINCPAC to JCS, 070232Z Aug 63; PACAF Ops Plan 32-65 (as of Aug 63); memo, 4 Nov 63, Col L. W. Bray, Ofc of Dep Dir of Plans for War Plans to CSAF, subj: Consideration of CINCPAC Oplan 99-64; *Gravel Pentagon Papers*, Vol II, p 752; McNamara and VanDeMark, *In Retrospect*, pp 70–80.

20. Van Staaveren, *USAF Plans and Policies in SVN, 1961–1963*, pp 72–74; McNamara and VanDeMark, *In Retrospect*, pp 81–87.

21. *New York Times Pentagon Papers*, pp 232–33; Johnson, *The Vantage Point*, p 45.

22. *New York Times Pentagon Papers*, pp 271–74; Johnson, *The Vantage Point*, pp 63–64; Jt COMUSMACV Oplan 34A and Saigon Oplan Tiger, 15 Dec 63, subj: Operations in NVN; msg, CIA to State Dept (Jt State-DOD-CIA msg), 162215Z Jan 64.

23. Msg, McNamara to SECSTATE and Director CIA, no subj, Jan 3, 64, with attached copy of draft memo to Pres, subj: Covert Ops Against NVN; msg, CIA to State Dept, White House, JCS (personal for Lodge, Harkins, and CIA Chief, Saigon), 162215Z Jan 64.

24. Hist, MACV, Annex A, 14 Jan 66.

25. Msg, Saigon 3943 to Washington,

Honolulu (from Lodge to SECSTATE, JCS, CINCPAC Pol Adviser (POL AD), 21 Jan 64; msg, CIA Wash to SECSTATE, OSD, JCS, White House, 250250Z Jan 64; hist, SAC, Jan–Jun 64, Vol III, p 417; Kenneth Sams, *Escalation of the War in SEA, Jul–Dec 64* (Proj CHECO, 1965), pp 92–93; William R. Greenhalgh, Jr., ms, *US Air Force Reconnaissance in Southeast Asia, 1960–1975*, (AF Hist Research Cent, 1977), pp 118–21; Van Staaveren, *Interdiction in Southern Laos*, p 22.

26. Hist, CINCPAC, 1964, p 367; *DOD Pentagon Papers*, Bk 4, IV, C. 2, pp 2–3.

27. COMUSMACV Oplan 34A, 15 Dec 63; msg, Saigon to SECSTATE, OSD, JCS, White House, 14 Mar 64; msg, COMUSMACV to SECSTATE, OSD, White House, CIA, JCS, 060515Z Apr 65; *New York Times Pentagon Papers*, pp 234–40.

28. Msg, State-Def to Amembassy Saigon, Paris, et al, Feb 23, 64; msg, CIA to SECSTATE, OSD, JCS, ISA, White House, Mar 16, 64; msgs, State Dept to Amembassy Saigon 155, 1581, and 1587, Mar 28, Apr 1 and 2, 64; msg, Vientiane to SECSTATE 1083, Apr 64.

29. *Gravel Pentagon Papers*, Vol III, pp 496–99.

30. *Facts on File*, SVN 1961–1965, Vol I, pp 88–89; *Gravel Pentagon Papers*, Vol III, p 42; Taylor, *Swords and Plowshares*, p 308.

31. Msg AFCVC, USAF to PACAF (personal Gen McKee to Gen Smart), 1 Mar 64; memo, SECDEF to Chmn JCS, 21 Feb 64, subj: Vietnam.

32. *Book of Actions in SEA, 1961–74*, Dir/Ops, HQ USAF (hereafter cited as *Bk of Actions, SEA, 1961–1974*), Tab K.

33. *Ibid.*

34. *Gravel Pentagon Papers*, Vol II, pp 121 and 499–510; memo, SECDEF to SA, SAF, SN, et al, 17 Mar 65, subj: Implementation of SVN Program; hist, Dir/Plans, Hqs USAF, Jan–Jun 64, pp 17–18; Robert F. Futrell, ms, *The Advisory Years to 1965*, Ofc AF Hist, 1979, pp 406–07; Mark Clodfelter, *The Limits of Air Power: The Bombing of North Vietnam* (New York: Free Press, 1989), pp 45–46; McNamara and VanDeMark, *In Retrospect*, p 274.

35. Msg, State Dept to Amembassy Saigon 1484 (from the President to Amb Lodge), Mar 20, 64; *Gravel Pentagon Papers*, Vol IV, p 511; Futrell, *The Advisory Years*, pp 406–07; Johnson, *The Vantage Point*, pp 65–67, and 189.

36. Msg, Saigon to SECSTATE 1594 (from Lodge to Pres), Feb 20, 64; Futrell, *The Advisory Years*, pp 406–07; Johnson, *The Vantage Point*, pp 66–67.

37. Memo, Chmn JCS to SECDEF, subj: Alternative Courses of Action, 14 Apr 65.

38. CSAFM-549-64, 28 May 64; JCSM-471-64, 2 Jun 64; *Bk of Actions in SEA, 1961–74*, pt IV, tabs O and P; Futrell, *The Advisory Years*, p 409.

39. CM-451-64, 5 Jun 64; Futrell, *The Advisory Years*, p 418.

40. Taylor, *Swords and Plowshares*, p 316; Jacob Van Staaveren, *USAF Plans and Policies in South Vietnam and Laos, 1964* (USA Hist Div Liaison Ofc, 1965), pp 19–21; *Gravel Pentagon Papers*, Vol II, pp 172–76; *New York Times*, May 31, 64.

41. *Gravel Pentagon Papers*, Vol IV, pp 172–78; MR, by Brig Gen Richard A. Yudkin, Dep Dir of Plans for Policy, DCS/P&C, Hq USAF (based on Gen Smart's notes), subj: Honolulu Conference, 1–2 Jun 64; MR, Gen Yudkin, subj: SECDEF Conf, 1–2 Jun 64, with attached MR by Lt Col Walter M. Pickard, Ofc of Dir/Plans, 24 Jun 64, no subj; Van Staaveren, *USAF Plans and Policies in SVN and Laos*, 1964, pp 19–21; *New York Times*, May 31 and Jun 3, 64; Taylor, *Swords and Plowshares*, pp 312–13.

42. Msg, JCS to CINCPAC, 162144Z Jun 64, and 21 Jun 64; hist, CINCPAC, 1964, pp 61–62; Futrell, *The Advisory Years*, p 410; *Gravel Pentagon Papers*, Vol III, p 177; Van Staaveren, *USAF Plans and Policies in SVN and Laos*, 1964, pp 19–21; *New York Times*, May 31, and Jun 3, 64.

43. Msg, CINCPAC to COMUS-MACV, 180800Z Jun 64; msg, JCS to

CINCPAC, 02211 5Z and 081414Z Jul 64; JCS 2343/423, 11 Jul 64, with atchd memo, Col R.E. Phelan, Asst Dep Dir of Plans for Policy to CSAF, 9 Mar 65, subj: Proposal for a Settlement of SEA, with atchd list of key 1964 JCS Papers; study, *Outcountry Strike Operations in Southeast Asia, 1 Jan 65–31 Mar 68, Plans, Concepts, Doctrine*, Vol V, pt 1, 30 Sep 70, pp 11–12; msg, JCS to CINCPAC, 0211 Jul 64.

44. Msg, PACAF to CINCPAC, 042151Z Jul 64.

45. Ltr, Gen Smart to Dep SECDEF Vance, 18 Jul 64, no subj.

46. Memo, Phelan to CSAF, 9 Mar 65, subj: Proposals for a Settlement of the SEA Conflict with atchd key 1964 JCS Papers.

47. Futrell, *The Advisory Years*, p 452; hist, CINCPAC, 1964, p 354; *New York Times*, Jul 20, 23, and 24, 64 (all p 1).

48. Futrell, *The Advisory Years*, p 452; *Gravel Pentagon Papers*, Vol III, pp 512–17; Taylor, *Swords and Plowshares*, p 316.

49. *Gravel Pentagon Papers*, Vol III, pp 177–80; *DOD Pentagon Papers*, Bk 4, p 42ff; *Washington Post*, Jun 27, 72, p A-13; *New York Times*, Jun 28, 72.

50. Futrell, *The Advisory Years*, pp 451–56; Van Staaveren, *USAF Plans and Policies in SVN and Laos, 1964*, pp 24–27; hearing before the Committee on Foreign Relations, U.S. Senate, 90th Cong, 2d sess, subj: *The Gulf of Tonkin: The 1964 Incidents* (GPO, 20 Feb 1968), pp 9–19; *Gravel Pentagon Papers*, Vol III, p 575; msg, Bangkok to SECSTATE, 157 to DoD, JCS, White House, CIA, Saigon (Westmoreland) 7 Aug 64.

51. Futrell, *The Advisory Years*, pp 451–57; Johnson, *The Vantage Point*, pp 112–119; Van Staaveren, *USAF Plans and Policies in SVN and Laos, 1964*, pp 24–27; *Public Papers of the Presidents*, Johnson, Vol II, 1963–64, pp 927–41; Joint Hearing before the Committee on Foreign Relations and the Committee on Armed Services, U.S. Senate, 88th Cong, 2d sess, subj: *Southeast Asia Resolution* (GPO), 6 Aug 64; Supplementary Documents to February 20, 1968 Hearing with SECDEF Robert S. McNamara, Cmte on Foreign Relations, 90th Cong, 2d sess, subj: *The Gulf of Tonkin, The 1964 Incident*, part II, Dec 16, 1968, pp 2–3.

52. *New York Times*, Aug 7, 8, 9, 10, 11, 64.

53. Futrell, *The Advisory Years*, p 456.

54. *Gravel Pentagon Papers*, Vol III, pp 530–33; Futrell, *The Advisory Years*, p 45; msg, Saigon to SECSTATE 132, 7 Aug 64.

55. *Gravel Pentagon Papers*, Vol III, pp 524–37; Futrell, *The Advisory Years*, pp 456–67.

56. Van Staaveren, *USAF Plans and Policies in SVN and Laos, 1964*, pp 34–35.

57. Msgs, Amembassy Bangkok to SECSTATE 133, Aug 5, 64 and 157, Aug 7, 64; msg, CINCPAC to CINCPACFLT, CINCPACAF, COMUSMACV, 1122272 Aug 64.

58. *Gravel Pentagon Papers*, Vol III, pp 524–39.

59. *Ibid.*, pp 539–42 and 537–55; JCSM-729-64, 24 Aug 64; JCS Armed Reconnaissance Study Group Report, *Analysis of the Armed Reconnaissance Program in NVN*, 15 Nov 65, Tab A to app 1 to annex C, p 2.

60. *Gravel Pentagon Papers*, Vol III, pp 555–56; JCSM-729-64, 24 Aug 64.

61. *Gravel Pentagon Papers*, Vol III, pp 542–45, 550–52; msg, CINCPACAF to CSAF, 29 Aug 64.

62. *Gravel Pentagon Papers*, Vol III, pp 192–93, 560–66; Johnson, *The Vantage Point*, pp 120–21; Taylor, *Swords and Plowshares*, pp 320–21; *New York Times*, Sep 8, 64.

63. *Gravel Pentagon Papers*, Vol III, pp 565–66.

64. JCS 2343/450, 31 Aug 64; hist, Dir/Plans, Hq USAF, Jul–Dec 64, pp 50–51, 58–59; *New York Times*, Aug 25, 64; *Baltimore Sun*, Aug 25, 64; *Chicago Tribune* Sep 1, 64.

65. *New York Times*, Sep 13–16, 64;

Facts on File, *South Vietnam*, 1961–65, Vol I, p 104; Taylor, *Swords and Plowshares*, p 321.

66. *Gravel Pentagon Papers*, Vol III, pp 194–95; Futrell, *The Advisory Years*, p 460.

67. *Gravel Pentagon Papers*, Vol III, pp 133–34; Facts on File, *South Vietnam*, 1961–65, Vol I, p 107.

68. *Gravel Pentagon Papers*, Vol III, pp 569–70; Van Staaveren, *USAF Plans and Policies in SVN and Laos, 1965*, p 32.

69. *Gravel Pentagon Papers*, Vol III, pp 133–34; *New York Times Pentagon Papers*, p 319; Van Staaveren, *Interdiction in Southern Laos*, chap. III.

70. *Gravel Pentagon Papers*, Vol III, p 134; JCSM-893-64, 21 Oct 64; JCSM-902-64, 27 Oct 64: Book of Actions in SEA, pt II tab W; *DOD Pentagon Papers*, 4, pp 2–3; McNamara and VanDeMark, *In Retrospect*, p 159.

71. Taylor, *Swords and Plowshares*, pp 323–25; Van Staaveren, *USAF Plans and Policies in SVN and Laos, 1964*, pp 36–38.

72. Johnson, The Vantage Point, p 121; Van Staaveren, *USAF Plans and Policies in SVN and Laos, 1964*, pp 36–37; Taylor, *Swords and Plowshares*, p 323–25.

73. William C. Westmoreland, *A Soldier Reports*, (New York: Dell, 1976), p 111; Sharp, *Strategy for Defeat*, pp 48–49; Taylor, *Swords and Plowshares*, p 324.

74. Taylor, *Swords and Plowshares*, p 324; Westmoreland, *A Soldier Reports*, p 111; Sharp, *Strategy for Defeat*, pp 40–45.

75. Van Staaveren, *USAF Plans and Ops in SVN and Laos, 1964*, pp 39–41.

76. Lt Col Roger P. Fox, draft study, *Air Base Defense in the Republic of Vietnam* (Ofc AF Hist, undated), pp 20–36; Van Staaveren, *USAF Plans and Policies in SVN and Laos, 1964*, pp 39–41.

77. CSAFM-K-73-74, 23 Nov 64; JCSM-997-64, 28 Nov 64; *Bk of Actions in SEA, 1961–74*, pt V, Tab H; *USAF Mgt Sum SEA*, 16 Jul 65.

78. Futrell, *The Advisory Years*, pp 493–95; Van Staaveren, *USAF Plans and Policies in SVN and Laos*, 1964, pp 42–43.

79. *Gravel Pentagon Papers*, Vol III, pp 210–36; Van Staaveren, *USAF Plans and Policies in SVN and Laos*, 1964, pp 42–43; Clodfelter, *The Limits of Air Power*, pp 52–56; McNamara and VanDeMark, *In Retrospect*, pp 159–61.

80. Van Staaveren, *USAF Plans and Policies in SVN and Laos*, 1964, pp 42–43; Taylor, *Swords and Plowshares*, pp 326–27; *Gravel Pentagon Papers*, Vol III, pp 236–51.

81. Van Staaveren, *USAF Plans and Policies in SVN and Laos*, 1964, pp 43–44; *Gravel Pentagon Papers*, Vol III, pp 248–55, 677–83; Futrell, *The Advisory Years*, pp 495–96.

82. Futrell, *The Advisory Years*, pp 495–96; *Gravel Pentagon Papers*, Vol III, pp 258–263; Taylor, *Swords and Plowshares*, pp 329–32.

83. Futrell, *The Advisory Years*, pp 495–96; Sams, *Escalation of the War in SEA, Jul–Dec 64*, pp 79–80, 201–06; Van Staaveren, *USAF Plans and Policies in SVN and Laos, 1964*, pp 44, 79; *Gravel Pentagon Papers*, Vol III, pp 251–57; memo, SAF to SECDEF, *Use of Infra-Red Equipped Acft for Locating Targets in Laos at Night*, 11 Jan 65; 1st Lt Robert L. MacNaughton, *Yankee Team*, May 64–Jun 65, (Proj CHECO, 1966), p 34.

84. Futrell, *The Advisory Years*, pp 502–5; Johnson, *The Vantage Point*, p 121; Kenneth Sams, *The Battle for Binh Gia* (Proj CHECO, 1965), p 1; Taylor, *Swords and Plowshares*, pp 322–34.

85. Taylor, *Swords and Plowshares*, pp 326, 329–32.

86. Intvw, Dr. Alfred E. Goldberg and Arthur M. Marmor, AF Hist Liaison Ofc, with Gen LeMay, 12 Jan 65.

87. Johnson, *The Vantage Point*, pp 123–24.

88. *Ibid.*, pp 122–23.

89. *Ibid.*, p 123.

Chapter 3

1. Hist, MACV, 1965, pp 46 and 269; hist, CINCPAC, 1965, An B, p 22.

2. CINCPACFLT rpt, *U.S. Navy in the Pacific*, 1965, p 214–15; Van Staaveren, *Interdiction in Southern Laos*, p 5.

3. Msg, PACAF to Thirteenth AF, Fifth AF, 2d AD, 313th AD, 109334Z, Feb 65.

4. Msg, JCS to SAC, 111440Z Feb 65.

5. Hist, 2d AD, Jan–Jun 65, Vol II, p 2.

6. *Ibid.*

7. DIA Bull-6-65, 3 Feb 65.

8. PACOM WID No 9-65, 26 Feb 65.

9. Harrison, pp 11, 27–28, 53, 73, and 78; PACAF rpt, *Climatology in Southeast Asia*, p 5; hist, 355th TFW, Jan–Jun 66, p 12.

10. Robert F. Futrell and Martin Blumenson, *The Advisory Years to 1965* (Ofc AF Hist, 1978), chap IX; William W. Momyer, *Air Power in Three Wars (WW II, Korea, Vietnam)* (GPO, 1978), pp 70–71.

11. Van Staaveren, *USAF Plans and Policies in SVN, 1961–1963*, pp 14–19; Momyer, *Air Power in Three Wars*, pp 70–71.

12. Hist, 2d AD, Jan–Jun 64, p 12; Van Staaveren, *USAF Plans and Policies in SVN, 1961–1963*, pp 14–19; Van Staaveren, *USAF Plans and Policies in SVN and Laos, 1964*, pp 65–68; Momyer, *Air Power in Three Wars*, pp 70–71; Futrell and Blumenson, *Air Force Ops In SEA*, Chap IX.

13. PACAF rpt, *Plans, Concepts, and Doctrine*, pt 1, pp 102 and 114–17; Kenneth Sams, *Command and Control, 1965* (Proj CHECO, 1966), pp 1–2; msg, CINCPACAF to CSAF 110645Z Feb 65; hist, MACV, 1965, p 101; hist, CINCPAC, 1965, Vol II, p 393.

14. *Ibid.*; MSgt Robert T. Helmka and TSgt Beverly Hale, *USAF Operations from Thailand, 1964–65* (Proj CHECO, 1966), pp 10–11.

15. Van Staaveren, *USAF Plans and Ops in SEA*, 1965, pp 65–68; Momyer, *Air Power in Three Wars*, Chap III.

16. Hist, MACV, 1964, p 9; McConnell notebook, Item 75, 5 Apr 65; intvw, Maj Samuel E. Riddlebarger and Lt Col Valentino Castillina with Gen Moore, 22 Nov 69, p 27; Sharp and Westmoreland, *Report on the War*, pp 83 and 279.

17. Intvw, Maj Samuel E. Riddlebarger and Lt Col Valentino Castillina with Gen Moore, 22 Nov 69, p 27.

18. Intvw, Maj Richard B. Clement and Capt Ralph G. Swentson with Maj Gen Gilbert L. Meyers, 20 May 70, pp 36–38.

19. Msg, CINCPACAF to CSAF, 110645Z Feb 65; intvws, Maj Riddlebarger and Lt Col Castillina with Gen Moore, 29 Nov 69, p 29, and Maj Clement and Capt Swentson with Gen Meyers, 27 May 70, pp 46–48.

20. Msg, CINCPACAF to Fifth AF, Thirteenth AF, 315th AD, PACAF-BASECOM, 140340Z Feb 65.

21. Msg, 2d AD to PACAF, 110748Z Feb 65.

22. Msg, CINCPAC to JCS, 110942Z Feb 65.

23. Msg, CINCPAC to JCS, 132220Z Feb 65.

24. Msg, COMUSMACV to CINCPAC, 131250Z Feb 65.

25. David Kraslow and Stuart H. Loory, *The Secret Search for Peace*, (New York: Random House, 1968) pp 114–15. JCSM-100-65, 11 Feb 65; James C. Thompson, "How Could Vietnam Happen?" *Atlantic Monthly* Apr 68, p 51.

26. JCSM-100-65, 11 Feb 65; *Gravel Pentagon Papers*, Vol III, pp 318–21; PACAF Corona Harvest Rpt, *Strike Operations in NVN*, 12 Feb–23 Dec 65, pp 16–17.

27. Memo, Maj Gen J. W. Carpenter III, Asst DCS/Plans and Ops for NCS Matters to CSAF, 28 Mar 65, subj: Recent Actions by JCS and Recommendations to Higher Authority Re SEA; JCS Rpt, Night Song Study Gp Rpt, prepared by Jt Staff, 30 Mar 65, Vol III, p C-27; *Gravel Pentagon Papers*, Vol III, pp 320–21.

28. *Gravel Pentagon Papers*, Vol III, pp 340–41; *DOD Pentagon Papers*, Vol IV, p 75; CM-438-65, 19 Feb 65; memo, Carpenter to CSAF, 1 Mar 65, subj: Air

Strikes Against NVN Transportation System.

29. Johnson, *The Vantage Point*, p 310; *Gravel Pentagon Papers*, Vol III, pp 308–18; Senate Rpt, *Background Information Relating to SEA and VN*, p 19; Taylor, *Swords and Plowshares*, p 336.

30. Johnson, *The Vantage Point*, pp 130–31.

31. *Gravel Pentagon Papers*, Vol III, pp 325–30.

32. Msg, JCS to CINCPAC, 162215Z Feb 65; msg, CINCPAC to JCS, 180045Z Feb 65; Johnson, *The Vantage Point*, p 132.

33. Msg, JCS to CINCPAC, 182327Z Feb 65.

34. Msg, Hq PACAF to CINCPACFLT et al, 190835Z Feb 65; msg, CINCPACAF to Comdr Thirteenth AF, 19001Z Feb 65; *Gravel Pentagon Papers*, Vol III, p 325; Kenneth Sams, *Nguyen Cao Ky* (Proj CHECO, 1965), pp 13–15.

35. *Gravel Pentagon Papers*, Vol III, p 325; Sams, *Nguyen Cao Ky*, pp 13–15.

36. Msg, CINCPAC to JCS, 190754Z Feb 65; *Gravel Pentagon Papers*, Vol III, p 325.

37. Msg, COMUSMACV to CINCPAC, 240220Z Feb 65; Sams, *Nguyen Cao Ky*, pp 13–14; *Analysis of Air Ops*, 26 Mar 65, Vol I, pp 4-1 to 4-2.

38. *Gravel Pentagon Papers*, Vol III, pp 325–40.

39. *New York Times*, Feb 26, 65, p 1.

40. *Ibid.*, Mar 1, 65.

41. Rpt, *Aggression from the North: The Record of North Vietnam's Campaign to Conquer South Vietnam* (Dept of State Publ 7839 of Media Services, Bureau of Public Affairs, Feb 64) pp 133.

42. *New York Times*, Mar 17, 65.

43. Jon M. Van Dyke, *North Vietnam's Strategy for Survival* (Palo Alto, Pacific Books, 1972), pp 30 and 126–27.

44. Msg, JCS to CINCPAC, 011840Z Mar 65.

45. *Ibid.*

46. *Ibid.*; *Analysis of Air Ops*, May 64–5 Apr 65, Vol I, , pp 4-1 to 4-2; *Rolling Thunder,* 26 Mar 65, p 22.

47. Msg, JCS to CINCPAC, 011840Z Mar 65; hist, CINCPAC, 1965, Vol I, p 326.

48. Msg, COMUSMACV to CINCPAC, JCS, 041120Z Mar 65; *Analysis of Air Ops,* 26 Mar 65, Vol I, pp 4-1 to 4-2; *Rolling Thunder*. Personal Notebook on Significant Events, by Gen John P. McConnell, CSAF (hereafter cited as McConnell Notebook), item 33.

49. *Baltimore Sun*, Mar 3, 65.

50. Stmt, by Secy McNamara on Mar 2, 65, Hearings before the House Subcmte on Appns, 89th Cong, 1st sess, DOD Approps for 1966, pp 3 and 80.

51. Msgs, JCS to CINCPAC, 092251Z Mar 65, and 111624Z Mar 65.

52. Msg, COMUSMACV to CINCPAC, NMCC, 120825Z Mar 65; msgs, Amembassy Saigon to SECSTATE, 130245Z Mar 65; MACV J-3 to CINCPAC, NMCC, 130050Z Mar 65; MACV to CINCPAC, CINCPACAF, 130310Z Mar 65; JCS to CINCPAC, 131548Z Mar 65.

53. PACAF Working Paper, subj: *Sequence of Events (Feb 65–Jan 67)*, undtd; msg, JCS to CINCPAC, 131548Z Mar 65; *Analysis of Air Ops,* May 64–Apr 65, Vol I, pp 4-4 to 4-6; *New York Times*, Mar 15, 65; *Washington Post*, May 15 and 16, 65.

54. *Analysis of Air Ops,* Vol I, pp 4-1 to 4-3; *Rolling Thunder,* pp 22–23.

55. Memo, Gen W.H. Blanchard, Vice CSAF to TAC (Maj Gen Graham), 4 Mar 65, subj: Ltr of Instruction; msg, CSAF to PACAF (Personal Gen Blanchard to Gen Harris), 040034Z Mar 65; hist, TAC, Jan–Jun 65, pp 794–95.

56. Msg, 313th AD, Kadena AB, Okinawa to CINCPACAF, 060927Z; msg, CINCPAC to JCS, 040710Z Mar 65; hist, TAC, Jan–Jun 65, pp 794–95; msg, COMUSMACV to CINCPAC, 041120Z Mar 65.

57. Memo, Vice Adm L. Mustin, Dir/Ops J-3, Joint Staff to Vice Dir/Ops, J-3 Jt Staff, 3 Mar 65, subj: Analysis of Acft Losses in SEA; CM-469-65, 10 Mar 65.

58. Memo, H. Brown to SAF, SN, et al, 15 Mar 65, subj: Acft Combat Losses in VN.

59. Msgs AFIN 40725 and 40735, 2d AD to CSAF, 15 Mar 65; msg, 2d AD to CSAF 160535Z Mar 65; memo, Brig Gen R.A. Yudkin, to AFXOPL, 25 Mar 65, subj: USAF Analysis Team; memo, SAF to SECDEF, 15 Mar 65, no subj; rpt, *Advanced Flying Training in TAC in Support Southeast Asia Operations, 1965–1969* (Ofc TAC Hist, Jun 71), pp 22–26.

60. Memo, SAF to SECDEF, 22 May 65, subj: Rpt of USAF Combat Ops in SEA.

61. *New York Times*, Mar 4 and 5, 65; *Washington Post*, Mar 4, 65.

62. *Washington Post*, Mar 8, 65, p 1; CINCPACFLT rpt, *The United States Navy in the Pacific*, 1965, pp 58–59; *Communist Policy Towards Southeast Asia, 1954–1969, A Chronological Compendium* (Aerospace Studies Institute, Maxwell AFB, Ala., 1970), pp 228–29.

63. Senate rpt, *Background Info Relating to SEA and VN*, p 20.

64. Memo, Legal Basis for United States Actions Against North Vietnam: Department of State Memorandum, March 8, 1965; Senate rpt, *Background Info Relating to SEA and VN*, Jun 70, pp 220–24.

65. Msg, CINCPAC to JCS, 040304Z Mar 65.

66. *Gravel Pentagon Papers*, Vol III, pp 334–36; JCS-180-65, 15 Mar 65.

67. Rpt, Gen Harold K. Johnson, CSA to SECDEF, et al, 14 Mar 65, subj: *VN Trip from 5–12 Mar 65*; *Gravel Pentagon Papers*, Vol III pp 337–40; JCSM-197-65, 17 Mar 65.

68. Msg, JCS to CINCPAC, 160119Z Mar 65; msg, State Dept to Amembassy Saigon, 2000, Mar 16, 65.

69. Msg, JCS to CINCPAC, 162346Z; msg, CINCPACAF to CINCPAC, 140315Z Mar 65; msg, CINCPAC to CINCPACAF, 162259Z Mar 65; Greenhalgh, *USAF Reconnaissance in SEA, 1960–1975*, p 171.

70. CSAF-J-78-65, 17 Mar 65; Momyer, *Air Power in Three Wars*, p 19.

71. Momyer, *Air Power in Three Wars*, p 19.

72. Hist, JCS Historical Office, *The Joint Chiefs of Staff and the War in Vietnam, 1960–1968* (JCS Hist Ofc, 1970) (hereafter cited as *The JCS and the War in VN*), p II, pp 18-21 to 18-24; msg, CINCPAC to JCS, 210525Z Mar 65.

73. Msg, JCS to CINCPAC, 162142Z Mar 65; msg, CINCPAC to JCS, 172219Z Mar 65; msg, CSAF to CINCPACAF, 181322Z Mar 65; hist, CINCPAC, 1965, Vol II, p 332.

74. Msg, JCS to CINCPAC, 162143Z Mar 65; *Analysis of Air Ops*, Vol I, pp 4-7 and 4-9; Vol III, pp 3–28.

75. *Analysis of Air Ops, SEA*, Vol I, 26 Mar 65, pp 4-8 to 4-11; memo, Col H. L. Price, Ofc Dir/Ops 2d AD to AFB GP (ODC), subj: *Rolling Thunder* VII, 18 Mar 65.

76. *Analysis of Air Ops*, Vol 1, 26 Mar 65, pp 4-11 to 4-12.

77. *Ibid*., pp 4-12 to 4-14.

78. Msg, JCS to CINCPAC, CINCSAC, 240057Z Mar 65; msg, CINPAC to CINCPACFLT, CINCPACAF, COMUSMACV, 24084Z Mar 65; msg, CINCPACAF to Thirteenth AF, 2d AD, 241054Z Mar 65.

79. *Analysis of Air Ops*, Vol I, 26 Mar 65, pp 4-14A to 4-14M; hist, CINCPAC, 1965, Vol II, p 332.

80. *Analysis of Air Ops,* Vol I, 6 Mar 65, pp 4-14A to 4-14M.

81. DIA Bull, 5 Apr 65, pp F-3 and F-4.

82. Van Staaveren, *USAF Plans and Ops in SEA, 1965,* p 24.

83. Msg, CINCPAC to JCS, 210515Z Mar 65; msg, JCS to CINCPAC, 300059Z Mar 65; *The JCS and the War in VN*, pt II, pp 18–25.

84. Msg, JCS to CINCPAC, 300059Z Mar 65.

85. Greenhalgh, *USAF Reconnaissance in SEA, 1960–1975*, pp 181–82; Helmka and Hale, *USAF Operations from Thailand, 1964–1965*, pp 112–13; *Analysis of Air Ops*, 6–12 Apr 65, Vol II, p 1-1.

86. JCSM-202-65, 20 Mar 65; msg, CSAF to PACAF, TAC, 312215Z Mar 65; memo, SECDEF to Chmn JCS, 1 Apr 65, subj: Immediate Deployment of an F–4C Squadron to Thailand; hist, CINCPAC, 1965, Vol I, p 285; hist, 8th TFW, Jul–Dec 65, pp 5 and 11; Robert F. Futrell, *Chron of Significant Air Power Events in Southeast Asia, 1950–1968* (Maxwell AFB, Ala: Aerospace Studies Institute, 1969) p 91.

87. Msg, CSAF to PACAF, 312215Z Mar 65; Helmka and Hale, *USAF Operations from Thailand 1964–1965*, p 114.

88. Msg, CINCPAC to COMUS-MACV, CINCPACAF et al, 060127Z, Mar 65; msg, COMUSMACV to CINCPAC, 150645Z Mar 65; memo, McKee to DCS/P&O, 31 Mar 65, subj: Interagency Psywar Ops Subcmte; hist, MACV, 1965, p 458.

89. *Analysis of Air Ops*, May 64–5 Apr 65, Vol I, pp 2-15a to 2-20a.

90. *Gravel Pentagon Papers*, Vol III, pp 319–20.

91. *Ibid.*

92. CM-481-65, 11 Mar 65.

93. Memo, Germeraad to CSAF, 12 Mar 65, subj: Contingency Planning for SEA/WESTPAC; CM-481-65, 11 Mar 65.

94. CSAFM-J-67-65, 12 Mar 65; Germeraad to CSAF, 12 Mar 65.

95. Msg, CINCPACAF to CSAF, 2d AD, 090117 Mar 65 (Personnel for Gens Carpenter, Preston, Moore, Maddux, and Ellis from Moorman); 2d AD (personal) to Gen Compton (from Harris), 12 Mar 65.

96. Memo, McKee to CSAF, 18 Mar 65, subj: Briefing on Views of Amb Taylor, CINCPAC, and COMUSMACV on Certain Proposals made by Chmn JCS.

97. CMCN-27-65, subj: U.S. Deployments to SEA, 18 Mar 65; McKee to CSAF, 19 Mar 65, subj: VSMC Plan for U.S. Deployments into SEA; memo, McKee to CSAF, 18 Mar 65, subj: Briefing on Views of Amb Taylor, CINC-PAC and COMUSMACV on Certain Proposals Made by Chmn JCS; memo, McKee to CSAF, 19 Mar 65, subj: USMC Plan for U.S. Deployments into SEA.

Chapter 4

1. JCSM-204-65, 20 Mar 65.

2. Johnson, *The Vantage Point*, p 140; *New York Times Pentagon Papers*, pp 440–43.

3. Msg, COMUSMACV to CINCPAC, 271338Z Mar 65; *New York Times Pentagon Papers*, pp 398–400.

4. *New York Times Pentagon Papers*, pp 394–400; *New York Times*, Mar 29, 65; *The JCS and the War in VN*, pt II, pp 18–25.

5. *Gravel Pentagon Papers*, Vol III, pp 695–702; and *New York Times Pentagon Papers*, pp 432–440.

6. Johnson, *The Vantage Point*, p 147.

7. McNamara and VanDeMark, *In Retrospect*, pp 171–77.

8. *Ibid.*, pp 139–40 and 147; *Gravel Pentagon Papers*, Vol III, p 407.

9. *Gravel Pentagon Papers*, Vol III, pp 702–03; *Public Papers of the President, Johnson, 1965*, Vol I, p 370; *New York Times*, Apr 2 and 3, 65; McNamara and VanDeMark, *In Retrospect*, pp 185–87; Clodfelter, *The Limits of Air Power*, pp 66–67; Van Staaveren, *Interdiction in Southern Laos*, pp 56–61.

10. Facts on File, *South Vietnam 1961–65*, p 170.

11. *New York Herald Tribune*, Apr 5, 65.

12. Johnson, *The Vantage Point*, pp 132–33.

13. Chester L. Cooper, *The Lost Crusade: America in Vietnam* (New York: Dodd, Mead, 1970), pp 272–75.

14. *Gravel Pentagon Papers*, Vol III, p 356.

15. Msg, JCS to CINCPAC, 311717Z Mar 65; *Analysis of Air Ops*, 26 Mar 65, Vol I, pp 4-14N to 4-14W; Vol II, 6–12 Apr 65, p 3-3; and Vol II, tab 3; Asst SECDEF (PA) News Release 206–65, 4 Apr 65; Maj A.J.C. Lavalle, ed, *The Tale*

of Two Bridges and *The Battle for the Skies Over North Vietnam* (Air University, 1976), pp 31–38; Ofc Asst SECDEF (PA) News Release No 206-65, 4 Apr 65.

16. *Analysis of Air Ops,* 26 Mar 65, Vol I, pp 4-14N to 4-14Q; Hq PACAF Working Paper, *Sequence of Events,* 4 Feb 65–24 Feb 67; CINCPACFLT rpt, *The U.S. Navy in the Pacific, 1965,* p 49; *Washington Post,* May 15, 72; hist, 313th AD, Jul–Dec 65, p 187.

17. *Analysis of Air Ops,* 26 Mar 65, Vol I, pp 4-14N to 4-14R; *Rolling Thunder,* pp 31–35; Asst SECDEF (PA), News Release 206-65, 4 Apr 65; hist, 313th AD, Jul–Dec 65, p 187; hist, 67th TFS, 1 Jan–30 Jun 65, chap IV; Lt Charles H. Heffron, *Air to Air Encounters Over NVN* (Proj CHECO, 1967), p 1; *New York Times,* Apr 5, 65; *Washington Post,* Apr 5, 65; memo, L. Unger, Dep Asst SECSTATE for Far Eastern Affairs and Chmn of VN Coordinating Cmte to George Ball, Acting SECSTATE, subj: Recent U.S. Mil Engagements in NVN and Vicinity; msg, Wheeler to Sharp, 061616Z Apr 65; McConnell Notebook, Item 68, 3 Apr 65, and Item 93, 13 Apr 65; Lavalle, *Tale of Two Bridges,* pp 38–40.

18. Msg, 18th TFW to 2d AD, 051740Z Apr 65; *Rolling Thunder,* pp 32–35; McConnell Notebook, Items 70, 4 Apr 65, and 84, 9 Apr 65; *New York Times,* Apr 4, 65; *Washington Post,* Apr 5, 65.

19. *Analysis of Air Ops,* Vol I, p 4-14S, Vol II, p 3-3.

20. *Ibid.,* Vol I, pp 4-14S to 4-14U, Vol II, p 3-3.

21. CM-534-65, 6 Apr 65.

22. Memo, Maj Gen J.W. Carpenter III, Asst DCS/Plans, and Ops for JCS to CSAF, 15 Apr 65, subj: Overall Appraisal of Air Strikes in NVN, 7 Feb–4 Apr 65.

23. *Analysis of Air Ops,* 6–12 Apr 65, Vol II, pp 3-4 to 3-9, and Vol III, 13-19 Apr 65, pp 3-3 to 3-10.

24. CINCPACFLT rpt, *The United States Navy in the Pacific, 1965,* pp 49–50; *Aviation Week and Space Technology,* Apr 26 65, p 30; *New York Times,* Apr 10, 65.

25. Memo, L. Unger, Dep Asst SECSTATE for Far Eastern Affairs to Acting SECSTATE, Apr 9, 65.

26. *Analysis of Air Ops,* Vol II, pp 3-8 to 3-9 and Vol IV, pp 3-3 to 3-10.

27. Msg, CINCPACAF to 13th AF, 2d AD, 161012Z Apr 65; *Analysis of Air Ops,* Vol III, p 3-28, Vol IV, pp 3-1 to 3-20.

28. *Ibid.*

29. *Analysis of Air Ops,* Vol III, p 3-28; and Vol IV, pp 3-1 to 3-20.

30. *New York Times,* Apr 17, 65; David A. McCormack, *Summary of Source Materiel on the Indochina War 1965–1973,* in the Joint Publications Research Series (Special Report prepared for Ofc AF Hist, 3 Aug 76).

31. CSAFM-R-40-65, 12 Feb 65.

32. CM-519-65, 2 Mar 65; JCSM-275-65, 14 Apr 65.

33. Memo, SECDEF to Chmn JCS, 19 Apr 65, subj: SA–2 Sites.

34. Ltr, Lt Gen Joseph H. Moore, Jr., Comdr, 2d AD to Maj Gen Robert N. Ginsburgh, Chief, Ofc AF Hist, 15 Apr 65.

35. Memo, by the J-3 for the JCS on Air Attack of SA–2 SAM Installations, annex A to App B (JCS 2343/599-5), 26 Jul 65.

36. Hist, SAC, Jul–Dec 64, Vol II, p 124.

37. Maj Paul W. Elder, *Buffalo Hunter, 1970–1972* (Proj CHECO, 1970), p 1.

38. Msg, 2d AD to all R/T addressees, 050840Z May 65; msg, PACAF to 2d AD, 120208Z Oct 65; msg, CINCPACAF to 2d AD, et al, 150201Z Apr 65; Capt Mark E. Smith, *USAF Reconnaissance in SEA, 1961–1966,* (Proj CHECO, 1967), p 37; Rpt, *Jt Study of Theater ELINT ECM Ops,* JCS 2031/376-17, 18 Oct 65; hist, 363d Tac Reconnaissance Wing, Jul–Dec 65, pp 31–32 and 38–40; hist, 355th TFW, Jul–Dec 65, p 28; ltr, CG, Marine Composite Reconnaissance Sq 1, Marine Acft Gp 11, 1st Marine Acft Wing (adv), III Marine Amphibious Force to CMS via Marine Acft Gp 11, 1st Marine Acft Wing and Fleet Marine Force, Pacific, subj: Electronic Warfare Special Action Rpt,

period 29 Apr 65 to 31 Aug 65; Futrell, *Chron of Significant Air Power Events in SEA, 1954–1967*, p 63; rpt, JCS Prong Tong Study Report, *Surface-to-Air Missile Problems in North Vietnam*, 15 Oct 65 (hereafter cited as *JCS Prong Tong Study Rpt*), Vol I, Foreword; Lt Col Robert M. Burch, *Tactical Electronic Warfare Operations in SEA, 1962–1968* (Proj CHECO, 1969), pp 18–19.

39. Capt Melvin F. Porter, *Air Tactics Against NVN Air-Ground Defenses* (Proj CHECO, 1967), pp 14–15.

40. CSAFM-J-77-65, 17 Mar 65; JCSM-202-65, 20 Mar 65; memo, SECDEF Chmn JCS, 1 Apr 65, subj: Immediate Deployment of an F–86 Sq to Thailand.

41. Msg, CINCPACAF to CINCPAC, (Personal, Harris to Sharp), 18 Mar 65; msg, CSAF to PACAF, 232009Z Mar 65; msg, CINCPACAF to 13 AF, 2d AD, 23 Mar 65.

42. Msg, JCS to CINCONAD, CINCPAC, CSAF, *et al*, 4 Apr 65.

43. Hist, CINCPAC, 1965, Vol II, p 285; *Analysis of Air Ops*, 6–12 Apr 65, Vol II, p 3-6, 14 May–3 Jun 65, Vol VI, p 3-55; hist, 8th TFW, Jul–Dec 65, pp 5 and 11.

44. Hist rcrd, *Big Eye Task Force MOB and FOB for period ending 10 Jul 65*, in hist, 552d AEW&C Wing (ADC), 1 Apr 65–30 Jun 65; msg, CINCPACAF to CINCPAC, 18 Mar 65; Porter, *Air Tactics Against NVN Air-Ground Defenses*, pp 21–11; msg, CINCPACAF to 13th AF, 2d AD, 161012Z Apr 65; memo, Background Info, Project 5-52/5111, 10 Jun 65 and Oct 65.

45. Futrell, *Chron of Significant Air Power Events in SEA, 1954–1967*, p 62.

46. CSAFM-R-65, 12 Apr 65; msg, CINCPAC to CINCPACAF, 170018Z Apr 65; JCSM-300-65, 22 Apr 65; msg, JCS to CINCPAC, 130049Z May 65.

47. Momyer, *Air Power in Three Wars*, p 140.

48. *Gravel Pentagon Papers*, Vol III, pp 411, 436–37, 704–05; Taylor, *Swords and Plowshares*, pp 341–42.

49. *Gravel Pentagon Papers*, Vol III, pp 367–58, 411, 436–37, 704–05.

50. *Ibid.*, pp 705–6; minutes of 20 Apr 65 Honolulu Mtg by John T. McNaughton, Asst SECDEF (ISA), 20 Apr 65; McNamara and VanDeMark, *In Retrospect*, pp 184–87; Clodfelter, *The Limits of Air Power*, pp 66–67.

51. Msg, CINCPAC to COMUSMACV, 230412Z Apr 65.

52. Ltr, Gen Harris to Gen McConnell, 13 May 65, no subj.

53. Johnson, *The Vantage Point*, p 142; *Public Papers of the President*, Johnson, 1965, Vol I, pp 448–49, and 454; *New York Times*, Apr 28, 65.

54. Transcripts of McNamara's News Conferences in Honolulu, Apr 20, 65, and Andrews AFB, Wash, Apr 22, 65, and at the White House, Apr 22, 65; News Release 261–65 by Ofc Asst SECDEF (PA), Apr 26, 65, *Washington Post*, Apr 22, 65, *New York Times*, Apr 27, 65, pp 1 and 12.

55. Msg, CINCPAC to CINCPACFLT, CINCPACAF, COMUSMACV, 212339Z Apr 65; msg, CINCPACAF to 13th AF, 2d AD 221031Z Apr 65; msg, PACAF to 13th CC and 2d AD CC, 210340Z Apr 65; Sharp, *Strategy for Defeat*, pp 86–87.

56. *Analysis of Air Ops*, Vol IV, 20-29 Apr 65, pp 3-10 and 3-57 to 3-61, Vol V, 30 Apr30–May 65, p 3-20, Vol VI, 14 May–3 Jun 65, p 3-82, Vol VII, 4-10 Jun 65, pp 3-38, 3-44; hist rpt, Chief, Ops Plans Div, PACAF, Apr 65, in hist, PACAF, Vol II, 1 Jul 64–30 Jun 65; hist, 34th Tac Gp, 1 Jan–8 Jul 65, pp 10–11.

57. *Analysis of Air Ops*, Vol IV, pp 3-21 to 3-95.

58. Msg, PACAF to 13th AF, 2d AD, 210340Z Apr 65; Lavalle, *Tale of Two Bridges*, p 42.

59. Msg, JCS to CINCPAC, 290056Z Apr 65 and 051832Z May 65; msg, CINCPAC to CINCPACFLT, CINCPACAF, *et al*, 29081Z Apr 65; msg, CINCPACAF to 13th AF, 2d AD 291940Z Apr 65.

60. *Analysis of Air Ops*, Vol V, 30 Apr–13 May 65, pp 3-7, 3-8, 3-31 to 3-36,

3-64 to 3-69; hist, 313th AD, Jul–Dec 65, pp 162–64; *New York Times* May 9, 65.

61. Msgs, PACAF to 13th AF, 2d AD, 140505Z May 65 and 13th AF to CINCPACAF, 150500Z May 65.

62. *Analysis of Air Ops*, Vol V, 30 Apr–13 May 65, pp 3-7, 3-8, 3-31 to 3-36, 3-64 to 3-69.

63. *Ibid.*, 3-76 to 3-77; memos, Wm P. Bundy, Asst SECSTATE for Far Eastern Affairs to SECSTATE, Apr 19, 65, subj: Planning for R/T 12, Action Memo, Apr 26, 65.

64. Memos, Seymour Weiss, Director for Combined Policy, Bureau of Political-Military Affairs Llewellyn E. Thompson, Jr., Amb-at-Large, Ofc, SECSTATE, Apr 23, 65, subj: VN Mil Actions, and Weiss to Lewis Hoffacker, Dep Executive Secy, Director, Ops Center, State Dept, Apr 27, 65, subj: Tuesday Luncheon Item.

65. Msg, PACAF to 13th AF, 2d AD, 140505Z May 65; msg, 13th AF to CINCPACAF, 150500Z May 65.

66. Memo, SECDEF to Chmn JCS, 26 Apr 65, subj: Interdiction of Dredging Ops in Haiphong Harbor; msg, CINCPAC to CNO, 290743Z Apr 65; JCSM-350-65, 12 May 65.

67. Memo, SECDEF to Chmn JCS, 18 May 65, subj: Dredging Ops in NVN.

68. NSAM-328, 6 Apr 65.

69. Msg, Jt MACV-USIS-Embassy Saigon (Taylor) to Secy State 260930Z Mar 65; *Rolling Thunder*, p 74; *New York Times* Apr 18 and 20 65; msg, 2d AD to All Rolling Thunder Addressees 110950Z Apr 65; *New York Times*, Apr 15, 65, p 1; *Philadelphia Inquirer*, Apr 29, 65.

70. Intvw, Hearst Papers Newspaper Panel with McNamara, *New York Journal American*, May 9, 65.

71. Msg, CINCPAC to JCS, 120314Z May 65; msg, PACAF to 2d AD, 162355Z May 65; PACAF DI rpt, *Effects of Air Ops, SEA* (as of 12 May 65), 1965, pp 1–6.

72. *Analysis of Air Ops*, Vol V, 30 Apr–13 May 65, pp 3-7, 3-8; Clodfelter, *The Limits of Air Power*, p 132.

73. Clodfelter, *The Limits of Air Power*, pp 130–31.

Chapter 5

1. *Gravel Pentagon Papers*, Vol III, pp 362–68; McNamara and VanDeMark, *In Restrospect*, pp 184–86; Sharp, *Strategy for Defeat*, pp 81–84.

2. *Gravel Pentagon Papers*, Vol III, pp 366–68.

3. Msgs, OSD (State-Def msg) to CINCPAC, Amb Taylor, 112359Z May 65 and CINCPAC to CINCARPAC, CINCPACFLT, and CINCPACAF, 122318Z May 65.

4. Msg, CINCPAC to JCS, 162031Z May 65; hist, 313th AD, 1 Jan–30 Jun 65, p 311; Greenhalgh, *USAF Reconnaissance in SEA, 1960–1975*, p 182.

5. *Gravel Pentagon Papers*, Vol II, pp 369–74; Johnson, *The Vantage Point*, pp 136–37; *New York Times* Jun 28, 72, p 19; *Public Papers of the Presidents*, Johnson, Vol I, p 522; msg, OSD-State-Def to Amb Taylor, CINCPAC, 112359Z May 65.

6. Msg, CINCPAC to JCS 162031Z May 65; hist, 313th AD, 1 Jan–30 Jun 65, p 311.

7. Msg, CINCPACAF to CINCPAC, 180141Z May 65; Hq USAF rpt, *Stat Sum of Air Ops, SEA*, Vol VI, 14 May–3 Jun 65, pp 1-1 to 1-2; DIA Bull, 18 May 65, p F-2.

8. *Gravel Pentagon Papers*, Vol III, pp 371–74.

9. *Ibid.*; *Washington Post*, May 17, 65, p 1; and May 19, 65, p 1, *New York Times*, May 19, 65, p 1; Johnson, *The Vantage Point*, p 137.

10. *New York Times*, May 19, 65, p 1.

11. Johnson, *The Vantage Point*, p 137; *Gravel Pentagon Papers*, Vol III, pp 375, 378; memo, Maj Gen J.W. Carpenter III, Asst DCS/Plans & Ops for JCS Letters to CSAF, subj: Modification of Rolling Thunder Program; 19 May 65; Clodfelter,

The Limits of Air Power, p 67.

12. *Gravel Pentagon Papers*, Vol III, p 375; memo, Carpenter to CSAF, Modification of Rolling Thunder Program, 19 May 65.

13. Memo, Carpenter to CSAF, subj: Modification of Rolling Thunder Program, 19 May 65; JCSM-394-65, 20 May 65; JCSM-404-65, 22 May 65; Sharp, *Strategy for Defeat*, pp 77–80.

14. *Gravel Pentagon Papers*, Vol III, pp 381–82

15. Hq USAF rpt, *Stat Sum of Air Ops, SEA*, Vol VI, 14 May–3 Jun 65, pp 1-1; msg, JCS to CINCPAC, 171201Z May 65; *Gravel Pentagon Papers*, Vol III, p 378; memo, W.P. Bundy to SECSTATE, May 10, 65, subj: FE/INR Comments on R/T 15.

16. Hq USAF rpt, *Stat Sum of Air Ops, SEA*, Vol VI, 14 May–3 Jun 65, pp 3-1 to 3-11, 3-14 to 3-47; *New York Times*, May 21, 22, and 23, 65.

17. Msg, JCS to CINCPAC, 222235Z May 65; msg, CINCPACAF to 13th AF, 2d AD, 231517Z May 65; msg, PACAF to 13th AF and 2d AD, 282345Z May 65; msg, JCS to CINCPAC, 272233Z May 65; memo, W.P. Bundy to SECSTATE, May 25, 65, subj: FE/INR Comments on R/T: msg, COMUSMACV to CINCPAC, 240105Z Jun 65.

18. Hq USAF rpt, *Stat Sum Or Air Ops, SEA*, Vol VI, 14 May–3 Jun 65, pp 3-10 to 3-13, 3-49 to 3-74.

19. Msg, JCS to CINCPAC, 111659Z and 152030Z Jun 65; msg, CINCPAC TO CINCPACFLT, CINCPACAF, COMUSMACV, 161814Z Jun 65; msg, CINCPACAF to 13th AF, 2d AD, 240755Z and 240331Z Jun 65; msg, CINCPACAF to CINCPAC, 120235Z Jun 65; msg, JCS to CINCPAC, 292236Z Jun 65; msg, CINCPACAF to 13th AF, 2d AD, 301700Z Jun 65; hist, CINCPAC, 1965, Vol II, p 333; Hq USAF rpts, *Stat Sum of Air Ops, SEA*, Vol VIII, 11–24 Jun 65, pp 3-5 to 3-8, Vol IX, 25 Jun–8 Jul 65, pp 3-1 to 3-11; *Baltimore Sun*, Jun 24, 65.

20. Hist, 12th TFS, 1 Jul–31 Dec 65, pp 3–4.

21. Abstract from Ops Analysis Working Paper 27, subj: An Analysis of Air Strikes Against Bridges in NVN, prepared by Ops Analysis Ofc, Hqs PACAF, 6 Aug 65.

22. Hq USAF rpt, *Stat Sum of Air Ops, SEA*, Vol VIII, 11–24 Jun 65, pp 3-123 to 3-128, tab 3B.

23. *Ibid.*, Vol IX, 25 Jun–8 Jul 65, pp 3-1 to 3-11; *New York Times*, Jun 29, 65.

24. *Stat Sum of Air Ops,* Vol VIII, 11–24 Jun 65, pp 3-123 to 3-128, and tab 3B; Hearings before Senate Committee on Armed Services, *Fiscal Year 1974 Authorization for Military Procurement, Research, and Development ... and Active Duty and Selected Reserve Strengths*.

25. DIA Bull, 24 May 65; PACOM WID No 9-65, 26 Feb 65 and No 20-65, 14 May 65.

26. Msg, CINCPAC to COMUSMACV, CINCPACFLT, CINCPACAF, et al, 292320Z May 65; msgs, 2d AD to 13th AF, 011259Z, 011300Z, 011000Z, 011006Z Jun 65; msg, CINCPACAF to CINCPAC, 030235Z Jun 65; msg, CINCPACFLT to CINCPAC 040027Z Jun 65; *Rolling Thunder*, pp 55–56.

27. Msg, CINCPACAF to CINCPAC, 030235Z Jun 65; msg, CINCPACFLT to CINCPAC, 040027Z Jun 65; msg, COMUSMACV to CINCPAC, 101024z Jun 65; JCSM-415-65, 27 May 65; *USAF Mgt Digest, SEA*, 7 Jun 65, p 39.

28. JCSM-442-65, 7 Jun 65.

29. Memo, SECDEF to Chmn JCS, 15 Jun 65; memo, Col Frank F. Kaufman, Ofc Dir/Plans to CSAF, 28 Aug 65, subj: Ops Against NVN.

30. CINCPACFLT rpt, *The U.S. Navy in the Pacific, 1965*, pp 90–92; hist, 313th AD, Jul 64–Jun 65, Vol I, p xi; *New York Times*, Jun 18, 65, p 2.

31. CINCPACFLT rpt, *The U.S. Navy in the Pacific, 1965*, pp 92–96; *New York Times*, Jun 22, 65.

32. Hq USAF rpt, *Stat Sum of Air Ops, SEA*, Vol VII, 11–24 Jun 65, p 3-6.

33. Hist, CINCPAC, 1965, An B, USMACTHAI, pp 22–24; EOT rpt by

Brig Gen John R. Murphy, 15 Jun 66; EOT rpt, by Brig Gen Murphy, 15 Jun 66; Helmka and Hale, *USAF Ops from Thailand, 1964–1965*, pp 7–9; hist, CINCPAC, An B, USMACTHAI, pp 22–24; Futrell, *Chron of Significant Air Power Events in SEA, 1954–1967*, pp 35 and 60.

34. *USAF Mgt Digest, SEA*, 16 Jul 65, p 14 and 3 Sep 65, pp 8 and 9.

35. *Ibid.*, 16 Jul 65, pp 4–5; EOT rpt by Capt George W. Baker, 13th Recon Tech Sq, 1 Dec 65.

36. Futrell, *Chron of Significant Air Power Events*, pp 59–69.

37. Helmka and Hale, *USAF Ops from Thailand, 1964–1965*, pp 8–9; Van Staaveren, *USAF Plans and Ops in SEA, 1965*, p 49; memo, SECDEF to Pres, Sep 22 65, no subj.

38. Helmka and Hale, *USAF Ops from Thailand, 1964–1965*, pp 9–13; msg, CINCPACAF TO 5th AF, 13th AF, *et al*, 250216Z Jun 665; hist, 2d AD, Jan–Jun 65, Vol I, pp 12–14; hist, MACV, 1965, p 50; Momyer, *Air Power in Three Wars*, pp 82–83; Records of Regular and Reserve Officer Matters, Ofc of Asst Dep COFS For Manpower and Personnel, Hqs USAF.

39. Hist, CINCPAC, 1965, Vol II, p 313; hist, MACV, 1965, pp 92–93; Van Staaveren, *USAF Plans and Policies in SVN, 1961–1963*, pp 14–17.

40. Hist, MACV, 1965, pp 92–93; Van Staaveren, *USAF Plans and Ops in SEA, 1965*, pp 43–44.

41. Memo, Ofc, Combined Plans Div, Dir/Plans, Dir/Plans, Hqs USAF to CSAF, 27 Apr 65; JCS 2448/3, 26 May 65; JCSM-319-65, 28 Apr 65; hist, MACV,1965, pp 102–3; hist, CINCPAC, 1965, Vol II, p 313, An B; hist, USMACTHAI, 1965, apps F3 and F4; Momyer, *Air Power in Three Wars*, p 82; Van Staaveren, *USAF Plans and Ops in SEA, 1965*, p 44.

42. Memo, Maj Gen S.J. McKee, Dir/Plans, Hq USAF to CSAF, 19 Jul 65, subj: Issue Raised by SECDEF As a Result of Trip to VN.

43. Msg, Amembassy Saigon to State No 108, Jul 11 65; CIA Weekly Sum, Jun 11 65, p 1.

44. Taylor, *Swords and Plowshares*, p 345; *Baltimore Sun*, Jun 8, 65; John Schlight, *The War In South Vietnam: The Years of the Offensive* (Ofc AF Hist, 1988), pp 58–60; Westmoreland, *A Soldier Reports*, p 178.

45. Hist, MACV, 1965, p 35; Sharp and Westmoreland, *Report on the War*, p 98; msgs 17988 and 19995, CINCPACAF to CSAF, 8 Jun 65; msg, CINCPAC to COMUSMACV, 130083Z Jun 65; memo, Germeraad to CSAF, 24 Jun 65, subj: Additional Deployments to SVN; JCSM-457-65, 11 Jun 65; Taylor, *Swords and Plowshares*, pp 344; Westmoreland, *A Soldier Reports*, pp 180–81; McNamara and VanDemark, *In Retrospect*, pp 186–90.

46. Msgs 17988 and 17995, CINCPACAF to CSAF, 8 Jun 65.

47. *New York Times*, Jun 17, 65.

48. Memo, Carpenter to CSAF, 20 Jun 65, subj: Targeting in NVN; CSAFM-86-65, 21 Jun 65.

49. Col F. L. Kaufman, Asst Dep Dir, DCS/Plans to CSAF, 27 Jun 65, subj: Air Strikes Against NVN, with atch Background Paper on Air strikes in NVN.

50. CSAFM-M-105-65, 30 Jun 65.

51. McConnell Notebook, Item 186, 26 Jun 65.

52. *Gravel Pentagon Papers*, Vol IV, pp 1 and 24.

53. Record of Questions and Answers at Mtg between Secy McNamara and His Party, Ambassador Taylor and His Staff, and COMUSMACV and his Staff, Jul 16, 65; Taylor, *Swords and Plowshares*, p 288; Johnson, *The Vantage Point*, p 144; Van Staaveren, *USAF Plans and Ops in SEA, 1965*, pp 45–47; hist, MACV, 1965, pp 42–43; *DOD Pentagon Papers*, Bk 4, p 110; transcript of SECDEF questions and Taylor's Replies in JCS 2343/637, 22 Jul 65; msg, CINCPAC to Amembassy Vientiane, COMUSMACV, 260330Z Jun 65; McNamara and VanDeMark, *In Retrospect*, pp 200–03.

54. *Gravel Pentagon Papers*, Vol IV, pp 26–32, 619–22; McNamara and

VanDeMark, *In Retrospect*, pp 203–05.

55. Jack Valenti, *A Very Human President* (New York: W. W. Norton, 1975), pp 319–56.

56. *Public Papers of the Presidents, Johnson*, 1965, Vol II, pp 794–803; Westmoreland, *A Soldier Reports*, pp 182–85; McNamara and VanDeMark, *In Retrospect*, pp 201–06.

57. Msg, CINCPAC to JCS, 050300Z Jun 65; msg, COMUSMACV to CINCPAC, 201207Z Jun 65; msg, JCS to CINCPAC et al, 062224Z Jul 65; msg, CINCPAC to CINCPACFLT, CINCPACAF, and COMUSMACV, 070320Z Jul 65; hist, CINCPAC, Vol II, 1965, p 333.

58. Msgs JCS to CINCPAC *et al*, 062224Z Jul 65; msg, CINCPAC to CINCPACFLT, CINCPACAF, and COMUSMACV, 070320Z Jul 65; Hq USAF rpt, *Stat Sum of Air Ops, SEA*, Vol IX, 9–22 Jul 65, pp 3–6; Hq PACAF rpt, *Summary of Air Ops, SEA*, Vol II, 9–22 Jul 65, p 3-1; msg, JCS to CINCPAC, 082113Z Jul 65.

59. Hq USAF rpt, *Stat Sum of Air Ops, SEA*, Vol X, 9–22 Jul 65, pp 3-1 to 3-8 and p 3-38; *Washington Post*, Jul 13, 65, p 1.

60. *New York Times*, Jul 13, 65, and Jul 14, 65, p 5; hist, 12th TFS, 1 Jul–31 Dec 65, pp 4–5.

61. *Washington Post*, Jul 15, 65, p A8.

62. Hq PACAF rpt, *Sum of Air Ops, SEA*, Vol II, 9–22 Jul 65, pp 3-A-3, to 3-A-16.

63. Hist, Dir/Ops, Jan–Jun 65, pp 63–64; hist, 8th TFW, 1 Jul–31 Dec 65, p 5; *New York Times*, Jul 11, 65, p 1; R. Frank Futrell, ed, *Aces and Aerial Victories* (The Albert F. Simpson Hist Research Center and Ofc AF Hist, 1976), pp 22–26, 118.

64. Hq USAF rpt, *Stat Sum of Air Ops, SEA*, Vol X, 9–22 Jul 65, pp 3–132.

65. *Ibid*., pp 3-126 to 3-131.

66. *New York Times*, Jul 11, 65, p 3.

67. Hqs MATS S. O. G-81, 25 Jun 65; hist, 38th Air Rescue Sq 1 Jul–30 Sep 65; USAF Fact Sheet on USAF in SEA, Nov 1965, p 27.

68. Msg, COMUSMACV to CINCPAC, 271315Z Oct 65; msg, CINCPAC to DIA 312209Z Oct 65; NMCC OPSUM-169-65, 22 Jul 65; *Rolling Thunder*, pp 74–75.

69. Memo by J-3 for the JCS on Air Attack on SA–2 SAM Installations, An A to App B (JCS 2343/599-5), 26 Jul 65.

70. DIA Bull, 6 Jul 65, p F-4; CSAFM-F-34-65, 2 Jul 65; JCSM-529-65, 3 Jul 65; CSAFM-F-40-65, 7 Jul 65; *New York Herald Tribune*, Jul 12, 65.

Chapter 6

1. Hist, CINCPAC, 1965, Vol II, 377-78; Burch, *Tactical Electronic Warfare Operations in SEA, 1962–1968*, p 28; msg, CINCPAC to AIG 830, 280210Z Jul 65; Hq USAF rpt, *Stat Sum of Air Ops, SEA*, 23 Jul–5 Aug 65, Vol XI, pp 3-25, 3-26, 3-29; *USAF Mgt Digest, SEA*, 13 Aug 65, p 16; *New York Times*, Jul 28, 65, p 1; *Washington Post*, Aug 7, 65, pp 1, A-13; NMCC OPSUM-174-65, 28 Jul 65; msg, Wheeler to Sharp and Westmoreland, 301641Z Jul 65; Earl H. Tilford, *Crosswinds: The Air Force's Setup in Vietnam* (College Station: Texas A&M University, Press, 1993), p 82.

2. Msg, Amembassy Bangkok to Amembassy Saigon, 290529Z Jul 65.

3. Msg AFIN 40776, CINCPACAF to CSAF, 30 Jul 65.

4. PACAF DI rpt, *Effects of Air Ops, SEA*, 6th ed, 5 Jul 65, p 9; CIA Weekly Sum, Aug 13, 65, p 5; msg, CINCPAC to CINCPACAF, 292344Z Jul 65.

5. Msg, CINCPAC to CINCPACFLT, CINCPACAF, 292125Z Jul 65.

6. Hist, CINCPAC, 1965, Vol II, p 378; *JCS Prong Tong Study Rpt*, Vol II, App 1; Tilford, *Crosswinds*, pp 81–83.

7. Hist, CINCPAC, 1965, Vol II, p 378; Greenhalgh, *USAF Reconnaissance in SEA, 1960–1975*, p 194.

8. Hq PACAF rpt, *Sum of Air Ops, SEA*, Vol IV, pp 3-1 and 3-10 and 3-11; CINCPACFLT rpt, *The U.S. Navy in the Pacific, 1965*, p 128; hist, 313th AD, Jul–Dec 65, pp 168–70.

9. Hist, CINCPAC, 1965, Vol II, pp 378–79.

10. Hq PACAF rpt, *Sum of Air Ops, SEA*, Vol IV, 6–19 Aug 65, pp 3-1, 3-A-2, 3-A-10.

11. *Ibid.*, p 3-2, 3-11, 3-A-10; CINCPACFLT rpt, *U.S. Navy in the Pacific, 1965*, pp 129–31; *New York Times*, Aug 13, 65; DIA Bull 156-65, 12 Aug 65; hist, CINCPAC, 1965, Vol II, pp 379–80; *Aviation Week and Space Digest*, Aug 16, 65, p 43.

12. DJSM-964-65, 20 Aug 65; ltr, Gen W. H. Blanchard, Vice CSAF to Deputies, Dirs, and Chiefs Of Comparable Ofcs, 13 Aug 65, subj: Acft Attrition; hist, Dir/Ops, Jul–Dec 65, p 146.

13. Hist, CINCPAC, 1965, Vol II, p 379; PACAF DI rpt, *Effects of Air Ops, SEA*, 8th ed, 19 Aug 65, p 5 and 9th ed, 2 Sep 65, p 8; Hq PACAF rpt, *Sum of Air Ops, SEA*, Vol IV, 6–19 Aug 65, pp 3-A-2 to 3-A-3.

14. Hist, CINCPAC, 1965, Vol II, p 379; memo, Rear Adm John J. Hyland, Ofc CNO to SN, 26 Aug 65, subj: Navy Air Ops, SEA, in *JCS Prong Tong Study Rpt*, App 2.

15. Hq PACAF rpt, *Sum of Air Ops, SEA*, Vol IV, 6–19 Aug 65, pp 3-1, 3-A-2, 3-A-10.

16. *Ibid.*, p 3-2, 3-11, and 3-A-10; CINCPACFLT rpt, *U.S. Navy in the Pacific, 1965*, pp 129–31; *New York Times*, Aug 13, 65; DIA Bull 156-65, 12 Aug 65; hist, CINCPAC, 1965, Vol II, pp 379–80; *Aviation Week and Space Digest*, Aug 16, 65, p 43.

17. DJSM-964-65, 20 Aug 65; ltr, Gen W. H. Blanchard, Vice CSAF to Deputies, Dirs, and Chiefs Of Comparable Ofcs, 13 Aug 65, subj: Acft Attrition; hist, Dir/Ops, Jul–Dec 65, p 146.

18. Hist, CINCPAC, 1965, Vol II, p 379; PACAF DI rpt, *Effects of Air Ops, SEA*, 8th ed, 19 Aug 65, p 5 and 9th ed, 2 Sep 65, p 8; Hq PACAF rpt, *Sum of Air Ops, SEA*, Vol IV, 6–19 Aug 65, pp 3-A-2 to 3-A-3.

19. Hist, CINCPAC, 1965, Vol II, p 379; memo, Rear Adm John J. Hyland, Ofc, CNO to SN, 26 Aug, 65, subj: Navy Air Ops, SEA, in *JCS Prong Tong Study Rpt*, App 2.

20. Msg, JCS to CINCPAC, 172220Z Aug 65; msg, CINCPACAF to 2d AD, 181637Z Aug 65.

21. Hq PACAF rpt, *Sum of Air Ops, SEA*, Vol V, 20 Aug–2 Sep 65, pp 3-1, 3-A-5.

22. CINCPACFLT rpt, *The U.S. Navy in the Pacific, 1965*, p 132; DIA Bull 163-65, 23 Aug 65; PACAF rpt, *Sum of Air Ops, SEA*, Vol V, 20 Aug–2 Sep 65, pp 3-1 to 3-A-5; *New York Times*, Aug 26, 65.

23. CINCPACFLT rpt, *The U.S. Navy in the Pacific, 1965*, p 132; CIA Weekly Sum, Aug 27, 65, p 5.

24. PACOM WID No 47-65, 19 Nov 65, p 7.

25. *Ibid.*

26. PACAF DI rpt, *Effects of Air OPS, SEA*, 9th ed, 2 Sep 65, pp 1, 8, and 19; PACAF rpt, *Sum of Air Ops, SEA*, Vol IV, pp 3-1 thru 3-6, Vol V, 20 Aug–2 Sep 65, pp 3-1 to 3-7; Wesley R.C. Melyan and Lee Bonetti, *Rolling Thunder, Jul 65–Dec 66* (Project CHECO, 1967), p 6; *New York Times*, Sep 1, 65, p 4; DIA Bull 187-65, 17 Sep 65, p F-3.

27. Msg, NMCC-216-65, 16 Sep 65; and NMCC 217-65, 17 Sep 65; *JCS Prong Tong Study Rpt*, Vol II, App 3, Tab A, App 5 to Annex B; PACAF DI rpt, *Effects of Air Ops, SEA*, 10th ed, 16 Sep 65, p 7, 11th ed, 30 Sep 65, pp 11–12; PACAF rpt, *Sum of Air Ops, SEA*, 3–16 Sep 65, Vol VI, pp 3-A-12 to 3-A-19, 17 30 Sep 65, Vol XI, pp 3-A-1 to 3-A-12.

28. Robinson Risner, *The Passing of the Night: My Seven Years as a Prisoner of the North Vietnamese* (New York: Random House, 1973), pp 7–10.

29. *JCS Prong Tong Study Rpt*, Vol II, App 3, Tab A, App 5 to Annex B; PACAF DI rpt, *Effects of Air Ops, SEA*, 10th ed, 16 Sep 65, p 7, 11th ed, 30 Sep 65, pp 11–12.

30. PACAF DI rpt, *Effects of Air Ops, SEA*, 11th ed, 30 Sep 65, pp 11–12.

31. Msg, 2d AD to PACAF, 191276Z Sep 65; PACAF rpt, *Stat Sum of Air Ops, SEA*, Vol VI, 3–16 Sep 65, p 3-2.

32. PACAF DI rpt, *Effects of Air Ops, SEA*, 11th ed, 30 Sep 65, p 12.

33. Msg, JCS to CINCPAC, 032148Z Aug 65; and msg, CINCPAC to CINC- PACFLT, CINCPACAF, 040315Z Aug 65.

34. Msg, CINCPAC to COMUS- MACV, CINCPACAF, 2d AD, FMFPAC, et al, 151942Z Aug 65.

35. *JCS Prong Tong Study Rpt*, Vol II, Tab A to App 3 to An B; JCS Armed Reconnaissance Study Group Rpt, subj: An Analysis of Armed Reconnaissance Program in NVN, 15 Nov 65, App 3 to Annex A, p 1; PACAF rpt, *Sum of Air Ops, SEA*, Vol V, 20 Aug–2 Sep 65; msg, PACAF to CINCPAC, 221054Z Aug 65.

36. *JCS Prong Tong Study Rpt*, Vol II, Tab A to App B to Annex B; Greenhalgh, *USAF Reconnaissance in SEA, 1960–1975*, pp 194–95.

37. Greenhalgh, *USAF Reconnaissance in SEA, 1960–1975*, p 195.

38. Msg, JCS to CINCPAC, 312141Z Aug 65.

39. Msgs, 2d AD to CINCPACAF, 291323Z Jul 65, Amembassy Bangkok to 13th AF, 200847Z Aug 65, and JCS to CINCPAC, 302142Z Aug 65.

40. Futrell, *Chron of Significant Air Power Events in SEA, 1954–1967*, p 75; CINCPACFLT rpt, *The U.S. Navy in the Pacific, 1965*, pp 129, 160–61, and 208; Hq USAF DCS/P&O rpt, *Southeast Asia Counter Air Alternatives*, 20 Apr 66, p B-29.

41. Msg, JCS to CINCPAC, 212259Z Jul 65; msg, CINCPAC to CINCPACFLT, CINCPACAF, COMUSMACV, 220100Z Jul 65.

42. Hq PACAF rpt, *Sum of Air Ops, SEA*, 23 Jul–5 Aug 65, Vol III, pp 3-A-1 to 3-A-13; PACAF DI rpt, *Effects of Air Ops, SEA*, 7th ed, 5 Aug 65, p 23; Hq USAF rpt, *Stat Sum of Air Ops, SEA*, 23 Jul–5 Aug 65, Vol XI, p 3-8; PACAF rpt, *Out-Country Strike Operations in SEA, 12 Feb 65–23 Dec 65*, Subtask 1b, 23 Oct 70, pp 128–29 (hereafter cited as *Out-Country Strike Ops, SEA, 12 Feb 65–23 Dec 65*); hist, 12th TFS, 1 Jul–31 Dec 65, p 6; msg, NMCC OPSUM 176-65, 30 Jul 65; msg, NMCC OPSUM-177-65, 31 Jul 65.

43. Hq PACAF rpt, *Sum of Air Ops, SEA*; Vol IV, 6–19 Aug 65, pp 3-1 to 3-5, 3-A-1 to 3-A-12; CM-863-65, 25 Sep 65.

44. Msg, JCS to CINCPAC, 172200Z Aug 65; msg, CINCPACAF to 2d AD, 181637Z Aug 65.

45. PACAF rpt, *Sum of Air Ops, SEA*, Vol V, 19 Aug–2 Sep 65, pp 3-1 to 3-13; *New York Times*, Aug 24, 65; *Baltimore Sun*, Aug 24, 65.

46. PACAF rpt, *Sum of Air Ops, SEA*, Vol IV, 6–19 Aug 65, pp 3-2 to 3-6, Vol V, 20 Aug–2 Sep 65, pp 3-1 to 3-5; Futrell, *Chron of Significant Air Power Events in SEA, 1954–1967*, p 72; Herman S. Wolk, *USAF Logistic Plans and Policies in SEA, 1965* (USAF Hist Div Liaison Ofc, 1967), pp 38–45.

47. PACAF rpt, *Sum of Air Ops, SEA*, Vol IV, 6–19 Aug 65, pp 3-1 to 3-6, Vol V, 20 Aug–2 Sep 65, pp 3-1 to 3-5.

48. Memo, Col J. C. Berger, Asst for Jt Matters, Dir of Ops, DCS/Plans and Ops Hqs USAF to CSAF, 2 Sept 65, subj: Second Supplemental Brief; msg, CINC- PACAF to 2d AD, 040214Z Sep 65.

49. *New York Herald Tribune*, Sep 27, 65.

50. PACAF rpt, *Sum of Air Ops, SEA*, Vol VI, 3–16 Sep 65, pp 3-A-1 and 3-A-2; hist, 313th AD, Jul–Dec 65, Vol I, pp 182–87.

51. PACAF rpt, *Sum of Air Ops, SEA*, Vol VI, 3–16 Sep 65, pp 3-2, 3-B-1, Vol VII, 17–30 Sep 65, pp 3-3, 3-B-1; msg, CSAF to AFSC, TAC, AFLC, 13 Sep 65.

52. Maj Victor B. Anthony, *Tactics and Techniques of Night Operations, 1961–1970*, (Ofc AF Hist, 1976), p 114ff; 2AD Study, *A Preliminary Comparison of Night Operations*.

53. *Washington Post*, Sep 18, 65, p 1 and Sep 20, 65, p 8; *Baltimore Sun*, Sep 20, 65; *Chicago Tribune*, Sep 20, 65; hist,

MACV, 1965, p 204; PACAF DI rpt, *Effects of Air Ops, SEA*, 30 Sep 65, p 4; msg, 2d Ad to PACAF.

54. *Washington Post*, Sep 21, 65, p 1 and Sep 22, 65, p A16.

55. Msg, PACAF to CINCPAC, 201223Z Sep 65; msg, 2d AD to CINCPAC, 200511Z Sep 65; msg, PACAF to CINCPAC, 200626; msg, PACAF to CINCPAC, 201340Z Sep 65 (in CINCPAC microfilm collection for Sep 65); *Washington Post*, Sep 21, 65, p 1, Sep 22, 65, p A16; Smith, *USAF Reconnaissance in SEA, 1961–1966*, pp 55–56.

56. Memo, William P. Bundy to John T. McNaughton, Asst SECDEF (ISA), 16 Sep 65, subj: Rolling Thunder; memo, McNaughton to Chmn JCS, 22 Sep 65, subj: Rolling Thunder.

57. CM-876-65, 24 Sep 65; msg, JCS to CINCPAC, 281858Z Oct 65.

58. Msg, CINCPACAF to 2d AD and CSAF (Personal, Harris to Gens Moore and McConnell), 300546Z Sep 65.

59. Minutes of Air Force Commanders Conference (Edited Excerpts), Nov 65.

60. Intvw, Col Franklin D. Lown, Jr., Dir/Intel, Hqs 2d AD, Apr 65–May 66, by Capt Robert M. Snakenberg and Lt Col James C. Enney (Proj Corona Harvest Oral Hist Intvw No 319), 4 Nov 69.

61. CM-863, 23 Sep 65 (JCS 2343/598-4), 27 Sep 65.

62. PACAF DI rpts, *Effects of Air Ops, SEA*, 16 Sep 65, pp 4–11, 30 Sep 65, pp 1–14.

63. PACAF rpt, *Sum of Air Ops, SEA*, Vol VI, 3–16 Sep 65, pp 3-2, 3-B-1, Vol VI, 17–30 Sep 65, pp 3-3, 3-B-1, Vol X, 29 Oct–11 Nov 65, p 9-C-1; msg, CSAF to AFSC, TAC, AFLC, 13 Sep 65; hist, MACV, 1965, p 203.

64. PACAF DI rpts, *Effects Of Air Ops, SEA*, 6 Jul 65, p 9, 30 Sep 65, p 12; DIA Bull-214-65, 3 Nov 65; U.S. ARPAC Bull, Apr 65; PACOM WID-32-65, 6 Aug 65; PACOM WID 24-66, 24 Jun 66; JCS Study Gp rpt, *An Analysis of the Armed Reconnaissance Program in NVN*, 15 Nov 65, Annex F, p 8.

65. JCS Study Gp rpt, *An Analysis of the Armed Reconnaissance Program in NVN*, 15 Nov 65; App 1 to Annex F; Tab D to Annex D to App A to Sec II.

66. Memo, Adm David L. McDonald, CNO to Chmn JCS, 20 Sep 65, subj: Air Strikes on NVN; memo, Col Heath Bottomley, Asst Secy JCS, 20 Sep 65, subj: Note to Control Div on CNO's Trip Rpt; msg, CINCPAC to COMUSMACV, 240855Z Sep 65.

67. Memo, McKee to CSAF, 3 Aug 65, subj: R/T 26/27; USAF Mgt Sum, SEA, 27 Aug 65, p 7.

68. Msg 90300, CSAF to CINCPACAF (Personal, McKee to Harris), 31 Jul 65.

69. Msg, CINCPAC to JCS, 220043Z Aug 65.

70. JCSM-670-65, 2 Sep 65; PACAF rpt, *Out-Country Strike Ops in SEA, 12 Feb 65–23 Dec 65*, Vol I, Subtask 1b, pp 134–35.

71. PACAF rpt, *Sum of Air Ops, SEA*, Vol VI, 3–16 Sep 65, pp 3-0 through 3-16.

72. Hist, CINCPAC, 1965, Vol II, p 334.

73. *Baltimore Sun*, Sep 10, 65; msgs, Sharp to Wheeler, 100004Z Sep 65, Sharp to Westmoreland, 100002Z Sep 65, and Westmoreland to Sharp, 110115Z Sep 65.

74. Talking Paper for Chmn JCS on an Item to be Discussed at JCS Mtg, 10 Sep 65, subj: Air Strikes on NVN; JCSM-686-65, 11 Sep 65; memo, SECDEF to Chmn JCS, 15 Sep 65, subj: Air Strikes Against NVN; memo, SECDEF to DIA, 15 Sep 65, no subj.

75. Intvw, Secys McNamara and Rusk on CBS Face the Nation, Aug 9, 65.

76. Hq PACAF rpt, *Sum of Air Ops, SEA*, Vol VII, 1–14 Oct 65, pp 3-1 to 3-5, Vol IX, 15–28 Oct 65, pp 1-1 to 1-2; CINCPACFLT rpt, 5 Oct 65; NMCC OPSUM-232-65, 6 Oct 65; hist, CINCPAC 1965, Vol II, pp 380–81; *Washington Post*, Oct 6, 65, p A10; *New York Herald Tribune*, Oct 6, 65; *New York Times*, Oct 18, 65, p 1.

77. PACAF rpt, *Sum of Air Ops, SEA*, Vol X, 29 Oct–11 Nov 65, pp 2-A-3 thru

2-A-11; CINCPACFLT rpt, *The U.S. Navy in the Pacific, 1965*, p 160; hist, 355th TFW, 1 Jul 65–31 Dec 65, pp 31–33; Burch, *Tactical Electronic Warfare Operations in SEA, 1962–1968*, pp 28–29; *Washington Post*, Nov 2, 65.

78. Msgs, NMCC OPSUMS-259-65, 5 Nov 65, 260-65, 6 Nov 65, and 261-65, 8 Nov 65; msg, CINCPAC to NMCC (Lt Gen Emerick to Vice Adm Mustin), 10 Nov 65; msg, NMCC to CINCPAC (Vice Adm Mustin to Lt Gen Emerick), 102119Z Nov 65; *Aviation Week and Space Technology*, Nov 22, 65, *New York Times*, Nov 7, 65, p 1, and Nov 8, 65; *Baltimore Sun*, Nov 9, 65, p 2.

79. PACAF rpt, *Sum of Air Ops, SEA*, Vol XI, 12–25 Nov 65, 2-2 to 2-4, 2-A-2 and 2-A-8; Weekly Sum, 19 Nov 65, p 4; *Washington Post*, Nov 17, 65; *New York Times*, Nov 18, 65; *Baltimore Sun*, Nov 23, 65.

80. PACAF rpt, *Sum of Air Ops, SEA*, Vol XII, 26 Nov–9 Dec 65, pp 2-2 and 2-A-1; msg, NMCC Ops Sum-277-65, 29 Nov 65; *New York Times*, Nov 28, 65.

81. PACAF rpt, *Sum of Air Ops, SEA*, Vol VII, 10–23 Dec 65, pp 2-4, 2-A-2.

82. *Report of Air Staff Task Force on Surface-to-Surface Missiles*, 23 Sep 65; *JCS Prong Tong Study Rpt*, Vol I, pp 28–3, Vol II, App 1, Vol III, Tab 1; memo, Maj L.G. Sorrell, Electronic Warfare Div, Dir/Ops, Hq USAF to CSAF, 9 Oct 65, subj: Jamming Capability.

83. McConnell Notebook, Item 302, 5 Oct 66; Greenhalgh, *USAF Reconnaissance in SEA, 1960–1975*, pp 195–96.

84. PACAF rpt, *In-Country and Out-Country Strike Ops in SEA*, Vol IV, *Support: Electronic Warfare*, 30 Sep 70, pp 38–39; *USAF Mgt Sum, SEA*, 1 Oct 65, p 9, 5 Nov 65, p 43; hist, 355th TFW, Jul–Dec 65, p 33, doc 22.

85. Briefing Bk on SEA, subj: Trip Brochure for Secy Brown's Visit to SEA (prepared by Dir/Plans and Ops, Hq USAF), 29 Dec 65, Bk I, p 74; Hq 2d AD OPORD 525-65, 4 Nov 65; Porter, *Air Tactics Against NVN Air-Ground Defenses*, pp 18–21; Col Gordon E. Danforth, *Iron Hand/Wild Weasel* (Special Proj Corona Harvest Rpt, 1970), p 5.

86. Msg, 6234th TFW, Korat RTAFB to 2d AD, 21 Dec 65; msg, 2d AD to 6234th TFW, 300645Z Dec 65; PACAF rpt, *Sum of Air Ops, SEA*, Vol XII, 10–23 Dec 65, p 2-A-8; trip rpt, Air Staff Anti-SAM Task Force Field Trip to SEA, 5–14 Dec 65 (undated).

87. Bernard C. Nalty, *Tactics and Techniques in Electronic Warfare: Electronic Countermeasures in the Air War Against North Vietnam* (Ofc AF Hist, 1967), pp 40–41; Momyer, *Air Power in Three Wars*, pp 130–31.

Chapter 7

1. Msg, CINCPAC to CINCPACAF, CINCPACFLT, COMUSMACV, 300347Z Sep 65; msg, JCS to CINCPAC, 131846Z and 132345Z Oct 65; msg, CINCPAC to CINCPACFLT, CINCPACAF, et al, 140015Z Oct 65; msg, CINCPACAF to 2d AD, 1400945Z Oct 65; msg, JCS to CINCPAC, 281858Z Oct 65; msg, JCS to CINCPAC, 232227Z Nov 65; msg, JCS to CINCPAC, 090002Z Dec 65; PACAF DI rpt, *Effects of Air Ops, SEA*, 25 Nov 65, p 22; hist, CINCPAC, 1965, Vol II, pp 364–376.

2. PACAF rpt, *Sum of Air Ops, SEA*, Vol VII, 1–14 Oct 65, pp 3-1 to 3-5, Vol IX, 15–28 Oct 65, pp 1-1 to 1-2; CINCPACFLT rpt, *U.S. Navy in the Pacific, 1965*, pp 133–35, 210; hist, CINCPAC, 1965, Vol II, pp 380–81; msgs, NMCC OPSUM-232-54, 5 Oct 65 and OPSUM-233-65, 6 Oct 65; *Washington Post*, Oct 6, 65, p A-10; *New York Herald Tribune*, Oct 6, 65; and *New York Times*, Oct 18, 65, p 1; msg, CINCPACAF to 2d AD, 5 Oct 68; msg, JCS to CINCPAC, 1222151 Jul 65.

3. DIA Bull-277-65, 8 Nov 65; PACAF rpt, *Sum of Air Ops, SEA*, Vol VIII, 1–14 Oct 65, p 3-28, Vol IX, 15–28 Oct 65, pp 1-2 to 1-5; Vol X, 29 Oct–11 Nov 65, p 2-9, and Vol XI, 12–15 Nov 65, p 2-9.

4. Msgs, NMCC OPSUM 267-65, 16 Nov 65 and 276-65, 27 Nov 65; PACAF rpt, *Sum of Air Ops, SEA*, Vol XI, 12–25 Nov 65, pp 2-3, 2-4, 2-A-13, 6-6; Weekly WID Sum, 19 Nov 65; Porter, *Air Tactics Against NVN Air-Ground Defenses*, pp 22–24.

5. Msg, CINCPAC to CINCPACFLT and CINCPACAF, 201945Z Nov 65.

6. Memo, McKee, Dir/Plans to CSAF, 10 Nov 65, subj: Air Ops Against NVN POL System; JCSM-910-65; JCSM-811-65, 10 Nov 65; PACAF rpt, *Out-Country Ops in SEA, 12 Feb–23 Dec 65*, Subtask 1b, pp 40–42.

7. *Gravel Pentagon Papers*, Vol IV, pp 622–23.

8. Kraslow and Loory, *The Secret Search for Peace in Vietnam*, pp 129–35.

9. Msg, JCS to CINCPAC, 090002 Dec 65; memo, Lt Gen F. Carroll, Dir DIA to SECDEF, 21 Jan 66, subj: An Appraisal of Bombing in NVN; Facts on File, *South Vietnam, 1961–65*, pp 141–42; *New York Times*, Dec 16, 65.

10. PACAF rpt, *Sum of Air Ops, SEA*, Vol XIII, 10–23 Dec 65, pp 2-A-1 thru 2-A-27.

11. PACAF DI rpt, *Effects of Air Ops, SEA*, 23 Dec 65, p 13; PACAF rpt, *Sum of Air Ops, SEA*, Vol XIII, pp 2-2 and 2-4 and 2-A-1, 2-A-21, and 2-A-22; msg, CINCPAC to JCS, 140147Z Dec 65; msg, JCS to CINCPAC, 16 Dec 65; *New York Times*, Dec 16, 65, p 11, Dec 21, 65, p 1, Dec 24, 65, p 3; *Washington Post*, Dec 17, 65; memo, Carroll to SECDEF, 21 Jan 66, subj: An Appraisal of the Bombing of NVN.

12. Memo, Col J. C. Berger, Asst Dir for Jt Matters, Dir/Ops to CSAF, 21 Dec 65, subj: Jt Staff Actions Concerning Restrike of Target 82.

13. Hist, 363d Tac Reconnaissance Wing, Jul–Dec 65, pp 31–41; PACAF rpt, *Sum of Air Ops, SEA*, Vol XI, 12–25 Nov 65, pp 6-4 to 6-6; Statement by Gen McConnell in Hearings before House Cmte on Armed Services: *Military Posture, Executive Session*, Mar 31, 66, p 1079; hist, TAC, Jan–Dec 65, pp 562–64; memo, Brown to CSAF 30 Nov 65, subj: Improved Intelligence Handling in SEA; USAF Mgt Digest, SEA, 7 Jan 66, pp 23, 24, and 36.

14. Smith, *USAF Reconnaissance in SEA, 1961–66*, pp 31–56, 70–71, 77–78; PACAF rpt, *Sum of Air Ops, SEA*, Vol XII, 26 Nov–9 Dec 65, p 6-3, Vol XIII, 10–23 Dec 65, pp 6-5 to 6-6, Vol XIII, 24 Dec 65–6 Jan 66, pp 6-4 to 6-6.

15. James Cameron, *Here is Your Enemy* (New York: Holt, Rinehart, and Winston, 1966), pp 53–57.

16. JCS Rolling Thunder Study Group rpt, *Air Ops Against NVN*, 6 Apr 66, Annex D to App A to Section II, pp 8–10, 19; msg, CINCPACAF to CSAF, 062135Z Sep 66; EOT rpt by Brig Gen G.B. Simler, DCS/Plans and Ops, 2d AD/7th AF, 13 Jul 66; intvw, Riddlebarger and Castellina with Gen Moore, 22 Nov 69, pp 17–18.

17. Futrell, *Chron of Significant Air Power Events in SEA, 1954–1967*, p 85; hist, 355th TFW, 1 Jul–31 Dec 65, p 36; *Personnel Support, Phase I* (DCS/P, Hqs USAF, Proj Corona Harvest), 1 Feb 68, p 59.

18. Sharp and Westmoreland, *Rpt on the War in VN*, pp 20–21.

19. Msg, CINCPAC to DIA, 312209Z Oct 65.

20. Sharp and Westmoreland, *Rpt on the War in VN*, p 21; *New York Times*, Dec 2, 65.

21. Msg, JCS to CINCPAC, 230038Z Dec 65; Johnson, *The Vantage Point*, pp 233–38.

22. Msg, Amembassy Vientiane to SECDEF, 230525Z Dec 65; msg, COMUSMACV to 2d AD, 250807Z Dec 65; msg, COMUSMACV to CINCPAC, JCS (Exclusive from Westmoreland to McConnell and Sharp), 260936Z Dec 65; msg, SECDEF to Principal Defense Agencies, 230013Z Dec 65; Capt Melvin F. Porter, *Tiger Hound* (Project CHECO, 1966), pp 17–18; Van Staaveren,

Interdiction in Southern Laos, pp 102–03.

23. Msg, CINCPAC to CINCPACFLT, CINCPACAF, 272158Z Dec 65.

24. McConnell Notebook, Item 372, 27 Dec 67; Johnson, *The Vantage Point*, pp 237–239; Westmoreland, *A Soldier Reports*, p 256; Van Staaveren, *Interdiction in Southern Laos*, pp 80, 85, 96–105.

25. *Gravel Pentagon Papers*, Vol IV, pp 32–39.

26. *Ibid.*, Vol IV, pp 32–39, 623; talking paper for Chmn JCS on an item to be discussed at JCS mtg, subj: Resumption of R/T 46/47, 26 Dec 65; Sharp, *Strategy for Defeat*, pp 105–8; Clodfelter, *The Limits of Air Power*, pp 91–92; George C. Herring, *LBJ and Vietnam: A Different Kind of War* (Austin: University of Texas Press, 1994), pp 99–100.

27. Msg, SECDEF to Westmoreland, Wheeler, Sharp, McConnell; McNamara and VanDeMark, *In Retrospect*, pp 222–226; Johnson, *The Vantage Point*, pp 233–23, *Gravel Pentagon Papers*, pp 32–36.

28. Msg, McNamara to Westmoreland, Wheeler, Sharp, McConnell, Abrams, Greene, 28 Dec 65; msg, McNamara to Westmoreland, 282350Z.

Chapter 8

1. Kraslow and Loory, *The Secret Search for Peace*, Chap 9; Janos Radvanyi, *Delusion and Reality: Gambits, Hoaxes, and Diplomatic One-upmanship in Vietnam* (South Bend: Gateway Editions, 1978), pp 101–112; Cooper, *The Lost Crusade: America in Vietnam*, pp 292–94; Allen E. Goodman, *The Lost Peace: America's Search for a Negotiated Settlement of the War* (Stanford: Hoover Institution Press, 1978), pp 34–35; Herring, *LBJ and Vietnam: A Different Kind of War*, p 100.

2. Cooper, *The Lost Crusade*, pp 293–94.

3. Senate Foreign Relations Committee Print, *Background Information Relating to Southeast Asia and Vietnam* (7th Rev ed, 93d Cong, 2d Sess, GPO, Dec 74), pp 24–26; Goodman, *The Lost Peace*, p 35; Ranvanyi, *Delusion and Reality*, p 42.

4. PACAF reports, *Sum of Air Ops, SEA*, Vols XIV, XV, XVI, (24 Dec 65 through 3 Feb 66), section 6 of each report and p 7-C-1 in Vol XVI.

5. *Ibid.*; hearings of Jt Session of Senate Armed Services and Appropriations Cmtes in FY 1966 Supplemental, *Background Paper on Pertinent Testimony by SECDEF and JCS*, 20 Jan 66; intvw, McConnell with Hearst Panel, 21 Mar 66; *Test of Gen Wheeler before House Cmte on Armed Services*, 3 Feb 66, pp 135–66; hist, CINCPAC, 1966, Vol II, pp 490–91; McNamara and VanDeMark, *In Retrospect*, pp 227–229.

6. Msg, CSAF to AU, 5 Jan 66; memo, Lt Gen Glen W. Martin, IG Hq USAF to CSAF, 10 Jan 66.

7. Memo, Martin to CSAF, 10 Jan 66.

8. Memo, CSAF to SAF, 6 Jan 66, subj: Reprogrammed Rqmts for CY 1966; McNamara and VanDeMark, *In Retrospect*, pp 218–22.

9. Memos, SAF to SECDEF, 10 Jan 66, subj: Reprogrammed Rqmts for CY 1966, and 17 Jan 66, subj: AF Capability to meet CINCPAC's Rqmts.

10. Memo, Col J.H. Germeraad, Asst Dep Dir/Plans for War Plans to CSAF, 25 Jan 66, subj: Deployments to SVN w/atch *Background Paper on SEA Strategy Against Deployments*; hearings of Jt session of Senate Armed Services and Approps Cmtes on FY 1966 Supplemental, *Background Paper on Pertinent Testimony by SECDEF and JCS*, 20 Jan 66.

11. JCSM-16-66, subj: Air Ops Against NVN, 8 Jan 66; Sharp, *Strategy for Defeat*, pp 107–110.

12. CASFM-Y-32-66, 12 Jan 66, subj: Future Air Ops Against NVN; msg, CINCPAC to JCS, 120205Z Jan 66; JCSM-41-66, 18 Jan 66, and CM-1134-66, 25 Jan 66.

13. Memo, SECDEF to Pres, 24 Jan 66, subj: The Mil Outlook in SVN; *Gravel Pentagon Papers*, Vol IV, p 51.

14. Test of Secy McNamara on 26 Jan 66 before the House Subcmte on Appns, 89th Cong, 2d sess, *Supplemental Def Appns for 1966*, p 31; Jacob Van Staaveren, *The Air Campaign Against NVN* (Ofc AF Hist, 1966), p 13.

15. Senate Foreign Relations Cmte Print, *Background Info Relating to SEA and VN*, 7th Rev Ed, Dec 74, p 25; *Gravel Pentagon Papers*, Vol IV, pp 67–68.

16. *Gravel Pentagon Papers*, Vol IV, p 67; memo, George C. Denney, Jr., Intelligence and Research Ofc, State Dept to SECSTATE, 26 Jan 66, subj: Infiltration-Oriented Bombing: The Song Ca River Line.

17. JCS-56-66, subj: Air Ops Against NVN, 25 Jan 66; msgs, JCS to CINCPAC, 250209Z Jan 66; and ADMINO CINCPAC to CINCPACFLT, CINCPACAF, COMUSMACTHAI, 260037Z Jan 66; msg, CINCPAC to NMCC (Lt Gen Emerick to Maj Gen McPherson), 272153Z Jan 66; Tilford, *Crosswinds*, pp 77–78.

18. Msg, CINCPAC to CINCPACAF, CINCPACFLT, COMUSMACV, 300305Z, Jan 66; Johnson, *The Vantage Point*, p 240; Sharp, *Strategy for Defeat*, p 111.

19. Msg, CINCPAC to CINCPACAF, CINCPACFLT, COMUSMACV, 300305Z Jan 66.

20. PACAF rpts, *Sum of Air Ops, SEA*, Vol XVII, 21 Jan–3 Feb 66, 11 Jul 65–31 Dec 65, pp 2-1 and 2-2, and sections 2-B-5 and 2-B-14; Melyan and Bonetti, *Rolling Thunder Jul 65–Dec 66*, p 33.

21. Msg, JCS to CINCPACAF, CINCPACFLT, COMUSMACV, 300305Z Jan 66; *New York Times*, Feb 1, 66; *Washington Post*, Feb 1, 66.

22. Melyan and Bonetti, *Rolling Thunder, Jul 65–Dec 66*, pp 33–34; PACAF rpt, *Sum of Air Ops, SEA*, Vol XVI, 21 Jan–3 Feb 66, pp 2-2 and 2-3, and section 2B.

23. Melyan and Bonetti, *Rolling Thunder, Jul 65–Dec 66*, pp 33–34; PACAF report, *Sum of Air Ops SEA*, Vol XVI, 21 Jan–3 Feb 66, pp 2-2, 2-3, and section 2B; Vol XIX, 4–17 Mar 66, pp 6-3 and 6-4.

24. Msgs, CINCPAC to Amembassy Vientiane, 010405Z Feb 66, and JCS to CINCPAC, 030125Z Feb 66; msg, CINCPAC to CINCPACAF and CINCPACFLT, 030522Z Feb 66.

25. Msgs, CJCS to ACJCS (Personal, Wheeler to Adm McDonald), 090021Z Feb 66; PACAF rpt, *Sum of Air Ops, SEA*, Vol XVII, 4–17 Feb 66, pp 2-B-8, 2-B-9, 2-B-22, and 2-B-23.

26. Telecon, 2d AD to PACAF Comd Center, 21 Feb 66.

27. PACAF rpt, *Sum of Air Ops, SEA*, Vol XVII 4–17 Feb 66, p 2-B-1.

28. Hearings before Senate Cmte on Armed Services, *Fiscal Year 1974 Authorization for Military Procurement, Research and Development*, p 427; William R. Greenhalgh, Jr, ms, *USAF in Southeast Asia, Feb 1965–Nov 68* (AF Hist Research Cent, 1969), Chap VII, pp 7–5 and 7–6; PACAF rpt, *Sum of Air Ops, SEA*, Vols XVI, XVII, XVIII, from 21 Jan–3 Mar 66, section 2 of each rpt; *USAF Mgt Sum, SEA*, 11 Mar 66, pp 35, and 37.

29. Van Staaveren, *USAF Plans and Ops in SEA, 1965*, p 74.

30. Jacob Van Staaveren, *USAF Deployment Planning in Southeast Asia, 1966*, (USAF Hist Div Liaison Ofc, 1967), pp 17–18.

31. *Ibid.*; McConnell Notebook Item 399, 3 Feb 66, and Item 400, 5 Feb 66; Wolk, *USAF Logistic Plans and Policies in Southeast Asia, 1965*, chap IV.

32. Van Staaveren, *USAF Plans and Ops in SEA, 1965*, pp 64–70.

33. Van Staaveren, *USAF Deployment Planning for SEA, 1966*, pp 10–12.

34. *Ibid.*; memo, CSAF to SAF, 6 Jan 66; *Gravel Pentagon Papers*, Vol IV, pp 309–15.

35. Ltr, Maj Gen John W. Vogt, DCS/P&O, Hq PACAF to Hq USAF, 12 Feb 66, subj: Phase IIA Evaluations.

36. *Ibid.*, p 14; ltr, CINCPAC 310 Ser 00055, CINCPAC to JCS, 12 Feb 66, subj: CY 66 Capabilities Program.

37. JCS 2343/772, 18 Feb 66, subj: Ops and Force Deployments with Respect to the War in VN.

38. Van Staaveren, *USAF Deployment Planning for SEA, 1966*, pp 15–16.

39. Memo, MacDonald to CSAF, 25 Feb 66.

40. Ltr, Vogt to Hqs USAF, 12 Feb 66.

41. McConnell Notebook, Item 402, 8 Feb 66; Col. E.F. MacDonald, Asst Chief, Combined Plans Div, DCS/P&O to CSAF, 25 Feb 66, subj: Deployment Schedule for SEA and other PACOM areas.

42. Memo, Secy Brown to SECDEF, 19 Feb 66, subj: Decisions Required Associated with SEA Deployment Planning Assumptions; memo, Secy Brown to SECDEF, 3 Mar 66, subj: SEA Deployment Planning; JCSM-130-66 with Apps A and B, 1 Mar 66.

43. Memo, SECDEF to Secys of Mil Depts and JCS, 10 Mar 66 subj: Deployments to SEA; memo, SECDEF to Chmn JCS, 26 Mar 66, subj: Tac acft Rqmts for SEA.

44. JCSM-113-55, 19 Feb 66.

45. *Ibid.*; memo, McKee to CSAF, 18 Feb 66, subj: Air Ops Against NVN.

46. Msg, JCS to CINCPAC, 260025Z Feb 66.

47. *Ibid.*; msg, Wheeler to Sharp, 262219Z Feb 66; unsigned memo for JCS chmn, 25 Feb 66, in JCS folder R/T 51, sec 12; PACAF rpt, *Out-Country Strike Operations in SEA, 24 Dec 65–21 Jul 67*, Vol I, Subtask 1C, subj: Air Operations Against North Vietnam, pp 24–25.

48. *Ibid.*

49. PACAF rpts, *Sum of Air Ops, SEA*, Vol XIX, 4–17 Mar 66, pp 2–9, 2–10, Vol XX, 18–31 Mar 66, p 2–8.

50. *Ibid.*, Vols XVIII, XIX, XXX, 18 Feb–31 Mar 66, section 2 of each rpt.

51. *Ibid.*

52. PACAF rpts, *Sum of Air Ops, SEA*, Vol IX, 4–17 Mar 66, p 2–8, Vol XX, 18–31 Mar 66, p 2–3.

53. *Ibid.*, Vol IX, 4–17 Mar 66, p 2-B-1, Vol XX, 18–31 Mar 66, p 2-B-0.

54. *Ibid.*, Vol XIX, 4–17 Mar 66, pp 2-2, 2-3, 2-B-1, Vol XX, 18–31 Mar 66, p 2-B-0; Annual Report, *CINCPACFLT, FY 1966*, 19 Sep 66, pp 1 and 32.

55. PACAF rpt, *Sum of Air Ops, SEA*, Vol IX, 4–17 Mar 66, pp 2–5, 2–8, Vol XX, 18–31 Mar 66, pp 2-9 to 2-12; *USAF Mgt Sum, SEA*, 1 Apr 66, pp 35–39.

56. PACAF rpt, *Sum of Air Ops*, SEA, Vol IX, 4–17 Mar, pp 2-5 to 2-8, Vol XX, 18–31 Mar 66, pp 2-9 to 2-12.

57. *Ibid.*, Vol XIX, 4–17 Mar 66, p 2-8, and Vol XX, 18–31 Mar 66, p 29.

58. Memo, McKee to Blanchard, 23 Mar 66, subj: Air Ops Against Aflds in NVN; draft memo, SAF to SECDEF, Mar 66, subj: Buildup of Ftr Acft in NVN; Dir/Plans Talking Paper on the Growing MiG Threat in NVN, 28 Mar 66; PACAF rpt, *Sum of Air Ops, SEA*, Vol XX, 18–31 Mar 66, pp 2-9 to 1-12.

Chapter 9

1. Msgs, COMUSMACV to CINCPAC, 170652Z Nar 66, and COMUSMACV to CINCPAC and JCS (Westmoreland to Sharp and Wheeler), 1710372 Mar 66.

2. Msgs, COMUSMACV to CINCPAC, 170652Z Mar 66, and Westmoreland to Sharp, 171210Z Mar 66, and 220220Z Mar 66.

3. Msg, CINCPAC to COMUSMACV, 190452Z Mar 66; Sharp, *Strategy for Defeat*, pp 114–15.

4. 4. Msg, CINCPAC TO 2d AD (Exclusive Harris to Moore), 252132Z

Mar 66.

5. Msg, CINCPACAF to 2d AD, 252132 (Exclusive Harris to Moore), 252032Z Mar 66; msg, 2d AD AFSSO to PACAFAFSSO (Exclusive Gen Simler to Gen Vogt), 281030Z Mar 66; Gen Westmoreland's Hist Briefing, 3 Apr 66.

6. Msgs, Wheeler to Sharp, 222345Z Mar 66 and SECDEF to CINCPAC, CINCSAC, COMUSMACV, CNO, AND CSAF, 162229Z Apr 66; *The JCS and the War in VN*, Vol II, p 31–13.

7. Msg, CINCPAC to COMUSMACV, CINCPACFLT, CINCPACAF, 262337Z Mar 66; msgs, Wheeler to Sharp, 222345Z Mar 66, and SECDEF to CINCPAC, CINCSAC, COMUSMACV, CNO, CSPF, 162229Z Apr 66; Sharp, *Strategy for Defeat*, pp 114–15.

8. 8. Msg, CINCPAC to CINCPACFLT, CINCPACAF, COMUSMACV, CINCUSARPAC, 280003Z MAR 66.

9. Msg, 2d PD AFSSO to PACAF AFSSO (Exclusive Gen Simler to Gen Vogt), 281030Z Mar 66; end of tour rpt, Brig Gen G.B. Simler, DCS/P&O Hqs 7th AF, 13 Jul 66; PACAF rpt, *Air Ops Against NVN*, 24 Dec 65–21 Jul 67, p 51.

10. Msg, Wheeler to Sharp, 222345Z Mar 66; Air Staff rpt, *Analysis of Actions by JCS: Air Ops Against NVN*, 25 Mar 66; JCS 2343/799, 24 Mar 66; *The JCS and the War in VN*, Vol II, p 31-13.

11. JCSM 189-66; memo, McKee to William H. Blanchard, Vice COFS, 23 Mar 66, subj: Air Ops Against Airfields in NVN.

12. *Gravel Pentagon Papers*, Vol IV, pp 77–78.

13. *Ibid.*, pp 78–79.

14. *Ibid.*; Goodman, *The Lost Peace*, p 37; Cooper, *The Lost Crusade*, p 304; Johnson, *The Vantage Point*, 246–47; Clodfelter, *The Limits of Air Power*, p 95; *Washington Post*, Mar 31, 65; *New York Times*, Apr 3, 66.

15. Msg, JCS to CINCPAC, 010112Z Mar 66.

16. Msgs, CINCPAC to CINCPACFLT, CINCPACAF, COMUSMACV, 010835Z Apr 66, and 010200Z Apr 66.

17. Msgs, CINCPAC to CINCPACFLT, CINCPACAF, COMUSMACV, 010200Z Apr 66, and CINCPAC to COMUSMACV, 302305Z Apr 66.

18. PACAF rpt, *Air Ops Against NVN*, 24 Dec 65–21 Jul 67, pp 25–26; Van Staaveren, *The Air Campaign Against NVN, 1966*, pp 23–25.

19. Van Staaveren, *The Air Campaign Against NVN, 1966*, pp 22–25.

20. *Gravel Pentagon Papers*, Vol IV, pp 95–98; Senate rpt, Committee on Foreign Relations, *Background Info Relating to SEA and VN* (7th ed, 1974), pp 29–30; Goodman, *The Lost Peace*, p 38.

21. *New York Times*, May 23, 66.

22. Msgs, CINCPAC to CINCPACFLT, CINCPACAF, COMUSMACV, 010835Z Apr 66, and SECDEF to CINCPAC, COMUSMACV, CNO, CSPF, 162229Z Apr 66; PACAF rpt, *Sum of Air Ops, SEA*, Vol XXI, Apr 66, section 1.

23. PACAF rpt, *Sum of Air Ops, SEA*, Vols XXII and XXIII, May and Jun 66, section 1 of each rpt.

24. Van Staaveren, *The Air Campaign Against NVN, 1966*, pp 24–28; and Van Staaveren, *Interdiction in Southern Laos*, pp 107, and 118–20.

25. Van Staaveren, *The Air Campaign Against NVN, 1966*, pp 25–28.

26. PACAF rpts, *Sum of Air Ops, SEA*, Vols XXI, XXII, and XXIII, Apr, May, Jun 66, section 1 of each rpt.

27. *Ibid.*

28. Msgs, CINCPACAF to CINCPAC, 050155Z and 130255Z Apr 66, and 032046Z Jun 66, and CINCPAC to CINCPACAF and CINCPACFLT, 15041Z Apr 66; PACAF rpts, *Sum of Air Ops, SEA*, Vol XXI, Apr 66, p 1-15; and Data Addendum, Vol XXI Apr 66, pp 1-A-78 and 1-A-79.

29. Msgs, CINCPAC to JCS, 052329Z May 66, and CINCPACAF to 7th AF, 072255Z May 66; memo, Adm L.M. Mustin, Dir for Ops, Jt Staff to Dir for Jt Staff, 12 May 66, subj: CINCPAC's Request for Strike of SAM Support Facilities; msg, Wheeler to Sharp,

162306Z May 66.

30. PACAF rpts, *Sum of Air Ops, SEA*, Vols XXII and XXIII, May and Jun 66, Section 1 of each rpt.

31. Msg, CINCPAC to JCS, 04044722 May 66; PACAF rpt, *Sum of Air Ops, SEA*, Vol XXI, Apr 66, pp 1-5 to 1-17, Vol XXIII, Jun 66, p 1-31.

32. Lavalle, *Tale of Two Bridges*.

33. *Ibid.*; memo, Brig Gen Woodrow P. Swancutt, Dep Dir for Forces, Dir Ops to Dep COFS, Plans and Ops, Hqs USAF, subj: Recapitulation of Carolina Noon Activities, 6 Jun 66.

34. Lavalle, *Tale of Two Bridges*, pp 52–56; Hqs 7th AF Folder on Carolina Moon, 29–30 May 66.

35. Lavalle, *Tale of Two Bridges*, pp 52–56.

36. *Ibid.*; msg, PACAF to TAC, TAWC, Eglin 110150Z Jun 66; memo, Swancutt to Dep COFS Plans and Ops, 6 Jun 66; *New York Times*, Mar 25, 72.

37. Gen Westmoreland's Hist Briefing; Wesley R. C. Melyan, *Arc Light, 1965–1966* (Proj CHECO, 1967), pp 127–32.

38. Hist, SAC, Jan–Jun 66, Vol I, p 126.

39. *New York Times*, Apr 13, 66.

40. Gen Westmoreland's Hist Briefing, 26 Apr 66; Melyan, *Arc Light, 1965–1966*, pp 137–41.

41. Hist, SAC, Jan–Jun 66, Vol I, pp 128–29; Melyan, *Arc Light, 1965–1966*, p 141.

42. Msg, COMUSMACV to AIG 7241, Amembassy Vientiane, 290745Z Apr 66; hist, SAC, Jan–Jun 66 Vol I, p 129.

43. Msg, Amembassy Vientiane 1121 to SECSTATE 26 Apr 66; msg, CINCPAC to JCS, COMUSMACV, 300405Z Apr 66.

44. Msg, CINCPAC to JCS, COMUSMACV, CINCSAC, 30 Apr 66.

45. Msg, SAC to CINCPAC, 071650Z May 66; msgs, PDMINO CINCPAC to CINCPAC, 11 May and 130925Z May 66; msg, Amembassy Vientiane to SECSTATE, 028330Z May 66; msg, Amembassy Vientiane to SECSTATE, 30302Z May 66; msg, CINCPAC to COMUSMACV, CINCSAC, 310110Z May 66; Melyan, *Arc Light, 1965–1966*, pp 145–46.

46. PACAF rpts, *Sum of Air Ops, SEA*, Vols, XXI, XXII, and XXIII, Apr, May, and Jun 66, section 1 of each report.

47. Wolk, *USAF Logistic Plans and Policies in Southeast Asia, 1966*, Chap II.

48. Hist, MACV, 1966, pp 259–66; Wolk, *USAF Logistic Plans and Policies in SEA, 1966*, Chap II.

49. Wolk, *USAF Logistic Plans and Policies in SEA, 1966*, pp 15–17.

50. Memo, SECDEF to JCS Chmn, subj: Air Munitions and Sortie Plan, 24 May 66; Van Staaveren, *Interdiction in Southern Laos*, pp 140–43.

51. Wolk, *USAF Logistic Plans and Policies in SVN, 1966*, pp 15–17; hist, CINCPAC, Vol II, pp 761–63; msg, SECDEF to COMUSMACV, 081853Z Apr 66; Van Staaveren, *Interdiction in Southern Laos*, pp 140–43.

52. Greenhalgh, *USAF in SEA, Feb 65–Nov 68*, pp 457–58.

53. Stmt by Gen McConnell on 9 May in hearings before the Senate Preparedness Investigating Subcommittee of the Committee on Armed Services, 89th Cong. 2d sess, Tactical Air Operations and Readiness, 9 May 66, pp 62–63.

54. PACAF rpt, *Sum of Air Ops, SEA*, Vol XXI, Apr 66, pp 4 and 1-16 and 1-17, Vol XXII May, 66, pp 1-12 and 1-13, and Vol XXII, Jun 66, pp 1-14 and 1-15; msg, CINCPAC to CINCPACAF, CINCPACFLT, and COMUSMACV, 290225Z Apr 66; msg, CINCPAC to CINCPACFLT, COMUSHACVL 150419Z Apr 66.

55. Maj Richard A. D. Durkee, *Combat Skyspot* (Proj. CHECO, 1967), p 4; and Van Staaveren, *The Air Campaign Against NVN*, 1966, p 28.

56. Durkee, *Combat Skyspot*, pp 4 and 25.

57. *Ibid.*, pp 10–11.

58. PACAF rpts, *Sum of Air Ops, SEA*,

Vol XXIV, Jun 66, p 1-8 and Vol XII Jul 66, pp 7-B-2 and 7-B-3; MACV Monthly Eval Rpt, Jul 66, p 4.

59. PACAF rpts, *Sum of Air Ops, SEA*, Vol XXI, Apr 66, pp 1-31 and 1-32, Vol XXII, May 66, pp 1-18 and 1-19, Vol XXIII, Jun 66, pp 1-19 and 1-20.

60. *Ibid.*, Vol XXI, Apr 66, p 54; Greenhalgh, *USAF in SEA, Feb 65–Nov 68*, p 467.

61. PACAF rpt, *Sum of Air Ops, SEA*, Vol XXI, Apr 66, p 1-28.

62. *Ibid.*, Vol XXIII, Jun 66, pp 1–9; stmt by Gen McConnell on 31 Mar 66 in hearings before the House Armed Services Cmte, p 1,053.

63. *USAF Mgt Sum, SEA*, 15 Jul 66, pp 45 and 78; CINCPAC briefing for SECDEF, 8 Jul 66; PACAF rpts, *Sum of Air Ops, SEA*, Vols XXII, May 66, p 1-15 and Vol XXIII, Jun 66, p 1-17.

64. PACAF rpt, *Sum of Air Ops, SEA*, Vol XXI, Apr 66, pp 1-24 to 1-28.

65. Hist, 355th TFW, 1 Jul–31 Dec 66, p 32; msgs, 355th Takhli to 13th AF, 030730 Jul 66; and TAC to CINCPACAF, 12th AF Waco, Tex. *et al*, 171548Z Jun 66; *USAF Mgt Sum, SEA*, 10 Jun 66, p 22; Nalty, *Electronic Countermeasures*, pp 40–42.

66. Intvw, Capt Snakenberg with Lt Col David P. Blackbird, 9 Nov 69; PACAF rpt, *Sum of Air Ops SEA*, Vol XXI, Apr 66, pp 1-19 and 1-24 to 1-26, Vol XXI, Apr 66, Data Addendum, p 1-A-36, Vol XXII, May 66, p 1-16; Nalty, *Electronic Countermeasures*, pp 40–42.

67. PACAF rpts, *Sum of Air Ops, SEA*, Vol XXII, May 66 and Vol XXIII, Jun 66, pt 1, subsection 3 of each rpt; memo, Col Richard E, Gaspard, Ops Intel Div, Hqs 7th AFI to Brig Gen G.B. Simler, DCS Plans and Ops, 7th AF, with atchd rpt, 23 Jun 66, subj: SA–2 Deployment and Tactics in NVN; Nalty, *Electronic Countermeasures*, p 43.

68. Fact sheet, subj: Wild Weasel, 22 Apr 66, in Notebook on CINCPACAF and Vice COFS USAF Conference, 25–26 Apr 66 at Hickam AFB, Hawaii; msg, 7th AF to PACAF, 280856Z May 66.

69. Msg, Sharp to Westmoreland, 302239Z Apr 66; PACAF rpts, *Sum of Air Ops SEA*, Vol XXI, Apr 66, pp 1-24 and 1-25 and Vol XXII, May 66, p 1-16.

70. Melyan and Bonetti, *Rolling Thunder, Jul 65–Dec 66*, pp 105–06; hist, 355th TFW, Jul–Dec 66, p 30.

71. Msgs, CINCPAC to CINCPACFLT, CINCPACAF, CINCSAC, 090505Z Apr 66; 7th AF to PACAF, 1113457, Apr 66. and SAC to JCS, CINCPAC, 122335Z Apr 66.

72. PACAF rpt, *Sum of Air Ops, SEA*, Vol XXI, Apr 66, pp 1-20, 1-23.

73. Futrell, et al, *Aces and Aerial Victories*, pp 27–29.

74. *Ibid.*, pp 27–29; *New York Times*, Apr 25, 66, and Apr 28, 66.

75. Futrell, et al, *Aces and Aerial Victories*, pp 27–29.

76. *Ibid.*, pp 29–30.

77. *Ibid.*, p 30.

78. *New York Times*, May 13 and 27, 66.

79. PACAF rpt, *Sum of Air Ops, SEA*, Vol XXIII, Jun 66, pp 1–16.

80. Futrell, et al, *Aces and Aerial Victories*, pp 30–31; hist, TACC-NS, Oct 67, p 7.

81. *USAF Mgt Sum, SEA*, 8 Jul 66, p 79.

82. Hist, TACC-NS, p 30; msg, ADMINO CINCPAC to COMUSMACV, CINCPACAF, CINCPACFLT, 180412Z May 66; msg, SSO MACV to AFSSO 7th AF, 18013OZ May 66.

83. Msg, AFSSO MACV to 7th AF, 18013OZ May 66; msg, 7th AF to Hq USAF, PACAF 180715Z Jun 66; hist, 7th AF Tactical Air Control Center, North Sector (TACC-NS), Oct 67, p 4; Melyan and Bonetti, *The War in VN*, 1966, pp 25–27.

84. Hist, 7th AF TACC-NS, Oct 67, pp 4 and 7; msg, AFSSO MACV to AFSSO 7th AF, 180130Z May 66; Air Force rpt, SEA Items, Item No. 37A; msg, NMCC to CINCPAC (Adm Mustin to Gen Everick), 070040Z Jul 66.

85. Hist, 7th AF TACC-NS, pp 4–5.

86. *Ibid.*; Air Force rpt, SEA Items No.

37A, Jul 66; memo, Lt Gen K.K. Compton, DCS/Plans and Ops to Lt Gen James Furgeson, DCS/R&D, 9 Jun 66, subj: Enhanced Control Capability SEA; msg, CSAF to PACAF, 2914327 Jun 66.

87. Msgs, CINCPAC to JCS, 040206Z Sep 66; JCS to CSAF, 102244Z Sep 66; hist, 7th IF TACC, p 7.

Chapter 10

1. Msgs USAF Dir/Plan memo, Background Paper on CSAF Recommendations Regarding Attacks on NVN POL, Jun 66; *Gravel Pentagon Papers,* Vol IV, pp 60–63; Clodfelter, *The Limits of Air Power,* pp 92–95.

2. JCSM-910-65, 10 Nov 65; *Gravel Pentagon Papers*, Vol VI, pp 59–62.

3. *Gravel Pentagon Papers*, Vol IV, p 61.

4. *Ibid.*, pp 62–66.

5. *Ibid.*, pp 66–67; *The JCS and the War in VN,* pt II, 31-4 and 31-5.

6. JCSM-16-66, 8 Jan 66; JCSM-41-66, 18 Jan 66; msg, CINCPAC to CINCPACFLT, COMUSMACV, 300305 Jan 66. Sharp, *Strategy for Defeat,* pp 108–111; Tilford, *Crosswinds,* p 78.

7. JCSM-15-66, 8 Jan 66; JCSM-41-66, 18 Jan 66; *Gravel Pentagon Papers,* Vol IV, pp 68–70.

8. *Gravel Pentagon Papers*, Vol IV, pp 74–76.

9. Msg, Wheeler to Sharp, 222345Z Mar 66; *Gravel Pentagon Papers,* Vol IV, p 77; Sharp, *Strategy for Defeat,* pp 116–17; Clodfelter, *The Limits of Air Power,* pp 94–95.

10. Msg, Wheeler to Sharp, 222345Z Mar 66; *Gravel Pentagon Papers,* Vol IV, p 77.

11. *Gravel Pentagon Papers*, Vol IV, pp 77–78.

12. Goodman, *The Lost Peace,* pp 36–38; *Gravel Pentagon Papers,* Vol IV, pp 94–95.

13. Memo, Walt W. Rostow, Special Asst to President for National Security Affairs to Secys State and Def, 6 May 66; *Gravel Pentagon Papers,* Vol IV, pp 100–101; Van Staaveren, *The Air Campaign Against NVN, 1966,* p 31.

14. *Gravel Pentagon Papers*, Vol IV, p 102.

15. *Ibid.*, pp 102–3.

16. Msg, COMUSMACV to CINCPAC, 051201Z Jun 66; PACAF rpt, *Sum of Air Ops, SEA,* Vol XXII, May 66, pp 1-7 to 1-10, *Data Addendum,* pp 1-A-78 to 1-A-83, 1-A-175 to 1-A-181; *Gravel Pentagon Papers,* Vol IV pp 102–3; *New York Times,* Jun 1, 66.

17. Msgs, CINCPAC to JCS, 060805Z Jun 66; memo, Maj Gen Robert N. Smith, Dir/Plans, DCS P&O to CSAF, subj: NVN Air Strike Program, 16 Jun 66; *Gravel Pentagon Papers,* Vol IV, p 102.

18. *Gravel Pentagon Papers*, Vol IV, pp 103–05.

19. *Ibid.*; Kraslow and Loory, *The Secret Search for Peace,* pp 155–57.

20. Msg, SECDEF to CINCPAC (Adm Mustin to Gens Hutchins, Hutchinson, and Brown), 130384Z Jun 66.

21. Msg, JCS to CINCPAC (Adm Mustin to Gens Hutchins, Hutchinson, and Brown), 130384Z Jun 66.

22. Msg, CINCPAC to SECDEF (Exclusive Sharp to McNamara), 140659Z Jun 66; msg, SECDEF to CINCPAC (personal SECDEF to Sharp), 152000Z Jun 66; *Gravel Pentagon Papers,* Vol IV, p 105.

23. Msg, JCS to CINCPAC, 1522552 Jun 66; msg, CINCPAC to CINCPACFLT, CINCPACAF, COMUSMACV, 160922Z Jun 66; msg, CINCPACFLT to COMSEVENTHFLT, 162227Z Jun 66; msg, CINCPAC to CINCPACFLT, 180006Z; msg, CSAFM-W-53-66, 20 Jun 66, subj: NVN Strike Program.

24. Goodman, *The Lost Peace,* p 38; *Gravel Pentagon Papers,* Vol IV, pp 104–05.

25. *Public Papers of the Presidents,* Johnson, Vol I, p 629; *Baltimore Sun,* Jun 19, 66; *New York Times,* Jun 19 and 24,

66; *Chicago Tribune,* Jun 24, 66; *New York Post,* Jun 24, 66; intvw, Capt Snakenberg with Lt Col David P. Blackbird, 9 Nov 69; PACAF rpt, *Sum of Air Ops, SEA,* Vol XIII, Jun 66, pp 1-9 to 1-13.

26. Msg, NMCC to CINCPAC, 231747Z Jun 66.

27. Msg, JCS to CINCPAC, 222044Z Jun 66; msg, CINCPAC to CINCPACFLT, CINCPACAF, 222044Z Jun 66; Melyan and Bonetti, *Rolling Thunder, Jul 65–Dec 66,* p 60; Sharp, *Strategy for Defeat,* p 117.

28. Msg, JCS to CINCPAC, 251859Z Jun 66; *Gravel Pentagon Papers,* Vol IV, p 105; *The JCS and the War in VN,* Pt II, p 31-30; *Washington Post,* Jun 26, 66.

29. Msg, CJCS to CINCPAC, 281254Z Jun 66; *Gravel Pentagon Papers,* Vol IV, p 106.

30. Msgs, CINCPAC to CINCPACAF and CINCPACFLT, 230943Z Jun 66 and 281932Z Jun 66; UPI dispatch (in Current News, Early Bird ed), Jun 29, 66, p 6; Clodfelter, *The Limits of Air Power,* p 98.

31. PACAF rpt, *Sum of Air Ops, SEA,* Vol XXIII, Jun 66, p 1-4; UPI dispatch, Jun 29, 66 (in Current News, Jun 29, 66); msgs, JCS to CINCPAC 052249Z and 052249Z Jul 66 and CINCPAC to CINCPACFLT, CINCPACAF, et al, 060845Z Jul 66.

32. PACAF rpts, *Sum of Air Ops, SEA,* Vol XXIII, Jun 66, pp 1-3 and 1-4; Facts on File, SVN, 1966–67, p 90; *Washington Post,* Jun 30, 66; Melyan and Bonetti, *Rolling Thunder Jul 65–Dec 66,* p 64.

33. Futrell, et al, *Aces and Aerial Victories,* pp 30–31; PACAF rpt, *Sum of Air Ops, SEA,* Vol XXIII, Jun 66, pp 1–3; *Aviation Week,* Jul 4, 66, pp 22–23; *Baltimore Sun,* Jun 30, 66; *Washington Post,* Jul 2, 66.

34. Text of McNamara's Stmt and Questions and Answers on the Bombing of Hanoi and Haiphong Depots, in the *New York Times* Jun 30 66; *Baltimore Sun,* Jun 30, 66.

35. Text of McNamara's Stmt and Questions and Answers, Jun 29, 66; *Baltimore Sun,* Jul 1, 66.

36. PACAF rpt, *Sum of Air Ops, SEA,* Vol XXIII, Jun 66, pp 1-4 and 1-5; *Washington Post,* Jul 1, 66.

37. *Ibid.*

38. Msgs, JCS to CINCPAC 052249Z Jul 66 and CINCPAC to CINCPACFLT, CINCPACAF *et al*, 060845Z Jul 66; Van Staaveren, *The Air Campaign Against NVN,* 1966, p 33; Facts on File, SVN, 1966–67, pp 102–03; *Philadelphia Inquirer,* Jun 12, 66.

39. Facts on File, SVN, 1966–67, pp 90–91; Oleg Hoeffding, *The Bombing of North Vietnam: An Appraisal of Economic and Military Effects* (RM-5213, Dec 66), p 25.

40. *Baltimore Sun,* Jul 1, 66; *Gravel Pentagon Papers,* Vol IV, p 108; Facts on File, SVN, 1966–67, pp 90–100.

41. Baltimore Sun, Jul 1, 66; Philadelphia Inquirer, Jul 4, 66; *Gravel Pentagon Papers,* Vol IV, pp 107–08; Facts on File, SVN, 1966–67, pp 99–101.

42. MR by Maj Gen George Brown, Spec Asst to Chmn JCS, 8 Jul 66, subj: Highlights of SECDEF Conf; Van Staaveren, *USAF Deployment Planning for SEA,* 1966, pp 39–45.

43. NIE 14-3-66, 7 Jul 66; *USAF Mgt Sum, SEA* rpts, 1 and 8, Jul 66.

44. Van Staaveren, *The Air Campaign Against NVN, 1966,* pp 33–35; Van Staaveren, *USAF Deployment Planning for SEA, 1966,* p 39.

45. Van Staaveren, *USAF Deployment Planning for SEA, 1966,* p 41.

46. MR, Maj Gen George Brown, Spec Asst to Chmn JCS, 8 July 66, subj: Highlights of SECDEF Conference; msgs, AFIN 10036OZ and 100625Z, CINCPACAF to CSAF, 10 Jul 66.

47. Hist, CINCPAC, 1966, pp 500–01; msg, JCS to CINCPAC, 061949Z; *Sum of Air Ops, SEA, 1966,* Vol XXIV, pp 1-4 and 1-8.

48. Msg, PACAF to 7th AF, 070323Z Jul 66; PACAF rpt, *Sum of Air Ops, SEA, 1966,* Vol XXIV, p 1-4.

49. Msgs, CINCPAC to Chmn JCS (to

Gen Wheeler) 230909Z Jul 66; CINCPAC to CINCPACFLT, CINCPACAF, COMUSMACV, 242059Z Jul 66; hist, CINCPAC, 1966, Vol II, pp 500–01.

50. Msg, CINCPAC to CINCPACFLT, CINCPACAF, COMUSMACV, 242059Z Jul 66.

51. CM-1638, 23 Jul 66; msg, COMUSMACV to 7th AF, 300222Z Jul 66; PACAF rpt, *Sum of Air Ops, SEA,* Aug 66, Vol XXV, p 1-B-4.

52. PACAF rpt, *Sum of Air Ops, SEA,* 1966, Vol XXIV, p 1-40 and 1-43.

53. *Ibid.,* Jul 66, Vol XXI, section 1.

54. Msg, CINCPAC to JCS, 081937Z Aug 66; Melyan and Bonetti, *Rolling Thunder, Jul 65–Dec 66,* p 82; McNamara and VanDeMark, *In Retrospect,* pp 245–46.

55. Memo, VN Task Force, State Dept to William P. Bundy, Asst Secy, Far Eastern Affairs, 25 Aug 66, subj: Proposed Rolling Thunder Program and Escalation Generally: Melyan and Bonetti, *Rolling Thunder, Jul 65–Dec 66*, pp 84–87.

56. Msg, 7th AF to CINCPACAF, CSAF (Personal, Gen Momyer to Gens Harris and McConnell), 120430Z Aug 66; msgs, 7th AF to CINCPACAF, 120430Z Aug 66.

57. Msg, CINCPAC to CINCPACFLT, CINCPACAF, 150135Z, Aug 66.

58. Msg, JCS to CINCPAC 111813Z Aug 66; msg, CINCPAC to DIA, 110015Z Aug 66; msgs, 7th AF to CINCPAC, 130845Z Aug 66 and to PACAF, 300940Z Aug 66.

59. Msg, CINCPAC to CINCPACFLT, CINCPACAF, COMUSMACV, 260412Z Aug 66; *The JCS and the War in VN*, pt II, pp 36-2 and 36-3.

60. PACAF rpts, *Sum of Air Ops, SEA,* Aug 66, Vol XXV, pp 1-B-4 and 1-B-19.

61. Msg, CINCPAC to CINCPACFLT, CINCPACAF, COMUSMACV, 260412Z, Aug 66; *The JCS and the War in VN*, pp 36-2 and 36-3; Sharp, *Strategy for Defeat,* pp 118–19.

62. Msg, 7th AF to CINCPACAF, 231143Z Sep 66; PACAF rpts, *Sum of Air Ops, SEA,* 1966, Vol XXV, Sep 66, pp 3, 1-B-11, 1-B-17 and 1-B-18, Vol XXVII, pp 1-A-l and 1-A-12.

63. Msgs, 7th AF to CINCPACAF, 231143Z Sep 66; CINCPAC to JCS, 282258Z, Sep 66; undated memo for Chmn, JCS, subj: R/T 52 Strike Objectives.

64. Hist, CINCPAC, 1966, Vol II p 502; *Gravel Pentagon Papers,* Vol II, pp 110–12; McNamara and VanDeMark, *In Retrospect*, pp 245–46.

65. *Gravel Pentagon Papers*, Vol IV, 110–16 and 123; Clodfelter, *The Limits of Air Power*, p 99.

66. PACAF rpts, *Sum of Air Ops, SEA,* Oct 1966, Vol XXVII, pp 1-1 and 1-A-2; *Gravel Pentagon Papers,* Vol IV, pp 110–12 and 124–26.

67. *Gravel Pentagon Papers,* Vol IV, pp 110–12 and 125–26; memo, Col Fred W. Vetter, Jr., Mil Asst to SAF, 9–14 Oct 66, subj: Air Staff Activities as a Result of SECDEF trip to SEA; test of SECDEF McNamara on January 23, 1967 before Senate Armed Services Cmte and the Subcmte on DOD Approps, 90th Cong., 1st Sess, *Supplemental Military Procurement and Construction Authorizations, FY 1967,* pp 70–72.

68. *Gravel Pentagon Papers,* Vol IV, pp 125–26; Tilford, *Crosswinds,* p 80.

69. *Gravel Pentagon Papers*, Vol I, pp 125–26; Clodfelter, *The Limits of Air Power*, pp 99–100.

70. Msg, CINCPAC to JCS, 261920Z Oct 66.

Glossary

AB	Air Base
ABCCC	Airborne Battlefield Command and Control Center
Acft	Aircraft
AD	Air Division
AFI	Air Force Intelligence
AFLC	Air Force Logistics Command
AFSC	Air Force Systems Command
AFSSO	Air Force Security Service Office
AFTAC	Air Force Tactical Air Command
AGM	Air-Ground Missile
AOC	Air Operations Center
ARPAC	Army Pacific
AU	Air University
BDA	Bomb Damage Assessment
CAP	Combat Air Patrol
CEP	Circular Error Probable
CHECO	Comparative Historical Evaluation of Counterinsurgency Operations (later Contemporary Historical Evaluation of Combat Operations)
CIA	Central Intelligence Agency
CINCPAC	Commander in Chief, Pacific
CINCPACFLT	Commander in Chief, Pacific Fleet
CINCSAC	Commander in Chief, Strategic Air Command
COMUSMACTHAI	Commander, U. S. Military Assistance Command, Thailand
COMUSMACV	Commander, U. S. Military Assistance Command, Vietnam
COMUSSEVENTHFLT	Commander, U. S. Seventh Fleet
CNO	Chief of Naval Operations
CSAF	Chief of Staff, Air Force
CSAFM	Chief of Staff, Air Force Memo
DI	Director of Intelligence
DIA	Defense Intelligence Agency
DMZ	Demilitarized Zone
EOTR	End of Tour Report
FAC	Forward Air Controller
Flak	Antiaircraft artillery

Iron Hand	Code name for specially equipped aircraft engaged in attacking SA–2 surface-to-air missiles
JCS	Joint Chiefs of Staff
JCSM	Joint Chiefs of Staff Memo
Jt	Joint
LIMDIS	Limited Distribution
LOC	Line of Communication
MACV	Military Assistance Command, Vietnam
NASM	National Action Security Memo
n.m.	Nautical Mile
NMCC	National Military Command Center
NIE	National Intelligence Estimate
NSC	National Security Council
NVA	North Vietnamese Army
NVAF	North Vietnamese Air Force
OSD	Office of the Secretary of Defense
PACAF	Pacific Air Force
PACFLT	Pacific Fleet
PACOM	Pacific Command
PCS	Permanent Change of Station
PL	Pathet Lao
POL	Petroleum, Oil, and Lubricants
RAND	Research and development (the RAND Corporation, Santa Monica, California)
RLAF	Royal Laotian Air Force
RM	Research Memo
RTAF	Royal Thai Air Force
RVNAF	Republic of Vietnam Air Force
SAC	Strategic Air Command
SAF	Secretary of the Air Force
SAM	Surface-to-Air Missile
SEA	Southeast Asia
SEACORD	Southeast Asia Coordination (Committee)
SECDEF	Secretary of Defense
SLAR	Side-Looking Airborne Radar
SNIE	Special National Intelligence Estimate
Sortie	A single aircraft mission
SVG	South Vietnamese government
TAC	Tactical Air Command
TACC	Tactical Air Control Center

TDY	Temporary Duty
TFS	Tactical Fighter Squadron
TFW	Tactical Fighter Wing
TIC	Tactical Intelligence Center
TRS	Tactical Reconnaissance Squadron
UHF	Ultra High Frequency
USA	United States Army
USAFE	United States Air Force, Europe
USIA	United States Information Agency
USMACTHAI	United States Military Assistance Command, Thailand
USMACV	United States Military Assistance Command, Vietnam
VNAF	Vietnamese Air Force
WID	Weekly Intelligence Digest

Bibliography

The Washington National Records Center in Suitland, Maryland, held many of the Air Force's records used in this study, pending their eventual transfer to the National Archives at College Park, Maryland. These included records of Air Staff directorates (e.g. plans, operations, and intelligence), the Chief of Staff, the Secretary of the Air Force, and Pacific Air Forces.

During the Vietnam war, the Air Force's Project CHECO (Contemporary Historical Evaluation of Combat Operations) microfilmed records in Southeast Asia. More than a thousand rolls of this microfilm are held by the Air Force Historical Research Agency at Maxwell Air Force Base, Alabama, together with thousands of relevant rolls filmed in the United States under the auspices of the Air Force's Project Corona Harvest. Unfortunately, these microfilming projects did not get fully underway until 1968, and the researcher must look elsewhere for much of the documentation of early operations over North Vietnam.

A rich collection of documents on the early months of air operations over North Vietnam was maintained by the Naval Historical Center in Washington, D.C. These included records of the Commanders in Chief Pacific, Pacific Fleet, and Seventh Fleet.

Statistical data on the war can be found in the following multivolume Headquarters USAF Reports: *Analysis of Air Operations, Southeast Asia*; *Statistical Summaries of Air Operations, Southeast Asia*; and *USAF Management Digests*. Headquarters, Pacific Air Forces issued its own monthly *Summary of Air Operations*.

The National Archives facility at College Park now holds the voluminous records of the Military Assistance Command in Saigon. Most of these documents deal with the air-ground war in South Vietnam. Many duplicate those found in the records of the Pacific Command and Pacific Air Forces.

The Pentagon Papers (leaked to the press in 1972) are available in three separate editions (Department of Defense, Gravel, and New York Times), no one of which is complete; they contain a lode of high-level planning for the air war in North Vietnam and air-ground operations in South Vietnam. *The Public Papers of the Presidents of the United States: John F. Kennedy (1961–1963)* and *Lyndon Baines Johnson (1963–1969)* also contain material on how the Southeast Asian war unfolded and expanded, including the air war in North Vietnam.

Separate House and Senate hearings, especially by their respective armed services committees and subcommittees, contain large amounts of material on the air war in North Vietnam, particularly periodic testimony by the Secretary of Defense and by other ranking defense officials. Also very useful are the House and Senate hearings and reports of their foreign relations committees and subcommittees.

The most important contemporary official studies of Air Force operations in North Vietnam were written by civilian historians and a few military officers assigned to the United States Air Force Historical Division Liaison Office in Washington and in Southeast Asia by military and civilian historians of Project CHECO. Other chronologies, special studies, and evaluations of the air war in North Vietnam were written by military and civilian personnel at various Air Force commands (especially Pacific Air Forces) under the aegis of Project Corona Harvest. All of these reports can be consulted at the Air Force Historical Research Agency, Maxwell AFB, Alabama, together with periodic histories of the commands and units involved. Although of varying quality, many command and unit histories contain details on the progress and problems of air operations in North Vietnam as well as supporting documents.

In no previous war have newspapers played so prominent a role as in Southeast Asia. By far the most useful for this book has been the *New York Times*. Also helpful have been memoirs penned by former military officers and civilians who played prominent roles early in the period under study: two volumes by General Maxwell D. Taylor, *The Uncertain Trumpet* and *Swords and Plowshares*; General Curtis E. LeMay with MacKinley Kantor, *Mission With LeMay*; William W. Momyer, *Air Power in Three Wars (World War II, Korean War, and Vietnam)*; Admiral U. S. Grant Sharp, *Strategy for Defeat*; General William W. Westmoreland, *A Soldier Reports*; Robert S. McNamara and Brian VanDeMark, *In Retrospect: The Lessons and Tragedy of Vietnam*; and Lyndon Baines Johnson, *The Vantage Point: Perspectives of the Presidency*.

Published accounts of the air war in North Vietnam include Mark Clodfelter's *The Limits of Air Power* and Earl H. Tilford's *Crosswinds: The Air Force's Setup in Vietnam*. The most comprehensive single volume on the Southeast Asia War is Stanley Karnow's *Vietnam: The First Complete Account of Vietnam at War*; while his book lacks footnotes, Karnow obviously consulted a wide array of sources, Vietnamese as well as American.

BOOKS

Berger, Carl, ed. *The United States Air Force in Southeast Asia, 1961–1973: An Illustrated Account*. Washington: Office of Air Force History, 1977. Rev., 1984.

Cameron, James. *Here Is Your Enemy*. New York: Holt, Rinehart and Winston, 1966.

Clodfelter, Mark. *The Limits of Air Power: The American Bombing of North Vietnam*. New York: The Free Press, 1989.

Colby, William E. and Peter Forbath. *My Life in the CIA*. New York: Simon and Schuster, 1978.

Cooper, Chester L. *The Lost Crusade: America in Vietnam*. New York: Dodd, Mead, 1970.

Dommen, Arthur J. *Conflict in Laos: The Politics of Neutralization*. Rev. ed., New York: Frederick A. Praeger, 1971.

Ely, John Hart. *War and Responsibility: Constitutional Lessons of Vietnam and its Aftermath*. Princeton: Princeton University Press, 1993.

Facts on File. *South Vietnam: U. S.-Communist Confrontation in Southeast Asia, 1961–1965*.

———. *South Vietnam: U.S.-Communist Confrontation in Southeast Asia, 1966–1967*.

Futrell, Robert F. with the Assistance of Martin Blumenson. *The United States Air Force in Southeast Asia: The Advisory Years to 1965*. Washington: Office of Air Force History, 1981.

Goodman, Allen E. *The Lost Peace: America's Search for a Negotiated Settlement of the War*. Stanford: Hoover Institution Press, 1978.

Herring, George C. *LBJ and Vietnam: A Different Kind of War*. Austin: University of Texas Press, 1994.

Johnson, Lyndon Baines. *The Vantage Point: Perspectives of the Presidency, 1963–1969*. New York: Holt, Rinehart and Winston, 1971.

Karnow, Stanley. *Vietnam: The First Complete Account of Vietnam at War*. New York: The Viking Press, 1983.

Kraslow, David and Stuart H. Loory. *The Secret Search for Peace*. New York: Random House, 1968.

LeMay, Curtis E. with MacKinlay Kantor. *Mission With LeMay: My Story*. New York: Doubleday, 1965.

McNamara, Robert S. and Brian VanDeMark. *In Retrospect: The Tragedy and Lessons of Vietnam*. New York: Times Books/Random House, 1995.

Momyer, William W. *Air Power in Three Wars*. Washington: Government Printing Office, 1978.

The Pentagon Papers as Published by the New York Times. New York: Bantam Books, 1971.

The Pentagon Papers: The Senator Gravel Edition. 4 vols. Boston: Beacon Press, 1971.

Radvanyi, Janos. *Delusion and Reality: Gambits, Hoaxes, and Diplomatic One-upmanship in Vietnam*. South Bend: Gateway Editions, 1978.

Risner, Robinson. *The Passing of the Night: My Seven Years as a Prisoner of the North Vietnamese*. New York: Random House, 1973.

Schlight, John. *The War in South Vietnam: The Years of the Offensive, 1965–1968*. Washington: Office of Air Force History, 1988.

Sharp, U. S. Grant. *Strategy for Defeat: Vietnam in Retrospect*. San Rafael: Presidio Press, 1978.

Taylor, Maxwell D. *Swords and Plowshares*. New York: W. W. Norton and Company, 1972.

———. *The Uncertain Trumpet.* New York: Harper and Brothers, 1959.
Thompson, James Clay. *Rolling Thunder: Understanding Policy and Program Failure.* University of North Carolina Press, 1980.
Tilford, Earl H. *Crosswinds: The Air Force's Setup in Vietnam.* College Station: Texas A&M University Press, 1993.
Valenti, Jack. *A Very Human President.* New York: W. W. Norton, 1975.
Van Dyke, Jon M. *North Vietnam's Strategy for Survival.* Palo Alto, Calif.: Pacific Books, 1972.
Van Staaveren, Jacob. *Interdiction in Southern Laos, 1960–1968.* Washington: Center for Air Force History, 1993.
Westmoreland, William C. *A Soldier Reports.* New York: Dell, 1976.

AIR FORCE STUDIES AND REPORTS

In addition to periodic historical reports submitted by Air Force units (major commands, numbered air forces, wings and squadrons), the author consulted the following:

Analysis of Air Operations, Southeast Asia. 5 vols. Washington, 1965.
Analysis of the War in Southeast Asia. HQ USAF, 1965 and 1966.
Anthony, Maj. Victor B. *Tactics and Techniques of Night Operations, 1961–1966.* Washington: Office of Air Force History, 1976.
Book of Actions in Southeast Asia, 1961–1974. Directorate of Operations, Headquarters, USAF, n.d.
Burch, Lt. Col. Robert M. *Tactical Electronic Warfare Operations in Southeast Asia, 1962–1968.* Project CHECO, 1969.
Danforth, Col Gordon. *Iron Hand/Wild Weasel.* Project Corona Harvest, 1970.
Durkee, Maj. Richard A. *Combat Skyspot.* Project CHECO, 1968.
Effects of Air Operations, Southeast Asia. PACAF, Directorate of Intelligence, quarterly.
Elder, Maj. Paul W. *Buffalo Hunter, 1970–1972.* Project CHECO, 1973.
Futrell, Robert F. *A Chronology of Significant Air Power Events in Southeast Asia, 1950–1968.* Maxwell AFB, Ala: Aerospace Studies Institute, 1969.
———. *A Chronology of Significant Air Power Events in Southeast Asia, 1954–1967.* Maxwell AFB, Ala: Aerospace Studies Institute, 1968.
Futrell, R. Frank, et al. *Aces and Aerial Victories.* Washington: Office of Air Force History, 1976.
Greenhalgh, William H., Jr. *U. S. Air Force Reconnaissance in Southeast Asia, 1960–1975.* Manuscript. Albert Simpson Historical Research Center: Maxwell AFB, Ala., 1977.
———. *USAF in Southeast Asia, February 1965–November 1968.* Manuscript. Albert Simpson Historical Research Center: Maxwell AFB, Ala., 1969.

Hefron, Lt Charles H. *Air to Air Encounters Over North Vietnam.* Project CHECO, 1967.

Helmka, MSgt Robert T. and TSgt Beverly Hale. *USAF Operations from Thailand, 1964–1965.* Project CHECO, 1966.

In-Country and Out-Country Strike Operations in Southeast Asia. Project Corona Harvest: Headquarters, Pacific Air Forces, n.d.

Lavalle, Maj. A. J. C. *The Tale of Two Bridges and the Battle for the Skies Over North Vietnam.* Maxwell AFB, Ala., Air University, 1976.

McCormack, David A. *Summary of Source Material on the Indochina War, 1965–1973.* Joint Publication Research Series. A Special Report for the Office of Air Force History, 1976.

MacNaughton, 1st Lt. Robert L. *Yankee Team, May 1964–June 1965.* Project CHECO, 1966.

Management Digest, Southeast Asia. HQ USAF, 1965 and 1966.

Melyan, Wesley R.C. *Arc Light, 1965–1966.* Project CHECO, 1967.

Melyan, Wesley R.C. and Lee Bonetti. *Rolling Thunder, 1 July 1965–31 December 1965.* Project CHECO, 1966.

———. *The War in North Vietnam, 1966.* Project CHECO, 1967.

Nalty, Bernard. *Tactics and Techniques of Electronic Warfare: Electronic Countermeasures in the Air War Against North Vietnam, 1956–1973.* Washington: USAF Historical Division Liaison Office, 1977.

Porter, Capt. Melvin. *Air Tactics Against North Vietnam's Air-Ground Defenses.* Project CHECO, 1967.

———. *Interdiction in Southeast Asia, 1965–1966.* Project CHECO, 1966.

———. *Tiger Hound.* Project CHECO, 1966.

Rolling Thunder, March–June 1965. Southeast Asia Team, Pacific Air Forces, 1966.

Sams, Kenneth. *Command and Control,* Project CHECO, 1965.

———. *Escalation of the War in Southeast Asia, July–December 1964.* Project CHECO, 1965.

Nguyen Cao Ky. Project CHECO, 1965.

Smith, Capt. Mark E. *USAF Reconnaissance in Southeast Asia, 1961–1966.* Project CHECO, 1967.

Statistical Summaries of Air Operations. HQ USAF, 1965 and 1966.

Strike Operations in North Vietnam, 12 February–23 December 1965. Project Corona Harvest, PACAF, 1966.

Summary of Air Operations. PACAF, monthly.

Van Staaveren, Jacob. *The Air Campaign Against North Vietnam, 1966.* Washington: USAF Historical Division Liaison Office, 1967.

———. *USAF Deployment Planning for Southeast Asia, 1966.* Washington: USAF Historical Division Liaison Office, 1967.

———. *USAF Logistic Plans and Operations in Southeast Asia, 1966.* Washington: USAF Historical Division Liaison Office, 1967.
———. *USAF Plans and Operations in Southeast Asia, 1965.* Washington: USAF Historical Division Liaison Office, 1966.
———. *USAF Plans and Policies in South Vietnam, 1961–1963.* Washington: USAF Historical Division Liaison Office, 1965.
———. *USAF Plans and Policies in South Vietnam and Laos, 1964.* Washington: USAF Historical Division Liaison Office, 1965.
Wolk, Herman S. *USAF Logistic Plans and Operations in Southeast Asia, 1965.* Washington: USAF Historical Division Liaison Office, 1967.

OTHER DEFENSE DEPARTMENT REPORTS

Aggression from the North: The Record of North Vietnam's Campaign to Conquer South Vietnam. Washington: Department of State, 1965.
Air Operations Against North Vietnam. Rolling Thunder Study Group, Joint Chiefs of Staff, 1966.
CINCPAC Histories, 1965, 1966.
CINCPACFLT, *The U.S. Navy in the Pacific*, 1965, 1966.
Defense Intelligence Agency Bulletins.
Defense Intelligence Digest. Monthly.
Hoeffding, Oleg. *The Bombing of North Vietnam: An Appraisal of Economic and Military Effects.* RAND RM-5213, December 1966.
The Joint Chiefs of Staff and the War in Vietnam, 1960–1968. Washington: JCS Historical Office, 1970.
MACV Histories, 1965 and 1966.
Sharp, U.S. Grant and William C. Westmoreland. *Report on the War in Vietnam.* Washington: Government Printing Office, 1969.

CONGRESSIONAL HEARINGS AND REPORTS

House. Hearings Before the Subcommittee on Appropriations. *Supplemental Defense Appropriations for 1966.* 89th Cong., 2d sess. Washington: Government Printing Office, 1966.
House. Committee on Armed Services. *United States-Vietnam Relations, 1945–1967.* Washington: Government Printing Office, 1971.
House. Hearings before the Committee on Armed Services. *Military Posture, Executive Session.* 89th Cong., 2d sess. Washington: Government Printing Office, 1966.
Senate. Hearings before the Subcommittee on United States Security Agreements and Commitments Abroad of the Committee on Foreign Relations. *United States Security Agreements and Commitments Abroad: The Kingdom of Laos.* 91st Cong., 1st sess. Washington: Government Printing Office, 1968.

Senate. Foreign Relations Committee. *Background Information Relating to Southeast Asia and Vietnam*. 7th Rev. ed., 93d Cong., 2d sess. Washington: Government Printing Office, 1974.

Senate. Final Report of the Select Committee Study on Governmental Operations with Respect to Intelligence Activities, Together with Additional Supplemental and Separate Views. *Foreign Military Intelligence*. Report No. 94-755. Washington: 94th Cong., 2d sess. 1976.

Senate. Hearings before the Committee on Foreign Relations. *The 1964 Gulf of Tonkin Incidents*. 90th Cong., 2d sess. Washington: Government Printing Office, 1968.

Senate. Joint Hearing before the Committee on Foreign Relations and the Committee on Armed Services. *Southeast Asia Resolution*. 88th Cong., 2d sess. Washington: Government Printing Office, 1964.

Senate. Committee on Foreign Relations. Supplementary Documents to February 20, 1968 Hearing with Secretary of Defense Robert S. McNamara. *The Gulf of Tonkin: The 1964 Incident*. 90th Cong., 2d sess. Washington: Government Printing Office, 1968.

Senate. Hearings before the Committee on Armed Services. *Fiscal Year 1974 Authorization for Military Procurement, Research and Development, Construction Authorization for the Safeguard ABM, and Active Duty and Reserve Strength*. 93d Cong., 2d sess. Washington: Government Printing Office, 1973.

Senate. Hearings before a Joint Session of the Armed Services and Appropriations Committees on Fiscal Year 1966 Supplemental. *Background Paper on Pertinent Testimony of the Secretary of Defense and the Joint Chiefs of Staff*. 89th Cong., 2d sess. Washington: Government Printing Office, 1966.

Senate. Hearings before the Preparedness Investigating Subcommittee of the Committee on the Armed Services. *Tactical Air Operations and Readiness*. 89th Cong., 2d sess. Washington: Government Printing Office, 1966.

Senate. Hearings before the Armed Services Committee and the Subcommittee on Department of Defense Appropriations. *Supplemental Military Procurement and Construction Authorizations, Fiscal Year 1967*. 90th Cong., 1st sess. Washington: Government Printing Office, 1967.

Index

Index

(numbers in **bold** indicate illustrations)

ADVON (advanced echelon). *See* Air Forces, numbered, Thirteenth, 2d ADVON.
Aerial engagements: 315, 320–21
  with Chinese 111, 183n, 274–75, 314.
    See also Airspace violations.
  with North Vietnamese: 110–11, 144–45, 158–59, 273–74
Airborne Battlefield Command and Control Center: 173, 241, 254
Aircraft, China
  MiG–17: 111
Aircraft, Laos
  T–28: 52, 56, 58, 60, 61, 63, **65**
Aircraft, North Korea
  PO–2: 31n
Aircraft, North Vietnam
  Il–28: 143, **143**, 188, 190, 241, 276
  MiG–15: 52, 70, 96, 106, 143, 145, 188, 241, 276, 313, 320
  MiG–17: 52, 70, **71**, 96, 108, 143, 159, **223**, 241, 273, **273**, 274, 276, 291, 313, 320
    attacks on U.S. aircraft: 108, 109, 144, 201, 273, 275–76, 291
  MiG–21: 241, **244**, 276, 313, 319, 320
    attacks on U.S. aircraft: 273
    introduction of: 241
Aircraft, South Vietnam
  A–1: 17, 18, 22, **26**, 38, 42, 69, 84, 85, 108, 110, 112, 113, 125, 137, 140, 161
    losses at Bien Hoa: 59
  C–47: 38
    losses at Bien Hoa: 59
  H–34: 38
  O–1F: 9
  RC–47: 38
  RT–28: 38
  T–28: **26**, 38, 42
Aircraft, U.S.
  A–1: 49, 110, 228
  A–1: 17, 22, 49, 63–64, 69–70, 86, 95, 110, 140, 193, 228, 265
    engagement with North Vietnamese MiGs: 144–45
  A–4: 16, **16**, 24, 49, 63, 86, 95, 106, 110, 140, 168, 170, 173, 201, 204, 225, 226, **299**, 315
    first destruction of SAM: 192
    Iron Hand: 193
    loss to SAM: 166–69:
    loss in Flaming Dart: 16
  A–5A: 195
  A–6: 168, **202**, 227, 289, 315
    Iron Hand: 192
    night radar equipment: 204
  B–26: **21**, 38
  B–52: 22n, 59, 69, 84, 143, **180**, **181**, 226, 232, 243, 244, 262, **262**, 263, **263**, 266, 272, 289
    Arc Light: 179
    operations halt: 212
    ordnance depletion: 263
    Rock Kick II: 260, 320
    vulnerability: 271
  B–57: **41**, 42, **43**, 46, 50, 78, 84, 265
    buddy bombing: 266
    deployments of: 22n, 50, 77
    destroyed at Bien Hoa: **58**, 59
    night armed reconnaissance: 97, 125, 181–82
    training for VNAF pilots: 47n
  B–66: 5, 234, 238, 261
    buddy bombing: 226–27, 266
  C–47: 38, 59, **127**
  C–123: 38, 258
  C–130: 48, **102**, 182, 210, 265, 315, 316
    Blindbat operations: 97, 125, 181–82
    Carolina Moon: 258–59, 320
    deployments: 51
    flare dropping: 254
    night reconnaissance: 125
  CH–3: 193
  DC–130: 115, **124**, 174
  EA–1F: 115
  EA–3: 174, 269
  EB–66: 88n, 116, 174, **175**, 195, 199, 200, 203, 206, 217, 229, 239, 254, 259, **264**, 269, 273, 274, 289, 315. *See also* RB–66.
    Chinese airspace violations: 276, 277
    equipment improvements: 196
    Iron Hand missions: 269
  EC–121: 5, **6**, 164, **164**, 173

369

Big Eye: 117–18, 159–60, 173, 174, 195, 201, 241
   fitted with AN/APS–95 search radar: 118
EC–121M: 269
EF–10: 164, 174, 239, 269
F–4: 96, 114, **117**, 117–18, 125, 138, **138**, 139, 140, 147, 158, **159**, 174, 193, 199, 203, **209**, 216, 225, 228, 230, 241, 265, 273, 274, 277, 289, 313, 320
   anti-SAM operations: 163, 164
   buddy bombing: 226, 266
   deployments: 77, 145, 234
   down MiGs: 273–74
   first armed reconnaissance: 179
   first arrivals on PCS: 210
   first bombing missions: 314
   losses: 114, 163, 173, 195, 199, 239, 259
   Night Owl: 182
F–4B: 63–64, 111, 144, **226**
   losses: 110, 170, 226
F– 5: 235
F–8: 24, 48, 106, **115**, 117, 170, 275
   losses: 95, 200
   Pierce Arrow: 49
F–100: 5, 17–18, 22, 58, 64, 78, 84, 85, **96**, 106, 107, 112, 125, 182, 195, 235, 239, 265, 313
   deployments of: 22n, 50, 51, 77
   leaflet missions: 129–30
   losses: 60, 84
F–100F: **196**, 196–97, 269–70, 315, 320
F–102: 17, **17**, 50, 235
   deployments of: 50
F–104: 118, **119**, 164, 265, 289–90
   shootdown by Chinese MiG: 182–83
F–105: **4**, 15, **23**, **70**, **75**, 94, 106, **106**, **107**, 110, 112, 113, 125, 126, **132**, 135, 138, 145, 147, 158, 163, 164, 171, 179, 182, **183**, **189**, 199, 201, 225, 230, **238**, 257, **264**, 265, **270**, 273, **306**, **308**, 313
   accidental civilian strike: 316
   deployments: 22–23n, 50, 77–78, 145, 147
   Barrel Roll: 63–64
   buddy bombing: 226, 261, 266
   drone escort: 174–75
   first arrivals at Da Nang: 22–23

   first landmine drop: 158
   first Rolling Thunder strikes: 84–86
   hunter-killer missions: 168n, 192, 193, 196, 270
   improved rotation arrangements: 210
   Iron Hand: 168–69, 197, 275, 291, 315
   leaflet missions: 137, 210
   losses: 95, 107–8, 109, 116, 117, 128, 159, 173, 193, 194, 203–4, 226, 229, 239–40, 267–68
   need for improved equipment: 195
   POL strikes: 289
   SAM strikes: 165, 194, **303**
   Thanh Hoa bridge: 106–7
   Wild Weasel testing and training: 196–97
F–105F: 6, 197, 269–71, 320
   Wild Weasel II: 269n
   Wild Weasel III: 269, 270
H–43
   losses at Bien Hoa: 59
HU–16: **228**, 229, **229**, 239
KB–50: 50
KC–135: 63, 84, 106, **107**, **132**, **138**, 158, 164, 174, 181, 197, 203, **227**, 228, **308**
   Combat Lighting: 277
   deployments of: 22n, 51, 69
   Rock Kick II: 260
O–1: 9, 234, **253**, 254
RA–5: 195, 204
RB–47: 56, 174
RB–57E: **176**, 206, 217,
RB–57F: 175
RB–66: 5, 88, 88n, 96, 116, 234. See also EB–66.
RF–4: 205–6, **208**, 216, 234
RF–101: 17, 22, 33n, 58, 61, 63, 84, 106, **110**, 115, 116, 145, 147, 164, 201, 216, 217, 241, 254, 315. See also Yankee Team.
   Blue Tree: 134:
   deployments: 50, 51, 96, 234
   losses: 128, 199, 239–40
Ryan 147 reconnaissance drone: 114–15, **124**, 174–75, 256, 315
T–6: **21**
T–28: **21**
U–2: 37, 38, 42, 71, 78, 113, 113n, **114**, 128, 143, 311

370

deployment: 38
discovery of first SAM sites: 161, 163
Trojan Horse: 14
UH–1B: 9
Aircraft losses, China: 111, 144, 274–75.
Aircraft losses, North Vietnam: 110–11, 144, 159, 273, 274–76, 320–21
Aircraft losses, South Vietnam: 18, 59, 86, 141, 186, 267–68, 314, 317
Aircraft losses, U.S.: 6, 7, 59, 60–61, 107–8, 109, 110, 111, 113, 116, 117, 141, 159, 160, 165–66, 171, 173, 183n, 186–87, 193, 194, 197, 204, 226, 229, 239, 241, 267–68, 316, 317. *See also* Air defense, North Vietnam; Bien Hoa Air Base, attacks at; Surface-to-air missiles.
  to SAMs: 163–64, 169, 194, 195, 272
  studies of: 86–89
  weather-related: 313–14
Aircraft technology: 315. *See also* Electronics technology; Missiles, U.S.
  infrared imaging: 196, 217, 315
  AN/AAS–18: 205–6
  reconnaissance drones: 114–15, 174–75
  weapons systems: 176, 178
  Wild Weasels: 6, 196–97, 269, 320
Air defense, North Vietnam: 31, 86, 113–17, 161, 186–87, 196, 201, 217, 222, 236, 241, 263, 272–74, 280, 295–96, 318. *See also* Radar improvements, North Vietnam; Surface-to-air missiles.
  antiaircraft artillery: 5, 6, 7, 16, 31n, 61, 86–88, 97, 107, 129, 130, 159, 165–67, 169, 173, 175, **187, 188**, 193, 195, 197, 202, 204, 205, 206, 217, 236, 248, 254, **269, 272**, 290, 295, 313, 314, 315, 318, 320, 322, 324
  estimates of strength: 70, 141, 166n, 186n
  ground controlled intercept: 31, 141, 176, 295
  losses to: 141, 186, 226, 317
  searchlight use: 177
  tactics to counter: 267–68
  weaponry: 141
Air Divisions
  2d: 22, 37, 76, 84, 88, 96, 107, 173, 175, 314. *See also* Air Forces, numbered, Thirteenth.
air defense conferences: 143
air operations centers: 75
anti-SAM radar tactics: 196
command post, Tan Son Nhut: 51
command reporting post, Udorn: 75
coordination of ECM efforts: 115
growth of: 147, 320
Intelligence Directorate: 185. *See also* Target Intelligence Center.
mission coordination: 22, 312
organization and subordination: 15, 72–73, 314
outcountry operations: 74–75, 145
redesignation: 252n, 320
relationship to MACV: 74, 244–45
Task Force 77 coordinating committee: 209. *See also* Rolling Thunder Armed Reconnaissance Coordination Committee.
2d Air Division/Thirteenth Air Force: 148, 252n, 320
3d Air Division: 261
Airfields, North Vietnamese
  Dien Bien Phu: 138–39, **139**, 158, 227–28
  Gia Lam: **143**
  Kep: 192, 197, 272, **275**, 276
  Phuc Yen: 22n, 52, 59, 61, 70, 95, 96, 101, 117, 118, 121, 143–44, 164, 188, 190, 222, **223**, 237, 241, 272, 276, 300, 302, 315
  perceived threat from: 77–78, 143–44, 248
  protected status: 118–19, 138, 144, 178, 237, 241, 272–73, 300, 315
Air Force Tactical Air Warfare Center: 147, 258
Air Forces, numbered
  Thirteenth: 14, 22, 72, 74, 76, 81, 147, 148, 252n. 312, 320
  2d ADVON: 32, 72–73, 310
Air Operations Centers: 75, 76
Airspace violations: 4, 111, 274–75, 182–83, 314, 320–21. *See also* Buffer zones; Shootdowns, by China.
  study of: 276–77
Air Staff: 147, 148, 150, 236, 241, 276,

277. *See also* Command and control issues; Personnel expansion.
airbase construction planning: 218–19, 230, 233–35
defense of Rolling Thunder: 109
deployment planning: 235–36
discontent with administration-led strategy: 188–90, 205
Air University: 218
Alden, William A.: 163
ALQ–51. *See* Electronics technology, electronic countermeasures.
Alverez, Everett, Jr.: 49
AN/AAS–18. *See* Aircraft technology.
AN/APS–95. *See* Radar improvements, U.S.
Andersen AFB, Guam: 22–23, 23n, 51, 260
Anderson, Ronald C.: 159, **160**
Anthis, Rollen H.: 32, 310, 312
APS–20. *See* Radar improvements, U.S.
Arc Light. *See* Bombing techniques and procedures.
Argent Fletcher Company: 275
Armament Development Laboratory. *See* Eglin AFB, Florida, Tactical Air Warfare Center.
Armed Forces Council: 81
Assembly of nonaligned nations: 103
Australian troops. *See* Personnel expansion, with foreign forces.

Bach Long Island: 94–95
Bai Thuong: 130, 255
Ball, George: 11, 21, 62, 101, 111, 222, 293
Bangkok: 23, 53, 75, 92, 93, 145, 148, 149, 165
Barksdale AFB, Louisiana: 22n
Barrel Roll: 4, 63–64, 87, 89, 91, 190, 311–12. *See also* Laos, infiltration routes.
in coordination with other programs: 77–78, 121, 185
division of effort: 63–64, 250, 252
Barrier combat air patrol: 111, 170
Barrier concept: 7, 304–5, 324
Barthelemy Pass: 239, 255, 299
Base congestion: 230
Bassac River: 54
Batson, E.D.: 144n

Bay of Pigs operation: 30, 30n
Bedcheck Charlie flights: 31
Ben Hai river: 182
Berlin: 42, 98
Bien Hoa Air Base: 16n, **21**, 22n, 38, **114**, 115, 125. *See also* Farm Gate.
attacks at: **58**, 59–60, 312
deployments to: 50, 113, 160
MSQ–77 ground installation: 266n
response options to attacks: 61–62
VNAF presence: 69
Big Eye/College Eye: 117–18, 118n, 158, 173, 195, 201, 241, 275, 276–77
Big Kite: 261
Big Look: 173. *See also* Big Eye/College Eye.
Binh Gia: 64. *See also* Viet Cong, military engagements.
Binh Thuy: 266n
Black Sea: 279
Blake, Robert E.: 273
Blanchard, William H.: 221
Bleakley, Robert A.: 274
Blue Spring: 115, 256
Blue Tree: 85, 92, 96, 134, 205, 251
Bomb damage assessment: 16, 17, 24, 109, 128, 131, 142, 158, 193, 301, 355
Bombing, international view of: 103, 293
Bombing halts. *See also* Peace initiatives.
five-day: 133–35, 313
thirty-seven day: 191, 199, 211–13, 215–17, 218, 225, 317–18
opinions of effects: 217, 221, 228
Bombing policy: 13, 46, 92, 128, 135, 141, 179, 224, 225, 238, 256, 299. *See also* Command and control issues.
allocations: 232, 264, 297–98
effectiveness of: 155, 187, 265
gradual relaxation of rules: 123, 138, 166, 174, 190, 211, 237–38, 318
limits: 4, 6, 83, 95–96, 110, 112, 125, 126, 136, 157, 168, 174, 176, 222, 225, 226, 237, 250, 265, 300–301, 316, 318
loss rate analysis: 86–87, 268
Navy-USAF division of effort: 157, 159, 170, 180–81, 199, 216–17, 225, 228, 250, 255, 318
Rolling Thunder statistics: 142, 152, 153, 180, 295, 316

Bombing techniques and procedures. *See also* Aircraft technology; Targeting; Reconnaissance.
   Arc Light: 23n, 179, 260, 262
   buddy bombing: 226–27, 238–39, 261, 266
      K–5 bombing navigation system: 226, 266
   dive bombing: 86, 88, 172, 192–93
   hunter-killer teams: 168n, 192, 193, 197, 269
   skip bombing: 127
Brezhnev, Leonid I.: 66,
Bridge busting: 104–13, 130–31. *See also* Targets, bridges, Thanh Hoa.
Brink Hotel bombing: 64, 312
British Consul, Hong Kong: 134
Brown, Harold: 87, **205**, 206, 219, 221, 223, 230, **232**, 234–36, **246**, 252,
Buddy bombing. 226–27, 238–39, 261, 266
Buffer zones: 151, 168, 211, 237–38, 250, 251, 286, 323, 312, 315, 318, 321, 322. *See also* Airspace violations.
   Chinese border: 38, 111, 180, 200, 237, 277, 297
   Hanoi-Haiphong sanctuary: 6, 37, 95–96, 114, 118, 121, 128, 151, 164, 166, 168, 170, 184, 188, 191, 193, 203, 222, 224, 248, 250, 273, 279, 283–84, 297, 315
Bundy, McGeorge: 10–11, 12, 80, 103, 284, 321
   search for diplomatic solution: 215
   position on Vietnamese policy: 19–21, 66–67, 78
Bundy, William P.: 101, 120, 223, 287
   NSC working group: 61
   influence on Rolling Thunder bombing policy: 183–84, 224
   policy paper following retaliatory air strike: 52, 53–54
   preparation of Gulf of Tonkin Resolution: 47–48
Burchinal, David A.: 32
Burma: 98, 216n

Cambodia: 27, 32, 33, 38, 40, 42, 54, 113n, 309
Cameron, James: 206
Cameron, Max F.: 273
Camp Holloway: 9–10, 67

Cam Ranh Bay Air Base: 230, **233**
Canada: 27, 91, 252, 284, 286. *See also* International Control Commission; Peace initiatives, by foreign agencies.
Canton Military Region, China: 70
Carroll, Joseph F.: 213
Case, Thomas F.: 258–60
Castro, Fidel: 30
Casualties: 62, 84, 143, 149, 156, 190, 280, 286
CBS: 289, 293
Central Intelligence Agency: 29, 30, 35, 37, 45, 56, 62, 310. *See also* Covert operations.
   bombing policy position: 43, 66, 101, 249, 319
   covert operation support: 38
   joint reports with DIA: 185, 304, 323
   leaks: 56
   POL strikes, position on: 281, 283, 286
   Saigon Military Mission: 28–29
Chambley, France: 196
Chan Ching, China: 282
Chapman, Andrew H.: 17–18
Chen Yi: 103
China, People's Republic of: 19, 27, 52, 66, 72, 89, 97, 101, 103, 129, 134–35, 136, 199, 228, 309. *See also* Airspace violations; Buffer zones.
   influence on plans and policy: 3, 7, 12, 25, 32, 37, 40, 45–46, 57, 61, 69, 93, 97–99, 144, 155, 156, 166, 184, 189, 191, 219–20, 222, 223, 224, 233, 241, 249, 293, 300, 306, 310, 314, 315, 318, 321–22, 324
   relations with Soviet Union: 42, 213
   supplies to Viet Cong: 122, 158, 295
   support for North Vietnam: 71, 130, 140, 236, 298, 319
Chinese air force: 70, 313
Chinese nationalists: 36, 37. *See also* Covert operations.
Chou En-lai: 103
Civilian casualties: 285–86, 290, 321–22.
   Ben Hai River: 182
   concerns: 4, 7, 83, 130, 202, 254, 286, 289, 303, 307, 312, 323
Clark, Arthur C.: 159
Clements, Richard: 127n

373

Colby, William E.: 29–30, 30n
College Eye/Big Eye: 117–18, 118n, 158, 173, 195, 201, 241, 275, 276–77
Combat Air Patrol: 17, 22, 62, 84, 92, 94, 96, 106–7, 117–18, 141, 167, 170, 179, 181, 199, 237, 241, 274, 275, 290, 318
Combat Lighting: 277
Combat Skyspot. *See* MSQ-77 radar bombing guidance.
Command and control issues: 5, 14–15, 72–76, 88–89, 147–49, 312–13. *See also* Bombing policy; Joint Chiefs of Staff; McNamara, Robert S.; Johnson, Lyndon B.
  civilian control of operations: 4, 6, 83, 83n, 137, 138, 188, 199, 236, 248, 286
  complex coordination for 2d Air Division: 22–23
  role of MACV: 245–46, 245n
  Rolling Thunder: 245
  Sharp's attitude to Navy-Air Force roles: 209–10
  system study of: 276–77
  troop rotation planning: 146–47
  Westmoreland's extended battlefield area: 243–44
Conferences
  1954 Geneva: 81
  1965 CINCPAC deployment:147
  1965 Honolulu: 52, 119–23
    conclusions of: 120–21
  1966 deployment: 230–36, 318
  1966 Honolulu: 294–97
  1966 Manila: **214**
  Saigon air defense: 143, 210
Cossard, Hulbert: 274
Counterinsurgency operations: 3, 40–41, 70, 73, 157, 355
Covert operations: 29–30, 35, 37–38, 56n. *See also* Central Intelligence Agency; Operations plans.
Crum, William J.: 261
C. Turner Joy, USS: 48–49
Cuban Missile crisis: 98
Cultural Revolution: 300, 322

Da Lat: 266n.
Da Nang Air Base: 17, 18, **19**, 23, **23**, **43**, 69, **119**, 143, 183, 190
  Barrel Roll missions from: 63–64

deployments to: 22n, 50, 77, 118, 160, 182, 210, 258
  Carolina Moon missions from: 258–59
  emergency landings at: 106, 199
  Flaming Dart missions from: 23, 69–70
  Marines at: 65n, 89, 115, 119, 143
  MSQ–77 installation: 277
  security for: 18, 60, 89
  VNAF presence: 69, 85
Decorations
  Air Force Cross: 107, 167, 171, 181
  Distinguished Flying Cross: 159
  Silver Star: 126–27 159, 167, 181
Defense Intelligence Agency: 131, 141, 144, 186, 301. *See also* Central Intelligence Agency; Joint Chiefs of Staff.
  bombing effects, assessment of: 151
  DIA-CIA reports: 185, 304, 323
  import study: 222n
  McNamara disputes Chinese assessment: 191
  South Vietnam stabilization recommendations: 53–54
  target list: 46
De Gaulle, Charles: 40
Demilitarized Zone: 7, 16, 44, 243, 314
  accidental strike in: 316
  barrier to prevent infiltration: 7, 304–5, 307, 324
  infiltration through: 254, 300, 320, 324.
Democratic Republic of Vietnam. *See* North Vietnamese government.
Dempster, K.C.: 195.
De Soto patrols: 11, 38, 38n, 48, 52, 56, 78–79. *See also* Flaming Dart; Seventh Fleet; Ships, U.S. Navy.
  Flaming Dart intelligence: 13
  suspensions and resumptions: 54, 55, 56n, 61, 311,
Diem, Ngo Dinh. *See* Ngo Dinh Diem.
Dien Bien Phu: 44, 138–39, 158, 177–78, 309
Dixie Station: 299
Dong Em: 195
Dong Ha: 266, **269**
Dong Phuong Thuong: 109, 140
Dong Xoai: 154
Don Muang Royal Thai Air Force Base: 48, 145
Donovan, John E.: 197
Dowell, William B. P.: 274

374

Draft calls: 157
Drones. *See* Reconnaissance drones.
Dudley, William B.: 274
Duong Minh (Big Minh): 36–37, 38, 40, 310–11

Easterbrook, Ernest F.: 148, 148n
Eckhardt, George S.: 245n
Edmundson, William: 259
Eglin AFB, Florida: 259
   Tactical Air Warfare Center: 147, 258
      Armament Development Laboratory: 258.
   Wild Weasels: 196, 197, 269
Eisenhower, Dwight D.: 25, 81
Electronics technology: 195–96
   electronic countermeasures: 88n, 114–16, 195, 217, 229, 239, 273, 286
      ALQ–51: 173
      QRC–160–1 pods: 115–16
   electronic intelligence: 96, 167, 168, 169, 193, 195, 209
   radio relay
      KC–135: 271–72, 277
   SAM detection and jamming: 172, 196–97, 239. *See also* Aircraft, U.S, EB–66; EC–121.
Emerick, Paul S.: 277
Enney, James C.: 185
Evans, Robert E.: 273
Extended battlefield area. *See* Westmoreland, William C.

Fact Sheet. *See* Operation Fact Sheet.
Fanfani, Amitore: 203
Farm Gate: 16n, 17–18, 22, 31–32, 34, 38, 40, 42, 46, 84, 87, 94, 310
Fan Song radar. *See* Surface-to-air missiles.
Felt, Harry D.: 32, 33, 34, 35, 36, 42, 45, 49, 74
Fifth Air Force: 115
Fire Can radar. *See* Radar improvements, North Vietnam.
First Fleet: 51
Fish Net: 78
Flaming Dart: 3, 60, 86, 89, 313
Flaming Dart I: 13–19, 67, 70, 312
Flaming Dart II: 22–25, 67, 70, 312
Flaming Dart III: 78
Fobair, Roscoe H.: 163–64

Formosa Strait crisis resolution: 51
Forward Air Controllers: 72, 243, **253**, 254
Four-point peace plan. *See* Peace initiatives.
France: 28, 89, 103, 293
French-Viet Minh war: 3, 27, 44, 71, 105, 138, 309. *See also* Dien Bien Phu.
Fulbright, J. William: 293

Gate Guard: 253–54, 254n
Geneva Agreements
   1954: 3, 27, 89, 104, 161, 182, 216, 309
   1962: 47, 64, 216
Geneva conference, 1954: 81
George AFB, California: 117, 118, 182
George, S. W.: 273
Geyelin, Philip: 289
Gilmore, Paul J.: 273
Goldberg, Arthur: 157, 203, 215, 216
Goldberg, Lawrence H.: 274
Goldwater, Barry: 42. *See also* Johnson, Lyndon B., presidential elections.
Goure, Leon: 154n
Graham, Gordon M.: 86, 87–89
Great Britain: 28, 47, 81, 252, 284. *See also* Peace initiatives, by foreign agencies.
   position on bombing policy: 285
Greathouse, Edwin A.: 144–45
Greece: 136
Green Python: 96
Greene, Wallace M. Jr.: 41, 43, 53, **54**, 55–56, 59, 92, 93
Groom, John F.: 253
Ground controlled intercept. *See* Air defense, North Vietnam.
Groups, U.S., Air Force
   34th Tactical: 17–18, 125
   35th Tactical Control: 75, 145
      detachment 2: 75
   6234th Combat Support: 145
   6235th Combat Support: 145
   6250th Combat: 175
Guam: 59, 69, 84. *See also* Andersen AFB, Guam.
Gulf of Tonkin Resolution: 4, 47–48, 49, 49n, 51, 311
Gulf of Tonkin: 111, 126, 145, 173, 183n, 201, 202, 224, 229, 230, 232, 258, 259, 277, 288n, 299, 311, 312

Hainan Island: 110–11, 144, 182, 183n, 314, 316. *See also* Airspace violations.
Haiphong: 23n, 34, 37, 71, 83, 96, 118, 169, 184, 190, 193, 200, 203, 222, 257, 279, 283, 315. *See also* Buffer zones, Hanoi-Haiphong sanctuary; POL strangulation campaign; Targets.
Haiphong harbor: 7, 34, **44**, 45–46, 101, 223, 282, 288, 300, 303, 307
 plans to block: 128–29, 300
Hall, Richard: 158–59, **160**
Hancock, USS: **16**, **115**
Hargrove, Gerald D.: 274
Harkins, Paul D.: 32, 34, 37, 41, 72–74, **73**, 310, 311
Harriman, W. Averell: 215
Harris, Hunter, Jr.: 14–15, 46n, **57**, 74n, 81, 95, 98, 120, 133, 143, 163, 165, 168, 184, 225, 227, 237. *See also* Bien Hoa Air Base, attacks at; Pacific Air Forces; Tonkin Gulf Incident.
 calls for more vigorous armed responses: 49, 52, 60, 150, 282
 command and control: 148–49, 312, 314. *See also* Command and control issues.
 extended battlefield area: 245
 planning for troops expansion: 77–78, 121, 147
 proposal to counter MiG threat: 117
 view of POL bombing campaign: 300, 303
 views of Air Force role in theater operations: 76, 247
Harris public opinion poll: 293
Hartke, Vance: 293
Hartman, Charles W.: 144–45
Heavy repair units: 234
Heyman, Victor K.: 233–34
Ho Chi Minh: 32, 105, 216
Ho Chi Minh Trail: 39, 58, 239, 313, 321
Holcombe, Kenneth E.: 159
Holt, William H.: 272
Hon Gai: 300
Hon Gio (Tiger) Island: 85, 105, 125, 126, 225
Hon Matt Island: 94–95, 110–11, 126, 137, 177
Hon Me Island: 48

Hon Ngu Island: 48, 94–95
Hon Nieu Island: 126
Hong Rong (the Dragon's Jaw). *See* Targets, bridges, Thanh Hoa.
Honolulu: 31, 34–35, 45, 322.
 munitions meeting: 264
 meeting between U.S. and South Vietnamese presidents: 222–23
Honolulu Conferences. *See* Conferences.
Hosmer, William J.: 167
Hue: 250
Huong, Tran Van. *See* Tran Van Huong.
Humphrey, Hubert H.: 21, 215, 216
Hungary: 215n
Hunter-killer missions: 168n, 192, 193, 196, 270. *See also* Iron Hand.

Igloo White: 305, 307
Ignatius, Paul R.: 264
Infiltration, barrier to prevent: 7, 304–5, 307, 324
Infiltration routes: **5**, 37, 62, 91, 202, 213, 225, 227, 280
International Control Commission: 27, 48, 64, 91, 158, 182
Interservice deployment conference. *See* Honolulu, deployment conference.
Iron Hand: 166–68, 170. *See also* Surface-to-air missiles.
Itazuke Air Base, Japan: 77

Japan: 22n, 42, 48, 50, 77, 115, 182, 219, 231
Jarret, Grover C.: 118n
Johns Hopkins University: 103
Johnson, Clinton B.: 144–45
Johnson, Harold K.: 41, 43, **54**, 91, 97
Johnson, Lyndon B.: 10, **10**, **14**, 36, 37, 50, 80, 81, 92, **150**, 155, **213**, **214**, 215, 283, 286, 294, 311, 313, 323. *See also* Command and control issues; McNamara, Robert S.; National Security Memoranda.
 alarm about South Vietnam instability: 119–20, 250
 bombing halts: 133–35, 211–12, 282, 317
 domestic considerations: 42, 47
 Eisenhower's advice: 25, 81
 escalation reluctance: 20–21, 25, 27, 40, 59, 60, 62–64, 67, 102, 309
 ground war decision: 318

increased deployments: 147
meeting with South Vietnamese
    premier: 222–23
McNamara's report on Saigon: 37
munitions production priority: 254, 321
negotiation stance: 103, 293
NSAM 288: 42
Oplan 34A approval: 37
POL strike authorization: 288
presidential elections: 42
retaliatory bombing approval: 67, 164
Rolling Thunder approval: 92
Rolling Thunder resumption: 224–25,
    318
Steel Tiger approval: 97, 103
Tonkin Gulf Resolution: 51, 311
withdrawal of U.S. dependents: 18
Johnson, Roy L.: 133, 237, 250
Johnson, U. Alexis: 10, 64, 144, 156
Joint Chiefs of Staff: 11, 20, 35, 40, **54**,
    59, 79, 97, 135, 144, 184, 190,
    221, 224, 238, 249, 279
  aircraft loss analyses: 86–87
  barrier concept opposition: 304
  bombing halt views: 212, 221
  and bombing rextrictions: 128
  border violations investigation: 276–77
  differences with administration: 58,
    224, 236, 237
  eight-week bombing program: 78–79,
    97
  Iron Hand authorization: 168–67
  J–3 operations: 276
  low-altitude photoreconnaissance
    authorization: 174
  McNamara and JCS target requests:
    188, 191
  and North Vietnamese aircraft threat:
    143–44
  and NSAM 314: 55
  political dilemma alarm: 65
  POL strike recommendation: 6, 202–3,
    282, 287
  retaliation recommended: 39–41
  sortie increase recommended: 202–3
  sortie limit proposals: 202, 222, 249
  three-phase air attack plan: 46
  VNAF B–57 training: 47n
  Weapons Systems Evaluation Group: 87

Kadena Air Base, Okinawa: 115
  deployments to: 23n, 50, 51, 77, 277

Keirn, Richard P.: 163
Keith, Larry R.: 274
Kennedy, John F.: 30, 30n, 31–32, **33**, 34,
    36, 310–11
Khe Kiem: 110
Kitty Hawk, USS: **202**
Kong Le: 28
Korat Royal Thai Air Force base: **75**, 84,
    126, 145, 147
  deployments to: 22n, 50, 77, 160, 182,
    196, 269
Korean War: 31, 31n, 221
  comparisons with: 86, 103
Kosygin, Alexsei N.: 12, 56n
  visits to Hanoi: 11, 21, 66
Krafka, Edward: 160
Kringelis, Imants: 274
Krulak, Victor H.: 37
Khrushchev, Nikita: 66
Kung Kuan Air Base, Taiwan: 77, 118
Kunming Military region, China: 70
Kunsan Air Base, Korea: 77
Kwangsi Province, China: 199
Ky, Nguyen Cao. *See* Nguyen Cao Ky.

Lam Van Phat: 81–82
Lamb, Allen T.: 197
Lang Luang: 199
Lansdale, Edward G.: 28–29
Lao Cai: 71, 158, 228, 238–39, 241, 246,
    248, 255
Lao Dong (Labor) Party: 83. *See also*
    North Vietnamese government.
Laos: 5, 15, 22, 23, 23n, 30, 33n, 36, 38,
    40, 45, 55, 60, 71, 72, 78, 91, 96,
    113n, 130, 254n, 309. *See also*
    Barrel Roll; Steel Tiger; Tiger
    Hound; Yankee Team.
  concerns for stability: 3, 27–28, 32, 39
  deniability: 63
  infiltration routes: 4, **5**, 7, 27–28, 30,
    33, 34, 35, 37, 42–43, 46–47,
    52, 53, 54, 58, 61, 62, 103, 105,
    111–12, 122, 129, 206, 227,
    243, 260, 261, 299, 313, 320
  napalm ban: 243
  North Vietnamese influence in: 40, 139,
    251
  reconnaissance: 310, 311
  sensors: 324
  strike missions: 73, 74, 87–89, 148,
    149, 157, 209, 222, 225, 232,

377

236, 295, 311, 322
Lavalle, John D.: 234
Lazy Dog containers. *See* Munitions and ordnance, U.S.
Leaflet distribution: 29, 38, 96–97, 129–30, 137, 140–41, 160–61, 210–11, 313. *See also* Psychological warfare, U.S..
LeMay, Curtis E.: 11, 11n, **12**, 35, 41, 43, 44, 46–47, 55, 59, 60, 61, 73, **73**, 74, 310, 311
   speech to House of Representatives: 40
   view of NCS' approach: 53
   view of U.S. policy: 56, 65–66
Lifsey, Truman: 197
Lindemuth, Leslie J: 197
Lockheed Corporation: 117
Lodge, Henry Cabot: **36**, 37, 41, 42–43, 45, 47, 153, 153n, 156, 157, 212–13, 221, 285
Lucky Dragon: 38

Maddox, USS: 48–49. *See also* Tonkin Gulf incident.
Maddux, Sam, Jr.: 14, 147
Malaysia: 32, 136
Manor, Leroy J.: 234
Mansfield, Mike: 11–12
Mao Tse-tung: 219
Marsten, Hallet F.: 290–91
Martin, Glen W.: 218–19
Martin, Graham A.: 23, 49, 53, 165
Mather AFB, California: 22n
McClellan AFB, California: 117
McCone, John: 37, 43, 45, 62, 66, 101, 157
McConnell, John P.: **54**, 79, **79**, 86, 92, 98, 106, 107, 121, 144, 147, 153, 161, 164, 206, 217, 251, 268, 287, 300, 311,
   Air Force command and control study: 276–77
   on bombing policy: 92–93, 151, 153, 314
   bombing proposal: 92–93
   deployment planning: 219, 233, 235
   ground-oriented campaign views: 318
   maximum sorties for pilots: 210
   munitions shortage: 264, 265
   POL strikes: 284, 321
   Rolling Thunder resumption: 221
   on thirty-seven day bombing halt: 221

McCreery, John H.: 75, 145
McDonald, David L.: 43, **54**, 187, 252–53
McKee, Seth J.: 188–89
McNamara, Robert S.: 11, **14**, **36**, **84**, 222, 249, 279, 288, 315–16, 323. *See also* Command and control issues; Johnson, Lyndon B.; Joint Chiefs of Staff.
   anti-SAM operations extension: 188
   barrier concept: 7, 304–5, 307, 324
   bombing halts: 191, 212–13, 217
   bombing strategy changes: 283
   Contingency Planning Facilities List: 53
   control of air operations: 236, 248, 249, 264–65, 297, 312, 319
   deployment plans: 235–36
   escalation: 121, 324
      concerns over communist response: 42, 191, 318
   extended battlefield area: 242–43, 246, 283
   initial recommendations: 37, 41–42
   JCS relations: 236
   Laos operations approval: 53
   munitions shortage: 264–65
   negotiations: 317
   POL strangulation campaign: 283, 300, 309, 321
   Rolling Thunder: 122–23, 191, 246
   Saigon visit: 311
   Southeast Asia Program Team: 233
   South Vietnamese stability: 119–20
   strategic options for Johnson: 155–57
McNaughton, John T.: 101, 114, 120, 223, 285
Mekong Delta: 46
Mekong River: 46, 54
Meo forces: 28, 30n
Meyers, Gilbert L.: 147, 291
   bomber crew training: 127n
   control from Washington: 76
Middle East: 42, 51
Military Assistance Command, Thailand: 148
Military Assistance Command, Vietnam: 15, 35, 37, 40, 60, 81, 93, 310, 319, 320, 323. *See also* Air Division, 2d; Command and control issues; Westmoreland, William C., extended battlefield area.
   battlefield command and control authority: 243

command and control complexity: 72–74
covert operations: 30, 32–33
  Operations Plan 34A: 39, 129, 311
  responsibility from CIA: 37
  Special Operations Group: 38. *See also* Central Intelligence Agency; Covert operations.
strike coordination complexity: 22
Viet Cong attack on: 9–10, 67
Military Assistance Command, Vietnam/Thailand: 148
Minh, Ho Chi. *See* Ho Chi Minh.
Misawa Air Base, Japan: 115
  deployments to: 50, 77
Missile guidance warning receiver. *See* Radar, improvements, U.S.
Missiles, U.S.:
  AGM–45 Shrike: 176, 239, 269–70
    use by Air Force: 176, 238, 270–71, **270**, 320
  Bullpup–12B: 106, **106**, 112, **113**, 127, 138, 140, 178
  Matador: 235n
  Sidewinder: 111, 159, 273, 274–75
  Sparrow III: 144
MK–24 flare: 182, 192
Moc Chau: 158
Momyer, William W.: 300, **301**, 323
Monkey Mountain: 277
Montagnard tribes: 10
Moore, Joseph H., Jr.: 14, 77, 109, 173, 210, 228, 258–59, 320
  bombing policy: 78, 314
  coordination with Navy: 276
  deputy MACV commander for air operations: 147
  operational authority: 15, 74, 81
  Thanh Hoa bridge: 106–7, 126–27
  thirty-seven day bombing halt opinion: 228
Moorer, Thomas H.: 14, 57, 133
Moscow: 17, 19, 31, 89, 104, 133, 293, 18
MSQ–77 radar bombing guidance: 265–67, 320. *See also* radar improvements, U.S.
  ground installations: 266n, **268**
  success of: 267
  X-band radar: 266
Mu Gia Pass: 58, 60, 78, 111–12, 239, **242**, 260–62, 260n, **261**, **264**, 320
Munitions and ordnance, U.S.

3,000 pound bomb: 177
BLU–3: 273
CBU–2: 263
CBU–24: 292
CBU–2A fragmentation bomblets: 84, 142
Dragon Tooth: 88
Gravel: 88
MLU–10 land mine: 158, 239
safety problems: 179
napalm: 88, 164, 165, 171, 172, 197
  effectiveness of: 95
  lifting of restrictions: 86, 87
  restrictions on use: 16, 83, 243
Zuni rockets: 16, 142, 239
Munitions improvements, U.S. *See also* Eglin AFB, Florida, Tactical Warfare Center.
  5,000 pound bomb: 258–60. *See also* Operation Carolina Moon.
  Bullpup development: 138, 140 178
  Lazy Dog: 88
  MK–82 Snake Eye: 88, 170, 192
Murphy, John R.: 145, 147, 148
Mustin, Lloyd M.: 277, 286, 288

Naha Air Base, Okinawa: 50, 77
Nakhon Phanom Royal Thai Air Force Base: 160, 266, 266n
Nam Dinh: 161, 280
Nape Pass: 109, 299
National Leadership Council: 149
National Liberation Army of the North: 33. *See also* Covert operations.
National Liberation Front: 103, 104, 216, 250. *See also* Viet Cong.
National Security Agency: 276
National Security Council: 10, 101, 224–25
  working group recommendations: 61–62
National Security Memoranda:
  NSAM 273: 36–37
  NSAM 288: 42
  NSAM 310: 58
  NSAM 314: 55–56, 63
  NSAM 319: 63
  NSAM 328: 102–5, 109, 119, 129
National Shame Day: 47
Nazzaro, Joseph J.: 252, 260
Neal, Murphy: 291
New Zealand troops: 120, 231, 313. *See*

also Personnel expansion, with foreign forces.
Ngo Dinh Diem: 25, **29**, 30, 310–11
 government weakness and U.S. policy: 30–32, 310
 internal opposition: 35
 overthrow: 27, 36, 250, 310
Nguyen Cao Ky: 17, 29, 81–82, 149, **150**, 214, 223, **232**, 250, 284, 314
Nguyen Chanh Thi: 82, **249**, 250, 283–84
Nguyen Khe: 280, 285, 288–89, 292, 298
Nguyen Van Thieu: 149, **150**, **217**, **249**, 314
Nha Trang: 9, 18
Nhan Dan: 216
Night armed reconnaissance: 111, 125–26, 222–23
Night Owl: 125, 182
Night Wind: 181–82
Ninh Binh: 137, 161, 173
Nix, C. Glen: **256**
Nixon, Richard M.: 129
Nolting, Frederick C.: 34, 37
North Korea: 57, 309
North Vietnamese air force: 70, 91, 272
 strength of: 70, 241, 276, 295, 313
North Vietnamese army: 38, 39,
 units:
  270th Regiment: 17
  316th Infantry Brigade: 139
  352d Division: 16
North Vietnamese government: 27, 31, 55, 57, 78, 81, 91, 97, 98. *See also* Lao Dong (Labor) Party.
 bombing effects: 185
 civilian protection measures: 109
 communist superpowers relations: 130
 four-point plan: 104, 135, 313, 317–18
 Pathet Lao/Viet Cong support: 34, 35, 43, 120, 130, 202, 221
 peace initiatives, response to: 135
 propaganda results: 210
North Vietnamese infrastructure. *See also* Bridge busting; POL strangulation campaign.
 night operations: 206–8
 repair efforts: 131, 178, **207**, 217, 296

Office of the Secretary of Defense: 31, 60, 76, 138, 179, 203, 230
 Southeast Asia Program team: 233–34, 236

Operation Carolina Moon: 258–60. *See also* Targets, bridges, Thanh Hoa.
Operation Fact Sheet: 129–30. *See also* Leaflet distribution; Psychological warfare, U.S.
Operation Hardnose: 39. *See also* Covert operations.
Operation Marigold. *See* Bombing halts, thirty-seven day.
Operation Mayflower. *See* Bombing halts, five-day.
Operations Plans: 32–36, 97–99
 32-64: 32, 45–46, 97–98
 32-65: 98n
 33-62: 32, 33, 35
 34A: 37, 38–40, 48, 52, 54–55, 61, 62–63, 78–79, 129, 311
 37-64: 45–46, 53, 54
 39-64: 57, 97–99
 39-65: 57, 77, 98n, 219
 99-64: 32, 35–36, 53
Operations Review Group: 234n. *See also* Air Staff.
Osan Air Base, Korea: 77
Owens, Robert G.: 276–77. *See also* Airspace violations.

Pacific Air Forces: 11, 14, 15, 22, 23, 32, 36, 46, 76. *See also* Smart, Jacob E.
Pacific Air Rescue Center: 160
Pacific Command: 57, 72–73, 74, 75–76, 90, 93, 95, 130, 141, 143, 149, 168, 202, 219, 224, 230, 232, 243. *See also* Sharp, U.S. Grant.
 command and control to MACV: 245
 POL strangulation campaign: 294, 322–23
Pacification programs: 30, 38, 41, 52, 54
Page, Louis C.: 144n
Pathet Lao: 27, 28, 43, 44, 52, 54, 64, 130, 138, 139, 158, 185, 256
Pathfinders: 94, 124, 192, 226, 261, 266
 replaced by Combat Skyspot: 267
Paul Doumer bridge: 105n
Peace initiatives. *See also* Bombing halts.
 by foreign agencies: 81, 252, 284, 286, 293, 321
 by the U.S. *See* Johnson, Lyndon B.
 four-point peace plan: 104, 135, 313, 317–18
Pentagon: 44, 285, 288, 292
Peoples Army, Vietnam: 57

Personnel expansion: 145–51, 157, 229–36
  with foreign forces: 101, 120, 150, 231, 313
Pham Ngoc Thao: 81–82
Pham Van Dong: 104, 104n, 287
Phan Huy Quat: 82, 120
Phan Khac Suii: 149
Phan Rang Air Base: 230
Philpott, Jammie M.: 251
Photoanalysis: **176**, 209
Photoreconnaissance: 21, 31, 33, 43, 50, 72, 95, 106, 133, 166, 174, 185, 213, 241, 254, 257, 259, 261, 270, 283. *See also* Blue Tree.
Pierce Arrow: 49, 288, 288n
Ping Hsiang, China: 199
Pitchford, John J.: 197. *See also* Prisoners of war.
Plain of Jars: 38, 109
Pleiku: 9–11, 13, 18, 67, 99, 150, 266n.
POL strangulation campaign: 294, 296, 297–307, 322, 323, 324. *See also* Rolling Thunder 50; Targets, POL facilities.
  concerns for civilian casualties: 286, 289, 290, 303, 307, 316, 321
Potter, Melvin: 165n
Powers, Richard: 192–93
Prisoners of war: 49, 154, 163, 171, 192, 197, 291
Propaganda, China: 182–83, 199
Propaganda, North Vietnam: 113, 135, 186
Psychological warfare, U.S.: 137, 140–41. *See also* Leaflet distribution.
  attempts to exploit Viet Cong vulnerabilities: 154n
Pyle, Jesse: 9

Queen Bee: 48
Quat, Phan Huy. *See* Phan Huy Quat.

Radio Hanoi: 216
Radar improvements, North Vietnam: 115, 116–17, 141. *See also* Air defense, North Vietnam.
  artillery controlled by: 226
  Fan Song:
  Fire Can: 116, 226–27
Radar improvements, U.S: 238–39, 277
  ALQ–51: 173

AN/APS–95: 118
APS–20: 173
jamming techniques and equipment: 196
night bombing equipment: 204
panoramic SCA Receiver: 196–97
Radar homing and warning system: 196
S-band jammer: 226
Side-Looking Air borne Radar: 205
skin painting: 266
techniques and equipment to neutralize SAMs: 196
RAND bombing study: 154
Reconnaissance drones: 114–15, **124**, 161, 164, 174–75, 192, 256, 315
  against SAM locations: 115, 174–75
  Ryan 147B: 114
  Ryan 147D: 114–15
Reconnaissance programs
  Blue Spring: 115, 256
  Blue Tree: 85, 92, 96, 134, 205, 251
  Yankee Team: 60–61, 96
Red River: 71, 238
Red River Delta: 158, 179, 208, 211
Refueling: 22n, 50–51, 63, 71, 84, **107**, 131, **132**, **138**, 158, 170, 181, 182, 197, 274, **308**
Remer, Richard T.: 258–60
Reserve units: 157
Risner, Robinson: 106, 107, 107n, 171, **172**, 181. *See also* Prisoners of war.
  account of capture: 171–73.
Roberts, Thomas S.: 159, **160**
Rock Kick II: 260–61. *See also* Aircraft, U.S., B–52; Strategic Air Command.
Rolling Thunder: 3, 4, 5, 6, 7, 13, 47n, 60, 69–83, 12. *See also* Bridge busting; Iron Hand; Night armed reconnaissance; Night Owl; POL strangulation campaign; Route packages; Steel Tiger; Targets.
  first strike: 84
  planning for: 188–89
  Planning Group: 247
  programs 1–4: 81, 82
  program 5: 83–84, 128
  program 6: 85–86
  program 7: 93–94
  program 8: 94–95
  program 9: 95, 104–9, 125

381

program 10: 110–11
program 11: 111–13
program 12: 123–25
program 13/14: 125–29
program 15: 136–37
program 16: 137–38
program 20: 138–39
program 21: 138–39
program 22/23: 157–58, 159
program 24/25: 176–77
program 26/27: 167, 177–78, 188
program 28/29: 170, 178–79
program 30/31: 180–82, 190–91
program 33: 182
program 34/35: 199
program 37/38: 199
program 38/39: 183, 199
program 44/45: 203
program 48: 224–28, 236, 237, 238, 318
program 49: 236–38, 241, 243, 318–19
program 50: 243–77, 283, 319–20
  first use of B–52s in North Vietnam: 319
program 51: 297, 305, 322
Rolling Thunder Armed Reconnaissance Coordination Committee: 208–9
Ronning, Chester: 286–87, 293
Rostow, Walt W.: 30, 31, 136, 157, 321
  POL facilities bombing: 284, 293
Route packages: 209–10, 225, 239, **240**, 250, 251, 255, 299, 301, 319
  route package 1: 246, 247, 252, 253, 254, 266, 267, 299, 300, 302, 320, 323, 2
  route package 2: 246, 266, 300
  route package 3: 258, 266, 300
  route package 4: 266, 300
  route package 5: 228, 237
  route package 6a: 302, 267
  route package 6b: 256, 266
Rowland, Robert R.: 82
Royal Laotian air force: 52, 56, 58, 60, 61, 63, 64. *See also* Aircraft, Laos.
Rusk, Dean: 11, **14**, **24**, 25, 34, 42, 64, 67, 82, 83, 123, 128, 133, 161, 203, **213**, 215, 223, 284, 286, 321

Saigon
  air defense conference: 143, 210
  attack on: **66**
  2d Air Division Air Operations Center: 75

Sam Neua, Laos: 138
Sattahip Royal Thai Air Force Base: 230
S-band jammer. *See* Radar improvements, U.S.
Seaborn, J. Blair: 48, 91n
Security leaks: 56, 165, 260, 286, 289, 321
Seismic sensors: 7, 92, 116, 304–5, 324. *See also* Barrier concept.
Seventh Air Force: 184, 226, 239, 243, 252n, 320, 323. *See also* Air Divisions, 2d.
Seventh Fleet: 11, 38–39, 48, 52, 69, 74, 312. *See also* Ships, U.S. Navy.
  De Soto patrols: 11n
Sharp, U.S. Grant :14–15, 89, 129, 166, 187, 200, 201–2, 271, 286, 289, 294, **301**. *See also* Pacific Command.
  air base defense resources recommended: 60
  barrier concept opposed: 304, 324
  bombing escalation recommended: 78, 90, 93, 130, 136, 189, 236–37
  bombing halt opposed: 135, 212, 317
  bombing sorties allocated: 157, 169, 170, 209, 225, 228, 250–51, 264, 297, 301
  EC–121 request approved: 117
  extended battlefield opposed: 244–45, 319
  force size increase recommended and planned: 219–20, 221, 230–33, 296, 307, 318
  Mu Gia Pass bombing opposed: 262
  Oplan 39–64 completed: 57
  POL bombing campaign: 282, 285, 322–23
  reconnaissance collaboration directed: 133–34, 174
  reconnaissance increase recommended: 92, 95
  retaliatory strikes recommended: 49, 52, 53, 59, 64
  route packages devised: 209, 316
  route packages responsibilities reassigned: 247–48, 251, 299, 319
  SAM strikes recommended: 163–64
  strategies for winning the war: 120, 143
  on Tonkin Gulf incident: 49n
Shaw AFB, South Carolina: 116, 196, 205

Shelepin, Alexander S.: 216, 221
Ships, Soviet:
   Komsomol: 288
   Buguruslan: **295**
Ships, U.S. Navy. *See also* De Soto patrols; Seventh Fleet.
   C. Turner Joy: 48–49. *See also* Tonkin Gulf Incident
   Constellation: 49, 289
   Coral Sea: 11, 15, 16, 22, 169,
   Craig: 38
   Franklin Roosevelt: **226**
   Hancock: 11, 15, 16, **16**, 22, **115**, 292
   Independence: 192
   Kitty Hawk: **202**
   Maddox: 48–49. *See also* Tonkin Gulf Incident.
   Midway: 169
   Oriskany: **194**
   Ranger: 11, 16, 22, 51, 111, 289
   Ticonderoga: **15**, 48–49. *See also* Tonkin Gulf Incident.
Shootdowns, by China: 182–83, 316. *See also* Airspace violations.
Shootdowns, by North Vietnam: 110–11
Shootdowns, by U.S.: 110–11, 158–59, 273–74, 320–21
   by propeller aircraft: 144–45
   of Chinese aircraft: 144
   of MiG-21: 273–74
Shoup, David M.: 41
Side-looking Airborne Radar. *See* Radar improvements, U.S.
Silver Dawn: 182
Simler, George B.: 248
Singapore: 32
Skoshi Tiger: 235
Smart, Jacob E.: 2, 46, 46n, 74. *See also* Pacific Air Forces.
Smith, John C., Jr.: 144n
Smith, Philip E.: 182–83
Smith, William T.: 273–74
Snake Eye. *See* Munitions and ordnance, U.S.
Song Ca River: 224
Song Ma River: 105, 258. *See also* Targets, bridges, Thanh Hoa.
Southeast Asia Program Division. *See* Office of the Secretary of Defense.
Southeast Asia Resolution. *See* Gulf of Tonkin Resolution.
Southeast Asia Treaty Organization: 99
South Korea: 57, 98, 99, 231, 309, 313.
   See also Personnel expansion, with foreign troops.
South Vietnamese army: 10, 82, 149
   I Corps: 40, 320, 323
   II Corps: 9, 312
   special forces: 31, 37
South Vietnamese elections: 216, 300, 323
Souphanouvong: 28
Souvanna Phouma: 27–28, 47, 63, 262
Soviet Union: 7, 47, 76, 191, 309, 321, 323
   influence on U.S. policy: 3, 35, 42, 52, 61, 97, 98, 144, 166, 191, 309–10, 314, 318, 319, 324,
   peace moves: 81, 89, 156, 213
   relations with China: 42, 213
   relations with North Vietnam: 130
   support for North Vietnam: 7, 19, 114, 163, 300, 303, 318, 322
   support for North Vietnam's air force: 69, 117
Special air warfare unit. *See* Farm Gate.
Special National Intelligence Estimates: 281, 282
SNIE 53264: 57
Spring High: 164–66
Squadrons, U.S. Air Force:
   1st Air Commando: 69
   4th Air Commando: **217**
   8th Bomb: 50
   9th Tactical Reconnaissance: 196
   12th Tactical Fighter: 147, 167, 177
   landmine drops: 158
   13th Bomb: 50, **58**
   13th Reconnaissance: 185
   15th Tactical Reconnaissance: 50, 96. *See also* Blue Tree; Yankee Team.
   16th Tactical Fighter: 50
   16th Tactical Reconnaissance: 205
   18th Tactical Fighter: 86
   25th Tactical Reconnaissance: 196
   35th Tactical Fighter: 147
   36th Tactical Fighter: 50
   38th Air Rescue: 160
   41st Tactical Reconnaissance: 196
   44th Tactical Fighter: 147
   45th Tactical Fighter: 96, 117, 138, 158–59, 179
   47th Tactical Fighter: 147, 179
   67th Tactical Fighter: 106, 181
   68th Tactical Fighter: 125, 182. *See also*

Night Owl.
80th Tactical Fighter: 147
90th Tactical Fighter: 17
333d Tactical Fighter: 210
354th Tactical Fighter: 126, 147
357th Tactical Fighter: 147
390th Tactical Fighter: 210
421st Air Refueling Squadron: 50
469th Tactical Fighter: 86
476th Tactical Fighter: 118
509th Tactical Fighter: 50
522d Tactical Fighter: 51
555th Tactical Fighter: 273
563d Tactical Fighter: 147
602d Air Commando: 69
614 Tactical Fighter: 51
615 Tactical Fighter: 50
904th Refueling: 23n
913th Refueling: 23n
6091st Reconnaissance: 48, 182–83. *See also* Queen Bee.
6234th Tactical Fighter: 196–97
Starboard, Alfred D.: 304–5
State Department: 37, 47, 82, 89, 111, 114, 128, 135, 136, 138, 157, 179, 183, 188, 215, 224, 285, 286, 293, 300
Steel Tiger: 4, 97, 101, 103, 105, 121, 130, 190, 211–12, 225, 250, 252
Strategic Air Command. *See also* Arc Light; Reconnaissance programs.
    bomber strikes: 119, 243, 260–63, 320
    tankers: 49, 84, 106, 180, 181
    U–2 flights: 14, 37, 38, 42, 71, 113n, 114, 128, 143, 311
Subic Bay, the Philippines: 11
Suii, Phan Khac. *See* Phan Khac Suii.
Sullivan, William H.: 23, 63, 64, 211–12, 227, 260, 261–62
Surface-to-air missiles: 113–14, 173, **162, 163**, 163–167, 169, 192, **271**, 303. *See also* Air defense, North Vietnam.
    anti-SAM operations: 164–73, 174, 192–97, 239, 269–71, 320. *See also* Electronics technology; Iron Hand; Radar improvements, U.S.
    Fan Song radar: 163, 165, 171–75, 192, 197
    tactics and equipment to defeat: 114, 115, 171–75, 271

SA–2: **162, 163**, 318
    diminishing threat from: 268, 269, 272
    discovery of first sites: 161, 163
    estimates of numbers: 241
    guidance radar: 176
    shootdowns by: 195, 204
    sites: **166, 167, 177**
    skill at hiding and protecting: 167, 170
SA–3: 171
Swatow boats: 48–49, **50**
Sweden: 103

Tactical Air Command: 51, 86, 88, 96, 235
Tactical Air Control Center: 277
Tactical Control Party: 234
Tainan Air Base, Taiwan: 77, 117–18
Taiwan: 29, 77, 118, 219
Takhli Royal Thai Air Force base: **70**, 84, 145, 160, 192, **227**
    deployments to: 22n, 50, 77, 116, 147, 196, 210
Tally-Ho: 254, 254n
Tan Son Nhut Air Base: **6**, 15, **17**, 36, 69, **80**, 82, 96, 160, 216, **228**
    2d Air Division command post: 51, 74, 148
    attacks at: **126, 127**
    deployments to: 50, 116, 118, 175, 205
    security for: 7, 60
    VNAF presence: 69
Target and photo ELINT panels. *See* Rolling Thunder Armed Reconnaissance Coordination Committee.
Target Intelligence Center: 185
Targets: 13–14. *See also* Airfields, North Vietnamese; Bridge busting; Route packages; POL strangulation campaign; Weather.
    ammunition depots: 45, 123, 181, 280, 294, 314
    Ban Nuoc Chieu: 138, 145, 178
    Haiphong: 70
    Hoai An: 138
    Long Het: 199
    Phu Qui: 85, 137
    Phu Van: 94
    Tai Xouan: 173
    Xom Bang: 84

384

Xom Rung: 177
Yen Bai: 158
Yen Khaoi: 181
Yen Son: 158
barracks: **7**, 58, 63, **68**, 95, 139, 150, 312, 315
  Bai Thuong: 177, 178
  Ban Na Pew: 170
  Ban Xom Lam: 158
  Binh Linh: 169
  Cam Doi:165
  Chanh Hoi: 21–24
  Chap Le: 15, 17–18, 21–24
  Dien Bien Phu: 138–39, 177
  Dong Hoi: 15, 16, 21, 177, 302
  Hanoi: 256, 290
  Hoan Lao: 137
  Hon Gio: 85
  Kim Cuong: 179
  Phu Le: 137
  Phu Nieu: 165
  Quang Soui: 136–37, 177
  Son La: 138, 144, 158, 177
  Thanh Chai: 178
  Vinh: 177, 178
  Vit Thu Lu: 15, 16, 94
  Vu Con: 16, 17, 21, 22, 81, 94
  Vu San: 137
  Xom Bang: 84, 170
  Xom Trung Hoa: 126, 128, 178
  Yen Khaoi: 181
bridges: **5**, 21, 34, 39, 40, 58, 61, 70, **100**, 110–11, 112, **178**, 189, 204, **207**, **211**, **220**, 256, 286, 302. *See also* Bridge busting.
  Bac Can: 192, 199, **200**, 201
  Bac Giang: 257, **257**, 273, 274, 320
  Ban Phu Lat: 177
  Chieu Ung: **304–5**
  Choi Moi: 199
  Dong Hoi: 105, 108
  Dong Lac: **218**
  Dong Phuong Thuong: 105, **105**, 106
  Kep: 192, 200
  Kim Cuong: **104**, 110, 112
  Lang Met: **168**
  Long Ban: 178
  Long Het: 197, 199
  Me Xa: 193, 201
  My Duc: 112, **123**
  Ninh Binh: 173
  Phu Dien Chau: **122**
  Phu Huong: 177
  Phu Ly: 193, **247**, 248, 257
  Qui Vinh: **108**, 110
  Roa Leky: 177
  Thai Nguyen: 192, 199, 200
  Thanh Hoa: 13, 105–7, 117, 126–27, 138, 139, 158, 177, 258, **258**, 315, 320
  Trai Hoi: **151**
  Tri Dong: 158
  Vu Chua: 199
  Xom Ca Trang: 112, **112**
  Xom Phuong: 199
  Yen Bai: 178
cement plants: 248, 286
locks and dams: 178–79
Mu Gia Pass: 58, 60, 78, 111–12, 239, **242**, 260–62, 260n, **261**, **264**, 320
munitions facilities
  Lang Tai: 163
  Long Chi: 177
ordnance depots
  Yen Bai: 158
  Yen Son: 158
POL facilities: 6–7, 34, 40, 53, 134, 151, 153, 202, 212, 223, 224, 233, 243, 244, 248, 249, 250, 252, 253, 255, 256, 278, 279–93, **281**, 298–304, 309, 316, 319–20, 321–23, 324. *See also* POL strangulation campaign.
  Bac Giang: 285, 288, 289, 292, 298, 299, 305
  Ba Don: **296–97**
  Bai Thuong: 288
  Da Loc: 285
  Dao Quan: 299
  Dong Hoi: **294**
  Don Son: 285, 286, 288, 289, 292, 298, 299
  Duong Nham: 285, 286–87, 288, 289, 299
  Haiphong: 22n, 169, 170, 190, 279, 285, 286, 288, 289, 292, 298, 299, 321
  Hanoi: 285, 286, 288, 289, **290–92**, 298, 299, 321
  Kep: 300, 302
  Nam Dinh: 177
  Nguyen Khe: 285, 288, 289, 292, 298, 299

Phuc Loi: 285
Phuc Yen: 285, 300, 302
Phu Qui: 137, 285, 298
Son Chau: 255
Thang Ha: 288
Viet Tri: 285, 292, 298
Vinh: 285
Yen Duong: 285
Yen Hau: 288
power stations: 178–79, 195, 203–5
   Haiphong: 34
   Nam Dinh: 177
   Thanh Hoa: 107, 177
radar facilities: 48, 93, 94, 109, 110–11, 129, 137, 177, 255
   Dong Hoi: 93
   Cuo Lao: 111
   Kep: 248, 287, 288, 289, 292
   Vinh: 56n
railroads and railyards: 71, 140, 178, **194**, 199, 228, 250, 273–74, **298, 306**
   Thai Nguyen: **255**, 255–56, 320
   Yen Bai: 228, **254**, 255
river, marine and naval facilities: 13, 49, 81, 84, 137, 158, **204**, 223, 255, 285
   Cam Pha: 300
   Haiphong: 7, 34, **44**, 45–46, 101, 223, 282, 288, 300, 303, 307
   Hamp Rong: 158
   Hai Yen: 255
   Hon Gai: 300
   Phuc Loi: 255
roads and highways: 169, 257
supply areas: 230, 237, 239, 295, 313, 314
   Bai Thuong: 255
   Dang Thanh: 177
   Hanoi: 290
   Long Giam Da: 177
   Phi Din: 255
   Phu Qui: 255
   Than Hoa: 255
   Vinh: 178, 255
   Vin Son: 94, 255
   Yen Bai: 255
   Yen Son: 158
surface-to-air missile launch sites: 6, 113–14, 164–65, 166, 167–69, 170, 171, **177, 190**, 192, 193–95, 224, 239, 251, 269, 201. See *also* Wild Weasels.
   Kep: 192–93, 197, 200
   Than Hoa: 181
missile support areas
   Dong Em: 195
trucks/truck parks: 90, 96, 108, 109, 111, 112, 123, 125, 126, 128, 130, 133, 139, 141, 142, 158, 179, 182, 225, **245**, 288, 312
Tass: 291
Taylor, Maxwell D.: 10, **14**, 17, 19, 25, **36, 39**, 56, 60, 63, 82, 85, 89, 90, 101, 119, 120, **134**, 135, 149, 153n, 154, 156, 164. *See also* Command and control issues; Bombing policy; Joint Chiefs of Staff
   ambassador to South Vietnam: 19
   Brink Hotel bombing: 64
   CIA responsibility transfer: 30, 30n
   on Flaming Dart: 24
   flexible bombing proposal: 135
   gradual approach advocate: 20, 52
   change of approach: 53
   influence: 47n, 54–55, 62
   request to cancel Rolling Thunder 1: 82
   on Rolling Thunder: 95, 101, 154
   worsening military situation warning: 64–65
Techepone, Laos: 31, 45
Temporary tour of duty: 146–47. *See also* Command and control issues.
Tet celebrations: 10
Thai Nguyen: 187, 299, 300
Thailand: 11, 15, 23, 32, 34, 49, 56, 75, 81, 84, 92, 93, 96, 98, 99, 106, 116, 121, 145, 148–49, 157, 165, 190, 196, 202, 219, 236, 260, 276, 297, 309, 312, 318, 320
   neutrality: 53, 74
   deployments and planning: 50–51, 229–30, 231, 232, 234, 296, 322
   troops and equipment in: 77, 146–47
Thanh Hoa: 107, 129, 135, 140, 171–72, 181, 187, 255
Thanon Kittikachorn: **214**
Thant, U. *See* U Thant.
Thao, Pham Ngoc. *See* Pham Ngoc Thao.
Thi, Nguyen Chanh. *See* Nguyen Chanh Thi.
Thieu, Nguyen Van. *See* Nguyen Van Thieu.
Thompson, Llewellyn: 21

Ticonderoga, USS: **15**, 48–49. *See also* Tonkin Gulf Incident.
Tiger Hound: 212, 212n, 243, 246, 253–54, 298
Tiger Island: 85, 105, 125, 126, 225
Tokyo: 89
Tonkin Gulf Incident: 4, 48–51, 117, 159n, 312
Tracy, Fred: 275–76, 291
Tran Van Huong: 57, 65
Tran Van Minh (Little Minh): 82
Triantafellu, Rockly: 185
Tribal road watch teams: 262
Trier, Robert D.: 197
Tuy Hoa Air Base
  attack on: 18
  construction: 230

Ubon Royal Thai Air Base: 158, 159
  deployments to: 77, 160, 179
Udorn Royal Thai Air Base: 75, 134, 145, 148, 160, 165, 198, 201, 216, 252, 274
  2d Air Division Command Reporting Post: 75
  data processing facility: 277
  deployments to: 96, 117, 175
Unger, Leonard: 47, 53, 63
United Nations Security Council: 80
United States Air Force, Europe: 196, 235, 239
United States Army Pacific: 32, 36, 73, 247
United States Army units
  1st Cavalry Division (Air Mobile): 150
  52d Aviation Battalion: 9
  173d Airborne Brigade: 15, 120
United States Congress: 4, 25, 47, 49n, 51, 103, 104, 156, 212, 224, 250, 293, 311, 321, 323. *See also* Johnson, Lyndon B.; McNamara, Robert S.
United States Embassy, Bangkok: 75, 92, 93, 145
United States Embassy, Moscow: 19, 134
United States Embassy, Saigon: 78, 153
United States Embassy, Vientiane: 75, 145
United States Information Agency: 102
United States Information Service: 129
United States Marine Corps: 41, 44, 99, 121, 148, 153, 174, 264
  deployment planning: 230–32
  sortie allocation: 239
  units
    1st Marine Air Wing: 143
    9th Marine Expeditionary Brigade: 89
    Composite Reconnaissance Squadron: 115
    Hawk air defense battalion: 18
United States Military Assistance Command. *See* Military Assistance Command, Thailand; Military Assistance Command, Vietnam; Military Assistance Command, Vietnam/Thailand.
United States National Board of Estimates: 37
Uong Bi: 195, 203–5
USAF Analysis Team: 86, 87–88
U-Tapao Royal Thai Air Base: 277
U Thant: 19, 252

Vance, Cyrus R.: 63, 111, 221, 253
Vang Pao: 28, **28**, 30n
Vientiane, Laos: 23, 27–28, 39, 47, 63, 75, 145, 148, 227, 243, 260
Viet Cong: 9, 20, 43, 45, 55, 90, 98, 102, 120, 129, 131, 149, 151, 185, 203, 218, 222, 226, 235, 243, 281, 295, 304
  attacks in South Vietnam: 18, **66**, 312. *See also* Bien Hoa Air Base; Camp Holloway; Pleiku; Saigon; Tan Son Nhut Air Base.
  Brink Hotel bombing: 312
  military engagements: 64, 154
  strength of: 153
  supply needs: 153–14
  vulnerabilities: 154n
Viet Tri: 248, 280, 285, 288,
Vietnamese Air Transport, Inc.: 29. *See also* Covert operations.
Vietnamese Navy. *See* Covert operations.
Vit Thu Lu: 13, 15, 16, 94, 95;
Vladivostok, Soviet Union: 98
Vogt, John W.: 235
  flying prohibitions: 184

Wall Street Journal: 289
Watry, Charles A.: 126–27
Weapons Systems Evaluation Group. *See* Joint Chiefs of Staff.
Weather: 179, 182, 201, 253, 265
Westmoreland, William C.: 10, 13, 15, 17,

19, **20**, 45, 53, 59, 60, 79, 81, 91,
119, 120, 133, **134**, 143, 148, **150**,
157, 224, **246**, 235, 311, 317, 320.
See also Command and control
issues.
airfield strikes opposition: 144
Brink Hotel bombing: 312
bombing halt: 212
extended battlefield area: 243–46, 248,
266, 283, 297–98, 299, 302, 319
flexible bombing proposal: 135
graduated reprisals: 78, 93, 153
ground war emphasis: 314
JCS differences: 136
McNamara meeting: 305
pacification program: 213
Rolling Thunder pessimisim: 305
sortie allocations in Laos: 237
on troop expansion: 101
on withdrawal of civilians: 65n
Wheeler, Earle G.: 11, **34**, 35, 47n, 55, 62,
79, 80, 87, 88, 98, 107, 109, 120,
153, 156, 183, 217, 227, 236, 243,
256, 282, 285, 289
evaluation of bombing campaign: 109
JCS investigative team: 32
on thirty-seven day bombing halt: 133,
217
Whitehouse, Thomas B.: 148, 148n
Wild Weasel. *See* Aircraft, U.S., F–100F;
F–105F
Willard, Garry A., Jr.: 196–97
Williams, Charles E. Jr.: 276–77
Wilson, Harold: 285
Wilson, James: 147
Wings, U.S. Air Force
2d Bomber: 22n

3d Bombardment: 125
3d Tactical Fighter: 17
8th Tactical Fighter: 117, 158, 273
15th Tactical Fighter: 96
314th Tactical Combat: 51
320th Bomb: 22n
354th Tactical Fighter: 126
355th Tactical Fighter: 192, 210, 272
363d Composite Reconnaissance Unit:
51
388th Tactical Fighter: 269
405th Tactical Fighter: 50
463d Tactical Combat: 51
479th Tactical Fighter: 118
516th Tactical Combat: 51
552d Airborne Early Warning and
Control: 117–18
555th Tactical Fighter: 274
4080th Strategic: 38, 113n, 114–15
6234th Tactical Fighter: 145, 147
6252d Tactical Fighter: 210
Mace Missile: 235
Withdrawal of U.S. civilians: 18
World War II: 75, 86, 87, 260, 284, 321,
324

Yalu River: 150
Yankee Station: 11, 15, 145n, 202, 299
Yankee Team. *See* Reconnaissance
programs.
Yen Bai: 159, 187, 197

ZSU self-propelled gun. *See* Antiaircraft
defense, North Vietnamese,
weapons and tactics.
Zuckert, Eugene M.: 86, **87**, 88, 206

Printed in Great Britain
by Amazon